THE GREEN GUIDE

Ph. Gajic/MICHELIN

Paris

Travel Publications

Hannay House, 39 Clarendon Road
Watford, Herts WD17 1JA, UK
☎ 01923 205 240 - Fax 01923 205 241
www.ViaMichelin.com
TheGreenGuide-uk@uk.michelin.com

Manufacture française des pneumatiques Michelin
Société en commandite par actions au capital de 304 000 000 EUR
Place des Carmes-Déchaux – 63 Clermont-Ferrand (France)
R.C.S. Clermont-Fd B 855 200 507

No part of this publication may be reproduced in any form
without the prior permission of the publisher

© Michelin et Cie, Propriétaires-éditeurs, 2001
Dépôt légal avril 2003 – ISBN 2-06-000873-5 – ISSN 0763-1383
Printed in France 05-03/4.3

Typesetting: EURONUMÉRIQUE, Ligugé
Printing: MAURY IMPRIMEUR, Malesherbes
Binding: AUBIN, Ligugé

Graphics: Christiane Beylier, Paris 12ᵉ arr.
Cover design: Carré Noir, Paris 17ᵉ arr.

THE GREEN GUIDE:
The Spirit of Discovery

*The exhilaration of new horizons,
the fun of seeing the world,
the excitement of discovery:
this is what we seek to share with you.
To help you make the most
of your travel experience, we offer
first-hand knowledge and turn
a discerning eye on places to visit.
This wealth of information gives
you the expertise to plan
your own enriching adventure.
With THE GREEN GUIDE showing you
the way, you can explore new destinations
with confidence or rediscover old ones.
Leisure time spent with THE GREEN GUIDE
is also a time for refreshing your spirit,
enjoying yourself, and taking advantage
of our selection of fine restaurants,
hotels and other places for relaxing.
So turn the page and open a window
on the world. Join THE GREEN GUIDE
in the spirit of discovery.*

Contents

Introduction

Sights

Admission times and charges   379

Index   390

Wallace fountain

Grande Arche de la Défense

Maps and plans

Thematic maps

Neighbourhoods

Monuments, gardens, parks

Walking tours

Window in Notre-Dame

E. Baret

Luxembourg Gardens

Ph. Gajic/MICHELIN

5

Michelin maps and plans

Make the most of your trip to Paris by keeping a good map to hand as you discover the city. Each of the places described in this guide is associated with the references which correspond to Michelin map 10, a fold-out street map. Other formats are also available for your convenience:

● No 106, Paris and environs (scale 1:100 000), which covers the road network as far as Fontainebleau to the south and Senlis to the north, provides tourist information.

● No 101, the suburbs of Paris scale (1:53 000).

● No 18, north-west suburbs, no 20 south-west suburbs, no 22 south-east suburbs (scale 1:15 000).
For getting around Paris, you have a choice of:

● Paris Tourisme, no 8, which shows monuments, museums, shopping, shows, practical information, tourist plan and metro (scale 1:20 000).

● Paris Transport, no 9, with a plan of the bus, metro and RER routes and taxi ranks, as well as numbers for car rental and railway station information.

● Paris no 10 shows one-way streets and car parks; it is very useful if you are driving a car.

● Paris Atlas no 11, with a street index, one-way streets, car parks, and metro – RER – bus routes.

● Paris no 12, which is the same as no 10, but with an index.

● Paris Atlas no 16, with street index, one-way streets, car parks, and metro – RER – bus routes.

● Paris Plan Poche no 3 is the newest arrival, small enough to fit in your pocket, you can carry it everywhere (includes a map of the metro).

● And of course, the map of France no 721 shows a view of all of the Paris region, and how to travel to and from the city by road. The whole country is mapped on a scale of 1:1 000 000.

● If you are travelling elsewhere in France, the Michelin web site, www.ViaMichelin.com can help you plan an itinerary.

Using this guide

- The **summary maps** on the following pages are designed to assist you in planning your discovery of Paris and getting around with ease: **Selected sights** highlights the major things to see and the **Walking tours** can guide you through the city's neighbourhoods.

- The **Practical information** section offers useful addresses for planning your trip, enjoying current activities in Paris and more.

- We have **selected hotels and restaurants**, and other places for **entertainment** and going out. Turn to the pages bordered in blue immediately following the Practical information for an overview of all the districts. In the Sights section, we have also included a few nice addresses and tips for having a good time.

- We recommend that you read the **Introduction** before setting out on your trip. The background information it contains on history, the arts and culture is interesting and can make your visit more meaningful.

- The main monuments and most interesting neighbourhoods and attractions are presented in alphabetical order in the **Sights** section. In order to ensure quick, easy identification, original place names have been used throughout the guide. The clock symbol ⊘, placed after monuments or other sights, refers to the **Admission times and charges** section at the end of the guide, where you will find information on opening hours, prices and useful telephone numbers.

- The **Index** lists attractions, famous people and events, and other subjects covered in the guide.

Let us hear from you. We are interested in your reaction to our guide, in any ideas you have to offer or good addresses you would like to share. Send your comments to Michelin Travel Publications, Hannay House, 39 Clarendon Road, Watford, Herts WD17 IJA, U.K. or by e-mail to TheGreenGuide-uk@uk.michelin.com.

S. Sauvignier/MICHELIN

Key

Selected monuments and sights

	Tour - Departure point
	Catholic church
	Protestant church, other temple
	Synagogue - Mosque
	Building
	Statue, small building
	Calvary, wayside cross
	Fountain
	Rampart - Tower - Gate
	Château, castle, historic house
	Ruins
	Dam
	Factory, power plant
	Fort
	Cave
	Troglodyte dwelling
	Prehistoric site
	Viewing table
	Viewpoint
	Other place of interest

Special symbols

	Metro station
R.E.R	R.E.R. station (Regional Express Rail)
	Boarding for boat tours
	Batobus
	Guignol marionettes
	Carousel or other ride
	Children's play area
	Court for playing "boules"

Sports and recreation

	Racecourse
	Skating rink
	Outdoor, indoor swimming pool
	Multiplex Cinema
	Marina, sailing centre
	Trail refuge hut
	Cable cars, gondolas
	Funicular, rack railway
	Tourist train
	Recreation area, park
	Theme, amusement park
	Wildlife park, zoo
	Gardens, park, arboretum
	Bird sanctuary, aviary
	Walking tour, footpath
	Of special interest to children

Abbreviations

A^{ée}	Allée
Arr.	Arrondissement
Bd	Boulevard
C^r	Cour
Ch^{ée}	Chaussée
Ch^{elle}	Chapelle
G^{al}	Général
Gal^e	Galerie
F^g	Faubourg
F^{ne}	Fontaine
M^{al}	Maréchal
M^{ée}	Musée
M^t	Monument
N.-D.	Notre-Dame
P^{ge}	Passage
Prés^t	Président
P^{te}	Porte
R^d P^t	Rond-Point
R^{te}	Route
S^t/St, S^{te}/Ste	Saint, Sainte

Highly recommended	★★★
Recommended	★★
Interesting	★

Additional symbols

🛈	Tourist information
▬▬ ▬▬	Motorway or other primary route
❶ ❶	Junction: complete, limited
⬌	Pedestrian street
I═════I	Unsuitable for traffic, street subject to restrictions
▥▥▥ ╌╌╌	Steps - Footpath
🚆 🚉	Train station - Auto-train station
🚌 SNCF	Coach (bus) station
─┼─	Tram
Ⓜ	Metro, underground
P/R	Park-and-Ride
♿	Access for the disabled
✉	Post office
☎	Telephone
⬚	Covered market
⁺×⁺	Barracks
△	Drawbridge
∪	Quarry
✕	Mine
B F	Car ferry (river or lake)
🛥	Ferry service: cars and passengers
⛴	Foot passengers only
③	Access route number common to Michelin maps and town plans
Bert (R.)...	Main shopping street
AZ B	Map co-ordinates
►►	Visit if time permits

Hotels and restaurants

20 rooms: *53.27/106.55 €*	Number of rooms: price for one person/ double room
⊐ 7.61 €	Price of breakfast
120 sites: *22.68 €*	Number of camp sites and cost for 2 people with a car
12.18€ lunch- *16.74/38.05 €*	Restaurant: fixed-price menus served at lunch only – mini/maxi price fixed menu (lunch and dinner) or à la carte
rest. *16.74/38.05 €*	Lodging where meals are served mini/maxi price fixed menu or à la carte
reserv	Reservation recommended
🚫	No credit cards accepted
P	Reserved parking for hotel patrons

The prices correspond to the higher rates of the tourist season

Principal sights

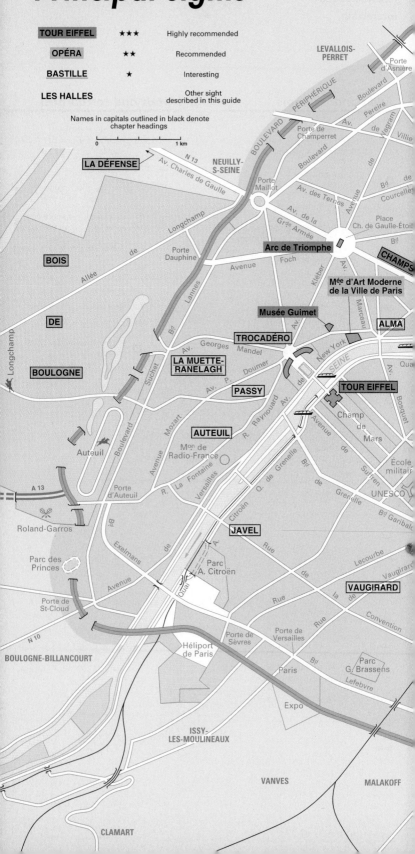

TOUR EIFFEL	★★★	Highly recommended
OPÉRA	★★	Recommended
BASTILLE	★	Interesting
LES HALLES		Other sight described in this guide

Names in capitals outlined in black denote chapter headings

0   1 km

LA DÉFENSE

N 13

NEUILLY-S-SEINE

Av. Charles de Gaulle

BOULEVARD PÉRIPHÉRIQUE

LEVALLOIS-PERRET

Porte d'Asnière

Boulevard

Pereire

Av.

de Wagram

Villie

Porte de Champerret

Boulevard

Bd

de

Courcelle

Longchamp

Porte Maillot

Av. des Ternes

Avenue

Place Ch. de Gaulle-Étoile

Porte Dauphine

Av. de la Grde Armée

Bd

BOIS

Avenue

Foch

Arc de Triomphe

CHAMPS

Kléber

Av.

DE

Allée

Lannes

Bd

Mée d'Art Moderne de la Ville de Paris

Longchamp

Suchet

Georges

Av.

Mandel

Musée Guimet

Manceau

New York

ALMA

BOULOGNE

LA MUETTE-RANELAGH

TROCADÉRO

Doumer

de

SEINE

Quai

Av. P.

Av.

PASSY

Mozart

R. Raynouard

Av.

de

TOUR EIFFEL

Auteuil

Boulevard

AUTEUIL

Mon de Radio-France

R. La Fontaine

Versailles

Av.

Champ de Mars

Avenue

de

Suffren

École militair

A 13

Avenue

Porte d'Auteuil

Q. de Grenelle

Bd

Grenelle

UNESCO

Bd Garibal

Citroën

Roland-Garros

Bd

de

JAVEL

Rue

de

Lecourbe

Vaugirar

Parc des Princes

Exelmans

Parc A. Citroën

Quai

A

Rue

la

VAUGIRARD

de

Porte de St-Cloud

Avenue

Rue

Rue

Convention

N 10

Porte de Versailles

Porte de Sèvres

Bd

Parc G. Brassens

BOULOGNE-BILLANCOURT

Héliport de Paris

Paris

Lefebvre

Expo

ISSY-LES-MOULINEAUX

VANVES

MALAKOFF

CLAMART

Br J. Jau

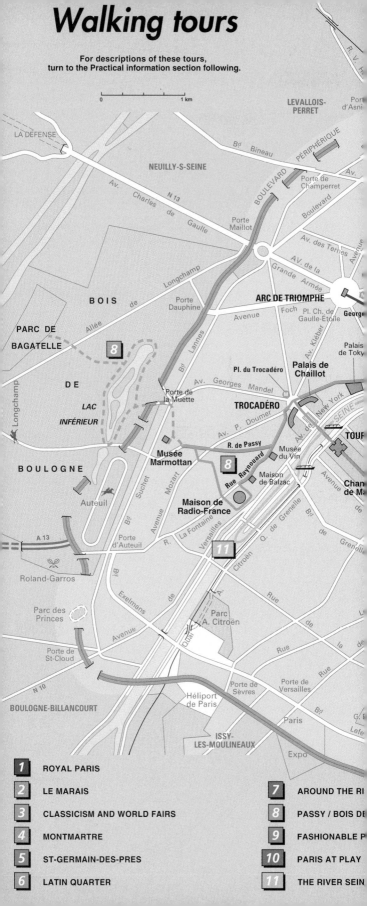

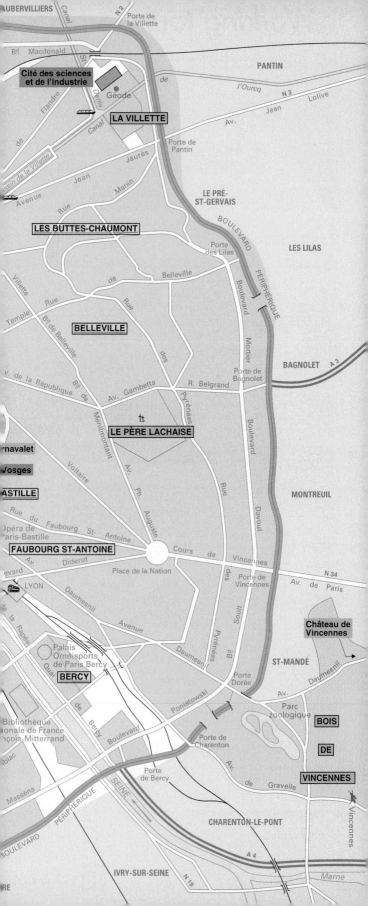

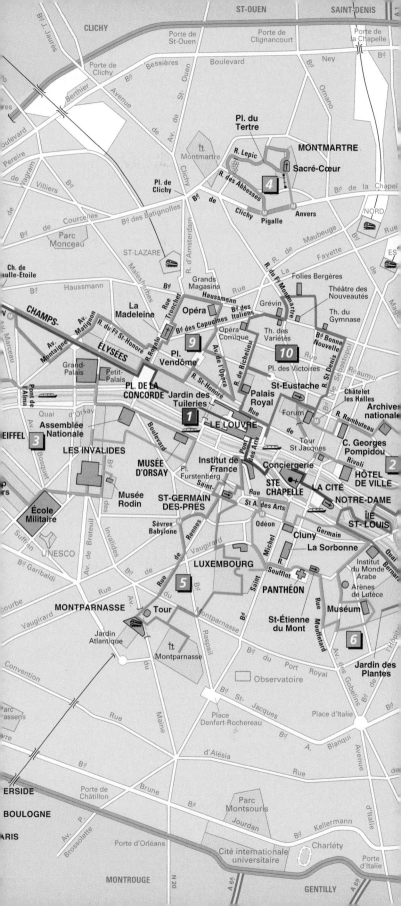

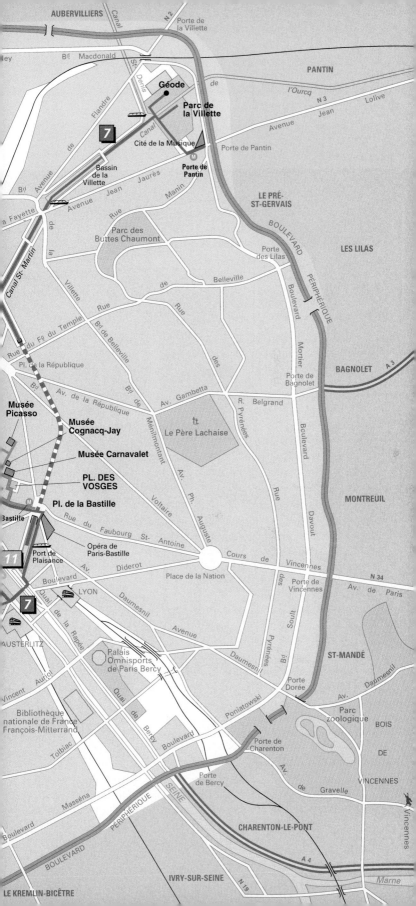

Metro line no 5

Practical
information

Planning your trip

Cyberspace

www.info.france-usa.org
The French Embassy's web site provides basic information (geography, demographics, history), a news digest and business-related information. It offers special pages for children, and pages devoted to culture, language study and travel, and you can reach other selected French sites (regions, cities, ministries) with a hypertext link.

www.ottowa.ambafrance.org
The Cultural Service of the French Embassy in Ottawa has a bright and varied site with many links to other sites for French literature, news updates and E-texts in both French and English.

www.fr-holidaystore.co.uk
The new Travel Centre in London has gone on-line with this service, providing information on all of the regions of France, including updated special travel offers and details on available accommodation.

www.visiteurope.com
The European Travel Commission provides useful information on travelling to and around 27 European countries, and includes links to some commercial booking services (ie vehicle hire), rail schedules, weather reports and more.

www.paris.org
The Paris Pages is a collection of everything useful for visiting Paris, lively and well-illustrated. Categories include museums, cafés, hotels, restaurants, current events and exhibits, stores and shops, public transportation and a discussion group. Almost as good as being there!

French tourist offices abroad

For information, brochures, maps and assistance in planning a trip to France travellers should apply to the official French tourist office in their own country:

Australia – New Zealand
Sydney – BNP Building, 12 Castlereagh Street
Sydney, New South Wales 2000
☎ (02) 9 231 52 44, Fax: (02) 9 221 86 82.

Canada
Toronto – 30 St Patrick's Street, Suite 700, Toronto, ONT M5T 3A3,
☎ (416) 979 7587.
Montreal – 1981 McGill College Avenue, Suite 490,
Montreal PQ H3A 2W9
☎ (514) 288-4264, Fax: (514) 845 48 68.

Eire
Dublin – 10 Suffolk St, Dublin 2
☎ (1) 679 0813, Fax: (1) 679 0814.

United Kingdom
London – 178 Piccadilly, London WI
☎ (09068) 244 123, Fax: (020) 793 6594.

United States
East Coast: New York – 444 Madison Avenue, NY 10022
☎ 212-838-7800, Fax: (212) 838 7855.
Midwest: Chicago – 676 North Michigan Avenue, Suite 3360
Chicago, IL 60611
☎ (312) 751 7800, Fax: (312) 337 6339.
West Coast: Los Angeles – 9454 Wilshire Boulevard, Suite 715
Beverly Hills, CA 90212.
☎ (310) 271 6665, Fax: (310) 276 2835.

Local tourist offices

Office du Tourisme et des Congrès de Paris, 127 avenue des Champs-Élysées, 75008 Paris, Ⓜ Charles-de-Gaulle/Étoile. ☎ 08 92 68 31 12; www.paris-touristoffice.com.

Espace du tourisme d'île-de-France, place de la Pyramide-Inversée, Carrousel du Louvre, 99 rue de Rivoli, 75001 Paris, Ⓜ Palais-Royal/Musée du Louvre. ☎ 0 826 166 666; www.paris-iledefrance.com.

Embassies and consulates

Australia	Embassy	4, rue Jean-Rey, 75015 Paris, ☎ 01 40 59 33 00; Fax 01 40 59 33 10
Canada	Embassy	35, avenue Montaigne, 75008 Paris, ☎ 01 44 43 29 00; Fax 01 44 43 29 99
Eire	Embassy	4, rue Rude, 75016 Paris, ☎ 01 44 17 67 00; Fax 01 44 17 67 60
New Zealand	Embassy	7 ter, rue Léonard-de-Vinci, 75016 Paris, ☎ 01 45 01 43 43; Fax 01 45 01 43 44
UK	Embassy	35, rue du Faubourg-St-Honoré, 75008 Paris, ☎ 01 44 51 31 00; Fax 01 44 51 31 27
	Consulate	16, rue d'Anjou, 75008 Paris, ☎ 01 44 51 31 01 (visas)
USA	Embassy	2, avenue Gabriel, 75008 Paris, ☎ 01 43 12 22 22; Fax 01 42 66 97 83
	Consulate	2 , rue St-Florentin, 75001 Paris, ☎ 01 42 96 14 88

TRAVELLERS WITH SPECIAL NEEDS

The sights described in this guide which are easily accessible to people of reduced mobility are indicated in the Admission times and charges section by the symbol &.
For information on transportation, holidaymaking and sports associations for the disabled apply to the **Office du tourisme et des congrès de Paris** *(see address above)*.
Web-surfers can find information for slow walkers, mature travellers and others with special needs at www.access-able.com. For information on museum access for the disabled contact La Direction, *Les Musées de France, Service Accueil des Publics Spécifiques*, 6 rue des Pyramides, 75041 Paris Cedex 1, ☎ 01 40 15 80 72.
The Red Guide France and the **Michelin Camping Caravaning France** indicate hotels and camp sites with facilities suitable for physically handicapped people.

SEASONS AND WEATHER

Paris enjoys a typical temperate climate: cold winters, hot summers, spring and autumn both have their unpredictable share of glorious sunny days and gloomy wet ones.

Mean Temperatures						
	January	February	March	April	May	June
Min/max °F	21/59	23/59	30/70	34/75	41/81	46/88
Min/max °C	-6/15	-5/15	-1/21	1/24	5/27	8/31
	July	August	September	October	November	December
Min/max °F	52/91	50/88	45/84	34/75	28/63	25/55
Min/max °C	11/33	10/31	7/29	1/24	-2/17	-4/13

When to go

Paris is a wonderful city to visit at any time of year. In summer, you can sit beneath the trees with a long cold drink to take a break from seeing the sights, or idle away an evening on a café terrace, or go on an open boat on the Seine. The heat can be stifling at times: this is when Parisians converge towards the Paris-Arsenal marina, the riverside and open-air swimming pools which tend to become overcrowded. Autumn weather is generally grey with intermittent sunny periods; the grape-harvest on Montmartre hill offers visitors a picturesque spectacle. Parisians are back from their own holidays and there is an air of energy and bustle.Winter can be severe although there is rarely any snow and when the sun lights up the sky. Paris is most attractive. In December the streets and shop windows are bright with Christmas illuminations. As for Paris in the spring, it is a legendary delight.

Weather forecast

National forecast: ☎ 08 36 68 00 00.
Local forecast: ☎ 08 36 68 02 followed by the number of the *département* (☎ 08 36 68 02 75 for Paris).

This information is also available on www.meteo.fr.

FORMALITIES

Documents

Passport – Nationals of countries within the European Union entering France need only a national identity card. Nationals of other countries must be in possession of a valid national **passport**. In case of loss or theft report to the embassy or consulate and the local police.

Visa – An **entry visa** is required for Canadian and US citizens who intend to stay for more than three months and for Australian and New Zealand citizens. Apply to the French Consulate.

US citizens should obtain the booklet *Safe Trip Abroad* ($1), which provides useful information on visa requirements, customs regulations, medical care etc for international travellers. Published by the Government Printing Office, it can be ordered by phone – ☎ (202) 512-1800 – or consulted on-line (www.access.gpo.gov).

> *Remember to take some passport-size photos with you if you want to purchase a public transport and museum pass on arrival. Student and teacher IDs may also help you obtain discounts.*

Customs

Apply to the Customs Office (UK) for a Customs guide for travellers; available from HM Customs and Excise, Dorset House, Stamford Street, London SE1 9PS, ☎ 020 7865 3100. The US Customs Service offers a publication *Know Before You Go* for US citizens: for the office nearest you, consult the phone book, Federal Government, US Treasury (www.customs.ustreas.gov).

Americans can bring home, tax-free, up to US$400 worth of goods; Canadians up to CND$300; Australians up to AUS$400 and New Zealanders up to NZ$700. Persons living in a Member State of the European Union are not restricted in regard to purchasing goods for private use, but the recommended allowances for alcoholic beverages and tobacco are as follows:

Spirits (whisky, gin, vodka etc)	10l	Cigarettes	800
Fortified wines (vermouth, ports etc)	20l	Cigarillos	400
Wine (not more than 60 sparkling)	90l	Cigars	200
Beer	110l	Smoking tobacco	1kg

Health

It is advisable to take out comprehensive insurance cover as the recipient of medical treatment in French hospitals or clinics must pay the bill. Nationals of non-EU countries should check with their insurance companies about policy limitations. Reimbursement can then be negotiated with the insurance company according to the policy held.

All prescription drugs should be clearly labelled; it is recommended that you carry a copy of the prescription.

Americans concerned about travel and health can contact the International Association for Medical Assitance to Travelers on ☎ 716 754-4883.

British and Irish citizens should apply to the Department of Health and Social Security for **Form E111**, which entitles the holder to urgent treatment for accident or sudden illness in EU countries. A refund of part of the cost of treatment can be obtained on application in person or by post to the local Social Security Offices *(Caisse Primaire d'Assurance Maladie)*.

WHERE TO STAY

See page 48 for a list of hotels by neighbourhood.

For a comprehensive list including prices of hotels and restaurants, look in **The Red Guide Paris and Environs** (an extract from The Red Guide France).

Economy Chain Hotels

These can be useful, as they are inexpensive (under 40€ for a double room) and generally located near the main road. While breakfast is available, there may not be a restaurant; rooms are small, with a television and bathroom. See p 48 for central reservation numbers.

Bed and Breakfast

Bed & Breakfast (France), International reservations centre, PO Box 66, Henley-on-Thames, Oxon RG9 1XS, ☎ 01491 578 803, Fax 01491 410 806.

Alcôve et Agapes, 8 bis rue Coysevox, 75018 Paris, ☎ 01 44 85 06 05; www.bed-and-breakfast-in-paris.com.

There are several youth and student organisations – apply to the French Government Tourist Office *(address above)*, the French Consulate General, 21 Cromwell Road, London SW7 2EN, ☎ 020 7838 2000 or the Central Bureau for Educational Visits and Exchanges, 10 Spring Gardens, London, SW1A 2BN, ☎ 020 7389 4004.

Youth Hostels

There are two main youth hostel *(auberge de jeunesse)* associations in France.
– **Ligue Française pour les Auberges de Jeunesse**, 67 rue Vergniaud, 75013 Paris, ☎ 01 44 16 78 78, www.auberges-de-jeunesse.com;
– **Fédération Unie des Auberges de Jeunesse**, 4 boulevard Jules-Ferry, 75011 Paris, ☎ 01 43 57 02 60.

Holders of an International Youth Hostel Federation card should contact the IYHF in their own country for information and membership applications (US ☎ 202 783 6161; UK ☎ 01727 855 215).

Parlez-vous anglais?

If your French is rusty or non-existent, where can you turn for current information about what's on in Paris?
The weekly *Pariscope* guide, offering comprehensive listings of the city's myriad cultural happenings, includes a Paris in English section *(available wherever newspapers are sold)*. The monthly newspaper *The Paris Free Voice* features general-interest articles and reviews written from the expatriate point of view and contains listings of the month's cultural events. It is available at various English-American haunts throughout the city (bookstores, cafés, restaurants).

Fontaine Wallace

Getting there

By air

Paris is served by two major international airports: **Roissy-Charles de Gaulle** 23km/14mi to the north of Paris on the A1, and **Orly** 11km/7mi to the south along the A6. Internal flights are handled by Orly. Public services giving access to and from the city include Air France coaches, public transport (RATP) buses, private minibuses, RER trains and taxis.

> *Check whether the train or bus is running before buying your ticket from an automatic ticket machine – these are not refundable!*

From Roissy-Charles de Gaulle – **Les Cars Air France** run every 12min from 5.45am to 11pm to Porte Maillot (bd Gouvion St-Cyr) and Place Charles de Gaulle-Étoile *(corner with avenue Carnot)*. Approximate journey time: 35min. Cost 10€. Alternatively, buses run to Gare de Lyon (20 bis bd Diderot) and Montparnasse (rue du Commandant Mouchotte, in front of the Meridien Hotel) every half hour, from 7am to 9pm. Approximate journey time: 50min. Cost 11.50€. ☎ 01 41 56 89 00, on-line: www.cars.airfrance.fr.

Bus RATP run the ROISSYBUS to rue Scribe *(corner with rue Auber, Metro Opéra)* between Roissy-CDG and Paris from 6am to 11pm, and from Paris to Roissy-CDG from 5.45am to 11pm. Departures every 15-20min. Approximate journey time: 45min. ☎ 08 36 68 77 14. Cost 8€.

Underground trains RER line B run every 15min from Roissy-CDG to Paris from 5am to 11.30pm, and from Paris to Roissy-CDG from 5am to midnight. Average journey time to Gare du Nord: 30min. Cost 7.60€.

Taxis are subject to road traffic conditions; it is best to allow 1hr journey time to the centre of town, which will cost about 36€.

Shuttle services offer a good alternative to expensive cabs and to lugging baggage on the RER: Paris Airports Service (29€ for 2 people from Roissy-CGD; 22€ from Orly; degressive rates depend on the number of people in your party) ☎ 01 55 98 10 80; www.parisairportservice.com. ParisShuttle (15€ per person, minimum 2 people; 23€ for 1 person). ☎ 0143 90 91 91, Fax 01 43 90 91 10, www.parishuttle.com. It is essential to book ahead, for your trip into town and for your trip from the hotel back to the airport.

Useful numbers – Airport Information ☎ 08 36 68 15 15. Tourist information for hotel reservations etc (7am-11pm) ☎ 01 48 62 27 29. Luggage service: ☎ 01 48 62 10 46; on-line: www.adp.fr

From Orly – **Les Cars Air France** run every 12min from 6am to 11.30pm to Les Invalides and Gare Montparnasse (rue du Commandant Mouchotte), and from 5.45am to 11pm from Les Invalides to Orly. Approximate journey time to Montparnasse: 30min. Cost 7.62€. ☎ 01 41 56 89 00.

Bus RATP run the ORLYBUS to place Denfert-Rochereau *(outside RER station)* between Orly Sud and Orly Ouest terminals and Paris from 6.30am to 11.30pm and from Paris to Orly Sud and Orly Ouest from 6am to 11pm. Departures every 12min. Average journey time: 25min. Cost 5.64€. ☎ 08 36 68 77 14, on-line: www.ratp.fr.

Underground trains RER line C run from Pont-de-Rungis. Connection with the air-terminals is by shuttle. Trains run every 15min to Paris from 5.30am to 11.15pm, and from Paris between 5.50am and 10.50pm. Average journey time to Gare d'Austerlitz: 35min. Cost 4.95€.

Underground trains RER line B run as far as Antony and connect with ORLYVAL, automated trains to the air-terminals. Scheduled departures in both directions from Orly Sud or Antony, every 7min, between 6am and 10.30pm (7am and 11pm Sunday and public holidays). Average journey time between Châtelet and Orly: 35min (40min to Etoile). Cost 8.69€. ☎ 08 36 68 77 14.

Taxis are subject to traffic conditions. Allow at least a 45min journey time to the centre of town at a minimum cost of around 24€.

Useful numbers – Airport information (24hr): Orly Sud ☎ 01 49 75 77 48. Orly Ouest ☎ 01 49 75 78 48; on-line: www.adp.fr.

Airline Offices – **Air France**: 119 avenue des Champs-Élysées, 75008, ☎ 01 42 99 21 01; flight information ☎ 08 36 68 10 48.

Air Canada – 10 rue de la Paix, 75002, ☎ 0 8 25 88 08 81.

Aer Lingus – 52-54 Belle Feuille, 92100 Boulogne-Billancourt, ☎ 01 55 38 38 55.

American Airlines – 109 rue du Fbg St-Honoré, 75008, ☎ 08 10 87 28 72.

British Midland Airways – 18 boulevard Malesherbes, 75008, ☎ 01 53 43 25 27.

By rail

Eurostar runs via the Channel Tunnel between **London** (Waterloo) and **Paris** (Gare du Nord) in 3hr (bookings and information ☎ 0345 303 030 in the UK; ☎ 1-888-EUROSTAR in the US).

Eurailpass, Flexipass and **Saverpass** are travel passes which may be purchased in the US. Conact your travel agent or **Rail Europe** 2100 Central Ave. Boulder, CO, 80301, ☎ 1-800-4-EURAIL and in the UK 179 Piccadilly London W1V OBA, ☎ 0990 848 848 or **Europrail International** ☎ 1-888-667-9731. Information on schedules can be obtained on web sites for these agencies and the **SNCF**, respectively: www.raileurop.com.us, www.eurail.on.ca, www.sncf.fr.

Tickets bought in France must be validated *(composter)* by using the orange automatic date-stamping machines at the platform entrance (failure to do so may result in a fine).

The French railway company SNCF operates a telephone information, reservation and prepayment service in English from 7am to 10pm (French time). In France call ☎ 08 36 35 35 39 (when calling from outside France, drop the initial 0).

Paris has six mainline stations: **Gare du Nord** (for northern France, Belgium, Denmark, Germany, Holland, Scandinavia and the UK); **Gare de l'Est** (for eastern France, Austria, Germany, Luxembourg); **Gare de Lyon** (for eastern and southern France, the Alps, Greece, Italy, Switzerland); **Gare d'Austerlitz** (for south-west France, Portugal, Spain); **Gare Montparnasse** (for western France and TGV to south-west France); **Gare St-Lazare** (for regional lines to north-west France).

By coach

Eurolines (UK), 4 Cardiff Road, Luton, Bedfordshire, LU1 1PP, ☎ 08705 143219, Fax 01582 400694.

Eurolines (Paris), 22 rue Malmaison 93177 Bagnolet, ☎ 01 49 72 57 80, Fax 01 49 72 57 99.

www.eurolines.com is the international web site with information about travelling all over Europe by coach (bus).

By car

Documents – Travellers from other European Union countries and North America can drive in France with a valid national or home-state **driving licence**. An **international driving licence** is useful because the information on it appears in nine languages (keep in mind that traffic officers are empowered to fine motorists). A permit is available (US$10) from the National Automobile Club, 1151 East Hillsdale Blvd, Foster City, CA 94404 ☎ 650-294-7000; or contact your local branch of the American Automobile Association. For the vehicle it is necessary to have the registration papers (logbook) and a nationality plate of the approved size.

Insurance – Certain motoring organisations (AAA, AA, RAC) offer accident insurance and breakdown service schemes for members. Check with your current insurance company in regard to coverage while abroad. If you plan to hire a car using your credit card, check with the company, which may provide liability insurance automatically (and thus save you having to pay the cost for optimum coverage).

Highway Code – The minimum driving age is 18. Traffic drives on the right. It is compulsory for the front-seat passengers to wear **seat belts** and it is also compulsory for the back-seat passengers when the car is fitted with them. Children under the age of 10 must travel in the back seat of the vehicle. Full or dipped headlights must be switched on in poor visibility and at night; use side-lights only when the vehicle is stationary.

In the case of a **breakdown** a red warning triangle or hazard warning lights are obligatory. In the absence of stop signs at intersections, cars must **yield to the right**. Traffic on main roads outside built-up areas (priority indicated by a yellow diamond sign) and on roundabouts has right of way. Vehicles must stop when the lights turn red at road junctions and may filter to the right only when indicated by an amber arrow.

The regulations on **drinking and driving** (limited to 0.50g/l) and **speeding** are strictly enforced – usually by an on-the-spot fine and/or confiscation of the vehicle.

Speed limits – Although liable to modification, these are as follows:
– toll motorways *(péage)* 130kph/80mph (110kph/68mph when raining);
– dual carriageways and motorways without tolls 110kph/68mph (100kph/62mph when raining);
– other roads 90kph/56mph (80kph/50mph when raining) and in towns 50kph/31mph;
–outside lane on motorways during daylight, on level ground and with good visibility – minimum speed limit of 80kph/50mph.

Petrol (US: gas) – French service stations dispense: *sans plomb 98* (super unleaded 98), *sans plomb 95* (super unleaded 95), *diesel/gazole* (diesel) and some have GPL (LPG). Petrol is considerably more expensive in France than in the USA, but slightly cheaper than in the UK. Prices are listed on signboards on the motorways; it is usually cheaper to fill up after leaving the motorway, check the large hypermarkets on the outskirts of town.

Tolls – In France, most motorway sections are subject to a toll *(péage)*. You can pay in cash or with a credit card (Visa, Mastercard).

Car Rental

Car rental agencies can be found at airports, air terminals and railway stations. European cars usually have manual transmission but automatic cars are available on request (advance reservation recommended). It is relatively expensive to hire a car in France; Americans in particular will notice the difference and should consider booking a car from home before leaving or taking advantage of fly-drive schemes. If you rent a car in the UK, make sure to inform the car hire company that you intend to take the car to France, for insurance purposes. Most car rental firms will not rent to those under 21 and make an extra charge for any drivers aged between 21 and 25. If you have a young person with you who may take the wheel, be sure that this is authorized and covered by insurance.

Central Reservation in France:

Avis:	☎ 08 02 05 05 05	Europcar:	☎ 08 25 352 352
Budget France:	☎ 08 00 10 00 01	Hertz France:	☎ 01 39 38 38 38
SIXT-Eurorent:	☎ 01 40 65 01 00	National-CITER:	☎ 01 45 22 88 40
Baron's Limousine and Driver:	☎ 01 45 30 21 21		

Arriving by sea from the UK or Ireland

There are numerous **cross-Channel services** (passenger and car ferries, hovercraft) from the United Kingdom and Ireland and also the rail Shuttle through the Channel Tunnel (**Le Shuttle-Eurotunnel**, ☎ 0990 353-535). To choose the most suitable route between your port of arrival and your destination use the Michelin Tourist and Motoring Atlas France, Michelin map 911 (which gives travel times and mileages) or Michelin maps from the 1:200 000 series (with the yellow cover). For details apply to travel agencies or to:

P & O Stena Line Ferries	Channel House, Channel View Road, Dover CT17 9JT, ☎ 0990 980 980 or 01304 863 000 (Switchboard), www.p-and-o.com
Hoverspeed	International Hoverport, Marine Parade, Dover, Kent CT17 9TG, ☎ 0990 240 241, Fax 01304 240088, www.hoverspeed.co.uk
Brittany Ferries	Millbay Docks; Plymouth, Devon. PL1 3EW. ☎ 0990 360 360, www.brittany-ferries.com
Portsmouth Commercial Port (and ferry information)	George Byng Way, Portsmouth, Hampshire PO2 8SP, ☎ 01705 297391, Fax 01705 861165
Irish Ferries	50 West Norland Street, Dublin 2. ☎ (353) 16-610-511, www.irishferries.com
Seafrance	Eastern Docks, Dover, Kent. CT16 1JA ☎ 01304 212696, Fax 01304 240033, www.seafrance.fr

Getting around

Public transport

Paris is justly renowned for its excellent and inexpensive public transport system. The **RATP** – Independent Paris Transport Authority – was created in 1949 to manage the urban metro, bus, tram and RER (Regional Express Rail) networks. It is heir to the 17C carriage network envisioned by the philosopher Blaise Pascal and the 18C General Omnibus Company, which operated cabs with such fanciful names as *Josephines*, *Gazelles*, *Carolines* and *Hirondelles*. Today, there are 14 Metro lines, 66 stops on the regional express lines, and around 7 000 bus stops in Paris and the suburbs.

Best fares – A book of 10 tickets *(un carnet)* costs 9.60€: use one for each metro or bus ride within Paris and keep it with you (inspectors may ask to see it). Children under age 4 ride for free on a lap; under 10's pay half fare *(demi-tarif)*. Passes may be purchased for different travel zones (zones 1-2, Paris; 3, near suburbs including St-Denis, La Défense, Le Bourget; 5, the airports, Disneyland, Versailles; 8, Provins). **Paris Visite** is a 1, 2, 3 or 5 day pass valid on all modes of transport. Advantages: access to first class on SNCF trains in the valid zones; half-fare for children under age 12; no photo required; discounts for tourist attractions. Cost varies from 8.35€ (adult, 1 day, 3 zones) to 45.70€ (adult, 5 days, 5 zones). The monthly and weekly **Carte Orange** passes are valid from the first of the month or from Monday to Sunday, at an advantageous rate (eg 2 zones for one week, 13.75€); photograph required. **Mobilis** is a one-day pass valid for unlimited travel in the zones selected (but does not include services to airports), costing from 5€ (1-2 zones) to 17.95€ (8 zones).

Ticket windows in stations open at 6.30am (first train around 5.30am depending on the station) but tickets can also be purchased from machines in stations and in *tabacs* and other shops with the RATP sign outside. The last metro leaves the end of the line around 12.30am. Insert your metro ticket in the turnstile and recover it.

There is a map of the Metro on the inside back cover of this book. For information in English ☎ 08 36 68 41 14. While access for physically impaired people is limited, it is improving, and an itinerary planning service is available, ☎ 01 45 83 67 77. You can also plan ahead with the RATP itinerary service on the Internet: www.ratp.fr.

Construction – Parisians first took the metro on 19 July 1900. The first Paris line was on the Right Bank, from Porte de Vincennes to Porte Maillot.
The engineer responsible was Fulgence Bienvenüe and Guimard designed the emblematic Art Nouveau metro entrance, in the so-called noodle style.

Facts and figures – There are over 200km/124mi of track for the 14 lines, not including the RER, and 380 stations of which 90 are interchanges. No point in the capital is more than 500m/550 yd from a metro station.

RER – The Regional Express Network includes five lines: **line A** runs from St-Germain-en-Laye, Poissy and Cergy to Boissy-St-Léger and Marne-la-Vallée; **line B** from Robinson and St-Rémy-lès-Chevreuse to Roissy-Charles-de-Gaulle, and Mitry-Claye; **line C** links Versailles (left bank), St-Quentin-en-Yvelines, Argenteuil and Pontoise to Dourdan, Massy-Palaiseau and St-Martin d'Etampes; **line D** runs from Orry-la-Ville and Coye to Corbeille, Melun and Malesherbes; **line E** from St-Lazare to Villiers-sur-Marne and Chelles-Gournay. Regular services run between approximately 5am and 1.15am. Metro tickets may be used for RER trains within the Metro system – outside these, special fares and tickets apply (including to airports, Versailles and Disneyland-Paris).

Buses – References in the main text will help you to find the stop to look for on the bus itineraries. Bus-routes are displayed in bus shelters as well as inside the buses themselves. Buses normally operate between 6.30am and 9.30pm (Mon-Sat); designated lines operate until around 12.30am and on Sundays and holidays *(service assuré les dimanches et fêtes)*; 18 night buses *(Noctambus)* operate between 1am and 5.30am; departures every hour (every half-hour at weekends). On the bus, punch a single ticket in the machine by the door, but **do not punch a pass**, simply show it to the driver.

Taxis – There are some 14 900 taxis in Paris, cruising the streets day and night and parked in the 745 ranks alongside the kerb close to road junctions and other frequented points beneath the signs labelled *Tête de Station*. Taxis may also be hailed in the street when the white taxi sign is fully lit. The rate varies according to the zone and time of day (higher rates between 8pm and 6.30am). The white, orange or blue lights correspond to the three different rates A, B and C and these appear on the meter inside the cab. A supplementary charge is made for taxi pick-up at train stations, air terminals and for heavy baggage or unwieldy parcels as well as for a fourth person and domestic animals.

Radio-taxis – Taxis Bleus ☎ 08 91 70 10 10; Artaxi ☎ 08 91 70 25 50; Taxi G7 ☎ 01 47 39 47 39 (credit cards); Alpha Taxis: for immediate use ☎ 01 45 85 85 85; to book a taxi for the next day ☎ 08 92 16 08 92; Taxis G-Space (large vehicles for up to five passengers and their luggage) ☎ 01 47 39 47 39.

Driving and parking in Paris

Everything you have heard about driving in Paris is true. Avoid it! Parking is restricted and while parking garages are well indicated on Michelin maps and on street signs, they are expensive. The metro and bus are usually faster than driving at busy times of day (almost all day long). Taxis are abundant. Parking on the street, when authorized, is subject to a fee; tickets should be obtained from the ticket machines (*horodateurs* – small change necessary) and displayed inside the windscreen on the driver's side; failure to display may result in a fine, or towing and impoundment. For a stress-free holiday, get out of the car! That said, visitors who arrive in August will find that it is easier to drive around the city then – Parisians traditionally desert town for holidays – but the riverside expressways may be closed to traffic.

Beware of *axes rouges* or red routes along main thoroughfares where parking is prohibited in order to maintain free flow of traffic (between Gare de Lyon and Gare de l'Est, via Bastille, République, quai des Célestins and quai de la Rapée). NEVER – even in congested traffic – use the lanes reserved for buses and taxis. Severe fines are enforced.

Paris is served by a six-lane outer ring-road, the **boulevard périphérique** (35km/22mi) built in 1919 along the line of the Thiers fortifications. Traffic from the motorways into Paris all merges onto the *périphérique* before filtering into the city centre via the *Portes*. As traffic can move at considerable speed during off-peak periods, it is advisable to have pin-pointed which exit you require before getting onto the ring-road system. Once on the *périphérique*, cross onto the central lanes allowing traffic to join from the right-hand side, and cross back onto the far right lane before leaving the ring road. This may be particularly hazardous for left-hand drive vehicles. If in doubt, try to avoid tackling the *périphérique* during rush hours! Parking sites have been built near the outlying stations to promote the use of public transport.

Once inside Paris, a west-to-east expressway (**Georges Pompidou expressway**, 13km/8mi) runs along the Right Bank, facilitating the flow of cars through the capital.

> *Do not leave anything of value in unattended vehicles at any time.*

Breakdown and towing – If you need an emergency tow, try one of the following (24hr/7days): **Abac** ☎ 0 800 00 8000, **Abaca Auto** ☎ 0 800 25 10 00 or **A.D.A.** 01 45 31 16 20.

Basic information

CURRENCY

There are no restrictions on the amount of currency visitors can take into France, however, the amount of cash you may take out of France is subject to a limit, so visitors carrying a lot of cash should complete a currency declaration form on arrival.

Notes and coins

Since 17 February 2002, the **euro** has been the only currency accepted as a means of payment in France, as in the 11 other European countries participating in the monetary union. It is divided into 100 cents or centimes. Old notes and coins in French francs can only be exchanged at the Banque de France (3 years for coins and 10 years for notes).

Prices and Tipping

Since a service charge is automatically included in the prices of meals and accommodation in France, it is not necessary to tip in restaurants and hotels. However if the service in a restaurant is especially good or if you have enjoyed a fine meal, an extra tip (this is the *pourboire*, rather than the *service*) is a well-appreciated gesture. Usually 1.50 to 3.50 euros is enough, but if the bill is big (a large party or a luxury restaurant), it is not uncommon to leave 7 to 8 euros or more.

As a rule, the cost of staying in a hotel and eating in restaurants is significantly higher in Paris than in the French regions. However, by reserving a hotel room well in advance and taking advantage of the wide choice of restaurants, you can enjoy your trip without breaking the bank.

Here are a few indicative prices, based on surveys conducted by French authorities in 2001. Exchange rates change regularly so you will have to check before you leave for an exact calculation. At the time of going to press, the exchange rate for one euro (€1) was: USD 1.07; GBP 0.64; CAD 1.59; AUD 1.80.

Hotel rooms (based on double occupancy) in a city	Euros
1 star (French Tourist Board standards)	28-54
2 star	54-77
3 star	77-122
4 star	140-230
4 star (luxury)	230-400

Food and entertainment	Euros
Movie ticket	8
River cruise	7-10
Dinner cruise	70-80
Expresso coffee	1.83
Café au lait	3.35
Soda	3.35
Beer	3.05
Mineral water	3.05
Ice cream	4.88
Ham sandwich	3.20
Baguette of bread	0.69
Soda (1 litre in a shop)	2.13
Restaurant meal (3 courses, no wine)	22.87
Big Mac menu meal	5.34
French daily newspaper	0.91
Foreign newspaper	1.50-2.30
Compact disc	12.00-21.00
Telephone card (50 units)	7.47
Telephone card (120 units)	14.86
Cigarettes (pack of 20)	2.50-3.50
Public transportation	**Euros**
Bus, metro ticket	1.30
Book of ten tickets	9.60
Taxi (5km + tip)	10

Restaurants usually charge for meals in two ways: a menu that is a fixed price menu with 2 or 3 courses, sometimes a small pitcher of wine, all for a stated price, or à la carte, the more expensive way, with each course ordered separately.

Cafés have very different prices, depending on where they are located. The price of a drink or a coffee is cheaper if you stand at the counter (comptoir) than if you sit down (salle) and sometimes it is even more expensive if you sit outdoors (terrasse).

Banks

Banks are usually open from 9am to noon and 2pm to 5pm and are closed on Mondays or Saturdays (except on market days); some branches open for limited transactions on Saturdays. Banks close early on the day before a bank holiday.

A passport is necessary as identification when cashing cheques in banks. Commission charges vary and hotels usually charge more than banks for cashing cheques for non-residents.

Most banks have **cash dispensers** (ATM) which accept international credit or debit cards and are easily recognised by the logo showing a hand holding a card. American Express cards can be used only in dispensers operated by the Crédit Lyonnais Bank or by American Express.

Credit cards – American Express, Visa (Carte Bleue), Mastercard/Eurocard and Diners Club are widely accepted in shops, hotels and restaurants and petrol stations. Before you leave home, learn you bank's emergency policies. Carry account numbers and emergency phone numbers separate from your wallet. Leave a copy with someone easily reachable. In the case of a lost or stolen credit card, ring one of the following 24-hour numbers:

American Express	☎ 01 47 77 72 00	**Visa**	☎ 01 42 77 11 90
Mastercard/Eurocard	☎ 01 45 67 47 67	**Diners Club**	☎ 01 47 62 75 75

Such loss or theft must also be reported to the local police who will issue a certificate to show to the credit card company.

Discounts

Significant discounts are available for senior citizens, students, youth under age 25, teachers, and groups for public transportation, museums and monuments and for some leisure activities such as the cinema (at certain times of day). Bring student or senior cards with you, and bring along some extra passport-size photos for discount travel cards. The *Carte Musées-Monuments* is available from the Paris tourist office, from museums and monuments as well as from the main metro stations. *For details, see the chapter Discovering Paris, p 33.*

ELECTRICITY

The electric current is 220 volts. Circular two-pin plugs are the rule. Adapters and converters (for hairdryers, for example) should be bought before you leave home; they are on sale in most airports. If you have a rechargeable device (video camera, portable computer, battery charger), read the instructions carefully or contact the manufacturer or shop. Sometimes these items only require a plug adapter, in other cases you must use a voltage converter as well or risk ruining your appliance.

LOST PROPERTY

Lost property office: Préfecture de Police, Objets trouvés, *36 rue des Morillons, 75015 Paris; Metro Convention.* ☎ 01 55 76 20 20. Open 8.30am to 5pm Monday and Wednesday, to 5.30pm Friday and to 8pm Tuesday and Thursday.

MEDICAL TREATMENT

First aid, medical advice and chemists' night service rota are available from chemists/drugstores (*pharmacie* – identified by the green cross sign).

Useful numbers – **SOS Medecins**, ☎ 01 47 07 77 77 (for emergencies).

Pharmacie Les Champs, 84 avenue des Champs-Élysées (Galerie des Champs-Élysées) Metro George-V. Open around the clock, seven days a week. ☎ 01 45 62 02 41.

Pharmacie Européenne de la place de Clichy, 6 place de Clichy. Open around the clock, seven days a week. ☎ 01 48 74 65 18.

American Hospital, 63 bd Victor-Hugo, 93 Neuilly-sur-Seine (7.5km/5mi from central Paris). ☎ 01 46 41 25 25.

British Hospital, 3 rue Barbès, 92 Levallois-Perret (7.5km/5mi). ☎ 01 46 39 22 22.

POST AND TELEPHONE

Post offices open Mondays to Fridays, 8am to 7pm, Saturdays, 8am to noon. Smaller branch post offices often close at lunchtime between noon and 2pm and in the afternoon at 4pm. Postage via air mail to
– UK letter (20g) €0.46
– US letter (20g) €0.67
– US postcard €0.67
– Australia and New Zealand letter (20g) €0.79
Stamps are also available from newsagents and tobacconists.
Stamp collectors should ask for *timbres de collection* in any post office.
Poste Restante (General Delivery) mail should be addressed as follows: Name, Poste Restante, Poste Centrale, postal code of the *département* followed by town name, France. *The Red Guide France* gives local postal codes.

Public Telephones

Most public phones in France use prepaid phone cards *(télécartes)*, rather than coins. Some telephone booths accept credit cards (Visa, Mastercard/Eurocard).

Télécartes (50 or 120 units) can be bought in post offices, branches of France Télécom, *bureaux de tabac* (cafés that sell cigarettes) and newsagents and can be used to make calls in France and abroad. Calls can be received at phone boxes where the blue bell sign is shown; the phone will not ring, so keep your eye on the little message screen.

Notes and coins

The euro banknotes were designed by Robert Kalinan, an Austrian artist. His designs were inspired by the theme "Ages and styles of European Architecture". Windows and gateways feature on the front of the banknotes, bridges feature on the reverse, symbolising the European spirit of openness and co-operation.
The images are stylised representations of the typical architectural style of each period, rather than specific structures.

Classical

Baroque and Rococo

Romanesque

19C iron and glass

Gothic

Renaissance

20C modern

Euro coins have one face common to all 12 countries in the European single currency area or "Eurozone" (currently Austria, Belgium, Finland, France, Germany, Greece, Ireland, Italy, Luxembourg, The Netherlands, Portugal and Spain) and a reverse side specific to each country, created by their own national artists.

Euro banknotes look the same throughout the Eurozone. All Euro banknotes and coins can be used anywhere in this area.

National calls

French telephone numbers have 10 digits. Paris and Paris region numbers begin with 01; 02 in north-west France; 03 in north-east France; 04 in south-east France and Corsica; 05 in south-west France.

International calls

To call France from abroad, dial the country code (33) + 9-digit number (omit the initial 0). When calling abroad from France dial 00, then dial the country code followed by the area code and number of your correspondent.

International dialling codes (00 + code):

Australia	☎ 61	New Zealand	☎ 64
Canada	☎ 1	United Kingdom	☎ 44
Eire	☎ 353	United States	☎ 1

To use your **personal calling card** dial:

AT&T . . .	☎ 0-800 99 00 11	Sprint	☎ 0-800 99 00 87
MCI	☎ 0-800 99 00 19	Canada Direct	☎ 0-800 99 00 16

International Information, US/Canada: 00 33 12 11

International operator: 00 33 12 + country code

Local directory assistance: 12

Special rate numbers in France begin with 0 800 (calls from within France only).

Emergency numbers

Police: 17   **Fire** *(Pompiers)*: 18   **SAMU** (Paramedics): 15

Minitel

France Télécom operates a system offering directory enquiries (free of charge up to 3min), travel and entertainment reservations, and other services (cost per minute varies). These small computer-like terminals can be found in some post offices, hotels and France Télécom agencies and in many French homes. 3614 PAGES E is the code for directory assistance in English (turn on the unit, dial 3614, hit the connexion button when you get the tone, type in "PAGES E", and follow the instructions on the screen).

Cellular phones

In France these have numbers which begin with 06. Two-watt (lighter, shorter reach) and eight-watt models are on the market, using the Itinéris (France Télécom) or SFR network. *Mobicartes* are prepaid phone cards that fit into mobile units. Cell phone rentals (delivery or airport pickup provided):

A.L.T. Rent A Phone   ☎ 01 48 00 06 06, E-mail altloc@jve.fr
Rent a Cell Express   ☎ 01 53 93 78 00, Fax 01 53 93 78 09

PUBLIC HOLIDAYS

Museums and other monuments may be closed or may vary their hours of admission on the following public holidays:

1	January	New Year's Day *(Jour de l'An)*
Easter Day and Easter Monday		*(Pâques)*
1	May	May Day
8	May	VE Day
40 days after Easter		Ascension Day *(Ascension)*
7th Sun after Easter		Whitsun *(Pentecôte)*
14	July	France's National Day (Bastille Day)
15	August	Assumption *(Assomption)*
1	November	All Saints' Day *(Toussaint)*
11	November	Armistice Day
25	December	Christmas Day *(Noël)*

In addition to the usual school holidays at Christmas and in the spring and summer, there are long mid-term breaks (10 days to a fortnight) in February and early November.

Conversion Tables

Weights and measures

1 kilogram (kg)	2.2 pounds (lb)	2.2 pounds
1 metric ton (tn)	1.1 tons	1.1 tons

to convert kilograms to pounds, multiply by 2.2

1 litre (l)	2.1 pints (pt)	1.8 pints
1 litre	0.3 gallon (gal)	0.2 gallon

to convert litres to gallons, multiply by 0.26 (US) or 0.22 (UK)

1 hectare (ha)	2.5 acres	2.5 acres
1 square kilometre (km²)	0.4 square miles (sq mi)	0.4 square miles

to convert hectares to acres, multiply by 2.4

1centimetre (cm)	0.4 inches (in)	0.4 inches
1 metre (m)	3.3 feet (ft) - 39.4 inches - 1.1 yards (yd)	
1 kilometre (km)	0.6 miles (mi)	0.6 miles

to convert metres to feet, multiply by 3.28 . kilometres to miles, multiply by 0.6

Clothing

Women							Men
	35	4	2½	40	7½	7	
	36	5	3½	41	8½	8	
	37	6	4½	42	9½	9	
Shoes	38	7	5½	43	10½	10	Shoes
	39	8	6½	44	11½	11	
	40	9	7½	45	12½	12	
	41	10	8½	46	13½	13	
	36	4	8	46	36	36	
	38	6	10	48	38	38	
Dresses &	40	8	12	50	40	40	Suits
Suits	42	12	14	52	42	42	
	44	14	16	54	44	44	
	46	16	18	56	46	48	
	36	08	30	37	14½	14,5	
	38	10	32	38	15	15	
Blouses &	40	12	14	39	15½	15½	Shirts
sweaters	42	14	36	40	15¾	15¾	
	44	16	38	41	16	16	
	46	18	40	42	16½	16½	

Sizes often vary depending on the designer. These equivalents are given for guidance only.

Speed

kph	10	30	50	70	80	90	100	110	120	130
mph	6	19	31	43	50	56	62	68	75	81

Temperature

Celsius (°C)	0°	5°	10°	15°	20°	25°	30°	40°	60°	80°	100°
Fahrenheit (°F)	32°	41°	50°	59°	68°	77°	86°	104°	140°	176°	212°

To convert Celsius into Fahrenheit, multiply °C by 9, divide by 5, and add 32.
To convert Fahrenheit into Celsius, subtract 32 from °F, multiply by 5, and divide by 9.

TIME

France is 1hr ahead of Greenwich Mean Time (GMT).

When it is **noon in France**, it is

3am	in Los Angeles
6am	in New York
11am	in Dublin
11am	in London
7pm	in Perth
9pm	in Sydney
11pm	in Auckland

In France am and pm are not used but the 24-hour clock is widely applied

Shopping

Most of the larger shops are open Monday to Saturday from 9am to 6.30pm or 7.30pm. Smaller, individual shops may close during the lunch hour. Food shops – grocers, wine merchants and bakeries – are open from around 7am to 7.30pm; some open on Sundays. Many food shops close for an hour or two between noon and 2pm and on Mondays. Hypermarkets stay usually open until 9pm or 10pm.

People travelling to the USA cannot import plant products or fresh food, including fruit, cheeses and nuts. It is alright to carry tinned products or preserves.

Recovering VAT

In France a sales tax (*TVA* or Value Added Tax ranging from 5.5% to 19.6%) is added to almost all retail goods – it can be worth your while to recover it. VAT refunds are available to visitors from outside the EU only if purchases exceed US$200 per store, but repeat visits to a store can be combined. The system works in large stores which cater to tourists, in luxury stores and other shops advertising "Duty Free". Show your passport, and the store will complete a form which is to be stamped (at the airport) by a European customs agents. The refund is paid into your credit card account.

Markets

Food markets – These take place year-round, whatever the weather, usually from 7am to 2.30pm. In Paris, there are 65 open-air markets (one, two or three times a week) and 13 covered markets (daily). Here is a list of the most interesting:

Monge, place Monge, 75005, Ⓜ Place-Monge; Wed, Fri, Sun;

Raspail, boulevard Raspail, 75006, Ⓜ Rennes; Tue, Fri, Sun: organic produce;

Bastille, boulevard Richard-Lenoir, 75011, Ⓜ Bastille; Thu, Sun;

Belleville, boulevard de Belleville, 75011, Ⓜ Belleville; Tue, Fri;

Aligre, place d'Aligre, 75012, Ⓜ Ledru-Rollin; daily except Mon;

Brancusi, place Brancusi, 75014, Ⓜ Gaité; Sat: organic produce;

Batignolles, boulevard des Batignolles, 75017, Ⓜ Rome; Sat: organic produce.

In addition, a number of picturesque street markets take place all day on a daily basis: **rue Montorgueil** (75002), **rue Mouffetard** (75005), **rue de Buci** and **rue de Seine** (75006), rue Cler (75007), rue des Martyrs (75009), rue Daguerre (75014), rue St-Charles and rue du Commerce (75015), rue de Passy and rue de l'Annonciation (75016), **rue Poncelet**, **rue de Lévis** and rue de Tocqueville (75017), and rue de Belleville (75019).

Specialised markets – Flea markets: Porte de Vanves (75014), Ⓜ Porte-de-Vanves, weekends from 7am to 7.30pm; Porte de Clignancourt (75018), Ⓜ Porte-de-Clignancourt, Sat-Mon from 8am to 6pm; and Porte de Montreuil (75020), Ⓜ Porte-de-Montreuil, Sat-Mon from 8am to 6pm.

Flower markets: place Louis-Lépine (75004), Ⓜ Cité, daily except Sun 8am-7pm; place de la Madeleine (75008), Ⓜ Madeleine, daily except Sun 8am-7.30pm; place des Ternes (75017), Ⓜ Ternes, daily except Mon 8am-7.30pm.

Bird market: place Louis-Lépine (75004), Ⓜ Cité, Sun 8am-7pm.

Book market: parc Georges-Brassens (75015 entrance along rue Brancion), Ⓜ Porte de Vanves, weekends.

Stamp market: Carré Marigny (75008 on the corner of avenue Marigny and avenue Gabriel), Ⓜ Champs-Élysées-Clémenceau, Thu, weekends and holidays 9am-7pm.

Art market (Marché parisien de la Création): boulevard Edgar-Quinet (75014), Ⓜ Montparnasse or Edgar-Quinet, Sun 10am-7pm.

Clothes and leather market: Carreau du Temple (75003), Ⓜ Temple or Arts-et-Métiers, daily except Mon 9am-noon, Sat 9am-6pm.

Department stores

Galeries Lafayette de Paris, 40 boulevard Haussmann, 75008 Paris, Ⓜ Chaussée-d'Antin, ☎ 01 42 82 34 56, www.galerieslafayette.com; daily 9.30am-7pm (Thu 9pm).

Printemps, 64 boulevard Haussmann, 75008 Paris, Ⓜ Havre-Caumartin, RER Auber, ☎ 01 42 82 50 00, www.printemps.fr; daily 9.35am-7pm (Thu 10pm).

Le Bon Marché, 24 rue de Sèvres, 75007 Paris, Ⓜ Sèvres-Babylone, ☎ 01 44 39 80 00; daily 9.30am-7pm (Thu 9pm, Sat 8pm).

La Samaritaine, 19 rue de la Monnaie, 75001 Paris, Ⓜ Pont-Neuf, ☎ 01 40 41 20 20; daily 9.30pm-7pm (Thu 10pm).

Le Bazar de l'Hôtel-de-Ville, 55 rue de la Verrerie, 75004 Paris, Ⓜ Hôtel-de-Ville, ☎ 01 42 74 90 00, www.bhv.fr; daily 9.30am-7pm (Wed and Sat 8.30pm).

Shopping centres

Carrousel du Louvre, 75001 Paris, Ⓜ Palais-Royal, ☎ 01 43 16 47 10; more than 30 boutiques selling high-quality products sometimes connected with the museum.

Centre commercial Maine-Montparnasse, place du 18-juin-1940, 75014 Paris, Ⓜ Gare Montparnasse; multi-level complex with some 60 fashion boutiques are grouped round larger shops such as Galeries Lafayette, C & A and Habitat.

Les Trois Quartiers, 23 boulevard de la Madeleine, 75008 Paris, Ⓜ Madeleine; Mon-Sat 10am-7pm; luxury shops (fashion, jewellery, household goods, sport...).

There is a selection of individual boutiques in the Sights section (blue-bordered pages).

Bouquinistes' stalls

The *bouquinistes'* dark-green boxes lining the embankment on both sides of the river (between Pont du Carrousel and Pont de la Tournelle) form part of Paris' cityscape, their lids propped up to reveal odd collections of second-hand books and prints; among the tattered volumes and the suspiciously new-looking ones, it is still possible to find a genuinely old leather-bound copy of one of the French classics... Arm yourself with patience!

Discovering Paris

'If you are lucky enough to have lived in Paris as a young man, then wherever you go for the rest of your life, it stays with you, for Paris is a moveable feast'
Ernest Hemingway to a friend, 1950.

FOR A VIRTUAL TOUR...

If you would like to dream ahead, or to plan your own walk around Paris, there are some web sites to help you: **parisbalades.com** covers a lot of ground, and has especially good information about architecture from all periods with links to the museums of Paris and other useful sites; **pariswalkabout.com** offers a selection of guided tours through different neighbourhoods with well-qualified group leaders, and includes wine-tasting stops. Put on your travelling shoes!

IN A HURRY?

If, alas, you only have a few days to spend in Paris, here are our suggestions for discovering the best of the city in a minimum of time.

The musts

Tour Eiffel – One of the most famous monuments in the world affording superb views of the city.

Triumphal Way – Vista extending from the Arche de la Défense to the Arc de Triomphe then on to the Concorde along the Champs-Élysées, right through to the Louvre.

Louvre Museum – One of the largest and most prestigious European art collections in the world from Antiquity to 1850.

Invalides and Army Museum – Masterpiece of 17C architecture housing Napoleon's tomb.

Orsay Museum and Faubourg St-Germain – 19C and 20C national art collections (including Impressionist painting) housed in a former 19C railway station surrounded by elegant 18C mansions.

Île de la Cité and banks of the Seine – Notre-Dame and Sainte-Chapelle, two jewels of Gothic architecture in the historic centre of Paris.

Montmartre Hill – Crowned by the Sacré-Coeur Basilica, it symbolises the 19C artistic world and bohemian life.

Latin Quarter – Lively students' district.

Le Marais and its museums – One of the oldest districts of Paris, tastefully restored: Musée Picasso, Musée Carnavalet, Musée d'Art et d'Histoire du Judaïsme etc.

Centre Georges Pompidou and Beaubourg district – The futuristic National Museum of Modern Art in the heart of one of the capital's oldest districts.

Rue du Faubourg-St-Honoré, Madeleine, Opéra Garnier – Luxury boutiques and imposing buildings.

La Villette, Cité des sciences et de l'industrie – Fascinating interactive museum complex.

Trocadéro and Alma district – Wide avenues lined with fashion boutiques and a wealth of museums (Musée des Arts Asiatiques-Guimet, Musée d'Art Moderne de la Ville de Paris, Musée de la Marine).

Make up your own itinerary from the list above or follow one of the itineraries suggested below.

In four days

1. Morning: Notre-Dame, the banks of the Seine, Sainte-Chapelle.

Afternoon: Louvre (closed Tue), Tuileries (lunch in the museum or in the gardens); a stroll around place Vendôme, La Madeleine, Concorde and to the Opéra Garnier.

2. Morning: Quartier Latin / Luxembourg, Musée d'Orsay (closed Mon).

Afternoon: La Villette (closed Mon), lunch at the Café de la Musique, Montmartre in the evening.

3. Morning: Versailles Château (closed Mon), park and gardens (bring a picnic or eat at the restaurant by the Grand Canal).

Return to town in the afternoon via the RER, get off at Alma station, and enjoy a river tour aboard a bateau-mouche.

4. Morning: place des Vosges and the Marais, Centre Pompidou (closed Tue – lunch in the museum or in the neighbourhood).

Afternoon: Invalides, Tour Eiffel, Trocadéro, Champs-Élysées.

In two days

1. Morning: Notre-Dame, Les Quais, Sainte-Chapelle.

Afternoon: Louvre (closed Tue) or the Orsay Museum (closed Mon), walk through the Tuileries Gardens and on to place de la Concorde, Champs-Élysées, Eiffel Tower.

2. Morning: Le Marais, place des Vosges, Centre Pompidou (closed Tue).

Afternoon: Boat tour starting from Pont Neuf, Latin Quarter, Luxembourg Gardens. Take the metro at Notre-Dame-des-Champs (line 12) to Montmartre to finish the evening.

VISITING MUSEUMS AND MONUMENTS

Detailed descriptions of Paris' museums are found in the Sights section, while the admission times and charges are in a separate section following, with museums and other sights listed in alphabetical order.

There is no admission charge for museums owned by the city of Paris (the catacombs are an exception). Admission to state-owned museums and historic monuments is free for travellers with special needs, such as the handicapped – as well as those accompanying them – but the rules require that you show an identification card. In practice, foreign visitors accompanying handicapped individuals may or may not benefit from this advantage, as the application of discounts to foreign visitors is not always made. There are currently debates in the EU about standardising policies. Admission is free for all visitors on the first Sunday in every month.

In Paris, national museums and art galleries are closed on Tuesdays; municipal museums are generally closed on Mondays.

Carte Musées-Monuments

This is a Museums and Monuments Pass that allows free access, without queueing, to 70 museums and monuments in the capital. It may be purchased at participating museums and monuments, main metro stations, FNAC shops, the Office du Tourisme de Paris, the Espace du Tourisme Île-de-France (Carrousel du Louvre), at Batobus stops or from travel agents before leaving home. Cost: 15€, 30€ or 45€ for 1, 3 and 5 days respectively. Information is available from Association InterMusées, 4 rue Brantôme, 75003 Paris, ☏ 01 44 61 96 60; www.intermusees.com.

Guided tours

Guided tours of monuments, districts and exhibitions are organised by the following organisations:

Centre des monuments nationaux – Service visites-conférences, 7 boulevard Morland, 75004, ☏ 01 44 54 19 30/35. Open weekdays from 9am to noon and 2pm to 6pm (to 5pm on Fridays).

Association pour la Sauvegarde et la mise en valeur du Paris historique – 44-46 rue François-Miron, 75004, ☏ 01 48 87 74 31. Open daily 2pm to 6pm. www.chez.com/parishistorique

Paris et son Histoire – 82 rue Taitbout, 75009, ☏ 01 45 26 26 77 or 01 45 26 16 14.

Fédération pour la connaissance de Paris et le rayonnement du Tourisme – 21 rue du Repos, 75020, ☏ 01 43 70 70 87.

Fédération internationale de Tourisme culturel – 78 av. des Champs-Elysées, 75008, ☏ 01 42 25 41 27 (on request only).

Ecoute du Passé – 77 av. de St-Mandé, 75012, ☏ 01 43 44 49 86 or 01 42 82 11 81.

Communautés d'accueil dans les sites artistiques – ☏ 01 42 34 56 10; www.cathedralede-paris.com. Free guided tours.

These guided tours, which are on offer on a daily basis in Paris, are publicised in weekly entertainment guides (such as Pariscope), and are also listed on Web sites such as The Paris Pages, Paris-Anglophone and Bienvenu sur Pariscope. You can also find them posted at the entrance to the monuments themselves.

For children

⊚ This symbol is intended to draw attention to the sights and museums listed in this guide that are particularly suitable for children.

Some museums propose supervised educational activities such as quizzes and treasure hunts, whereas workshops give children the opportunity to try out artistic techniques for themselves. These sessions are generally held on Wednesdays and during school holidays and last between one and three hours.

Looking for something in particular?

(see the index for the page number)

Art

Antiquities: Louvre; Musée de Cluny; Musée de l'Homme; Arènes de Lutèce.

Painting: Louvre; Musée d'Orsay; Musée National d'Art Moderne; Centre Georges Pompidou; Château de Versailles; Musée d'Art Moderne de la Ville de Paris (Palais de Tokyo); Musée Carnavalet; Musée Picasso; Musée Marmottan-Monet; Musée Maillol; Musée du Petit Palais; Musée Gustave-Moreau; Musée Eugène-Delacroix; Musée Henner; Musée Hébert; Musée de l'Orangerie; Musée de Montmartre; Musée d'Art naïf Max-Fourny.

Sculpture: Louvre; Notre-Dame de Paris; Musée d'Orsay; Basilique St-Denis; Musée des Monuments Français; Musée Rodin; Musée Maillol; Musée Bourdelle; Musée Bouchard; Musée Zadkine; Espace Dali; Fontaine Stravinski; Jardin des Tuileries.

Literature: Maison de Balzac; Maison de Victor Hugo; Musée de la Vie Romantique; Musée Adam-Mickiewicz.

Furniture: Louvre; Musée de Cluny; Musée des Arts Décoratifs; Musée Cognacq-Jay; Musée Jacquemart-André; Musée Nissim de Camondo; Hôtel de Soubise; Faubourg St-Antoine; Mobilier National (Gobelins).

Tapestries: Louvre; Musée de Cluny; Musée Nissim de Camondo; Manufacture des Gobelins.

Silver, Glass and China: Château de Vincennes; Musée Baccarat; Musée Bouilhet-Christofle; Petit Musée de l'Argenterie Insolite.

Fashion: Musée des Arts Décoratifs; Musée de la Mode et du Costume; Faubourg St-Honoré; Musée des Lunettes et des Lorgnettes; Musée de l'Éventail; Musée Fragonard; Musée de la Contrefaçon.

Music: Musée de l'Opéra-Garnier; Cité de la Musique.

Ethnic: Musée des Arts asiatiques-Guimet; Musée de l'Homme; Musée Cernuschi; Institut du Monde Arabe; Musée Dapper; Musée Arménien; Musée d'Ennery; Centre Bouddhique du Bois de Vincennes; Musée d'Art et d'Histoire du Judaïsme.

Science

Natural History: Musée d'Histoire Naturelle, Jardin des Plantes.

Astronomy: Palais de la Découverte; Musée des Arts et Métiers; l'Observatoire; La Villette Planetarium.

Medicine: Hôpital Militaire du Val-de-Grâce; La Salpêtrière; Musée de l'Assistance Publique; Institut Pasteur; Musée des Moulages de l'Hôpital Saint-Louis.

Mineralogy: École Supérieure des Mines; Musée de Minéralogie; Galerie de Minéralogie.

Technology: Cité des Sciences et de l'Industrie; Palais de la Découverte; Musée National des Techniques; Musée Marie-Curie.

WALKING TOURS

These tours are mapped out on pages 12-13.

1 Royal Paris **Start from the Étoile (place Charles-de-Gaulle)**

Begin by admiring the view from atop the Arc de Triomphe, down the Champs-Élysées and into the Tuileries Gardens. Beyond the palace, the Île de la Cité is the oldest part of Paris, and the site of some of its most beautiful monuments: the Conciergerie, Notre-Dame, La Sainte-Chapelle.

2 Le Marais **Start from place de la Bastille**

This walk takes you through the centuries from the Middle Ages to the golden age of the monarchy and into modern Paris. From beautiful Renaissance town houses to the stunning contemporary architecture of the Pompidou Centre, from the sublime symmetry of place des Vosges to the adventurous art of Pablo Picasso, this neighbourhood is always lively and entertaining.

3 Classicism and world fairs **Start from Les Invalides**

Monumental inspiration is the order of the day as you stroll by the sumptuously restored Musée d'Orsay and the Palais Bourbon on the riverside, or cross the elaborate Pont Alexandre III to the Grand and Petit Palais. Continue to Trocadéro, where the view reveals curving flights of stone stairs and a cascade of fountains and pools leading to the river. Directly in front of you rises Paris' most unmissable tower, a long swathe of green park stretching out behind it.

4 Montmartre **Start from place Pigalle**

Little streets twist upwards past the local vineyard, leading you from the noise and neon of naughty Pigalle to the village-like quiet of old Montmartre. Although there is always a crowd of tourists around the Sacré-Coeur and place du Tertre, the view from the steps in front of the church is memorable.

5 St-Germain-des-Prés **Start from St-Germain-des-Prés**

The church, the Café des Deux Magots and the Café de Flore make a cosy corner of town where the literary are wont to gather. The pedestrian Pont des Arts is a favourite bridge for painting and contemplation; you can also watch the world go by from a chair in the beautiful Luxembourg Gardens. Thus restored, you are ready to face the hubbub of the Montparnasse district, its shops, restaurants and cinemas.

6 Latin Quarter **Start from Luxembourg Gardens**

This neighbourhood has long been the favoured haunt of students, and the atmosphere is appropriately animated. All kinds of shops and restaurants attract visitors, and there are plenty of historic places to discover too, such as the Cluny Museum, the Panthéon, the Jardin des Plantes and its natural history collections.

⁊ The river banks **Start from Sully-Morland**

Wander from one bank of the Seine to the other, discover the islands at the heart of the city's history and complete your tour at the modern marina by the Bastille.

⑧ Passy/Bois de Boulogne **Start from the Bois de Boulogne**

For a change of pace from the busy city centre, head for the woods and soothe your spirit with a visit to the Marmottan-Monet Museum, where Claude Monet's inspired paintings of the flowers in his garden are like so many rays of sunshine. On your way home stop to see Balzac's house and the Musée du Vin.

⑨ Fashionable Paris **Start from place Vendôme**

If your money is burning a hole in your pocket, or if you like to dream in front of elegant shop window displays, don your finery and play millionaire on avenue Montaigne and faubourg St-Honoré… before heading for the big department stores around the Opéra to pick up something special to take home.

⑩ Paris at play **Start from St-Germain-l'Auxerrois**

Walk along the Grands Boulevards to see what Parisians are up to, the films they're watching, the singers they prefer. Some of the covered passages in this neighbourhood seem to be lost in the 19C, with their charming shops and tearooms. But you'll have no doubts about the date when you reach the Forum des Halles. Young people gather here to scour the shops and enjoy the street theatre.

⑪ The River Seine **Start from the Eiffel Tower or the Pont Neuf**

And why not make this tour aboard a boat? It is delightful to cruise below the distinctive bridges of Paris and to admire the many prestigious buildings on the waterfront. Rain or shine, day or night, this is a trip that everyone can enjoy.

THEMATIC VISITS

Historic Paris

Ancient Paris – The oldest part of Paris, historically speaking, includes the **île de la Cité** (place Dauphine, Palais de Justice, Sainte-Chapelle, Conciergerie) and the **Marais** (place des Vosges, rue des Francs-Bourgeois lined with fine mansions, a wealth of museums).

Monumental Paris – This itinerary includes two magnificent vistas: one encompasses the Trocadéro, the Eiffel Tower, the Champ de Mars and the École Militaire next to the Invalides, the other extends from Tuileries Gardens and place de la Concorde along the Champs-Élysées to the Arc de Triomphe; the River Seine provides an inspiring link between the two!

Right-bank Paris – The right bank is dominated by the extensive buildings of the Louvre. Just north across rue de Rivoli is the Palais-Royal and its peaceful gardens. To the west is avenue de l'Opéra heading towards the Opéra Garnier, rue de la Paix and place Vendôme home to prestigious jewellery shops, rue St-Honoré and rue Royale, lined with leading fashion houses, and the Madeleine. From there, metro line 12 will take you directly to Lamarck-Caulaincourt station at the foot of Montmartre hill. As a reward for climbing to the top, you will enjoy a superb view from the Sacré Coeur Basilica.

Left-bank Paris – Strolling through the Odéon, St-Germain-des-Prés and St-Sulpice districts then across Luxembourg Gardens to the south, you will get the feel of the left-bank atmosphere. Further east stand the Panthéon and the Sorbonne overlooking the Latin Quarter. At the heart of this lively university district, the Musée de Cluny takes visitors on a delightful journey back to medieval times. Heading west along the embankment, you will walk past the *bouquinistes*' stalls displaying second-hand books and old prints. Walk as far as the Musée d'Orsay for fine views of the right-bank monuments including the Louvre.

Riverside Paris

Along the Seine – The river banks are the favourite haunt of Parisians in summer and winter alike. They like to stroll along past lovers oblivious to the world around them, musicians who practise their instruments, unperturbed by onlookers, and anglers convinced that the Seine abounds with fish. Many strollers browse through the old books and prints displayed on the *bouquinistes*' stalls, hoping to find a rare copy or manuscript, although they know it is most unlikely nowadays.

Right bank – The Voie Express Georges Pompidou carries fast-flowing traffic from west to east along the river, through the city centre and past the capital's most prestigious monuments. Walk east along the embankment lined with *bouquinistes'* stalls from quai du Louvre to quai de Gesvres, then continue along quai de l'Hôtel-de-Ville and quai des Célestins for fine views of Île Saint-Louis and its mansions.

Around île Saint-Louis – Quai de Bourbon and quai d'Anjou running along the northern edge of the island offer a peaceful stroll past elegant 17C mansions full of old-world charm. Anyone venturing along rue Saint-Louis-en-l'île finds it hard to resist Berthillon's delicious ice cream! From quai de Béthune and quai d'Orléans, the east end of Notre-Dame looks breathtakingly lovely and Pont Louis-Philippe affords a beautiful view of the Panthéon.

Left bank – The bouquinistes' familiar dark-green boxes line the embankment from Pont du Carrousel to Pont de la Tournelle. Admire the view up and down river from Pont des Arts (restricted to pedestrians) then walk down to the river's edge away from the noise and bustle to take in the splendid view of the Pont Neuf with the twin towers of Notre-Dame beyond. The busy place St-Michel is the favourite meeting place of young people in the Latin Quarter; take time to wander through the nearby narrow streets, past the Flamboyant Gothic church of St-Séverin and the quaint Shakespeare & Company bookshop. Back to the river, walk along the water's edge by Pont au Double to admire the south side of Notre-Dame and the charming square Jean-XXIII.

Around the Paris-Arsenal marina – Green terraces, floating gangways and colourful sailing boats in the heart of the capital... Get a glimpse of this unusual scene from the platform of the Bastille metro station.

Along the Canal St-Martin – Dainty metallic footbridges spanning the canal at regular intervals, barges negotiating the locks and anglers lost in their thoughts form the peaceful setting of the Canal St-Martin linking the Bassin de la Villette and the Paris-Arsenal marina.

Fashion and luxury

Paris is generally acknowledged as the capital of fashion. Fashion houses and luxury boutiques are located in well-defined areas.

On the right bank: south of the Champs-Élysées, along avenue Montaigne, avenue George-V, avenue Marceau and rue François-I (fashion houses); along rue du Faubourg St-Honoré leading to place Vendôme and rue de la Paix (fashion, jewellery); place des Victoires, rue des Francs-Bourgeois and place des Vosges (fashion boutiques); department stores along boulevard Haussmann, around the Madeleine (Old England, Madelios, Les Trois Quartiers); rue de Rivoli (department stores and boutiques).

On the left bank: Le Bon Marché (department store) along rue de Sèvres and boutiques along rue du Bac, rue du Dragon, rue des Saints-Pères, rue du Vieux Colombier, rue du Cherche-Midi, rue du Four, rue de Rennes and rue Bonaparte leading to boulevard Saint-Germain.

Unusual Paris

Some districts have retained their old-world charm and atmosphere: Montmartre hill with its vineyard and windmill, Canal St-Martin and its metallic footbridges, rue des Rosiers in the Marais, the St-Séverin Quarter near place St-Michel....

Other districts, on the contrary, look so modern that they stand out against the traditional Parisian townscape: the Beaugrenelle district along the Seine (15th *arrondissement*), place de Catalogne (14th *arrondissement*) and La Défense.

Some museums and monuments can also be termed unusual: Musée de la Curiosité et de la Magie (Marais district), Musée Cernuschi (Parc Monceau), Cathédrale St-Alexandre-Nevski (Monceau), Musée du Vin (Passy), Les Catacombes (Denfert-Rochereau), the Paris sewers (Alma).

Green Paris

Parks and gardens

Paris has evolved into a city of trees and flowers, boasting almost 400 parks, public and private gardens, little squares, and, of course, its two vast stretches of woodland (Bois de Boulogne and Bois de Vincennes – 846 and 995 hectares respectively) where lakes and waterfalls complement fountains and ponds.
A new style of urban landscape gardening has been developed integrating water, stone, glass and varieties of plants that appeal to all the senses. These are places to stroll, relax, play, feed the birds, read, have lunch and a gossip or enjoy a bit of peace and quiet.
Thanks to its varied landscape of woods, parks and gardens, Paris allows a surprising diversity of flora and fauna to thrive in the very heart of this urban metropolis. Who would have thought that rare wildlife such as the hedge sparrow could be present in even the smallest of the capital's parks?

Wrens, chaffinches and tits can be heard singing in spring, whereas the swift's song resounds in the summer sky. After dusk, some 20 pairs of tawny owls are known to wing their way through the Parisian night, and many of the city's monuments, including Notre-Dame, are home to the kestrel.

In Paris' streets and gardens grows a whole variety of trees: planes, chestnuts and maples, as well as ash and elms, among others, whereas in the parks grow paulownias, cedrelas, gingkgoes, walnut and tulip trees.

Some of the gardens provide a setting for a range of temporary or year-round exhibitions: flower shows, classic car-meets, classical and avant-garde artwork (for information, ☎ 01 42 76 50 00, or contact the local town hall).

Here is a list, with metro stations, of some of the nicest parks in town:

Bagatelle (Ⓜ Sablons) for its irises and rose garden; the botanical gardens and greenhouses of the **Jardin des Plantes** (Ⓜ Jussieu); **Parc Montsouris** (Ⓜ Cité Universitaire) and the **Square des Batignolles** (Ⓜ Brochant) with their English-style gardens; the most picturesque of the landscaped parks, the **Buttes-Chaumont** (Ⓜ Buttes-Chaumont); the calm, elegant **Palais-Royal** Gardens (Ⓜ Palais-Royal); the **Unesco** Japanese Gardens (Ⓜ Cambronne); the cherry trees in the gardens of the university halls of residence (Ⓜ Cité Universitaire). The **Luxembourg Gardens** (Ⓜ Luxembourg, Port Royal, Rennes) where courting couples and students from the Latin Quarter come to relax in the sunshine; the gardens of the **Rodin Museum** (Ⓜ Varenne) where a visit to the museum can be prolonged to take in its outdoor sculpture exhibition and the spectacular view of the dome of Les Invalides; Parc **Monceau** whose wrought-iron gates open on to a collection of statues of Musset, Maupassant and Chopin (Ⓜ Monceau); the botanical **Auteuil** Greenhouses and, just next to them, the Poets' Garden where you can wander among the memorials engraved with famous lines written by some of France's greatest poets (Ⓜ Porte d'Auteuil); the sophisticated Parc André-Citroën gardens complete with hi-tech glasshouses (Ⓜ Javel); the **Parc Georges-Brassens** with its grassy slopes, vineyard and beehives in the heart of a quiet urban district (Ⓜ Porte de Vanves); and the largest park in Paris *intra-muros*, **Parc de la Villette**, dotted with futuristic buildings (Ⓜ Porte de la Villette/Porte de Pantin).

As if this wealth of greenery were not enough, several new parks have sprung up on the cityscape in recent years: the magnificent **Parc de Bercy** (12th arr.); the **Jardin de l'Atlantique** (15th arr.) laid out on a huge concrete slab over the tracks of Gare Montparnasse; the **Promenade along boulevard Richard-Lenoir** (11th arr.); the **Promenade plantée** from Bastille to the Vincennes woods; meanwhile the **Tuileries Gardens** (1st arr.) have been restored to their former glory.

Vineyards – The area occupied by vineyards in the Île de France region as a whole remained considerable until the 18C and, even today, Paris boasts nine vineyards producing red and white wines. The most interesting are listed below.

Montmartre – Rue des Saules, 75018; Ⓜ Lamarck-Caulaincourt. This is the oldest vineyard in Paris since it was originally planted during the Gallo-Roman period. Today it consists of 1 762 vines which can yield up to 1 000kg/2 205lb of grapes. The harvest is always a festive occasion.

Parc de Belleville – Rue des Couronnes, rue Piat, rue Julien-Lacroix or rue Jouye-Rouve 75020; Ⓜ Couronnes. This slightly more recent vineyard, dating from the Carolingian period, consists of only 140 vines tucked away inside the Parc de Belleville.

Jardin du Luxembourg

Parc Georges-Brassens – Rue des Morillons, rue des Périchaux or rue Brancion 75015; Ⓜ Porte-de-Vanves. The southern part of Vaugirard village was still covered with vineyards in the 18C; 700 vines were planted inside the park in 1983 and the first harvest took place in 1985.

Parc de Bercy – 41 rue Paul-Belmondo, 75012; Ⓜ Cour Saint-Émilion. The Bercy cellars were once famous; this long-standing tradition is perpetuated by 350 vines producing some 250 litres!

The **Musée du Vin** is situated in a quiet street of the 16th *arrondissement (see Passy)*.

FROM ANOTHER ANGLE

Paris by night

The city is floodlit throughout the year from nightfall (between 5.15pm and 9.20pm according to the season) to midnight, (1am on Saturdays, the eve of bank holidays and during the summer months). The fountains are turned off during the cold weather from 1 January to 1 April.

As the sky darkens, the bright monuments imbue the city with glamorous splendour. Architectural contours, the details of fountains and sculptures are picked out by an interplay of highlight and deep shadow. At Christmas, the city sparkles and glistens with sequins of brightness; the Champs-Élysées, avenue Montaigne, rue Royale or boulevard Haussmann take on a magical quality with trees and shop windows decked in seasonal lights.

On foot or by car, the main sights line the **banks of the Seine**: place de la Concorde with its two fountains; the **Champs-Élysées** climbing up to the **Arc de Triomphe**; **Cour Napoléon** and **Pei's Pyramid** which, together with the majestic walls of the Louvre are reflected in the rippling waters of the flat fountains; place André-Malraux and the arcades fronting the **Comédie-Française**; the area around the abbey of **Saint-Germain-des-Prés** although not as white as the limestone of the **Sacré-Cœur**, takes on a paler hue beneath the lights; the **Invalides** with its striking gilded dome; **Notre-Dame** which is even more impressive when the floodlights of the river boats pick out the exquisite detail of its sculpted façade, and the **Esplanade du Palais de Chaillot** from which there is a wonderful view of the Champ-de-Mars and the École Militaire, while fountains play below in the **Trocadéro** Gardens. On the other bank of the Seine, stop directly underneath the **Eiffel Tower** to gaze upward at the latticed ironwork, monumental and yet surprisingly delicate.

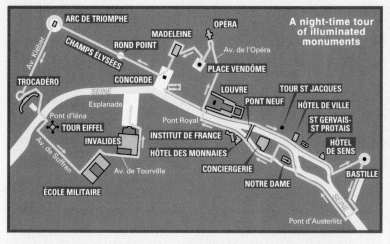

Paris for pedestrians

See the map of walking tours at the beginning of the guide and their description above. Paris' neighbourhoods *(quartiers)* are perhaps best explored on foot. In addition to the tours mapped at the beginning of this book and in certain neighbourhoods, you may want to try the two signposted walks that cross Paris: one from east to west, from the Bois de Boulogne to the Bois de Vincennes, the other from north to south, from Porte de la Villette to Parc Montsouris. Each of these routes totals about 20km/12mi. Detailed information about walks in Paris is provided in *Paris à pied*, a guide published by the **Fédération française de randonnée pédestre**, 14 rue Riquet 75019, ☎ 01 44 89 93 90. **Moveable Feast** offers three regular guided walks entitled Paris is a Woman, The Medieval Soul of Paris and The Belly of Paris in English in the summer months. ☎ 06 66 92 34 12 or visit www.moveablefeast.com.

Paris by bus

The bus is another excellent means of exploring Paris. There are several different tourist buses and coaches (with or without commentary), and, alternatively, Parisian RATP buses. Riding the regular transportation system is a good way to see historic Paris in the company of the locals, for only a modest sum of money.

Balabus crosses Paris from east to west, from Gare de Lyon to La Défense. (*Balabus Bb* is indicated on bus stops). The buses only run on Sundays and public holidays, from the last Sunday in April to the last Sunday in September, between 1.30pm and 8pm.

Montmartobus takes you on a tour around Montmartre between the town hall of the 18th *arrondissement* and place Pigalle. Standard bus fare.

Les cars rouges (Parisbus) – ☎ 01 53 95 39 53.
– **Stops**: Eiffel Tower, Champ-de-Mars, the Louvre, Notre-Dame, Musée d'Orsay, Opéra, Champs-Elysées-Etoile, Grand Palais, Trocadéro. Bus tour with running commentary.
– **Duration**: 2hr 15min for the complete circuit, although it is possible to get on or off at any stop on the route.
– **Prices**: 21€/adult, 10€/child. Tickets can be bought on the bus and are valid for two consecutive days.
– **Departure**: every 20min from the Eiffel Tower, starting at 9.45am.

Paris-Vision Plus – 214 rue de Rivoli, 75001, Ⓜ Tuileries. ☎ 01 42 60 86 00; www.parisvision.com. Tour of the city aboard an 8-seater minibus which collects you from and takes you back to your hotel.

Les cars rouges

Cityrama – 4 place des Pyramides, 75001, Ⓜ Pyramides. ☎ 01 44 55 61 00. Tour of the city aboard panoramic buses.

L'Open Tour – 13 rue Auber, 75009, Ⓜ Opéra or Havre-Caumartin. ☎ 01 42 66 56 56. Designated stops are marked "OpenTour".

Paris grand tour: starting at 13 rue Auber, via Opéra, the Louvre, Notre-Dame, the Luxembourg Gardens, Musée d'Orsay, place de la Concorde, the Champs-Elysées, the Arc de Triomphe and Trocadéro, La Madeleine (every 10 to 20min; duration: 2hr 15min).

Montmartre – Tour of romantic Paris; the bus stops near the Sacré Coeur Basilica (every 10 to 30min; duration: 1hr 15min).

Bastille-Bercy – Tour of modern Paris starting from Notre-Dame, then on to place de la Bastille, Gare de Lyon, Parc de Bercy (every 30min; duration: 1hr).
Commentary in English and French.

Price: 26€/adult for two consecutive days or 24€ for one day, 12€/child. The "Pass OpenTour" can be bought on the coach or from the stands situated at the Malesherbes and Anvers stops.

RATP buses

Like all forms of public transport, Parisian buses – depending to some extent on the line – can be slightly unpredictable in terms of punctuality and comfort: they can get extremely crowded so it is best to avoid rush hours if possible. Nonetheless, the bus remains an excellent way to see Paris. All bus trips in Paris and the immediate suburbs require one ticket (no transfers). These are the same as the tickets used in the metro, and you can save money by buying a pass *(see p 24)* or a book of 10 tickets ahead of time. On board the bus, you can buy tickets individually from the driver, at a higher price.

Line 21 (Gare St-Lazare – Porte-de-Gentilly) – Opéra, Palais-Royal, the Louvre, then along the Seine, before crossing the river towards the Latin Quarter and Luxembourg Gardens.

Line 52 (Opéra – Pont-de-St-Cloud) – Madeleine, place de la Concorde, the Rond-Point des Champs-Elysées, the Eglise St-Philippe-du-Roule, the Arc de Triomphe, avenue Victor-Hugo, rue de la Pompe and Auteuil.

Line 72 (Pont-de-St-Cloud – Hôtel-de-Ville) – the right bank of the Seine: Alma-Marceau, the Grand Palais, place de la Concorde, Palais-Royal, the Louvre, Place du Châtelet and the Hôtel de Ville.

Line 73 (La Défense – Musée d'Orsay) – Place de l'Etoile, the Champs-Elysées, place de la Concorde and the Musée d'Orsay.

Line 82 (Luxembourg – Pont-de-Neuilly-Hôpital Américain) – Round the magnificent Luxembourg Gardens before heading towards Montparnasse, Les Invalides, the Ecole Militaire and the Eiffel Tower. The bus crosses avenue Victor-Hugo and avenue Foch before reaching Porte Maillot and continuing on to Neuilly.

Line 92 (Gare Montparnasse – Porte de Champerret) – Via Les Invalides, the Ecole Militaire, Alma-Marceau, place de l'Etoile, Wagram and place du Maréchal-Juin.
Line 96 (Gare Montparnasse – Porte-des-Lilas) – The St-Sulpice area, Odéon, the Latin Quarter, Île de la Cité, Châtelet-Hôtel de Ville, the Marais and finally Belleville.
In good weather, The RATP brings a few platform buses out of retirement. You can stand out back in the open air **(lines 29 and 56)**.

Paris by bicycle… or on rollerblades

Paris has some 230km/138mi of cycle lanes and many more are currently under construction due to a concern for cyclists' safety.
A north-south axis links the cycle path at Canal de l'Ourcq and place de la Bataille-de-Stalingrad to Porte de Vanves. Another, running from east to west joins the Bois de Vincennes and the Bois de Boulogne, both of which have a network of cycle paths complete with signposts. A cycle track around the circumference of Paris is currently being built; a sort of ring-road for cyclists!
Designated areas where cyclists can leave their bikes are dotted around the capital; the French railway SNCF facilitates the free entry of bikes on the RER lines B, C and D, although only at particular times and in particular stations.
On Sundays, pedestrians and cyclists are given priority on certain roads:

– the roads which run parallel to the Seine from 9am to 5pm (quai des Tuileries, quai Henri-IV, quai Anatole-France and quai Branly);
– Canal St-Martin from 9am to 5pm (quai de Jemmapes, quai de Valmy);
– in the Mouffetard area from 10am to 6pm (place Marcelin-Berthelot, rue de Cluny, rue de l'Ecole Polytechnique, rue de Lanneau, rue Mouffetard, rue Descartes), the only drawback is that it is uphill!
You can also look in English publications such as the Paris Free Voice and FUSAC, available in many bookshops and restaurants, for information on guided bike tours of the city, or try the on-line magazine paris-anglo.com for rentals and tours or meeting points for informal clubs.

Cycling along the banks of the Seine

Remember: Parisian motorists do not always take much notice of cyclists even though, theoretically, both groups share the same status on the roads. It is therefore advisable to be extremely careful, especially of parked cars as inconsiderate drivers may open car doors without prior warning. Remember that all road-users, including cyclists, must adhere to the Highway Code. Always keep an eye on your bicycle – even if it is equipped with a padlock, detachable parts such as the saddle and the front wheel are easily stolen and re-sold.

Obligatory:
– Bell and lights.
– Use of designated parking areas.
– Wearing of a cycle helmet (soon to be a requisite).
– Use of cycle paths where they exist.

Bicycle hire
Below are some useful addresses; for further information, you can consult the *Paris à vélo* map, published by the **Mairie de Paris** and available from town halls and the **Office de Tourisme de Paris**. Always carry your passport with you, as it will be essential for hiring anything in Paris. A cycle helmet, basket and bike lock – and sometimes baby seats – are included in the price.

Paris à vélo, c'est sympa! – 37 bd Bourdon, 75004, Ⓜ Bastille. ☎ 01 48 87 60 01. www.parisvelosympa.com;12.50€ per day, tandem 25€ per day. Offers guided tours (26€ to 30€). Baby seats can be provided. Convenient location; reservation necessary.
Paris Vélo – 2 rue du Fer-à-Moulin, 75005, Ⓜ Censier-Daubenton. ☎ 01 43 37 59 22. 14€/day (10am to 7pm), 12€/half-day. 300€ deposit.
Bike 'n' Roller – 137 rue St-Dominique, 75007. Ⓜ Pont de l'Alma. ☎ 01 44 18 30 39. Bikes: 12€/half-day, 17€/day. Deposit required. Baby-seats available. Reservation recommended; Rollers: 9€/half day, 12€/day. Deposit required.
Roue libre (RATP) – 1 passage Mondétour, 75001 ☎ 08 10 44 15 34. Mon to Fri: 4.60€/day. Weekend and public holidays: 3.10€/hr, 7.60€/half day, 11.50€/day. Reservation and deposit required. Baby seats available. Bike hire is also available in the Bois de Boulogne, Bois de Vincennes, Bercy and Auteuil bus stations and at Châtelet (same prices).

Rollerblading in Paris

Every Friday evening a rollerblading rally takes place in Paris, following a different itinerary on each occasion. The event is overseen by policemen, themselves on rollerblades, who prevent the traffic accessing the roads used by the rollerbladers. Several thousand people now gather every week in front of the Gare Montparnasse, the starting point. Relaxed, fun atmosphere. A good way to meet people! Not suitable for beginners as a good breaking technique is essential. Contact **Pari Roller**, 33 rue de Tocqueville, 75017, ☎ 01 43 36 89 81; www.pari-roller.com.

Roller skating tours

Rollers et Coquillages, 75004, Ⓜ Bastille. ☎ 01 44 54 94 42. www.rollers-coquillages.org. Meeting on Sundays at 2.30pm in front of 37 boulevard Bourdon. Duration: 3hr. For beginners and experienced skaters; the itinerary is different on each occasion.

Rollers Squad Institut (RSI), 7 rue Jean-Giono, 75013, Ⓜ Quai-de-la-Gare. ☎ 01 56 61 99 61. www.rsi.asso.fr. Mon to Thu 10am-1pm and 2-6pm. This association organises various roller skating tours such as:
– **Rando skating initiation**: meeting point at Les Invalides in front of Pont Alexandre-III at 2.30pm on Sun. Duration: 2hr. Ability: beginners and competent skaters. Venue: the roads running parallel to the banks of the Seine.
Contact the association for information on other tours.
Skaters are accompanied by instructors with the recognised French Roller Skating Federation qualification.

Boat trips

Paris would not be Paris without its *bateaux-mouches*. These riverboats have become quite an institution. No visit is complete without taking in Notre-Dame, the Eiffel Tower, and the rest of the sights along the riverside from on board one of these now-legendary boats. Something of a Parisian cliché, but nonetheless an unforgettable experience

On the Seine

Bateaux-mouches: boarding point: Pont de l'Alma (Right Bank), 75008, Ⓜ Alma-Marceau. ☎ 01 42 25 96 10; Itinerary: from Pont de l'Alma to Notre-Dame.

Les Vedettes du Pont-Neuf: boarding point: square du Vert-Galant, 75001, Ⓜ Pont-Neuf. ☎ 01 46 33 98 38. Itinerary: from Pont-Neuf to Pont d'Iéna, including a circuit around Île de la Cité and Île St-Louis. Commentary. Duration: 1hr. Price: 9€/adult, 4.50€/child.

Les Bateaux parisiens: boarding point: Port de la Bourdonnais, 75007, RER Champs-de-Mars-Tour-Eiffel or Ⓜ Bir-Hakeim. ☎ 01 44 11 33 44.
Boarding point: quai de Montebello, opposite Notre-Dame (end March to early November), Metro/RER C Saint-Michel. ☎ 01 43 26 92 55. Duration: 1hr. Departures every 30min from 10am to 10pm from April to October; every hour from November to March.

Batobus: Port de la Bourdonnais, 75007, RER C Champs-de-Mars-Tour-Eiffel or Ⓜ Bir-Hakeim, ☎ 01 44 11 33 99. Stops: Eiffel Tower (Port de la Bourdonnais), Musée d'Orsay (quai de Solférino), St-Germain-des-Prés (quai Malaquais), Notre-Dame (quai de Montebello), Jardin des Plantes (quai St-Bernard), Hôtel de Ville (quai de l'Hôtel de Ville), Louvre (quai du Louvre), Champs-Elysées (Port des Champs-Elysées, near Pont Alexandre-III). Times: from mid-April to the beginning of November; from 10am to 7pm (9pm in June, July, August and September). Departures every 25min. 9.91€/adult and 5.34€/child for the day; 12.20€/adult and 6.10€/child for two days.

Canal St-Martin

Canauxrama: boarding point at Port de Plaisance-Paris-Arsenal, opposite no 50 boulevard de la Bastille, 75011, Ⓜ Bastille. Departure times: 9.45am and 2.30pm. Another boarding point at Bassin-de-la-Villette, 13 quai de la Loire, 75019, Ⓜ Jaurès. Departure times: 9.45am and 2.45pm. Reservation recommended by calling ☎ 01 42 39 15 00 or on-line: www.canauxrama.com. This 3hr barge trip takes you from Port de Plaisance to Parc de la Villette or vice versa, crossing four locks and two swing bridges. Commentary. 13€/adult, 8€/children under 12, free for children under 6 (Saturday and Sunday afternoons and public holidays: 13€/person).

Paris Canal: reservation essential, ☎ 01 42 40 96 97. Half-day cruise along the Seine in the centre of Paris (Louvre, Notre-Dame, Île Saint-Louis) and along Canal St-Martin: negotiating locks and swing bridges and navigating through a 2km/1.2mi-long tunnel beneath the Bastille. Two departures daily from mid-March to mid-November at 9.30am in front of the Musée d'Orsay (Ⓜ Solférino) and at 2.30pm from the Parc de la Villette (Ⓜ Porte-de-Pantin). Duration: 2hr 45min. Price: 16€ (children 9€).

Canal de l'Ourcq

Canauxrama – Reservation recommended by calling ☎ 01 42 39 15 00 or on-line: www.canauxrama.com. Departure from Paris-Arsenal marina, 75012, Ⓜ Bastille at 9am. All-day cruise to Bry-sur-Marne. Price: 33€/person. Not recommended for children.

Views

The Eiffel Tower is of course the place from which to view Paris, but by no means is it the only one. Here are some ideas of places which offer unexpectedly stunning views over the City of Light, by day or by night.

A few of our favourite perspectives…

View from Altitude 95,
restaurant on the Eiffel Tower

Here is the editors' informal selection of some of the prettiest views in town – all you have to do is find the right street corner:

Montmartre: from in front of the Sacré-Coeur, place Emile-Goudeau.

Belleville and Ménilmontant: from the summit of the Parc de Belleville, at the end of rue Piat.

The Butte-aux-Cailles: as you go down avenue des Gobelins to place d'Italie.

The Montagne Ste-Geneviève: rue Soufflot.

Passy: place du Trocadéro.

"Mont Parnasse": place des Cinq-Martyrs-du-Lycée-Buffon, place du 18-Juin-1940 (rue de Rennes as far as St-Germain-des-Prés).

Parvis de la Défense: looking towards Paris from the Grande Arche.

Favourite tourist views

Montparnasse Tower – Ⓜ Montparnasse-Bienvenüe *(see MONTPARNASSE).*

The Eiffel Tower – Ⓜ Bir-Hakeim *(see Tour EIFFEL).*

The Arc de Triomphe – Ⓜ Charles-de-Gaulle-Etoile *(see Les CHAMPS-ÉLYSÉES).*

Notre-Dame (towers) – Ⓜ Cité *(see Cathédrale NOTRE-DAME).*

Panthéon (upper parts) – RER Luxembourg *(see Quartier Latin).*

Georges-Pompidou Centre (5th floor terrace) – Ⓜ Rambuteau or Hôtel-de-Ville or RER Châtelet-Les Halles. ☎ 01 44 78 12 33. Museum and exhibitions: daily from 11am to 9pm (last admission 1hr before closing). Closed Tuesdays. Access to the terrace requires a ticket to the museum or to an exhibition.

Sacré-Coeur (dome) – Ⓜ Anvers or Abesses *(see MONTMARTRE).*

La Samaritaine (terrace of shop no. 2) – Ⓜ Louvre-Rivoli. Daily (except Sunday) from 9.30am to 7pm (10pm on Thursdays). 2€.

Printemps – Ⓜ Havre-Caumartin. Daily (except Sundays) 9.30am to 7pm (10pm on Thursdays). Free entry via the escalator.

Institut du Monde arabe (9th floor terrace) – Ⓜ Jussieu. No charge *(see JUSSIEU).*

Hôtel Concorde-Lafayette (bar with panoramic view) – Ⓜ Porte-Maillot.

The Grande Arche at La Défense – Ⓜ and RER La Défense *(see La DÉFENSE).*

Calendar of events

Traditional Fêtes and events

April – October
Flower displays (tulips, rhododendrons, irises, dahlias) Parc floral de Vincennes

21 June
Fête de la Musique........... Venues throughout the capital and in the streets (21 June)

13 and 14 July
Dancing .... Various districts across Paris
Military parade .... Champs-Élysées (14 July)
Fireworks display .... Trocadéro (14 July)

September
Journées du Patrimoine .... Various sites (third weekend in September)

October
Fête des vendanges .... Montmartre (first Saturday of October)

December – February
Outdoor skating rink .... In front of Notre-Dame Cathedral

Festivals

Early February
Festival mondial du Cirque de demain .... Circus festival; Cirque d'hiver Bouglione, ☎ 01 56 29 19 10

End March – early April
Festival du Film de Paris... Gaumont Marignan cinema (Champs-Élysées), ☎ 01 45 72 96 40

May – July
Paris Jazz Festival .... Parc floral de Vincennes: free concerts Sat and Sun afternoons; ☎ 01 55 94 20 20

May – September
Musique côté jardin .... Free concerts in the city's parks and gardens; ☎ 08 20 00 75 75 PIM

First fortnight in June
Music festival................... Institut du Monde arabe, ☎ 01 40 51 38 38

End June – early July
La Villette Jazz Festival .... Parc de La Villette

Mid-July – mid-August
Paris quartier d'été (music, theatre...)............ Various venues around town; ☎ 01 44 94 98 00

Mid-September – end December
Festival d'automne (theatre, cinema...) .... Different theatres around town; ☎ 01 53 45 17 00

October
Festival d'Art sacré .... Churches and cultural centres throughout the capital; ☎ 01 44 70 64 05/06

November
Month of the Photo.......... Museums and galleries throughout the capital (even years); ☎ 01 44 78 75 10

Fairs, shows and exhibitions

Late February
International Agricultural Show .... Parc des Expositions, Porte de Versailles; www.salon-agriculture.com

March
Salon du Livre (Paris Bookfair) .... Parc des Expositions, Porte de Versailles; www.salondulivreparis.com

End April – early May
Foire de Paris .... Parc des Expositions, Porte de Versailles; www.comexpo-paris.com

Last fortnight in September
Biennale internationale des Antiquaires .... Carrousel du Louvre (even years)

End September – early October
Mondial du deux-roues Paris (international two-wheel show).............. Parc des Expositions, Porte de Versailles; www.mondial-deuxroues.com

October
**Paris International
Motor Show**...................... Parc des Expositions, Porte de Versailles (even years);
www.mondial-automobile.com

**FIAC (International
Contemporay Art Fair)**...... Parc des Expositions, Porte de Versailles

Early December
Salon nautique................. Boat show. Parc des Expositions,
Porte de Versailles; www.salonnautiqueparis.com

**Salon du cheval,
du poney et de l'âne** .... Horse, pony and donkey fair, Parc des Expositions,
Porte de Versailles; www.salon-cheval.com

Sporting events

Last Sunday in January
Prix d'Amérique horse race   Hippodrome de Vincennes

February – March
Six Nations Rugby............ Stade de France, St-Denis

April
Paris Marathon .... Through the streets of the capital
**Prix du Président
de la République** .... Hippodrome d'Auteuil (Sunday in the first fortnight);
www.france-galop.com

May
Vintage-car race............... Montmartre (mid-May)
French Football Cup Final . Parc des Princes (end of May)

End May – early June
French Open Tennis.......... Roland Garros Stadium

June
Paris Grand Prix .... Hippodrome de Longchamp (last Sunday in June);
www.france-galop.com

Late July (Sunday)
Tour de France................. Final stage on the Champs-Élysées

September
Prix d'Ete .... Hippodrome de Vincennes (mid-September)

October
Prix de l'Arc de Triomphe . Hippodrome de Longchamp (first Sunday);
www.france-galop.com
Les 20km de Paris .... Eiffel Tower (mid-October)

Pont Alexandre III

J.-P. Clapham/MICHELIN

Paris Directory

The addresses in this directory have been listed by district for the hotels and restaurants, and by theme for theatre and entertainment.

For an even wider selection of hotels and restaurants in Paris, The Red Guide Paris is Michelin's annual guide to dining and accommodation, with the famous star-rating system and pictograms to help you choose the place that best suits your needs and desires.

Selected hotels by district

To make your stay in Paris a success, we have included a wide range of select establishments. You'll be able to choose between hotels, an organisation that specialises in bed and breakfast type lodgings and even a campsite in the shade of the trees of the Bois de Boulogne. Whether in bustling, lively neighbourhoods or close to the main monuments, from the most sophisticated to the simplest, there is something for every budget, enabling visitors to get a real sense of life in the capital.

Obviously, comfort and quality were essential selection criteria. Each and every establishment was visited and inspected. It is, of course, possible that things have changed since our last stay. Please let us know – we truly appreciate your comments and suggestions!

For each neighbourhood described in the **Sights** section, the corresponding *arrondissement* is always mentioned, so that you can choose among the establishments listed there.

A price for every budget...

Are you on a budget of less than 65€? The **"Budget"** category has a selection of hotels and a campground.

If you have a slightly larger budget – up to 120€ – choose among the hotels in the **"Moderate"** category. More comfortable than the former, with nicer furnishings, many of these are also quite picturesque.

Do you wish to pamper yourself for a night, or prefer to travel as comfortably as possible? Our **"Luxury"** category is for you. You may also enjoy the posh decor and atmosphere of these mythical palaces by dropping in for brunch or a cup of tea... But please remember: correct attire is often *de rigueur* in these elegant places.

Something for everyone

Hotels – We have presented a very wide range of establishments in terms of comfort. Rooms are rented per night and breakfast is extra unless otherwise stated. Some establishments have restaurant facilities that are also open to non-residents. It is recommended to reserve ahead – Parisian hotels are often fully booked. Keep in mind that you are expected to reconfirm if you plan to arrive after 5 or 6pm. This is essential in many hotels, where your room may be given away if you fail to call or fax your confirmation and your time of arrival.

Bed & Breakfast – **Alcôve et Agapes** – 8 bis r. Coysevox – 75018 Paris – ☎ 01 44 85 06 05 – www.bed-and-breakfast-in-paris.com – This innovative organisation co-ordinates stopovers at French hosts' homes in Paris. The atmosphere, friendlier than in a hotel, requires a mutual desire to communicate: misanthropes would do better to seek a more traditional solution! Accommodation as a paying guest is often very reasonably priced (from 45€ to 115€), depending on the comfort available, and the choice of neighbourhoods is quite varied. Given the success of this option, bookings should be made well in advance.

Cut-price hotel chains – Cut-price hotels may prove useful on occasion. Although the decoration is generally minimal, all rooms are fully equipped with a private bathroom and television. Located around the outskirts of Paris, these establishments do not offer restaurant facilities. Their prices, however, are hard to beat (less than 38€ for a double room). Should the need arise, here is a list of central booking services for a few chains:

B&B – ☎ 0 803 00 29 29 in France; from abroad (0) 2 98 33 75 00
Mister Bed – ☎ 01 46 14 38 00
Etap Hôtel – ☎ 08 36 68 89 00 in France; online reservations wwwetaphotel.com
Villages Hôtel – ☎ 03 80 60 92 70
NB: Some establishments won't accept pets, while others will put them up for a fee. Remember to enquire when you reserve.

And don't forget ...

The Red Guide to hotels and restaurants in Paris – If, by chance, you can't find what you're looking for in our address book, then do try **The Red Guide** to Hotels and Restaurants in Paris, which is full of excellent addresses in the capital. The category in terms of comfort and price is indicated for each establishment, together with a wealth of practical information.

1st arrondissement

CHÂTELET-HÔTEL DE VILLE – CONCORDE – HALLES – LOUVRE – MADELEINE – PALAIS-ROYAL – TUILERIES

Moderate

Hôtel Place du Louvre – *21 r. des Prêtres-St-Germain-l'Auxerrois* – Ⓜ *Pont-Neuf or Louvre-Rivoli* – ☎ *01 42 33 78 68* – *hotel.place.louvre@wanadoo.fr* – *20 rms: 87/141€* – ☐ *9.15€*. An excellent address for Louvre lovers. At a minute's walk from the museum, one could easily spend one's days visiting its every corner from top to bottom and from morning 'til night, if so desired. The hotel's other strong points are its central location, shipshape rooms and 5th floor duplexes.

Luxury

Hôtel Ducs de Bourgogne – *19 r. du Pont-Neuf* – Ⓜ *Pont-Neuf* – ☎ *01 42 33 95 64* – *Mail@hotel-paris-bourgogne.com* – *50 rms: 98/168€* – ☐ *11€*. This 19C building halfway between the Pont Neuf and the Forum des Halles is set right in the heart of the capital. Antique furniture and a tasteful colour scheme give the lobby a plush feel, while the rooms, of varying sizes, are more sober.

Hôtel Britannique – *20 av. Victoria* – Ⓜ *Châtelet* – ☎ *01 42 33 74 59* – *Mailbox@hotel-britannique.fr* – *40 rms: 124/171€* – ☐ *11€*. How very British! Reminiscent of a scene from an Agatha Christie novel, the English flavour of this hotel located just behind Châtelet is further accentuated by the copies of Turner paintings hanging on the walls. Rooms, though less representative, are nonetheless pleasant and breakfasts are ample.

2nd arrondissement

GRANDS BOULEVARDS – HALLES – PLACE DES VICTOIRES – SENTIER

Budget

Hôtel Tiquetonne – *6 r. Tiquetonne* – Ⓜ *Étienne-Marcel* – ☎ *01 42 36 94 58* – *closed Aug and Christmas school holidays* – *46 rms: 23.46/41.92€* – ☐ *5€*. A modest family hotel in a semi-pedestrian street a few steps from Les Halles and Rue Montorgueil. *The bright rooms, with their old-fashioned charm, are quite well kept and, above all, very inexpensive.*

Moderate

Hôtel Vivienne – *40 r. Vivienne* – Ⓜ *Bourse* – ☎ *01 42 33 13 26* – *paris@hotel-vivienne.com* – *44 rms: 63/84€* – ☐ *6€. Two minutes from the stock exchange and the Palais-Royal, this tidy little establishment enables visitors to discover Paris on foot: the Grands Boulevards, department stores and Opéra Garnier are all just a few strides away. Simple rooms and a pleasant welcome.*

Hôtel Favart – *5 r. Marivaux* – Ⓜ *Richelieu-Drouot* – ☎ *01 42 97 59 83* – *favart.hotel@wanadoo.fr* – *37 rms: 83.85/105.95€* – ☐ *3.05€*. Goya, the artist, stayed here in 1824 while sketching life *à la Parisienne*. And what better glimpse could one have? Located just opposite the Opéra-Comique, this hotel is set in a very lively neighbourhood. Some rooms have period furniture and exposed beams overhead.

3rd arrondissement

MARAIS – RÉPUBLIQUE

Luxury

Meslay République – *3 r. Meslay* – Ⓜ *République* – ☎ *01 42 72 79 79* – *hotel.meslay@wanadoo.fr* – *39 rms: 115/131€* – ☐ *7.20€*. Situated in a quiet street a stone's throw from the Place de la République, this hotel with a listed façade lays Paris at your feet. A few steps from the Marais, not far from the Bastille and close to the business districts, it is perfect for those looking to combine business and tourist pleasure.

Hôtel Little Palace – *4 r. Salomon-de-Caus* – Ⓜ *Réaumur-Sébastopol* – ☎ *01 42 72 08 15 – littlepalacehotel@compuserve.com – 57 rms: 153/190€ – ☐ 11€ – restaurant 30/42€*. Set in an early 20C building opposite a small public park, this colonnaded hotel with a sculpted façade has been entirely renovated. The restaurant, with its art nouveau chairs and the original glass-roofed bar, has lost nothing of its original pizzazz.

Hôtel Pavillon de la Reine – *28 pl. des Vosges* – Ⓜ *Chemin-Vert* – ☎ *01 40 29 19 19 – pavillon@club-internet.fr – 31 rms: 330/385€* – ☐ *20€*. Set in a courtyard garden on the Place des Vosges, this is one the most beautiful hotels in the city. Protected from the commotion of the capital, you'll delight in the refined decor where handsome woodwork, old stones, beautiful fabrics and antique furniture all create a posh, cosy atmosphere.

4th arrondissement

BASTILLE – BEAUBOURG – CHÂTELET-HÔTEL DE VILLE – ÎLE SAINT-LOUIS – MARAIS – NOTRE-DAME

Budget

Sansonnet – *48 r. de la Verrerie* – Ⓜ *Hôtel-de-Ville or Châtelet-les-Halles* – ☎ *01 48 87 96 14 – www.hotel-sansonnet.com – 26 rms: 53/76€* – ☐ *6.50€*. This small, tidy hotel is the ideal stopover for those who are torn between shopping on the Rue de Rivoli and visiting the Marais. There are rooms on four floors with efficient double-glazed windows, and the prices are quite reasonable.

Andréa Rivoli – *3 r. St-Bon* – Ⓜ *Châtelet or Hôtel-de-Ville* – ☎ *01 42 78 43 93 – hotelandrea@aol.com – 32 rms: 58/94€* – ☐ *6€*. You won't regret having chosen this extremely well located, central hotel: from the reception desk to the bedrooms, while passing through the breakfast room, everything here is spanking new. Up-to-the-minute decor and air-conditioning throughout. A sure bet.

Grand Hôtel Jeanne d'Arc – *3 r. de Jarente* – Ⓜ *Saint-Paul or Bastille* – ☎ *01 48 87 62 11 – www.parishotel – 36 rms: 64/92€*. This hotel located behind the Place du Marché-Ste-Catherine was built in the 17C. The lobby is adorned with a unique mirror framed by mosaics. The prices are reasonable and the degree of comfort very satisfactory, so think to book ahead. The colourful renovated rooms are the best; the others are more ordinary.

Moderate

Hôtel du 7e Art – *20 r. St-Paul* – Ⓜ *Saint-Paul* – ☎ *01 44 54 85 00 – hotel7art@wanadoo.fr – 23 rms: 70/120€* – ☐ *7€*. The name says it all: cinema, and more particularly the films of 1940-60, is the underlying theme of this hotel's interior design. Ask for a room with exposed beams on the 3rd or 4th floor. Guest laundry room.

Acacias – Hôtel-de-Ville – *20 r. du Temple* – Ⓜ *Hôtel-de-Ville* – ☎ *01 48 87 07 70 – www.acacias-hotel.com – 33 rms: 73.94/94.52€* – ☐ *7.62€*. This old building is not particularly attractive, but the location is excellent. The well fitted-out bedrooms are decorated in a simple, modern spirit. The rustic appeal of the breakfast room is most pleasant.

St-Louis Marais – *1 r. Charles-V* – Ⓜ *Bastille* – ☎ *01 48 87 87 04 – saintlouismarais.com – 16 rms: 75/120€* – ☐ *7.50€*. A most charming little establishment, this hotel is housed in a building dating from 1740. The smallish rooms are stylish, with their ceilings crossed by time-worn beams. Rustic, carefully thought-out decor in the reception area.

Hôtel de la Place des Vosges – *12 r. de Birague* – Ⓜ *Bastille* – ☎ *01 42 72 60 46 – hôtel.place.des.vosges@gofornet.com – 16 rms: 76/120€* – ☐ *6€*. Here's a hotel with character. Built in the 17C, its reasonably-sized rooms are simply furnished, while the reception area blends old stones, exposed beams and tapestries. A sophisticated stopover next to one of the most beautiful squares in Paris.

Grand Hôtel Malher – *5 r. Malher* – Ⓜ *Saint-Paul* – ☎ *01 42 72 60 92 – www.grandhotelmalher.com – 31 rms: 86/128€* – ☐ *8€*. Conveniently situated for strolling around the Marais, this hotel shows an ancient façade that conceals modern rooms decorated with painted wood furniture and colourful fabrics. Pleasantly quiet on the courtyard side; well-soundproofed on the street side.

Hôtel Bretonnerie – *22 r. Ste-Croix-de-la-Bretonnerie* – Ⓜ *Hôtel-de-Ville* – ☎ *01 48 87 77 63 – hotel@bretonnerie.com – closed 29 Jul to 27 Aug – 22 rms: 108/140€ – ☐ 9.50€*. Treat yourself to a sojourn in this private 17C mansion in the bosom of the Marais. The peaceful environment, beamed ceilings and old-fashioned fabrics all contribute to the warm appeal of its rooms.

5th arrondissement

JARDIN DES PLANTES – JUSSIEU – LUXEMBOURG – MAUBERT – MOUFFETARD – QUARTIER LATIN

Budget

Hôtel Les Argonautes – *12 r. de la Huchette* – Ⓜ *Saint-Michel* – ☎ *01 43 54 09 82 – 25 rms: 44/70€ – ☐ 4€ – restaurant 20/45€*. African masks, objects, drawings: a rich decor from the colonies greets you as soon as you walk in. The halls are also quite colourful, contrasting with the sobriety of the bare-walled bedrooms. All around the hotel, various and sundry bars and restaurants teem with life.

Hôtel du Mont-Blanc – *28 r. de la Huchette* – Ⓜ *Saint-Michel* – ☎ *01 43 54 49 44 – www.france-hotel-guide.com – 42 rms: 55/80€ – ☐ 6€ – restaurant 18€*. Located in a little street lined with bars and Greek restaurants, this hotel opposite the legendary Théâtre de la Huchette is perfect for all those looking to stay in a neighbourhood as lively by night as by day. The rooms are functional and suitably fitted-out; those in back are quieter. Reasonably-priced for the capital.

Hôtel Sunny – *48 bd du Port-Royal* – Ⓜ *Les Gobelins* – ☎ *01 43 31 79 86 – www.hotelsunny.com – 37 rms: 60/74€ – ☐ 5.90€*. What are the assets of this hotel hidden behind a façade of the Haussmann style? The functional rooms, with their old rose textiles (ask for one on the courtyard side), the impeccable orderliness and the location just ten minutes' walk from the Panthéon and the Luxembourg gardens.

Moderate

Hôtel St-Jacques – *35 r. des Écoles* – Ⓜ *Maubert-Mutualité* – ☎ *01 44 07 45 45 – hotelsaintjacques@wanadoo.fr – 35 rms: 67.84/102.14€ – ☐ 6.10€*. Situated in the heart of the Latin Quarter, here's a hospitable stopover in a 19C building that has retained all of its original plaster mouldings. The bedrooms are spacious, decorated with tasteful furniture and well soundproofed; some are endowed with fireplaces. Reasonably priced.

Hôtel de L'Espérance – *15 r. Pascal* – Ⓜ *Les Gobelins or Censier-Daubenton* – ☎ *01 47 07 10 99 – hotel.esperance@wanadoo.fr – 38 rms: 68/84€ – ☐ 6€*. Two strides from Rue Mouffetard and its picturesque fruit and vegetable market, this charming little establishment is decked with flowers, both in window boxes and on the patio. The comfortable, relatively peaceful rooms are decorated in cheerful colours.

Hôtel Familia – *11 r. des Écoles* – Ⓜ *Cardinal-Lemoine* – ☎ *01 43 54 55 27 – familia.hotel@libertysurf.fr – 30 rms: 68.60/106€ – ☐ 6.10€*. This modest little hotel is just a stone's throw from the Mouffetard quarter. Despite its rather out-of-date pseudo-Italian interior, complete with frescoes in the corridors and some of the rooms, it remains a practical, unassuming address. Reasonably priced.

Hôtel des Grandes Écoles – *75 r. du Cardinal-Lemoine* – Ⓜ *Cardinal-Lemoine* – ☎ *01 43 26 79 23 – www.hotel-grandes-ecoles.com – 🄿 – 51 rms: 95/125€ – ☐ 7€*. These three houses resembling rural cottages feature a pretty garden that provides a welcome island of quietude. The main building has retained its somewhat archaic charm, while the other two have been tastefully renovated. Very sought after...

Luxury

Hôtel Select – *1 pl. de la Sorbonne* – Ⓜ *Cluny – La Sorbonne* – ☎ *01 46 34 14 80 – select.hotel@wanadoo.fr – 68 rms: 137€ – ☐ 6€*. Situated on the Place de la Sorbonne, this hotel unifies old stones and new tastes. The drawing rooms are laid out in a gallery around a patio-cum-greenhouse, the staircase, lined with tropical plants, leads up to corridors of bare granite and breakfast is served in a room with stone arches...

Grand Hôtel St-Michel – *19 r. Cujas* – Ⓜ *Luxembourg* – ☎ *01 46 33 33 02* – *grand.hotel@st.michel.com* – *45 rms: 160€* – ☕ *10€*. Located near the Sorbonne and the Luxembourg Gardens, this entirely renovated hotel is pleasant indeed. The rooms, with their painted furniture and fluffy feather quilts, are cosy; some have a balcony with a view. Vaulted breakfast room.

6th arrondissement

INSTITUT DE FRANÇE – LUXEMBOURG – MONTPARNASSE – ODÉON – QUARTIER LATIN – SAINT-GERMAIN-DES-PRÉS – SAINT-SULPICE – SÈVRES-BABYLONE

Budget

St-Placide – *6 r. St-Placide* – Ⓜ *Sèvres-Babylone* – ☎ *01 45 48 80 08* – *20 rms: 42.62/57.84€* – ☕ *5.34€*. A minute's walk from the Le Bon Marché department store, here's an acceptably well-soundproofed establishment offering simple rooms fitted out with good, comfortable beds; those on the uppermost floor have a small balcony. Those on a shoestring budget take note.

Hôtel de Nesle – *7 r. de Nesle* – Ⓜ *Odéon* – ☎ *01 43 54 62 41* – *hoteldenesle.com* – *20 rms: 50/100€*. A minor miracle right in the centre of the Latin Quarter. Each room is decorated according to a different theme, including the colonies, the Orient, the countryside, Molière. The result is surprisingly successful. The garden, planted with Tunisian palm trees, soothes the eyes and the soul.

Hôtel Delhy's – *22 r. de l'Hirondelle* – Ⓜ *Saint-Michel* – *Notre-Dame* – ☎ *01 43 26 58 25* – *21 rms: 41/73€*. This little gem in the heart of Paris will delight those on mini budgets. Hidden behind a porch on the place St-Michel, this charmingly old-fashioned family hotel provides quiet accommodation for tired travellers. Most rooms have shared shower and WC.

Moderate

Grand Hôtel des Balcons – *3 r. Casimir-Delavigne* – Ⓜ *Odéon* – ☎ *01 46 34 78 50* – *www.balcons.com* – *50 rms: 72/150€* – ☕ *10€*. "Paris is planted in my heart," wrote the Hungarian poet André Ady after a stay here. Downstairs, an enchanting art nouveau style; upstairs, more standardised rooms with small balconies overlooking the street. Reasonable prices for the neighbourhood. Plentiful buffet breakfast.

Hôtel Sèvres Azur – *22 r. de l'Abbé-Grégoire* – Ⓜ *Saint-Placide* – ☎ *01 45 48 84 07* – *sevres.azur@wanadoo.fr* – *31 rms: 74/89€* – ☕ *7€*. Located in a quiet street near the Bon Marché department store, this charming hotel with a tiny flower-filled courtyard has sunny yellow rooms and attractive waxed-wood furniture. Perfect for putting oneself in a Parisian's shoes and strolling about St-Germain-des-Prés and Montparnasse.

Luxury

Millésime Hôtel – *15 r. Jacob* – Ⓜ *Saint-Germain-des-Prés* – ☎ *01 44 07 97 97* – *reservation@millesimehotel.com* – *22 rms: 150/210€* – ☕ *12€*. This 17C hotel right in the heart of St-Germain des Près has a spectacular (listed) period staircase. It offers its guests top-quality comfort in a charming setting. The modern bedrooms have sunshine-coloured walls.

7th arrondissement

TOUR EIFFEL – FAUBOURG SAINT-GERMAIN – INVALIDES – ORSAY

Budget

Hôtel du Palais-Bourbon – *49 r. de Bourgogne* – Ⓜ *Varenne* – ☎ *01 44 11 30 70* – *www.hotel-palais-bourbon.com* – *32 rms: 65/120€*. Built in 1730, this hotel near the Rodin museum and the Invalides is a pleasant surprise. The attractive rooms have parquet floors, wood furniture and air conditioning. Single rooms are small but very good value; doubles are spacious. There are also several family rooms. Breakfast is included in the price.

Hôtel Lévêque – *29 r. Clerc* – Ⓜ *École-Militaire* – ☏ *01 47 05 49 15* – *info@hotel-leveque.com* – *50 rms: 53/91€* – 🍽 *7€*. A rare find – jot down the address! This hotel located in a small, lively street in the shadow of the École Militaire offers sober, well-furnished, bright rooms at very affordable prices. Given its solid reputation, advance booking is most recommended.

Moderate

Hôtel L'Empereur – *2 r. Chevert* – Ⓜ *École-Militaire or La Tour-Maubourg* – ☏ *01 45 55 88 02* – *contact@hotelempereur.com* – *38 rms: 75/85€* – 🍽 *7€*. The Empire style comes as no surprise in this hotel located just opposite the Invalides: consider it a tip of the hat to Napoleon, who is buried under the Dome... Ask for a refurbished room; they echo the establishment's historic flavour and are more pleasant.

Hôtel Muguet – *11 r. Chevert* – Ⓜ *École-Militaire or La Tour-Maubourg* – ☏ *01 47 05 05 93* – *muguet@wanadoo.fr* – *48 rms: 83/100€* – 🍽 *7.50€*. Small, basic and discreet, this hotel is set in a quiet side street half-way between the École Militaire and the Invalides. The well-maintained rooms are spotless and comfortable. Little flower-decked courtyard at the rear where breakfasts are served summers. Reasonable rates for Paris.

Hôtel Malar – *29 r. Malar* – Ⓜ *École-Militaire or La Tour-Maubourg* – ☏ *01 45 51 38 46* – *www.eiffeltower-paris-hotel.com* – *22 rms: 83/100€* – 🍽 *7€*. These two buildings constructed under Louis-Philippe have been renovated many times over. The rooms, fitted out with handsome furniture, come with pretty two-toned bathrooms. Summers, breakfasts are served in the small inner courtyard.

Hôtel St-Thomas-d'Aquin – *3 r. du Pré-aux-Clercs* – Ⓜ *Rue du Bac or Saint-Germain-des-Prés* – ☏ *01 42 61 01 22* – *hotel-st-thomas-daquin.com* – *20 rms: 90/110€* – 🍽 *8€*. Chic boutiques, antique shops, art galleries and literary cafés: Left Bank Paris is yours for the taking, just a minute's walk from this hotel, which is gradually being renovated. Comfortable, modern bedrooms; bathrooms reminiscent of ships' cabins.

Hôtel Lindbergh – *5 r. Chomel* – Ⓜ *Sèvres-Babylone or Saint-Sulpice* – ☏ *01 45 48 35 53* – *www.hotellindbergh.com* – *26 rms: 90/130€* – 🍽 *8€*. One of the men who designed Lindbergh's famous monoplane, The Spirit of St. Louis, supposedly stayed in this 19C hotel right near the Bon Marché department store. The rooms are being progressively redecorated in a 1930s-40s style. Very hospitable welcome.

Hôtel de la Tulipe – *33 r. Malar* – Ⓜ *Pont-de-l'Alma or La Tour-Maubourg* – ☏ *01 45 51 67 21* – *www.hoteldelatulipe.com* – *20 rms: 95/119€* – 🍽 *8€*. Built in the 17C, this yellow residence is now home to a small, charming hotel with a Provençal slant. The paved, tree-covered courtyard is pretty and the small bedrooms are tastefully decorated: wicker, stone and beams complement each other to a tee.

Luxury

Hôtel Verneuil – *8 r. de Verneuil* – Ⓜ *Solférino or Musée-d'Orsay* – ☏ *01 42 60 82 14* – *verneuil@noos.fr* – *26 rms: 115/175€* – 🍽 *10€*. A delightful stopover just a few steps from St-Germain-des-Prés, this hotel wants for nothing. Although the bedrooms are a bit cramped, their refined, elegant interior decoration gives them an incomparable charm. An entrancing halt, well worth discovering.

8th arrondissement

CHAMPS-ÉLYSÉES – CONCORDE – FAUBOURG-SAINT-HONORÉ – SAINT-LAZARE

Budget

Modern Élysée – *9 r. Washington* – Ⓜ *George-V* – ☏ *01 45 63 27 33* – *closed Aug* – *26 rms: 57.93/65.55€* – 🍽 *4.57€*. The name gives the game away: this hotel is situated right near the Champs-Elysées. The reasonably spacious rooms are impeccably maintained; those overlooking the small inner courtyard are quieter. Reasonable prices, given the location.

Moderate

Hôtel New Orient – *16 r. de Constantinople* – Ⓜ *Europe or Villiers* – ☏ *01 45 22 21 64* – *new.orient.hotel@wanadoo.fr* – *30 rms: 69/102€* – 🍽 *7€*. This hotel's inviting façade is in perfect keeping with the smart interior. The wooden staircase and immaculate rooms complement the warm, hospitable ambience. An establishment after our own hearts, just minutes from the Place de l'Europe.

Champs-Élysées – *2 r. d'Artois* – Ⓜ *Saint-Philippe-du-Roule* – ☎ *01 43 59 11 42 – 36 rms: 81/99€ –* ☐ *7€.* A convivial establishment housed in a late 19C building that has been modernised. The entrance and bedrooms have been revamped in the art deco spirit. Breakfast room under handsome stone arches.

Hôtel d'Albion – *15 r. de Penthièvre* – Ⓜ *Miromesnil* – ☎ *01 42 65 84 15 – www.hoteldalbion.net –* ▣ *– 26 rms: 95/115€ –* ☐ *8€.* Midway between the Champs-Élysées and La Madeleine, here's a hotel located in an unexpectedly calm street. The commodious rooms each have their own pleasant personality; ask for one on the courtyard if possible. Summertime, breakfast is served in a pleasant mini-garden.

Luxury

Hôtel Powers – *52 r. François-ler* – Ⓜ *George-V or Alma-Marceau* – ☎ *01 47 23 91 05 – contact@hotel-powers.com – 55 rms: 100/300€ –* ☐ *13€.* This discreet, agreeable establishment is situated just a stone's throw from the world's most celebrated avenue. The reasonably spacious yellow rooms are cosy, with their antique furniture and elegant ceiling mouldings reminiscent of an English manor. Sauna.

9th arrondissement

FAUBOURG POISSONNIÈRE – GRANDS BOULEVARDS – OPÉRA – PIGALLE – SAINT-LAZARE

Budget

Hôtel Chopin – *10 bd Montmartre, 46 passage Jouffroy* – Ⓜ *Richelieu-Drouot* – ☎ *01 47 70 58 10 – 35 rms: 62/80€ –* ☐ *7€.* Located in a covered passage dating from 1846, also home to the Grévin wax museum, this little hotel is surprisingly calm, considering the effervescent neighbourhood. The colourfully painted rooms must be booked well in advance.

Moderate

Résidence du Pré – *15 r. Pierre-Sémard* – Ⓜ *Poissonnière* – ☎ *01 48 78 26 72 – reservation@leshotelsdupre.com – 40 rms: 75/90€ –* ☐ *9€.* Two minutes from the Gare du Nord, this modest establishment situated in an old building is well-maintained: the practical rooms are clean and functional, if not wildly original. Useful for those on tight budgets.

Hôtel des Croisés – *63 r. St-Lazare* – Ⓜ *Trinité* – ☎ *01 48 74 78 24 – hotel-des-croisés@wanadoo.fr – reserv. recommended – 27 rms: 77/94€ –* ☐ *7.50€.* Two kinds of rooms may be found in this late-19C edifice. The larger have a delicious old-fashioned charm – some even have a fireplace, art deco or art nouveau furniture – while the others, more sober, come with renovated bathrooms. Remember to reserve as early as possible.

Luxury

Hôtel Alba – *34 ter r. de La Tour-d'Auvergne* – Ⓜ *Poissonnière* – ☎ *01 48 78 80 22 – 24 rms: 90/121€ –* ☐ *7€.* The rather old-fashioned furniture and quaint rooms give this tidy hotel located in a cul-de-sac the ambience of a family *pension.* Each room is equipped with a kitchenette, and there is also a laundry room on the premises.

10th arrondissement

FAUBOURG POISSONNIÈRE – GRANDS BOULEVARDS – CANAL SAINT-MARTIN

Budget

République Hôtel – *31 r. Albert-Thomas* – Ⓜ *République* – ☎ *01 42 39 19 03 – www.republiquehotel.com – 40 rms: 55/65€ –* ☐ *6€.* Situated in a rather quiet street between the Place de la République and the Saint-Martin Canal, this hotel lodges guests in small white rooms. Simple comfort and decor – at these prices, one shouldn't expect too much fuss.

Moderate

Hôtel Français – *13 r. du 8-Mai-1945* – Ⓜ *Gare-de-l'Est* – ☎ *01 40 35 94 14 – hotelfrancais@wanadoo.fr – 71 rms: 73/81€ –* ☐ *7.50€.* This hotel, located opposite the Gare de l'Est in a busy area, offers excellent value for money. The rooms, decorated in a 1970s veneered furniture style, are clean, well-fitted out and soundproofed. Turn-of-the-century drawing room and reception area.

Hôtel Caravelle – *41 r. des Petites Écuries* – Ⓜ *Bonne-Nouvelle or Poissonnière* – ☎ *01 45 23 08 22* – *38 rms: 79/84€* – ☲ *5.40€*. Here's a good address for travellers looking to stay in the capital, in the heart of a lively quarter with a spicy aroma. The bedrooms, admittedly small, are immaculate and rather merry, with their multi-coloured curtains and bedcovers.

Hôtel Albert 1er – *162 r. Lafayette* – Ⓜ *Le Peletier or Cadet* – ☎ *01 40 36 82 40* – *resa@hotel-albert1er-paris.com* – *55 rms: 85/101€* – ☲ *9€*. A few short steps from the Gare du Nord, here's a practical address that puts Sacré-Cœur and the St-Martin Canal almost at your doorstep. The bright rooms are well-maintained, air-conditioned and sound-proofed. Marble bathrooms and cane furniture.

11th arrondissement

BASTILLE – BELLEVILLE – FAUBOURG SAINT-ANTOINE – RÉPUBLIQUE

Budget

Hôtel Nord et Est – *49 r. de Malte* – Ⓜ *Oberkampf* – ☎ *01 47 00 71 70* – *closed Aug and 24 Dec to 2 Jan* – *45 rms: 53.36/59.46€* – ☲ *5.34€*. This small, unassuming hotel is well-situated in a quiet street near République. Run by the same family since 1929, the cheerful welcome makes one feel at home, even if the facilities are rather basic.

Hôtel Grand Prieuré – *20 r. du Grand-Prieuré* – Ⓜ *Oberkampf* – ☎ *01 47 00 74 14* – *32 rms: 54.90/62.60€* – ☲ *5€*. A hotel not far from République offering clean, functional rooms with a bath or shower. Trendy travellers will be interested to learn that it is just a minute from Rue Oberkampf, known for its succession of fashionable restaurants and cafés.

Moderate

Hôtel Beaumarchais – *3 r. Oberkampf* – Ⓜ *Filles-du-Calvaire* – ☎ *01 53 36 86 86* – *hotel.beaumarchais@libertysurf.fr* – *31 rms: 69/99€* – ☲ *9€*. This century-old, flower-decked building has recently been rejuvenated. The rooms, painted with vivid colours and endowed with gracefully curved furniture, are as charming as can be. The verdant inner courtyard is a welcome summer refuge.

Hôtel Campanile – *9 r. du Chemin-Vert* – Ⓜ *Chemin-Vert* – ☎ *01 43 38 58 08* – *157 rms: 80€* – ☲ *6.49€*. A chain hotel housed in a modern building between Bastille and République. Its assets: all rooms have air conditioning, those on the uppermost floor have a terrace and, when the weather is fine, breakfast is served in the tiny garden.

Grand Hôtel Français – *223 bd Voltaire* – Ⓜ *Nation* – ☎ *01 43 71 27 57* – *40 rms: 83.85/114.34€* – ☲ *6.10€*. Its location a stone's throw from the Place de la Nation and the principal Metro and RER lines is one of the chief advantages of this handsome, fully restored hotel. The bedrooms, decorated with colourful fabrics, are new and well-soundproofed. Hospitable welcome.

12th arrondissement

BASTILLE – BERCY – FAUBOURG SAINT-ANTOINE

Budget

Lux Hôtel Picpus – *74 bd Picpus* – Ⓜ *Picpus* – ☎ *01 43 43 08 46* – *lux-hotel@wanadoo.fr* – *38 rms: 43/60€* – ☲ *5.50€*. Close to the Place de la Nation, this building of cut stone is not luxurious, but it has been freshly renovated. The rooms, a bit on the small side, have been personalised with a pleasing choice of textiles.

Hôtel Amadeus – *39 r. Claude-Tillier* – Ⓜ *Reuilly-Diderot or Nation* – ☎ *01 43 48 53 48* – *22 rms: 47.26/59.45€* – ☲ *3.05€*. Seen from the outside, this small hotel is nothing special. Don't let that stop you – the newly renovated interior wants for nothing. The very quiet bedrooms, furnished in wicker, change colour with every floor.

Venise Hôtel – *4 r. Chaligny* – Ⓜ *Reuilly-Diderot* – ☎ *01 43 43 63 45* – *28 rms: 55/62€* – ☲ *6€*. This family-run establishment is located near the original Viaduc des Arts and its landscaped promenade. The rooms, practical above all, change colours at each floor; the washrooms all come with a bathtub. Warm reception.

Inter Hôtel – *17 r. de Prague* – Ⓜ *Ledru-Rollin* – ☎ *01 43 43 66 35* – *hotel-alcyon@wanadoo.fr* – 🅿 – *37 rms: 60.22/75.46€* – ⛾ *6.10€* – *restaurant 11.43/17.53€*. This hotel's location within reach of the Bastille is ideal for night owls. The rooms, some of which are rather narrow, have been decorated without too much fuss; the bathrooms are well equipped. The restaurant offers a modern setting and simple cuisine at affordable prices.

Hôtel de Reuilly – *33 bd de Reuilly* – Ⓜ *Daumesnil or Dugommier* – ☎ *01 44 87 09 09* – *hotreuilly@aol.com* – *61 rms: 71.35/82€* – ⛾ *7.20€*. Although it is located in the heart of Paris, this hotel is a peaceful port in the city storm. Most of the rooms, smallish but neat and tidy, give onto one of the two verdant inner courtyards. Breakfasts served outdoors in summer, on the veranda in winter.

Ibis Gare de Lyon – *43 av. Ledru-Rollin* – Ⓜ *Ledru-Rollin or Quai-de-la-Rapée* – ☎ *01 53 02 30 30* – *h1937@accor-hotels.com* – ⟗ – *119 rms: 84€* – ⛾ *6€*. Not far from the lively neighbourhoods of the Rue du Faubourg St-Antoine and the Place de la Bastille, this modern chain hotel has well-equipped rooms with white roughcast walls, quite spacious for an Ibis hotel. Buffet breakfast.

13th arrondissement

GOBELINS

Résidence Les Gobelins – *9 r. des Gobelins* – Ⓜ *Les Gobelins* – ☎ *01 47 07 26 90* – *www.hotelgobelins.com* – *32 rms: 52/70€* – ⛾ *6€*. Situated on a little paved road just next-door to the Manufacture des Gobelins, this hotel looks as though it belongs in a village. The small, basic rooms are quiet; some are colourful. A pretty, flower-decked patio livens up the breakfast room.

Touring Hôtel Magendie – *6 r. Corvisart* – Ⓜ *Corvisart* – ☎ *01 43 36 13 61* – *magendie@vvf-vacances.fr* – *112 rms: 56/65€* – ⛾ *5.34€*. Located in a small street behind Boulevard Arago, this hotel should please those on tight budgets, with particularly attractive rates for the many single rooms. Refurbished, they are somewhat cramped but quiet; those overlooking the courtyard are particularly peaceful.

Hôtel Résidence Vert Galant – *43 r. Croulebarbe* – Ⓜ *Les Gobelins* – ☎ *01 44 08 83 50* – *15 rms: 80/90€* – ⛾ *7€*. A little garden in town. Such is the added bonus of this modern residence located in a quiet street, behind the Manufacture des Gobelins. The ground-floor rooms are particularly pleasant, their large French windows opening onto the greenery.

Hôtel Manufacture – *8 r. Philippe-de-Champagne* – Ⓜ *Place-d'Italie* – ☎ *01 45 35 45 25* – *lamanufacturehot@aol.com* – *57 rms: 119/128€* – ⛾ *7€*. Very close to the Place d'Italie, the rooms of this recent establishment are practical and well-fitted out. All are sound-proofed and air-conditioned; five of the rooms on the top floor are bigger.

14th arrondissement

DENFERT-ROCHEREAU – MONTPARNASSE – MONTSOURIS

Hôtel Daguerre – *94 r. Daguerre* – Ⓜ *Denfert-Rochereau* – ☎ *01 43 22 43 54* – *hotel.daguerre.paris14@gofornet.com* – *30 rms: 69/104€* – ⛾ *8€*. Although entirely refurbished in 1994, evidence of the hotel's 1920s architecture can still be glimpsed, such as the façade or the amusing fountain at the entrance. Near to Montparnasse, this hotel in a busy shopping street has rooms that are soberly decorated but immaculate, and the prices are reasonable.

Hôtel Moulin Vert – *74 r. du Moulin-Vert* – Ⓜ *Pernéty* – ☎ *01 45 43 65 38* – *www.hotel-moulinvert.com* – 🅿 – *28 rms: 79/89€* – ⛾ *6.50€*. This small hotel has been undergoing a gradual transformation since it changed hands recently. The façade has just been redone, the entrance is sparkling new, and the bedrooms, while a bit compact, are well maintained and soon to be renovated.

Hôtel Delambre – *35 r. Delambre* – Ⓜ *Vavin or Edgar-Quinet* – ☎ *01 43 20 66 31* – *30 rms: 80/90€* – ⌷ *8€*. This fully refurbished modern establishment is just a few minutes from Montparnasse. The bright, functional rooms and cheerful welcome have already resulted in a regular clientele of guests, happy to have found lodgings for a reasonable price in this neighbourhood.

Hôtel Istria – *29 r. Campagne-Première* – Ⓜ *Raspail* – ☎ *01 43 20 91 82* – *hotelistria@wanadoo.fr* – *26 rms: 90/100€* – ⌷ *8€*. Man Ray stayed here, Elsa Triolet and Aragon loved here, Raymond Radiguet was unfaithful to Cocteau here... This small hotel, popular with many artists of Montparnasse's golden era, has retained all the charm of its rich, colourful past. Refurbished rooms.

Hôtel Lenox Montparnasse – *15 r. Delambre* – Ⓜ *Vavin or Edgar-Quinet* – ☎ *01 43 35 34 50* – *52 rms: 102/122€* – ⌷ *9€*. The early 20C façade of this building situated in a popular side-street off Montparnasse is most attractive. Behind it lies a pleasant establishment, particularly the large suites on the 6th floor. All rooms are decorated with handsome antique mirrors.

Hôtel L'Aiglon – *232 bd Raspail* – Ⓜ *Denfert-Rochereau or Raspail* – ☎ *01 43 20 82 42* – *hotelaiglon@wanadoo.fr* – *34 rms: 104/138€* – ⌷ *6.50€*. Two minutes from the Cartier foundation and just behind the Montparnasse cemetery, this hotel sports a decidedly Napoleonic personality. Cherry or softwood furniture and appealing fabrics give the rooms their pleasant feel.

Luxury

Hôtel Raspail Montparnasse – *203 bd Raspail* – Ⓜ *Denfert-Rochereau or Raspail* – ☎ *01 43 20 62 86* – *raspailm@aol.com* – *38 rms: 96/199€* – ⌷ *9€*. Set in the shadow of the Montparnasse tower, this hotel – renovated a few years ago – offers attractive, colourful rooms. The lobby and small bar-drawing room done in an art deco style are quite inviting.

15th arrondissement

JAVEL – MONTPARNASSE – TOUR EIFFEL – VAUGIRARD

Budget

Hôtel de l'Avre – *21 r. de l'Avre* – Ⓜ *La Motte-Picquet-Grenelle* – ☎ *01 45 75 31 03* – *26 rms: 59/77€* – ⌷ *6.50€*. Very colourful indeed. A bright yellow lobby in memory of Provence and a luscious green garden to enjoy at breakfast. The white, yellow or blue bedrooms promise snug, quiet nights in a simple yet cosy ambience.

Hôtel Printania – *55 r. Olivier-de-Serres* – Ⓜ *Convention* – ☎ *01 45 33 96 77* – *hotelprintania.paris15@wanadoo.fr* – *21 rms: 65/84€* – ⌷ *6€*. Right next door to the Parc des Expositions, here's a small hotel whose bedrooms, practical and very well looked after, have all just been redone. The breakfast room, repainted in the shades of southern France, is delightful.

Saphir Hôtel – *10 r. du Commerce* – Ⓜ *La Motte-Picquet - Grenelle* – ☎ *01 45 75 12 23* – *32 rms: 65/85€* – ⌷ *7€*. You're just a minute's walk from the Eiffel Tower when you stay in this small, very well-kept establishment without airs. Functional, tidy rooms; ask for one overlooking the inner courtyard where breakfasts may be taken in summer.

Moderate

Lutèce Hôtel – *5 r. Langeac* – Ⓜ *Convention or Porte-de-Versailles* – ☎ *01 48 28 56 95* – *closed 23 Jul to 1 Sep and 21 Dec to 3 Jan* – *35 rms: 69/92€* – ⌷ *7€*. Built between the World Wars, this building has just been freshened up. All of the bedrooms have been renovated; those on the 6th and 7th floors, many with balconies, offer a view of the roofs of Paris. Summertime, breakfast is served in the inner courtyard.

Hôtel Avia – *181 r. de Vaugirard* – Ⓜ *Pasteur* – ☎ *01 43 06 43 80* – *40 rms: 72/85€* – ⌷ *7€*. The well-conceived, well-run restaurant rounds out this hotel with every modern comfort. Bedrooms are spacious, suitably fitted out and decorated with fabric chosen to match the furniture and wallpaper. Breakfast room with a modern flair.

Hôtel Arès – *7 r. du Gén.-de-Larminat* – Ⓜ *La Motte-Picquet - Grenelle* – ☎ *01 47 34 74 04* – *aresotel@easynet.fr* – *42 rms: 97.56/190.55€* – ⌷ *7.16€*. Here's a hotel for seekers of second-hand treasures. Just a few strides from the Village Suisse and its antique shops, the hotel is set in a quiet, little-travelled street. The rather plush lounge is inviting; the rooms, in vivid colours, are more ordinary.

Hôtel Tour Eiffel Dupleix – *11 r. Juge* – Ⓜ *Dupleix* – ☎ *01 45 78 29 29* – *39 rms: 106.71€* – ☐ *7.62€*. This spruce-looking hotel has worked hard in order to appeal to younger travellers. The fashionable interior decoration with wood-panelling, comfortable wicker furniture and brightly coloured curtains and convenient metro links to the centre of Paris suit their needs admirably.

16th arrondissement

AUTEUIL – BOIS DE BOULOGNE – MUETTE-RANELAGH – PASSY – TROCADÉRO

Budget

Camping Le Bois de Boulogne – *Allée du Bord-de-l'Eau (between the Suresnes Bridge and the Puteaux Bridge)* – ☎ *01 45 24 30 00* – *resa@mobilhome-paris.com* – *reserv. recommended* – *460 sites: 29€* – *food service (evenings only)*. Located in the Bois de Boulogne, this campground, which is only for those residing outside of greater Paris, is predictably noisy, but the prices can't be beat. Sites closest to the Seine are the quietest. The price indicated is for a tent site for one night and for two people. Mobile home rentals. In summer there's a shuttle service to and from the Porte-Maillot metro station every quarter of an hour.

Moderate

Queen's Hôtel – *4 r. Bastien-Lepage* – Ⓜ *Michel-Ange – Auteuil* – ☎ *01 42 88 89 85* – *contact@queens-hotel.fr* – *22 rms: 68/120€* – ☐ *6.10€*. Tucked away in a quiet street, this small hotel run by an ex-journalist is being refurbished bit by bit. Modern paintings from the owner's private collection hang in each well-maintained, if smallish, bedroom. Six of the rooms have a jacuzzi.

Hôtel Ambassade – *79 r. Lauriston* – Ⓜ *Boissière or Kléber* – ☎ *01 45 53 41 15* – *38 rms: 73/105€* – ☐ *8.50€*. This newly refaced hotel benefits from the quietude of the surrounding residential neighbourhood although it is only a few hundred metres from the Champs-Élysées. The comfort level of the wicker-furnished rooms is variable; the least expensive are rather cramped.

Hôtel Hameau de Passy – *48 r. de Passy* – Ⓜ *La Muette* – ☎ *01 42 88 47 55* – *hameau.passy@wanadoo.fr* – *32 rms: 89.20/101.40€* – ☐ *4.57€*. A stone's throw from the Trocadéro in a little pedestrian side-street, this hotel is a salutary refuge where the commotion of the capital fades away. The small, white, modern rooms all open onto a tree-filled park: true luxury amidst the hustle and bustle of the capital.

Hôtel Gavarni – *5 r. Gavarni* – Ⓜ *Passy* – ☎ *01 45 24 52 82* – *reservation@gavarni.com* – *25 rms: 92/145€* – ☐ *8.50€*. Two minutes from the Rue de Passy, beloved of all fashion and shopping addicts, this hotel with a spruce red brick façade and refurbished interior is rather simple. The rooms are small, smart and well fitted out. Very hospitable welcome.

Luxury

Régina de Passy – *6 r. de La Tour* – Ⓜ *Passy* – ☎ *01 55 74 75 75* – *regina@gofornet.com* – *63 rms: 140/275€* – ☐ *10€*. The architecture of this 1930s residence located in the chic shopping district around Passy is interesting. The hotel's regular guests appreciate the warm reception, spacious rooms and, from the fifth floor up, balconies whence one can gaze at the Eiffel Tower. The prices are reasonable considering all that's offered.

17th arrondissement

CHAMPS-ÉLYSÉES – MONCEAU

Budget

Hôtel de Paris – *17 r. Biot* – Ⓜ *Place-de-Clichy* – ☎ *01 42 94 02 50* – *hotelde-paris@yahoo.fr* – *30 rms: 45.73/56.40€* – ☐ *4.57€*. In close proximity to the very lively Place de Clichy, this establishment has been overhauled from A to Z. The small rooms all come with well-equipped bathrooms attached. Breakfasts served on the patio in summer.

Hôtel Prince Albert – *28 passage Cardinet, access via 11 r. Jouffroy –* Ⓜ *Villiers-Malesherbes –* ☎ *01 47 54 06 00 – resapaw@free.fr – 32 rms: 61/77€ –* 🖵 *6€.* Hidden in an alley, this hotel has just undergone a major restoration. The highly practical rooms are a wee bit tight but very well maintained. Go downstairs to find the breakfast room.

Hôtel Flaubert – *19 r. Rennequin –* Ⓜ *Ternes –* ☎ *01 46 22 44 35 – 40 rms: 86/99€ –* 🖵 *7.50€.* What a lovely surprise! Behind the very ordinary looking facade of this hotel there's a pocket-sized, verdant courtyard giving onto a few of the rooms. Simple but well maintained, this appealing establishment combines a certain charm with affordable prices.

Résidence Malesherbes – *129 r. Cardinet –* Ⓜ *Villiers or Malesherbes –* ☎ *01 44 15 85 00 – 21 rms: 88/119€ –* 🖵 *8€.* A small, very pleasant hotel with a family feel. The cosy bedrooms all follow the same theme: warm colours, curtains and bedspreads matching the carpet, and a practical corner kitchenette. Breakfast is served in your room.

Luxury

Hôtel Banville – *166 bd Berthier –* Ⓜ *Porte-de-Champerret –* ☎ *01 42 67 70 16 – hotelbanville@wanadoo.fr – 38 rms: 127/183€ –* 🖵 *11€.* Terribly romantic, this small hotel with its 1926 façade is an invitation to stay in and laze about. From Amélie's Room, complete with terrace, to Marie's Apartment, adorned with lace and trimmings, four-poster bed and soft lighting, all of the renovated rooms – our favourites – are simply delightful.

18th arrondissement

MONTMARTRE

Budget

Hôtel des Arts – *5 r. Tholozé –* Ⓜ *Abbesses or Blanche –* ☎ *01 46 06 30 52 – 50 rms: 64/80€ –* 🖵 *6.50€.* A noteworthy address near the Moulin de la Galette and the Place du Tertre. In the lobby, visitors can admire paintings by Roland Dubuc, an artist from Montmartre. All of the rooms have been renovated and are attractive and colourful. We suggest you book well in advance.

Moderate

Ermitage Hôtel – *24 r. Lamarck –* Ⓜ *Lamarck-Caulaincourt –* ☎ *01 42 64 79 22 –* 🖅 *– 12 rms: 74/84€.* This private residence dating from the Second Empire was built by a wealthy gentleman for his mistress. Rooms with a personal touch; four of them overlook the roofs of Paris, while those with a terrace giving onto the garden are the most popular.

Hôtel Roma Sacré Cœur – *101 r. Caulaincourt –* Ⓜ *Lamarck-Caulaincourt –* ☎ *01 42 62 02 02 – 57 rms: 75/86€ –* 🖵 *6€.* Two minutes from the Sacré-Cœur in one of Montmartre's livelier streets, this hotel provides accommodation in the heart of the artists' quarter. The clean, functional rooms are reasonably well-soundproofed.

Les Relais de Paris – Sacré-Cœur – *16 r. Tholozé –* Ⓜ *Abbesses or Blanche –* ☎ *01 42 55 05 06 – Sacré-Cœur@lesrelaisdeparis.fr – 46 rms: 88.42€ –* 🖵 *7.47€.* A top-rate location between the Moulin de la Galette and the Rue des Abbesses for this entirely refurbished hotel. The practical rooms, enlivened by colourful carpets, curtains and bedspreads, benefit from the peaceful surroundings.

19th arrondissement

BELLEVILLE – CANAL SAINT-MARTIN – LA VILLETTE

Budget

Balladins – *219 r. de Crimée –* Ⓜ *Crimée –* ☎ *01 40 38 91 00 – rmhhotel.parisxix@worldonline.fr – 36 rms: 45/60€ –* 🖵 *6€.* Those visiting La Villette and its many attractions will appreciate the proximity of this hotel. The progressively renovated rooms have light wood furniture and bright bedspreads. Agreeable breakfast room.

Kyriad – *147 av. de Flandre* – Ⓜ *Corentin-Cariou* – ☎ *01 44 72 46 46* – *kyriad-paris-villette@wanadoo.fr* – *207 rms: 65/90€* – ⌲ *6€* – *restaurant 11.50€*. The Parc de la Villette is virtually at your feet, should you care to visit an exhibition, listen to a concert or see a film in La Géode. The hotel is of the same stuff: modern and practical, although the rooms are not very spacious. Grilled fish and meat in the restaurant.

Moderate

Hôtel Parc des Buttes Chaumont – *1 pl. Armand-Carrel* – Ⓜ *Jaurès* – ☎ *01 42 08 08 37* – *hpbc@wanadoo.fr* – *45 rms: 84/124€* – ⌲ *8€*. A simplissimo hotel whose location is its forte: opposite the Buttes-Chaumont park, some of the bedrooms open their windows onto a view of the trees. Recently renovated, they are solemn, but well fitted out.

20th arrondissement

BELLEVILLE – PÈRE-LACHAISE

Budget

Hôtel Pyrénées-Gambetta – *12 av. du Père-Lachaise* – Ⓜ *Gambetta* – ☎ *01 47 97 76 57* – *29 rms: 50/75€* – ⌲ *5.50€*. This appealing hotel near the Père-Lachaise cemetery is a tranquil stopover in a quiet street shielded from the urban fracas. Well-soundproofed rooms furnished in the 1980s style.

Hôtel Lilas-Gambetta – *223 av. Gambetta* – Ⓜ *Porte-des-Lilas* – ☎ *01 40 31 85 60* – *hotel-lilas-gambetta@wanadoo.fr* – *34 rms: 55/64€* – ⌲ *6.25€*. The 1925 façade of brick and cut stone conceals a contemporary interior repainted in pretty shades of pastel yellow and almond green. The quietest rooms give onto a charming little courtyard where breakfast is served in summer.

Moderate

Hôtel Palma – *77 av. Gambetta* – Ⓜ *Gambetta* – ☎ *01 46 36 13 65* – *hotel.palma@wanadoo.fr* – *32 rms: 58/73€* – ⌲ *5.65€*. Situated on a noisy avenue right near the Père-Lachaise, this hotel offers small, soundproofed rooms at very reasonable prices. Well managed and spotless, it is outfitted with furniture from the 1970s and 80s that will charm fans of the genre.

Selected restaurants
by district

For all budgets ...

The selected restaurants are listed by neighbourhood and by price range. The metro station nearest to each entry is indicated so that it will be easy to find.
In addition, each of the neighbourhood descriptions in the **Sights** section tells you which arrondissement to look for in this directory.
Looking for a meal under 23€? Have a look at the restaurants in the "Budget" category.
If your budget is as much as 46€, choose one from the "Moderate" category, where you'll find lists of fashionable, choice establishments.
Nothing but the best will do? The "Luxury" category is for you. The restaurants listed here are top-rate, offering Epicurean feasts and magnificent decors. You'll want to remember that correct attire is generally *de rigueur* in these stylish places.

... and for all tastes

In order to provide you with as many choices as possible, we have selected typically Parisian restaurants such as *brasseries* and *bistros*, as well as traditional, exotic or otherwise distinctive establishments. You'll also find simple venues where you can stop in for a salad, a bit of quiche or a sweet snack.
A few fervent defenders of France's regional cuisines are included as well, giving you the opportunity to sample the diversity of the country's culinary heritage. Yearning for something yet further afield? Follow the guide. to Italian, Spanish, Argentinian, Japanese, Thai and other cuisines of the world. There's something for everyone.

Many restaurants in Paris serve lunch from 12.30pm to mid-afternoon and dinner from 7.30pm to 10pm. Some *brasseries* are open all day without a break, while other establishments continue serving until midnight and beyond. Remember to reserve your table, especially in the evening.

For even more choices ...

If perchance you have not been able to find exactly what you're looking for among our many hotel and restaurant listings, do consult **The Red Guide Paris**. It offers a varied list of Parisian addresses, including those that have been awarded the famous Michelin stars. The "Bib Gourmand" symbol designates establishments serving fine food at reasonable prices.
Bon appétit!

1st arrondissement

CHÂTELET-HÔTEL DE VILLE – CONCORDE – HALLES – LOUVRE – MADELEINE – PALAIS-ROYAL – TUILERIES

Budget

Toupary – *2 quai du Louvre (in the Samaritaine, 2nd store)* – Ⓜ *Pont-Neuf* – ☎ *01 40 41 29 29 – le.toupary.rv@elior.com – closed Sun – reserv. recommended evenings– 25.20€ lunch – 12.20/53€.* What an absolutely splendid view from the 5th floor of the Samaritaine. With the Seine at your feet and the great monuments as a backdrop, have a seat in the distinctly modern decor of this colourful restaurant. Evenings, the lighting is muted and the cuisine more sophisticated.

Habitat Restaurant and Café – *8 r. du Pont-Neuf* – Ⓜ *Pont-Neuf or Châtelet* – ☎ *01 45 08 14 90 – closed evenings and Sun – 15/23€.* Belonging to the "food-in-shop" genre, Habitat's restaurant and café may be found on the store's first floor. Habitat furnishings and decor. Traditional cuisine and a small assortment of pastries to be sampled in the afternoon.

Saudade – *34 r. des Bourdonnais* – Ⓜ *Pont-Neuf or Châtelet* – ☎ *01 42 36 30 71* – *closed Sun* – *19.66€*. This small Portuguese restaurant near Les Halles is well appreciated by fans of southern cuisine. Typical dishes cooked in olive oil are served in a simple setting decorated with traditional enamelled wall tiles. The fixed-price lunch menu is tempting; the atmosphere is livelier in the evening.

Lescure – *7 r. Mondovi* – Ⓜ *Concorde* – ☎ *01 42 60 18 91* – *closed 1-23 Aug, 24 Dec to 1 Jan and weekends* – *19.82€*. This little neighbourhood bistro has been run by the same family since 1919. Popular among the locals, one must force one's way into the tiny dining room with its closely-placed tables in order to savour tasty fare served at very reasonable prices.

Chez Clovis – *33 r. Berger* – Ⓜ *Les Halles or Châtelet* – ☎ *01 42 33 97 07* – *closed Sun and public holidays* – *20/32€*. This little bistro set in the Halles Quarter seems to belong to the past, with its handful of tables surrounding the bar and its old photos on the walls. Calf's head, *blanquette* (veal stew in white stock), steak and long-simmered dishes recall the Paris of yester-year with a sigh of nostalgia. The terrace offers a view of the Saint-Eustache church.

Café de l'Époque – *2 r. du Bouloi* – *Galerie Véro-Dodat* – Ⓜ *Palais-Royal* – *Musée-du-Louvre* – ☎ *01 42 33 40 70* – *20.58/32.01€*. Midway between Les Halles and the Louvre, this 1826 café at the entrance to the Véro-Dodat Gallery is now a restaurant. The authentic Parisian bistro decor is elegant and subdued, while the fare is traditional: salads, terrines, foie gras, andouillette and home-made pastries.

Le Relais du Pont-Neuf – *18 quai du Louvre* – Ⓜ *Pont-Neuf or Louvre-Rivoli* – ☎ *01 42 33 98 17* – *pontrelay@aol.com* – *22.10€*. Located on the docks along the Seine, here's a little neighbourhood address where you can hang up your hat and relax. The modern decor, with its pink pastel walls, is agreeable and the menu has an original flair. Make yourself at home.

La Potée des Halles – *3 r. Étienne-Marcel* – Ⓜ *Étienne-Marcel* – ☎ *01 40 41 98 15* – *closed Aug, Sat lunch, Sun lunch and Mon evening* – *20€ lunch* – *28/29€*. This old Halles bistro serves unpretentious meals and has a very afford-able fixed-price menu. Tourists, regulars and the trendy set mingle here, enjoy-ing the handsome art nouveau wall tiles and the cheerful atmosphere. Unfussy service.

Brasserie Le Louvre – *Pl. André-Malraux* – Ⓜ *Palais-Royal* – *Musée-du-Louvre* – ☎ *01 42 96 27 98* – *hoteldulouvre@hoteldulouvre.com* – *30€*. Between the Louvre and the Palais-Royal, this restaurant is remarkably well situated within the gates of the Louvre Hotel. Inaugurated in 1855 by Napoleon III himself, its terrace is set under the arcades of the Place du Palais-Royal when weather permits. Brasserie-style decor and affordable fixed-price menus.

Moderate

Le Fumoir – *6 r. de l'Amiral-Coligny* – Ⓜ *Louvre-Rivoli* – ☎ *01 42 92 00 24* – *http://lefumoir.com* – *closed 24-26 Dec, 31 Dec to 2 Jan* – *26€*. Opposite the Louvre, this fashionable bistro with its brown lacquered tones has an old-fash-ioned café appeal. Enticed by the city-style fare, cosy bar and summer terrace, patrons come here to chat, read the paper or borrow a book from the library. Sunday brunch.

Café Ruc – *159 r. St-Honoré* – Ⓜ *Palais-Royal* – ☎ *01 42 60 97 54* – *reserv. recommended* – *28.97/40€*. Halfway between the Louvre and the Palais-Royal, the atmosphere of this café-restaurant is warm and welcoming. Decorated by Jacques Garcia in a neo-baroque style with green walls and red velvet, it offers an eclectic menu and modern cuisine. During fashion-show season, reporters, designers and mode people fill the place to the brim.

Café Marly – *93 r. de Rivoli* – Ⓜ *Palais-Royal* – *Musée-du-Louvre* – ☎ *01 49 26 06 60* – *31/57€*. Opposite the pyramid and under the Louvre's arcades, this hip restaurant serves contemporary cuisine in a setting that suc-cessfully melds moulded ceilings, wooden floors and modern furniture. Summertime, have a drink on the terrace – it's one of Paris's prettiest. Serves until 1am.

Palais Royal – *110 Galerie de Valois* – Ⓜ *Palais-Royal* – *Musée-du-Louvre* – ☎ *01 40 20 00 27* – *palaisrest@aol.com* – *closed 15 Dec to 30 Jan, Sat from Oct to May and Sun* – *43/80€*. What could be more delightful than taking a seat here in the gardens of the Palais-Royal for lunch, dinner or just an afternoon drink? In winter, the room under the arcades is very pleasant; its art deco theme and the contemporary cuisine are well-matched.

Luxury

Le Grand Vefour – *17 r. de Beaujolais* – Ⓜ *Palais-Royal* – *Musée-du-Louvre* – ☎ *01 42 96 56 27* – *grand.vefour@wanadoo.fr* – *closed 1-7 Apr, 2 Aug to 2 Sep, 23-31 Dec, Fri evening and weekends* – *73.17€ lunch* – *221.05€*. Located beneath the arches of the Palais-Royal, this former 18C café is luxuriously decorated with woodwork, mirrors and frescoes, setting the stage for an exquisite meal. Gourmet diners come here to indulge in the famous *ravioles de foie gras* in truffled cream sauce or any of their other justly celebrated specialities. More moderately-priced lunch menu.

2nd arrondissement

GRANDS BOULEVARDS – HALLES – PLACE DES VICTOIRES – SENTIER

Budget

Domaine de Lintillac – *10 r. St-Augustin* – Ⓜ *Quatre-Septembre* – ☎ *01 40 20 96 27* – *lintillac@free.fr* – *closed 10 days in Aug, Sat lunch and Sun* – *reserv. recommended* – *11.74/23.78€*. Flavours of Southwest France abound in this restaurant located between the Bourse and the Opéra Garnier. The prices are quite low because many ingredients come straight from the owner's canned goods factory in Corrèze. The decor is simple and the service pleasant. It's always packed.

Petite France – *14 r. de la Banque* – Ⓜ *Bourse* – ☎ *01 42 96 17 19* – *closed Sat* – *13.72/21.34€*. Here's a convivial, down-to-earth address where one can have a quick, tasty meal at reasonable prices. The decor is of the simple, natural sort: ochre walls, parquet floor, beech wood furniture and big tables. Cooking with a focus on regional produce.

L'Arbre à Cannelle – *57 passage des Panoramas* – Ⓜ *Grands-Boulevards* – ☎ *01 45 08 55 87* – *closed Sun and evenings* – *15.24/22.87€*. This former *chocolaterie* situated in the Passage des Panoramas has Napoleon III woodwork and a tea room. If tempted by quiches, pies, salads, gourmand platters or the daily special, ask for a table in the room with the beautiful ornamental ceiling.

La Cocarde – *7 r. Marie-Stuart* – Ⓜ *Étienne-Marcel* – ☎ *01 40 39 05 09* – *brunococarde@wanadoo.fr* – *closed Sat lunch and Sun* – *reserv. recommended* – *12.30€ lunch* – *16/30€*. What does this little place hidden in a pedestrian street of the Halles district have to recommend it? The warm-toned decor, the young, enthusiastic service, healthy servings of traditional fare and very reasonable prices, no less.

À La Grille Montorgueil – *50 r. Montorgueil* – Ⓜ *Châtelet-les-Halles or Sentier* – ☎ *01 42 33 21 21* – *20.12/35.27€*. A butcher's shop during the Halles' golden era, this old house tucked away in Rue Montorgueil is now home to an attractive 1920s-style bistro. A superb bar stands proudly at the entrance and there is a vaulted cellar. Typical bistro cookery.

Moderate

Le Grand Colbert – *2 r. Vivienne* – Ⓜ *Bourse* – ☎ *01 42 86 87 88* – *le.grand.colbert@wanadoo.fr* – *24.40€*. Worthy of a film-set, with its mosaics, murals, fine high ceiling, long wall seats and vast bar, this 19C brasserie is frequented more for the setting than the food. Attractive fixed-priced menu. Serves until 1am.

Le Gallopin – *40 r. N.-D.-des-Victoires* – Ⓜ *Bourse* – ☎ *01 42 36 45 38* – *closed Sun* – *25.50/30.50€*. Monsieur Gallopin had the Cuban mahogany bar that stands in this brasserie built to seduce his beloved in 1900. Restored with brio, Le Gallopin is still a most pleasurable place to have a meal served by the staff in white aprons, as is only befitting. Service until 12:30am.

Café Drouant – *pl. Gaillon* – Ⓜ *Opéra or Quatre-Septembre* – ☎ *01 42 65 15 16* – *closed Aug and weekends* – *38€*. This Parisian institution, home of the Académie Goncourt since 1914, offers two possibilities. The 'Café Drouant' menu is served in a more sober dining room, while the restaurant boasts a characteristic art deco decor. An opportunity to try this mythical citadel without risking bankruptcy.

MARAIS – RÉPUBLIQUE

Budget

L'Apparement – 18 r. des Coutures-St-Gervais – Ⓜ St-Sébastien-Froissart – ☎ 01 48 87 12 22 – closed Sat lunch – reserv. requested evenings – 12.50/18.30€. The little rooms of this café just opposite the Picasso Museum garden are appealingly homey. Lined in wood and decorated with a varied array of paintings and furniture, they're are cosy as can be. Fine selection of salads at lunchtime; cocktails and cold plates in the evening.

Trattoria Amici Miei – 53 bd Beaumarchais – Ⓜ Chemin-Vert – ☎ 01 42 71 82 62 – closed Easter school holidays, 6-30 Aug, 23 Dec to 2 Jan, Mon lunch and Sun – ⌿ – 17/20€. Aficionados of real Italian cooking just like la mamma's will discover this simple establishment between the Place des Vosges and Bastille with great pleasure. Pasta, pizzas and, of course, a first rate buffalo mozzarella are on the agenda. Often very crowded, but worth the wait.

Caves St-Gilles – 4 r. St-Gilles – Ⓜ Chemin-Vert – ☎ 01 48 87 22 62 – ⌿ – reserv. requested – 18.29/35€. Wine, beer and sherry flow freely in this lively tapas and wine bar, washing down the hors d'oeuvres and mixed plates sampled at the small bistro tables. Spanish decor, accordingly noisy and friendly atmosphere.

Chez Omar – 47 r. de Bretagne – Ⓜ Arts-et-Métiers – ☎ 01 42 72 36 26 – closed Sun lunch and evenings of 24 and 31 Dec – ⌿ – 19.85/32.85€. The couscous served in this old neighbourhood bistro-style eatery has been delighting fans for over twenty years. With its noisy, casual atmosphere, this has been the 'in' place to dine since its discovery by the capital's top models a few years ago.

Chez Jenny – 39 bd du Temple – Ⓜ République – ☎ 01 44 54 39 00 – www.chez-jenny.com – 22.50€. Jean-Charles Spindler, a marquetry craftsman, accomplished a tour de force when he decorated this Alsatian brasserie founded in 1932. The marquetry artwork in different species of wood and the sculptures in the upper floor rooms are well worth a visit. Brasserie-style cuisine.

Chez Janou – 2 r. Roger-Verlomme – Ⓜ Chemin-Vert – ☎ 01 42 72 28 41 – ⌿ – 22.87€. This charming 1900s bistro, which has retained its original decor, features a superb ceramic-covered wall. The menu has been replaced with an attractive lunch special and dishes of Provençal inspiration listed on the hallowed slate bill of fare.

Moderate

Ambassade d'Auvergne – 22 r. du Grenier-St-Lazare – Ⓜ Rambuteau or Étienne-Marcel – ☎ 01 42 72 31 22 – info@ambassade-auvergne.com – 25.92€. Local flavour guaranteed: the rustic ground-floor dining room is sure to transport you to the hilly reaches of this rural region of central France. Hams and sausages hang above the large communal table that reunites fans of typical fare from Auvergne.

4th arrondissement

BASTILLE – BEAUBOURG – CHÂTELET-HÔTEL DE VILLE – ÎLE SAINT-LOUIS – MARAIS – NOTRE-DAME

Budget

Le Pain Quotidien – 20 r. des Archives – Ⓜ Hôtel-de-Ville – ☎ 01 44 54 03 07 – closed 1 Jan, 25 Dec and evenings from May to Sep – 9.15/18.29€. Located in the heart of Paris's gay district, the terrace of this bakery-grocery-tea room under a canopy of horse-chestnut trees is all the rage. You may also take a seat at one of the large communal tables indoors to enjoy a salad or an open-faced sandwich.

Chez Marianne – 2 r. des Hospitalières-St-Gervais – Ⓜ Saint-Paul – ☎ 01 42 72 18 86 – reserv. requested – 12.96/27.44€. This restaurant-cum-delicatessen on the Rue des Rosiers in the Jewish quarter serves a blend of Mediterranean and Central European food. Clients compose their own meals from a selection of victuals on display. Ask for a table in the room opposite the wine racks or, in summer, on the terrace.

Le Franc Pinot – *1 quai de Bourbon* – Ⓜ *Pont-Marie or Hôtel-de-Ville* – ☎ *01 46 33 60 64 – closed Christmas school holidays, lunch (except Sun), Sun evening and Mon – 19.82/30.49€.* Well-situated on the Ile St-Louis opposite the Pont-Marie, this bar-bistro hidden in a blue house serves food without airs. Come Friday or Saturday night – the vaulted cellars fill up fast as patrons crowd in to dine to the tune of jazz concerts organised by the proprietor.

Vins des Pyrénées – *25 r. Beautreillis* – Ⓜ *Bastille or Sully-Morland* – ☎ *01 42 72 64 94 – closed 10-25 Aug, Sun in summer and Sat lunch – 22.87/30.49€.* How very inviting, this former wine merchant's boutique with its elderly bottle racks, collection of labels from the past, old-fashioned postcards, handsome marble bar and oilskin tablecloths. Bistro fare and very relaxed service.

Moderate

Le Petit Bofinger – *6 r. de la Bastille* – Ⓜ *Bastille* – ☎ *01 42 72 05 23 – 18€ lunch – 24.39/27€.* Opposite the famous Bofinger brasserie, this little bistro run by the same team offers a simpler menu in an amusing 1950s decor with wall frescoes, tube chairs and woodwork. The reasonable fixed-price menus are popular with the regular clientele. Serves until midnight.

La Brasserie de l'Isle St-Louis – *55 quai de Bourbon* – Ⓜ *Pont-Marie or Cité* – ☎ *01 43 54 02 59 – closed 1 wk in Feb, Aug, Thu lunch and Wed – no reserv. – 25.92/38.11€.* After visiting Notre-Dame, cross over the Pont St-Louis and take a seat in this traditional brasserie with its well-worn wooden furniture. Indoors or on the terrace in summer, amidst regulars and tourists, you'll enjoy the street artists and musicians playing in front of the bridge.

Thanksgiving's Bayou la Seine – *20 r. St-Paul* – Ⓜ *Saint-Paul* – ☎ *01 42 77 68 28 – www.thanksgivingparis.com – closed 30 Apr to 9 May, 23 Jul to 17 Aug, Sun evening and Mon – 27.50/36.50€.* Ever tasted Louisiana cooking? This little restaurant in the Marais provides an opportunity to discover real Cajun dishes in a small, simple dining room. There is also an American grocery just next-door for homesick Yankees.

L'Enoteca – *25 r. Charles-V* – Ⓜ *Sully-Morland or Saint-Paul* – ☎ *01 42 78 91 44 – closed 12-20 Aug – reserv. recommended – 30€.* This Italian restaurant has acquired a fine reputation thanks to its superior Italian wine list and creative cuisine. Set in a charming 17C house, the decoration is a pleasing combination of old beams, ochre-coloured walls and hand-blown Murano lamps.

Bofinger – *5 r. de la Bastille* – Ⓜ *Bastille* – ☎ *01 42 72 87 82 – 30.50€.* Founded in 1864, this restaurant is a Parisian landmark. The venerable seats of its Belle Époque decor have cushioned the bottoms of some of the most famous politicians, writers, artists and musicians of the 20C. The brasserie, with its handsome glass roof, remains as crowded today as ever before. Reservations recommended. Serves until 1am.

Au Bourguignon du Marais – *52 r. François-Miron* – Ⓜ *Saint-Paul* – ☎ *01 48 87 15 40 – Au.Bourguignon.Du.Marais@wanadoo.fr – closed Sat evening and Sun – 38/53€.* This restaurant and wine merchant's gives Burgundy the starring role, both in your wine glass and on your plate with such delectable recipes as the parsleyed house ham or the *andouillette à l'aligoté*. All is served in a pleasant, contemporary setting. Mini-terrace.

5th arrondissement

JARDIN DES PLANTES – JUSSIEU – LUXEMBOURG – MAUBERT – MOUFFETARD – QUARTIER LATIN

Budget

Au Piano Muet – *48 r. Mouffetard* – Ⓜ *Place-Monge* – ☎ *01 43 31 45 15 – closed lunch except weekends – 15€.* The perfect place to come in from the cold, here's a nourishing halt that offers traditional dishes as well as the house specialities, raclettes and fondues. The decor – exposed beams and stone walls – is inviting and the atmosphere convivial.

Mirama – *17 r. St-Jacques* – Ⓜ *Maubert-Mutualité, Cluny or Saint-Michel* – ☎ *01 43 54 71 77 – 15.24/19.82€.* This little Chinese restaurant in the Latin Quarter is popular with everyone: Asians, tourists and Parisians cluster at its doors for one of the tightly-packed tables upstairs or in the cave-like cellar. Serves generous helpings of well-prepared food at reasonable prices.

Le Reminet – *3 r. des Grands-Degrés* – Ⓜ *Maubert-Mutualité* – ☎ *01 44 07 04 24* – *closed 18 Feb to 3 Mar, 12 Aug to 1 Sep, Tue-Wed* – *13€ lunch* – *17€*. This terrific address close by Notre-Dame has everything to attract diners and keep them coming back: a young chef at the ovens, toothsome cuisine, a fixed-price lunch menu and a very affordable weekday dinner menu. The wine list is as tempting as the food.

Café Littéraire – *1 r. des Fossés-St-Bernard, in the Institut du Monde Arabe (ground floor)* – Ⓜ *Cardinal-Lemoine or Jussieu* – ☎ *01 40 51 34 69* – *jf.bouquillon@sodexho-prestige.fr* – *closed evenings and Mon* – *reserv. recommended* – *18/23€*. This small restaurant with Moorish benches proposes salads, a daily special and a buffet of Mid-Eastern pastries. It's basic and inexpensive; there's a (mint) tea room in the afternoons. Those with more ample means can go upstairs to the Ziryab and enjoy a wider choice and an unforgettable view.

Le Perraudin – *157 r. St-Jacques* – Ⓜ *Luxembourg* – ☎ *01 46 33 15 75* – *closed 3 wks in Aug, Christmas school holidays, Mon lunch and weekends* – ✝ – *10.37€ lunch* – *18.29/27.44€*. Worthy of a scene from a Maigret detective novel, the feel of this former coal merchant's with its bistro chairs, chequered table-cloths, bar and old mirrors is utterly authentic. Appetising bistro cuisine full of old-fashioned flavours and *Tarte Tatin* for those with a sweet tooth. No reservations.

Moissonnier – *28 r. des Fossés-St-Bernard* – Ⓜ *Cardinal-Lemoine* – ☎ *01 43 29 87 65* – *closed 1 Aug to 1 Sep, Sun and Mon* – *22.90€ lunch* – *31/47€*. In a somewhat outdated but impeccably managed bistro décor, this little restaurant, a stone's throw from the Institut du Monde Arabe, serves healthy portions of traditionally prepared Lyonnais specialities. Affordable fixed-price lunch and dinner menus.

Moderate

Ma Cuisine – *26 bd St-Germain* – Ⓜ *Maubert-Mutualité* – ☎ *01 40 51 08 27* – *closed Sun* – *24.39€*. The dining room, entirely renovated, is light and merry, with white walls allowing a stone to peek through here and there, blue beams and round tables set comfortably apart from one another. Traditional cuisine prepared with fresh ingredients.

El Palenque – *5 r. de la Montagne-Ste-Geneviève* – Ⓜ *Maubert-Mutualité* – ☎ *01 43 54 08 99* – *closed Aug, 24 Dec to 2 Jan and Sun* – ✝ – *25.31/32.01€*. Take a trip to faraway Argentina without leaving Paris. Try succulent meat dishes from the pampa accompanied by the fruits of South American vineyards, all served in a *rancho* setting. Quite an adventure!

Le Buisson Ardent – *25 r. Jussieu* – Ⓜ *Jussieu* – ☎ *01 43 54 93 02* – *closed 1 Aug to 2 Sep and weekends* – *14.50€ lunch* – *27€*. This little house opposite Jussieu university with its 1923 frescoes and neighbourhood bistro flair is always crowded. If the lunchtime menu is excellent value, the evening menu is just as good. Relaxed, friendly atmosphere and good food.

Les Bouchons de François Clerc – *12 r. de l'Hôtel-Colbert* – Ⓜ *Maubert-Mutualité* – ☎ *01 43 54 15 34* – *closed Sat lunch and Sun* – *40.86€*. Two minutes from Notre-Dame, this restaurant located in a traditional old Parisian house continues to lure customers back with its list of wines sold at store price. In either the pleasant dining room or the romantic vaulted cellar, choose one of the fixed-priced menus and enjoy your pick of reds, whites and rosés.

6th arrondissement

INSTITUT DE FRANCE – LUXEMBOURG – MONTPARNASSE ODÉON – QUARTIER LATIN – SAINT-GERMAIN-DES-PRÉS SAINT-SULPICE – SÈVRES-BABYLONE

Budget

Crêperie St-Germain – *33 r. St-André-des-Arts* – Ⓜ *Saint-Michel* – ☎ *01 43 54 24 41* – *8.70€ lunch* – *11/19€*. Fancy a snack near the Place St-Michel? This crêperie with an original Moorish decor has two sister-restaurants at no 27 of this busy little street: "Les Pêcheurs" for the maritime ambience and "Les Arts" which has little alcoves. Spoilt for choice?

Le Bistrot d'Opio – *9 r. Guisarde* – Ⓜ *Mabillon or Saint-Germain-des-Prés* – ☎ *01 43 29 01 84* – *www.bistrot-opio.com* – *14.20/23.80€*. Sunny colours, wrought-iron, bistro tables, scents of the south and the song of cicadas in the background: both of the small dining rooms of this pleasant restaurant exude the charm of the south. Mediterranean cuisine prepared with olive oil, *naturellement*.

Gustavia – *26 r. des Grands-Augustins* – Ⓜ *Saint-Michel* – ☎ *01 40 46 86 70 – closed 1-15 Aug, Mon evening and Sun – 10.40€ lunch – 17.53/24.39€*. The Swedish flag flies proudly in front of this little establishment serving marinated salmon, herring, salads and daily specials, delighting all those who appreciate simple Nordic flavours. Subdued Scandinavian decor and gentle prices.

Le Machon d'Henri – *8 r. Guisarde* – Ⓜ *Mabillon* – ☎ *01 43 29 08 70 – 21.34/25.92€*. This bistro, with its classy dark green facade, is often full at lunch. Seated elbow to elbow, customers enjoy tasty little dishes of Lyonnais inspiration in a decor of exposed beams, painted stones and well-stocked shelves displaying bottles of wine. Lively atmosphere.

Chez Marcel – *7 r. Stanislas* – Ⓜ *Vavin* – ☎ *01 45 48 29 94 – closed Aug and weekends – 27/43€*. Yet to be overrun by Montparnasse's hungry hordes, this Lyonnais bistro founded in 1905 has a comfortable old feel to it. Knick-knacks, copper pots, pictures and benches, it's all there. Generous helpings of good, solid food. Excellent value for money at lunchtime. Go through the kitchen to find the washrooms ...

Chez Maître Paul – *12 r. Monsieur-le-Prince* – Ⓜ *Odéon* – ☎ *01 43 54 74 59 – chezmaitrepaul@aol.com – closed 20-27 Dec, Sun and Mon Jul-Aug – 26/31€*. A few steps from the Théâtre de l'Odéon, this rustic-looking restaurant is renowned for its cuisine from the Franche-Comté (a mountainous region in the east of France). Connoisseurs will enjoy a glass of the famous *vin jaune* (yellow wine), vinified on the slopes of the Jura.

Bouillon Racine – *3 r. Racine* – Ⓜ *Odéon or Cluny-la-Sorbonne* – ☎ *01 44 32 15 60 – bouillon.racine@wanadoo.fr – 20€ lunch – 27.29€*. A bastion of Belgian cuisine in St-Michel: beer and local fare take pride of place in this former soup kitchen with a surprising art nouveau decor. Brasserie menu upstairs, simpler fare to be sampled facing the bar on the ground floor. Serves until midnight.

Le Bistrot d'Alex – *2 r. Clément* – Ⓜ *Mabillon* – ☎ *01 43 54 09 53 – closed 11-18 Aug and Sun evening – 28/70€*. After a stroll around the St-Germain-des-Prés market, rest your weary bones at one of the tables of this little bistro offering a choice of specialities from Lyon and Provence with a southern lilt. Simply-decorated dining room with tables set close together.

Casa Bini – *36 r. Grégoire-de-Tours* – Ⓜ *Odéon* – ☎ *01 46 34 05 60 – closed 12-19 Aug and 23-25 Dec – 21€ lunch – 30/40€*. Located in a side street off St-Germain-des-Prés, this Italian restaurant serves a fine selection of antipasti, toast with mozzarella, carpaccios and pasta. Decorated with sobriety in the modern bistro style; the upstairs dining room features enormous beams. Attractive lunchtime menu.

7th arrondissement

TOUR EIFFEL – FAUBOURG SAINT-GERMAIN – INVALIDES – ORSAY

Chez Germaine – *30 r. Pierre-Leroux* – Ⓜ *Duroc or Vaneau* – ☎ *01 42 73 28 34 – closed Aug, Sat evening and Sun – ✁ – reserv. requested – 12/19€*. At lunch this restaurant is filled with fans of the hard-boiled eggs with mayonnaise, grated carrot salad, calf's liver, rabbit and other dishes whipped up 'just like at home'. Inviting interior and efficient service. Warning: neither washrooms nor coffee.

Sancerre – *22 av. Rapp* – Ⓜ *Pont-de-l'Alma* – ☎ *01 45 51 75 91 – closed Aug, Sat evening and Sun – 15.24/25.92€*. This countrified restaurant is a genuine ambassador for the village of Sancerre in the Berry region. Opening at 8am, it offers ample snacks such as terrines, omelettes, *andouillette* cooked in Sancerre wine, *crottins de Chavignol* (aged goat's cheese) and home-made pies. All liberally washed down with a glass of the region's best – *à votre santé!*

Restaurant Domaine de Lintillac – *20 r. Rousselet* – Ⓜ *Duroc or Vaneau* – ☎ *01 45 66 88 23 – closed 1-15 Aug, Sat lunch and Sun – 15.24/22.87€*. Yearning for a morsel of *confit*, some *cassoulet* or *foie gras* without busting your budget? Come taste produce shipped directly from the proprietor's own premises in Corrèze served in a simple, no-frills decor blending beamed ceilings and roughcast walls. This convivial restaurant is one of the best values for the euro in Paris.

Les Jardins de Varenne in the Musée Rodin – *77 r. de Varenne* – Ⓜ *Varenne* – ☎ *01 45 50 42 34 – rodin@soustart-horeto.com – closed evenings and Mon* – *15.25/22.87€*. Visitors and regulars looking for a bite to eat convene under the trees of the delightful terrace belonging to this pavilion hidden in a lovely garden. Simple salads, mixed platters and sandwiches available from the self-service section. Divine.

L'Auvergne Gourmande – *127 r. St-Dominique* – Ⓜ *École-Militaire* – ☎ *01 47 05 60 79 – closed Sun* – ✝ – *19.82/28€*. Two guest tables for five and eight diners separated by a bookshelf filled with wine bottles, old porcelain on the walls, slate place settings: what an imaginative decor for this restaurant housed in an old butcher shop. Cuisine essentially from Auvergne.

La Poule au Pot – *121 r. de l'Université* – Ⓜ *La Tour-Maubourg* – ☎ *01 47 05 16 36 – closed Sat lunch and Sun – 22.50€*. The brown façade, so typical of the old Parisian bistros, sets the tone of this eatery with its 1930s ambience. Pleasant interior with red leather wall seats, a ceiling edged with crown moulding and decorative windows. Traditional cuisine.

Thoumieux – *79 r. St-Dominique* – Ⓜ *Solférino* – ☎ *01 47 05 49 75 – 30.49€*. Half-way between the Eiffel Tower and the Invalides, this busy, old-fashioned bistro with red velvet seats and art nouveau chairs serves generous helpings at reasonable prices: *cassoulet*, duck *confit*, leeks and lentils in vinaigrette all feature prominently. Serves until midnight.

Ribe – *15 av. de Suffren* – Ⓜ *Champ-de-Mars, Tour-Eiffel or Bir-Hakeim* – ☎ *01 45 66 53 79 – 16.90€ lunch – 24.90€*. A short distance from the Eiffel Tower, this restaurant now sports an interior inspired by colonial England. Parisians and tourists alike appreciate the reasonable prices as well as the traditional French fare: onion soup, terrines, and steak in pepper sauce.

Le P'tit Troquet – *28 r. de l'Exposition* – Ⓜ *École-Militaire* – ☎ *01 47 05 80 39 – closed 1-23 Aug, 23 Dec to 2 Feb, Sat lunch, Mon lunch and Sun – reserv. requested – 26.50€*. This little bistro, just a few minutes from the Champ-de-Mars, will delight second-hand treasure hunters: bottles, mirrors, lace, lamps and other odds-and-bobs grace the dining room. Epicureans will savour the market-fresh fare, chalked up on a slate. Popular among Parisians.

Au Bon Accueil – *14 r. de Monttessuy* – Ⓜ *Pont-de-l'Alma* – ☎ *01 47 05 46 11 – closed 10-25 Aug and weekends – 25.20€ lunch – 28.20€*. Just down the road from the Eiffel Tower, this restaurant lives up to its name: the Pleasant Welcome. Two small, cheerful dining rooms and friendly service with a smile. The decoration is elegant and refined, the menu is simple, and the cooking is flavoursome and inventive. Add reasonable prices, and you have an unbeatable recipe.

Le Vauban – *7 pl. Vauban* – Ⓜ *Saint-François-Xavier* – ☎ *01 47 05 52 67 – 30€*. For a wonderful view of the church of the Dôme des Invalides, take a seat on the very popular terrace of this brasserie or in the stylish dining room featuring trompe l'œil marble work. A well-thought-out menu awaits diners lunch and evening.

La Maison de l'Amérique Latine – *217 bd St-Germain* – Ⓜ *Solférino or Rue-du-Bac* – ☎ *01 49 54 75 10 – commercial@mal217.org – closed Aug, 20 Dec to 1 Jan, weekends and evenings from Oct to Apr – 37€*. A garden in the bosom of Paris. As soon as the weather becomes warm enough, this is where the restaurant's lovely terrace is set up. A refreshing haven from the summer heat, this private 18C mansion on Boulevard St-Germain is a rare find.

CHAMPS-ÉLYSÉES – CONCORDE – FAUBOURG-SAINT-HONORÉ – SAINT-LAZARE

Le Griffonnier – *8 r. des Saussaies* – Ⓜ *Miromesnil* – ☎ *01 42 65 17 17 – 13.57/22.87€*. A 17C house is the setting for this wine bar serving appetising little dishes of the bistro genre. Rustic and something of a tight squeeze but quite jolly all the same. The cream of the Beaujolais crop is savoured here every year.

Théâtre du Rond-Point – *2 bis av. Franklin-D.-Roosevelt* – Ⓜ *Franklin-D.-Roosevelt* – ☎ *01 44 95 98 44 – closed Aug and Sun evening – 18€*. To reach this red and grey-toned restaurant, adorned with posters and other mementoes from former shows, you have to cross the lobby of the attractive theatre just alongside the Champs-Elysées. The terrace in the shade of horse chestnut trees is popular when the weather is fine.

Bar à Vin Nicolas – *31 pl. de la Madeleine* – Ⓜ *Madeleine* – ☎ *01 44 51 90 22 – closed Sun – 18.29€*. The Nicolas wine stores are a familiar Parisian sight; this one also has a restaurant where you can enjoy a fine glass of wine and a light meal of salad, quiche, delicatessen, cheese or a prepared dish. Modern setting and rather impersonal service.

Le Bistrot de Jean-Luc – *41 r. de Penthièvre* – Ⓜ *Miromesnil* – ☎ *01 43 59 23 99 – closed 1-20 Aug and weekends – 19/30€*. The small dining room with its big mirror is as simple as they come, but never mind. The tempting bistro menu and wide choice of wines by the glass are the main draw of this likeable little neighbourhood restaurant. Easy on the wallet.

Granterroirs – *30 r. de Miromesnil* – Ⓜ *Villiers* – ☎ *01 47 42 18 18 – closed 5-15 Aug and weekends – 22.71€*. Big oak tables, shelves stocked with local products, baskets garnished with small-label wines and specialities of different regions. The French countryside has come to Paris via this deluxe grocery store-cum-restaurant. Delectable salads, open-faced sandwiches, assorted gourmand dishes and house desserts. No smoking.

Moderate

Lô Sushi – *8 r. de Berri* – Ⓜ *George-V* – ☎ *01 45 62 01 00 – 25/40€*. A simple formula: sushi served in a minimalist setting created by the famous decorator Andrée Putman. Designed for fun, the idea is simple: you take a seat at the bar and take your sushi from a little conveyor belt. Much favoured by the jet-set who flock here every night.

La Fermette Marbeuf 1900 – *5 r. Marbeuf* – Ⓜ *Alma-Marceau* – ☎ *01 53 23 08 00 – 27.90€*. A minute's walk from Avenue Georges-V, the 1900s decor of this brasserie featuring ceramics and period windows will appeal to fans of classic Parisian restaurants. A period glass roof illuminates the second dining room. Traditional cuisine.

L'Appart' – *9 r. du Colisée* – Ⓜ *Franklin-D.-Roosevelt* – ☎ *01 53 75 16 34 – restapart@aol.com – 29/39.60€*. An engaging address right near the Champs-Élysées. Whether in the living room, den or kitchen of this restaurant pretending to be an apartment, you'll sample contemporary cuisine in a relaxed ambience. Service until midnight; Sunday brunch.

Mollard – *115 r. St-Lazare* – Ⓜ *Saint-Lazare* – ☎ *01 43 87 50 22 – 30.49/120€*. The nothing-special exterior leads to a gem of the art nouveau period in its large, listed dining room designed by Edouard Niermans. Superb mosaics and decorated wall tiles from Sarreguemines. Straightforward brasserie cuisine.

Ladurée – Champs-Élysées – *75 av. des Champs-Élysées* – Ⓜ *George-V* – ☎ *01 40 75 08 75 – 38.50€*. Can one possibly resist such gourmand temptations? In addition to the forty or so house pastries, the menu offers such savoury treats as salads, sample platters and traditional dishes, all served in a magnificent Napoleon III decor with charming drawing rooms upstairs. *Très chic!*

9th arrondissement

FAUBOURG POISSONNIÈRE – GRANDS BOULEVARDS – OPÉRA – PIGALLE – SAINT-LAZARE

Budget

L'Auberge du Clou – *30 av. Trudaine* – Ⓜ *Pigalle or Anvers* – ☎ *01 48 78 22 48 – aubergeduclou@wanadoo.fr – closed Mon – reserv. recommended – 12.20€ lunch – 14.94/45€*. We're not the first to discover this inn: Toulouse-Lautrec, Courteline and Debussy used to come here too. Wintertime, have a seat upstairs and enjoy the fireplace; summertime it's difficult to pull oneself away from the delightful terrace. Traditional cuisine with a hint of the exotic.

Au Bonheur de Sophie – *63 r. de Provence* – Ⓜ *Chaussée-d'Antin* – ☎ *01 48 78 67 00 – closed weekends, evenings except Thu – reserv. recommended – 15.30€*. This little bistro hidden behind the big department stores is the perfect place to take a break between two shopping sprees. The dining room, albeit somewhat cramped, is pleasant with its beige walls, old photos and advertising posters. The menu offers a wide variety of dishes.

Café Flo – *60 bd Haussmann – Printemps de la Mode store, 6th floor* – Ⓜ *Havre-Caumartin* – ☎ *01 42 82 58 84 – closed Sun and evenings except Thu – 16.77/25.92€*. You have to go up to the 6th floor of the Printemps department store to admire the vast glass roof of this restaurant built in 1923, now a listed monument. Simple fare served from morning to teatime under the 3,185 panes of glass.

Menthe et Basilic – *6 r. Lamartine* – Ⓜ *Cadet* – ☎ *01 48 78 12 20* – *closed Sat lunch, Mon evening and Sun* – *reserv. requested* – *20/30€*. The decor and cuisine of this pleasant sienna-walled restaurant conjure up southern France. The clever lighting system creates an intimate ambience and the nicely presented, delectable food is served with a smile.

Au Petit Riche – *25 r. Le Peletier* – Ⓜ *Le Peletier* – ☎ *01 47 70 68 68* – *closed Sun* – *25.15€ lunch* – *27.45€*. An institution in this business district. Since 1858, bankers and stock-brokers have convened in the cosy comfort of this handsome room, plotting the course of the universe. Excellent selection of Loire wines. Serves until 12:15am.

Moderate

Paprika – *28 av. Trudaine* – Ⓜ *Anvers* – ☎ *01 44 63 02 91* – *closed 1-20 Aug* – *13€ lunch* – *19.80/38€*. On the same spot as the Âne Rouge, where socialist radicals rallied in the early 20C, this restaurant is now a citadel of Hungarian cooking. Try the cold meats, national dishes and Hungarian wines. Live music in the evening.

I Golosi – *6 r. de la Grange-Batelière* – Ⓜ *Grands-Boulevards* – ☎ *01 48 24 18 63* – *i.golosi@wanadoo.fr* – *closed Aug, Sat evening and Sun* – *28/42€*. At the entrance to the Passage Verdeau, this Venetian bistro serves cuisine with a decidedly Italian accent in a modern, elegant interior graced with Murano lamps, furniture from Trevise and a Venetian tiled floor. The entry has a small wine bar and shop, plus a few tables at lunchtime.

Le Barramundi – *3 r. Taitbout* – Ⓜ *Richelieu-Drouot* – ☎ *01 47 70 21 21* – *closed Sun* – *20€ lunch* – *38/53€*. The bar-lounge on the ground floor plays popular 'world music', whilst downstairs the spacious restaurant, a blend of Indian and African influences, is very popular with the business lunch bunch. Mediterranean cuisine with a spicy tang.

10th arrondissement

FAUBOURG POISSONNIÈRE – GRANDS BOULEVARDS – CANAL SAINT-MARTIN

Budget

Hôtel du Nord – *102 quai de Jemmapes* – Ⓜ *Jacques-Bonsergent or République* – ☎ *01 40 40 78 78* – *closed 13-28 Aug* – *14€ lunch* – *18/22€*. It was in front of this very façade alongside the canal St-Martin that Arletty huskily said the now-famous words *"atmosphère, atmosphère"* to Jean Gabin in Marcel Carné's classic film *Hôtel du Nord*. Now a café-restaurant with a retro feel, it serves classic cuisine and organises live music in the evenings.

Moderate

Brasserie Flo – *7 cour des Petites-Écuries* – Ⓜ *Château-d'Eau* – ☎ *01 47 70 13 59* – *29€ lunch* – *30.50€*. Set in a paved cul-de-sac, this turn-of-the-century brasserie takes you back to a Paris of yore. Benches overhung with gleaming copper coat-hooks, old paintings and stained-glass windows: a picturesque setting for the appetising cuisine. Serves until 1.30am.

Julien – *16 r. du Fg-St-Denis* – Ⓜ *Strasbourg-Saint-Denis or Château-d'Eau* – ☎ *01 47 70 12 06* – *21.50€ lunch* – *30.50€*. The discreet façade of this brasserie hides a splendid gem of art nouveau decoration that's quite unexpected in this neighbourhood. The noisy, exuberant dining room has been in favour for over a century with customers who dine side by side, enjoying the generous portions and the seafood. Serves until 1.30am.

11th arrondissement

BASTILLE – BELLEVILLE – FAUBOURG SAINT-ANTOINE – RÉPUBLIQUE

Budget

Haïku – *63 r. Jean-Pierre-Timbaud* – Ⓜ *Parmentier* – ☎ *01 56 98 11 67* – *closed 9-26 Aug and Mon evening* – *14.40/21€*. In Japan, a "haiku" is a short poem that seeks to capture the essence and harmony of nature. This restaurant's concise menu illustrates this philosophy: organic ingredients, crudités and fresh pasta sautéed with vegetables. The healthful food is prepared in front of diners in a smart bistro setting.

Chez Paul – *13 r. de Charonne* – Ⓜ *Bastille* – ☎ *01 47 00 34 57* – *reserv. recommended evenings* – *19.82/27.44€*. Chez Paul is truly as old as it feels. A century ago it sold coffee, coal and lemonade; today the regular clientele contributes to the family spirit of the place. Old mirrors, advertising posters and pictures on the walls; well-prepared bistro-style cuisine on the plate.

Taco Loco – *116 r. Amelot* – Ⓜ *Filles-du-Calvaire* – ☎ *01 43 57 90 24* – *closed 12-26 Aug, Mon lunch and Sun* – *22.44€*. Aficionados appreciate this simple Mexican restaurant, with its typical decor and authentic, family-style dishes prepared in the cooking space in the middle of the dining room. A convivial meal at affordable prices.

Le Souk – *1 r. Keller* – Ⓜ *Ledru-Rollin or Bastille* – ☎ *01 49 29 05 08* – *closed Mon* – *reserv. recommended evenings* – *22.87/30.49€*. Go beyond the spice shop and enter this Moroccan house featuring sculpted woodwork, Oriental-style paintings and North African music to experience a meal from the southern side of the Mediterranean. Enjoy the generous helpings of couscous and the subtly spiced tajines.

Bistrot Les Sans Culottes – *27 r. de Lappe* – Ⓜ *Bastille or Ledru-Rollin* – ☎ *01 48 05 42 92* – *closed Mon* – *20€ lunch* – *24/29€*. Before venturing into the nocturnal throng of the Rue de Lappe, stop off here and savour the turn-of-the-century flavour of this bistro. Complete with bar, percolator, woodwork and moulded ceiling, menu on a chalk-slate and delicious chocolate cake, it's the perfect lair for party-goers. A few rooms available.

Blue Elephant – *43 r. de la Roquette* – Ⓜ *Bastille or Voltaire* – ☎ *01 47 00 42 00* – *closed Sat lunch* – *18.29€ lunch* – *25.15/48€*. A little corner of Thailand in the shadow of the Bastille. Set in the bustle of a lively street, this restaurant's doors open to reveal an exotic decor of green plants, wicker furniture and typical tablecloths. It's like stepping into another world – a world rich with a thousand flavours. Serves until midnight.

Bodega La Plancha – *34 r. Keller* – Ⓜ *Voltaire* – ☎ *01 48 05 20 30* – *closed 11-18 Aug, lunch, Sun and Mon* – 🚭 – *26.67/38.11€*. Be prepared for a lively evening in the 12 sq m of this Basque restaurant plastered with posters, old photos and postcards. Seated elbow-to-elbow, diners cheerfully tuck into Basque specialities: *pimientos, chipirons à l'encre* (squid in ink sauce) and Basque cake.

Mansouria – *11 r. Faidherbe* – Ⓜ *Faidherbe-Chaligny* – ☎ *01 43 71 00 16* – *closed 12-19 Aug, Mon lunch, Tue lunch and Sun* – *29/43.50€*. Former ethnologist Fatima Hal is a Parisian reference in the field of Moroccan cooking, especially since her works featuring her country's recipes were published. This restaurant serves food cooked by women, in accordance with tradition, and served in a typical Moroccan decor.

Le Chardenoux – *1 r. Jules-Vallès* – Ⓜ *Charonne* – ☎ *01 43 71 49 52* – *closed Feb school holidays, Aug, Sat lunch and Sun* – *30.49/48€*. A real live Parisian café. With its authentic decor from 1904, venerable furniture and old paintings, this little restaurant is as inviting as can be. Customers gladly squeeze into the narrow dining room to savour the delicious, revitalising cuisine.

12th arrondissement

BASTILLE – BERCY – FAUBOURG SAINT-ANTOINE

L'Aubergeade – *17 r. Chaligny* – Ⓜ *Reuilly-Diderot* – ☎ *01 43 44 33 36* – *closed 23 Dec to 2 Jan* – *10.60€ lunch* – *14/20€*. Keep this address in your note pad. You'll appreciate the pretty varnished wood decor, the tables nearly touching one another, the relaxed atmosphere and the generous portions of traditional dishes that are easy on the wallet.

Le Vinéa Café – *26-28 cour St-Émilion* – Ⓜ *Cour-Saint-Émilion* – ☎ *01 44 74 09 09* – *vinea-cafe.fr* – *23/29€*. The spirit of wine still haunts Bercy: witness this former warehouse where old beams and stone walls cohabit with a hip menu, a few bistro-style dishes and a revamped decor. A quick drink at the striped bar or on the terrace before heading for the nearby cinemas is also an option.

Jean-Pierre Frelet – 25 r. Montgallet – Ⓜ Montgallet – ☎ 01 43 43 76 65 – frelet@infonie.fr – closed Feb school holidays, Aug, Sat lunch and Sun – 24€. Although one could almost miss the narrow facade of this restaurant next-door to the busy shops of this little street, it is well worth crossing the threshold to take a seat and savour the luscious cooking. The owner-chef worked for years in the country's best restaurants before opening his own establishment.

Le Grand Bleu – Bd de la Bastille, Arsenal yacht harbour – Ⓜ Bastille – ☎ 01 43 45 19 99 – closed Feb – 13.72€ lunch – 27.44/45.73€. No, you're not dreaming – you're still in the heart of Paris! Seated at the terrace overlooking the capital's charming yacht harbour and garden, you're beneath the Bastille, scarcely 50m from its Génie-topped column. Meals are served on the veranda when the sun is playing hard to get. Fish menu.

L'Ébauchoir – 45 r. de Citeaux – Ⓜ Reuilly-Diderot – ☎ 01 43 42 49 31 – closed Sun and Mon – reserv. recommended evenings – 17€ lunch – 28€. Lunchtime, this is the neighbourhood eatery where locals come enjoy unequivocally traditional fare in a veritable bistro setting. Oak tables, painted walls and a large fresco. Evenings, the atmosphere is more intimate and serene.

Quincy – 28 av. Ledru-Rollin – Ⓜ Ledru-Rollin – ☎ 01 46 28 46 76 – closed 10 Aug to 10 Sep, Sat-Mon – 🚫 – 40/69€. This establishment's forte is savoury, substantial, regional fare with no unnecessary fuss. The decoration is reminiscent of a country inn with wood panelled walls, wooden beams, chequered tablecloths and straw chairs. The atmosphere is jovial and the menu enticing.

Le Train Bleu – At the Gare de Lyon (1st floor) – Ⓜ Gare-de-Lyon – ☎ 01 43 43 09 06 – isabell.car@compass-group.fr – 40€. A must! This opulent 1900 brasserie with its luxurious frescoes and gold-leaf covered mouldings belongs to Paris's historic heritage. Like a ticket to continents yet to be discovered, the landscape murals transport one afar.

13th arrondissement

GOBELINS

Le Jardin des Pâtes – 33 bd Arago – Ⓜ Les Gobelins – ☎ 01 45 35 93 67 – closed 23 Dec to 6 Jan and Sun – 13.26/21.19€. A few minutes' walk from the Manufacture des Gobelins, this terrace under the boulevard's horse chestnut trees prolongs the flower-decked façade of a tiny wood-furnished dining room. The menu features original pasta dishes made from organic and freshly-milled flours.

Nouveau Village Tao-Tao – 159 bd Vincent-Auriol – Ⓜ Nationale or Place-d'Italie – ☎ 01 45 86 40 08 – 10.67€ lunch – 19.82/24.39€. Just a few strides from Chinatown, here's a stopover for those who wish to continue their Asian adventure. Chinese food, of course, but also Thai dishes are served in the typically orientalist decor; the fixed-price lunch menus are a particularly good value; evening meals are à la carte.

L'Avant Goût – 26 r. Bobillot – Ⓜ Place-d'Italie – ☎ 01 53 80 24 00 – closed 1-7 Jan, 1-7 May, 7-27 Aug, Sun and Mon – reserv. required – 26/40.40€. Close to the Place d'Italie, a little bistro specialising in simple, gourmand dishes. Thanks to the solid reputation and very appetising menu, this inviting, cheery establishment is full at lunch and dinner.

14th arrondissement

DENFERT-ROCHEREAU – MONTPARNASSE – MONTSOURIS

Crêperie Le Petit Josselin – 59 r. du Montparnasse – Ⓜ Edgar-Quinet or Notre-Dame-des-Champs – ☎ 01 43 22 91 81 – closed Jul and Sun – 15€. Crêperies have flourished in the area around the Gare Montparnasse, where Bretons used to arrive in the capital and settle down. In this one – a culinary ambassador of Brittany – crêpes are prepared under the eyes of on-looking diners, just like back east. Carved wood art and Quimper porcelain on the walls.

Au 14 Juillet il y a toujours des lampions – *99 r. Didot* – Ⓜ *Plaisance* – ☎ *01 40 44 91 19* – *10.52€ lunch* – *16.01/27.44€*. Second-hand bric-a-brac here and there, walls covered with old posters, an aged wood-burning stove, porcelain lights and coloured lamps illuminating the bar make up the decor of this bistro sporting a singular, festive name: 'There are always lanterns on 14 July'. Slate menu du jour.

Au Moulin Vert – *34 bis r. des Plantes* – Ⓜ *Plaisance or Alésia* – ☎ *01 45 39 31 31* – *www.aumoulinvert.com* – *30€*. A spot of greenery in the heart of Paris. Green furniture, white tablecloths and vigorous house plants on the veranda; imposing deciduous trees and an arborvitae hedge by the terrace. The traditional fare is good value for the money.

Moderate

Monsieur Lapin – *11 r. Raymond-Losserand* – Ⓜ *Gaîté* – ☎ *01 43 20 21 39* – *closed Aug, Tue lunch and Mon* – *reserv. requested* – *28.20/45.73€*. Behind the amusing façade evoking a flower-decked country inn, Mister Rabbit has pride of place. He is celebrated both through the decor and on the menu, where he is prepared in every imaginable manner. Pleasant, retro interior. The gourmand menu is easy on the budget.

La Contre-Allée – *83 av. Denfert-Rochereau* – Ⓜ *Denfert-Rochereau* – ☎ *01 43 54 99 86* – *closed Sat lunch* – *28.96/34.30€*. The regular clientele enjoys congregating here, right near the roaring lion of the Place Denfert-Rochereau. Whether on the terrace or in the warm, pleasant dining room with its modern bistro allure, patrons enjoy tasty little dishes with a contemporary slant.

La Régalade – *49 av. J.-Moulin* – Ⓜ *Alésia* – ☎ *01 45 45 68 58* – *closed Aug, Sat lunch, Sun and Mon* – *reserv. required* – *30€*. This Parisian bistro, located on a busy avenue, welcomes guests cheerfully and offers first-rate meals in the crowded dining room. Quite popular with the regulars, the restorative fare spotlights regional flavours.

La Coupole – *102 bd du Montparnasse* – Ⓜ *Vavin* – ☎ *01 43 20 14 20* – *29€ lunch* – *31€*. A temple of Parisian nightlife that needs no introduction. A famous night-club in the early 20C, this 1920s brasserie has retained its splendid original decor featuring frescoes, a superb bar and long bay windows. It continues to cater to late-night patrons in a noisy, lively atmosphere until 2am.

15th arrondissement

JAVEL – MONTPARNASSE –
TOUR EIFFEL – VAUGIRARD

Budget

L'Infinithé – *8 r. Desnouettes* – Ⓜ *Convention* – ☎ *01 40 43 14 23* – *www.infinithe.com* – *closed evenings and weekends except the 1st Sun of each month* – *reserv. recommended* – *16/20€*. This tiny *salon de thé* does a fine job of reviving the 1930s. Infini-tea's interior has been carefully chosen – woodwork, dressers, small pedestal tables, embroidered tablecloths and sugar bowls found in second-hand shops contribute to the upbeat atmosphere. Delicious house pastries.

Au Soleil de Minuit – *15 r. Desnouettes* – Ⓜ *Convention* – ☎ *01 48 28 15 15* – *closed 28 Jul to 19 Aug, 23-26 Dec, Sun evening and Mon* – *20/42€*. The blue and white tones of the Finnish flag adorn this little establishment off the beaten tourist track, but close to the exhibition halls of the Porte de Versailles. After a glass of Aquavit, sample one of Finland's specialities, such as marinated herring or elk or reindeer steak with cranberries.

Le Sept/Quinze – *29 av. de Lowendal* – Ⓜ *Cambronne* – ☎ *01 43 06 23 06* – *closed 8-26 Aug and Sun* – *21€ lunch* – *23.30/29.40€*. Close to the École Militaire and the Unesco headquarters, this former bistro now boasts bright colours and original works of art. Diners jostle gaily in the noisy ambience, as they tuck into a delectable selection of carefully-prepared meals at very gentle prices.

Moderate

Le Beau Violet – *92 r. des Entrepreneurs* – Ⓜ *Commerce* – ☎ *01 45 78 93 44* – *closed Aug and Sun* – *reserv. required evenings* – *30.49/38.11€*. The perfect place for taking a culinary trip to Corsica without leaving Paris. The dishes, simmered in the hearth and served in copper ovenware, are heavenly; the decor and music give voice to the Corsican spirit. You can almost feel the ocean beckon.

AUTEUIL – BOIS DE BOULOGNE – MUETTE-RANELAGH – PASSY – TROCADÉRO

Budget

Brasserie de la Poste – *54 r. de Longchamp* – Ⓜ *Trocadéro* – ☎ *01 47 55 01 31 – closed Sat lunch – 20/40€.* This neighbourhood brasserie has acquired a regular clientele that appreciates the accessible prices and generous helpings served in the long, narrow dining room. The hospitable atmosphere and 1930s-style decor have undoubtedly contributed to its success.

Le Bistrot des Vignes – *1 r. Jean-Bologne* – Ⓜ *La Muette* – ☎ *01 45 27 76 64 – reserv. recommended – 13€ lunch – 22.56/38.11€.* Hurry to this bistro, then relax and settle in for a while. The colourful decor of stained wood is very inviting, and the cuisine – between Provence and Aveyron down south – is absolutely delicious. Warm reception; young, efficient service.

Moderate

La Gare – *19 Chaussée de la Muette* – Ⓜ *La Muette* – ☎ *01 42 15 15 31 – 29/47€.* Dinner on the platform or a quick lunch in the waiting room: you're dining in the old Passy-La Muette train station. Built in 1854, it now houses a restaurant frequented by the district's jet set. Surprising decor, lively cuisine and terrace in summer. Serves until midnight.

Le Petit Rétro – *5 r. Mesnil* – Ⓜ *Victor-Hugo* – ☎ *01 44 05 06 05 – www.petitretro.fr – closed 29 Jul to 27 Aug, Sat lunch and Sun – reserv. recommended evenings– 30/35€.* Elegant art nouveau tiles grace this charming little bistro set in an ultra-chic neighbourhood. Try the first room, with its lovely old bar, or discover the new dining room. The lunch *menu du jour* is more affordable than the evening menu. Skilfully prepared cuisine.

Le Totem – *17 pl. du Trocadéro, Musée de l'Homme, Palais de Chaillot* – Ⓜ *Trocadéro* – ☎ *01 47 27 28 29 – www.letotem.fr – 38/55€.* Opposite the Eiffel Tower, here is one of the capital's most beautiful terraces. The Palais de Chaillot's spacious dining room is also very alluring, with its striking totem poles, Native American artefacts and warm colours. Reservations recommended. Tea room in the afternoon.

Al Mounia – *16 r. de Magdebourg* – Ⓜ *Trocadéro or Iéna* – ☎ *01 47 27 57 28 – www.almounia.com – closed Sun – reserv. required evenings – 38.11/61€.* Carvings and oriental friezes are part of the authentic Moroccan decor of this restaurant which serves *pastillas*, *couscous* and *tajines* on gigantic copper platters to guests comfortably seated on low sofas. The staff are all in traditional dress. Order ahead for *méchoui* (spit-roasted lamb).

Luxury

Le Pré Catelan – *rte de Suresnes in the Bois de Boulogne* – *from Porte Maillot take the Allée de Longchamp, then the Allée de la Reine* – ☎ *01 44 14 41 14 – closed 1-24 Feb, 27 Oct to 5 Nov, Sun except lunch from 6 May to 26 Oct and Mon – 55€ lunch – 87/115€.* Situated in the Bois de Boulogne on the edge of the enchanting Pré-Catelan garden, this Second Empire pavilion is a marvellous site indeed. The luxurious interior, winter garden and beautiful summer terrace beguile the Paris elite who continue to flock here to savour the exceptional (Michelin-starred) cuisine. Attractive lunch menu.

CHAMPS-ÉLYSÉES – MONCEAU

Budget

O & Co – *8 r. de Lévis* – Ⓜ *Villiers* – ☎ *01 53 42 18 04 – levis@oliviers-co.com – closed Aug – 13.72/22€.* This new restaurant-cum-grocer's is an idea whose time has come. Wooden shelves displaying foodstuffs sharing an olive oil theme surround one big, common dining table where original savoury and sweet victuals are served.

Le Morosophe – *83 r. Legendre* – Ⓜ *Rome* – ☎ *01 53 06 82 82 – closed Sun – 22.87/38.11€.* Raspberry hues, woodwork, statuettes and bistro furniture comprise the decor of this restaurant whose name is defined as "wise madman" in the Rabelaisian dictionary. The imaginative fare is presented with flair. Interesting wine list.

Café d'Angel – *16 r. Brey* – Ⓜ *Charles-de-Gaulle* – *Étoile or Ternes* – ☏ *01 47 54 03 33* – *closed Aug, Christmas to New Year's and weekends* – *19.06/30.49€*. An old-fashioned look for the latest cuisine, flavoursome and gourmand, defines this little bistro close to the Étoile. You can view the establishment's young chef working in the kitchen from your table in the dining room where leatherette benches, old tiles and a slate menu set the tone. Quite reasonably priced at lunchtime.

Caves Petrissans – *30 bis av. Niel* – Ⓜ *Pereire or Ternes* – ☏ *01 42 27 52 03* – *cavespetrissans@noos.fr* – *closed 27 Jul to 25 Aug, 28 Dec to 5 Jan and weekends* – *29€*. Over 100 years old, this establishment is a Parisian institution. The familiar bistro atmosphere, refreshing cuisine and noteworthy wine cellar contribute to its success. The leatherette booth seats and terrace on the pavement in summer are ever in demand.

Graindorge – *15 r. de l'Arc-de-Triomphe* – Ⓜ *Charles-de-Gaulle* – *Étoile* – ☏ *01 47 54 00 28* – *closed Sat lunch and Sun* – *27€ lunch* – *32€*. The young chef's native Flanders inspires the menu here. Two minutes from the Étoile, the red velvet wall seats, large decorative mirrors and handsome bar define the amusing art deco style. Wine list enhanced by a choice of beers…

Les Béatilles – *11 bis r. Villebois-Mareuil* – Ⓜ *Charles-de-Gaulle-Étoile* – ☏ *01 45 74 43 80* – *closed 30 Jul to 26 Aug, 24-30 Dec and weekends* – *38.20€ lunch* – *44.20/65.60€*. Genuine gourmets take note: here's an establishment worthy of your attention! Beguiled by the mouth-watering menu, you'll be conquered by the excellent cuisine served in the tastefully modern, attractive dining room. Add the particularly attentive reception, tuck in your serviette and enjoy.

18th arrondissement

MONTMARTRE

Budget

La Chouette – *113 r. de Crimée* – Ⓜ *Laumière* – ☏ *01 42 45 60 15* – *closed 8-20 Aug, Sat lunch and Sun* – ✍ – *8.23/8.69€*. This little neighbourhood restaurant is a veritable godsend. The menu, based on what's fresh at the market, offers a varied choice of very reasonably priced dishes. The minimalist decor is restricted to a few photos and paintings; the welcome is very hospitable.

L'Été en Pente Douce – *23 r. Muller* – Ⓜ *Anvers* – ☏ *01 42 64 02 67* – *paris-resto.com* – *closed 24-25, 31 Dec and 2 Jan* – *14.18/21.34€*. From Sacré-Cœur, walk down a few steps into this side street and take a seat on the charming terrace of this former baker's shop, now a restaurant-cum-tea room. You'll savour salads, mixed platters and pastries just opposite a pretty public garden.

Le Vieux Chalet – *14 bis r. Norvins* – Ⓜ *Abbesses or Anvers* – ☏ *01 46 06 21 44* – *closed Dec, Sun evening and Mon* – ✍ – *14.50/38€*. Yes, it is possible to sample simple fare without risking wrack and ruin just 50m from the exclusive Place du Tertre. Venture into this hundred-year old countrified inn and enjoy its heavenly terrace-garden far from the madding crowd, as did Apollinaire and Picasso in their day. Unpretentious home-style cooking.

La Mère Catherine – *6 pl. du Tertre* – Ⓜ *Abbesses* – ☏ *01 46 06 32 69* – *14.94/37.35€*. One of Montmartre's pride and joys. In addition to its legendary location, this 17C establishment became famous after housing Danton and his disciples. Decidedly rustic interior and a terrace that's assailed by enthusiasts whenever the sun shines.

Le Verger de Montmartre – *37 r. Lamarck* – Ⓜ *Lamarck* – ☏ *01 42 62 62 67* – *10.37€ lunch* – *14.94/17.99€*. Beyond the discreet façade lies a soothing interior of brown and orange tints, furnished with a mind to originality. Traditional cuisine and very nice welcome. A philosophical dinner-debate *(en français)* is held the first Thursday of the month.

Aux Négociants – *27 r. Lambert* – Ⓜ *Château-Rouge* – ☏ *01 46 06 15 11* – *closed weekends and Mon evening* – *19.82/25.92€*. Located at the foot of the Butte Montmartre, this establishment dedicated to wine is immediately likeable. Simple decor with a handsome bar and photos by Doisneau immortalising bistro life. Nourishing, traditional fare on the menu.

Moderate

Per Bacco – *10 r. Lambert* – Ⓜ *Château-Rouge* – ☎ *01 42 52 22 40* – *closed Sat lunch and Sun* – *18.29€ lunch* – *27.44€*. Somewhat removed from the crowds of Montmartre, here's a small Italian restaurant whose reputation extends far beyond the neighbourhood boundaries. With a mind to preserving authenticity, the Neapolitan proprietor imports tasty ingredients from the homeland. The lunch menu is a steal; fine selection of Italian wines.

Rughetta – *41 r. Lepic* – Ⓜ *Blanche* – ☎ *01 42 23 41 70* – *larughetta@wanadoo.fr* – *closed Christmas and New Year's* – *reserv. recommended* – *30.49€*. This cheerful, colourful little Italian restaurant in one of Montmartre's lively streets is truly delightful. The closely set tables are generally besieged as the chef skilfully whips up dishes from his native land.

19th arrondissement

BELLEVILLE – CANAL SAINT-MARTIN – LA VILLETTE

Budget

Le Fleuve Rouge – *1 r. Pradier* – Ⓜ *Pyrénées* – ☎ *01 42 06 25 04* – *closed weekends* – *9.45/18.60€*. It's no surprise that this little restaurant, as simple as they come, is so popular with the natives: the atmosphere is always convivial and the portions of home-style cookery are ever generous. Vietnamese dishes on demand; unfussy, friendly service.

Le Pacifique – *29/35 r. de Belleville* – Ⓜ *Belleville* – ☎ *01 42 49 66 80* – *15€ lunch* – *20/25€*. Situated in the centre of Belleville, this Chinese restaurant is a favourite with locals and Asians who come share the steamed specialities and other typical dishes. Local events can be followed and commented on without leaving the table thanks to the large picture windows. Open until 2am.

Le Rendez-Vous des Quais – *10 quai de la Seine* – *Cinémas MK2* – Ⓜ *Stalingrad* – ☎ *01 40 37 02 81* – *21.34/25.15€*. A holiday spirit inhabits this restaurant on the banks of the Bassin de la Villette, just next-door to the cinemas. Before or after your film, stop here and enjoy the superb terrace, especially delightful during the summer. Much frequented by Parisians. The wine list is put together by Claude Chabrol, the film director.

L'Hermès – *23 r. Mélingue* – Ⓜ *Pyrénées* – ☎ *01 42 39 94 70* – *closed Sun, Mon and public holidays* – *12.20€ lunch* – *22.10€*. Finding the discreet blue façade of this small restaurant near the Buttes-Chaumont takes some doing, but it's worth the effort. The dining rooms have been renovated, the lunch menu is a bargain, and each month a new exhibition is on show.

20th arrondissement

BELLEVILLE – PÈRE-LACHAISE

Budget

Le Vieux Belleville – *12 r. des Envierges* – Ⓜ *Pyrénées* – ☎ *01 44 62 92 66* – *closed Sat lunch, Mon evening and Sun* – *10.37/18.29€*. This establishment rings with the inimitable Parisian twang of days gone by. The decor, principally black and white photos and vinyl, sings the praises of songsters from the 1940s and 50s. Homey cooking and no-frills service.

Pascaline – *49 r. de Pixérécourt* – Ⓜ *Télégraphe* – ☎ *01 44 62 22 80* – *closed 2 wks in Aug, Mon evening, Sat lunch and Sun* – *11.50/20€*. A small neighbourhood restaurant where wine reigns supreme. The owner has a rare talent for bringing unjustly overlooked vintages to light while the cuisine reveals the flavours of Auvergne. Nice terrace in pleasant weather.

Le Rez-de-Chaussée – *10 r. Sorbier* – Ⓜ *Ménilmontant or Gambetta* – ☎ *01 43 58 30 14* – *www.sortir.net* – *16.77/21.34€*. A retro bistro with an agreeable second-hand shop atmosphere. Tables on wrought iron stands, frosted glass wall lights, aged clocks and black and white photos: the imaginative decor tips its hat to the 1930s and 40s. Progressive cuisine.

Bistro Chantefable – *93 av. Gambetta* – Ⓜ *Gambetta* – ☎ *01 46 36 81 76* – *closed 24-25 Dec* – *20.12/38.11€*. After paying your respects at the Père-Lachaise cemetery, come join the living in this bistro situated behind the 20th *arrondissement* town hall. The crown moulding, fine bar, old sheen, healthy selection of wines by the glass, seafood and palatable dishes are a hit with the local population. Convivial ambience.

Zéphyr – *1 r. du Jourdain* – Ⓜ *Jourdain* – ☎ *01 46 36 65 81* – *closed 8-21 Aug, 23 Dec to 4 Jan, Sat lunch and Sun* – *reserv. recommended* – *11.89€ lunch* – *25.61/45€*. Rediscover the mood of 1930s Paris in this pretty period bistro. The original art deco interior, featuring frescoes of cubist inspiration, woodwork and old light fixtures, has been carefully preserved. Reigning good humour, inventive cuisine and an ample choice of wines. Often packed.

Moderate

Les Allobroges – *71 r. des Grands-Champs* – Ⓜ *Maraîchers* – ☎ *01 43 73 40 00* – *closed 28 Jul to 28 Aug, Sun and Mon* – *15.24/28.97€*. Granted, this restaurant is far from the heart of Paris, but it is well worth a visit nonetheless. Behind the handsome light wood façade, you'll savour food from menus devised by the proprietor, a self-taught enthusiast, in an animated, convivial setting. A must if you're in the neighbourhood.

La Défense

Moderate

Le Café Malongo – *15 pl. de la Défense* – Ⓜ *La Défense* – ☎ *01 55 91 96 96* – *cafemalongo@libertysurf.fr* – *closed weekends and evenings* – *reserv. recommended* – *29.42€*. Amidst the glass and concrete towers of La Défense, here's an exotic islet created by Malongo, a well-known brand of coffee. The boutique sells a vast selection of coffees and teas from the world over; the restaurant offers foreign flavours served in a decor that hints of the colonies, ornamented with tropical plants.

Theatre and entertainment

Kiosque Théâtre – *Pl. de la Madeleine – Tue-Sat 12.30pm-7.45pm, Sun 12.30pm-3.45pm.* Theatre tickets can be bought here on the day of the performance for half the normal price (for the most expensive shows). You can choose from over 100 shows and 120 plays (more private than state-run theatres). You'll want to go with alternative choices in mind, as you may not get what you want. No credit cards.

Comédie-Française – *Pl. Colette –* ☎ *01 40 15 00 15 – www.comedie-francaise.fr – tickets: 11am-1pm – closed end Jul to Sep and 1 May.* Founded in 1860 by Louis XIV, the repertoire consists principally of traditional drama composed by the classical French playwrights. Theatregoers can admire the famous seated figure of Voltaire by Houdon in the public foyer, as well as the chair in which Molière himself fell ill while playing *Le Malade Imaginaire* on 17 February, 1673.

Théâtre National de Chaillot – *1 pl. du Trocadéro –* ☎ *01 53 65 30 00 – www.theatre-chaillot.fr – tickets: Mon-Sat 11am-7pm, Sun 11am-5pm.* Inaugurated in November 1920, from 1930 to 1972 this stage was home to the Théâtre National Populaire (TNP) under the supervision of some of the world's finest directors, including Jean Vilar and Georges Wilson. It was here that Gérard Philipe gave unforgettable performances as the lead roles in *El Cid* and *Lorenzaccio*. Certain shows are accessible to those with impaired sight or hearing.

Odéon Théâtre de l'Europe – During renovations, the theatre has moved to 8 bd Berthier (reopening in 2004) – Ⓜ Porte-de-Clichy – Tickets: ☎ 01 44 85 40 40. Jean-Louis Barrault and Madeleine Renaud made this one of Paris's premier playhouses up until 1968. Productions of Paul Claudel's *Tête d'Or*, Ionesco's *Rhinoceros* and Samuel Beckett's *Waiting for Godot* and *Happy Days* were staged here. Since 1990, Odéon's mission has been to stage European productions.

Théâtre National de la Colline – *15 r. Malte-Brun –* ☎ *01 44 62 52 52 – www.colline.fr – reserv. by phone: Mon-Tue 11am-6pm, Wed-Fri 11am-7pm – closed Jul-Aug.* The staging of modern drama is this national theatre's vocation. Alain Françon has been the director since 1997.

Théâtre du Rond-Point – *2 bis av. Franklin-Roosevelt –* ☎ *01 44 95 98 00 – tickets: Tue-Sat noon-7pm – closed summer.* First a panoramic view-point, then a skating rink, Rond-Point has been a playhouse since 1981. Its current director, Marcel Maréchal, alternates repertory theatre and contemporary creations.

Théâtre Marigny – *Av. de Marigny –* ☎ *01 53 96 70 00 – www.theatre marigny.fr – performances Tue-Sat 8.30pm, Sun 4pm; matinee certain Saturdays – closed Jul-Aug.* *Amadeus* produced by Roman Polanski, *Cyrano de Bergerac* by Robert Hossein, *Les Variations Enigmatiques* with Alain Delon and *La Dame aux Camélias* starring Isabelle Adjani have been some of this prestigious theatre's finest moments. Long directed by the Compagnie Renauld-Barrault, followed by Elvire Popesco and Robert Manuel.

Théâtre de la Renaissance – *20 bd St-Martin –* ☎ *01 42 08 18 50 or 01 42 02 47 35 – performance schedule variable.* *Ma sœur est un chic type* and *Un air de famille* (Family Resemblances) by Bacri and Jaoui are two of this theatre's greatest hits to date. Guy Bedos and Fabrice Lucchini have also graced the stage of this playhouse dedicated to quality entertainment. A cut above the usual boulevard fare.

Théâtre Mogador – *25 r. Mogador –* ☎ *01 53 32 32 00 – www.mogador.net – Mon 10am-7pm, Tue-Sat 10am-8.30pm, Sun 10am-3pm.* Built in 1914 along the lines of the Palladium in London, this is Paris's largest private theatre (1,805 seats). Over the years, the programme has featured variety shows, operettas, drama *(Cyrano de Bergerac, La Femme du Boulanger)* and films. Currently dedicated to musicals, Jérôme Savary, Jeanne Moreau and Dee Dee Bridgewater have worked wonders here.

Comédie Caumartin – *25 r. Caumartin –* ☎ *01 47 42 43 41.* Sartre's *Huis-Clos* (No Exit) was created in this small century-old theatre. Nowadays, the programme is not nearly so intellectually demanding; it specializes in comedies with long-running hits such as *Bœing-Bœing* or *Reviens dormir à l' Élysée!* This is also where young talents like Anne Roumanoff and Bratsch are given the opportunity to show their stuff.

Théâtre des Variétés – *7 bd Montmartre* – ☎ *01 42 33 09 92* – *Tue-Sat 11am-7pm* – *closed Jul-Aug.* Feydeau's *La Puce à l' oreille* (Meet me at the Pussycat), Marcel Pagnol's *Topaze*, Jean Poiret's *La Cage aux folles (Birds of a Feather)*, and, more recently, *Le Dîner de cons* (The Dinner Game) were all created in this theatre, one of Paris's oldest.

Théâtre de l' Est Parisien (TEP) – *159 av. Gambetta* – ☎ *01 43 64 80 80* – *Mon-Fri 10am-6pm.* Located in a blue-collar neighbourhood, TEP produces theatre for the people. Modern and classical plays (Musset, Marivaux, Brecht, Lorca) are staged with the intention of making culture available to all; TEP goes a step further by reaching beyond theatre walls and taking drama to the public. It also organizes festivals featuring works by young authors and directors.

Théâtre Hébertot – *78 bis bd des Batignolles* – ☎ *01 43 87 23 23* – *tickets: Mon 11am-6pm, Tue-Sat 11am-7pm, Sun 11am-2pm.* This handsome playhouse *à l'italienne* built in the late 19C produces contemporary and classical drama, including works by Thomas Bernhard, Milan Kundera and Carlo Goldoni... Celebrated thespians Gérard Philipe and Jean Marais have graced this stage with their magical presence.

La Cartoucherie – *Rte du Champ-de-Manœuvres, Bois de Vincennes* – ☎ *01 48 08 39 74.* This group of theatres, composed of five independent playhouses (Théâtre du Soleil, Théâtre du Chaudron, Épée de bois, Théâtre de l'Aquarium and Théâtre de la Tempête), was created in the 1970s on land formerly belonging to the army. The woody, peaceful setting and the quality and variety of its shows have contributed greatly to its success.

Opera and dance

Opéra-Bastille – *Pl. de la Bastille* – ☎ *01 40 01 17 89* – *www.opera-de-paris.fr* – *Mon-Sat 11am-6.30pm* – *closed mid-Jul to mid-Sep.* Designed by Carlos Ott, this opera house marries technical prowess and public outreach. Inaugurated in 1989 by François Mitterrand, it began its first season in spring, 1990, with a revival of Hector Berlioz' *Les Troyens*, under the direction of the conductor Myung-Whun Chung.

Opéra-Comique (Salle Favart) – *5 r. Favart* – ☎ *08 25 00 00 58 or 01 42 44 45 50* – *www.opera-comique.com* – *Mon-Sat 9am-9pm, Sun 11am-7pm* – *closed Aug.* The Opéra-Comique is also known as the **Salle Favart**, its original name. Operas such as Bizet's *Carmen* (1875), Léo Delibes's *Lakmé* (1883), and *Pelléas et Mélisande*, which dazed the world of opera in 1902, all made their débuts here.

Palais Garnier – *8 r. Scribe* – *RER Auber* – ☎ *01 40 01 17 89 or 08 36 69 78 68* – *www.opera-de-paris.fr* – *tickets: Mon-Sat 11am-6.30pm* – *closed mid-Jul to early Sep.* Built from 1862 to 1875 by Garnier, a young architect, this theatre's impressive size and luxurious decoration make it a fine example of Second Empire architecture. It has been the home of the National Academy of Music since 1875. One can admire the magnificence of the stairwell and foyer, along with the splendid hall, embellished in 1964 by a ceiling painted by Chagall.

Théâtre de la Ville – *2 pl. du Châtelet* – ☎ *01 42 74 22 77* – *www.theatre-delaville-Paris.com.* A multidisciplinary people's theatre, featuring ballet, drama, and popular, traditional and classical music. With an eye to encouraging contemporary creativity, this stage has showcased many fine artists, from Pina Bausch to Nusrat Fateh Ali Kahn.

Classical and contemporary concerts

Châtelet-Théâtre Musical de Paris (TMP) – *Pl. du Châtelet* – ☎ *01 40 28 28 40* – *www.chatelet-theatre.com* – *10am-7pm.* In 1909, Serge de Diaghilev's Russian Ballet presented *Borodin's Prince Igor* here; the following year, Gustav Mahler conducted his own *Symphony No 2* and Caruso was acclaimed for his performance of Verdi's *Aïda.*

Cité de la Musique – *221 av. Jean-Jaurès* – ☎ *01 44 84 44 84* – *www.cite-musique.fr* – *Tue-Sat noon-6pm, Sun 10am-6pm* – *closed 1 May.* Inaugurated in 1995, this musical village complex designed by the architect Christian de Portzamparc contains a modular concert hall that adapts to the pieces given, an amphitheatre, documentation centres, musicians' workshops, a Music Museum, a bookshop and a café.

Maison de Radio-France – *116 av. du Prés.-Kennedy* – ☎ *01 56 40 15 16* – *Mon-Sat 11am-6pm* – *closed public holidays.* The Maison de Radio France holds a wide range of music concerts: jazz, classical, traditional and contemporary (the "Présences" festival in February, for example); performances are inexpensive or free. The Olivier-Messiaen hall also stages concerts by Radio-France's choir and orchestra.

Salle Gaveau – *45 r. La Boétie* – Ⓜ *Miromesnil* – ☎ *01 49 53 05 07 – tickets: Mon-Fri 11.30am-6pm; concert schedule variable: 8.30pm-11pm – closed Jul-Aug.* The conductors Pasdeloup and Lamoureux held concerts here, as did many of the world's greatest musicians. On 2 February, 1927, Yehudi Menhuin performed Lalo's *Symphonie Espagnole* at the age of 11, holding his Parisian audience spellbound.

Salle Pleyel – *252 r. du Fg-St-Honoré* – Ⓜ *Ternes* – ☎ *08 25 00 02 52 – salle-pleyel@salle-pleyel – 8am-9pm, for same-day concerts 8am-11pm – closed Jul-Aug and 1 May.* Paris's Symphony Orchestra, along with some of the world's most gifted conductors and musicians (Fedor Chaliapine, Arthur Rubinstein, R. Casadesus, Pablo Casals, Yehudi Menuhin, etc.), have given many dazzling performances here.

Théâtre des Champs-Élysées – *15 av. Montaigne* – Ⓜ *Alma-Marceau* – ☎ *01 49 52 50 50 – rpublic@theatrechampselysees.fr – tickets: Mon-Sat 1pm-7pm; for Sun morning concerts: tickets sold from 10am for the 11am concert – closed Jul-Aug.* Constructed in 1913 by the Perret brothers and belonging to the historical register since 1953, the Théâtre des Champs-Élysées offers music lovers a choice between the traditional evening programme and Sunday morning concerts. The world's greatest conductors, including Karl Bœhm, Herbert Von Karajan, and many others, have waved their batons here. In addition, some of the planet's finest ballet troupes have also performed here, such as the Russian Bolchoï and Kirov Ballets, Maurice Béjart, Roland Petit's Ballet de Paris and Josephine Baker's famous Revue Nègre.

Jazz-rock

Jazz-Club Lionel Hampton – *81 bd Gouvion-St-Cyr* – ☎ *01 40 68 30 42 – from 8pm.* Since 1976, all the greatest names in jazz have played here, including Count Basie and the Modern Jazz Quartet. Traditional jazz (New Orleans, Swing) concerts alternate with rhythm'n'blues. A modern club that remains true to its jazzy origins.

Le New Morning – *7-9 r. des Petites-Écuries* – ☎ *01 45 23 51 41 – 8pm-1am.* Jazz, world music, salsa, blues: the New Morning is an effervescent, eclectic club that has produced Chet Baker, Dexter Gordon, Art Blakey and James Carter as well as Compay Segundo, The Cranberries and The Fugees...

Le Petit Journal Montparnasse – *13 r. du Cdt-Mouchotte* – Ⓜ *Montparnasse-Bienvenüe or Gaîté* – ☎ *01 43 21 56 70 – Mon-Sat 8.30pm-2am, concerts: 10pm – closed mid-Jul to mid-Aug and certain public holidays.* A bastion of classical jazz boasting a lengthy inventory of great names: Baden Powell, Claude Bolling, Didier Lockwood, Eddy Louiss and Richard Galliano, in addition to songsters with a jazz, swing or blues slant, like Claude Nougaro, Manu Di Bango and Bill Deraime who appreciate the club's unique atmosphere.

Le Divan du Monde – *75 r. des Martyrs* – Ⓜ *Pigalle* – ☎ *01 44 92 77 66 – www.virtuel.cplus.fr/divan.htm – 7.30pm.* A musical crossroads (from salsa to electronic music), the Divan du Monde also puts on cabaret revues and other original happenings, such as the "Bal Grenadine" for 4 to 10 year olds (first Sunday of the month) and the "Bal à la Page" for their parents.

Élysée-Montmartre – *72 bd de Rochechouart* – Ⓜ *Anvers* – ☎ *01 55 07 06 00 – www.elyseemontmartre.com – 9pm-11pm.* The Élysée-Montmartre is as popular with artists as the public. Tricky, Metallica, Bjork, Burning Spear, David Bowie and Iggy Pop have played here, enjoying the close contact with fans and the charm of the hall. Enthusiasts are also keen on the theme evenings, especially the legendary ball held the 1st and 3rd Saturdays of each month.

Variety

Olympia – *28 bd des Capucines* – ☎ *01 47 42 25 49 – shows: 8.30pm – closed Aug.* The most popular music-hall performers have given shows in this concert hall formerly managed by Bruno Coquatrix, the outstanding talent scout. Demolished in 1997, the Olympia was entirely rebuilt just a few dozen metres from the original site.

Zénith – *211 av. Jean-Jaurès* – ☎ *01 42 08 60 00.* The Parc de la Villette's vast grey and red hall (6,335 seats) is appropriately named: many artists at the zenith of their careers play here, including the greatest names in rock and pop.

Palais Omnisports de Paris-Bercy (POPB) – *8 bd de Bercy* – ☎ *08 25 03 00 31 – www.bercy.com.* The POPB hosts the capital's biggest music and sports events. Rock and pop's greatest stars – Elton John, Bruce Springsteen, Sting and Madonna, to name but a few – fill the stadium. As for sports, tournaments include figure skating (the Lalique Trophy), go-karting, rollerblading, indoor cycling (Open des Nations), equestrian competitions and gymnastics.

Casino de Paris – *16 r. de Clichy –* ☎ *01 49 95 99 99 – Mon-Sat 11am-6pm.* Maurice Chevalier and Josephine Baker made their names in this century-old theatre that now produces contemporary stars like Jacques Higelin, Henri Salvador, Sylvie Vartan, Eddy Mitchell and the hit musical *Starmania.*

La Cigale – *120 bd Rochechouart –* ☎ *01 49 25 89 99.* Born in 1887, La Cigale (The Cicada) has vibrated to the tune of the great Mistinguett, Maurice Chevalier and Arletty. Redecorated in 1987 by Philippe Starck, the stage of its handsome Italian-style theatre now welcomes variety artists, together with international rock and pop musicians.

Le Bataclan – *50 bd Voltaire –* ☎ *01 43 14 35 35 – www.bataclan.fr – Mon-Sat 11am-7pm.* Built in 1864, the Bataclan was named after an Offenbach operetta. Successively a café-concert hall, a revue theatre and a cinema, it has hosted stars as dissimilar as Buffalo Bill and Edith Piaf. Today it is a well-established member of the rock circuit (The Cure and Elvis Costello have played here) and a theatre (repertory and musicals).

Palais des congrès de Paris – *2 pl. de la Porte-Maillot –* ☎ *01 40 68 25 07 – daily.* Opened in 1974, the Palais des Congrès saw the first performances of *Starmania* and *Notre-Dame de Paris,* as well as concerts by Ray Charles and Charles Aznavour. It doubles as an exhibition hall and a convention centre used for trade conventions and corporate general assemblies.

Cabarets, revues

Moulin-Rouge – *82 bd de Clichy –* ☎ *01 53 09 82 82 – www.moulin-rouge.com – tickets: 9am-1am.* Since 1889, the Moulin Rouge has enthralled spectators from all over the world with its sumptuous productions: from the French Cancan, immortalised by Toulouse-Lautrec, to Maurice Chevalier, from Colette to Mistinguett, from Ella Fitzgerald to Elton John. "Féerie", the Moulin Rouge's new revue, carries on the tradition with dancers who are as gorgeous as ever...

Chez Michou – *80 r. des Martyrs –* ☎ *01 46 06 16 04 – www.michou.com – reserv. only by phone: Mon-Fri 11am-5pm – closed Aug and 1 May.* Michou's loud jackets, huge glasses and passion for nightlife are well-known throughout Paris, even better, perhaps, than his cabaret in Montmartre. Cutting humour and satire are to be expected from his dinner-shows, in which men in drag impersonate the world's leading (female) stars of rock and show-biz. Correct attire a must.

Crazy Horse – *12 av. George-V –* ☎ *01 47 23 32 32 – www.lecrazy-horse.com – Sun-Fri 8.30pm-11pm, Sat 8pm, 10.15pm and 12.15am.* One of the capital's most beautiful revues. Magnificent dancers burn up this stage night after night performing original choreographed works.

Folies-Bergère – *32 r. Richer –* ☎ *01 44 79 98 98 – www.foliesbergere.com – tickets10am-6pm.* Loïe Fuller and Yvette Guilbert, Maurice Chevalier, Yvonne Printemps and Mistinguett, Josephine Baker and Charles Trenet – the legendary stars of yesteryear whose spirits now haunt this theatre all crossed paths here. Note the art deco façade and the gigantic hall of Hollywoodian proportions whose stage was immortalized by Maupassant in *Bel Ami.*

Le Lido – *116 bis av. des Champs-Élysées –* ☎ *01 40 76 56 10 – www.lido.fr – from 8pm.* Without a doubt Paris's most international revue show. The celebrated Bluebell Girls show off their feathers, glitter and stunning anatomy with panache. Over 600 costumes, dozens of decors, fountains and superb lighting effects combine to produce this ever popular show.

Le Paradis Latin – *28 r. du Card.-Lemoine –* Ⓜ *Jussieu or Cardinal-Lemoine –* ☎ *01 43 25 28 28 – www.paradis-latin.com – daily except Tue 8pm-midnight – 75€.* This fêted Parisian cabaret was designed by Gustave Eiffel and inaugurated in January 1889 to mark the World Fair. The dancers (male and female), lights, sets and music all participate in upholding the magic of this revue where the French Cancan still kicks up its heels.

Cafés-théâtres

Here is a list of a few of the lively *café-théâtres* which are a speciality of Paris, mixing humour, song and often a bit of late-night carousing. If you don't speak French, you're likely to feel left out, and would be better off taking in a show at one of the cabarets listed above.

Café d' Edgar-Théâtre d' Edgar – *58 bd Edgar-Quinet –* ☎ *01 42 79 97 97 – www.edgar.fr – Mon-Sat 2.30pm-7.30pm.* The Café d'Edgar is one of Paris's most famous café-théâtres with a reputation for comedy and original shows. Its *Babas-cadres* has been a hit for over 15 years and is still going strong.

Café de la Gare – *41 r. du Temple* – Ⓜ *Hôtel-de-Ville* – ☎ *01 42 78 52 51* – *www.cafe-de-la-gare.fr.st* – *8pm and 9.45pm, Sun 8.15pm.* Set in the heart of the Marais, this hallowed hall of merriment has been open for three decades. Patrick Dewaere and Coluche both started their careers here. Today, one comical creation after another is staged under the venerable beams of this old posting inn.

Le Caveau de la République – *1 bd St-Martin* – ☎ *01 42 78 44 45* – *www.caveau.fr* – *Tue-Fri 9pm, Sat 5pm and 9pm, Sun 3.30pm – closed early Apr to mid-Sep.* Open since 1901, this establishment continues to operate along the same lines as when Pierre Dac performed here: 6 or 7 comedians follow one another for 21/2 hours of stand-up comedy. Laurent Ruquier, François Morel, Smaïn and Patrick Sébastien are just a few of France's famous comedians whose illustrious careers began here.

Le Lapin Agile – *22 r. des Saules* – ☎ *01 46 06 85 87* – *www.au-lapin-agile.com* – *Tue-Sun 9pm-2am.* This cabaret located in a rustic little house looks surprisingly bucolic in the urban environment. It owes its name to the sign painted by André Gill in 1875 – still visible today – of a rabbit *(lapin)* leaping out of a stew-pot. Le Lapin has remained true to its origins, when Apollinaire, Bruant, Modigliani and Picasso used to spend an evening here: song, satire and poetry like in the old days – *sans* microphone.

Le Point-Virgule – *7 r. Ste-Croix-de-la-Bretonnerie* – Ⓜ *Hôtel-de-Ville* – ☎ *01 42 78 67 03* – *children's shows: Wed and Sun afternoons. Evening shows: 8pm, 9.15pm and 10.15pm.* The Semi-colon's programme gives laughter and songs pride of place. Young talents and seasoned artists come perform in the very convivial mini-hall. September's *Grand Festival de l'Humour* is exceedingly popular.

Les Blancs-Manteaux – *15 r. des Blancs-Manteaux* – ☎ *01 48 87 15 84* – *www.blancs manteaux.fr* – *7pm-11pm – closed 21 Jun and 14 Jul.* A hotbed of talent for the past thirty years, this café-théâtre gave many performers their first taste of fame (Renaud, Jacques Higelin, Bernard Lavilliers, Romain Bouteille, Anne Roumanoff, Michèle Laroque...). Several different artists share the stage every night: the show must go on!

Les Deux Ânes – *100 bd de Clichy* – ☎ *01 46 06 10 26* – *Tue-Sun show 8.30pm, Sat 4.30pm, Sun 3.30pm – closed Jul-Aug.* Since 1922, the tradition of French songs and Montmartre humour has been kept alive at the Two Donkeys in the form of biting satire targeting news and politics.

Cinemas

When consulting a cinema programme, it should be remembered that foreign films shown in France can be divided into two categories: V.O. or V.F. V.O. *(version originale)* means that the film is shown with its original soundtrack and subtitled in French. V.F. *(version française)* means that the film has been dubbed. This does not apply to French films which are in French, unless otherwise stated.

Cinéma L' Entrepôt – *9 r. Francis-de-Pressensé* – ☎ *01 45 40 78 38.* Film buffs appreciate this movie house's particularly thoughtful programme: films in V.O., experimental feature-length cinema, after-film debates, weekend concerts, etc. A vast bar and a restaurant – very popular when the weather warms up, thanks to the garden-terrace – keep the conversations going.

Cinéma Le Grand Rex – *1 bd Poissonnière* – Ⓜ *Bonne-Nouvelle* – ☎ *01 42 36 83 93* – *www.legrandrex.com.* 7 theatres, including one with 2,750 seats (on 3 levels), and another with 504 places. Two giant screens, one of which is 21m across; Dolby stereo sound. V.F. (dubbed) box-office type films. Bar. This cinema, built in 1932, is famous for its starry night-sky ceiling which rises 24m above the oriental/art deco interior.

Cinéma Mac-Mahon – *5 av. Mac-Mahon* – ☎ *01 41 34 23 00* – *closed Aug.* This cinema was a giant shrine to the Hollywood film goddess during the 1950s and 60s. Today the Mac-Mahon continues to present movies in their original format and context (with news reels of the period). One screen. Dolby stereo sound. Classic films, V.O. only. Cocktail bar.

Cinéma UGC Ciné Cité Bercy – *114 quai de Bercy* – ☎ *01 53 44 79 79* – *www.ugc.fr.* 18 theatres with giant screens, 4,500 seats, Dolby AS/R and DTS numeric sound. Films in V.O. Primarily box-office type films. Café and snacks. The capital's largest cinema complex is built on the site of Bercy's former wine warehouses.

Gaumont Grand Écran Italie – *30 pl. d' Italie* – ☎ *01 45 80 82 82.* 3 cinemas, one with 650 tiered seats equipped with a giant 24X10m screen. Dolby A/SR and numeric sound. Films in V.O. Primarily box-office type films. The capital's largest screen is here, in a designer building conceived by Kenzo Tange.

La Pagode – *57 bis r. de Babylone* – ☎ *01 45 55 48 48* – Ⓜ *Saint-François-Xavier.* The excellent programme of the 7th *arrondissement*'s only movie theatre puts the accent on artistic and independent films, while the oriental atmosphere transports one to a universe made of mystery and splendours of the past. This superb Japanese pagoda was a gift that the then director of the Bon Marché store gave his wife in 1896. The home of oriental galas for over 20 years, it became a cinema in the 1930s.

La Cinémathèque française-Salle Chaillot – *7 av. Albert-de-Mun* – Ⓜ *Iéna or Trocadéro* – ☏ *01 56 26 01 01* – *www.cinemathequefrancaise.com* – *general admission: 4.70€; members: 3€*. Founded in 1936 by Henri Langlois and Paul-Auguste Harlé, the Cinemathèque has been preserving and cataloguing films from all over the world, including the entire works of Marcel L'Herbier and René Clair, as well as a large number of short films and pre-war works.

La Cinémathèque française-Salle Grands Boulevards – *42 bd de Bonne-Nouvelle* – Ⓜ *Bonne-Nouvelle* – ☏ *01 56 26 01 01* – *www. cinemathequefran-caise.com* – Until such time as the new Maison du Cinéma at Bercy (12th *arr.*) is operational, this annex of the French Cinemathèque (Palais de Chaillot) is located in what used to be the heart of Paris's cinema district.

Max Linder Panorama – *24 bd Poissonnière* – Ⓜ *Grands-Boulevards* – ☏ *08 36 68 50 52* – *noon-10pm* – *8 €*. 1 giant screen, 615 seats (on 3 levels). THX Dolby stereo SR, DTS and SRD numeric sound. Excellent acoustics. V.O. films. Box-office pro-gramme featuring high-quality films with an accent on culture. Bar. Purchased by Max Linder himself, this cinema is the only one in Paris to bear the name of a film director.

Children's entertainment

The main public gardens have marionette shows, usually on Wednesday afternoon, Saturday and Sunday, and during the school holidays. You need to arrive before show time to buy your tickets in advance. Adults should sit in the back rows!

Guignol & Compagnie – *Jardin d' acclimatation – Bois de Boulogne* – Ⓜ *Sablons* – ☏ *01 45 01 53 52* – *www.guignol.fr* – *Wed, weekends, public and school hol-idays at 3pm and 4pm – 2.13€ (including park entrance fee)*.

Guignol Anatole – *Parc des Buttes-Chaumont* – Ⓜ *Laumière* – ☏ *01 43 98 10 95* – *outdoors theatre (Apr to late Oct): Wed, weekends and holidays at 3pm and 4.30pm – 3 yrs and older: 3€*.

La Vallée des Fleurs – *Parc floral de Paris – Bois de Vincennes* – Ⓜ *Château-de-Vincennes* – *park admission covers events*. Shows include theatre, mime, clowns and marionettes.

Marionnettes des Champs-Élysées – *Rond-Point des Champs-Élysées* – Ⓜ *Champs-Élysées* – ☏ *01 42 45 38 30* – *Wed, weekends and school holidays at 3pm, 4pm and 5pm – 2.90€*.

Marionnettes du Champs-de-Mars – *Av. du Gén.-Margueritte* – Ⓜ *École-Militaire* – ☏ *01 48 56 01 44* – *Wed and weekends at 3.15pm and 4.15pm – 2.59€*.

Marionnettes du Luxembourg – *Jardin du Luxembourg* – Ⓜ *Vavin* – ☏ *01 43 26 46 47 or 01 43 29 50 97* – *Wed, weekends, school and public holidays at 3pm, 4pm and 5pm (extra show at 11am weekends) – 3.81€*.

Marionnettes du parc Georges-Brassens – *Parc Georges-Brassens – r. Brancion* – Ⓜ *Porte-de-Vanves* – ☏ *01 48 42 51 80* – *summer: Wed, week-ends and school holidays at 3pm, 4pm and 5pm; winter: same days at 3.30pm and 4.30pm. Closed mid-Jul to mid-Aug – 2.59€*.

Mélo d' Amélie – *4 r. Marie-Stuart* – Ⓜ *Étienne-Marcel* – ☏ *01 40 26 11 11* – *7.62€*. 2 to 8 yrs old: a musical comedy combining magic, reality and fantasy.

Théâtre Astral – *Parc floral de Paris (Bois de Vincennes)* – Ⓜ *Château-de-Vincennes* – ☏ *01 43 71 31 10* – *Reserv. required. Shows Wed, weekends, pub-lic and school holidays– 5.34€. 3 to 8 yrs old*.

Métamorphosis – *55 quai de la Tournelle* – Ⓜ *Maubert-Mutualité* – ☏ *01 43 54 08 08* – *Tue-Sat at 9.30pm, Sun at 3pm – 24.39€ (price Sun and children: 9.15€)*. A show of magic and illusion aboard a barge.

Cirque Alexandra Bouglione – *Jardin d' acclimatation – Bois de Boulogne* – Ⓜ *Sablons* – ☏ *01 45 00 87 00* – *Wed at 2.30pm, weekends at 4pm*.

Cirque Diana Moreno Bormann – *1 bd du Bois-Lepretre* – Ⓜ *Porte-de-Clichy or Porte-de St-Ouen* – ☏ *01 64 05 36 25* – *Wed, weekends, school and public holidays at 3pm – 9.05€/27.44€*.

Cirque d' hiver Bouglione – *110 r. Amelot* – Ⓜ *Filles-du-Calvaire* – ☏ *01 47 00 12 25* – *late Oct to late Jan*. The Bouglione family enchants viewers of all ages with its traditional circus shows.

Cirque du Grand-Céleste – *13 av. de la Porte-des-Lilas* – Ⓜ *Porte-des-Lilas* – ☏ *01 53 19 99 13* – *Wed and school holidays (except Mon) at 3pm, Fri at 8.30pm, Sat at 3pm and 8.30pm, Sun at 3pm and 5pm*.

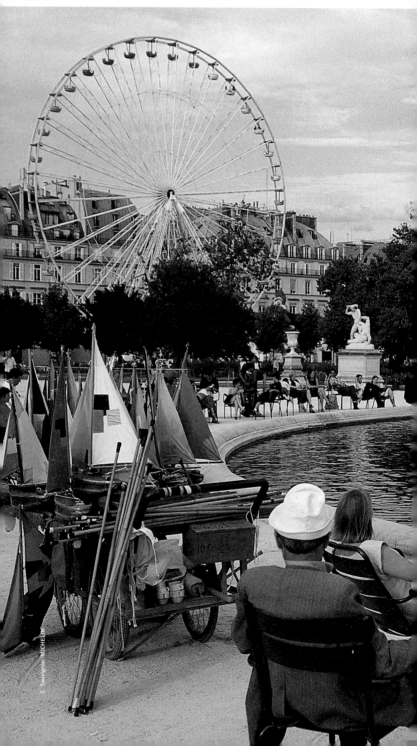
Tuileries Gardens

S. Sauvignier/MICHELIN

Introduction

The making of Paris

Paris has been forged throughout the centuries by the changing spirit and sensibility of each era, marked by the major events and upheavals that have occurred there during its long history. For a broader perspective of the city, here is a time capsule that takes you from its origins up to the present.

Gallo-Roman period

3C BC	The Parisii, a Celtic fishing tribe, settle on Lutetia, now the Île de la Cité.
52 BC	Labienus, Caesar's lieutenant, takes the city from the Gauls, who set fire to the Île de la Cité before fleeing.
1C AD	The Gallo-Romans build the city of Lutetia.
c 250	The martyrdom of St Denis, first Bishop of the city. Christianity takes hold and the first churches are built.
360	Julian the Apostate, prefect of the Gauls, is proclaimed Emperor of Rome by his soldiers. Lutetia is known henceforth as Paris.

Early Middle Ages

451	**St Geneviève** deflects Attila's attack on Paris.
508	Paris is taken over by Germanic tribes. Frankish king Clovis I makes it his capital, settling on the Cité.
8C	Paris declines in importance when Charlemagne makes Aix-la-Chapelle (Aachen) his main capital.
885	Paris, besieged by the Normans for the fifth time, is defended by Count Eudes who is made King of France in 888.

The Capetians

Early 12C	Trade picks up on the Cité. The Watermen's Guild is at its peak. Suger, Abbot of St-Denis and minister under Louis VI and Louis VII, rebuilds the abbey.
1163	Maurice de Sully begins construction of Notre-Dame.
1180-1223	Philippe Auguste erects a wall around Paris and builds the Louvre.
1215	The University of Paris is founded, turning the city into an important cultural centre.
1226-1270	Louis IX, called St Louis, commissions the building of the Sainte-Chapelle, Notre-Dame and St-Denis, and dispenses justice at Vincennes.
1253	Foundation of a college by Sorbon, later known as the Sorbonne.
1260	The dean of the Merchants' Guild becomes Provost of Paris.
1307	Philip the Fair dissolves the Order of the Knights Templars.

The Valois

1337	Beginning of the Hundred Years War. Upon the death of Philip the Fair and his three sons a problem of succession arises: the French barons prefer Philip the Fair's nephew, Philip de Valois, to his grandson, Edward III, King of England. The following century is marked by battles between the French and the English, who lay claim to the French Crown, between the Armagnacs, supporters of the family of Orléans, and the Burgundians, supporters of the dukes of Burgundy.
1358	Uprising under **Étienne Marcel**, Provost of Paris. The monarchs move to the Marais and the Louvre.
1364-1380	**Charles V** builds the Bastille and a new wall around Paris.
1382	During the troubled reign of Charles VI, the Parisians revolt against heavy taxes, but their loss strips them of earlier exemptions and severely weakens the Provost's power.
1407	Duke Louis of Orleans is assassinated on the order of John the Fearless.
1408-1420	Fighting breaks out between the Armagnacs and the Burgundians. The English take Paris.
1429	In vain Charles VII tries to lay siege to Paris; Joan of Arc is wounded at St-Honoré Gate.
1430	Henry VI of England is crowned King of France at Notre-Dame.
1437	Charles VII recaptures Paris.
1469	The first French printing works open in the Sorbonne.

1530	**François I** founds the Collège de France.
1534	Ignatius Loyola founds the Society of Jesus in Montmartre.
1559	Henri II is fatally wounded in a tourney.
1572	The struggle between Protestant and Roman Catholic factions leads to the St Bartholomew's Day Massacre.
1578-1604	Construction of the Pont Neuf.
1588	Paris strengthens its position as the centre of political power. The Catholic League turns against Henri III, and the citizens of Paris force him to flee after the Day of the Barricades (12 May).
1589	Returning to Paris with Henri of Navarre, Henri III is assassinated by a fanatical Dominican friar.

The Bourbons

1594	Paris opens its gates to Henri IV after he converts to Catholicism.
1594-1610	Place des Vosges is created. La Charité and St Louis Hospitals are founded.
14 May 1610	**Henri IV** is mortally wounded by Ravaillac.
1615-1625	Marie de Medici has Luxembourg Palace built.
1622	Paris becomes an episcopal see.
1629	The Palais-Royal is built.
1635	**Richelieu** founds the Académie Française.
1648-1653	The **Fronde** foments a rebellion in Paris against the Crown.
1661	Mazarin founds the College of Four Nations, the future Institut de France.
1667	Colbert establishes the Observatoire and restructures the Gobelins Tapestry Works.
17C	Louis XIV transfers the Court to Versailles, but increases royal control over Paris. Development of the Marais.
Late 17C	The Louvre Colonnade and the Invalides are built.
Early 18C	Construction of place Vendôme and development of the Faubourg St-Germain.
1717-1720	**John Law's Bank.**
1760-1780	Louis XV has the École Militaire, St-Geneviève (the future Panthéon) and place de la Concorde built.
1783	First balloon flights by Pilâtre de Rozier, and Charles and Robert.
1783	Treaty of Versailles: independence of the 13 American States.
1784-1791	Paris has nearly 500 000 inhabitants. To the dislike of the Parisians, the Farmers General Wall is erected, including the gateways and toll-houses by Ledoux.

Louis XIV Visits the Invalides

The Revolution and the First Empire

14 July 1789	Taking of the Bastille.
17 July 1789	Louis XVI at the Hôtel de Ville: the tricolour flag is adopted.
14 July 1790	Festival of Federation.
20 June 1792	A mob invades the Tuileries.
10 Aug 1792	Taking of the Tuileries and fall of the monarchy.
2-4 Sept 1792	September Massacres.
21 Sept 1792	Proclamation of the Republic.
21 Jan 1793	Execution of Louis XVI.
1793	Opening of the Louvre Museum and institution of the Natural History Museum.
1793-1794	The Terror.
8 June 1794	Festival of the Supreme Being.
5 Oct 1795	Royalist uprising suppressed by Napoleon.
9-10 Nov 1799	Fall of the Directory.
1800	Bonaparte creates the offices of Prefect of the Seine and of the Police.
2 Dec 1804	Napoleon's coronation at Notre-Dame.
1806-1814	Napoleon continues construction of the Louvre and erects the Arc de Triomphe and Vendôme Column. Gas lamps are used to light the city's streets.
31 March 1814	The Allies occupy Paris. First Treaty of Paris.

J.-L. CHARMET

Storming the Bastille

The Restoration

1815	Waterloo. Restoration of the Bourbons with Louis XVIII.
1824-1830	Charles X mounts the throne, but his ultra-conservative policies displease the Parisians, who take to the streets to defend their freedom in the July Revolution. Fall of Charles X, who flees to the Palace of Holyroodhouse in Edinburgh and is succeeded by Louis-Philippe.
1832	A cholera epidemic kills 19 000 Parisians.
1837	The first French railway line links Paris with St-Germain.
1840	Return of Napoleon's ashes from St Helena.
1841-1845	Construction of the Thiers fortifications.
February 1848	Fall of Louis-Philippe in the February Revolution; proclamation of the Second Republic.

ROGER-VIOLLET

Victor Hugo

From 1848 to 1870

June 1848	The suppression of the national workshops provokes socialist riots, signalling the failure of the Second Republic. Louis Napoleon is elected President of the Republic.
1852	Louis Napoleon becomes Napoleon III, creating the Second Empire. When the Parisians once again rise up in protest, the riots are violently repressed.
1852-1870	Huge urban planning projects are undertaken by Baron Haussmann: Les Halles, the railway stations, the Buttes-Chaumont, Bois de Boulogne and Bois de Vincennes, the Opéra, the sewers, completion of the Louvre, and construction of the new boulevards. Paris is divided into 20 *arrondissements*.
1855-1867	**World Exhibitions.**
4 Sept 1870	The Third Republic is proclaimed at the Hôtel de Ville.

ROGER-VIOLLET

Baron Haussmann

The Third Republic

Winter 1870-1871	Paris is besieged by the Prussians and capitulates. Napoleon III goes into exile in England.
March-May 1871	The Paris Commune is finally suppressed by the Men of Versailles during the Bloody Week (21-28 May); fire, destruction (Tuileries, Cour des Comptes, Hôtel de Ville, Vendôme Column) and massacres.
1879	Executive and legislative powers are returned from Versailles to Paris.
1882	Paris inaugurates its new Hôtel de Ville.
1889	World Exhibition at the foot of the new Eiffel Tower.
1892	First multi-storey building constructed of reinforced concrete.
1900	First metro line in operation between Maillot and Vincennes. The Grand and Petit Palais are built. Cubism is born at the Bateau-Lavoir. The Sacré-Cœur Basilica is erected on the Butte Montmartre.
1914-1918	At the outset of the war, the government leaves Paris for Bordeaux. Paris, under the threat of German attack, is saved by the Battle of the Marne. A shell hits the church of St-Gervais.
1920	Interment of the Unknown Soldier under the Arc de Triomphe.
Roaring Twenties	Paris is a cultural hub where new literary and artistic movements are born.
1927	Inauguration of Monet's *Nymphéas* series at the Orangerie.
1930s	The worldwide economic crisis hits Paris.
February 1934	Riots around the Chamber of Deputies end in a bloodbath.
June 1940	Paris is bombed, then occupied, by the Germans. Hostages and resistance fighters detained at Mont Valérien (Suresnes).
19-25 Aug 1944	Liberation of Paris.
27 October 1946	The Fourth Republic is proclaimed at the Hôtel de Ville.

The Fifth Republic

1958-1963	Construction of the UNESCO, CNIT, and Maison de Radio-France buildings.
1965	The Urban Development Plan for the greater Paris area is published.
May 1968	Strikes and demonstrations, triggered by students at the Sorbonne, spread to the whole of France within days, leading to the largest social movement in the country's history.
1969	Transfer of the wholesale markets from Les Halles to Rungis.
1970	Thirteen autonomous universities are created in the Paris Region. The RER (Réseau Express Régional) is launched to extend the metro system.
1973	Completion of the boulevard Périphérique (ring road) and Montparnasse Tower.
February 1974	Opening of the Palais des Congrès.
25 March 1977	The first election of a mayor of Paris (J Chirac), 11 predecessors between 1789 and 1871 having been appointed rather than elected.
1977	Opening of the Centre Georges-Pompidou.
1986	Inauguration of the Orsay Museum.
1989	The opening of the Louvre Pyramid, Grande Arche at La Défense and Opéra Bastille during bicentennial celebrations.
1995	Jacques Chirac is elected president.
1996	The Bibliothèque Nationale opens at Tolbiac.
1999	Severe windstorms damage parks and monuments in Paris on 26 December.
2002	Jacques Chirac is re-elected president.

Urban growth

The capital's site was carved out of the limestone and Tertiary sands by the Seine which flowed at a level of 35m/100ft, above its present course.

The Gallo-Roman Wall: – The Parisii, taking advantage of the *Pax romana*, emerged from Lutetia, built by the Gauls and defended by the river and surrounding swamps, to settle along the Left Bank of the river. The Barbarians later forced them to retreat to the Cité (c 276). On the island, they built houses, fortifications and a rampart wall to defend themselves against future invasions.

The Philippe Auguste Wall: – Between the 6C and 10C, the swamps were drained and cultivated, monasteries founded and a river harbour established near the place de Grève. Between 1180 and 1210 Philippe Auguste ordered that a massive wall be built, reinforced upstream by a chain barrage across the river and downstream by the Louvre Fortress and Nesle Tower.

The Charles V Rampart: – The Town, which was on the Right Bank (as opposed to the University on the Left Bank, and the Cité), prospered as roads were built connecting it with Montmartre, St-Denis, the Knights Templar Commandery and the castle at Vincennes. By the end of the 14C, Charles V had erected new fortifications, supported in the east by the Bastille. The Paris ramparts enclosed just under 440ha/1.75sq mi and protected 150 000 inhabitants.

The Louis XIII Wall: – Throughout the 16C, the Wars of Religion and the siege by Henri of Navarre maintained a threat to the city, forcing Charles IX and Louis XIII to extend the 14C wall westwards to include the Louvre Palace.

The Farmers General Wall: – The monarchy moved to Versailles as Paris encroached upon the surrounding countryside, its population 500 000 strong. The Invalides, Observatory, Salpêtrière, St-Denis and St-Martin Gates were erected; new city confines were required, calling for a new wall (1784-91) complete with 57 **toll-houses** to be designed by **Ledoux**.

The Thiers Fortifications: – During the Revolution many of the larger estates were broken up but little was built. Under the Empire, Paris faced problems of overcrowding and supply. The Restoration encouraged great industrial developments and social change: gas lighting was installed in the streets, and the railway allowed for growth and economic development in outlying villages (Austerlitz, Montrouge, Vaugirard, Passy, Montmartre, Belleville). Thiers determined the capital's perimeter with another wall (1841-45), reinforced at a cannon-ball's distance by 16 bastions, the official city confines from 1859. Subsequently, 20 *arrondissements* were created in the 7 800ha/30sq mi, as Haussmann began his transformation of the city (population in 1846: 1 050 000; in 1866: 1 800 000).

The present limits: – The forts remained intact (Mont Valérien, Romainville, Ivry, Bagneux...), but the walls, after serving in the city's defence in 1871, were razed by the Third Republic in 1919. Between 1925 and 1930 the confines of the city are redefined to include the Bois de Boulogne and Bois de Vincennes, but not extending elsewhere beyond a narrow circular belt to give an overall surface area of 10 540ha/40.75sq mi, for a population, in 1945, of 2 700 000.

ABC of architecture

Church of St-Germain-des-Prés

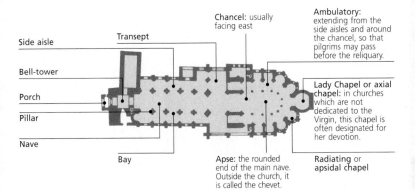

Side aisle

Transept

Bell-tower

Porch

Pillar

Nave

Bay

Chancel: usually facing east

Ambulatory: extending from the side aisles and around the chancel, so that pilgrims may pass before the reliquary.

Lady Chapel or axial chapel: in churches which are not dedicated to the Virgin, this chapel is often designated for her devotion.

Apse: the rounded end of the main nave. Outside the church, it is called the chevet.

Radiating or **apsidal chapel**

St-Séverin church: cross-section (from the east end looking towards the nave)

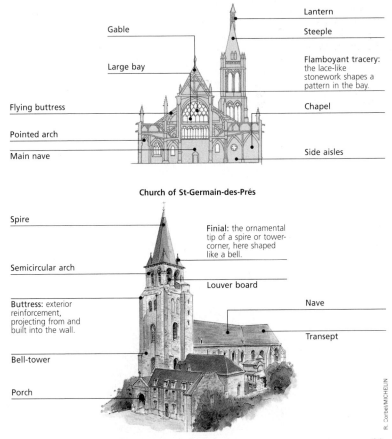

Gable

Large bay

Flying buttress

Pointed arch

Main nave

Lantern

Steeple

Flamboyant tracery: the lace-like stonework shapes a pattern in the bay.

Chapel

Side aisles

Church of St-Germain-des-Prés

Spire

Semicircular arch

Buttress: exterior reinforcement, projecting from and built into the wall.

Bell-tower

Porch

Finial: the ornamental tip of a spire or tower-corner, here shaped like a bell.

Louver board

Nave

Transept

Chevet of Notre-Dame Cathedral

The cathedral is exquisite for its well-proportioned volumes, the purity of its lines and the craftsmanship of the decorative elements. The remarkable flying buttresses span the double ambulatory and the galleries inside.

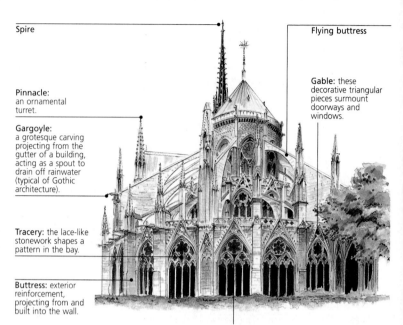

Spire

Flying buttress

Gable: these decorative triangular pieces surmount doorways and windows.

Pinnacle: an ornamental turret.

Gargoyle: a grotesque carving projecting from the gutter of a building, acting as a spout to drain off rainwater (typical of Gothic architecture).

Tracery: the lace-like stonework shapes a pattern in the bay.

Buttress: exterior reinforcement, projecting from and built into the wall.

Rose window

Church of the Sorbonne

The oldest part of the university, the church was built by Le Mercier between 1635-1642.

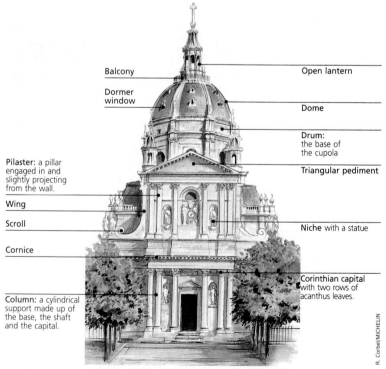

Balcony

Open lantern

Dormer window

Dome

Drum: the base of the cupola

Pilaster: a pillar engaged in and slightly projecting from the wall.

Triangular pediment

Wing

Scroll

Niche with a statue

Cornice

Corinthian capital with two rows of acanthus leaves.

Column: a cylindrical support made up of the base, the shaft and the capital.

R. Corbel/MICHELIN

PONT-NEUF

Despite its name – "new bridge" – it is the oldest in Paris. The 12 arches are embellished with amusing mascarons.

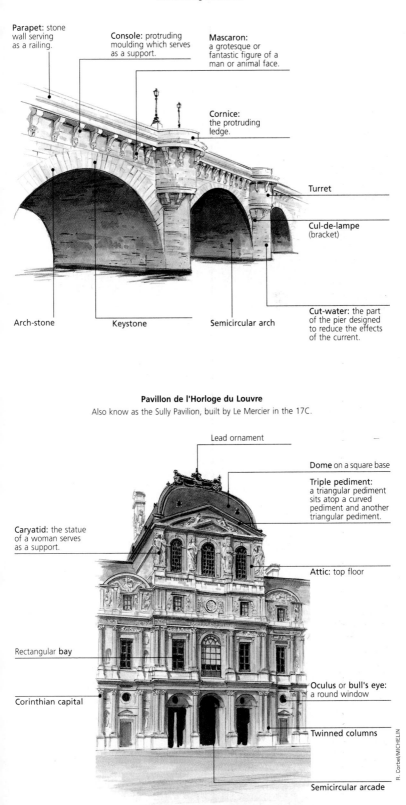

Parapet: stone wall serving as a railing.

Console: protruding moulding which serves as a support.

Mascaron: a grotesque or fantastic figure of a man or animal face.

Cornice: the protruding ledge.

Turret

Cul-de-lampe (bracket)

Arch-stone

Keystone

Semicircular arch

Cut-water: the part of the pier designed to reduce the effects of the current.

Pavillon de l'Horloge du Louvre

Also know as the Sully Pavilion, built by Le Mercier in the 17C.

Lead ornament

Dome on a square base

Triple pediment: a triangular pediment sits atop a curved pediment and another triangular pediment.

Caryatid: the statue of a woman serves as a support.

Attic: top floor

Rectangular **bay**

Oculus or bull's eye: a round window

Corinthian capital

Twinned columns

Semicircular arcade

R. Corbel/MICHELIN

93

INSTITUT DE FRANCE

The chapel with its dome is set between two semicircular wings which lead to two square pavilions.

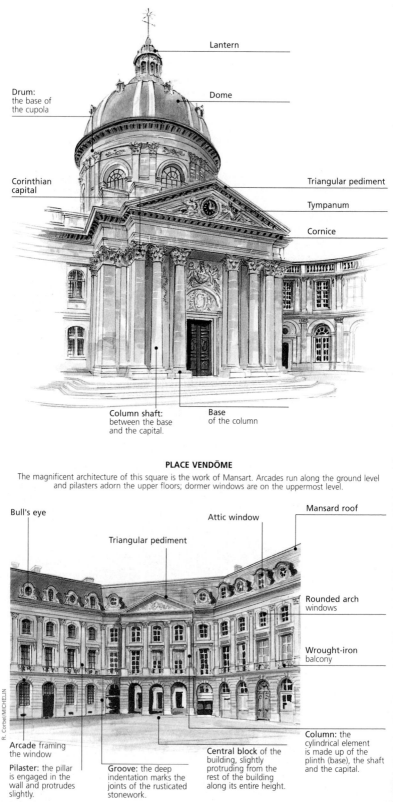

Lantern

Drum:
the base of
the cupola

Dome

Corinthian
capital

Triangular pediment

Tympanum

Cornice

Column shaft:
between the base
and the capital.

Base
of the column

PLACE VENDÔME

The magnificent architecture of this square is the work of Mansart. Arcades run along the ground level and pilasters adorn the upper floors; dormer windows are on the uppermost level.

Bull's eye

Attic window

Mansard roof

Triangular pediment

Rounded arch
windows

Wrought-iron
balcony

Column: the
cylindrical element
is made up of the
plinth (base), the shaft
and the capital.

Arcade framing
the window

Pilaster: the pillar
is engaged in the
wall and protrudes
slightly.

Groove: the deep
indentation marks the
joints of the rusticated
stonework.

Central block of the
building, slightly
protruding from the
rest of the building
along its entire height.

94

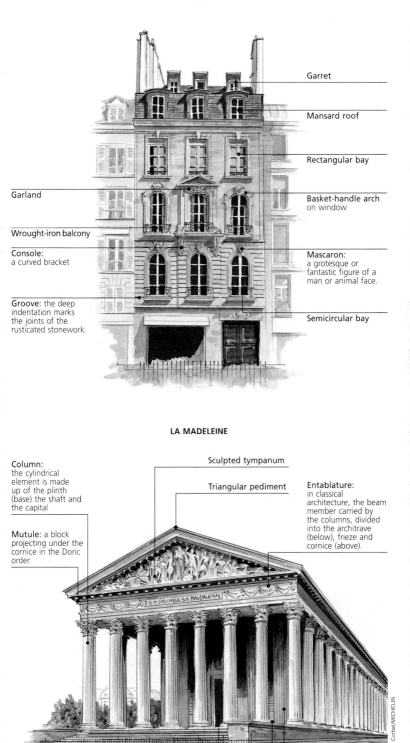

Building on rue de Seine
Louis XV façade with typical embellishments

Garret

Mansard roof

Rectangular bay

Garland

Basket-handle arch
on window

Wrought-iron balcony

Console:
a curved bracket

Mascaron:
a grotesque or
fantastic figure of a
man or animal face.

Groove: the deep
indentation marks
the joints of the
rusticated stonework.

Semicircular bay

LA MADELEINE

Column:
the cylindrical
element is made
up of the plinth
(base) the shaft and
the capital

Sculpted tympanum

Triangular pediment

Entablature:
in classical
architecture, the beam
member carried by
the columns, divided
into the architrave
(below), frieze and
cornice (above).

Mutule: a block
projecting under the
cornice in the Doric
order.

Plinth: the stone base
of the building.

Door leaf in bronze

Peristyle: the colonnade
surrounding the exterior.

The double row of
free-standing columns
makes this a **dipteral
colonnade.**

R. Corbel/MICHELIN

95

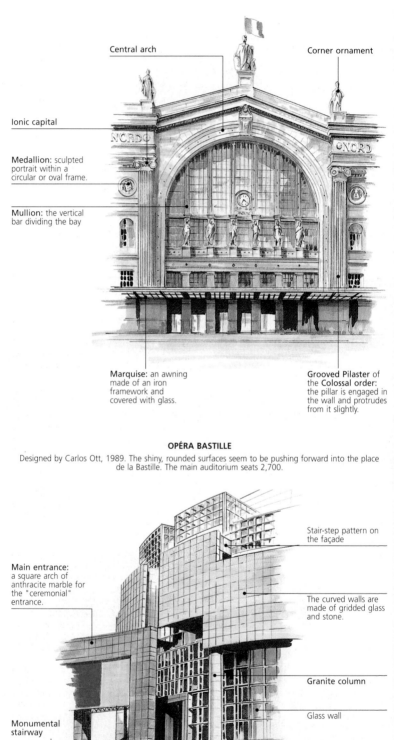

GARE DU NORD

Designed by the architect Hittorff, the train station was built between 1861-1868.

Central arch

Corner ornament

Ionic capital

Medallion: sculpted portrait within a circular or oval frame.

Mullion: the vertical bar dividing the bay

NORD

NORD

Marquise: an awning made of an iron framework and covered with glass.

Grooved Pilaster of the **Colossal order:** the pillar is engaged in the wall and protrudes from it slightly.

OPÉRA BASTILLE

Designed by Carlos Ott, 1989. The shiny, rounded surfaces seem to be pushing forward into the place de la Bastille. The main auditorium seats 2,700.

Stair-step pattern on the façade

Main entrance: a square arch of anthracite marble for the "ceremonial" entrance.

The curved walls are made of gridded glass and stone.

Granite column

Glass wall

Monumental stairway

R. Corbel/MICHELIN

Architecture and urban planning

The charm of the Parisian landscape is unquestionably due to its talented artists and craftsmen over the centuries; but it is also a result of its successful blending of styles from different periods, including contemporary buildings. Paris is a dynamic city whose contrasting faces never cease to astonish visitors and inhabitants alike.

Paris has acquired an impressive array of architectural masterpieces over its 2 000-year history.

Since its very beginnings, the city has been shaped by a myriad of social, political, commercial and artistic events.

Urban development has evolved constantly since the Middle Ages with the city's continuous population growth.

Of Gallo-Roman Paris only a few cradle-vaulted arches still stand in the Roman baths at the Hôtel de Cluny, along with remnants of the Lutetia arena that have been heavily restored.

Medieval Paris

From the 6C to the 10C marshy areas were dried up and cultivated, while the city's port and trade activities developed around place de Grève. Walls were built around the city, and its first streets constructed – extensions of the town's few bridges. Traffic and hygienic conditions improved when Philippe-Auguste had the streets paved. Soon, fountains began to dot the Parisian landscape, and springs – such as the one in Belleville – were tapped more frequently, providing a better water service.

Romanesque architecture, known as Norman style in England, didn't blossom in Paris as it did in the rest of France. Some rare examples include the chancel columns and bell-tower porch at St-Germain-des-Prés, the apse of St-Martin-des-Champs, and a few capitals in St-Pierre-de-Montmartre and St-Aignan Chapel.

Greater Paris was the cradle of **Gothic architecture**. Vast churches were built as tall and light as possible, using ogive or pointed arches and groin vaults (St-Germain-des-Prés chancel), whose thrust and weight are contained by side aisles and external buttressing (St-Julien-le-Pauvre apse).

Early Gothic (12C) architecture is best illustrated by Notre-Dame Cathedral, where the transition of building techniques and styles from the 12C to the early 14C can be seen in the vast chancel, slightly projecting transept and the dark triforium gallery. Capitals are decorated with motifs of plants and flowers from the greater Paris area. Sources of light are limited to narrow windows in the nave, topped by small round windows, or oculi, at the transept crossing.

Paris in the 15C

High or Rayonnant Gothic (13C-14C) is a style developed during the reign of Louis IX, when structural engineering reached new heights under architect Pierre de Montreuil. Walls are replaced by huge panels of glass, allowing light to flood in. Slender piers support the vault, reinforced externally by unobtrusive buttressing or flying buttresses (St-Martin-des-Champs refectory). With the new use of light, stained glass began to flourish. The *chevet* of Notre-Dame, Sainte-Chapelle and the Royal Chapel at Vincennes are Paris' masterpieces of **High Gothic** architecture. The gargoyles were another innovation, designed as spouts to drain off rainwater. It is this style, in particular, that was assimilated in England at Canterbury and London (St Stephen's, Westminster).

In the 15C a trend emerged towards more exaggerated decoration during the **Late or Flamboyant Gothic period (15C)** with an increase in purely decorative vaulting (St Merri transept, St-Germain-l'Auxerrois porch) – flame motifs flourish on window tracery; the triforium gives way to ever taller clerestory windows; piers culminating in ribs without capitals run straight to the ceiling (St-Séverin ambulatory), from which hang monumental vault bosses (St-Étienne-du-Mont).

With the outbreak of the Hundred Years War (1337-1453), civil architecture reverted to the sombre, massive style of feudal times (the Bastille and Men at Arms Hall in the Conciergerie).

Large residences with huge gardens such as the Hôtel St-Paul were built in the Marais district, along with many small half-timbered houses, a few of which can still be seen on rue François-Miron and on Île St-Louis.

In domestic architecture, defensive features – turrets, crenellations, wicket gates – blend with richly sculpted decorative elements such as balustrades and mullioned dormer windows.

The Renaissance

In the 16C, the war with Italy kindled the interest of French artists in Antiquity and non-religious decoration. Cradle or coffered ceilings (St-Nicolas-des-Champs) replaced ogive vaults, and architectural orders – especially Ionic and Corinthian – were reintroduced. The rood screen at St-Étienne-du-Mont and the stalls at St-Gervais are the finest examples of this style. However, Paris was not entirely loyal to the Italian influence. The capital preserved its own style, at least in terms of religious architecture.

A trio of Renaissance Parisian architects – The Renaissance in France is inextricably linked with the *châteaux de la Loire*. But Paris stands out for two majestic new edifices, the Louvre and the Tuileries, built by three men: Pierre Lescot (1515-78), Baptiste Androuët Du Cerceau (1560-1602) and Philibert Delorme (1517-70). All three were influenced by Italian architecture. The former two introduced from Italy the continuous façade broken by projecting bays with semicircular pediments. The Cour Carrée in the Louvre combines the splendour of Antiquity with rich decoration: statues nestling in niches between fluted pilasters; a frieze and cornices above doorways; and inside, coffered ceilings (Henri II staircase in the Clock Pavilion of the Louvre).

Work on the first Hôtel de Ville was begun in 1533 by Le Boccador and Pierre Chambiges.

Paris continued to expand, and new civil and religious edifices were always underway, despite the Wars of Religion and the siege of the city by Henri de Navarre. Charles IX and Louis XIII pushed the walls built by Philippe-Auguste further west. The right bank benefited from this dynamic urban development.

Classical architecture from Louis XIV to Louis XVI

Paris was transformed in the 17C with the rise of Classical art and architecture inspired by Antiquity. Rules were established by the Academy of Architecture, founded in 1671, and strengthened by an absolute monarchy, asserting the need to combine religion and Antiquity and leading Classical art to its pinnacle.

Religious architecture was modelled on Roman churches, with columns, pediments and statues competing for space.

The Jesuit style of the Counter-Reformation adopted for the design of St-Paul-St-Louis caught on and the Paris skyline was soon filled with domes. Lemercier built the Sorbonne and Val-de-Grâce (finished by Le Muet). The Sun King's architects demonstrated their progressive assimilation and mastery of the dome through the magnificent creations that beautified the city under Louis XIV – Hardouin-Mansart (Invalides, St-Roch), Libéral-Bruant (Salpêtrière), Le Vau (St-Louis-en-l'Île), Soufflot (Panthéon).

Public buildings were shaped by Classical symmetry and pure lines. Place des Vosges, place Dauphine and Hôpital St-Louis typify the Louis XIII style with

the use of brick and stone; whereas Salomon de Brosse blended French and Italian features in the Luxembourg Palace built for Marie de Medici. Mansart, Androuet Du Cerceau, Delamair and Le Muet created a new design in the Marais for the Parisian town house, or *hôtel particulier*, smaller than before and featuring a garden.

Classical architecture reached its height between 1650 and 1750 with magnificent buildings by Perrault (Louvre Colonnade), Le Vau (Institut de France) and Gabriel (place de la Concorde, École Militaire). Although originality was in vogue at the end of the 17C, the Rococo style (decorations on the Hôtel de Soubise) never was very popular in Paris. Under Louis XVI, taste gravitated towards the more elegant simplicity of Antiquity (Palais de la Légion d'Honneur) as epitomised by Ledoux (Farmers General Wall toll-houses).

Dome of the church, Les Invalides

S. Sauvignier/MICHELIN

Urban development – Construction work was ongoing throughout the 17C in Paris. François Mansart (1598-1666) designed the Val-de-Grâce, the Hôtel de la Vrillière (Banque de France), and the façade of the Hôtel Carnavalet. His nephew, **Jules Hardouin-Mansart** (1646-1708) built the Invalides dome, place Vendôme, place des Victoires and the Hôtel Conti.

Paris was fitted out with magnificent buildings and avenues. The right and left banks tried to outdo each other. The Palais Cardinal designed by Jacques Lemercier, as well as the Cours de la Reine (Champs-Elysées), and place Royale – a model of Classical symmetry – were constructed on the Right Bank. The Hôtel Lambert was built on Île St-Louis by **Le Vau** (1612-70), who also designed St-Sulpice and the Collège des Quatre Nations (now the Institut de France) on the Left Bank. The Manufacture des Gobelins and the Observatoire were erected in the late 17C.

The building frenzy continued into the 18C, when an impressive number of new monuments appeared on the Paris skyline: the Palais-Royal arcades, the Hôtel des Monnaies, the Palais de l'Élysée, the Palais-Bourbon, the Théâtre de l'Odéon, and the Palais de Bagatelle. After the Revolution, the city was divided into chic areas and the working-class districts west of the Marais, whose winding streets add a touch of charm from the past to present-day Paris (Latin Quarter and St-Merri Quarter).

Safety and cleanliness improved with the addition of lanterns that were lit until midnight, as well as a road maintenance service and fire brigade. Traffic problems were alleviated by ring-roads built around the capital. The banks of the Seine were remodelled and new bridges constructed, allowing fresh supplies to be brought in by boat on a daily basis. Finally, Paris adopted its current system of street names and numbers with no 1 being the house closest to the Seine.

Second Empire and innovation

The Empire and Restoration were not marked by any significant architectural achievements. Napoleon I continued construction of the Louvre and built monuments such as the Madeleine, the Arc de Triomphe and the Arc de Triomphe du Carrousel. But the real transformation of Paris took place during the Second Empire, when **Baron Haussmann**'s massive urban planning programme and the new application of cast iron in construction irrevocably altered the city. The technique of cladding metallic sub-structures was refined by Baltard (St Augustin, Pavillon Baltard at Nogent-sur-Marne), Labrouste (Bibliothèque Ste-Geneviève), and Hittorff (Gare du Nord), the most famous example of the new building method being **Gustave Eiffel**'s Tower.

Paris was enlarged to encompass some of its surrounding villages, and the current system of the 20 *arrondissements* was created. Haussmann's wide avenues enhance buildings such as the Opéra Garnier, one of the finer stone edifices of a period that was less preoccupied with monumental buildings.

Towards the end of the century, new trends developed that were different from the official style. Art Nouveau architects, the most well known being Guimard, defined a new decorative vocabulary for façades, interiors and furniture featuring stylised floral motifs, asymmetrical designs and materials such as glass and ceramics.

The 20C

The 20C marks a turning point in urban architecture. Architects and structural engineers collaborated on ever more economical and functional designs using industrially manufactured, thus cheaper, materials (cast iron, plate-glass, artificial stone) and improved building methods. Buildings in totally different styles have gone up side-by-side. While the Grand and Petit Palais, Pont Alexandre-III and Sacré-Cœur look to the past for their inspiration, the Théâtre des Champs-Elysées (Frères Perret), Palais de Chaillot and Palais de Tokyo, fashioned in reinforced concrete, look resolutely ahead to the modern age.

Contemporary developments – Since 1945, under the influence of **Le Corbusier** (Fondation, Cité Universitaire), architectural design has undergone a fundamental reappraisal. A wide variety of new forms, styles and lines strive to fit into the existing urban landscape, starting with social housing in the 1970s. Ricardo Bofill's buildings use elements of Classical architecture while employing modern materials such as glass and cement.

Glass has been used to cover most new constructions (La Défense, Institut du Monde Arabe, Bibliothèque de France, Palais de la culture du Japon), enabling architects to achieve stunning technical effects.

La Défense

Blending past and future – Architecture today falls within the wider scope of town planning, with new buildings designed as part of a larger scheme of renovations in a district (Maine-Montparnasse, Les Halles, La Villette, Bercy) or of newly created areas (La Défense, Tolbiac). Green spaces, pedestrian zones and bicycle paths have also been designed as part of the restructuring of the city.

The International Foundation for Human Rights in the Arche de La Défense, the Bibliothèque Nationale de France and the Palais Omnisports de Bercy are only a few examples of how the city's reputation as an important centre for culture and sports has been enhanced in recent years.

Paris has often chosen foreign architects to undertake its large-scale buildings. The Louvre Pyramide, one of the finest examples of a successful alliance of old and new, is the work of American architect **Ieoh Ming Pei**.

But the era of huge projects seems to be coming to an end. Today the accent is on improving and preserving existing monuments.

Some buildings from the past 30 years

The Forum des Halles, Centre Georges-Pompidou, Cité des Sciences et de l'Industrie and the nearby Cité de la Musique (La VILLETTE), Institut du Monde Arabe, Opéra Bastille, Pyramide du Louvre, the CNIT and the Grande Arche (La DÉFENSE), Palais Omnisports, Ministère des Finances, and the Bibliothèque de France-site Tolbiac (BERCY), the Fondation Cartier near place Denfert-Rochereau (MONTPARNASSE), and the reflective plastic forms of the Le Ponant apartment block built on the site of the old Citroën car factory (VAUGIRARD).

Paris and the arts

PAINTING and SCULPTURE

Painting and sculpture have always been closely interwoven into Parisian life. After centuries of working on commission from the monarchy, 19C and 20C artists began to reach levels of freedom and creativity acclaimed throughout the world.

In the Middle Ages

Painting and sculpture appeared within a religious context during this period, as Gothic buildings were gradually decorated. Stained glass, the main medium, reached stunning heights (Sainte-Chapelle, rose windows in Notre-Dame). The palette of colours was broadened and became increasingly suffused with light. The realism of painting from the Middle Ages is striking through its expressive faces and minutely detailed clothing. Painters from this period were given the name Primitives.

Gothic sculpture also flourished. Realism and a sense of drama combined to transform what was until then mere decoration into a true art form. Churches were covered with statues: little sculptures adorn the balustrade and the sides of the chancel at Notre-Dame, whereas the Portal of the Last Judgement marks the beginning of a more sober style that developed in the 13C into French Gothic.

The Renaissance

At the beginning of the 14C the Parisian schools of painting chose a style that was still realistic but more subdued. Expressions became finer and details more important, leading to a mannerist style. Painting evolved and adopted new themes such as mythology and portraits, as well as humanist themes with Antiquity as the ideal. The influence of Italian art is omnipresent in French painting, whereas sculpture preserved its own character.

The art of stained glass was at its peak. Jean Cousin the Younger (1522-94) delved deeper into colour techniques. The *Judgement of Solomon* and the *Story of the Virgin* in St-Gervais, and the *Story of St-Joseph* in St-Merri are like paintings made of stained glass.

Jean Goujon (1510-68) – The master of 16C French statuary. While he didn't reject Italian mannerism, nature was his fundamental ideal. His works combine grace and elegance despite their complex composition. Fitting into the architectural design, they provide a preliminary idea of French classicism. The Cariatides (Louvre) and bas-relief sculptures of the Fontaine des Innocents (1547-49) are his two greatest masterpieces.

The 17C

Italian influence continued during the early 17C. Paintings were designed mainly as decoration for royal palaces such as the Louvre and Luxembourg. Sculpture also adopted the Italian style, becoming strictly decorative for the niches designated by architects.

Window in St-Étienne-du-Mont

But Classical French art asserts itself under the king's patronage in the second half of the 17C; and despite competition from Versailles, Paris was its main beneficiary. The main purpose of painting and sculpture became the glorification of the French monarchy, which enriches its 'great city' with magnificent monuments decorated by the Court's best sculptors: Girardon (Richelieu's tomb), Coysevox (Tuileries Gardens), and Coustou (The Marly Horses).

In 1648, the Academy of Painting and Sculpture was founded; it was to be the most important French art school until 1793. Quarrelling between the corporatists, represented by Vouet, and the independents, represented by Le Brun, kept things lively.

Pierre Mignard (1612-95) – Succeeding Le Brun as First Painter to the King, he was instrumental in the transition from the 17C to the 18C. His little paintings imitating Raphael are known as *mignardes*. By introducing a lighter, more elegant and realistic touch in his compositions, he started the quarrel between the Poussinist and the Rubenists similar to the literary spat between Ancients and Moderns. The modern painters gave nature the place of honour (the Le Nain brothers' landscapes), rejecting the Academy's sobriety.

Between Baroque and Classic

18C French painting was characterised by a surfeit of detail embellishing the themes of religious paintings (Boucher, *Pastoral Scene*, Louvre) as well as by the humanization of mythology. This mannerist French style launched the "Fête Galante" genre illustrated by Watteau (1684-1721) in *Pilgrimage to the island of Cythera* (1717, Louvre). Portraitists such as La Tour (*Portrait of the Marquise de Pompadour*, 1752-55, Louvre)

101

prefered pastel techniques. Jean-Baptiste Siméon-Chardin (1699-1779), the great master of the French School, devoted himself to still-life paintings and portraits. Boucher's delicate landscapes herald the pre-Romantic period.

The late 18C wavered between the pre-Romantic J-H Fragonard (1732-1806) and neo-Classicism, typified by J-L David and his *Oath of the Horatii* (1784-85, Louvre).

Monumental sculptures were as numerous as in the 17C: Robert le Lorrain (*Les Chevaux du soleil*, Hôtel de Rohan), Bouchardon (Quatre-Saisons Fountain), and Peigalle (St-Sulpice).

The 19C and 20C

Mirroring the era's political movements, painting and sculpture reacted violently to the new trends. Bright colours and fantasy came into fashion. Géricault (1791-1824) launched Romanticism: through its bold composition, dynamism and the characters' striking expressions, *Raft of the Medusa* (1819, Louvre) is in total opposition to the Classical style. Delacroix carried on in the same spirit. The official Salons were the scenes of battles between the two major trends: one advocating the superiority of drawing, the other that of colour. Ingres (1780-1867), taking his inspiration from Antiquity, lost the battle when he exhibited *The Apotheosis of Homer* at the 1827 Salon. However, the return to Academic art was successful at the 1863 Salon.

In reaction, Manet organised the 1863 Group featuring all of the painters rejected by the Salon. Fantin-Latour (1836-1904) and Manet portray everyday pleasures on their canvases, sometimes in a provocative manner in their drawings of women (*Olympia*, 1863, Orsay). Like Courbet before them, they were the precursors of Impressionism.

From Impressionism to Expressionism – The Impressionists use the precepts of Realism (works based on nature) while adding a powerful luminosity to their paintings through the use of a chromatic palette. They also relied on the art of drawing. Edgar Degas' sketches of dancers show firm strokes. Above all, they had a strong penchant for landscapes (Claude Monet, *Argenteuil Bridge*, 1834, Orsay). Cézanne (1839-1906) and Pissarro (1830-1903) blended characters and landscapes or indoor scenes (Paul Cézanne, *The Card Players*, around 1890-95, Orsay).

The success of the genre opened up new possibilities: Seurat created scientific Impressionism in which characters are placed in a subtle balance; systematic juxtaposition of primary colours and their complementary tones gives rise to Pointillism. Nature becomes a symbol under the brush strokes of Puvis de Chavannes (1824-98). Gauguin (1848-1903) and Van Gogh (1853-90) had a different reaction to Impressionism: while not breaking off from it, their explorations were directed towards expressive intensity through the use of bright colours. The Expressionist movement was associated with a new concern over social problems prevalent at the beginning of the 20C, as illustrated by painters such as Rouault and Soutine.

From Fauvism to Cubism – The Fauvists were a new, modernist movement in the early 20C who had nothing left in common with the Realists or Symbolists. Their palette of colours and the shapes represented are often aggressive, which created a scandal at the 1905 Autumn Salon. Vlaminck, Matisse and Derain are the masters of this movement advocating freedom. They strove to free themselves of all constraints and conventions in their daily lives, living a bohemian existence in the Bateau-Lavoir in Montmartre.

Nevertheless, Matisse reintroduced the concept of rigour and constraints, with the idea that the emphasis on colour shouldn't lead to an overshadowing of form – however primitive – or composition. Picasso brought this trend to the fore with *Les Demoiselles d'Avignon* (1907). Braque applied it to landscape painting. But some preferred more creative impulses to this spirit of discipline. Modigliani, Soutine, Chagall, Zadkine and Léger settled in the La Ruche workshop in Montparnasse, where they gave free rein to their moods, reviving Expressionism. This was the golden age of the Paris School, which came to an end with the Second World War, when Surrealism burst upon the scene.

Sculpture – During the Second Empire and the Third Republic, Paris was gradually transformed into an open-air museum. Works by Carpeaux (Observatory Fountain) and Rude *(Marshal Ney, the Marseillaise on the Arc de Triomphe)* precede those of the great masters of the late 19C and the period between the two World Wars, including Rodin *(Balzac, Victor Hugo, Bronze Age)*, Dalou (place de la Nation), Bourdelle (Palais de Tokyo, Théâtre des Champs-Élysées), Maillol (Tuileries Gardens) and Landowski (*Ste-Geneviève* on the Pont de la Tournelle, *Animals* at the Porte de St-Cloud).

The Art Nouveau style is epitomised by Hector Guimard's famous wrought-iron metro entrances, created around 1900.

Abstract sculpture is also given its place: Calder's mobile *(see UNESCO and La DÉFENSE)*, Louis Leygue, and Agam (La Défense). Renewing a 19C tradition, sculptures were erected in streets and gardens: of famous people (Georges Pompidou, Jean Moulin, Arthur Rimbaud) along with Symbolist works, and sculpture-fountains (Fontaine Stravinski, by Jean Tinguely and Niki de Saint-Phalle, next to Beaubourg).

Paris in paintings

Paris began to be the subject or background in paintings at the time of the Wars of Religion. During the reigns of Henry IV and Louis XIII, it was used as a theme by Jacques Callot (1592-1635) in his engravings and by Dutch landscape painters (De Verwer, Zeeman) fascinated by the light and atmosphere on the banks of the Seine.
The urban landscape of Paris really came into its own with the Impressionists, who preferred painting outdoors rather than in a studio.
Corot painted the Paris quaysides and Ville d'Avray a few miles away. Lépine, Monet *(St-Germain-l'Auxerrois, Gare St-Lazare)*, Renoir *(Moulin de la Galette, Moulin Rouge)*, Sisley *(Île St-Louis)* and Pissarro *(The Pont Neuf)* depict light effects in the capital at all hours and in all seasons. Paris is also an important focus in works by Seurat *(The Eiffel Tower)*, Gauguin, Cézanne and Van Gogh *(Montmartre scenes)*. Toulouse-Lautrec portrays a totally different view of Paris life in his witty, intimate sketches of cabaret artists. Among the Nabi artists, Vuillard captures the peace of Paris squares and gardens in a more poetic vein. In the early 20C, Paris figured prominently in the work of Fauve painters Marquet and Utrillo with their scenes of unfashionable neighbourhoods. Views of the capital by the naïve painters are sensitive, imaginative and highly colourful.
Among contemporary artists, Balthus (Paris between the wars), Yves Brayer and Bernard Buffet have cast Paris in a new light.

La Gare St-Lazare, Claude Monet

PARIS IN PICTURES

Artists roaming through the streets of Paris have always tried to capture the atmosphere of this city of a thousand faces. Who hasn't caught himself daydreaming in front of an image of bygone Paris?

Photography

The indiscreet eye of the photographer is a witness to everyday life in Paris. **Eugène Atget**, one of the fathers of modern photography, immortalised street scenes and tradesmen in a Paris that no longer exists (cabbies, street singers, rag merchants, lace sellers etc).
In more recent times, **Edouard Boubat**, **izis**, **Brassaï** (known as the "Toulouse-Lautrec of the camera lens") and **Marcel Bovis** captured the magic of Paris at night; **Jacques-Henri Lartigue** recorded the Roaring Twenties; **Cartier-Bresson**, the archetypal globe-trotter and founding member of the Magnum agency, caught views of Paris that resemble watercolours *(Île de la Cité)*; **Willy Ronis** shot scenes of Belleville-Ménilmontant, now changed beyond all recognition.

Robert Doisneau (1912-94) – One of the great photographers of Paris, he specialised in humorous shots of ordinary people filled with depth and poetry: children playing, concierges, scenes of cafés and markets. *The Kiss*, taken in front of the Hôtel de Ville in 1950, remains his most famous work.

Film

In the late 19C and early 20C, Paris encourages the development of the cinema by helping some of its pioneers, who were inspired by photography and theatre.

1892 – Émile Reynaud opens the Optical Theatre in the Musée Grévin, holding a total of 12 000 showings attended by 500 000 spectators.

28 December 1895 – The Lumière Brothers hold their first public showing of the cinematograph on boulevard des Capucines.

1896-1897 – Georges Meliès (1861-1938) invents double exposure and presents his first films with scripts.

1898 – Charles Pathé creates his international firm and studios. First newsreels (Pathé-Journal).

1900 – The *cinéorama* (a 100m/110yd circular screen invented by Grimoin-Sanson) was presented at the Paris Exposition.

Les Frères Lumière

The Lumière Brothers and the cinematograph – In February 1895, Auguste (1862-1954) and Louis (1864-1948) Lumière registered the patent for the cinematograph, a machine that projects animated scenes at a speed of 18 frames per second. Their *Sortie des usines Lumière* (shot in 1894) was a success, and showings were held in the Salon Indien at the Grand-Café, boulevard des Capucines.

Léon Gaumont (1863-1946) – Pursuing the work begun by the Lumière Brothers with his *chronophone*, he added synchronised sound to films.

Early 20C – **Charles Pathé** created his studios on rue Francœur and turned the cinema into an industry.

POSTERS

Paris was the major source and beneficiary of this new art between painting and photography.

The French masters – Their goal was to depict the joys and sorrows of everyday life, and to combine Parisians' social and cultural demands. **Gavarni** (1804-66) evokes the seedier side of Paris in his black-and-white posters of street-walkers and poor neighbourhoods. He created posters based on *Selected Works* by Balzac, who also inspired Grandville's *Petites misères de la vie humaine*.
Chéret revolutionised the art of poster-designing in the second half of the 19C with his inflated, or Rococo, style and lively figures in colour.

Toulouse-Lautrec (1864-1901) – As a lithographer, he adopted the principles of his teachers Chéret and Bonnat, but with a more cutting style. He portrayed the poverty in certain areas of Paris and frequented cabarets, where he created some of his greatest pieces such as *La Goulue at the Moulin Rouge*. His illustrations – verging on caricature and the grotesque – stirred up many a scandal.

Alphonse Mucha – Arriving in Paris in 1887 from his native Prague, Mucha lived in the city during a time of cultural blossoming. While Toulouse-Lautrec sought to bring out the truth of his subjects, Mucha created figures surrounded by great decorative verve and an abundance of motifs. Like Lautrec, he made poster designs for theatre openings, notably for Sarah Bernhardt.

LITERATURE IN PARIS THROUGH THE AGES

The story of Paris as a literary capital began with the creation of its university, while the 18C saw the rise of the city's intellectual and cultural prestige. The history of French literature is closely linked with that of Paris.
Many writers who were born in the city have celebrated it in their books, giving Paris a special place in literature.

Middle Ages and Renaissance

12C-13C – The first Paris university opened its doors. It was the only university in northern France, and gave a boost to intellectual life. The Parisian dialect was adopted by the Court as its official language, putting Paris on the literary map.

15C-16C – Writers, and the heroes of their stories, "go up"' to Paris, the former in order to write, the latter to study. Low life on the streets was portrayed in epic poems and mystery plays, whereas Rutebœuf and Villon wrote poems about individuals and everyday life. Although Rabelais criticised the Parisian character, he had Gargantua and Pantagruel attend the Sorbonne; and he himself lived and died in the Marais (d 1553).

1530 – The Collège de France was founded by François I and Guillaume Budé.
As the city grows into its role as capital, many writers choose to make it their second home, including Montaigne, Ronsard and the Pleiade poets, as well as Agrippa d'Aubigné, who witnessed the religious conflicts that overtook Paris and the rest of France in the late 16C.

The 17C

As the city was embellished by Henri IV and Louis XIII, and agitated by the Fronde during Louis XIV's minority, writers and noted wits of the period developed the famous literary salons, first at the Hôtel de Rambouillet (17C) and later on in the homes of the Marquise de Lambert, Madame du Deffand, and Madame Geoffrin (18C).
After its role as a centre of humanism in the 16C, Paris promoted classicism in the 17C with the assertion of absolute monarchy. Writers during the reign of Louis XIV, such as Molière, went beyond prior conventions and were allowed to criticise society.

1634-1635 – The Académie Française was founded by Richelieu. Paris became the centre of French literature. Contrary to the salons, where open discussion was encouraged, the Académie sought to standardise the French language and exert a restraining influence on all branches of literature.

1680 – The Comédie Française was created under the king's patronage.

18C – Revival of the literary salons

In the 18C, Louis XV and Louis XVI showed little interest in literature. Society resorted to philosophy salons and cafés (Procope, La Régence), where new ideas developed and the fates of French writers were decided.

1710-1780 – Prominent authors such as Marivaux and Montesquieu attended the salons, where Voltaire and Diderot also congregated.
Marivaux and Beaumarchais *(Barber of Seville* and *Marriage of Figaro)* tinged their light comedies about Paris society and lifestyle with irony, whereas Jean-Jacques Rousseau (1712-78), a precursor of Romanticism who was born in the provinces, expressed disdain for the place so full of "noise, smoke and mud"! Others concerned with the dichotomy between ethics and society include the Abbé Prévost *(Manon Lescaut)*, Restif de la Bretonne *(Nights of Paris)* the Marquis de Sade and Choderlos de Laclos *(Dangerous Liaisons)*. It is Voltaire (1694-1778), master social critic, historian, novelist *(Candide)*, essayist, letter-writer, diarist, dramatist and Humanist philosopher, who perhaps epitomises the best of 18C writing in Paris: ironic and witty with a light touch and perfect turn of phrase.

During the Age of Enlightenment, Paris wielded a great deal of influence in international intellectual circles with emissaries such as d'Alembert and Diderot, who secured subscriptions to their 28-volume Encyclopedia from Catherine the Great of Russia among others.

Hobnobbing at Le Procope

The 19C and 20C

After the French Revolution, literature was no longer restricted to a small section of society. Writers were active in the social and political debates of their times through its major literary trends: Realism, Romanticism, Symbolism, Naturalism and Surrealism.

Paris has a double image, portrayed at times as rich and prestigious, and at others as a more popular city full of vices. Heroes in novels head for Paris, leaving behind their native provinces. In *Les Illusions perdues*, Lucien de Rubempré dies there. In *Les Misérables* and *La Comédie humaine*, by Hugo and Balzac respectively, the city is portrayed as a character with a personality of its own subject to moods and illness. Both Julien Sorel, the hero of Stendhal's *Le Rouge et le Noir*, and Léon the notary in Flaubert's *Madame Bovary* run away from Paris society; and some of Zola's novels depict certain circles and areas of the city as a kind of prison.

Parisian writers such as Dumas the Younger, Musset, the song-writer Béranger, Eugène Sue *(Mysteries of Paris)*, Murger *(Scenes of Bohemian Life)* and Nerval vacillate between the two images of the city. Contrasts in humour and reflections on life's contradictions are explored, against the back-drop of Haussmann's upheavals, in verse by Baudelaire, the Parnassian and Symbolist poets, and in the emerging social-history, realist novel by Émile Zola *(Les Rougon-Macquart)*.

Old Montmartre lives on in the **songs** of Bruant (1851-1925), the novels of Carco (1886-1958) and Marcel Aymé (1902-67), Montparnasse in the poems of Max Jacob (1876-1944) and Léon-Paul Fargue (1876-1947); still other writers and poets such as Colette and Cocteau, Simenon, Montherlant, Louise de Vilmorin, Aragon, Prévert, Sacha Guitry, Eluard, Sartre, Simone de Beauvoir and Beckett have celebrated Paris-as-muse in their many works.

Playwrights' reputations, like novelists', are made and broken in Paris. Vaudeville, the soul of boulevard theatre, was the 19C heir to the farces featuring dialogue and songs that were performed at the St-Germain and St-Laurent fairs in earlier days, as well as the bawdy tableaux and pastiches of scenes from well-known plays. Talented playwrights also wrote serious vaudeville. Light opera and revues emerged during the Second Empire, whereas dramas were another outgrowth of boulevard theatre.

MUSIC

Paris is rather like a grand orchestra where enchanting music is played. It has been both the theme and setting for a host of musical compositions, and its streets are often filled with the sounds of this art with its long-standing tradition in the city.

In the Middle Ages

Late 12C – A school of polyphony was established at Notre-Dame characterised by its refined expression of the deep religious faith of the period.

13C-14C – Musical works such as Machaut's Masses (c 1300-77) and motets by contrapuntist Dufay are composed of several parts.

Under François I – A national musical printing works was created, illustrated by narrative ballads written by Janequin *(Les Cris de Paris)*. Renaissance-style madrigals and courtly songs accompanied on the lute become popular.

1571 – The poet Baïf founded the Academy for Music and Poetry in an attempt to revive Classical verse-form and poetic rhyme.

The Renaissance

"That most noble and gallant art" developed naturally at the Royal Court, first at the Louvre and later at Versailles, where sovereigns, their consorts and companions disported themselves in masques, ballets, allegorical dances, recitals, opera and comedy. The first Parisian songs were published.

The 17C: a musical high point

Music, like literature, flourished under the renewed interest of the Court. Italian opera was welcomed, thanks to Mazarin, and major foreign operas such as the *Marriage of Orpheus and Eurydice* (1643) were staged in Paris.

Lully and lyric opera – Florentine composer **Jean-Baptiste Lully** (1632-87) settled in Paris, and Louis XIV appointed him to direct music first at Court, then at the Académie Royale de Musique (1672). He created operas and ballets *(Ballet des Bienvenus, Ballet de la naissance de Vénus)*, dominating every genre. In 1661, he collaborated with Molière, developing a new genre, *ballet-comédie (Les Fâcheux, Le Sicilien, Le Bourgeois gentilhomme)*. Religious music was also part of his repertory *(Te Deum, 1677)*, and he attained new heights in choral music at Notre-Dame (with *Campra*) and Notre-Dame-des-Victoires. Meanwhile, the Couperins held sway at St-Gervais and at the Sainte-Chapelle, while Charpentier was musical director at St-Paul-St-Louis.

New operatic forms in the 18C

After the prestigious operas of the 17C, music was made more accessible to the general public in the comic operas given at the St-Germain and St-Laurent fairs. However, Jean-Philippe Rameau (1683-1764) carried on in the tradition of Lully, while accentuating the orchestra's role. His opera-ballets *(Les Indes galantes)*, lyric tragedies *(Castor et Pollux, Dardanus)* and comedies *(Platée)* gave birth to the French style. Rameau moved away from the Italian tradition without renouncing it, prompting the so-called War of the Buffoons.

The Musical Wars – The War of the Buffoons (from the name of an Italian troupe that performed in Paris in 1752) was a quarrel over French and Italian opera in which Rameau was pitted against the Encyclopedists. The main protagonists in the quarrel were Diderot *(Le Neveu de Rameau)* and J-J Rousseau *(Le Devin de village, Lettre sur la musique française)*, who enumerated all of the flaws in French music, which Lully still dominated. The second war developed over the new genre, comic opera, which grew out of the Parisian fairs and was launched by Gluck and Puccini, two foreigners who had settled in Paris. Gluck stressed dramatic intensity in his operas, reformed the opera by reducing the action to three acts and replacing the harpsichord by the flute. His works *(Orphée et Eurydice, Iphigénie en Aulide* and *Alceste)* transformed the principles of French tragic opera.

The 19C

1795 – The Conservatoire de Musique de Paris was founded in 1795 and directed successively by Cherubini, Auber and Ambroise Thomas.

1801 – The Théâtre de Feydeau and the Théâtre de Favart joined to form the Opéra-Comique de Paris.
Music in Paris was associated with the political and military events that were taking place there: the Revolution produced many popular songs, the most famous being *La Carmagnole*, a satirical song from 1792. In the 19C the city became the international capital of music, attracting the greatest masters of the century.

1830 – Berlioz composed the *Symphonie Fantastique*, which still resounds as the manifesto-opus of the young Romantic school.

1866 – Premiere in Paris of Offenbach's *La Vie parisienne*.

From **1870**, symphonic composition and opera evolved through the work of Bizet, St-Saëns, Charpentier and Dukas, Parisians by birth or adoption. France was the leader in ballet music, which draws inspiration from history and mythology.

The turn of the century (19C-20C)

Debussy and Ravel were the two major French impressionist composers at the end of the 19C. Refusing all foreign influence (including Wagner) in symphonic music, they gave it a national character.
Debussy and Ravel collaborated with Diaghilev's Ballets Russes.

1894 – The Schola Cantorum was founded by Bordes, Guilmant and d'Indy.

1899 – Premiere of *La Prise de Troie* by Berlioz at the Opéra.

1902 – Premiere of *Pelléas et Mélisande* by Debussy at the Opéra-Comique.

The Group of Six – Founded by Auric, Durey, Honegger, Milhaud, Poulenc and Tailleferre in 1920, the group created a new musical aesthetic rejecting Romanticism and Impressionism. Music had to be pure, requiring a long creative gestation. While claiming to draw inspiration from Satie, they didn't practise spontaneous composition.

The Garde républicaine – A description of Parisian musical life wouldn't be complete without mentioning the Garde Républicaine, formed in 1871. Originating with the Garde de Paris, created in 1848, it is composed of 127 musicians. Its military marches *(Sambre et Meuse, Marche lorraine, La Fille du régiment)* are hymns to French victories.

Musician at the harpsichord by Duplessis

Cabarets – These popular venues were all the rage at the beginning of the century. The *chansonniers* (singers) performing in Montmartre's cabarets are portrayed by Toulouse-Lautrec in his famous posters and lithographs.

1885-1899 – The Chat Noir was the *chansonniers'* favourite cabaret.

1903 – The Lapin Agile opens its doors.

1936 – Writers such as Prévert, Aragon and Apollinaire flocked to the Bœuf sur le Toit, where their works were set to music.

During the First World War, Nadia Boulanger led a new Parisian movement known as the neo-Classical School. A number of French and foreign composers studied under her, and drew inspiration from Stravinsky and Latin music. After 1920 Paris continued to nurture new forms of musical expression. From the *ondes martenot* to the Jeune-France Group and its humanist music, Schaeffer and his concrete sounds, Henry, Boulez, Xénakis and Messiaen, each one made an important individual contribution to the musical scene. As major foreign musicians continued to arrive in Paris, the Paris School was created in 1951.

The piano sonatas, ballet (*Le Loup*, 1953), symphonies and orchestral pieces by composer Henri Dutilleux (b 1916) are among the greatest works from the second half of the 20C.

National orchestras – Paris possesses some internationally renowned orchestras. The Orchestre National de France, Orchestre Philharmonique de Radio-France and its Maîtrise (Choir School created in 1981), the Ensemble Intercontemporain, the Orchestre de Paris and Université de Paris-Sorbonne choirs and the Petits Chanteurs de la Croix de Bois interpret major works from their varied repertoires with brio.

Parisian organists – Marie-Madeleine Duruflé-Chevalier, Olivier Latry, Philippe Lefebvre, Jean-Pierre Leguay and Riccardo Miravet; each of these organ players – many of whom are known throughout the world – is connected to a particular church, where they fill the vaulted spaces with their delightful music. Organ music is also featured at the Festival d'Art Sacré in the autumn.

Major venues for music – While the Opéra Garnier (inaugurated in 1875) continues to be a highly prestigious opera house (home of the Paris Ballet), the Opéra Bastille (designed by Carlos Ott) has become the main venue for staging operas since it opened in 1989.

The **Théâtre des Champs-Élysées** has maintained its spirit of musical innovation since it was founded in 1913 by Gabriel Astruc. The Théâtre du Châtelet was a mecca for light opera fans from 1928 to 1970. Renamed the **Théâtre musical de Paris** in 1980, it presents prestigious concerts and opera productions.

The **Cité de la Musique** (Parc de la Villette), designed by Christian de Portzamparc, includes the Conservatoire National Supérieur de Musique, the Musée de la Musique, and the Institut National de Pédagogie Musicale, as well as a concert hall. **IRCAM** (Institute of Acoustic and Musical Research) is a department of the Centre Pompidou devoted to experimental music. Thanks to the fervour of composer Pierre Boulez and to sophisticated technology using computers, electronic laboratories and sound processors, IRCAM has won international acclaim.

ASSOCIATION WITH THE BRITISH

Many an Englishman has harboured a secret admiration for Paris, while regretting that so many Parisians live there – the French have a similar view of London!

The English capital is now a mere 3hr away by train. But in the realms of politics the instinct for self-preservation has maintained a certain distance, commonly known as the Entente Cordiale. This relationship has been reiterated through history with many treaties – 1763 terminating the Seven Years War, 1814 and 1815 ending the Napoleonic era, 1856 sealing the alliance at the end of the Crimean War, 1904-10 commercial treaties which concluded in the Entente Cordiale, and 1919 the Treaty of Versailles.

Since the 17C, Paris has been a major attraction for British travellers: artists on their way to Italy (Charles Dickens, John Ruskin), gentlemen on the Grand Tour (Lord Byron), public figures escaping from persecution at home (Oscar Wilde, Duke and Duchess of Windsor) or impoverished journalists (WM Thackeray) and students (Orwell).

By the mid-19C, Thomas Cook was organising what he called package holidays. As he stated in Cook's Excursionist and Advertiser of 15 May 1863, *"We would have every class of British subjects visit Paris, that they may emulate its excellencies, and shun the vices and errors which detract from the glory of the French capital. In matters of taste and courtesy we have much to learn from Parisians…"*

Lawrence Durrell wrote: *"the national characteristics... are the restless metaphysical curiosity, the tenderness of good living and the passionate individualism. This is the invisible constant in a place with which the ordinary tourist can get in touch just by sitting quite quietly over a glass of wine in a Paris bistrot".*

AMERICANS IN PARIS

The world's quintessential expatriate city, Paris has long held a special fascination for Americans. Offering an incomparable urban setting, a rich cultural legacy and a deep-rooted respect for artistic pursuits and individual freedom, the French capital has provided a stimulating environment for successive waves of celebrated American émigrés.

18C-19C – Franco-American ties developed out of shared conflict with the British and a steadfast commitment to Revolutionary ideals. Francophiles **Benjamin Franklin** and **Thomas Jefferson**, sent to France as official emissaries of the new republic, contributed to establishing early political, cultural and scientific links between the two countries.
Throughout the 19C Paris reigned as the cultural capital of the Western world and as such attracted numerous American artists including Whistler, Eakins and Impressionist Mary Cassatt. Many of America's leading architects – notably Richard Morris Hunt, Henry Hobson Richardson and Louis Sullivan – studied at the world-renowned **École des Beaux-Arts**, the supreme arbiter of neo-Classical 19C architectural trends.

"Where the 20C was" – Referring to the city's pivotal role in the birth and development of modern literary and artistic movements, **Gertrude Stein** asserted "Paris is where the twentieth century was".
Like two other prominent life-long expatriates – Natalie Clifford Barney and **Sylvia Beach** – Gertrude Stein was lured by the city's stimulating environment, which allowed a degree of artistic and sexual freedom unthinkable in early-20C America. Beach's **Shakespeare and Company** bookshop and the celebrated literary salons of Stein and Barney became important meeting places for the city's intelligentsia. Beach's bookshop stood on rue de l'Odéon from 1921 to 1941. The shop of the same name off quai de Montebello at no 37 rue de la Bûcherie, founded by American George Whitman in 1956, has no direct affiliation, but does carry on the spirit of the original, and is a pleasure to visit.
American expatriate life in Paris reached its heyday in the 1920s. The First World War was over, the exchange rate was favourable and Paris was the place to be. During that historic decade, the Left Bank was home to an astounding number of literary personalities: Ezra Pound, F Scott-Fitzgerald, Sherwood Anderson, Ford Madox-Ford and **Ernest Hemingway**, whose life and work is more intimately linked to Paris than that of any other American writer. This foremost Lost Generation novelist brilliantly captured the unbridled expatriate experience as played out in the legendary cafés, night spots and streets of Montparnasse and the Latin Quarter *(The Sun Also Rises* and *A Moveable Feast)*. The period's unprecedented literary production gave rise to a proliferation of avant-garde expatriate reviews *(Little Review, Transitions)* and publishers (Black Sun Press, Black Manikin Press and Hours Press founded by Nancy Cunard). The first uncensored edition of James Joyce's masterpiece *Ulysses* was published in France in 1922 by Sylvia Beach.
Simultaneously Paris played host to an international colony of prodigious artists including Picasso, Chagall, Modigliani, and Americans **Man Ray** and **Alexander Calder**. Among the expatriate performing artists were dancer **Isadora Duncan** and Revue Nègre star **Josephine Baker**, who cherished the racial equality and the international fame offered by France. The dizzying Paris scene was astutely observed by **Janet Flanner** who, under the pseudonym Genêt, authored the "Letter from Paris" column in *The New Yorker* from 1925 to 1975.
The 1930s were marked by the presence of **Henry Miller**. Like Hemingway, Miller came to Paris to become a writer and chose a Paris setting for his first novel. The quasi-autobiographical *Tropic of Cancer* (1934), banned in the US until the 1960s, explicitly depicts a seedy Paris well off the beaten expatriate trail. During his Paris years, Miller met his American protector, muse and lover, **Anaïs Nin**.

Post-Second World War to Present – Expatriate life in Paris was interrupted by the outbreak of the Second World War: most of the American writers of the 1920s and 30s had gone home or moved on to safer havens, while the international art scene had been partially transplanted to New York. Shakespeare and Company, a Left Bank institution, closed its doors in 1941 after 20 years of existence. During the late 1950s and 1960s, a new American-run bookstore and lending library opened in the Latin Quarter. This picturesque haunt (which took over the name Shakespeare and Company following Sylvia Beach's death in 1962) was frequented by Beat Generation writers Ginsberg and Burroughs, as well as by many of the newly arrived black writers. Lured by France's reputation as a nation fostering a non-racist cultural climate, a wave of black writers and musicians went abroad while McCarthyism was sweeping the US. The most influential member of this group was acclaimed writer and intellectual **Richard Wright** *(Native*

Son), whose self-imposed Paris exile began in 1947 and lasted until his death in 1960. Fellow-expatriate black American writers included **Chester Himes**, **William Gardner Smith** and **James Baldwin** *(Another Country, Giovanni's Room)*.

Although Paris' heyday as an avant-garde expatriate haven may be over, the City of Lights continues to entice Americans. For an idea of the range of activities and events organised for and by today's expatriate community, consult the monthly newspaper, *The Paris Free Voice*, (available in English-language haunts throughout the city).

Richard Wright: a writer in exile

American writer and intellectual Richard Wright lived at 14 rue Monsieur-le-Prince with his wife and two daughters from 1948 to 1959. Wright's novels *Black Boy*, *Native Son* and *American Hunger* and essays forcefully exposed racism in American society. Discontented with the racial and political climate in post Second World War America, Wright was finally granted an American passport thanks to the intervention of Gertrude Stein, who arranged to have the French Government extend him an official invitation. Among the haunts frequented by Wright and other members of the black intelligentsia was the nearby Café Tournon, 20 rue de Tournon. Martin Luther King visited the writer in his rue Monsieur-le-Prince apartment in 1959. Richard Wright died in Paris in 1960. His ashes are preserved in Père Lachaise cemetery *(see PERE-LACHAISE)*.

Paris today

Paris is the pivot of France's political, administrative, economic and cultural life.
In recent years, the city has attracted many multinational corporations and has become an important international business centre.
In 1960, a century after Baron Haussmann's large-scale urban restructuring, steps were taken to resolve some of the capital's congestion problems; but much remains to be done.

Paris' coat-of-arms

S. Sauvignier/MICHELIN

Local government – Since March 1977, the **Mairie de Paris** has had an elected mayor, chosen by the 163 councillors who make up the municipal council; municipal elections are held every six years. With the exception of the police force, headed by a *préfet*, the mayor has the same status and powers of mayors of other municipalities.

The Paris municipal authority works closely with the town halls of the 20 *arrondissements*, which are the main units of local government. Paris being both a *commune* and a *département*, its Council sits as a municipal authority and a general, or departmental, council.

The city's coat of arms features the boat motif from the armorial bearings of the watermen's guild whose members were appointed by Louis IX in 1260 to administer the township. In the 16C a motto was added: *Fluctuat nec mergitur* (though buffeted by the waves, she never sinks).

The **Île-de-France** region is composed of eight *départements* (Paris, Seine-et-Marne, Yvelines, Essonne, Hauts-de-Seine, Seine-St-Denis, Val-de-Marne and Val-d'Oise), each with its own prefecture, covering a total area of 12 011km²/4 637sq mi with a total population of 10 073 053 (Paris: 105km²/40sq mi; 2 176 243).

Metamorphosis – Paris' historic, architectural and archaeological treasures have been safeguarded by the enlightened policy of André Malraux and his successors, who instituted a programme of cleaning, restoration, and revitalisation of whole areas such as the Marais and preservation of archaeological finds. Meanwhile, structural engineers and planners wrestle with today's problems – traffic and transport (ring road, expressway, RER), supply (Rungis, Garonor), cultural centres (G Pompidou Centre), sports facilities (Bercy), commercial property development (La Défense, Front de Seine, Maine-Montparnasse) and urban renewal (place d'Italie, Belleville, Bercy); the emphasis being on the preservation and restoration of historic heritage.

Major cultural and architectural achievements include the Cité des Sciences et de l'Industrie and the Cité de la Musique at La Villette, the Musée d'Orsay, the Grand Louvre, the Opéra-Bastille, the Grande Arche at La Défense and the Bibliothèque Nationale at Tolbiac.

The transfer of the wholesale markets from Les Halles to Rungis, the division of the University into 13 autonomous parts, the decentralisation of the Higher Schools of learning, have all helped to relieve congestion in the city centre. Modern hospitals, both public and private, have been built. Green spaces (La Villette, André Citroën) have been created, old parks and gardens remodelled...

Population – With over 2 million inhabitants, Paris is one of the most densely populated cities in the world. Although the inner-city population is declining slightly, figures show a constant influx from the provinces and abroad. Some minority groups have adopted particular neighbourhoods over the years: Russians in Montparnasse, Spaniards in Passy, North Africans in Clignancourt, La Villette, Aubervilliers, Asians in Belleville, the 13th *arrondissement* etc.

But whatever their background, true Parisians are easy to pick out among the cosmopolitan crowd: hurried, tense, protesting, frivolous, quick-witted, ever ready to poke fun or play on words.

Paris neighbourhoods – Some neighbourhoods have retained their traditional association with a medieval trade or guild, thus preserving some of the atmosphere of past centuries: seed merchants on quai de la Mégisserie; publishing and bookshops in the Odéon area; cabinet-makers in rue du Faubourg-St-Antoine; bric-a-brac and second-hand clothes in the Temple and Sentier quarters; antique dealers on rue Bonaparte and rue La Boëtie; art galleries on avenue Matignon and rue du Faubourg-St-Honoré; *haute couture* houses on rue du Faubourg-St-Honoré, avenue Montaigne and rue François-Ier; luxury goods in the Opéra area; stringed instrument makers on rue de Rome; porcelain, crystal and glassware on rue de Paradis; jewellers on rue de la Paix and place Vendôme. Meanwhile government offices line rue de Grenelle; financial institutions are located in the Bourse, Opéra, Champs-Élysées, and La Défense areas; students gather around their university buildings in the Latin Quarter. All of these blend in with the schools, workshops, warehouses and small shops which, along with the many large firms, make up Paris' infinitely varied economy.

PARIS NEIGHBOURHOODS

Each neighbourhood of Paris is a bit like a village unto itself. One of the joys of wandering around the city is that the transition from one district to the next is seamless, so that you are always in an interesting place. Here are some of the neighbourhoods *(arrondissements)* you are likely to want to visit.

Palais-Royal – St-Roch *1st arrondissement*

The **Palais-Royal** gardens are among the finest in Paris. Treat yourself to an ice cream in the *Muscade* tearoom at the far end, or to window-shopping along the gallery for lead soldiers, medals or antiques. Note the old-fashioned feel. Pause by the sophisticated window display in the Salons du Palais-Royal Shiseido, the old bookshops, or the delightful little toy shop in the Beaujolais arcade on the corner with one of the passages leading onto the street of the same name. Saunter along the street from **place des Victoires**, a mecca of high fashion *(Kenzo)*, towards **avenue de l'Opéra** past the countless little restaurants, costume-jewellery or interior design shops, and a Japanese delicatessen *(Kioko)*.

Beaubourg – Les Halles *1st-2nd-3rd arrondissements*

Much of the erstwhile atmosphere of the belly of Paris went when Baltard's pavilions were removed. The Forum des Halles tunnels its way below ground like a rabbit-warren between the rotunda of the Bourse du Commerce and the brightly coloured tubes of the Centre Georges-Pompidou. Renovation of the area has opened up the space around the church of **St Eustache** which is now floodlit and the Stravinski Fountain brightens up the street.

The modern neighbourhood continues to bustle with people of all kinds converging upon the shops, sometimes from the provinces, drawing buskers, mime artists, and eccentrics of all kinds. During the day, the main crowds collect in the Forum,

Forum des Halles

thronging **place des Innocents**, rue Pierre-Lescot and the narrow streets lying perpendicular to it (rue des Prêcheurs, rue de la Grande-Truanderie), which are lined with shops selling jewellery, Art Nouveau bric-a-brac, and records and clothing. At night, the crowds move away to the east, between the church of St-Merri and the Fountain of the Innocents (rue des Lombards).

Le Marais 4th arrondissement

This old district was saved from destruction by the novelist and Arts Minister André Malraux. It accommodates both a well-established Jewish community in **rue des Rosiers** and a younger gay set. Trendy bars and coffee shops have flourished and offbeat fashion designers operate from around **rue des Francs-Bourgeois**. More traditional shops survive by the Blancs-Manteaux market, in and around rue St-Antoine. The delightful **place du Marché-Ste-Catherine** is surrounded by cafés. At the end of the gardens in the Hôtel de Sully, a narrow passageway leads beneath arcades to **place des Vosges**, where arcades shelter antique shops and art galleries. The north end of the Marais is quieter, with a large number of museums. Further north still is the **Temple** district, the mecca for tailored leather. It also includes a few of the best-known Parisian nightclubs.

Île Saint-Louis 4th arrondissement

Its aristocratic 17C residences provided inspiration for Baudelaire who stayed in the Hôtel Lauzun. A stroll along the river banks or quaysides on the island is one of the most romantic walks in Paris.

Latin Quarter 5th arrondissement

The student quarter boasts many cinemas, bars, cafés and restaurants drawing people from all walks of life like a magnet. The **Boul' Mich** (boulevard St-Michel) is a colourful succession of boutiques, cafés, sandwich and kebab bars, of pizzerias and couscous restaurants. Crowds loiter around the Fontaine St-Michel. **Rue St-André-des-Arts**, now rather touristy, leads to the Odéon district with its many cinemas (go through the picturesque **Cour du Commerce St-André**). The statue of Danton is another traditional meeting place.
The narrow pedestrianised streets on the east side of boulevard St-Michel, around rue de la Huchette, are packed with gaudy Greek restaurants catering almost exclusively to tourists.
A quieter atmosphere pervades place Maubert and **rue Dante** where all the specialist strip-cartoon dealers have their shops. Back towards the Panthéon, rue de la Montagne-Ste-Geneviève and rue Laplace are popular student haunts. Rue Mouffetard **(la Mouffe)** leads to the charming **place de la Contrescarpe** and the St-Médard district which is famous for its market. These are some of the most picturesque places in town.

Saint-Germain-des-Prés 6th arrondissement

The oldest bell-tower in Paris, across the square from the terrace of the *Deux Magots*, keeps watch over a district that ceaselessly hums with activity. The intellectual ferment of the golden days of the 1950s and the Existentialists may have gone, but the charm lives on. The ambience is sustained by famous cafés and brasseries on **boulevard St-Germain**, jazz clubs in rue St-Benoît and rue Jacob, pubs in rue Guisarde, rue Bernard-

Palissy and rue des Canettes, and the late-opening bookshops peppered about. Up-market designer shops, antique and art galleries lend a decidedly Left Bank elegance to the old streets, picturesque crossroads and tiny squares such as **place de Fürstemberg**. The main focus of the bustle is **carrefour de Buci** with its street market, basic stores and fine *traiteurs* or gourmet delicatessens.

Champs-Élysées *8th arrondissement*

A recent facelift has reinstated the avenue's identity as the place in which to be seen browsing in the arcades or the **Virgin Megastore**, loitering in a café or going to see a newly released film.
By day as by night, tourists mingle with visitors to the capital to dine out in a neighbouring street, enjoy one of the spectacular revues at the Lido or the Crazy Horse or while away the hours until dawn at a famous club.

Grands Boulevards and Opéra *2nd-9th-10th arrondissements*

This district basked in fame from the 19C through to the 1950s, providing prestigious locations for the headquarters of major banks (Crédit Lyonnais, BNP, Société Générale). The boulevards are busy throughout the day, drawing shoppers to **Printemps** and **Galeries Lafayette**, who might break for a drink on the terrace of the famous **Café de la Paix** before going on to one of the neighbourhood's many cinemas, including the **Grand Rex** and the **Max Linder**. At the end of the day, people meet in one of the brasseries for a bite maybe before a performance at the **Opéra**, the **Folies-Bergère** or **Olympia** to hear a favourite singer.

S. Sauvignier/MICHELIN

Opéra Garnier

Bastille and Faubourg-St-Antoine *11th arrondissement*

The **Opéra Bastille** has brought lustre to a district that had become rather run-down over the years, though never lacking in character. Furniture and clothes shops abound alongside contemporary art galleries and artists' studios in the labyrinth of little streets. The Bastoche is again a lively and popular neighbourhood. With its numerous brasseries, in particular **Bofinger** which was established in 1864, place de la Bastille has become a central meeting place between the Marais on one side, and rue de Charonne, rue de la Roquette, rue de Lappe, rue St-Sabin and rue Keller on the other, where restaurants, cafés, beer cellars, wine bars and dance halls proliferate. Tequila, claret or Valdepenas may be quaffed with *tapas* in a Spanish-style bar, or look for Japanese, North African, American and Thai speciality restaurants alongside French mainstays.

Gobelins – Butte-aux-Cailles – Tolbiac *13th arrondissement*

Like all the *buttes* or hills in Paris, Butte-aux-Cailles has its own distinctive character. The streets (rue Samson, rue des Cinq-Diamants, rue de la Butte-aux-Cailles) have the comfortable feel of a place where people still greet neighbours and shopkeepers, even though the high-rise developments at Glacière and place d'Italie have multiplied the population density. Nowadays, there is also an exotic air of Chinatown.

Montparnasse – Port-Royal – Alésia *14th arrondissement*

At the turn of the 20C, this rural district was favoured by the artists of the Paris School; between the two World Wars its bars were frequented by the Lost Generation of American writers; today, it is dominated by the huge **Maine-Montparnasse complex** and its skyscraper.

The streets of Montparnasse are busy day-in-day-out. Rue de Rennes is an artery for traffic and shoppers between St-Germain and Montparnasse; rue de la Gaîté is lined with theatres and peep shows; rue Montparnasse and rue d'Odessa accommodate endless *crêperies* selling pancakes and fried snacks to travellers coming through the Gare Montparnasse, the terminus for trains arriving from western France and Brittany. Big bins of shellfish on ice stand outside brasseries; café tables await the weary, and brightly lit posters attract film-lovers to the cinemas. There is a quieter part of the neighbourhood, too, beyond the cemetery along rue Daguerre, rue Didot, rue Raymond-Losserand and avenue du Général-Leclerc.

> In the early 1920s noted American poet Ezra Pound lived with his wife Dorothy at no 70 bis rue Notre-Dame-des-Champs above a working sawmill. In their modestly appointed apartment, Pound began writing his lifetime work, the *Cantos*.

Batignolles-Ternes *17th arrondissement*

The village of Les Batignolles, which was made famous by Verlaine and Mallarmé, marks the boundary between the working-class commercial neighbourhood of the 17th *arrondissement* and its residential sector. Large numbers of shops line rue des Moines and rue des Batignolles off the delightful **place du Docteur-Lobligeois** dominated by the distinctive white columns of the church of Ste-Marie-des-Batignolles. Further east, beyond avenue de Clichy is the **Cité des Fleurs** (rue Cardinet), one of the finest town houses in Paris.

West of Les Batignolles, on the other side of the railway tracks, the main attractions are the shops in rue Lévis and rue de Tocqueville, place and avenue des Ternes and rue Poncelet.

Ph. Galic/MICHELIN

Flea market by the Abesses Metro station

Montmartre-Pigalle *18th arrondissement*

In the late 19C, shortly after the village was incorporated into the city of Paris, a journalist wrote: "The local bars have closed, the lilac trees have been cut, the hedges replaced by stone walls and the gardens divided into building plots. However, of all the suburbs, Montmartre has its own special brand of charm, a varied and complex charm that is a combination of good and bad things". Many faces of Montmartre still exist today, glimpsed occasionally in what remains of the old provincial village.

Between **place Clichy**, one of the most crowded squares in the capital with its large number of restaurants and cinemas clustered around the unmistakable *Wepler* brasserie, and **place Pigalle**, the streets are populated with concert venues, theatres, nightclubs and sex shops. Along boulevard de Rochechouart you will find the forever-crowded Tati discount store and the noisy, cosmopolitan Barbès district.

At the foot of square Willette, the extraordinarily busy **St-Pierre Market** provides an opportunity to find fabrics and clothing at rock-bottom prices. On the other side of the boulevard, the **Goutte-d'Or** district proffers Arab and African fabrics, wholesale food shops, hardware, luggage and jewellery shops.

Belleville-Ménilmontant *20th arrondissement*

Like Montmartre, the Belleville and Ménilmontant neighbourhoods nestling on a hillside were annexed by Paris during the 19C. The urban redevelopment launched by Haussmann brought large numbers of working-class people to the area; these have been followed by thousands of immigrant Jews, Russians, Poles, North Africans, Turks, Yugoslavs, Pakistanis, and lately Asians. Most of the exotic restaurants are concentrated in **rue de Belleville**.

The district is slowly being rebuilt in concrete, with new buildings standing alongside the old houses of rue Ramponneau, rue des Envierges and rue des Cascades. To the north lies the romantic, English-style **Parc des Buttes-Chaumont**, which owes its steep hills to the former gypsum quarries on which it stands.

CULTURAL DIVERSITY

Paris is a cosmopolitan city with a large number of communities from outside France: Caribbean, African, Slav, Far-Eastern, Latin-American, Jewish, Indian, Pakistani... It is a pleasure to eat an exotic meal, to search for ethnic music recordings or find fabrics from the far corners of the world. You will soon discover that many different cultures flourish in the City of Lights.

Afro-Caribbean

African and West Indian communities (18th *arrondissement* or along the north side of the Paris ring road) have given us **zouk** music (a combination of African and West Indian musical rhythms), which evolved during the early 1980s with *Kassav*; Radio Nova (on 101.5 FM) fashioned the concept of "world sono" which finally took off under the English name of **World Music**.

Black Cinema – **Images d'ailleurs** at 21 rue de la Clef *(5th arr)* is the first and only cinema club to specialise in showing black culture films.

Books and Music – **L'Harmattan** at 16 rue des Écoles and **Présence africaine** at 25 bis rue des Écoles; Ⓜ *Maubert-Mutualité, Cardinal-Lemoine (5th arr)*. For tropical music, the **FNAC Forum** has a broader selection than other FNAC stores.

Art – **Musée des Arts d'Afrique et d'Océanie** at 293 avenue Dausmesnil; Ⓜ *Porte Dorée*. Permanent collection and contemporary exhibitions *(see BOIS DE VINCENNES)*. The **Musée Dapper**, at *50 avenue Victor-Hugo;* Ⓜ *Victor-Hugo*, is a tiny, intimate museum that organises biannual exhibitions of exquisite African artefacts, painting, textiles, carvings... accompanied by excellent catalogues.

Dealers specialising in African artefacts are grouped around Bastille (rue Keller) and St-Germain-des-Prés, including: **Argiles** *16 rue Guénégaud*; **Galerie Majestic** *27 rue Guénégaud*; **Galerie de Monbrisson** *2 rue des Beaux-Arts*; **Mazarine** *52 J-P Laprugne, 52 rue Mazarine*. For printed fabrics sold by weight or by the yard, try **Chez Toto** *50 rue Polonceau* and other locations around town; the prices can't be beat.

Special shops – Most exotic food stores are run by Orientals. **Izrael** *30 rue François-Miron (4th arr)* is perhaps the best-known grocery store in Paris and it is stacked high with goods, like Ali Baba's cave; **Aux Cinq Continents** *75 rue de la Roquette (11th arr)* is a delightful store that has been in existence for 60 years; **Au Jardin Créole** *18 rue d'Aligre (12th arr)* specialises in Caribbean goodies and is located near the Aligre market; **Marché Dejean** *rue Dejean*, between rue des Poissonniers and rue du Poulet *(18th arr)* sells fish, meat and fresh or ready-prepared African specialities sold by women from their market stalls – Saturday mornings only; **Spécialités antillaises** *14-16 boulevard de Belleville (20th arr)* has all the ingredients you need to make a fine Caribbean meal.

North African and Middle Eastern

Many writers and journalists have made Paris their home, keeping abreast of both their indigenous culture and that of their adopted land: Tahar Ben Jelloun, the comedian Smaïn, the singer Cheb Khaled, and dramatists Moussa Lebkiri or Fatima Gallaire are all an integral part of the Parisian cultural scene.

The metro line linking Nation to Porte Dauphine (no 2) crosses several important concentrations of Mediterranean culture: **Barbès** and **Goutte d'Or** *(18th arr)*, **Belleville** *(19th and 20th arr)*. The **Strasbourg-St-Denis** district between rue de Hauteville and passage Brady is predominantly Turkish (with public steam baths) and Indian.

La Grande Mosquée – 1-2 place du Puits-de-l'Ermite has been used for countless films. Mint tea is served in the Moorish café next door *(see JUSSIEU)*; the traditional baths are open on alternate days for men and women.

Raï

This rhythmic music from the working-class districts of Oran combines *fado* with *blues*. It has literally taken over Paris. The singer-poets are all **cheb** (ie young people) such as Cheb Khaled, the undisputed King of Raï, Cheb Kader, or Cheb Mami. Among the most popular is **New Raï**, *26 rue de la Montagne-Ste-Geneviève (5th arr)*. **Le Petit Lappe**, *20 rue de Lappe (11th arr)*, plays all the latest music from the Capital of Raï, Marseille.

Art and culture – The **Institut du Monde arabe** *(1 rue des Fossés-St-Bernard;* Ⓜ *Jussieu)* at the edge of the Latin Quarter, has a particularly useful library and reference section; other facilities include interesting temporary exhibitions, and an expensive roof-terrace restaurant with an excellent view. **Musée des Arts d'Afrique et d'Océanie** *(293 avenue Dausmesnil;* Ⓜ *Porte Dorée)* offers a permanent collection and contemporary exhibitions.

Books and theatre – Avicenne *(25 rue de Jussieu, 5th arr)*, is the best Arabic bookshop. For contemporary theatre from North Africa and the Middle East, check the programmes of the **Théâtre du Renard** *(rue du Renard, 4th arr)*, **Théâtre de l'Arcane** *(168 rue St-Maur, 11th arr)* and **Théâtre du Lierre** *(22 rue du Chevaleret, 13th arr)*.

Markets – **Marché d'Aligre** on *place de l'Aligre* (largest of all the Arab markets; daily except Mondays); **Marché de Belleville** (Tuesday and Friday mornings); **Marché de Barbès** (Wednesday and Saturday).

Jewish community

Historically, the Jewish quarter was the **Marais** *(4th arr)*, a community that was decimated during the German Occupation but whose numbers have swelled again with the arrival of North African immigrants; these have settled in the **Sentier** *(2nd arr)* and Belleville *(19th arr)*.

Synagogues – Liberal Synagogue, *24 rue Copernic 16th arr,* ☎ 01 47 04 37 27. Great Synagogue, *44 rue de la Victoire 9th arr,* ☎ 01 42 85 71 09 or *17 rue St-Georges 9th arr,* ☎ 01 40 82 26 26.

History and culture – The most significant commemorative monuments are the **Mémorial du Martyr Juif Inconnu** *(rue G.-L'Asnier, 4th arr)* and, in the Père-Lachaise Cemetery, the **Monument à la mémoire des déportés de Buna, Monowitz, Auschwitz III** by Tim. The **Musée d'Art juif** *(42 rue des Saules, 18th arr)* is in Montmartre. The collection centres around North African religious articles, models and casts and includes paintings by Chagall, Lipschitz, Mané-Katz and Benn.

Pastries – Kosher and other speciality shops and restaurants abound on rue des Rosiers, in the Marais *(4th arr)*; try the strudel at Sacha Finkelsztajn's.

In the Middle Ages, there were two main synagogues in rue de la Cité and rue de la Tâcherie (behind the Hôtel de Ville). By the 18C numbers had grown with settlers from Alsace and Lorraine moving to the Réamur Sébastopol area, especially around Hôtel du Chariot d'Or in rue de Turbigo. Confidence was high when all Jews were granted French nationality during the Revolution. Haussmann included two synagogues in his plans for urban development: rue de la Victoire founded in 1874 and rue des Tornelles founded in 1876. This was built with an iron substructure that was manufactured in Normandy, most probably under the auspices of Gustav Eiffel. The façade of the synagogue at 8 rue Pavée was designed by Guimard.

Chinese

Until 1975, the predominant waves of immigrants came from Southern China; the latter-day arrivals come from post-war homelands in Indo-China, Malaysia and the Philippines. Although not as famous as the Chinatowns of New York or San Francisco, the 13th *arrondissement* (between avenue d'Ivry, avenue de Choisy and rue de Tolbiac) boasts 150 restaurants and shops piled high with exotic produce. The district, its modern high-rises visible from afar, has succeeded in making a name for itself in tourist guidebooks. The Chinese population, the largest concentration in Europe, is particularly busy around the Chinese New Year (end of January – beginning of February).

In **Belleville**, there is a smaller group of Asian restaurants (including the huge, and hugely fun **Nioulaville** *32 rue de l'Orillon 11th arr*) and stores. A plaque on the wall of no 13 rue Maurice-Denis in this neighbourhood pays homage to the 120 000 Chinese who came to France during the First World War, 3 000 of whom decided to stay in Paris at the end of the war, forming the first Chinese community near the Gare de Lyon.

Books – Le Phénix *(72 boulevard de Sébastopol 3rd arr)* has generalist books on the Far East with a specialist section on China and Japan and **You Feng** *(45 rue Monsieur-le-Prince 6th arr)* is the largest specialist bookshop on China.

Art – Paris is home to a number of pre-eminent collections of Oriental art, including the **Musée des Arts asiatiques-Guimet** *6 place d'Iéna* and its annexe **Hôtel Heidelbach-Guimet** *15 avenue d'Iéna* (Asian art from the Caucasus to Japan – *see ALMA)*; the **Musée Cernuschi** *7 avenue Velasquez* (Chinese antiques – *see PARC MONCEAU)*.

> ### Cultural encounters
>
> The Chinese-American architect Ieoh Ming Pei is one of the most prolific contemporary architects. Pei stirred controversy with his design of a glass pyramid for the new main entrance of the Louvre Museum (completed in 1988), but it is now generally regarded with admiration for both its delightful use of light and form and for its efficient channelling of visitors to the museum.

Shops – **Tang Frères** *48 avenue d'Ivry (13th arr)* and at *168 avenue de Choisy (13th arr)*; **Paris Store** *44 avenue d'Ivry (13th arr)* and at *12 boulevard de la Villette (19th arr)*; **Ban Heng Store-Europasie** *15 avenue de Choisy (13th arr)*; **Mandarin du marché** *33 rue de Torcy (18th arr)*; **Hang Seng Heng** *18 rue de l'Odéon (6th arr)*; **Odimex** *17 rue de l'Odéon* (porcelain and ceramics); **Phu-Xuan** *8 rue Monsieur-le-Prince (6th arr)* specialises in Chinese herbs and medicinal products.

Japanese

The Japanese community (businessmen, employees of Japanese firms, students and artists) is concentrated in the area around the **Opéra** and **rue Ste-Anne** where opportunities abound to taste *sashimi, sushi* and *tempura*.

Art – The **Musée Guimet** and its annexe, **Hôtel Heidelbach-Guimet**, houses a rich collection of Buddhas and Bodhisattvas brought back to France by Émile Guimet; **Musée d'Ennery** *59 avenue Foch* (finest collection of *netsuke* in the world, laid out in a remarkable oriental decor). The **Musée départemental Albert-Kahn** *14 rue du Port, 92100 Boulogne-Billancourt (see The Green Guide Northern France and the Paris Region)* is also a must, with its Japanese garden, tea house and collection of autochrome plates.

Fashion – Japanese designers have acquired an international reputation. Most of their boutiques are located around place des Victoires and in the St-Germain-des-Prés district: **Kenzo** *3 place des Victoires (1st arr), 16-17 boulevard Raspail (7th arr)*, and *18 avenue George-V (8th arr)*; **Comme des garçons** *40-42 rue Étienne-Marcel (2nd arr)*; **Yohji Yamamoto** *47 rue Étienne-Marcel (1st arr)* and at *69 rue des Saint-Pères (6th arr)*; **Issey Miyake** *201 boulevard St-Germain (6th arr), 17 boulevard Raspail (7th arr), 3 place des Vosges (4th arr), 47 rue des Francs-Bourgeois (4th arr)*; **Irié** *8 rue du Pré-aux-Clercs (7th arr)*.

Books – **Junju Tokyo-Do** *(4 rue Ste-Anne 1st arr)* for all the Japanese newspapers or a selection from thousands of *bunko* (paperbacks) and *mangas* (comic books); **L'Harmattan** *(see Afro-Caribbean)* and **L'Asiathèque** *(see Chinese)* also have books on Japan.

Food stores – **Kioko** *(46 rue des Petits-Champs 2nd arr)* is brimming with multi-coloured bags of cocktail snacks, sauces, sake and frozen raw fish.

Indian and Pakistani sub-continent

Most immigrants from the Indian sub-continent are not actually Indian but Pakistani, Tamils from northern Sri Lanka or recently arrived Bangladeshis. India in Paris runs along rue St-Denis (between the Gare du Nord and Porte de la Chapelle, around rue Jarry, passage Brady, and place du Caire). There are numerous food shops and restaurants in rue Gérando at the foot of the Sacré-Cœur, and beside the Lycée Jacques-Decours; **Ⓜ** Anvers.

Art and Culture – **Centre culturel Mandapa** *(6 rue Wurtz 13th arr)* stages some 100 or more Indian plays, dance shows and music concerts every year. **Maison des cultures du monde** *(101 boulevard Raspail 6th arr)* features performances of traditional Indian, Pakistani and Bangladeshi music, dance and theatre.

Books – Librairie de l'Inde *20 rue Descartes 5th arr*. The **Musée Guimet** *(see above)* bookshop has an excellent section on India, its civilizations, the arts from the Gandhâra (Greco-Buddhist art from Pakistan and Afghanistan) and from throughout the Far East.

Food shops – Shah et Cie *(33 rue Notre-Dame-de-Lorette 9th arr)* is the oldest Indian grocery store in Paris; Mourougane *(71 passage Brady 10th arr)* sells Pakistani specialities.

And here is one more suggestion for a thematic tour of the town: seek out the Passages of Paris. These covered alleyways, mostly built in the 19C, were once popular shopping and meeting places, where Parisians could stroll peacefully and at a safe distance from the many horses in the streets. As times changed and the streets became cleaner, and pavements more prevalent, these lovely arcades slowly fell out of favour. But fortunately, many have been restored and new shops have opened in them, alongside the quaint older ones. Visitors can enjoy a respite from the clamour of a busy day, or from inclement weather by exploring these charming passages.

Galerie Vivienne – *4 rue des Petits-Champs;* Ⓜ *Bourse.* Built in 1823, this is one of the busiest arcades in Paris. Light pours in through the glass roof. Notice the half-moon win-

Gelerie Véro-Dodat

dows on the mezzanine, and the mosaics designed by the Italian artist Facchina who worked on the decoration of a number of the capital's buildings. There are old bookshops (nos 45 and 46, the Petit Siroux bookshop established in 1826), haberdashers selling fabrics, and a tearoom (A Priori Thé at no 35).

Galerie Colbert – *6 rue Vivienne;* Ⓜ *Bourse.* Built in 1826 by a group of speculators who were impressed with the success of the neighbouring Vivienne gallery, this arcade was totally rebuilt in the 1980s on behalf of the Bibliothèque Nationale (National Library) which organises exhibitions, conferences and debates here. The "BN" operates a nice shop which sells post cards, posters and books published by the library. The *Arts du Spectacle* department puts up exhibits of stage sets and costumes. The Grand Café Colbert has also been restored in the 1900 style.

Passage Choiseul – *23 rue St-Augustin;* Ⓜ *Quatre-Septembre.* This arcade, which is less lavish than the ones described above, first opened to the public in 1827. It contains several printers, clothes and costume jewellery shops running along the rear of the Bouffes-Parisiens Theatre. This arcade was immortalised by the writer, Louis-Ferdinand Céline, who lived here as a child and gave a fairly cutting description of it in his work *Mort à crédit (Death on the Instalment Plan).*

Passage des Panoramas – *11 boulevard Montmartre;* Ⓜ *Grands Boulevards.* Built in 1800, its name comes from the paintings created there by Fulton, which gave visitors the illusion of visiting London or Athens, as they stood inside a round room (destroyed in 1831). It was the first public space to benefit from gas lights (1817). Zola described it in his novel, *Nana.* There are several shops which deal in collectors' items, an engraver's shop (operating here since 1870) and a tearoom, l'Arbre à Canelle, with a Napoleon III decor.

Passage Jouffroy – *10 boulevard Montmartre;* Ⓜ *Grands Boulevards.* The Musée Grévin is in the middle of the passage, the first arcade in the city to be heated. There is an interesting second-hand bookshop which has some rare editions, a good, old-fashioned toy store, some clothing shops and a few shops which are useful for gift hunters.

Passage Verdeau – *6 rue de la Grange-Batelière;* Ⓜ *Richelieu-Drouot, Rue Montmartre.* This arcade extends beyond passage Jouffroy, not far from the Hôtel Drouot and stocks antiques and old books (La France Ancienne); **Roland Buret** boasts a vast collection of back-numbered comics.

Galerie Véro-Dodat – *19 rue Jean-Jacques-Rousseau;* Ⓜ *Palais-Royal.* Opened in 1826, this arcade undoubtedly boasts the finest interior decoration. High-quality shops with windows encased in brass surrounds have been rebuilt in the original style, their windows full of old-fashioned charm like the old toy shop (Robert Capia), the Gauguin bookshop or the violin maker's at no 17.

Passage du Grand-Cerf – *145 rue Saint-Denis;* Ⓜ *Étienne-Marcel.* This arcade was built between 1825 and 1835 on the site of the Grand-Cerf hostelry; it has recently been restored. Paved in marble, it boasts an elegant and very high glass roof, wrought-iron walkways, and wood-framed shop windows. The shops are all modern.

Passage Brady – *18 rue du Faubourg-Saint-Denis;* Ⓜ *Strasbourg-Saint-Denis.* Scents and perfumes of India waft through this arcade where you will find restaurants and food shops.

Parlez-vous Parisien?

AROUND TOWN

Rive Gauche (Left Bank) – This is the southern bank of the Seine, which flows roughly westwards through Paris. St Germain des Prés and the St Michel area are the heart of *rive gauche* chic. However, in other circumstances, gauche is not fashionable. For example if you call a person *gauche*, you mean the same thing as in English: *Que je suis gauche!* (How I am lacking in social experience and grace!)

Rive Droite (Right Bank) – The *rive droite* style is more elegant and sophisticated than the style of the bohemian south bank: think Champs Elysées, avenue Montaigne, rue de la Paix, place Vendôme.

Le Quartier Latin (The Latin Quarter) – This Left Bank neighbourhood is so named because it has been the center of Paris university life for over 700 years. Although the students no longer speak the eponymous Latin of scholars, you can hear just about every other language on earth spoken here on busy nights when tourists and young people flock to the restaurants, shops and cafés in the labyrinth of old streets around St Michel.

Bateaux Mouches – The origin of the common name for the tourist boats that travel up and down the Seine ("fly boats") is a subject of controversy. Some say the name comes from La Mouche, a district of Lyon where such tours were first popularised. Others say a man named "Mouche" was the owner of the first boats in Paris. Another theory is that they are named after little buzz-boats that served as lookouts to warships.

MORNING, NOON AND NIGHT

French calendars show the first day of the week as Monday *(lundi)*, and refer to a week as *une semaine* or, more confusingly, *huit jours, une huitaine* (eight days, an eight-day period). To further complicate matters, a two-week period is called *quinze jours* or *une quinzaine* (fifteen days). If you want to make a dinner reservation or check the cinema or theatre programme, here are a few helpful words:

Monday	lundi	**tomorrow**	demain
Tuesday	mardi	**morning**	matin
Wednesday	mercredi	**noon**	midi
Thursday	jeudi	**evening**	soir
Friday	vendredi	**Smoking or non-smoking?**	Fumeur ou non-fumeur?
Saturday	samedi	**an expresso**	un café
Sunday	dimanche	**an expresso with a touch of milk, a coffee with milk**	une noisette, un crème
today	aujourd'hui	**a decaffeinated coffee**	un déca

ANIMAL INSTINCTS

Parisians are especially adept at *argot* (slang) and enjoy employing colourful idioms. Here is a selection of a few expressions inspired by the animal kingdom:

Your French teacher told you that the suffix *-ment* makes a word into an adverb. So *vachement* would be … "cowly"? In fact it serves as an intensifier, meaning "really", as in, *Ce film est vachement chouette!* (*La chouette* is an owl, but never mind, it is also used as an adjective to describe something great, super, smashing.) Bad weather is *un temps de chien* ("dog weather"), and may leave you *malade comme un chien* (sick as a dog) with *un chat dans la gorge* (a cat – we would say a frog – in your throat) and *une fièvre de cheval* (a horse's fever). If you are *bête comme une oie* (stupid as a goose) you may be *pigeonné* (played for a pigeon), in which case you had better call a *poulet* (a chicken, slang for a policeman, but avoid calling him that to his face). If a fellow is *muet comme une carpe* and *têtu comme un âne* (silent as a carp and stubborn as a donkey) it may be that you'll get satisfaction from him *quand les poules auront les dents* (when hens have teeth). It is quite all right to call a sweet little child *ma petite puce* (my little flea), but if she has *le cafard* (the cockroach – the blues) she may shed *une larme de crocodile* (a crocodile tear). When you feel at ease in the city, Parisians will see that you are *comme un poisson dans l'eau* (like a fish in water)!

Port des Champs-Élysées

S. Sauvignier/MICHELIN

Sights

ALMA ★

Michelin plan 10: G 8, G 9
Ⓜ *Alma-Marceau or léna (line 9) – Buses: 63, 72, 80, 92.*
For plan of the neighbourhood with suggested walk, see CHAMPS-ÉLYSÉES.

The area around **place de l'Alma** is one of the most luxurious quarters of Paris, with something for all tastes: a concert at the Théâtre des Champs-Élysées, an evening out at the Crazy Horse, an exhibition at the Musée d'Art Moderne, or a stroll among the couturiers and perfumers at the heart of the refined world of fashion. The square and bridge, created in the time of Napoleon III, are named after the first Franco-British victory of the Crimean War (1854).

Nearby neighbourhoods: CHAMPS-ÉLYSÉES, TROCADÉRO, PLACE DE LA CONCORDE, FAUBOURG ST-GERMAIN.

ASIAN ART IN PARIS

★★★**Musée national des Arts asiatiques – Guimet** ⊙ – *6 place d'léna.* This museum, founded by Émile Guimet, a successful 19C industrialist from Lyon, contains superb Oriental works of art. An extensive restoration was completed in January 2001. The musuem shop and a restaurant on the garden level are open at the same times as the museum and do not require an admission ticket. Audio-guides (1hr 30min) are available at no extra cost.

South-East Asia *(ground floor)* - A colossal statue of Nâga, a seven-head stone serpent from Angkor, sets the scene on the way to the area dedicated to **Khmer art★★** (Cambodia), which is well represented by intricately carved temple pediments and the famous triad formed by Vishnu with his solar disc, Siva with his third eye and Brahma with his four heads...

Indian divinities are displayed in the room on the left: Durga, the supreme goddess, Kali, symbolising the destructive power of time, Skanda, the god of war... note in particular the graceful statue of **Vishnu Nataraja**, which epitomizes Indian sculpture.

The journey continues through Vietnam, Indonesia, Burma and Thailand with its splendid **heads of Buddha**, typically stylised with eyes half closed and a meditative smile. The seated Shiva with 10 arms is an example of central Vietnamese art.

Afghanistan and Pakistan *(first floor)* – The art of both Pakistan (represented here by the famous Bodhisattva from Shabaz-Garhi) and Afghanistan (the Begram treasure: sculptured ivories of Indian origin and Hellenistic plasters) are of special interest.

Tibet and Nepal *(first floor)* – This section includes a remarkable collection of Tibetan and Nepalese banners *(thanka)* as well as ceremonial objects and gilded bronzes; of the latter the most noteworthy is the graceful **dancing Dakini**.

China, Central Asia *(first floor)* – Ancient Chinese art is represented by terracotta ware dating from the 3C BC, bronze objects from the 13C to the 10C BC, bells from the Zhou dynasty, animal carvings in lacquered wood, fierce looking gods and fine paintings on silk depicting sutras and bodhisattvas.

Note a charming collection of Han and Tang **funerary objects★★** from northern China, displayed in a glass case at the end of the long room devoted to Chinese art.

India: decorative arts – Indian jewellery and fabrics (dyed cotton, embroidered taffeta, silk damask...) are displayed in rotation in the first-floor rotunda. The former library contains miniatures from the court of the Mughal princes.

Classical China *(second floor)* – Indian ink paintings, black and white stoneware, celadon pottery and above all **Ming porcelain★** (1368-1644) with polychrome or blue-and-white motifs are on display here together with lacquered, gilt or inlaid furniture (the two gilt imperial wardrobes are particularly striking).

Korea – Celadon pottery, 18C theatre masks, screens and an imposing **portrait of Cho Man-Yong**, a 19C dignitary.

Japan *(second floor)* – Although largely influenced by Chinese and Korean art, Japanese art shows an undeniable originality in its esthetic approach: particularly noteworthy are the *inro* (small lacquered boxes tied to kimono belts) and the statue of a zen monk in lacquered cypress wood; note also the gilt-lacquer screens dating from the Edo period and, above all, the collection of etchings by Utamaro (18C), Sharaku (actors' portraits – late 18C), Hiroshige (19C) and Hokusai (**Wave off the coast of Kanagawa★★**).

China from the Qing period *(third and fourth floors)* – This section marking the end of the visit exhibits Chinese porcelain from the Qing period and houses the lacquer rotunda where two impressive screens, an altar table and a cabinet are displayed.

Galeries du panthéon bouddhique de la Chine et du Japon ⊙ – *Hôtel Heidelbach, 19 avenue d'léna.* Housed in a superb neo-Classical mansion, this annexe of the Guimet Museum is essentially dedicated to Chinese and

Japanese Buddhism from the 5C to the 19C. It illustrates the evolution of this religion from its birthplace in India to China then to Japan from AD 1000 onwards.

At the rear there is an intimate Japanese garden, haven of peace and greenery, as intended by Guimet in his original designs.

EXPLORING THE NEIGHBOURHOOD

2 Round tour from place de l'Alma *See map p 148*

Pont de l'Alma – The original bridge, slowly undermined by the Seine, was replaced in 1970 by an asymmetrical steel structure with a 110m/361ft span. Only the **Zouave** (upstream by the single pile) remains of the four Second Empire soldier statues which decorated the old bridge; he serves as a high water marker and is much loved by Parisians – in January 1910, the water reached his chin.

Place de l'Alma – On the southern side of the square, at the beginning of avenue de New-York, stands a life-size gilded model of the flame held by the Statue of Liberty in New York. Since the tragic death of Diana, Princess of Wales (31 August 1997), the monument has been covered in flowers in her memory.

The Zouave stands below the Pont de l'Alma

Cours Albert-Ier – The statue by **Bourdelle** *(see MONTPARNASSE)* in the gardens parallel to the river shows the Polish poet and patriot, **Mickiewicz** (1798-1855). At no 40, note the fine René Lalique façade.

Avenue Montaigne – Formerly known as allée des Veuves (Widows' Alley) this disreputable area's main attraction was the Mabille Dance Hall, which closed in 1870. Today this street exudes wealth and chic, lined with elegant buildings accommodating banks, art galleries, exclusive luxury boutiques: Cartier, Versace, Pierre Balmain, Ted Lapidus, Gustave Jaunet, Rochas, Carven, Nina Ricci, Céline, Christian Dior, Lacroix, Thierry Mugler.

Théâtre des Champs-Élysées – The theatre, designed by the Perret brothers, is one of the first major monuments built in reinforced concrete (1912). The façade sculptures designed by Antoine Bourdelle *(see MONTPARNASSE: Musée Bourdelle)* depict: *Apollo Meditating, His Attendant Muses* in high relief and, on the ground floor, above the side doors, the allegories of *Sculpture* and *Architecture, Music, Tragedy, Comedy* and *Dance*. The main auditorium, with its ceiling decorated by **Maurice Denis**, is one of the finest in Paris; it has a seating capacity of 2 100 (there is a smaller hall with 750 seats).

It was here that Igor Stravinski first directed his *Rite of Spring* (1913), scandalising the audience with its musical and choreographic audacity; it caused such a furore that the composer had to flee from the auditorium. Since then, the Champs-Élysées Theatre has welcomed many great stars from the world of music and dance: Richard Strauss, Paganini, **Diaghilev** with his Ballets Russes; **Jean Cocteau** who produced *Les Mariés de la Tour Eiffel* in 1921; the Swedish Ballet Company who performed *The Creation of the World* in 1924 to a musical score by Darius Milhaud, a libretto by Blaise Cendrars, in costumes by Fernand Léger; in 1925, the *Negro Review* introduced Josephine Baker dancing half-naked to a Charleston and rhythms played on the saxophone by Sidney Bechet; **Rudolf Nureyev** starred in *Beauty and the Beast* with the Grand Ballet du Marquis de Cuevas in 1960; and six years later, Roland Petit's Ballet Company created *L'Éloge de la folie* in a decor by Niki de Saint-Phalle and Tinguely.

The **Hôtel Plaza-Athénée** *(25 avenue Montaigne)*, frequented by government ministers, royalty and diplomats was founded in 1867 and rebuilt in 1911.

Walk up avenue Montaigne then down rue François I to the square of the same name.

At 22 **rue Bayard** is the Radio-Télé-Luxembourg (RTL) station – note the façade of the building decorated by Vasarely. Opposite is the Scottish Kirk.

Follow rue François I and avenue Pierre-I-de Serbie to avenue George-V.

Avenue George-V – This street is famous for its grand **Hotel George V** at no 31, frequented by the smart and famous jet-set, and media people meeting over a working breakfast; the neo-Gothic **American Cathedral in Paris** which was consecrated at the same time as the Statue of Liberty was unveiled in New York Harbor (1886); the **Crazy-Horse** music hall at no 12, with its renowned programme of choreographed topless stage shows.

Église St-Pierre-de-Chaillot – *35 avenue Marceau, on the corner of avenue Marceau.* The church was rebuilt in the neo-Romanesque style in 1937. Overlooking its façade, on which the life of St Peter has been carved by Bouchard *(see AUTEUIL)*, is a 65m/213ft-high belfry.

Return to place de l'Alma along avenue Marceau.

Shopping

Noura – *29 av. Marceau – 16th arr* – Ⓜ *Alma-Marceau* – ☎ *01 47 23 02 20* – *www.noura.fr* – *9am-midnight.* Perhaps the best place to shop for Lebanese specialities in town. Taboule with parsley, humus, mustabal, grilled meat, baklavas and other delicious specialities, all of which presented superbly.

Avenue Montaigne – *Av. Montaigne – 8th arr.* Undoubtedly the smartest street in Paris. All the major fashion designers and luxury brands have an outlet here: Dupont, Calvin Klein, Vuitton, Barbara Bui, J-L Scherrer, Junko Shimada, Céline, Caron, Nina Ricci, Joseph, Ungaro...

MUSEUMS

Palais de Tokyo– Built for the 1937 World Exhibition, the monumental building houses the Musée d'Art moderne de la Ville de Paris and an exhibition centre, the **Palais de Tokyo-Site de création contemporaine** ⊙, opened at the end of 2001 and exclusively devoted to contemporary culture (Fine arts, design, fashion, literature, music, dance, cinema...). Neither a museum nor an art gallery in the usual sense, the space is a laboratory of emerging art. In this largely open and bare space, you can see performance art, installations, videos, paintings, fashions shows and hear music, debates and creative ranting. A must-see if you are interested in the contemporary art scene. (www.palaisdetokyo.com).

★★ **Musée d'Art moderne de la Ville de Paris** – *11 avenue du Président-Wilson, in one of the two wings of the Palais de Tokyo.* The collection, illustrating the main trends of 20C art, includes some of the century's major works: *France* by Bourdelle (on a terrace), *Les Disques* by Léger (1918), *L'Équipe de Cardiff* by Robert Delaunay (1912-13), *Pastorale* and **Danse de Paris★** by Matisse (1932), *Évocation* by Picasso and *Rêve* by Chagall.
Dufy's **Fée Électricité★** *(The Good Fairy Electricity)*, the biggest picture in the world comprising 250 panels (600m²/6 095sq ft), represents the civilization of Man from the times of the ancient Greek philosophers to the modern scientists who evolved this excitingly new form of energy.

Palais Galliera (Musée de la Mode de la ville de Paris) ⊙ – *10 avenue Pierre-Iᵉʳ-de-Serbie.* The Duchess of Galliera, wife of the Italian financier and philanthropist, had this edifice built (1878-94) in the Italian Renaissance style. The mansion houses a museum dedicated to **fashion** and costume, with thematic exhibitions drawn from a vast collection of almost 12 000 complete outfits and an additional 60 000 articles of men's, women's and children's fashion and dress from 1735 to the present day.

Musée des Égouts ⊙ – *On the left bank. Entrance at the corner of quai d'Orsay and pont de l'Alma.* The Paris **sewer** system was initially the giant undertaking of the engineer Belgrand at the time of Napoleon III, and now incorporates 2 100km/1 305mi of underground tunnels, some passing under the Seine.
The tour of part of the sewer system includes an overflow outlet, sand-filtering basins, a secondary conduit, holding and regulatory reservoirs. The larger mains also contain pipes for drinking and industrial water, telephone and telegraph cables. Remember to bring a sweater, as it is always cool underground.

AUTEUIL

Michelin plan 10: K 4, K 5, L 4
Ⓜ *Église-d'Auteuil, Michel-Ange-d'Auteuil (line 10)*
Buses: 32, 52, 70 for Maison de Radio-France.

It was only at the turn of the 20C that the last vineyards disappeared from Auteuil, although it became part of the City of Paris during the Second Empire. It still enjoys a village atmosphere, in contrast to the modern development and high-rise blocks across the river. Many of the houses of this desirable residential area have retained good-sized gardens, and the streets named after famous composers and writers recall the era of Salon society. Two bridges give access to the Left Bank: Pont de Grenelle and Pont Mirabeau.

Nearby neighbourhoods: TROCADÉRO, PASSY, BOIS DE BOULOGNE.

EXPLORING THE NEIGHBOURHOOD

Place d'Auteuil – The Church of Notre-Dame (1880) is a Romano-Byzantine pastiche. The obelisk opposite the chapel of Ste-Bernadette is the last remaining tomb from the one-time cemetery. The monument commemorates the chancellor Aguesseau and his wife (1753).

Rue d'Auteuil – *Follow rue d'Auteuil as far as place Jean-Lorrain.* At no 11bis the 17C château is now occupied by a school. Admire at no **16** the main front of the Hôtel de Puscher; no **43-47** is an 18C mansion. The modern building at no **59** marks the site of a literary salon of a certain Madame Helvétius, who was better known as Notre-Dame d'Auteuil. The salon was frequented by philosophers and writers in the period from 1762 to 1800, including the Americans Thomas Jefferson, **Benjamin Franklin** and John Adams.

In place Jean-Lorrain, turn left along rue Michel-Ange, then first left along rue Molitor. Turn right along rue Boileau, then left along rue Jouvenet.

Promenade des villas d'Auteuil – At no 38 rue Boileau, the **hameau Boileau**, and opposite, the **villa Molitor** are havens of peace and greenery in central Paris.

Cross boulevard Exelmans by taking rue Chardon-Lagache, then turn right along rue Charles-Marie-Widor and continue along rue Claude-Lorrain.

The **villa Mulhouse** is a group of small houses reminiscent of late-19C workers' housing in the city of Mulhouse.

Head northwards back along rue Michel-Ange to place Jean-Lorrain.

Ph. Gajic/MICHELIN

L'Âge d'Airain,
place Rodin

Rue La-Fontaine – Make a short detour via rue Leconte-de-Lisle and the picturesque **rue des Perchamps** *(left)* before rejoining rue La Fontaine. This street takes its name from the spring which supplied the village of Auteuil. Here, as in rue Agar, there are several buildings by **Hector Guimard**, the famous Art Nouveau architect. His best-known block of flats, **Castel Béranger**, is at no 14. No **60**, also designed by Guimard, was built in 1911.

Avenue Léopold-II leads to **place Rodin**, the setting for Rodin's allegory, The Age of Bronze (L'Âge d'Airain), which was greatly admired for its precision at the Salon of 1874.

Go towards the Maison de Radio-France, via avenue du Recteur-Poincaré, rue La-Fontaine and rue de Boulainvilliers.

As you face the river, on the midstream island, the **allée des Cygnes** *(see PASSY)*, below Pont de Grenelle, is a smaller version of Frédéric-Auguste Bartholdi's **Statue of Liberty**, which stands at the entrance to New York harbour. It was donated by the American colony in Paris in 1885 and placed on this spot four years later at the time of the 1889 Universal Exhibition.

Shopping

La Ferme La Fontaine – *75 rue La-Fontaine – 16th arr – ☎ 01 42 88 47 55.* This cheese shop is well-known to the residents of the 16th *arrondissement*. Since 1890 it has been home to five generations of cheese merchants.

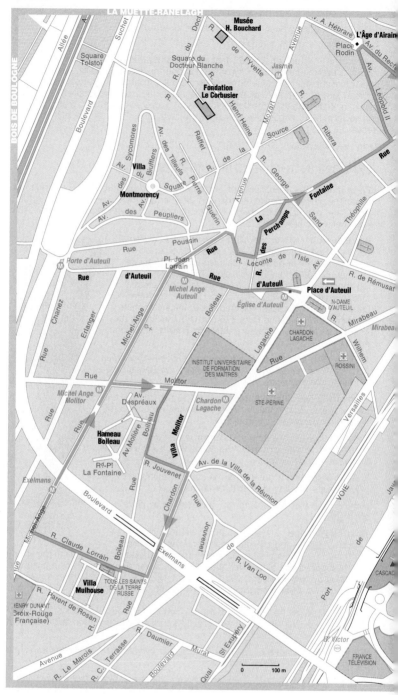

MUSEUMS AND OTHER ATTRACTIONS

★ Maison de Radio-France – *116 avenue du Président-Kennedy*. One concentric building 500m/547yd in circumference and a tower 68m/223ft tall go to make up Radio-
France House. It was designed by Henri Bernard in 1963 and it is here, in the 60 studios and the main auditorium, that the programmes of national radio have been produced since 1975. Free tickets for classical concerts are available in the entrance hall.
A museum traces the evolution of communication and the development of trans-
mitters and receivers from the 1793 **Chappe** telegraph and crystal sets to the latest
transistors.

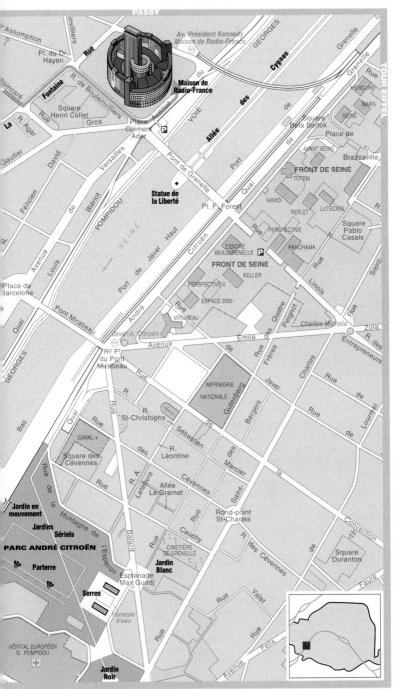

Fondation Le Corbusier ⊘ – *8-10 square du Dr-Blanche.* Two buildings, namely villas La Roche and its neighbour, dating from 1923, serve as a documentation centre for the work of the famous architect Charles Édouard Jeanneret, known as Le Corbusier (1887-1965). Villa La Roche houses a permanent exhibition, a library and photographic collection.

Musée Bouchard ⊘ – *25 rue de l'Yvette.* The work of sculptor Henri Bouchard (1875-1960), a contemporary of Rodin, varies from medals and statuettes to imposing memorials. Stone and bronze were his favourite materials. The studio display includes the plaster cast of *Apollo*, the monumental bronze in front of Chaillot Palace *(see TROCADÉRO),* and the materials used in the creation of low-relief sculptures, in particular those of the church of St-Pierre-de-Chaillot *(see ALMA).*

127

The vast crossroads, scene of the historic events of 1789, is dominated by the July Column. Today, the square remains a symbolic rallying point for demonstrations, marches and public celebrations as well as an informal meeting place for the young and trendy on a Friday night. It is also the busy meeting point of several major roads: boulevard Richard-Lenoir, boulevard Beaumarchais and boulevard de la Bastille, and rue du Faubourg-St-Antoine and rue St-Antoine.

Nearby neighbourhoods: FAUBOURG ST-ANTOINE, LE MARAIS.

Le Génie de la Bastille, atop the Colonne de Juillet

The Bastille prison – While Charles V lived at the Hôtel St-Paul *(see le MARAIS)*, he felt it necessary to have a fortified residence built in case of danger. The first stone of the Chastel St-Antoine – renamed La Bastille after the run-down, marshy area around – was laid in 1370. Construction lasted until 1382, and depended upon forced labour recruited by press-gangs from passers-by. Its history is, however, far from heroic: besieged seven times in periods of civil strife, it surrendered six times. An interesting episode occurred in 1652 when the Grande Mademoiselle Louis XIV's cousin, opened the St-Antoine gate to Condé's Fronde army who then turned against the royal guards. Renowned prisoners incarcerated here included the enigmatic Man in the Iron Mask, Bassompière, Mirabeau and Voltaire, usually detained under the notorious *lettre de cachet*. In 1784 these royal warrants were abolished: the Bastille was cleared leaving merely 32 Swiss guards and 82 invalid soldiers under the governor's command.

The taking of the Bastille – On 12 July 1789 trouble broke out: the popular Finance minister, Necker, was dismissed by the king; the Stock Exchange was closed as a militant crowd rallied. On the 14th, the mob marched first to the Invalides to capture arms, then on to the Arsenal and the Bastille. By late afternoon the Bastille had been seized and the prisoners – only seven in number, including a madman – were symbolically freed. The fortress was immediately demolished, 83 of its stones being carved into replicas and sent as dire reminders of the evil of despotism to the provinces. The following year there was dancing on the site.

EXPLORING THE NEIGHBOURHOOD

Start from the Arsenal marina.

Port de plaisance de Paris-Arsenal – After going through a tunnel beneath boulevard Richard-Lenoir, the Canal St-Martin ends its journey in this former moat of Charles V's fortifications.

Place de la Bastille – Paving stones mark out the ground plan of the former Bastille. The appearance of the square was modified first by the opening of rue de Lyon in 1847, subsequently by that of boulevard Henri-IV in 1866 and the building of a railway station in 1859.

Colonne de Juillet – A bronze column 52m/171ft high, crowned by the figure of Liberty (built between 1831 and 1840), stands in memory of Parisians killed during the uprisings of July 1830 and 1848. Many of those buried in a crypt beneath the column have their names on the shaft of the column.

Around Bastille – The area was traditionally famous for its dance halls and specialist shops selling produce from the Auvergne. The neighbourhood now hums with artists and contemporary art galleries, with open-days held when studios, workshops and galleries are open to the public. Many lively bars can be found along the narrow streets (rue St-Sabin, rue Daval and rue Keller). **Rue de Lappe** is particularly representative of this trendy neighbourhood.

A longer walk could incorporate a stroll along the Viaduc des Arts, a favourite Sunday occupation among Parisians *(see Faubourg ST-ANTOINE)*.

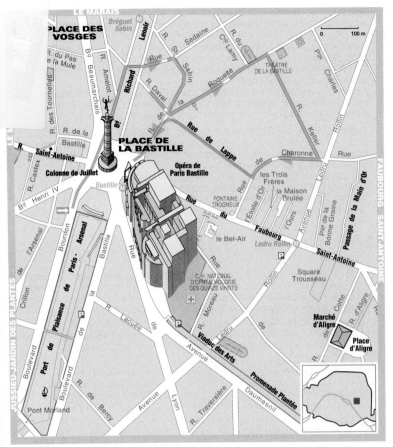

MUSEUMS AND OTHER ATTRACTIONS

★**Opéra de Paris-Bastille** ⓥ – On the site of the former station demolished in 1984 now rises a massive mirror-glass building often likened to a ship, designed by the Uruguay-born Canadian, Carlos Ott *(see illustration p 96)*. The curvilinear, utilitarian design accommodates a 2 700-seat auditorium with several revolving stages for quick scene changes, workshops housing 74 different trades and rehearsal rooms.

The opera was officially opened by President Mitterrand on Bastille Day 1989 to commemorate the Bicentenary of the French Revolution. *Les Troyens* by Berlioz directed by Myung-Whun Chung, its inaugural production, took place on 17 March 1990.

L'Arsenal – *(entrance: 1 rue de Sully)*. Note the cannon and mortar on the roof-top balustrade, recalling the original function of the building.

In 1512, the city requisitioned this riverside stretch of land to set up a cannon foundry. Henri II purloined the workshops and founded a royal arsenal: seven mills were built, producing gunpowder among other things. Destroyed in a famous explosion (1563) that was heard as far afield as Melun to the south, the Arsenal was rebuilt by Philibert Delorme before being taken over by Sully, Grand Master of Artillery, as his residence. Under Louis XIII the cannon works were discontinued and the production of gunpowder was transferred to the Salpêtrière.

Paris-Arsenal Marina

Bibliothèque de l'Arsenal – *20 boulevard Henri IV.* The library, created in 1757 and accommodated in what remained of the Arsenal building, was opened to the public in 1797. In the 19C it became the early meeting place of the Romantics: Lamartine, Hugo, Vigny, Musset, Dumas and the Parnassian Poets – Gautier, de Banville, de Lisle, Heredia. The library possesses more than 1.5 million volumes, 15 000 MSS, 120 000 prints and a large collection on the history of the theatre, which belongs to the Bibliothèque Nationale.

Access may be had to the manuscript room, the 18C Salon de Musique decorated with *grisaille* panels depicting Bouchardon's Fontaine des Quatre Saisons, and the 17C La Meilleraye apartments painted by a follower of Simon Vouet.

Pavillon de l'Arsenal ⊘– *21 boulevard Morland.* This late-19C iron and glass building accommodates an exhibition centre presenting the architecture and urban development of the capital from the earliest city walls to important contemporary projects (Bercy, La Défense and La Villette). A model of the city locates the various parks and open spaces, new development areas and public services.

In the square stands **Arthur Rimbaud's statue** by the sculptor Ipousteguy.

The barracks, **Caserne des Célestins** (1892), stand on the site of the monastery gardens, to the left of the Arsenal.

Going out

Bastille

Place de la Bastille, with its countless brasseries, particularly the Bofinger brasseries opened in 1864, has become a focal point for night-lovers on their way to and from the Marais and rue de Charonne, rue de la Roquette, rue de Lappe, rue St-Sabin, rue Keller which abound in restaurants, cafés, beer cellars, wine bars and nightclubs.

Bar sans Nom – *49 rue de Lappe – 11th arr – ☎ 01 48 05 59 36 – Mon-Sat 6pm-2am.* Torch-shaped lamps and walls covered in imitation tapestries give an idea of the look of this bar which serves delicious fresh fruit juices.

Café de l'Industrie – *16 rue St-Sabin – 11th arr – ☎ 01 47 00 13 53 – www.cafedelindustrie.com – daily (except Sat) 10am-3am.* The walls of this fine old café are covered in paintings and exotic bric-a-brac brought back by the owner from his extensive travels. Pleasant spot for a quiet cup of tea or coffee in the afternoon or for a drink in the evening, when it is livelier and trendier.

Café des Phares – *7 pl. de la Bastille – 11th arr – ☎ 01 42 72 04 70 – daily 7am-3am.* It was here that the philosopher Marc Sautet (now deceased) created the first Parisian *café philo* (philosophy café). Still very popular, it is particularly crowded on Sunday mornings when budding philosophers congregate to philosophise. Pleasant terrace.

La Chapelle des Lombards – *19 rue de Lappe – 11th arr – ☎ 01 43 57 24 24 – www.lachapelledeslombards.fr – Thu-Sat 10.30pm-dawn.* West-Indian, Latin-American and African music vie for pride of place (zouk, salsa etc). All age groups.

Le Balajo – *9 rue de Lappe – 11th arr – ☎ 01 47 00 07 87 – Tue, Wed and Thu (salsa); Thu and Sun afternoon (40s); Fri and Sat (disco) 9.30pm-dawn.* Founded in 1936 by Georges France (aka Jo), Balajo's is the oldest musette dance hall in Paris. Its old-fashioned atmosphere and preference for hits from the 1950s, 60s and 70s continue to attract crowds of all ages. Not to be missed on Mondays and Thursdays.

Pause Café – *41 rue de Charonne – 11th arr – ☎ 01 48 06 80 33 – Mon-Sat 7.45am-2am, Sun 9am-8pm – closed 25 Dec.* A traditional café with a fine U-shaped bar in the centre of the room. The soft lighting and subdued atmosphere make it a pleasant place for a quiet read.

Shopping

Caves Estève – *10 rue de la Cerisaie – 4th arr – Ⓜ Bastille – ☎ 01 42 72 33 05 – www.jcesteve.com – Tue-Sat 10am-8pm; daily in Dec.* Specialising in new wines, this establishment is run by young enthusiasts who publish a catalogue listing 1 300 wines and offer a selection of the best organically grown wines; tasting of 40 different wines sold in bulk.

Les Caprices de l'Instant – *12 rue Jacques-Cœur – 4th arr – Ⓜ Bastille – ☎ 01 40 27 89 00 – Thu-Tue 10am-1pm, 3-8pm – closed public holidays.* This wine merchant selects only vintages which uphold the spirit and traditions of their ancestry and makes it a point of honour to stock only wines which are ready for consumption. Anything suggested by the expert taste-buds of this wine enthusiast can be drunk with your eyes closed!

Art Galleries – The art galleries along rue de Charonne, rue de Lappe and rue Keller all exhibit the work of contemporary artists.

Eating out

Turn back to the Selected restaurants section at the beginning of the guide for a list of restaurants, bistros, cafés etc. This neighbourhood is spread over the 4th, 11th and 12th *arrondissements*.

BEAUBOURG★★★

Acrobats and fire-eaters, jugglers and pavement artists of all kinds are attracted to the hub of the Georges Pompidou Centre, where the sound of music and the movement of the crowds create a festive feel. Inside this modern art centre is a fine collection of 20C art, as well as changing contemporary exhibitions, and the urban renewal project for the Beaubourg plateau mingles zany, ultra-modern elements with medieval splendour – the Stravinski fountain and St-Merri.

Nearby neighbourhoods: CHÂTELET-HÔTEL DE VILLE, LES HALLES, LE MARAIS, RÉPUBLIQUE (Temple).

★★★ CENTRE GEORGES-POMPIDOU ☉ *Place Georges-Pompidou*

Architecture – Construction was completed in 1977. The architects **Richard Rogers** (British) and **Renzo Piano** (Italian) achieved a totally futuristic building. Innovative in conception, this gigantic steel structure boasts glass walls and bright colours. The façade appears a tangle of pipes and tubes latticed along its glass skin, giving the effect of a solid yet pliant superstructure.

Because its structure is apparent, Beaubourg has been called the inside-out museum, and indeed, the plaza in front of the building is as stimulating as the collection and activities inside.

Centre Georges-Pompidou, rue Beaubourg

S. Sauvignier/MICHELIN

A major restoration – Twenty years after its construction, the building, which had become one of the most visited attractions in the city, was ready for some improvements to help it recover from the wear and tear of its daily visitors. The centre reopened in 2000 after two years of renovation work to improve and extend the exhibition space yet further.

A unique cultural centre – Beaubourg is home to the **Musée national d'Art moderne** (National Museum of Modern Art, 4th and 5th levels), the **Bibliothèque publique d'information** (the public library known as the BPI, 1st, 2nd and 3rd levels), and the **IRCAM** (Institute for Acoustic and Musical Research beneath place Stravinski). In this way, the centre offers the public access to all forms of contemporary artistic creation, and explores modern artistic theories in all realms: painting, sculpture, photography, design, architecture, theatre, music, dance, film, new technologies, literature and philosophy. The centre also houses several **temporary exhibition halls** on the 1st (mezzanine) and 6th levels.

In addition, the centre provides **live entertainment** (dance, music, theatre), **cinema** performances and spoken reviews. Other services include learning-related activities, **children's workshops** and the provision of resources for teaching establishments, for example.

The library is especially popular with Parisians, thanks to its late hours, open access and up-to-date collection of printed and other resources.

Going out

Café Beaubourg – *43 rue St-Merri – 4th arr* – ☎ *01 48 87 63 96 – Sun-Thu 8am-1am, Fri-Sat 8am-2am.* This wonderful café, designed by Christian de Porzamparc, has a pleasant terrace overlooking the incessant toing-and-froing of visitors, buskers and fire-eaters on the esplanade in front of the Centre Georges-Pompidou. Magazines and a framed text by Philippe Sollers set the establishment's literary and artistic tone. The tables are beautifully decorated and the little alcoves upstairs are perfect for private conversations.

Le Petit Marcel – *65 rue Rambuteau – 4th arr* – ☎ *01 48 87 10 20 – Mon-Tue 7am-midnight, Wed-Sat 7am-2am, Sun noon-midnight – closed 1 Jan, 1 May and 25 Dec.* Visitors to this delightful turn-of-the-20C café may feel as if they've stepped back in time to when the nearby Halles was still the capital's fruit and vegetable market. Perfect for a coffee or a drink while waiting for friends.

Les Bains – *7 rue Bourg-l'Abbé – 3rd arr* – ☎ *01 48 87 01 80 – daily 9pm-dawn.* A temple to new wave very much in vogue in the 1980s, it is now devoted to house music under the auspices of the Guetta couple. Stars and top models gather here in a mutual admiration society in the upstairs VIP room or to dance downstairs to disco, house or funk music. It would be difficult to find anywhere in Paris that is more obsessed with fashion or appearance than here!

Shopping

La Boîte à perles – *194 rue St-Denis – 2nd arr* – Ⓜ *Réaumur-Sébastopol – Mon-Thu 8.45am-5.45pm, Fri 8.45am-4.45pm.* Tucked away in the rear of a little courtyard, this old-fashioned boutique has an amazing selection of hundreds of beads and pearls, together with all you could ever need to make your own jewellery.

Art

Rue Quincampoix – *Rue Quincampoix – 3rd arr* – Ⓜ *Rambuteau.* Among the many art galleries which are clustered at the top of this street, are *Tendance*, a gallery which displays rare works of well-known artists, *Clara Scremini* and her superb glass creations and *Aurus*, specialised in designer jewellery.

Eating out

Turn back to the Selected restaurants section at the beginning of the guide for a list of restaurants, bistros, cafés etc. This neighbourhood is in the 4th *arrondissement*.

There is a bookshop on level 0, a design shop and a nice café (view over the main entrance) on level one, and a good restaurant *(reservations required, see Eating Out)* on level 6.

★★★ **Musée national d'Art moderne** – This certainly ranks high among the most significant collections dedicated to modern art in the world (50 000 works and objects). It traces the evolution of art from Fauvism and Cubism to the contemporary art scene. The 20C Fine arts collection was substantially enriched in 1992 with a wide range of architectural motifs and design objects. The modern collection (1905-60) is housed on the fifth floor, whereas contemporary exhibitions from the 1960s onwards are held on the fourth floor.

On the ground floor, near the escalators, note the portrait of the centre's namesake by Vasarély. A clever design made of white slats, it hangs from the ceiling.

Outside the museum, **Constantin Brancusi's** (1876-1957) sculpture workshop has been restored by his bequest and is open to visitors.

The modern collection – *Fifth floor.* Forty galleries present around 900 works *(changed every 18 months)* of painting, sculpture, photographs, designs and architecture (models, objects, furniture, drawings).

Throughout the exhibition, the juxtaposition of painting and sculpture with the design and architecture of the same decade enables the visitor to obtain an overview of 20C creativity.

Galleries dedicated to a single artist (Matisse, Léger, Picasso, Rouault, Delaunay) alternate with thematic rooms, offering a lively and appealing presentation.

All the main movements of the first half of the 20C are represented here, such as **Fauvism** (1905-10), a reaction against methodical refraction of colour in Impressionism and the pastel tones of the Nabis, which is characterised by simplified form and strong colour (Derain, Marquet, Dufy and Matisse); or **Cubism**, founded by **Braque** and **Picasso** in 1907, which was to be a brief phase in their artistic development, translating their pictorial vision into refracted geometric planes and lines to suggest volume and texture.

On the periphery, **Georges Rouault** whose work reflects his spiritual quest and his deep concern for human misery, explored strongly religious subjects in a strangely sombre style.

Born during the First World War, **Dada** evolved as a violent counter-reaction to what its artists saw as the course of civilization towards its own self-destruction. They translated this debasement of values into anti-art. As early as 1913 **Marcel Duchamp** created his ready-made works of art, promoting everyday objects to the status of Art.

Between 1910 and 1930, Montparnasse harboured many foreign artists who gave birth to the **Paris School**, characterised by an expression of intense feeling. Such are the realms of **Soutine**'s tormented expressionist style, **Chagall**'s world of fantasy and **Modigliani**'s decorative arabesques. Other artists include Larionov and Gontcharova.

In a rejection of figurative representation, the Abstract School wished to find expression in an interplay of colour and line. The movement pioneered in 1910 by **Kandinsky** with his *Improvisations*, is sustained by **Kupka**and **Mondrian**, whereas **Klee**'s poetic compositions never quite ostracise themselves from reality. Close to this movement are Russian artists such as **Tatline** and **Malevitch** (author of the famous *Black Square* on a white background) and the **Bahaus School**.

Robert and Sonia Delaunay's fascination with colour and movement marks the intermediate stage between the geometric Cubist style and colourist experimentation.

Dada inevitably led to **Surrealism**, represented by De Chirico, **Salvador Dali**, Max Ernst, **Magritte**, Brauner, André Masson, Tanguy, Giacometti *(Woman with her throat cut*, 1932), Picasso and **Mirò**, who viewed painting and scupture as a means of expressing the subconscious mind. All verge on depicting the irrational and the incongruous. This movement inspired American artists such as **Gorky** and **Pollock**.

During the 1950s Abstract art appealed to many French and foreign artists: some emphasized line (Hartung), others divided surfaces into large blocks of colour (Poliakoff, De Staël) or added a three-dimensional element with tar and sand (Dubuffet). The **Cobra** movement (1948-51) advocated spontaneous expression through the free use of bold colour and energetic brush strokes (Alechinsky, Appel, Jorn). American art from the 1940s to the 1960s is represented by **Pollock**, **Rothko** and **Newman**.

Colour and purity of line are all-important to **Matisse**, in his distinctive gouache cut-outs or "drawing with scissors", as the artist put it, whereas in sculpture, **Brancusi** and Calder pursue abstraction for its own sake, paring down form to its most essential. **On the three terraces** are sculptures by Calder, Miró and Laurens.

The contemporary collection - *Fourth floor*. These exhibitions are regularly changed and present a wide diversity of media: painting, sculpture, installations, videos, design and architecture. The main artistic trends are represented, together with major personalities, combining to create a world of colour, form and movement linking art with everyday life.

Major works include *Requiem for a dead leaf* (Tinguely), *Red Rhinoceros* (Veilhan). **Pop Art** is represented by **Warhol** and Rauschenberg, **New Realism** by **Klein**, **Arman**, César, **Niki de Saint-Phalle**, **Op** and **Kinetic Art** by **Agam** *(Antechamber of the Élysée Palace private apartments)* and Vasarely, and there are installations by **Dubuffet** *(The Winter Garden)*, **Beuys** *(Plight)* and **Raynaud** *(Container Zero)*.

Three rooms contain examples of design and architecture from the 1960s to the present day (Starck, Nouvel, Perrault, Toto Ito).

Space is also devoted to the cinema **(Jean-Luc Godard)**, multimedia installations **(Ugo Rondinone)** and Happening (**Gutaï** and **Fluxu**s).

Sixth floor – A splendid **view**★★ extends over the Paris rooftops – from right to left: Montmartre dominated by the Sacré-Cœur, St-Eustache, the Eiffel Tower, Maine-Montparnasse Tower, St-Merri in the foreground with Notre-Dame behind.

EXPLORING THE NEIGHBOURHOOD

St Merri Quarter

Take the passageway to the south of the Fontaine des Innocents which joins rue de la Ferronnerie. *See map p 182.*

Rue de la Ferronnerie – It was while riding in this street in his carriage that **Henri IV** was assassinated on 14 May 1610 in front of no **11** (note the commemorative marble slab). The sign at no **13** was a crowned heart pierced by an arrow – the witnesses to the murder felt this to be an omen.

Rue St-Denis – The street, opened in the 8C to relieve the traffic on rue St-Martin, soon became the busiest and most prosperous in Paris. It became the main route for a king's grand entry processing with full pageantry to Notre-Dame. The lower end of the street is lined with clothes shops, whereas the top end is frequented by ladies of the night.

Rue de la Grande-Truanderie – Vagabonds' Row is contemporary with the medieval Court of Miracles, which gave sanctuary to miscreants up to the 17C *(see SENTIER)*.

Rue des Lombards – Its name recalls the Middle Ages when Lombard moneylenders monopolised banking transactions.

Rue Quincampoix – This was where the Scots financier, **John Law**'s South Sea Bubble was situated. Law founded a bank there in 1719, attracting all kinds of speculators, expanding into the neighbouring houses. The street became crowded with people making fortunes overnight – a hunchback was said to have been paid 150 000 livres for the use of his back as a desk. The frenzy lasted until 1720 when the bank crashed and the speculators fled. Law's house was razed when rue Rambuteau was built.

Several old houses *(nos 10, 12, 13, 14)* survive with unusual paved courtyards, mascarons (stone masks), intricate wrought-iron balconies and nailed or carved doors.

Continue north on this narrow pedestrianised street to discover a clutch of art galleries, boutiques and bars typifying the stylish urban atmosphere that has permeated the quarter since the construction of the Pompidou Centre.

⋆ **Église St-Merri** ⊘ – Access to the church is through the main façade on rue St-Martin or through the St Merri presbytery *(76 rue de la Verrerie)* with a fine 18C porch.

St Merry or Medericus who died here in the 7C used to be invoked to assist in the release of captives. The former parish church of the Lombard usurers, although dating from 1520 to 1612, curiously conforms to the 15C Flamboyant Gothic style.

Stravinski Fountain and St-Merri Church

Outside, the west front stands directly on the narrow rue St-Martin, crowded-in with small houses and shops, much as it might have been in the Middle Ages. The Flamboyant interior remodelled under Louis XV retains good 16C stained-glass windows in the first three bays of the chancel and transept, and fine ribbed vaulting at the transept crossing.

In addition to the majestic 17C organ loft – the organ at one time played by **Camille Saint-Saëns** – and beautiful wood panelling by the Slodtz brothers (pulpit, sacristy and the glory at the back of the choir), the church has interesting pictures.

One bell dating from 1331, probably the oldest in Paris, survives from the medieval chapel which stood on the site of the present church.

As you come out of the church, take rue de la Verrerie to the left and walk round the east end via rue des Juges-Consuls.

Note the restored 18C house on the corner of rue du Cloître-St-Merri.

Decorating place Stravinski, the **Stravinski fountain⋆** with black and coloured mobile sculptures by Tinguely and Niki de Saint-Phalle respectively illustrating the works of the great composer *(the Rite of Spring, Firebird...)* draw the crowds.

Rue St Merri – *On the north side of place Stravinski, this street is perpendidular to rue Beaubourg.* Note nos 9 and 12 with their fine frontages, and beyond, impasse du Bœuf, perhaps the oldest cul-de-sac in Paris.

Return to rue Beaubourg and follow it northwards. Turn left onto rue Rambuteau leading to the Beaubourg plateau.

Plateau de Beaubourg – The square takes its name from the old village included within the Philippe Auguste perimeter wall at the end of the 12C. Run-down and derelict, the old quarter was cleaned up in 1939 and subjected to major redevelopment in 1968. The Beaubourg plateau was to have been the site of a public library; however, in 1969, on the initiative of **Georges Pompidou** (1911-74), the then President of France, it was decided to create a multi-purpose cultural centre.

Explore the passages on the north side of the plateau.

Quartier de l'Horloge – **Le Défenseur du Temps**, an unusual brass and steel electronic clock with a Jack known as the Defender of Time, was designed by Jacques Monestier. On striking the hour, this life-size figure armed with a double-edged sword and shield, confronts one of three animals symbolising the elements: a dragon (earth), a bird (air) and a crab (water).

Musée de la Poupée ⊙ – *Impasse Berthaud.*
A fine collection of porcelain and modern dolls, from 1860 to 1960.

BELLEVILLE★

Michelin map 10: E 19 to G 21
Ⓜ *Belleville (lines 6 and 11), Pyrénées (line 11), Ménilmontant (line 2), Gambetta (lines 3 and 3 bis) – Buses: 26, 96*

Built on the highest hill in Paris after Montmartre (128m/420ft), Belleville owes part of its charm to the unexpectedly steep paths and winding streets. Despite the mushrooming of modern buildings, Belleville has, on the whole, kept its traditional atmosphere, its quiet streets and their secluded life, vacant lots and little snatches of greenery. The main streets, however, are full of popular ethnic restaurants (Chinese, Vietnamese).

A very old village – Once the country retreat of the Merovingian kings, then the property of several abbeys and priories, the hill and particularly the ancient hamlet of **Ménilmontant** were, for a long time, inhabited only by quarry workers and a handful of wine growers. In the 18C, it became known as Belleville, probably a corruption of *belle vue* or beautiful view, becoming a commune in 1789.
In 1860, the village, whose population had grown at an increasing pace, was annexed to Paris and allocated between the 19th and 20th *arrondissements*. Today, its territory is delimited by Buttes-Chaumont, Père-Lachaise and the outer boulevards.
A succession of different immigrant populations has resulted in a lively, popular place to live, particularly among the young.

EXPLORING THE NEIGHBOURHOOD

Starting from the Belleville metro station and following rue Belleville gives the walker a chance to appreciate the particularly lively character of the neighbourhood. **Belleville Insolite** is an association which organises 3hr tours of Belleville year-round, including meetings with artists *(bookings essential).*

Rue de Belleville – This lively shopping street stretches from Belleville metro station to the Porte des Lilas. Edith Piaf was born at no 72.

Retrace your steps and turn left along rue Piat.

On 19 December 1915, Giovanna Gassion was born to abject poverty on the steps of 72 rue de Belleville. She later sang in the streets, before becoming a radio, gramophone and music hall success in 1935 under the name of **Édith Piaf**. Beloved for the instinctive but deeply moving inflexions of her voice, she came to embody the spirit of France *(La Vie en rose, Les Cloches)*. A small private **museum** ⊙ in rue Crespin-du-Gast contains souvenirs of the great singer.
Another famous figure to come from this neighbourhood was **Maurice Chevalier** (1888-1974) – film star, entertainer and *chansonnier* – he paired with Jeanne Mistinguett at the Folies-Bergère (1909) and sang at the Casino de Paris between the wars. Before attaining fame on Broadway in black-tie and boater, he was known at home for songs that were rooted in Belleville: *Ma pomme, Prosper* and *Marche de Ménilmontant*.

★**Parc de Belleville** – Passage Julien-Lacroix, with its stone steps, is the main thoroughfare through this 4.5ha/11-acre park on Belleville Hill. The differences in ground level have been used to create tiered gardens, with cascades and waterfalls. From the top of the park, above the Maison de l'Air, there is a magnificent **view**★★ of Paris.

⊙ The park has several play areas for children.

Leave the park via rue Transvaal, taking the passage Plantin on the right, then turn right again onto rue des Couronnes, which overlooks the old railway line. Take rue de la Mare, then rue de Savies.

Rue des Cascades, narrow, winding and paved, is among the quaintest in the neighbourhood, reminiscent of a small provincial town. There is a magnificent view over Paris from the corner of the steps of rue Fernand-Raynaud.

The **Regard St-Martin** at no 42, opposite rue de Savies, is one of four buildings of its kind constructed in Belleville to channel the supply of water which is routed down to the capital by means of underground aqueducts. The building belonged to the priory of St-Martin-des-Champs.

The **Regard des Messiers** is at no 17. Descend the steps. The Messiers were the guards who kept watch over the vines and fields.

At the end of rue des Cascades, take rue Ménilmontant on the left, then rue de l'Ermitage.

Belleville villas and passages – Leave rue de l'Ermitage via **Villa de l'Ermitage**, a journey back in time through a picturesque village. Across rue des Pyrénées, rue de l'Est leads to **passage de la Duée**, one of the narrowest streets in Paris (1m/1yd).

Along rue de la Duée you will come to **villa Georgina** and rue Taclet, particularly pretty in the springtime.

A little further on, at no 40 **rue du Télégraphe**, on the site of the property once owned by a National Convention member, Pelletier de St-Fargeau, **Claude Chappe** (1763-1805) conducted his first experiments on the telegraph in 1793.

Mur des Otages – *53 rue du Borrégo*. In a courtyard near the church of Notre-Dame-des-Otages, built in 1936, can be seen a fragment of the wall in front of which 52 hostages (priests, nuns, Paris civilian guards) from Grande-Roquette prison were shot by the *communards* on 26 May 1871.

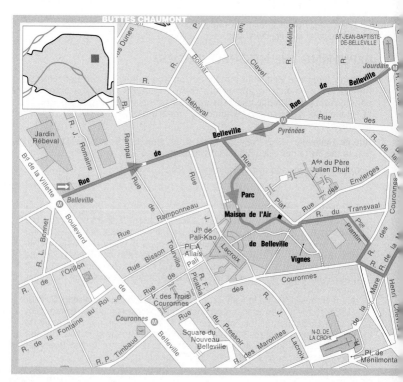

Going out

Au Vieux-Belleville – *12 rue des Envierges – 20th arr* – ☎ *01 44 62 92 66* – *Mon-Sat 10.30am-3.30pm, 6.30pm-2am.* Particularly friendly and welcoming; every evening songs circulate among the tables, often accompanied by an impromptu chorus of diners. Dancing and singing galore. (Tuesday and Saturdays: guitar, Fridays: accordion).

La Java – *105 rue du Fg-du-Temple – 10th arr* – ☎ *01 42 02 20 52* – *Thu-Sat 11pm-5am; Sun 4-8pm.* The Javanese flavour of this establishment has made it one of Paris' leading night-spots for Latin and Afro-Cuban music. On Thursdays (mainly) and Fridays, groups from all over Europe play here. Its charming, old-fashioned style is further accentuated by the Sunday 40s afternoons.

Le Baratin – *3 rue Jouye-Rouve – 20th arr* – ☎ *01 43 49 39 70* – *Tue-Fri noon-4.30pm, 6pm-1am, Sat until 1am – closed 2 weeks in Aug and the first week of Jan.* Only 2min from Belleville park and its Chinese restaurants, this unsophisticated wine bar is popular with the local artists.

Eating out

Turn back to the Selected restaurants section at the beginning of the guide for a list of restaurants, bistros, cafés etc. This neighbourhood covers the 11th, 19th and 20th *arrondissements*.

MUSEUM

Maison de l'Air ⊘ – *Parc de Belleville.*
On display is an attractive and educative permanent exhibition with games for children, explaining everything about the air which surrounds us.Taking examples from Paris, it explores the role of living creatures in the air, its quality, meteorological implements, the role of clouds and the risks of pollution.

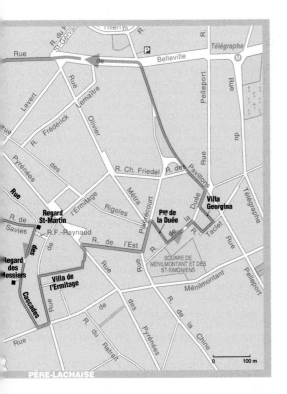

BERCY ★

Within the space of a few years, the wine warehouses have been replaced by a 13ha/32 acre riverside park flanked on its north-west side by a sports complex and on its south-east side by Bercy village and its cinemas; the massive new premises of the Ministry of Finance dominate the whole area.

Ministry of Finance

EXPLORING THE NEIGHBOUHOOD

The Ministry of Finance – Transferred from the traditional Rivoli wing of the Louvre, it is accommodated in a massive modern structure 300m/984ft long straddling the embankment expressway, sitting perpendicular to the river, with a foothold in the water. It was designed by architects Chemetov and Huidobro in 1989.

Palais omnisports de Paris-Bercy – This new sports complex was built to stage international indoor sporting events. Outside, grass-covered walls slope down at 45 degrees. The glass roof is sheathed with a network of girders. The design was a collaboration between the architects Andrault, Parat and Guvan.

Sport takes first place, with facilities catering to 22 different activities, but the centre's versatility is such that it can stage a variety of entertainment from opera, theatre and ballet to rock concerts. In addition to the adaptable main arena there are two multi-purpose halls and two warming-up or rehearsal halls.

In the square to the east of the stadium an unusual fountain with a deep gully, the Canyoneaustrate by Gérard Singer, recalls geological formations in the North-American continent.

Parc de Bercy memorial garden – This public space was designed to take the place of the old wine storehouses which once stood here; a few have been left standing as historical landmarks *(on the southern edge, around place des Vins-de-France)*. There are vast expanses of grass, used for football practice on Sundays, and eight different gardens: an orchard, a vegetable garden, a rose garden and one for aromatic plants, as well as one for each of the four seasons. Water meanders and cascades through the romantic garden which conceals small caves *(to the east)*.

Walk eastwards out of the park, cross rue François-Truffaut and walk beneath the arcades of the former wine warehouses.

★ **Cour St-Émilion** – Twenty years ago, the air was still filled with the smell of wine. The former brick warehouses have been converted and now house shops and wine bars. The railway line used for the transport of wine is still in place but is now a pleasant walkway.

Cross the river via the Tolbiac Bridge. A footbridge is planned to link the Parc de Bercy with the Bibliothèque Nationale.

Going out

Le Batofar – *Quai François-Mauriac – 13th arr –* ☎ *01 56 29 10 00 – Tue-Sun 8pm until at least 2am.* This former boat-lighthouse, painted red and moored opposite the François Mitterrand Library, is an invitation to travel around Europe's multiple cultures and forms of musical experimentation (electronic and avant-garde jazz). Visitors walk along the gangplanks, through cosy areas in living room-cabins to a dance floor playing house and techno music. An alternative approach to events, whatever they be.

Sport

Palais omnisports de Paris-Bercy (POPB) – *8 blvd de Bercy – 12th arr –* Ⓜ *Bercy* – ☎ *08 03 03 00 31 – www.bercy.com.* It is here that many of the major sporting and musical events of the capital take place. The sports range from ice-skating (Lalique trophy), go-carting and roller skating to cycling (Open des Nations), horse jumping and gymnastics. In terms of music, many international stars of pop, rock or variety have performed here: Elton John, Bruce Springsteen, Sting, Madonna.

Eating out

Turn back to the Selected restaurants section at the beginning of the guide for a list of restaurants, bistros, cafés etc. This neighbourhood covers the 12th *arrondissement*.

★ **Bibliothèque nationale de France: site François-Mitterand** ⊙ – Designed by architect Dominique Perrault, the library is set atop a vast rectangular esplanade planted with trees. The tall buildings represent the shapes of four open books, framing the central area. The glass façades (80m/262ft high) are lined with wooden blinds inside to protect the books from the light.

The **interior garden** resembles a pine grove, and is the backdrop for the different reading rooms devoted to literature and the arts; science and technology; law; economy and politics; philosophy; history; natural sciences; and audio-visual facilities. One room is devoted to periodicals and another to temporary exhibits.

Watch this space...

At 51 rue de Bercy stands a graceful limestone building designed by the influential contemporary architect Frank O Gehry. Pritzker Prize winner (1989) and designer of the Guggenheim Museum Bilbao, Gehry marks his work with powerful geometric forms, comfortable and inviting interior spaces, and strong links to the context and culture of each building site.

Why the cobwebs inside the rue de Bercy building? The American Center, a vibrant presence on the Parisian cultural scene since the 1930s, commissioned the building, completed in 1994 to be its new home. Sadly, after leaving its quaint old location, the Center was unable to generate enough interest to keep the performance and studio spaces occupied. Financial difficulties forced its closure in 1996. Recent plans to install a *Maison du Cinéma*, a film centre to be funded by the French government, appear to be compromised as well, and the building's fate is still up in the air...

Bois de BOULOGNE★★

Michelin plan 10: E 3 – E 5, F 1 – F 5, G 1 – G 4, H 1 – H 3, J 1 – J 3, K 1 – K 3
Ⓜ *Porte-Maillot (line 1), Sablons (line 1), Porte d'Auteuil (line 10) –*
RER: Porte-Maillot (line C) – Buses: 43, 52, 63, 73, 82, PC

This vast park of 846ha/2 100 acres is cut by wide shaded roads *(speed restriction)*, tracks for pedestrians, horses and cyclists; boating is allowed on the Lower Lake. There are lakes, waterfalls, gardens, lawns and woodland, two racecourses, cafés and restaurants for the enjoyment of the public. Race meetings at Longchamp and Auteuil attract large numbers of racegoers and roads tend to be busy. The best time for a pleasant stroll is on weekdays, in the morning, along one of the two waymarked paths.

Nearby neighbourhoods: AUTEUIL, PASSY.

A royal forest – In Merovingian times the forest was hunted for bear, deer, wolves and wild boar. It gets its present name from a pilgrimage made by Philippe IV in 1308 to Notre Dame at Boulogne-sur-Mer. On his return he built a church on the lines of that on the Channel coast, dedicating it to Our Lady of Boulogne the Lesser. Later, the royal forest became a refuge for bandits, and in 1556 Henri II enclosed it with a wall pierced by eight gates, including the Porte Maillot and Porte de la Muette.

In the 17C Colbert adapted it for hunting with a crisscross of straight rides marked at junction points with crosses. Louis XIV opened the wood to the public as a place for country walks, but its reputation soon left a lot to be desired! Judging from a contemporary chronicle, 'marriages from the Bois de Boulogne do not get celebrated by the priest'.

Decline – During the Revolution the forest provided refuge to those on the run, the destitute and poachers. In 1815, the English and Russian armies set up camp in the forest, devastating a great section. In the replanting, oaks were replaced by horse chestnuts, acacias, sycamores and maples, though sadly many of these were uprooted in the great storm of 26 December 1999.

The wood today – When Napoleon III gave the forest to the capital in 1852, Haussmann demolished the surrounding wall, landscaped the area creating winding paths, ornamental lakes and ponds, and built the Longchamp racecourse, restaurants, kiosks and pavilions. 1854 saw the opening of avenue de l'Impératrice (now avenue Foch); the wood became the fashionable place for a stroll. The Auteuil racecourse, famous for its jumps, was built after 1870. The 20C has seen the construction of the Paris ring road, of the Jardin des Serres, together with the **Parc des Princes** stadium.

> "*I will not describe the Bois de Boulogne. I cannot do it. It is simply a beautiful, cultivated, endless, wonderful wilderness. It is an enchanting place.*"
> Mark Twain.

IN AND AROUND THE PARK

Avenue Foch– This imposing avenue was one of the finest urban-planning projects completed by Haussmann. It is 120m/394ft wide and lined on both sides by lawns and side alleys,. As soon as it was inaugurated in 1854, it became the fashionable haunt of carriages on their way to the Bois de Boulogne. Private mansions and luxury blocks of flats were gradually built along the grass borders. It was named after Marshall Foch in 1929, soon after his death.

Route de Suresnes leads from place du Mar.-de-Lattre-de-Tassigny to the Lac Inférieur.

★**The Lakes** – **Lac Supérieur** is a pleasant recreation area, as is the larger **Lac Inférieur**, which is particularly popular on Sundays. It has a landing-stage for the motor boat to the islands *(café-restaurant)* and boats for hire.

From the Carrefour des Cascades, situated between the two lakes, skirt the west shore of the Lac Inférieur as far as route de la Grande-Cascade and turn left then shortly afterwards right onto chemin de la Croix-Catelan running past the Racing Club de France's sports complex. Proceed as far as the Carrefour Croix Catelan.

★**Pré Catelan** – This attractive well-kept park is named after a court minstrel from Provence murdered there in the reign of Philip IV. It includes a luxurious café-restaurant, lawns and shaded areas and a copper beech nearly 200 years old with the broadest spread of branches in Paris.

A **Shakespeare garden** ⊘ is planted with flowers, herbs and trees mentioned in the bard's plays. There is also an open-air theatre.

Continue westwards along route de la Cascade.

Longchamp – An abbey, dedicated to Our Lady of Humility, was founded in 1255 by St Isabel, sister to St Louis, on a site between Longchamp Pond and Carrefour des Tribunes. A picturesque although man-made waterfall (Grande Cascade) graces the crossroads **(carrefour de Longchamp)**. Beyond the pond is a monument to 35 young people shot by Nazis in 1944. A nearby oak is still visibly scarred by gunshot.

Bagatelle park and château

Château de Longchamp was given to Haussmann by Napoleon III and now houses the Centre International de l'Enfance. A tower, one of the few remains of the abbey, can be seen from rue des Moulins.

The **mill** at the far end of the racecourse has been rebuilt.

The famous racecourse, **Hippodrome de Longchamp**, which was opened by Napoleon III in 1857 hosts a number of important racing events. A panoramic restaurant *(open on race days only)* offers a good view of the course.

Near the Paris Polo Club, a **stele** marks one of the early aviation records established by the Brazilian **Santos-Dumont** on 12 November 1906.

From route de la Seine to the butte Mortemart, there is a good view out onto La Défense.

MUSEUMS AND OTHER ATTRACTIONS

Jardin d'Acclimatation ⊙ – 🔲 This park, primarily arranged as a children's amusement park (with enchanted river and miniature railway), includes a small zoo with a pets' corner, a typical Norman farm and an aviary. The **Musée en Herbe** ⊙ is an art-museum-cum-workshop designed for youngsters.

Explor@dome ⊙ – Under this dome lies a hands-on science and multimedia area offering interactive experiments, workshops and Internet facilities.

Jardin des Serres d'Auteuil ⊙ – *1 bis avenue de la Porte-d'Auteuil.* The formal garden which still retains its 19C charm is surrounded by hothouses cultivating azaleas, palm trees and ornamental plants for public buildings and official occasions.

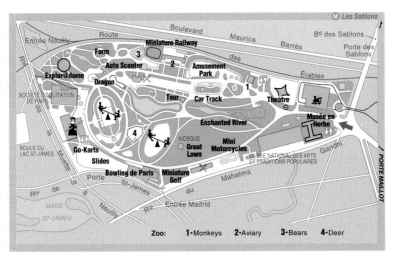

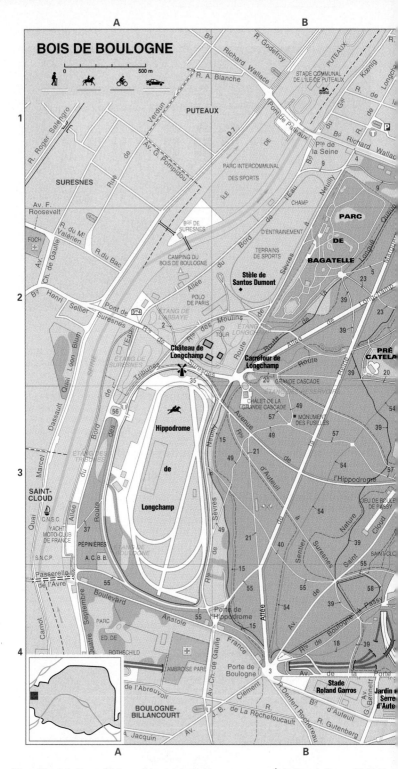

BOIS DE BOULOGNE

0   500 m

PUTEAUX

SURESNES

PARC INTERCOMMUNAL DES SPORTS

CAMPING DU BOIS DE BOULOGNE

POLO DE PARIS

Stèle de Santos Dumont

PARC DE BAGATELLE

PRÉ CATELAN

Château de Longchamp

Carrefour de Longchamp

GRANDE CASCADE

CHÂLET DE LA GRANDE CASCADE

MONUMENT DES FUSILLÉS

Hippodrome de Longchamp

SAINT-CLOUD

C.N.S.C.

YACHT MOTO-CLUB DE FRANCE

S.N.C.P.

PÉPINIÈRES

A.C.B.B.

Passerelle de l'Avre

JEU DE BOULE DE PASSY

Porte de l'Hippodrome

PARC ED. DE ROTHSCHILD

AMBROISE PARÉ

Porte de Boulogne

BOULOGNE-BILLANCOURT

Stade Roland Garros

Jardin Serre d'Aute

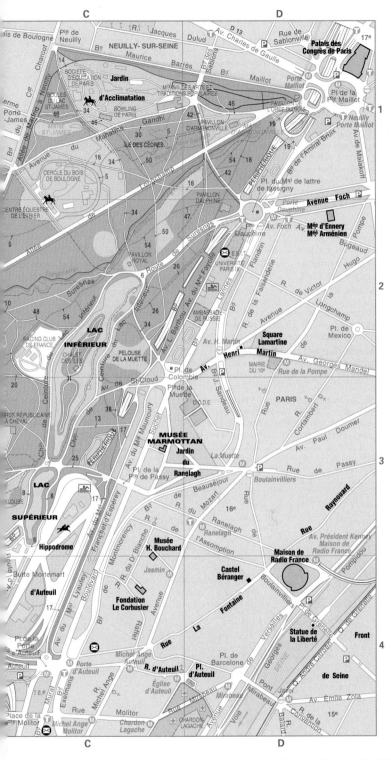

The central building contains a palm house and a tropical house with banana trees, papyrus plants and giant strelitzias. The other buildings house rare species (orchids, begonias...). The azalea and chrysanthemum displays draw large crowds.

Beyond the garden is the **Stade Roland-Garros** where the French Open Tennis Championships are held every year *(late May-early June)*.

★★Parc de Bagatelle 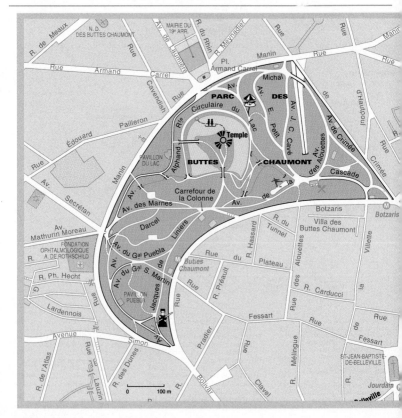 – *Route de Sèvres-à-Neuilly*. The first house to be built on the site was in 1720; it fell into ruin and in 1775 the Count of Artois – future Charles X – bought it, waging a bet with his sister-in-law, **Marie-Antoinette**, that he would have a house designed and built, complete with its landscaped garden, within three months. He won. Bagatelle survived the Revolution and in 1806 was acquired by Napoleon who at one time wanted to turn it into a palace. At the Restoration it reverted to the Duc de Berry before coming into the possession of the Hertford family. The third and fourth marquesses and the latter's son, **Sir Richard Wallace**, accumulated a large collection of 17C and 18C French paintings, furniture and objets d'art.

The art collection was transferred to London where, since 1897, it has been on view as the Wallace Collection at Hertford House. Bagatelle was sold to the City of Paris in 1905. Bagatelle is well known for its beautiful garden, particularly its walled iris garden *(May)*, roses *(June to October)* and water lilies *(August)*. Exhibitions of paintings and sculpture are held *(May to October)* in the Trianon and Orangery.

Musée Arménien – *59 avenue Foch*. The collection includes Armenian jewels, religious and folk art objects as well as modern paintings, sculpture and drawings.

Musée d'Ennery – *59 avenue Foch*. The rich collections of the dramatist and librettist, Adolphe d'Ennery (1811-99), are displayed in their original Second Empire setting. Chinese and Japanese furniture, ceramics, bronzes, lacquerwork, jade and several hundred **netsuke★** (small carved wood, ivory or bone belt ornaments) are displayed in showcases inlaid with mother-of-pearl.

Musée Dapper – *35 rue Paul-Valéry*. This museum holds fine temporary exhibitions. Objects drawn from an extensive private collection of artefacts from Africa and from other private or national collections are selected to illustrate tradition and craftsmanship. Friendly café situated beneath the entrance walkway.

Musée national des Arts et Traditions populaires – *6 avenue du Mahatma-Gandhi* *Sablons – Bus 73*. This museum of popular arts and culture offers a panorama of traditional society from the 1789 Revolution to the Second World War. There are galleries devoted to the environment, agriculture, crafts, local beliefs and customs, games, music and folklore.

BUTTES-CHAUMONT★

Michelin plan 10: D 19, E 20
Ⓜ *Buttes-Chaumont, Botzaris (line 7 bis) – Buses: 26, 60, 75*

Known as the *mont chauve*, the denuded (literally *bald*) rise of Chaumont, riddled with open quarrying and full of dumped rubbish, used to be a sinister place until **Haussmann** and Napoleon III transformed the area by creating the very first park on the northern edge of Paris between 1864 and 1867.

Nearby neighbourhood: LA VILLETTE.

★ The park – A lake was created, fed by water from the St-Martin Canal and landscaped with an island, built with huge rocks 50m/150ft high, half natural, half artificial. Access was provided by two bridges: one in brick, nicknamed the suicide bridge, the other a footbridge. A little temple on the island commands a good view over Montmartre and St-Denis. Additional folly features include a waterfall and cave encrusted with stalactites.

It was here that the invading Prussian armies were halted in 1814.

Quartier d'Amérique – *To the east of the park.* Hidden behind a screen of modern buildings, this area consists of charming small houses built at the end of the 19C for the workers of eastern Paris. Today, this maze of flower-decked villas looks like a provincial enclave within Paris.

Eating out

Turn back to the Selected restaurants section at the beginning of the guide for a list of restaurants, bistros, cafés etc. This neighbourhood covers the 19th *arrondissement*.

Leisure activities

There are many activities for children between 2pm and 5pm. Sport enthusiasts will appreciate the Sport Nature activity led by qualified instructors recognised by the Paris municipality; it takes place on Sundays from 9.30am to noon.

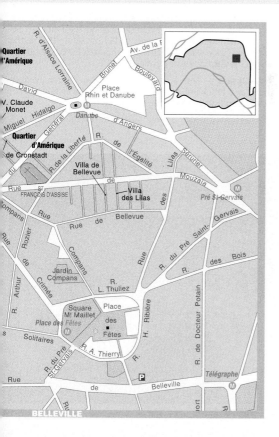

CHAMPS-ÉLYSÉES★★★

Michelin plan 10: F 8 – F 11, G 8 – G 11
Ⓜ Concorde (lines 1, 8 and 12), Champs-Élysées-Clemenceau (lines 1 and 13),
Franklin-D.-Roosevelt (lines 1 and 9), Georges-V (line 1), Charles-de-Gaulle-Étoile
(lines 1, 2 and 6) – Buses: 22, 28, 31, 42, 52, 73, 83, 84, 92, 94

The most famous thoroughfare in Paris is at once an avenue with a spectacular view, a place of entertainment and a street of smart luxury shops. The vista extending down the Champs-Élysées, with the Arc de Triomphe silhouetted against the sky, is known the world over. To Parisians it is the Voie Triomphale or **Triumphal Way**. On 14 July, military processions with musical bands draw immense crowds. At times of great patriotic fervour (as for the Tour de France), the triumphal avenue continues to be the spontaneous rallying point for the people of Paris: at the Liberation (26 August 1944), the demonstrations of 30 May 1968, the silent march in honour of General de Gaulle (12 November 1970) and the joyous celebration of the World Cup victory of the French football team (July 1998).

Nearby neighbourhoods: ALMA, PLACE DE LA CONCORDE, TUILERIES, FAUBOURG ST-HONORÉ, INVALIDES, TROCADÉRO, MONCEAU.

EXPLORING THE NEIGHBOUHOOD

1 Walking up the Champs-Élysées

This walk starts from the splendid place de la Concorde, through the gardens in the lower part of the avenue.

★**The gardens** – This section is landscaped with trees and bordered with avenues of grand old horse-chestnuts dotted with occasional pavilions. The gardens contain two theatres: **L'espace Pierre Cardin**, a venue for exhibitions, concerts, theatre and dance shows, and the **Théâtre Marigny**, designed by **Garnier** in 1853, and used almost exclusively by Jacques Offenbach from 1855 to amuse the Parisian public with his operettas. In Louis XVI's time **Restaurant Ledoyen** was a modest country inn where passers-by stopped to drink fresh milk drawn from the cows grazing outside. Four monuments evoke heroes of past wars: in place Clemenceau stands a bronze statue of the statesman **Georges Clemenceau**, *The Father of Victory*, by François Cogné (1932). Across avenue Winston-Churchill stands the statue of **Général de Gaulle** by J Cardot (2000). The monument on the corner with avenue Marigny is to the leader of the Resistance, **Jean Moulin**. Finally, near cours de la Reine is the statue of **Sir Winston Churchill**, looking as resolute as ever.

Avenue Gabriel – Shaded gardens on the northern side, running parallel to the Champs-Élysées, stretch along the back of smart mansions lining the faubourg St-Honoré: the **Elysée Palace** (fine wrought-iron gate with gilded cockerel, 1905), the British Embassy, the *Cercle de l'union interallié*, the United States Embassy (in the former home of the gastronome Grimod de la Reynière).

Rond-Point des Champs-Élysées – This is the meeting point of the avenues Champs-Élysées, Montaigne and Franklin-Roosevelt. Designed by **Le Nôtre** in 1670, the site offers a good view up and down the avenue.

Paris Tourist Office – *127 av. des Champs-Élysées – 8th arr –* ☎ *08 92 68 31 12 – daily.*

Looking up the Champs-Élysées to the Arc de Triomphe

Going out

B. Fly – *49 av. George-V - 8th arr - ☎ 01 53 67 84 60 - daily noon-3pm, 6.30pm-2am.* Contemporary photo exhibitions, loud hip-hop and funk background music, deep armchairs, soft lighting and a young, relatively well-to-do clique of regulars set the scene for this quintessential international bar and restaurant.

Café de Paris – *93 av. des Champs-Élysées - 8th arr - ☎ 01 47 23 54 37 - daily 8am-5am.* Very pleasant summer terrace. Inside, the room at the rear with its red moleskin seats and dignified atmosphere is somewhat reminiscent of a London club.

Chesterfield Café – *124 rue La-Boétie - 8th arr - ☎ 01 42 25 18 06 - daily 9am-5am.* A large American pub frequented by a young, cheerful crowd. Live rock'n roll and blues music. Good quality hamburgers and on Sundays, brunches are served to the sound of gospel hymns. Second basement bar open in the evenings from 8pm.

Fouquet's (Barrière) – *99 av. des Champs-Élysées - 8th arr - Ⓜ Georges-V - ☎ 01 47 23 50 00 - daily 8am-midnight.* Now a listed monument, Fouquet's has one of the few remaining historical terraces on the Champs-Elysées. It is equally in favour with TV and film celebrities as with the literary world. Renovated in 1999, Fouquet's now combines a brasserie-style menu with the inventive cuisine of Jean-François Lemercier, elected best craftsman of France in 1993.

Le Duplex – *2 bis av. Foch - 16th arr - ☎ 01 45 00 45 00 - Tue-Sun 11pm-dawn - closed end July to end Aug.* This distinctly hip and very fashionable spot, decorated in the style of an Italian theatre, alternates between eurodance music and the latest hits. Super smart with a marked preference for showy luxury. Correct dress only.

Montecristo café – *68 av. des Champs-Élysées - 8th arr - ☎ 01 45 62 30 86 - contact@montecristo-cafe.com - daily noon-6am.* One of the best places to enjoy the magic of Cuba in Paris. A smart crowd congregates here for a drink, lunch or dinner, and also to dance or smoke a cigar within the walls covered in Cuban graffiti and attractive mural frescoes. Salsa lessons available on Sunday afternoons and in the evenings from Tuesday to Friday. Very crowded at the weekends.

Sir Winston – *5 rue de Presbourg - 16th arr - ☎ 01 40 67 17 37 - Mon-Fri 9am-3am, Sat 10am-4am, Sun 10am-2am.* This large bar-restaurant stands behind a very British-looking façade. The interior decoration has combined a whole host of influences: a Chinese room, a leopard room and small partitioned tables. The place is bathed in soft lights, world music rhythms and hip-hop beats.

Shopping

Disney Store – *Ⓖ 44 av. des Champs-Élysées - 8th arr - Ⓜ Franklin-D.-Roosevelt - ☎ 01 45 61 45 25 - daily 10am-11pm - closed 1 May and 25 Dec.* Toys, clothes, disguises, accessories, music, videos etc. All of Disney's products are presented here in this vast children's bedroom, equipped with a giant screen which projects clips from all the latest cartoons all day long.

Guerlain – *68 av. des Champs-Élysées - 8th arr - Ⓜ Franklin-D.-Roosevelt - ☎ 01 45 62 52 57 - guerlain.com - Mon-Sat 10am-8.30pm, Sun 3pm-7pm.* The history of this illustrious family so acclaimed in the perfume world began back in 1828. Today the marble floors and walls of this perfumery and beauty institute are listed monuments. It sells all of Jean-Paul Guerlain's creations.

Virgin Mégastore – *52-60 av. des Champs-Élysées - 8th arr - Ⓜ Franklin-D.-Roosevelt - ☎ 01 49 53 50 00 - www.virgin.fr - Mon-Sat 10am-midnight, Sun noon-midnight.* The three floors of this mammoth record shop are always packed with young Parisian music lovers. It also has a large range of multimedia and video games together with a bookshop in the basement.

Stamp market – *Carré Marigny (on the corner of avenue de Marigny and avenue Gabriel) - 8th arr - Ⓜ Champs-Élysées-Clemenceau - Thu, weekends and holidays 9am-7pm.*

Eating out

Turn back to the Selected restaurants section at the beginning of the guide for a list of restaurants, bistros, cafés etc. This neighbourhood spreads over the 8th and the 17th *arrondissements*.

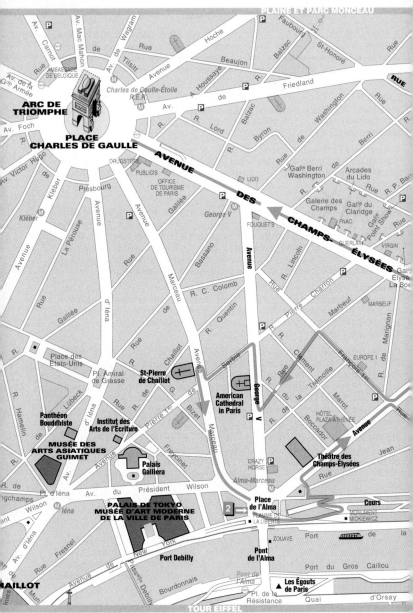

***Avenue des Champs-Élysées** – Along the Champs-Élysées today airline and tourist offices, motor-car showrooms and banks alternate with cinemas and big cafés. The fashion houses provide attractive and elegant window displays in the shopping arcades. The Second Empire private houses and amusement halls which once lined it have vanished, so the avenue appears without historical memories. The only exception is no **25**, a mansion built by La Païva, a Polish adventuress, whose house was famous for dinners attended by the Goncourt brothers and the philosophers Renan and Taine, the painter Delacroix and the writer Sainte-Beuve, and for its unique onyx staircase. **Le Colisée**, an amphitheatre built in 1770 to hold an audience of 40 000, has left its name to a street, a café and a cinema.

Today the avenue has lost much of its aristocratic dignity, none of its brightness and little of its appeal. Several foreign countries have their promotional house along the Champs-Élysées where their tourist attractions, gastronomic delights and handicraft specialities are promoted, thus adding to the avenue's cosmopolitan atmosphere.

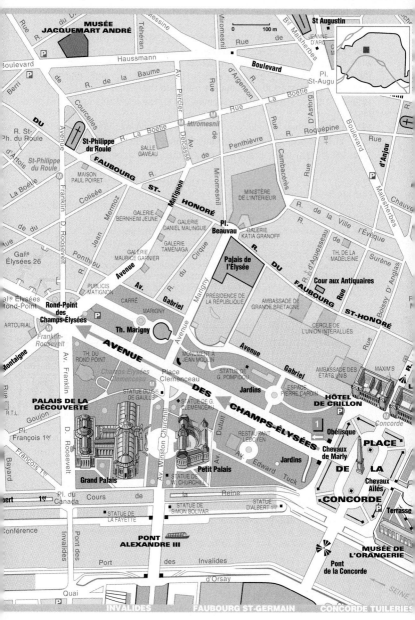

★★★Arc de Triomphe ⊘ – The arch and **place Charles-de-Gaulle★★★**, which surrounds it, form one of Paris' most famous landmarks. Twelve avenues radiate from the arch which explains why it is also called **place de l'Étoile** (*étoile* meaning star).

The arch commemorates Napoleon's victories, evoking at the same time imperial glory and the fate of the Unknown Soldier, whose tomb lies beneath. A Remembrance ceremony is held there on 11 November.

Historical notes – By the end of the 18C the square was already star-shaped despite having only five roads leading from it. At the centre was a semicircular lawn.

1806: Napoleon commissioned the construction of a giant arch. **Chalgrin** was appointed architect. It took two years to lay the foundations.

1810: With Empress Marie-Louise due to make her triumphal entry along the Champs-Élysées and the arch only a few feet above ground, Chalgrin had to erect a dummy arch of painted canvas mounted on scaffolding, to preserve appearances.

1832-1836: Construction, abandoned during the Restoration, was completed under **Louis-Philippe**.

1840: The carriage bearing the Emperor's body passed beneath the arch.

1854: **Haussmann** redesigned the square, creating a further seven radiating avenues, while Hittorff planned the uniform façades which surround it.

1885: **Victor Hugo**'s body lay in state for a night beneath the arch, draped in crepe, before being transported in a pauper's hearse to the Panthéon.

1919: On 14 July victorious Allied armies, led by the marshals, marched in procession.

1921: 11 November, an unknown soldier killed in the Great War was laid to rest.

1923: 11 November, the Flame of Remembrance was kindled.

1944: 26 August, Paris, liberated from German occupation, acclaimed General de Gaulle.

The arch – The arch's proportions and the relative scale of the sculpted reliefs are best appreciated from a distance.
Chalgrin's undertaking, inspired by Antiquity, is truly colossal, measuring 50m/164ft high by 45m/148ft wide, with massive high reliefs.

Rude was commissioned to carve the four main panels. Unfortunately, Etex and Cortot managed to influence President Thiers enough to steal work for three of the four groups – Rude's is the only inspired one. Pradier's Fames, four trumpet-blowing figures, abut the main arches. A frieze bustling with hundreds of figures, each 2m/6ft tall, encircles the arch; in the entablature above, a line of shields bear the names of the great victories of the Revolution and the Empire.

Facing the Champs-Élysées: **1** - *The Departure of the Volunteers in 1792*, commonly called **La Marseillaise**★★, Rude's sublime masterpiece represents the Nation leading her people to defend their independence; **2** - *General Marceau's Funeral*; **3** - *The Triumph of 1810* (by Cortot) celebrating the Treaty of Vienna; **4** - *The Battle of Aboukir*.
Facing avenue de Wagram: **5** - *The Battle of Austerlitz*.
Facing avenue de la Grande-Armée: **6** - *Resistance* (by Etex); **7** - *The Passage of the Bridge of Arcola*; **8** - *Peace* (by Etex); **9** - *The Capture of Alexandria*.
Facing avenue Kléber: **10** - *The Battle of Jemmapes*.

Beneath the monument, the Unknown Soldier rests under a plain slab; the flame of remembrance is rekindled each evening at 6.30pm. Lesser battles are engraved on the arch's inner walls together with the names of 558 generals – the names of those who died in the field are underlined.

Returning to the Champs-Élysées once more, take the underpass to the Arch platform, from the right pavement.

The Arch platform ⊙ – From here there is an excellent **view**★★★ of the capital: in the foreground the 12 avenues radiating from the square; you are halfway between the Louvre and La Défense, at the top of the Champs-Élysées.
Assembled in a small museum are mementoes of its construction and the celebratory and funerary ceremonies it has hosted. A documentary recalls the monument's moments of glory.

MUSEUMS AND OTHER ATTRACTIONS

★ **Musée du Petit Palais** ⊙ – *Avenue Winston-Churchill*. The museum owns and displays the Dutuit (antiques, medieval and Renaissance art objects, paintings, drawings, books, enamels, porcelain) and Tuck (18C furniture and objets d'art) bequests, alongside the city of Paris' collection of 19C paintings (**Ingres**, **Delacroix**, Courbet, Dalou, **Barbizon School**, Impressionists). Note in particular *The Good Samaritan* (1880) by A Morot and *Ascension* (1879) by **Gustave Doré**
The south gallery displays large historical and religious canvases and the north gallery contains works by Carpeaux.

★ **Grand Palais** – This great exhibition hall is formally fronted by an Ionic colonnade running the length of the building, before a mosaic frieze. Enormous quadrigae punctuate the corners; elsewhere turn-of-the-19C modern-style decorative elements are scattered. Inside, a single glazed space is covered by a flattened dome.

With an exhibition area of nearly 5 000m²/6 000sq yd, the Galleries du Grand Palais *(entrance: avenue du Général-Eisenhower)* has now become a cultural centre for temporary exhibitions.

Grand Palais

S. Sauvignier/MICHELIN

★★ **Palais de la Découverte** ⊘ – *Inside the Grand Palais; entrance on avenue Franklin-D.-Roosevelt.*

⊙ This museum, founded by a physicist in 1937 and dedicated to scientific discovery, is a centre both for higher scientific study and for popular enlightenment. *Allow half a day.*

Diagrams, lectures and demonstrations, experiments, documentary films and temporary exhibitions illustrate scientific invention and innovation. Many interactive attractions are specially intended for children, particularly in the field of biology. Other themes dealt with (mathematics, nuclear physics...) are intended for visitors who are already competent in these fields.

The domed **planetarium★** *(level 2)* presents a clear and fascinating introduction to the heavens including the course of the planets in the solar system.

CHÂTELET-HÔTEL DE VILLE★

Michelin plan 10: H 14, H 15, J 14, J 15
Ⓜ Châtelet (lines 1, 4, 7, 11 and 14), Hôtel-de-Ville (lines 1 and 11) –
RER: Châtelet (lines A, B, D) – Buses: 21, 69, 70, 72, 74, 75, 76, 81, 96

This is the heart of Paris, bounded to the south by the Seine and traversed by the busy rue de Rivoli. It is hard to believe that the history of France was often made here, today a centre of commerce, with historic shops such as the Samaritaine and the Bazar de l'Hôtel de Ville providing an invitation to visit the past as well as to buy.

Nearby neighbourhoods: BEAUBOURG, LES HALLES, ÎLE DE LA CITÉ, CONCIERGERIE, NOTRE-DAME, SAINTE-CHAPELLE, QUARTIER LATIN, ÎLE ST-LOUIS, LE MARAIS.

THE HÔTEL DE VILLE THROUGH THE CENTURIES

Maison aux Piliers – Paris was administered by a representative of the king until the 13C when Municipal government was introduced. The powerful watermen's guild held the monopoly over traffic on the rivers Seine, Oise, Marne and Yonne, and regulated levies thereon. In 1260, **Louis IX** appointed leading men of the guild to administer the township.

The municipal assembly was headed by a merchant provost and four aldermen who were elected by notables, who in turn nominated the town councillors. It moved from place du Châtelet to the Pillared House on place de Grève *(see below)* in 1357, at the instigation of Étienne Marcel.

The Hôtel de Ville – Under François I, the Pillared House fell into ruin. The king had plans drawn up by Domenico Bernabei (*Il Boccadoro* on account of his abundant golden moustache), and the first stone was laid in 1533. Building however continued until the early 17C. The central section of the present façade reproduces the original.

Étienne Marcel

This rich draper, a merchant provost, became leader of the States General in 1357 and came out in open revolt against royal power. By holding Paris, he tried to rally the whole of France to arms, allied himself with the peasants in revolt and allowed the English into the city. But Charles V who had taken refuge in the Hôtel St-Paul resisted victoriously, leaving Marcel to die a miserable death at the hands of the Parisians in 1358, just as he was about to open the city gates to Charles the Bad, King of Navarre.

Tour St-Jacques and the Hôtel de Ville

Until the Revolution the municipal authority was weak, the king making his own appointments – Pierre Lescaut, Guillaume Budet, François Miron and Étienne Turgot (who drew up the first maps of Paris) – on condition they be citizens of Paris.

July 1789 – After the fall of the Bastille, the rioters marched on to the town hall for arms. On 17 July 1789 Louis XVI appeared in the hall to kiss the newly adopted tricolour cockade. Between red and blue, the city colours since the provostship of Étienne Marcel in the 14C, La Fayette introduced the royal white.

The Commune – Throughout the Revolution the town hall was controlled by the Commune. The popular insurrection of 10 August 1792, which was led by Danton, Robespierre and Marat, forced the king to flee the Tuileries Palace and take refuge with the Legislative Assembly. The Montagnard faction, or deputies of the extreme left, was an offshoot of the Commune and dominated the National Convention (1793-94).

On 9 Thermidor (27 July 1794) the National Convention tired of Robespierre's tyrannical behaviour, had him imprisoned at the Luxembourg Palace. Released by the Commune, he was given refuge in the town hall where as a result of a suicide attempt or of disciplinary action he had his jaw shattered by a pistol shot. He was guillotined the following day.

In 1848, when Louis-Philippe was dismissed, it was in the Hôtel de Ville that the provisional government (led by Lamartine, Arago and Ledru-Rollin) was set up and from there that the Second Republic was proclaimed on 24 February 1848.

The Second Empire and Commune of 1871 – Louis Napoleon proclaimed himself emperor in 1851 and charged his Prefect of the Seine, Baron Haussmann, with replanning the area around the Hôtel de Ville. He razed the adjoining streets, enlarged the square and built the two barracks in rue de Lobau.

On 4 September 1870, after the defeat of the French Army at the Battle of Sedan, Gambetta, Jules Favre and Jules Ferry proclaimed the Third Republic from the Hôtel de Ville and instituted a National Defence Government. The capitulation of Paris on 28 January 1871, however, roused the citizens to revolt against the government, installing in its place the Paris Commune. In May during its final overthrow, the Hôtel de Ville, the Tuileries and several other buildings were set on fire by the Federalists.

25 August 1944 – It was from here that General de Gaulle made his famous speech "*Paris ! Paris outragé ! Paris brisé ! Paris martyrisé ! mais Paris libéré ! libéré par lui-même ! libéré par son peuple avec le concours des armées de la France...*".

In 1977, Paris became a municipality administered by a mayor like any other municipality in France and, today, the Hôtel de Ville is Paris' official reception and city government building.

EXPLORING THE NEIGHBOURHOOD

★★ **Église St-Germain-L'Auxerrois** – In what is now place du Louvre, the Roman Labienus pitched his camp when he crushed the Parisii in 52 BC, as did the Normans when they besieged Paris in 885. Until the Second Empire, fine mansions stood between the Louvre and the church, including the Petit Bourbon (demolished 1660).

On the northern side there is the neo-Renaissance town hall designed by Hittorff and a neo-Gothic bell-tower erected by Ballu, with a peal of 38 bells.

The church, named after St Germanus, Bishop of Auxerre in the 5C, spans five centuries of architectural development from the Romanesque (belfry) via High Gothic (chancel) and Flamboyant (porch and nave) to the Renaissance (doorway). Substantial restoration in the hands of Baltard and Lassus (1838-55) emphasised its composite nature further.

When the Valois moved into the Louvre in the 14C, St-Germain became the king's parish church and thereby received embellishments and endowments. On the night of 24 August 1572 the bells rang for matins giving the signal for the **St Bartholomew's Day Massacre** when thousands of Huguenots, invited to celebrate the marriage of Henri of Navarre to his cousin, Marguerite of Valois, were slaughtered according to a plan hatched by the Cardinal Duke of Guise, Catherine de' Medici, Charles IX and the future Henri III.

Many poets (Jodelle, Malherbe), painters (Coypel, Boucher, Nattier, Chardin, Van Loo), sculptors (Coysevox, the two Coustous), architects (Le Vau, Robert de Cotte, Gabriel the Elder, Soufflot) and others associated with the court and the Louvre are buried in the church.

Exterior – From the side of La Samaritaine there is a good view of the east end and the Romanesque belfry which abuts the transept.

Below the roof line along the chancel aisles are a series of small attic-like spaces in which were heaped the bones from tombs in the cloisters, which at one time surrounded the church. The apsidal chapel endowed by the Tronson family is decorated with a frieze of carp.

Porch – The porch is the building's most original feature dating from between 1435 and 1439. The column-statues are modern. The outermost, lowest, bays accommodate small chambers, covered with slate, in which the chapter placed the church archives and treasure.

The three middle bays have multi-ribbed Flamboyant vaults, flanked by a plain Gothic bay. The most interesting, central doorway is 13C. The figure in the right embrasure represents St Geneviève holding a candle which a small devil tries to snuff out, while an angel nearby, stands ready with a taper to rekindle it.

Interior – The restored 18C organ comes from the Sainte-Chapelle. The **churchwarden's pew**, dating from 1684, is thought to have been used by successive kings and their families. In the fourth chapel is a fine early-16C, Flemish **altarpiece** *(light switch)*.

The **stained glass** in the transept and the two rose windows date from the 16C. The multi-lierne vault in the south arm of the transept is typical of the Flamboyant style. The **chancel** is surrounded by an 18C grille before which stand 15C polychrome statues of St Germanus and St Vincent. In the 18C the fine Renaissance rood screen carved by Jean Goujon and Pierre Lescot was removed to allow for processions (the rescued low-relief panels are in the Louvre).

The **Chapel of the Holy Sacrament** *(on the right of the entrance)* contains a 14C polychrome stone statue of the Virgin; a 14C Crucifixion; one of the original statues from the main doorway, St Mary the Egyptian; a Last Supper by Theo Van Elsen (1954) and a 13C statue of St Germanus.

La Samaritaine – This department store overlooking the Pont Neuf is named after a pump (1602) under the bridge that drew water from the river to supply the Louvre and which, being decorated with a figure of the woman of Samaria giving Jesus water at the well, became known as the *Samaritaine*. From the terrace of shop No 2 there is an excellent **view★★** over the whole of Paris and around the back in rue de l'Arbre-Sec, there is a good view of the Gothic chevet of St-Germain-l'Auxerrois rippling across the rectilinear, glass lateral deco façade of the shop.

Quai de la Mégisserie – This section of the embankment gets its name from the stinking public slaughterhouse (*mégisserie* meaning tawing) that lined the river until the Revolution. Now there are rows of garden shops and pet-shops selling exotic birds in cages and fish in tanks. It was hereabouts that press-gangs operated, collecting volunteers for the armed forces. An attractive **view★★** extends over the law courts, Conciergerie, and the old houses along quai de l'Horloge on Île de la Cité and Pont Neuf.

Place du Châtelet

Place du Châtelet – The area gets its name from the Grand Châtelet, a great fortress which defended the northern entrance into the city, over the Pont au Change. This in turn accommodated the city notaries, surrounded by the halls of powerful guilds (butchers, sausage-makers, skinners and tanners). The Châtelet or **Palm Fountain** (1806-07) commemorates Napoleon's victories; the base was decorated with sphinxes in 1858.

The two theatres on either side were built by the architect Davioud in 1862. The Châtelet or Théâtre Musical de Paris (west side) staged performances by Diaghilev's Ballets Russes, Caruso, Mahler, Nijinski.... Opposite, the Théâtre de la Ville, formerly the Sarah Bernhardt Theatre, is a centre of popular culture (east side).

★ **Tour St-Jacques** – The tower is the former belfry of the church of St-Jacques-la-Boucherie, built in the 16C and one of the starting points for pilgrims journeying up rue St-Jacques and on to Santiago de Compostela in Spain. The church was pulled down in 1802 and the tower converted to a weather station.
The statue of Pascal, recalls the physicist-cum-philosopher's experiments into the weight of air carried out first in the Puy-de-Dôme, then, supposedly, on this spot in 1648.

Place de l'Hôtel-de-Ville – **Place de Grève**, as it was known until 1830, shelves gently down to the Seine. In the Middle Ages, the foreshore or *grève*, became a meeting place for those out of work, hence the expression *faire la grève* meaning not working or on strike. It was the place for popular fairs, where a huge bonfire was lit in midsummer for the feast day of St John the Baptist (24 June).
During the Ancien Régime, it was where *bourgeois* and commoners were hanged and where gentlemen were beheaded by the axe or the sword; witches and heretics were burnt at the stake; murderers were condemned to the wheel and punishment for treason consisted of being drawn and quartered.
Paved in granite, the square boasts modern rectangular fountains on either side of a boat-like form, representing the coat of arms of the 13C watermen's guild.

Going out

Le Petit Opportun – *15 rue des Lavandières – 1st arr* – ☎ *01 42 36 01 36 – Tue-Sat from 9pm – closed 1 Jan, Aug, 25 Dec.* One of oldest jazz clubs in Paris. On Tuesdays, *nuits blanches* sessions provide a stage for lesser-known musicians who have yet to record their first disc or who have never played live. All types of jazz, from the 1940s up until today.

Shopping

Rue de Rivoli – Built during the reigns of Napoleon I and Louis-Philippe, this street witnessed two important events: the proclamation of the Republic on 21 September 1792 and the arrest of General von Choltitz in August 1944. Today it is one of the main shopping streets in central Paris with several department stores.

La Samaritaine – *19 rue de la Monnaie – 1st arr* – Ⓜ *Pont-Neuf* – ☎ *01 40 41 20 20 – Mon-Sat 9.30am-7pm, Thu 9.30am-10pm.* Don't miss the terrace in store no 2 which has a superb view over Paris.

Le Bazar de l'Hôtel de Ville – *55 rue de la Verrerie – 4th arr* – Ⓜ *Hôtel-de-Ville* – ☎ *01 42 74 90 00 – Mon-Sat 9.30am-7pm (8.30pm on Wed and Fri).* This eternally packed department store can almost be said to be one of the capital's landmarks. If you're looking for something in the realms of decoration or home improvement, you will be hard-pressed not to find it here.

Eating out

Turn back to the Selected restaurants section at the beginning of the guide for a list of restaurants, bistros, cafés etc. This neighbourhood is in the 1st and the 4th *arrondissements*.

Hôtel de Ville – The Hôtel de Ville was entirely rebuilt between 1874 and 1882, following the fire during the fall of the Paris Commune in 1871, in the neo-Renaissance style by Ballu and Deperthes, complete with 146 statues of the illustrious and of French towns which adorn the building's façades.

Bazar de l'Hôtel de Ville – This store was founded in 1856 by Xavier Ruel, a street pedlar who had realised the commercial value of the site. Its decor dates from 1913. A major part of its stock has always consisted of home improvement and decoration materials.

Pont Notre-Dame – (1913) This was the Great Bridge in Roman times, as opposed to the Small Bridge (Petit Pont) on the far side of the island. Burnt down by the Normans and rebuilt on piles in 1413, it was the first to be given an official name, and the houses built on it were the first to be numbered in Paris. It fell down in Louis XII's reign (1499), but was rebuilt and lined with identical houses with richly decorated façades, since it was on the royal route of solemn entries into Paris. One of the houses belonged to the art collector Gersaint who befriended Watteau, figuring in Watteau's famous picture *L'Enseigne de Gersaint* (it now hangs in the Charlottenburg Museum in Berlin).

Pont au Change – The Money Changers' Bridge was established in the 9C by Charles the Bald. It was so tightly lined with workshops and houses all through the Middle Ages that one could cross the river without glimpsing it! These were cleared in 1788. Louis VII instituted a money exchange here in 1141, where all foreigners and visitors to Paris bartered for the best rate of exchange. The present bridge dates from 1860.

Île de la CITÉ★★★

Michelin plan 10: J 14, J 15, K 15
Ⓜ *Cité (line 4) – RER: St-Michel-Notre-Dame (line C) –*
Buses: 21, 27, 38, 58, 70, 96

The Île de la Cité is the cradle of Paris, geographically at the very heart of the capital. Its history, architecture and remarkable setting make it one of the city's principal attractions; its most impressive monument is undoubtedly the Cathedral of Notre-Dame *(see NOTRE-DAME)*, closely followed by the most exquisite Sainte-Chapelle *(see SAINTE-CHAPELLE)* and the Conciergerie *(see CONCIERGERIE)*.

Nearby neighbourhoods: ÎLE ST-LOUIS, CHÂTELET-HÔTEL DE VILLE, QUARTIER LATIN, MAUBERT.

Lutetia – Around 200 BC Gaulish fishermen and **boatmen** of the Parisii tribe discovered and set up their huts on the largest island in the Seine – Lutetia was born. The township, whose Celtic name meant boatyard on a river, was conquered by Labienus' Roman legions in 52 BC. The Gallo-Roman town prospered on shipping, so that the vessel which was later incorporated in the capital's coat of arms is a reminder both of the

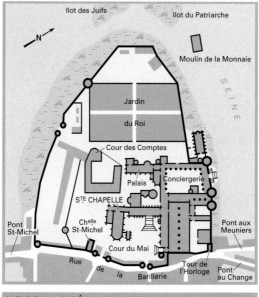

ILE DE LA CITÉ : DOWNSTREAM END IN THE 15C

shape of the island and of the way of life of its earliest inhabitants. The boatmen's existence has been confirmed by the discovery beneath Notre-Dame of one of their pagan altars.

In 360 the Roman prefect, Julian the Apostate, was here proclaimed emperor by his legions: at the same time Lutetia was renamed after its inhabitants and shortened to Paris.

Sainte Geneviève – In 451 Attila crossed the Rhine with 700 000 men; as he reached Laon the Parisians began to flee. Geneviève, a young girl from Nanterre who had dedicated her life to God, calmed them with the assurance that the town would be saved by heavenly intervention; the Huns approached, hesitated and turned away to advance on Orléans. Parisians adopted the girl as their protector and patron.

Ten years later when the island was besieged by the Franks and suffered famine, Geneviève escaped the enemy watch, loaded boats with victuals in Champagne and returned undetected as if by miracle. She died in 512 and was buried at King Clovis' side.

The Count of Paris becomes King – In 885, for the fifth time in 40 years, the Normans sailed up the Seine. The Cité – the name adopted in 506 when **Clovis** made it his capital – was confronted by 700 ships bearing 30 000 warriors bent on pillaging Burgundy. Assault and siege proving unsuccessful, the Normans beached their boats, mounted them on logs and rolled them to the upper reaches of Paris. Eudes, Count of Paris and the leader of the resistance, was thereupon elected king.

Cathedral and Parliament – During the Middle Ages the population grew, spilling onto both banks of the river. But while the episcopal see remained under Sens (Paris did not have its own archbishop until 1622), the number of schools around the cathedral proliferated, many becoming famous throughout Europe. Among the teachers were Alexander of Paris, creator of the 12-footed *alexandrine* line in poetry and, at the beginning of the 12C, the philosopher **Abelard**, whose moving romance with Héloïse, the niece of the canon Fulbert, began in the cloisters of Notre-Dame. Chapels and convents multiplied on the island: St-Denis-du-Pas (where St Denis' martyrdom is said to have begun), St-Pierre-aux-Bœufs (whose porch is now part of St-Séverin), St-Aignan, St-Jean-le-Rond (where unwanted children were abandoned). By the close of the 13C, there were at least 22 bell-towers!

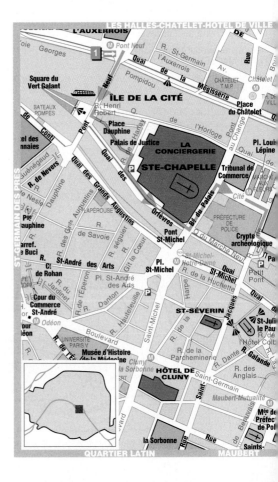

The Cité, the seat of Parliament, the highest judiciary in the kingdom was, inevitably, involved in revolutions and uprisings such as that attempted in the 14C by **Étienne Marcel** *(see CHÂTELET-HÔTEL DE VILLE)* and the **Fronde** in the 17C. During the Terror of 1793-94 the Conciergerie prisons were crowded, while next door, the Revolutionary Tribunal continued to sit in the law courts, endlessly pronouncing merciless sentences.

Transformation – Under Louis-Philippe and to an even greater extent, under Napoleon III, the entire centre of the island was demolished: 25 000 people were evacuated. Enormous administrative buildings were erected: the Hôtel-Dieu, barracks (now the police prefecture), the commercial courts; the Law Courts were doubled in size; place du Parvis before the cathedral was quadrupled in size; boulevard du Palais was built 10 times wider than before.

August 1944 – The Paris police barricaded themselves in the prefecture and hoisted the tricolour. For three days they held the Germans at bay until relieved by the arrival of the French Army Division under General Leclerc.

EXPLORING THE NEIGHBOUHOOD

⒈ From Pont Neuf to Notre-Dame

From Pont Neuf to Notre-Dame

★**Pont Neuf** – Pont Neuf *(see illustration p 93)* is the oldest of the Paris bridges, and was the first thoroughfare in Paris to benefit from pavements that separated pedestrians from the traffic. The original equestrian statue of **Henri IV** was melted down at the Revolution in 1792 and replaced during the Restoration with the present figure, made of bronze cast by a staunch Bonapartist who is said to have included in the monument a copy of Voltaire's epic poem *La Henriade* (on the League and Henri IV), a statuette of Napoleon and various written articles glorifying the Emperor!

Built in two halves between 1578 and 1604 to the designs of **Androuet Du Cerceau** the bridge is on a broken axis. The 12 rounded arches each have a keystone carved with humorous grotesques. In the olden days, it used to be crowded with stallholders,

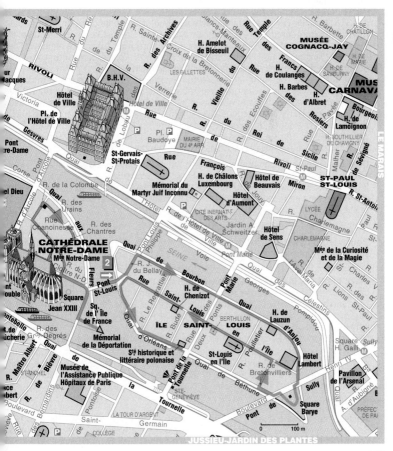

Île de la Cité

tooth pullers, comic characters such as Tabarin and the Italian Pantaloon, Scarlatini, the all-time charlatan and a host of gawpers and pickpockets. Today, the open view up and down the river is unobstructed by stalls and shops.

Square du Vert-Galant – Down the steps behind the Henri IV statue, this serene stretch of green below the hum of traffic is at its natural ground level, before the land was built up by **Henri III**. From the tip is a fine view of Pont Neuf, the Louvre and the Mint. Its name derives from the nickname given to Henri IV, alluding to his reputation as an amorous gentleman despite his age!

★ **Place Dauphine** – For a long time the western tip of the island gave way to a muddy marshy area broken by the river currents.
In 1314, **Philip the Fair** had a stake erected on one of the mounds of ground. It was there that he ordered the execution by fire of the Grand Master of the **Order of Templars, Jacques de Molay**. The king watched him burn from his palace window. The gardens (Jardin du Roi) which extended from the Conciergerie into the river became the first botanical garden under **Marie de Medici**.
At the end of the 16C Henri III decided to reorganise this untidy no man's land: the mud ditches were filled in, a great earth bank was amassed to support the future Pont Neuf, and the south bank was raised by some 6m/20ft. In 1607 Henri IV ceded the land between the Conciergerie and Pont Neuf for a triangular square to be built, surrounded by a series of houses constructed of brick, white stone and slate to a uniform design. The square was named after the Dauphin, in honour of the future Louis XIII. Only a few façades such as no **14** retain their original features.

. **Quai des Orfèvres** – The properties along the river front were during the 17C and 18C the jewellers' quarter: Strass, inventor of the synthetic diamond, Boehmer and Bassenge who fashioned Marie-Antoinette's celebrated necklace, had their shops in place Dauphine and along the quay. No **36** is today well known as the headquarters of the CID (Police Judiciaire).

Pont St-Michel – The present bridge (1857) replaced one dating from 1378.

Boulevard du Palais – The construction of this broad thoroughfare by **Haussmann** eliminated a sinister spot where individuals found guilty by the courts were publicly branded. Along the boulevard are the entrances to the Palais de Justice.

Place Louis-Lépine – A colourful **flower market** is held in front of the administrative offices of the Hôtel-Dieu, the police headquarters and the commercial court which have surrounded the square on three sides since the Second Empire. On Sundays a bird market replaces the flower stalls in the square named after the popular prefect, who instigated great changes in the force – policemen on bicycles, a road traffic system – and gave the Paris police their white truncheons and whistles.

The **Hôtel-Dieu** hospice, first mentioned as early as the 9C, moved into its present premises between 1864 and 1877 (the old building stood on the site of the small square overlooked by the statues of Charlemagne and his two valiant knights Roland and Olivier). The hall and inner court are of architectural interest.

★★★ **Notre-Dame** – see NOTRE-DAME.

Ancien quartier du Chapitre – The area extending north of Notre-Dame to the Seine belonged to the cathedral chapter. Enclosed in a wall with four gates, it was populated by the cathedral canons who each lodged their own students. Although considerably restored, the quarter is the only reminder of what the Cité looked like in the 11C and 12C when **Abelard**, St Bonaventure and St Dominic built up the reputation of the cathedral school which was later to merge with the **Sorbonne** *(see QUARTIER LATIN)*.

Rue Chanoinesse was the main thoroughfare of the former chapter. Nos **24** and **22** are the last two medieval canons' houses; note the stone posts in the courtyard. In **rue de la Colombe** traces of the Lutetian Gallo-Roman wall of Lutetia remain; note the curious tavern at the top of some steps. In laying rue d'Arcole, the chapel of Ste-Marie was razed, where deflowered brides could be married, sealing their vows with a ring made of straw. **Rue des Ursins** is level with the old banks of the Seine and Port St-Landry, Paris' first dock until the 12C when facilities on the Hôtel de Ville foreshore were established. At the end of the narrow street stand the last vestiges of the medieval chapel, St-Aignan, where priests celebrated mass secretly during the Revolution. At the picturesque corner with **rue des Chantres** stands a medieval mansion past which there is a fine view of Notre-Dame's skyline.

Quai aux Fleurs affords a vast panorama of St-Gervais and of the tip of the Île St-Louis.

Square Jean-XXIII – Until the beginning of the 19C, the area between Notre-Dame and the tip of the island was crowded with houses, chapels and the Archbishop's Palace. These were severely damaged in a riot and later razed to the ground (1831). The square opened as a formal garden with a neo-Gothic fountain in 1844.

Square de l'Île-de-France – **Napoleon III** built the Cité's municipal morgue on the upstream tip of the island, attracting until 1910 those with a morbid fascination.

Mémorial de la Déportation ⊙ – A modern crypt accommodates a metal sculpture by Desserprit, funerary urns and the tomb of the Unknown Deportee from Struthof, to commemorate the suffering and loss of so much life in the Nazi camps.

★ PALAIS DE JUSTICE ⊙

To balance the power of the Church, the Île de la Cité also accommodated the Law Courts – the pre-eminent seat of the civil and judicial authorities.

King's Palace – The stone buildings erected by the Roman governors for their administrative and military headquarters were requisitioned first by the Merovingian kings then by the early Capetian kings who fortified the palace with a keep and built a chapel in the precincts. Clovis died here.

In the 13C Louis IX lived in the Upper Chamber (today the First Civil Court), dispensed justice in the courtyard and built the Sainte-Chapelle; Philip the Fair constructed the Conciergerie, a sumptuous palace "more beautiful than anyone in France had ever seen". The Hall of the Men-at-Arms was the largest ever built in Europe. The former Chapelle St-Michel which gave its name to the bridge and boulevard on the left bank, was razed to the ground in the 18C.

On 22 February 1358, the mob under **Étienne Marcel** entered the apartments of the Dauphin, the future **Charles V**, and Regent whilst his father John the Good was being held in England. When the troubles had subsided, Charles V moved out of the palace where he had been compelled to witness the bloody slaughter of his counsellors, preferring to live at the Louvre, the Hôtel St-Paul or at Vincennes outside Paris. In the palace, he installed his Parliament.

It is interesting to note that Charles VII, **Henri IV** and **Louis XIV** all survived uprisings in Paris by fleeing the city; **Louis XVI**, **Charles X** and **Louis-Philippe** however, refused to abandon the palace, and all lost their thrones.

Judicial Palace – Parliament was the kingdom's supreme court of justice. Originally its members were nominated by the king, until 1522 when **François I** sold the rights for money on condition that the position become hereditary; thus the highest dignitaries in the land (the chancellor, peers of the realm, royal princes) secured their position by right or privilege.

In disputes between the officers of state and the king, matters were settled by courts presided over by the monarch, with offenders being sometimes sentenced to exile or imprisonment. Judges, barristers, clerks and a multitude of others populated the lesser courts in the palace. Bureaucracy proliferated.

Fires were frequent, damaging the Grande Salle (1618), Sainte-Chapelle spire (1630), the *Cour des Comptes* (Debtors' Court – 1737), and the Gallerie Marchande (1776). In 1788 Parliament demanded the convocation of the States General – not a good idea, because the General Assembly announced its suppression and the Convention sent the members to the guillotine.

The Law Courts – The Revolution overturned the judicial system. New courts were installed in the old buildings which took the name of Palais de Justice. Restoration lasted from 1840 to 1914, interrupted only by the Commune fire; the building was given its present façade overlooking place Dauphine and its extension along quai des Orfèvres.

Tour of the buildings – *Enter via the Cour du Mai.*

Cour du Mai – The Louis XVI wrought-iron grille is especially fine. The name *cour du Mai* is derived from a very old custom by which the clerks of the court – an important corporation – planted in the courtyard a tree from one of the Royal forests each year on 1 May. A similar practice prevailed in England often in honour of a particular person, often festooned in (yellow) ribbons.

The Galerie Marchande was once the most animated part of the building, bustling with plaintiffs, lawyers, clerks, court officials, souvenir peddlers and hangers-on. The ornate Première Chambre Civile de la Cour d'Appel (Chamber of the Civil Court of Appeal) and the Cour de Cassation (Chamber of the Court of Cassation) are decorated with frescoes and tapestries.

Enter the **Salle des Pas-Perdus** (Lobby), formerly the Gothic Grand'Salle of Philip the Fair, twice destroyed, and reconstructed most recently after the Commune of 1871. The two Classical aisles, crowded with plaintiffs, barristers in their gowns, clerks and officials, are now the busiest place in the building – Balzac called it "the cathedral of chicanery".

Notice the monument to the 19C barrister, Berryer, on the right, with the tortoise – maligning the delays in the law. At the end on the left is the former apartment of Louis IX, used as **Parliamentary Grand Chamber** when Louis XII had it decorated with a fine ceiling, and then by the Revolutionary Tribunal under Fouquier-Tinville (1793-94). It is now the First Civil Court.

CONCIERGERIE★★

Michelin plan 10: J 14

Ⓜ *Cité (line 4) – Buses: 21, 27, 38, 70, 85, 96*

The beauty of its medieval architecture conceals the bloody history of the Conciergerie. During the Revolution noblemen and ordinary citizens alike were imprisoned here, usually on their way to the guillotine.

See also ÎLE DE LA CITÉ, SAINTE-CHAPELLE, NOTRE-DAME. *Nearby neighbourhoods*: ÎLE ST-LOUIS, CHÂTELET-HÔTEL DE VILLE, QUARTIER LATIN.

A noble keeper – The name *Conciergerie* was given to a section of the old palace precinct controlled by a person of high degree: the *concierge* or keeper of the king's mansion – a remunerative office involving the licensing of the many shops within the palace walls.

It served as a prison from the 14C; among pre-Revolutionary prisoners were several who had made successful or unsuccessful attempts on successive kings' lives: Montgomery on Henri II; Ravaillac on Henri IV.

The guillotine's antechamber – At the time of the Revolution as many as 1 200 men and women were held at once in the Conciergerie; during the Terror the building became the antechamber to the Tribunal, which in nine cases out of ten meant the guillotine. Among those incarcerated here were Queen **Marie-Antoinette**; Madame Élisabeth, sister to Louis XVI; **Charlotte Corday** who stabbed Marat; **Madame du Barry**, the favourite of Louis XV; the poet André Chénier; Philippe-Égalité; the chemist Lavoisier; the 22 Girondins condemned by **Danton** who, with 15 of his companions, was in turn condemned by **Robespierre**, who was himself condemned with 20 of his followers by the Thermidor Convention; the public prosecutor Fouquier-Tinville; the judges of the Revolutionary Tribunal.

In all nearly 2 600 prisoners left the Conciergerie under the beady gaze of the *tricoteuses* between January 1793 and July 1794, for the guillotine which was erected successively on place du **Carrousel** in front of the Louvre, place de la **Concorde**, place de la **Bastille**, place de la **Nation** (where 1 306 heads rolled in 40 days), and lastly place de la Concorde.

★**Exterior** – The best view is from Mégisserie Quay on the Right Bank, with its four towers reflected in the Seine which originally flowed right up to their base. This is the oldest part of the palace built by the Capetian kings. The ground level was raised appreciably at the end of the 16C when quai de l'Horloge was built.

The oldest tower is the crenellated one on the right, Tour Bonbec. The twin towers in the centre of the 19C neo-Gothic façade flanked the palace entrance across the bridge of Charles the Bald. The Tour d'Argent on the right contained the royal treasure; the one on the left, Tour César, had apartments used during the Terror by the public prosecutor, Fouquier-Tinville.

The square **Tour de l'Horloge** has since 1370 housed the first public clock to be installed in Paris, and which has never ceased to mark time. The silver bell, having chimed golden hours for the monarchy, was melted down in 1793. The carvings on the face although much restored, are by **Germain Pilon** (16C).

★**Interior** ⊙ – *Entrance at 1 quai de l'horloge, through the vaulted archway, across the courtyard and down right, into the guard-room.*

Salle des Gardes – Stout pillars with interesting capitals support the Gothic vaulting in this dark room.

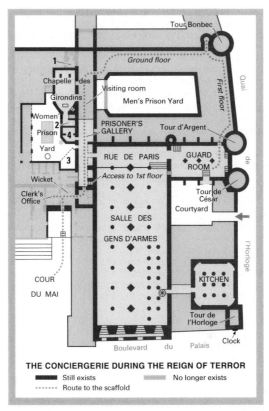

THE CONCIERGERIE DURING THE REIGN OF TERROR

- ▬▬ Still exists
- ▬▬ No longer exists
- ········ Route to the scaffold

★★ Salle des Gens d'Armes *(Hall of the Men-at-Arms)* – This magnificent four-aisled Gothic hall covers an area of 1 800m2/19 375sq ft, on a par with those of the Mont-St-Michel and the Palais des Papes in Avignon. Buildings erected in the May Courtyard in the 18C unfortunately block out much of the light. Above used to be the palace's Great Hall and royal apartments. On the first pillar in the central row is marked the level reached by the Seine in 1910.

The Revolutionary Tribunal sat in this hall from 1793 to 1795.

Cuisines – The four huge fireplaces in each corner of the old kitchens fulfilled a specific function: cooking enough meat, spit-roasted or boiled in cauldrons, to feed between 2 000 and 3 000 mouths, including the royal family. The canopies are supported by unusual buttresses.

Prison – Rue de Paris leads into the Galerie des Prisonniers, a corridor serving as the main axis of the prison, where penniless prisoners slept on the bare ground while the rich paid for their own cell and better food. It was the busiest part of the building, with a constant flow of prisoners arriving and departing, visitors, lawyers, police and gaolers. Flanked by police officers, prisoners were ushered from the Grande Chambre du Parlement on the first floor down a spiral staircase hidden in the Bonbec Tower, through the door (now walled up) at the far end of the gallery. This room gave onto the council room which on one side served as antechamber *(parloir)* to the men's prison yard (Préau des Hommes) and on the other opened onto a staircase (**1**) up to the Tribunal. The prisoners were most likely herded into the room now used as the kitchens for the law courts restaurant, from where, one by one, they passed into an

Conciergerie, Salle des Gens d'Armes

B. Kaufmann/MICHELIN

adjoining room. There, the prisoner sat on a stool, his or her hands were firmly tied behind the back, collars were cut away and hair was cut short. Batched up, the condemned crossed through the wicket gate *(guichet)* past the clerk of the court *(greffe* means register office) into the **May Courtyard** – and out to the tumbrils.

The history of the prison and important political prisoners is presented on the first floor. These include the Scots captain of the guard Montgomery who delivered a fatal blow to Henri II's eye during a tourney; Châtel who wounded Henri IV; Ravaillac who killed him; Louvel the assassin of the Duc de Berry and Robespierre.

Chapelle des Girondins – *Ground floor.* The chapel was transformed into a collective prison where prisoners heard mass through the grille on the upper storey. Twenty-two Girondins were held there together in 1793. The chapel was reconsecrated under the Restoration.

From here, one can visit the cell occupied by Marie-Antoinette (2 August to 16 October 1793) and transformed into an expiatory chapel (**2**) in 1816.

Cour des Femmes – In the centre, as in earlier times, is a pathetic patch of grass and a lonely tree. During the day the women prisoners were allowed out of their cells around the courtyard. The arcaded ground floor and the first floor accommodated different kinds of criminal; additional sections were added in the 19C.

The corridor known as the **Côté des Douzes** (**3**) was where prisoners of both sexes could talk through the bars, and from where daily the 12 inmates selected for the guillotine embarked on their final journey.

Back in the prison corridor a door on the right leads to a reconstruction of **Marie-Antoinette's cell** (**4**). The furniture consisted of a cot, a chair and a table. A screen separated the queen from watchmen, day and night.

Danton and Robespierre spent time in the adjacent cell, the latter just one night before his execution.

Place de la CONCORDE★★★

Michelin plan 10: G 11
Ⓜ *Concorde (lines 1, 8 and 12) – Buses: 31, 42, 72, 73, 84, 94*

Everything about this square – site, size, general elegance – is impressive, particularly the obelisk, which dominates the scene. Place de la Concorde is one of the most beautiful squares in Paris, but also one of the busiest… and now the largest sundial in the world since the shadow cast by the point of the obelisk indicates international time.

Nearby neighbourhoods: FAUBOURG ST-HONORÉ, CHAMPS-ÉLYSÉES, LA MADELEINE, LES TUILERIES, LE LOUVRE, FAUBOURG ST-GERMAIN, MUSÉE D'ORSAY.

History – Paris aldermen, wanting to find favour with Louis XV, commissioned **Bouchardon** to sculpt an equestrian statue of Le Bien-Aimé (the beloved) as he was known, and organised a competition to find an architect for the square. Servandoni, Soufflot and **Gabriel**, among others, submitted plans. Gabriel's designs for an octagon bordered by a dry moat and balustrade won. Eight massive paired pedestals intended to carry sculptures were to mark the oblique corners. Twin edifices with fine colonnades were to be constructed to flank the opening of rue Royale. Work began in 1755 and continued until 1775.

Place de la Concorde

Shopping

Bernardaud – *11 rue Royale – 8th arr* – Ⓜ *Concorde or Madeleine – other shop: Carrousel du Louvre 1st arr* – ☎ *01 47 42 82 86 – www.bernardaud.fr – Mon-Fri 9.30am-6.30pm, Sat 10am-7pm – closed 1Jan, Easter, 1 May, 4 Jun and 25 Dec.* From sumptuous re-editions of the Royal Manufacture of Limoges to dozens of original new creations, this shop is almost a living museum of porcelain and chinaware. Unusual gift ideas: engraved lithographs, jewellery etc.

Eating out

Turn back to the Selected restaurants section at the beginning of the guide for a list of restaurants, bistros, cafés etc. This neighbourhood is spread over the 8th *arrondissement*.

In 1792 the royal statue was toppled and the name of the square was changed from place Louis-XV to place de la Révolution. On Sunday 21 January 1793 a guillotine was erected in the north-west corner (near where the Brest statue now stands) for the execution of **Louis XVI**. On 13 May, the nation's razor, now installed near the grille to the Tuileries, began to claim a further 1 343 victims including Marie-Antoinette, Mme du Barry, Charlotte Corday, the Girondins, Danton and his friends, Mme Roland, Robespierre and his confederates. The last heads rolled in 1795. The Directory, hopeful of a better future, renamed the blood-soaked area place de la Concorde.

Under Louis-Philippe, the square's decoration was completed by the architect Hittorff. Wary of having a central statue that might become politically contentious, the king opted for a neutral symbol: an obelisk. To complete the design of the square, two fountains were added, inspired by those in St Peter's Square in Rome.

Eight statues representing eight French cities were commissioned for the pedestals provided by Gabriel. Cortot sculpted Brest and Rouen, Pradier Lille and Strasbourg. It was at the foot of this last figure that the poet-politician, Déroulède, rallied patriots after 1870 when the town of Strasbourg was under German rule. Lyons and Marseille are by Petitot, Bordeaux and Nantes by Caillouette.

EXPLORING THE NEIGHBOURHOOD

See map p 149

★★**Two mansions** – The colossal mansions on either side of the opening to rue Royale are impressive without being overbearing; the colonnades inspired by those of the Louvre are even more elegant than the original, and the mansions themselves, among the finest examples of the early Louis XVI style. Their architect, Jacques-Ange Gabriel succeeded his father, Jacques Gabriel, at the head of the Academy of Architecture. The right pavilion, the **Hôtel de la Marine**, was until 1792 the royal store; it then became the Admiralty Office. Today it houses the Navy Headquarters. The **Hôtel Crillon**, across the street, was at first occupied by four noblemen. It now accommodates the French Automobile Club and a famous hotel and is flanked on the left by the American Embassy across rue Boissy-d'Anglas.

To the right of the Hôtel de la Marine is the Hôtel Talleyrand, designed in the 18C by Chalgrin for the Duc de la Vrillière, and where the statesman and diplomat **Talleyrand** died in 1838.

★**Obelisk** – In the centre of the square stands the obelisk, which comes from the ruins of the temple at Luxor. It was given to France in 1831 by Mohammed Ali, Viceroy of Egypt, seeking support from the French. It reached Paris four years later and was erected in the centre of the square on 25 October 1836.

The monument in pink granite, 3 300 years old, is covered in hieroglyphics; it is 23m/75ft tall, and weighs more than 220t. Cleopatra's Needle in London, offered by the same ruler to Queen Victoria, comes from Heliopolis and is 2m/6ft 6in shorter.

★★★**Views** – The obelisk provides the best point from which to get a view of the Champs-Élysées, framed by the **Marly Horses** (commissioned from **Guillaume Coustou** for Marly, Louis XIV's superb château near Versailles) looking up the avenue towards the Arc de Triomphe. Coysevox's Winged Horses frame the view across the Tuileries towards the Louvre. Replicas have replaced the two original marble groups of horses, which are in the Louvre. There are good vistas also, north to the Madeleine beyond Gabriel's pavilions, and south to the Palais-Bourbon.

Fountain on the place de la Concorde

Pont de la Concorde – The bridge was designed in 1787 by the civil engineer, Perronet. It was completed by 1791, with the stones from the Bastille prison used in its construction so that, it was said, "the people could forever trample the ruins of the old fortress". During Louis-Philippe's reign the bridge was decorated with 12 colossal statues of famous men, but Parisians disliked them so that they were eventually dispersed to provincial towns! The bridge is classified as a UNESCO World Heritage Site, and offers a spectacular **view★★★** of the Seine and place de la Concorde, towards La Madeleine.

La DÉFENSE★★

Michelin plan 10: C 1, C 2
Central parking area: access road Défense 4 from the ring road
Ⓜ *Esplanade de la Défense (line 1),* Ⓜ*/RER: Grande Arche de la Défense (line 1/A)*
Buses: 73, 141, 144, 161, 174, 178, 258, 262, 272

The new business district of La Défense, juxtaposing traditional office space with highly experimental developments, is a truly exceptional environment. The Grande Arche stands at the extreme west of an axis along Champs-Élysées which starts at the Louvre and passes through the Arc de Triomphe.

The quarter gets its name from a monument commemorating the defence of Paris of 1871; the bronze statue by Barrias which once occupied the main roundabout before major development got under way.

The business sector – Divided into 11 zones, the 130ha/321 acre site falls within the **Puteaux, Nanterre** and **Courbevoie** districts. Since 1964 when the Esso building first opened, 48 towers have been completed and provide office space for over 900 companies.

The park area – Beyond the business area, a 90ha/222 acre site extends westwards in the Nanterre plain, to include offices, housing, sports facilities and the **parc André Malraux** (24ha/59 acres) with its botanical garden. Many of the surrounding buildings are highly original, designed by eminent architects (Théâtre des Amandiers and the Opéra Ballet School by Christian de Portzamparc).

★★ La Grande Arche ⊙ – Perhaps one of the most controversial of the *Grands Projets* instigated by President François Mitterrand, this development reaffirms the role of the French State as Patron of the Arts and design. At the western end of the podium towers the great arch, designed by Otto von Spreckelsen. It is the Danish architect's last project and the only one he completed in France. This gigantic open cube (110m/361ft wide) with its pre-stressed concrete frame, faced in glass and white Carrara marble, rises sheer without expansion joints. For technical reasons it is slightly out of alignment in relation to the La Défense-Louvre axis; the 300 000t weight is carried on 12 piles sunk in the below-ground area which is crisscrossed by communications systems. The cathedral of Notre-Dame with its spire could fit into the space between the walls of the arch.

Scenic lifts whisk visitors to the roof to enjoy a unique view of the Paris area from the terrace.

The top part of the arch is occupied by galleries, a presentation of the building of the monument, a library, a restaurant and... a belvedere offering exceptional views of **the capital's historic vista★★★** including the Arc de Triomphe, the Concorde and the Louvre.

The south vertical wall of the arch houses government ministry offices and the north wall major French and international companies.

EXPLORING THE NEIGHBOURHOOD

For all information refer to the **Info-Défense** ⊙ *in the main precinct or near the Esplanade-de-la-Défense metro exit.*

Esplanade de la Défense

This pedestrianised area provides the opportunity for a splendid **walk★★** to admire the modern architecture and 20C sculptures which are exhibited in this open-air gallery. Starting in place Carpeaux, is César's *Thumb* (**1**), whereas to the right of the Great Arch is a metal sculpture by the Japanese artist Miyawaki, consisting of 25 columns interwoven with a web of stainless-steel wire.

★ Palais de la Défense (CNIT) – The Centre for Industry and Technology, the first construction (1958) and one of the most famous of the complex, is remarkable for its sheer size and the boldness of its architecture. Its record breaking concrete vault (220m/722ft span) in the form of an inverted shell, has only three points of support, each poised on the apex of a triangle.

The building, originally designed as a venue for major trade fairs, is now a conference business centre accommodating offices, auditoriums, hotel accommodation, exhibition spaces and shopping arcades.

Further on, to the left, on place de la Défense is **Calder**'s last work, a red stabile (**2**) 15m/49ft high. Go through an opening on the left to the Fiat Tower.

Tour Framatome – Designed by a team of French and American architects, this, together with the Elf Tower, is the tallest building rising 45 storeys to 178m/584ft. Its stark form, dark, tinted windows and highly polished granite surfaces are particularly striking at night, when it appears chequered like a giant chess-board.

At the foot of the tower, *The Great Toscano* (**3**) a bronze bust by the Polish artist Mitoraj, evokes some antique giant. Pass round the tower to the left to see a sculpture (**4**) in polyester resin by Delfino inspired by the world of science fiction.

Tour Elf – This impressive building was designed by a team of French and Canadian architects. The three glass curtained towers of varying height are blue-tinted varying in intensity according to the brightness of the sky.

Return to the esplanade.

In the centre of the esplanade, the monumental **fountain by Agam** (**6**) interplays with music and floodlights at scheduled times.

The underground **Gallery** (**7**) holds art exhibitions. Pass in front of the *Midday-Midnight* pond (**8**) where the artist Clarus has decorated a ventilation shaft to represent the trajectory of the sun and moon in a *trompe-l'œil* rocky landscape.

Place des Corolles – Defined by the Europe and American International tower-blocks, this open space is named after its copper fountain, *Corolla* (**9**), sculpted by Louis Leygue. A ceramic fresco, *The Cloud Sculptor*, by Attila adorns a low wall introducing a vivid fanciful note to this concrete environment.

Les Reflets – Philolaos' *Mechanical Bird* (**12**) adorns the terrace, as he carefully folds his immense steel wings. Nearby is the **Moretti Tower**, covered in 672 differently coloured tubes. Beyond the Vision 80 Tower, built on stilts, is **place des Reflets** overlooked by and reflected in the shimmering **Aurore Tower**, in vibrant contrast with its neighbouring rose-coloured Manhattan Tower and the green GAN Tower. Note the allegory by Derbré of *The Earth* (**13**).

Tour Manhattan – This is one of the most original structures of the La Défense complex in terms of shape, colour and materials used. Designed as a series of curves and counter-curves, its smooth glazed façade mirrors the sky, its pure, elegant lines seeming cloaked in the colour of time. As restless reflections of light and movement lend a dimension of timelessness, its smooth forms and apparent weightlessness make this building truly mesmerising.

Esplanade de la Défense

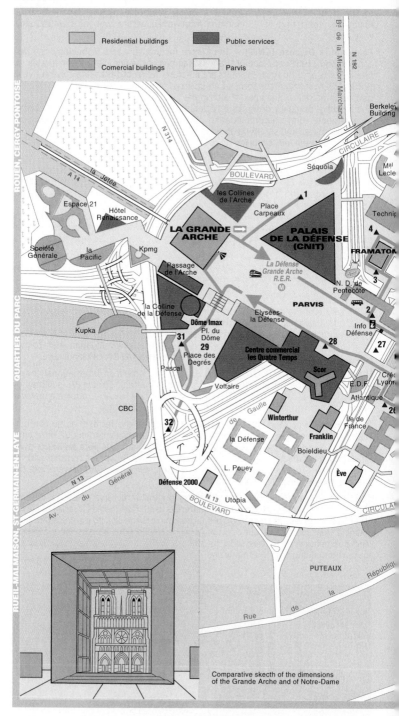

Comparative sketch of the dimensions
of the Grande Arche and of Notre-Dame

In place de l'Iris the slender silhouette of the *Sleepwalker* (**14**) balanced on a sphere poised on the ridge of a cuboid, is by H de Miller.

*Turn left in front of the **Tour GAN**, shaped like a Greek cross.*

Les Miroirs – This building is by Henri La Fonta: the fountain (**15**) in the courtyard consists of 10 cylinders decorated with mosaics. Known as the Grande Mosaïque, it is believed to be the largest mosaic in the world (2 500m²/2 990sq yd). From the patio area there is a view of the Poissons Tower with its giant clock-barometer that gives a weather reading for the Paris region (blue – variable, green – fine, red – inclement) and marks the hours with flashing lights.

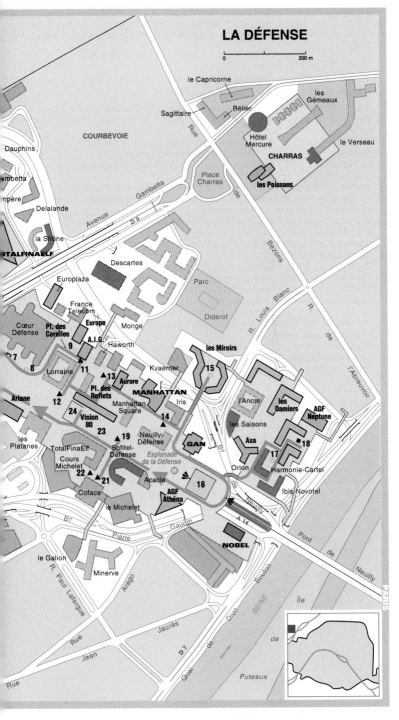

On the way note the unusual Assur Tower (UAP), shaped like a three-pronged star, designed by Pierre Dufau, and beyond the chequered layout of a residential development.

Bassin Takis (16) – East of the esplanade the Takis pond consists of a stretch of water on which the reflection of 49 multicoloured flexible light-tubes of different lengths seem to play. Pause to take in the wonderful views of the arch and of Paris.

On Square Vivaldi the *Conversation Fountain* (**17**) by Busato represents two bronze figures in animated conversation.

In place Napoleon-Ier at the foot of the Neptune Tower, a monument shaped like the Cross of the Légion d'Honneur medal (**18**) commemorates the return of the Emperor's remains from St Helena. The imperial eagle came from the railings of the Tuileries.

Return to the Takis pond.

Tour Hoechst-Marion-Roussel – This attractive blue-green, steel and glass highrise was the first to be built (1967) at La Défense.

South side – The triangular Athena Tower has sharp-angled curtain walls. The bronze low relief *Ophelia* (**19**) is by the Catalan sculptor Apel les Fenosa.

Go around the Sofitel Hotel on your left. From the terrace overlooking the square cours Michelet you can see Venet's 14m/46ft-high painted steel sculpture (**21**) and further on to the right Jakober's assemblage of welded iron resembling an American footballer's protective mask (**22**).

Further on stands a large frog-shaped fountain (**23**) with drinking water. In the square below the esplanade, 35 flower-planters (**24**) interspersed with faces and clasped hands are the work of Selinger.

The paler façade of the Ariane Tower decked in cruciform aluminium panels contrast with surrounding buildings.

A white-marble sculpture, *Lady Moon* (**26**) by Julio Silva, can be seen between the Atlantique and Crédit Lyonnais Towers; further to the right rise the tapering Défense 2000 and the white elliptical outline of the Eve Tower south of the Villon quarter.

The Scor Tower in the form of a tripod partly hides the fortress-like Winthertur and Franklin Towers (the latter comprises two abutting structures) with dark-glazed façades in a severe architectural style.

Barrias' bronze group entitled *La Défense* (**27**) has regained its original position at the foot of the monumental Agam fountain, facing westwards from where no invader has ever come.

The Quatre Temps shopping centre comprises department stores, over 250 shops, restaurants and cinemas on two levels. The building above, Élysées-La Défense, has indoor gardens.

In front of the centre is a brightly coloured monumental sculpture (**28**) of two figures by Miró.

Steps to the left of the Élysées-La Défense building lead up to the **Dôme IMAX**: at night, its lighting, designed by Yann Kersalé, is linked to road traffic by a computer device.

On place des Degrès, the sculptor Kowalski has created *a mineral landscape* (**29**): parts of pyramids, wave of granite...

A bronze *Icarus* (**31**) by César stands at the foot of the elegant IBM building.

A short distance away, *Slat* (**32**) a sculpture by R Serra consisting of five sheets of steel weighing 100t and rising 11m/36ft, has been installed at a crossroads.

DENFERT-ROCHEREAU

Michelin plan 10: M 12, M 13, N 12, N 13
Ⓜ Denfert-Rochereau (lines 4 and 6) – RER: Denfert-Rochereau (line B) –
Buses: 38, 68.

Underground are the disused quarries which became the catacombs, filled with several million skeletons... above ground is a pleasant district, with peaceful residential or commercial avenues, refashioned by Haussmann.

Nearby neighbourhoods: MONTPARNASSE, PORT-ROYAL, GOBELINS.

EXPLORING THE NEIGHBOURHOOD

The district gets its name from Colonel Denfert-Rochereau, who successfully defended Belfort in 1870-71; the event is commemorated by a reduced bronze version of Bartholdi's Lion in the middle of **place Denfert-Rochereau**.

The two elegantly proportioned buildings adorned by sculpted friezes are examples of Ledoux' city gates and toll-houses, which punctuated the wall built between 1784 and 1791.

Nearby, the partly pedestrianised **rue Daguerre** with its small shops is both attractive and lively.

Going out

Au Vin des rues – *21 rue Boulard – 14th arr – ☎ 01 43 22 19 78 – Tue, Sat 9am-11.30pm – closed two weeks in Feb, three weeks in Aug and public holidays.* This old-fashioned bistro continues to serve excellent wines in a traditional setting. The warm welcome and atmosphere make it very popular. Live accordion music on Thursday evenings.

Eating out

Turn back to the Selected restaurants section at the beginning of the guide for a list of restaurants, bistros, cafés etc. This neighbourhood is in the 14th *arrondissement.*

MUSEUMS AND OTHER ATTRACTIONS

★**Les Catacombes** ⊘ – *Entrance: 1 place Denfert-Rochereau. For access underground, a flashlight may be useful.*
These Gallo-Roman quarries were transformed into ossuaries between 1785 and 1810. Several million skeletons from the cemetery of the Innocents and other parish burial grounds were transferred here. Stacked against the walls, the skulls and crossed tibias form a macabre decoration.

At the liberation of Paris in August 1944 it was found that the Resistance Movement had established its headquarters within the catacombs.

Recent improvements have included the installation of air conditioning, dehumidifiers and better lighting.

Fondation Cartier ⊘ - *261 boulevard Raspail.* From the outside this building appears to float behind a larger panel of glass, sandwiched between street life and a garden with trees beyond. Designed by Jean Nouvel, it provides an airy, light and spacious venue for temporary exhibitions of contemporary art.

The Denfert Lion,
a well-known landmark for Parisians

EIFFEL TOWER ★★★

Michelin plan 10: J 7, J 8
Ⓜ *Bir-Hakeim (line 6), École Militaire (line 8)* –
RER: Champ-de-Mars-Tour-Eiffel (line C) – *Buses: 82, 92*

The best-loved monument in Paris, if not in the entire world, straddles the gardens that once were used for military parades, and nearby is a fine example of Classical French architecture, the École Militaire. The tower is the perfect place for a bird's-eye view of the city, to pause and enjoy the thrill of just being a part of this wonderful, beautiful and historic place!

Nearby neighbourhoods: INVALIDES, TROCADÉRO, ALMA, FAUBOURG ST-GERMAIN.

★★ EIFFEL TOWER ⊙

The Eiffel Tower, built for the Exposition Universelle of 1899, was the tallest construction in the world when it was erected, but since then its 300m/984ft have been topped by skyscrapers and telecommunication towers elsewhere. The addition of television transmitter aerials has increased its height by 20.75m/67ft.

Historical notes – The idea for a tower came to **Gustave Eiffel** (1832-1923) as a result of his study of high metal piles and their application to viaducts. The initial project dates from 1884; between 1887 and 1889 three hundred skyjacks pieced the tower together using 2.5 million rivets. Eiffel, in his enthusiasm, exclaimed "France will be the only country with a 300m flagpole!". Artists and writers, however, were appalled; the "Petition of the 300" was signed by **Charles Garnier**, architect of the Opéra, the composer Gounod, and the poets and writers François Coppée, Leconte de Lisle, Dumas the Younger and **Maupassant**. Despite the critics, its very boldness and novelty brought it also great acclaim. By the beginning of the new century it had become a subject for celebration by a new generation of poets (Apollinaire), dramatists (**Cocteau**) and painters (Pissarro, Dufy, **Utrillo**, Seurat, Marquet, Delaunay). Its distinctive outline, popularised by millions of souvenirs, is recognised the world over.

In 1909, when its planning concession expired, the tower was nearly pulled down – but saved on account of its huge antennae so vital to French radio telegraphy; from 1910 it became part of the International Time Service; by 1916 it had been made a terminal for the first radio telephone service across the Atlantic; from 1918 it was used as a transmitter for French radio and for television since 1957.

On 31 December 1999, the tower was ablaze with halogen lights and fireworks.

The tensile masterpiece – The tower weighs about 7 000t, giving a deadweight of 4kg per cm²/57lb per sq in – equal to that of a man sitting in a chair. A scale model made of steel 30cm/11.8in would weigh 7g or 1/4oz. At each re-painting, every seven years, 50t of paint are used. The sway at the top in the highest winds has never been more than 12cm/4.5in – whilst its height can vary by as much as 15cm/6in – depending on the temperature.

The visitor looking upwards through the intricate filigree of pig iron, gets an overwhelming feeling of the stupendous. There are three platforms – the first is at 57m/187ft; the second at 115m/377ft; the third at 276m/899ft – 1 652 steps in all to the top or lifts with specially designed brake attachments given the different angles of descent.

★★★ **View** – From the third platform, the view can extend 67km/42mi in ideal conditions, but it is more often hazy. Paris and its suburbs appear as on a giant map *(viewing tables)* – the best light is usually 1hr before sunset. At level 3, Eiffel's sitting room can be seen through a window. The second floor houses a restaurant, brasseries and boutiques.

An audio-visual presentation *(first floor)* retells the tower's history *(20min)*. Lift machinery from 1899 can be inspected when the corresponding lift operates in the east or west corner.

Beneath Eiffel's tower, by the north pillar, there is a bust by Bourdelle of the engineer who presented the country with one of the most visited monuments in France. At night the illuminated tower has a jewel-like quality.

Nobody now questions the tower's aesthetic appeal or its utility – it has taken its place on the capital's skyline and beckons to all who come to Paris. It is often the venue for artistic endeavours and publicity stunts.

EXPLORING THE NEIGHBOURHOOD

Once used for military parades, fairs and world exhibitions, the **Champ-de-Mars** is now a vast formal garden closed at one end by the École Militaire and at the other by the Trocadéro on Chaillot Hill. On your right, as you walk towards the École Militaire, is the **Village suisse** ⊙ *(54 avenue de la Motte-Piquet)*, a conglomeration of 150 antique and bric-a-brac shops.

The Eiffel Tower

A. ÉU/MICHELIN

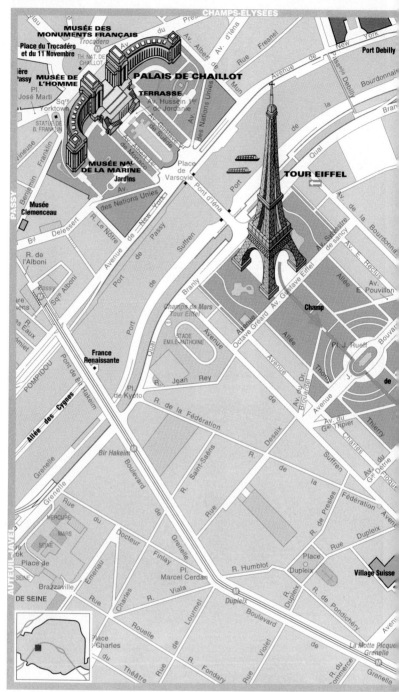

★**École militaire** – *1 place Joffre.* Thanks to **Mme de Pompadour**, Louis XV's favourite mistress, Pâris-Duverney – financier and supplier to the army – obtained permission in 1751 to found and to personally supervise the building of a Royal Military Academy where young gentlemen without means might be trained to become accomplished officers.

Jacques-Ange Gabriel, architect of the Petit Trianon at Versailles and of place de la Concorde, produced grandiose plans, which the financier duly modified. The final construction, nevertheless, remains truly magnificent when one remembers that it was designed as barracks for impoverished men!

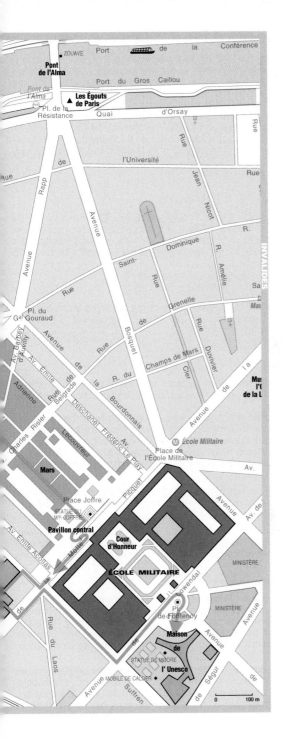

Thanks to Beaumarchais, money to pay for the building was later raised from a tax on playing cards and a lottery. In 1769 Louis XV laid the foundation stone for a chapel that was completed in 1772. Aged 15, the young cadet Bonaparte was formally sworn-in in the Academy chapel in 1784, and passed out as a lieutenant in the artillery with a report stating that he would "go far in favourable circumstances".

The military tradition – The institution was suppressed at the time of the Revolution, but the buildings have retained their status both as military quarters and as an army training centre. The Swiss Guards of the Ancien Régime, followed by the

Making the most of the tower

In summer, the best time to enjoy the view from the top is during a bright interval, immediately after a shower. However, visitors should bear in mind that the tower is the capital's prime tourist attraction and that it is therefore not always possible to plan one's visit for a specified time. There are two ways to climb the tower: up 1 652 steps... strenuous no doubt, but what a rewarding experience as one discovers the graceful architecture of the monument and gradually embraces the Champ-de-Mars, the surrounding buildings and Paris's rooftops. It is only possible to walk up to the second floor. The other way up is by the lifts, this time to the very top.

More information on www.tour-eiffel.fr.

Shopping

La Maison de l'escargot – *79 rue Fondary – 15th arr –* Ⓜ *Émile-Zola –* ☎ *01 45 75 31 09 – Tue-Sat 8.30am-7.30pm; Sun and holidays 10am-1pm – closed mid-July to end Aug.* Open since 1894, this shop only sells hand-prepared snails from Burgundy and Savoy for the *Bourgogne* and from Provence for the *petits gris.*

Eating out

Turn back to the Selected restaurants section at the beginning of the guide for a list of restaurants, bistros, cafés etc. This district is spread over the 7th and the 15th *arrondissements.*

National Guard of 1848, have been replaced by French and foreign officers attending the School of Advanced War Studies, and the Higher School for National Defence.

The impressive **central pavilion** which you see as you walk up from the Champ-de-Mars, is fronted by 10 superb Corinthian columns, each two storeys high supporting a carved pediment, with displayed trophies and allegorical figures. A fine dome crowns the whole. Low lateral wings frame the main building. The barracks on either side are 19C. Facing the central pavilion, is the equestrian statue of Marshal Joffre by Real del Sarte (1939).

Walk around the academy by way of avenue de Suffren and avenue de Lowendal to place de Fontenoy. (Lowendal commanded part of the French army, which defeated the British and Dutch at Fontenoy in 1745.)

From the semicircular square, look across the sports ground to the **main courtyard★**, lined on either side by beautiful porticoes with paired columns. At the back is the central pavilion, flanked by colonnaded buildings terminating in projecting wings.

Walk across place de Fontenoy to the right.

★ **Maison de l'UNESCO** Ⓥ **(United Nations Educational, Scientific and Cultural Organization HQ)** – *7 place de Fontenay.* The home of UNESCO was opened in 1958 and is the most truly international undertaking in Paris: the membership by 185 states and the construction of the buildings jointly by Breuer, Nervi and Zehrfuss, American, Italian and French architects respectively, demonstrate unique cooperation.

The buildings – The main building, in the form of a Y supported on piles, houses the Secretariat (sales counters in the entrance hall with souvenirs, newspapers, periodicals, coins and stamps). A second building with fluted concrete walls and an accordion-pleat-designed roof contains the conference halls and committee rooms. The small cubic construction, four storeys high, beside the Japanese garden is an administrative annexe. Additional accommodation was provided in 1965, by means of two basement floors underground, lit naturally by six low-level patios.

Decoration – The decoration is also the result of international artistic cooperation. There are frescoes by the Spaniard Picasso, and the Mexican Tamayo; tiled murals by the Spanish artists, Miró and Artigas; mosaics by the French, Bazaine and Herzell; a mosaic from El Jem in Tunisia (2C); a relief by Jean Arp; tapestries by Lurçat and by the Franco-Swiss **Le Corbusier**; a Japanese fountain by Noguchi and an angel's head from a Nagasaki church destroyed by the atom bomb in 1945. A monumental statue, *Figure in Repose* by **Henry Moore**, can be viewed from avenue de Suffren.

Les GOBELINS

You may have admired Gobelins tapestries hanging in many of the great museums and great houses, but the history of their manufacture is less well known. An opportunity to see these national treasures being made in the traditional style is not to be missed.

History – In about 1440 the dyer, Jean Gobelin, who specialised in scarlet, set up a workshop beside the River Bièvre. This continued through the generations until the reign of Henri IV when it was taken over by two Flemish craftsmen, summoned by the king (early 17C).

Colbert, charged by Louis XIV with the reorganisation of the tapestry and carpet-weaving industry, grouped the Paris and Maincy factories (at Vaux-le-Vicomte) around the Gobelins workshops thereby creating, in 1662, the Manufacture Royale des Tapisseries de la Couronne (Royal Factory of Tapestry and Carpet Weavers to the Crown). The artist, Charles Le Brun, was appointed as director. Five years later it became associated with the Manufacture Royale des Meubles (Royal Cabinet-Makers). The greatest craftsmen, including goldsmiths and gilders, thus worked side by side to decorate and furnish the sumptuous palaces of the Sun King and create a Louis XIV style.

Over the past 300 years more than 5 000 tapestries have been woven at the Gobelins factory from cartoons by the greatest painters – Le Brun, Poussin, Van Loo, Mignard, Boucher, Lurçat, **Picasso**...

The **Savonnerie** (1604-1826) and **Beauvais** (1664-1940) carpet and tapestry factories have also, over the years, been incorporated.

In 1989, the Manufacture des Gobelins accepted a commission from Denmark for 10 large tapestries illustrating the history of the country to be offered to Queen Margrethe as a birthday gift. It took the Manufacture 10 years to complete the order.

★MANUFACTURE DES GOBELINS ⊙

42 avenue des Gobelins

Working methods have changed little since the 17C: warp threads are set by daylight, the colours being selected from a range of over 14 000 tones. Each weaver, working with mirrors, completes from 1 to 8m²/1 to 8sq yd per year depending on the design. The workshop's entire production goes to the State.

The four great French Tapestry workshops

Aubusson: producing hangings for the lesser 17C and 18C aristocracy and bourgeoisie; subject matter includes floral and organic compositions, animals and beasts, Classical mythology and landscapes. Rococo Chinoiseries and pastoral scenes (after Huet) are also common.

Beauvais: very finely woven often with vivid coloured silks which, unfortunately, have faded. Motifs include grotesques, Fables after La Fontaine (by Oudry), Boucher's figures from the Commedia dell'Arte, Classical mythology, Chinoiseries, and pastoral scenes (after Huet). The use of 18C designs continued into the 19C.

Felletin: coarser weave hangings with rustic subject matter.

Gobelins: sumptuous hangings often interwoven with gold. Renowned for the originality of design, series include The Seasons and Elements, The Life of the King, The Royal Residences, Louis XV at the Hunt, as well as paintings by Oudry and Boucher (Loves of the Gods). Their most influential weaver during the late 18C was Neilson, a Scot.

EXPLORING THE NEIGHBOURHOOD

Starting in place d'Italie and finishing at the Gobelins workshop.

Place d'Italie – The square marks the site of one of the toll-houses built by **Ledoux**. Today it stands on the edge of an area bristling with high-rise buildings. At the corner of avenue d'Italie and rue Bobillot stands the audio-visual centre attached to the Italie 2 complex, housing one of France's largest cinema screens.

Take boulevard Blanqui, then follow rue du Moulin-des-Près (first left) as far as place Paul-Verlaine.

La Butte-aux-Cailles – On 21 November 1783, after taking off from the vicinity of La Muette, the physicist **Pilâtre de Rozier** landed his hot-air balloon on this mound, then occupied by several solitary windmills. This was the first free-flight in a hot-air balloon.

The Manufacture

It is most advisable to arrive 20min before your guided tour is due to depart because large groups are frequent, even during the week. The visit lasts some 2hr and there is nowhere to sit down. This tour is not very suitable for young children.

Going out

The Butte-aux-Cailles is a lively, Bohemian style district and abounds with little bars, cafés and restaurants.

La Folie en Tête – *33 rue de la Butte-aux-Cailles – 13th arr – ☎ 01 45 80 65 99 – daily 5pm-2am (except Sun)*. The musical instruments hung on the walls keep watch over this pleasant spot where visitors can play chess, draw, discuss or listen to music. Young crowd.

Shopping

Cave des Gobelins – *56 av. des Gobelins – 13th arr – Ⓜ Gobelins or Place d'Italie – ☎ 01 43 31 66 79 – ericmerlet@aol.com – Tue-Sat 9am-1pm, 3-8pm, public holidays 9am-1pm*. Following in the footsteps of his father, the equally friendly Eric Merlet has taken over the management of this exceptional wine cellar, with among others, a few very rare vintage spirits (including a cognac from 1809!) together with a selection of practically every fine wine produced over the last 40 years.

Eating out

Turn back to the Selected restaurants section at the beginning of the guide for a list of restaurants, bistros, cafés etc. This district is spread over the 5th and the 13th *arrondissements*.

Today the district is one of surprising contrasts as badly paved streets and low-lying houses slowly give way to modern blocks of flats with new urban development encroaching upon traditional village life.

Take rue de la Butte-aux-Cailles, then turn right along rue Barrault.

Square René-le-Gall – *Cross boulevard Auguste-Blanqui and take rue Corvisart.* Rue de Croulebarbe and rue Berbier-du-Mets drive the River **Bièvre** underground. Up to the 17C the willow-bordered stream was of sparkling clear water, and ice taken from the surrounding marshes during the winter was packed into wells and then covered with earth. It was this activity that gave the locality its name, **Glacière**, meaning ice house. Dyeing, tanning and bleaching turned the river into a murky evil-smelling stream and in 1910 it was filled in.

Exit via rue de Croulebarbe (north-west)

The **Mobilier national** building is by Auguste Perret (1935) and the two concrete hounds are by André Abbel. A plaque on the wall of an old house opposite the Mobilier National recalls the famous 15C Gobelins dye-works.

Follow the first street on the left, rue Berbier-du-Mets then continue along rue G.-Geffroy.

The **Hôtel de la Reine-Blanche** *(no 17; restoration work in progress)* was probably named after Blanche de Bourgogne, the unfaithful wife of Charles IV. It was here in 1393 that Charles VI was almost burnt alive at one of the many festivities organised on his physicians' orders in an attempt to cure his insanity.

Rue G.-Geffroy leads to avenue des Gobelins.

CHINA TOWN

On the southern side of place d'Italie, on the corner of avenue de Choisy and avenue Edison is the Tang Frères shop, a good introduction to the Asian quarter, which lies between avenue de Choisy, avenue d'Ivry and boulevard Masséna, and there are many Chinese, Japanese and Vietnamese restaurants nearby. The district may not quite have all the charms of Chinatown in San Francisco or London, but it is lively and entertaining.

Les GRANDS BOULEVARDS★

Michelin plan 10: G 11 – G 17
Ⓜ Richelieu Drouot (lines 8 and 9), Strasbourg-St Denis (lines 4, 8 and 9),
République (lines 3, 5, 8, 9 and 11) – Buses: 20, 38, 39, 47, 48

Thronged with pedestrians hurrying on business or idly window gazing, the broad tree-lined avenues full of cars, café tables spilling out onto the pavement, innumerable cinemas, theatres and a thousand shops, a profusion of signs, advertising slogans, glowing flashing neon at night: in short the Boulevards – the atmosphere lives on.

Nearby neighbourhoods: OPÉRA, FAUBOURG POISSONNIÈRE, RÉPUBLIQUE.

The ramparts transformed – Between the Bastille and Porte St-Denis stretched the city walls built by **Charles V**; between Porte St-Denis and the present Madeleine extended ramparts built by Charles IX and Louis XIII. By 1660, the fortifications rendered obsolete by **Louis XIV**'s victories had fallen into disrepair; these were dismantled and the ditches filled in. The land was terraced, a broad carriageway was built to accommodate four carriages riding abreast, two side roads for pedestrian traffic were laid flanking the carriageway, and planted with double rows of trees. Triumphal arches, symbols of Peace, replaced the fortified gates. Construction was completed in 1705.

The name boulevard was coined from the military term for a terreplein (sloping bank behind a rampart used by the artillery). At first the area surrounded by open countryside remained deserted; safe for the odd game of *boules* by day, unsafe after dark.

The fashionable stroll – Around 1750 the boulevard became fashionable: Parisians took to cane-seated chairs in the shade to watch out for the new glazed carriages and for gentry on horseback.

At the western end of the boulevard, the nobility and the well-heeled started to build themselves fine town houses. Under the Directoire, boulevard des Italiens, then boulevard Montmartre, began to be frequented by members of High Society; they became known as *Boulevardiers* – an epithet for ephemeral, superficial creatures that flirted with fad and fashion.

Improvements – The roads were paved in 1778, and gas lamps appeared in passage des Panoramas in 1817, and along the boulevard in 1826. The first omnibus appeared on 30 January 1828 linking the Madeleine to the Bastille. Finally, pavements were asphalted to reduce the quagmire on rainy days.

The modern boulevards – **Haussmann**'s radical urban planning transformed the area by inserting broad avenues between place de l'Opéra and place de la République. Street lighting, shop illuminations and other urban renovations further altered the area. The attributes of fashion changed ceaselessly through the years, but the colours, the noise and the bustle are constants. The area boasts a number of famous theatres and night spots.

EXPLORING THE NEIGHBOURHOOD

From place de l'Opéra to place de la République.

Boulevard des Italiens – The history of this thoroughfare is inextricably linked with that of fashion. At the time of the Directoire, the area was haunted by *Muscadins* – bow-legged and hunched fops in exaggerated garb; *Merveilleuses* dressed in high-waisted, transparent dresses in the style of Antiquity or with huge extravagant Turkish-style hats. During the Restoration, these were followed by the *Gandins*, moustachioed with side-whiskers, in top hat, cravat and jacket with broad turned-down collar. Under **Louis-Philippe**, the *Dandys* and the *Lions* followed the fashion from across the Channel: they began to smoke in public (1835). The Second Empire was a more sober age, waxed moustaches and close-cut goatee beards appeared, ladies sported crinolines and café society flourished.

Shopping

À la Mère de Famille – *35 rue du Fg-Montmartre – 9th arr* – Ⓜ *Le Peletier or Grands Boulevards* – ☎ *01 47 70 83 69 – Tue-Sat 9am-1.30pm, 3-7pm – closed public holidays and Aug.* This grocery-cum-sweet shop is steeped in history. The decoration, which has not changed since 1900, endows the place with a mysterious charm, enhanced by the odour of dried fruits and sugared almonds prepared at the back of the shop.

Eating out

Turn back to the Selected restaurants section at the beginning of the guide for a list of restaurants, bistros, cafés etc. This district is spread over the 2nd, 9th and the 10th *arrondissements*.

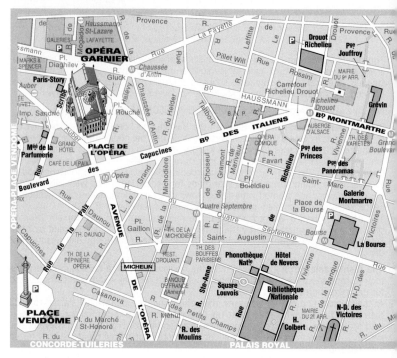

Today the area is popular for the proliferation of cinemas and chain restaurants, which have gradually slipped in between banking headquarters. The Crédit Lyonnais and BNP banks in particular have attractive façades (between rue Taitbout and Laffitte).

On reaching the latter, there is a good view★ of Sacré-Coeur.

Just off boulevard des Italiens, along rue Favart, stands the **Opéra-Comique**, its façade overlooking place Boeldieu. The present edifice was erected on the site of the theatre built in 1782 by the Duc de Choiseul for the company that had recently moved out of the ruined Hôtel de Bourgogne. The troupe became known as the Italians, hence the name of the boulevard. A couple of restaurants along rue Favart are the favourite haunt of music lovers.

Boulevard Montmartre – Particularly lively. On the right at no 11 is **passage des Panoramas** which was opened in 1799 and leads to the Stock Exchange (La Bourse). At no **47** in the arcade an engraver's shop retains its old-fashioned frontage. **Passage Jouffroy** at no 10 is also worth a visit. The street is full of small restaurants and interesting shops.

Follow boulevard Poissonnière and boulevard de Bonne-Nouvelle.

The atmosphere is slightly quieter, but a visit to the **Cinéma Grand Rex** is a must: a genuine temple to the glory of the silver screen, its baroque decor and its large screen make the building one of Europe's landmark cinemas.

 Les Étoiles du Rex, a walk-through feature, opened in 1997. This 50min interactive tour reveals the backstage legends and stars of Europe's most famous film theatre. Special effects, sounds, and sets all combine to put the visitor in the heart of the action – quite literally!

The cinema's annexe, the Cinémathèque Française, across the street at no 42, is also worth a look.

Just before Porte St-Denis, the **view★** of the crossroads of rue Cléry, rue Beauregard and rue de la Lune gives an idea of what Paris must have looked like in the 19C.

★**Porte St-Denis** – 24m/75ft high. The gate was erected at the city's expense in 1672 to celebrate Louis XIV's victorious campaigns on the Rhine when 40 strongholds were captured in less than two months. Along the top, pyramids are decked with trophies; then, on the boulevard side, allegorical figures represent Holland *(left)* and the Rhine *(right)* with panels depicting the crossing of the Rhine; and on the Faubourg side, the Fall of Maastricht.

★**Porte St-Martin** – The gate was erected in 1674 to commemorate the capture of Besançon and defeat of the German, Spanish and Dutch armies. A mere 17m/56ft high, the arch was designed by Pierre Bullet to bear carvings by

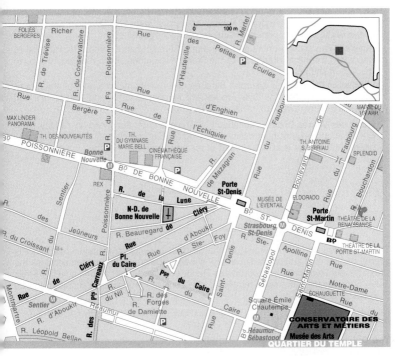

eminent artists who had worked at Versailles. Desjardins, Le Hongre, Marsy and Legros illustrate *(boulevard side)* the taking of Besançon, the breaking of the Triple Alliance, *(other side)* the capture of Limburg and the defeat of the Germans.

Boulevard St-Martin – This leads down to place de la République. The area was built up on an old rubbish dump, hence the undulations and the need for laying the road at a different gradient and level from the pavements. The boulevard runs past place J Strauss *(on the left)* adorned with a bust of the famous Viennese composer.

Porte St-Denis

MUSEUMS AND OTHER ATTRACTIONS

★ **Musée Grévin** ⊘ – *10 boulevard Montmartre.*

Grévin, a caricaturist, founded the museum in 1882. (The first waxworks were introduced to Paris in the 18C.) In addition to waxen effigies of famous politicians, artists and sports-people and re-creations of momentous historical and contemporary events in the form of tableaux, there is a hall of mirrors. Live conjuring sessions also add to the magical entertainment on offer.

Palais des Mirages – (Performances are announced by loudspeaker, but don't worry about getting a seat, as there is plenty of space). The sound and light show dates from 1900, but is still fascinating, with the coloured lights being infinitely reflected by 360° mirrors.

Le Théâtre du Tout-Paris – Prominent figures from the world of politics and cinema, including Gérard Depardieu and Roberto Begnini, are displayed in this late-19C theatre.

Paris Grévin Magazine – From the Élysée Palace, where all the major statesmen are gathered, to the artist's studio where Rodin can be seen at work, stars of yesterday and today are shown in their respective environments.

Les Clichés du 20e s. – Around 10 tableaux illustrate the main events of the 20C: the World Football Cup, the rise of Nazism, Man's first steps on the moon, the collapse of the Berlin Wall, the ascent of Anapurna, modern cuisine...

Histoire – This section offers an illustration of French history from Charlemagne to Napoleon, from the Inquisition to the French Revolution, from the Renaissance to the Age of the Enlightenment.

La Collection Grévin – This beautiful Baroque gallery is home to a host of stars, both living and dead, such as Elvis Presley and Marilyn Monroe, and also to real and imaginary characters such as Lara Croft.

Hôtel des Ventes Drouot Richelieu ⊘ – *9 rue Drouot*. Reopened on 13 May 1980 the 16 auction rooms hold business daily at 2pm in a lively and interesting atmosphere. Rue Drouot is also the haunt of stamp collectors.

Les HALLES

Michelin plan 10: H 14, H 15
Ⓜ *Les Halles (line 4) – RER: Châtelet-les-Halles (lines A, B and D) –*
Buses: 29, 38, 47

The demolition and displacement of the City's main wholesale market has radically altered the area's character. Today, a busy shopping centre with a garden occupies the site of the old trade halls, once known as The Belly of Paris (the title of a novel by Émile Zola). Some of the old streets remain, as does one of Paris' most beautiful churches, St-Eustache.

Nearby neighbourhoods: BEAUBOURG, CHÂTELET-HÔTEL DE VILLE, PALAIS-ROYAL, PLACE DES VICTOIRES, RÉPUBLIQUE (Temple).

The Old Halles – In 1135 there was already a twice-weekly market at Les Halles, where each street specialised in a particular trade. By the 16C, with a growing population of 300 000 in the capital, the trade in food-stuffs became of paramount importance, eventually replacing all other types of trade in the market. On the orders of Napoleon, the wine and leather markets were transferred to the Left Bank.
Until the Revolution, a pillory stood near St-Eustache crossroads; dishonest traders, thieves and prostitutes were publicly exposed there.
By the 19C the great market was in urgent need of reconstruction. As Rambuteau and Haussmann thrust wide avenues through the quarter (rue de Rivoli, rue du Pont-Neuf, rue du Louvre, rue des Halles, rue Étienne-Marcel), the architects **Baltard** and **Callet** designed plans for a hall of iron girders and skylight roofs, which were accepted by Napoleon III.
Ten halls in all were constructed (1854-74) and the buildings became the model for covered markets throughout France and abroad. The animated market scene and the rich variety of colour and smell are vividly described in Zola's novel. Locals enjoyed eating onion soup, snails and pig's trotters at 5am in simple but excellent restaurants with colourful names (Le Chien qui Fume, Le Pied de Cochon). As the old buildings became inadequate, they were demolished and removed, and the market was relocated to the outskirts of the city at Rungis (1969). One of the original buildings (the Pavillon Baltard) has been re-erected at Nogent-sur-Marne.

Forum des Halles and St-Eustache Church

Concerts

Église Saint-Eustache – Regular concerts *(see the posters outside)* of organ music played by today's masters Jean Guillou and André Fleury, directed by Father Martin.

Activities for children

⬚ **Le jardin des enfants** – *105 r. Rambuteau – 1st arr –* Ⓜ *Châtelet – ☎ 01 45 08 17 18 – children from 7 to 11 – school holidays: 9am-6pm; outside school holidays: Tue, Thu, Fri 9am-noon, 2-6pm, Wed and Sat 10am-6pm, Sun 1-6pm (except Nov-Mar: closes at 4pm).* As the name suggests, activities of all sorts for children take place here. It is also true that only children can actually find their way round the maze, swim in the ball pool etc.

Going out

Duc des Lombards – *42 rue des Lombards – 1st arr – ☎ 01 42 33 22 88 – daily 6.30pm, concert 9pm.* Modern jazz has pride of place in this small room on boulevard Sébastopol. Some of its regulars include the pianist Martial Solal, bass player Henri Texier, saxophonist Steve Lacy and drummer Aldo Romano.

Le Bistrot d'Eustache – *37 rue Berger – 1st arr – ☎ 01 40 26 23 20 – daily all night long.* Off the beaten track, this bistro-pub can seem a little forlorn at night, but its remoteness is more than compensated by the soft lights and good jazz: live music on Thursday, Friday and Saturday evenings.

Shopping

Agnès B. – *6 rue du Jour – 1st arr –* Ⓜ *Les Halles – ☎ 01 45 08 56 56 – agnesb.fr – Mon-Sat 10am-7pm in the winter, 10am-7.30pm in the summer – closed public holidays.* Clothes for men, women and children, accessories and jewellery. All of Agnès B's collections can be found behind one of the elegant windows of the five shops which line this little street.

La Droguerie – *9-11 rue du Jour – 1st arr –* Ⓜ *Les Halles – Mon 2-6.45pm, Tue-Sat 10.30am-6.45pm.* This shop stocks absolutely everything necessary for the budding dress or jewellery maker.

Eating out

Turn back to the Selected restaurants section at the beginning of the guide for a list of restaurants, bistros, cafés etc. This neighbourhood is spread over the 1st and the 2nd *arrondissements.*

EXPLORING THE NEIGHBOURHOOD

Galerie Véro-Dodat, just off rue Jean-Jacques-Rousseau, was one of the first streets in Paris to have gas lighting installed along it. It was created in 1826 by two eponymous pork butchers. Today the high-quality shops have an old-fashioned air.

Turn left along rue Jean-Jacques-Rousseau, to reach place des Deux-Écus, whose buildings still retain their original façades.

La Bourse du Commerce – *2 rue de Viarmes.* The circular Commercial Exchange building is hemmed in to the west by a semicircle of tall porticoed mansions and to the east by gardens and the Forum. A wheat market built in Louis XVI's reign was replaced in 1889 by the present rotunda. Inside, the vast circular hall lit by a glass dome is reserved for accredited commodity brokers.

Jardin des Halles – A garden (5ha/12 acres) includes pergolas along rue Berger, children's play areas and a tree-lined mall linking the semicircular area by St-Eustache, where a massive 70t stone head *(Écoute)* by H de Miller stands.

★★Church of St-Eustache – *Place du Jour.* Gothic in plan and structure, but Renaissance in decoration, this is one of Paris' most beautiful churches.
In 1214 a chapel dedicated to St Agnes was built on this spot. A few years later, the chapel was rededicated to St Eustace, a converted Roman general. But the Halles parish, which had become the biggest in Paris, dreamed of a church worthy of its new status. Grandiose plans were made and the foundation stone was laid in 1532. Construction was slow, however, in spite of liberal gifts and the church was not consecrated until a century later, in 1640. The **west front** was never completed but later rebuilt in the Classical style (1754). In 1844 the edifice was badly damaged by fire and subsequently restored by **Baltard**.

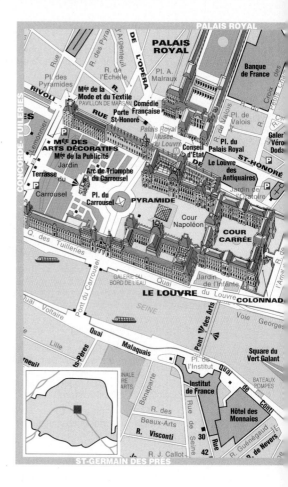

★ **North transept façade** – This fine Renaissance composition is flanked by twin staircase turrets ending in pinnacles. Beneath the gable point is a stag's head with a Cross between the antlers recalling St Eustace's conversion. The statues on the door shafts are modern. The pilasters, niches, mouldings, grotesques and roses are delicately fashioned.

Interior – St-Eustache measures 100x44x34m/328x144112ft. The church's majesty and rich decoration are striking.

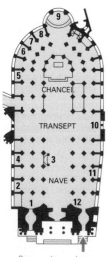

Rue   du   Jour

The plan is that of Notre-Dame with nave and chancel encircled by double aisles and flat transepts. The vaulting above the nave, transept and chancel is Flamboyant, adorned with numerous ribs and richly carved hanging keystones.

The elevation, however, is entirely different from the cathedral's. The aisles, devoid of galleries, rise very high, the arches being so tall that between them and the clerestory windows there is space only for a small Renaissance-style gallery.

The stained-glass windows in the chancel are after cartoons by Philippe de Champaigne (1631). St Eustace appears at the centre, surrounded by the Fathers of the Church and the Apostles.

The chapels are decorated with frescoes.

1) On the door tympanum: the *Martyrdom of St Eustace* by Simon Vouet (17C).

2) *Adoration of the Magi*, a copy of a painting by **Rubens**.

3) Churchwarden's pew presented by the Regent, Philippe of Orleans in 1720.

4) Colourful naïve sculpture by R Mason commemorating the fruit and vegetable market's move out of Paris on 28 February 1969.

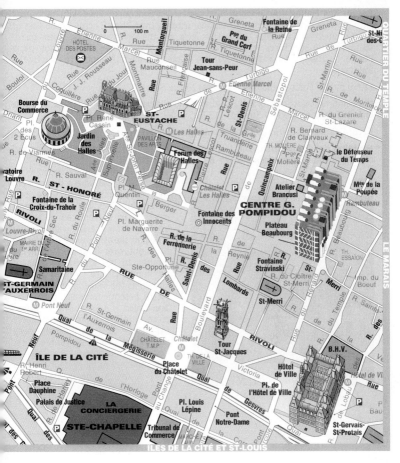

5) *Tobias and the Angel*, by Santi di Tito (16C).

6) *The Ecstasy of Mary Magdalen*, a painting by Manetti (17C).

7) *The Pilgrims at Emmaüs*, an early Rubens.

8) Colbert's tomb designed by **Le Brun**; **Coysevox** carved the statues of the minister and of Abundance; Tuby that of Fidelity (left).

9) Statue of the Virgin by **Pigalle**. Chapel frescoes by Thomas Couture (19C).

10) 16C statue of St John the Evangelist.

11) Bust of the composer **Jean-Philippe Rameau** who died in 1764.

12) Epitaph to 17C Lieutenant-General Chevert.

Walk down the narrow rue du Jour (no 4 once belonged to Montmorency-Bouteville who was beheaded in 1628 for contravening Richelieu's ban on duelling) *then turn right onto rue Montmartre.*

From no 3 and 4 rue Montmartre there are fine views of the church (east-end buttresses and Lady Chapel, restored spire surmounting the campanile).

At the end of rue Montmartre, turn left along rue Montorgueil, then take the first right.

Rue Mauconseil – In 1548 a theatre was built on land belonging to the Hôtel de Bourgogne to the left of the street. The troupe excluded women players until 1634 during which time female roles were played by men in masks. Racine first presented *Mithridate* and *Iphigénie* in this theatre. The last troupe to play in the theatre before it disappeared was the Comic-Opera (1716-82).

Turn left to reach rue Étienne-Marcel.

Tour de Jean-sans-Peur – At no 20 stands a square machicolated tower *(closed to the public)* built by John the Fearless for his own protection in 1409 following the assassination, on his orders, of the Duke of Orléans. The tower formed part of the **Hôtel de Bourgogne**. Note the carved vaulting of the staircase leading to the bedrooms.

Rue de Turbigo (on the right) leads to the Forum des Halles.

Forum des Halles – An underground pedestrian concourse, lined with shops and with direct access to the metro stations, extends over 7ha/17 acres to the east of the Commercial Exchange. At garden level, on the north and east sides, palm-shaped metal structures house public amenities (Pavillon des Arts, Maison de la Poésie...). There is a good view over the whole area from the upper terrace by the fountain.

Leave by the Porte du Louvre and cross to rue Sauval.

Opposite, on the corner of rue St-Honoré and rue de l'Arbre-Sec is the **Fontaine de la Croix-du-Trahoir** created by Soufflot (1775).

Return along rue St-Honoré to place Marguerite-de-Navarre.

★**Fontaine des Innocents** – The 19C square stands on the site of the cemetery and church of the Holy Innocents which dated back to the 12C.

The cemetery was once encircled by a charnel house where bones from the communal graves were collected. In 1786, the cemetery was closed – to be replaced by a fruit and vegetable market – and nearly 2 million skeletons were transferred by night over a period of many months to the former quarries of La Tombe-Issoire, which became known as the Catacombs.

Pierre Lescot's fountain, carved by **Jean Goujon**, is a Renaissance master-piece. In 1550, it stood at the corner of rue St-Denis against a wall requiring it to have only three sides; when the cemetery was closed, it was removed to its present site and given a fourth side by Pajou (the original low-relief sculptures are in the Louvre).

Fontaine des Innocents

INSTITUT DE FRANCE★★

Michelin plan 10: J 13
Ⓜ *Pont-Neuf (line 7), Odéon (lines 4 and 10) –
Buses: 24, 27, 58, 70*

The Institut is one of the gems of the Left Bank, though visiting this seat of learning is not easy; among the five academies housed within its walls is the renowned Académie Française. The building is best admired from the Pont des Arts, and the surrounding streets contain souvenirs of Molière, Racine and Balzac.

Nearby neighbourhoods: ODÉON, QUARTIER LATIN, ST-GERMAIN-DES-PRÉS, MUSÉE D'ORSAY, LE LOUVRE.

A prestigious legacy – The building we admire today came into being as a result of a legacy. In 1661, three days before he died, Cardinal Mazarin made final bequests from his immense wealth: he left 2 million *livres* for the foundation of a college for 60 scholars from the four provinces (Piedmont, Alsace, Artois and Roussillon) acquired by France under his ministry.

The Institute was founded in 1795 by the Convention, transferred from the Louvre by Napoleon in 1805. It consists of five academies: the Académie Française, founded by Richelieu in 1635 and the Académies des Inscriptions et Belles Lettres (1663), Sciences (1666), Beaux-Arts (1816) and Sciences morales et Politiques (1832).

Académie française – This is perhaps the most famous academy, best known by linguists for safeguarding the French language from *franglais*. The main activity of the 40 *immortels* is the constant revision of the definitive Dictionary of the French Language.

MUSEUMS AND OTHER ATTRACTIONS

★★ Institut de France – *23 quai de Conti. (See illustration page 94)*. A magnificent dome distinguishes the building from afar. The central Jesuit-styled chapel is flanked by two square pavilions designed by **Le Vau**, architect of the Louvre. The drum of the dome bears the Mazarin coat of arms: a lictor's fasces (a bundle of rods, among them an axe, used as a symbol of authority by ancient Roman magistrates), and a leather strap (his father was a saddler).

In the courtyard, to the left of the dome, is the **Mazarin Library★**.

Interior – The former chapel is now the formal audience chamber where members are sworn in. The Mazarin commemorative monument is by **Coysevox**.

A second courtyard is surrounded by the buildings where the scholars once lived; whereas the courtyard of the former kitchens still has its old well.

Stairway in the Hôtel des Monnaies

★ Hôtel des Monnaies et Médailles ⊘ – *11 quai Conti*. In the 18C Louis XV installed the Mint here, selecting the architect, **Antoine**, to design the workshops which were built between 1768 and 1775. The simplicity of line, sober rustication and restrained decoration was praised by the contemporary public, tired of excessive Classical orders and colonnades. Antoine's immediate success seconded him to the Academy of Architecture.

Before being transferred to Pessac (Gironde), the Ministry of Finance used to have all France's currency struck in the workshops. These still cast editions of collection pieces, dies for the Assay and Weights and Measures offices; medals and decorations are still produced here.

The **Coin Museum** *(back of main courtyard)* occupies the refurbished minting and milling halls. Exhibits retrace the history of French coin making and minting from 300 BC and includes the art of medal making which developed in the 16C under Italian influence. A fine collection of coins, medals, banking documentation, paintings, engravings and drawings illustrate various political, social and financial developments. In the laminating section, note the different weighing scales and the 1807 Uhlhorn steam-driven press.

EXPLORING THE NEIGHBOURHOOD

2 Around the Institut de France *See map p 321.*

Quai des Grands-Augustins – The oldest quay in Paris dates from 1313, and derives its name from the Great Augustine monastery established by St Louis in the 13C on a nearby site which extended across the waterfront between rue des Grands-Augustins and rue Dauphine. No 53 used to be the Paris Omnibus Co headquarters. Note, as you pass, two 17C mansions: no **51**, now the famous Lapérouse Restaurant, and no **35**, the former Hôtel Feydeau-Montholon.

At the beginning of quai de Conti, turn left onto rue de Nevers.

Rue de Nevers – Between nos **3** and **1** quai de Conti is this curious, picturesque alley created in the 13C which maintains its medieval character. It abuts a fragment of the old wall built by Philippe Auguste around the city.

Take rue de Nesle to rue Dauphine, then passage Dauphine, full of old-world charm, which comes out onto rue Mazarine.

Rue Mazarine – A narrow street containing small art galleries. As you leave the passage, look at the building opposite; it is decorated with statues perched on stilts. No **42**, formerly an indoor real tennis court converted into the **Guénégaud Theatre**, was where opera was presented for the first time in France in 1671.

At no **30**, the first Paris **fire station** was home to the capital's first fire brigade created in 1722 by François Dumouriez du Perrier.

INSTITUT DE FRANCE

Going out

Hôtel d'Aubusson (Café Laurent) – *33 rue Dauphine – 6th arr – ☎ 01 43 29 43 43 – www.hoteldaubusson.com – daily 7am-midnight.* Located in the former Grands Augustins convent, this café was very popular among 18C philosophers. Renamed the Café Tabou in 1946, it became one of the favourite haunts of Sartre and Camus. Today a modern room opens onto one of the former period rooms with original beams (1606) and hearthplace. For tea and a quiet read. Live music at weekends.

Art

Rue de Seine – *Rue de Seine – 6th arr –* Ⓜ *Mabillon.* A large number of art galleries line rue de Seine and neighbouring streets (rue des Beaux-Arts, rue Visconti, rue Jacob, rue Jacques-Callot etc). Maps can be obtained in each gallery.

Eating out

Turn back to the Selected restaurants section at the beginning of the guide for a list of restaurants, bistros, cafés etc. This neighbourhood is in the 6th *arrondissement.*

At no **12**, beyond square G.-Pierné stood a theatre where **Molière** made his first appearance as an actor; after his death, his troupe moved to no 42.
Take rue J.-Callot to reach rue Visconti.

Rue Visconti – This narrow alleyway was known in the 16C as Little Geneva because many Protestants, including the distinguished ceramist Bernard Palissy (c 1510-90), lived in its vicinity. 17C cabaret at no **26**. The playwright **Racine** died at no **24** in 1699. Two hundred years later, Balzac founded a printing house at no **17** (1826) which soon went bankrupt. Later still, **Delacroix** had his studio here from 1836 to 1844.

Rue Jacob – A street of old houses, home to antiques shops, publishers and interior decorators.
Take rue des Saints-Pères to reach quai Malaquais and turn right.

Quai Malaquais – The École nationale supérieure des Beaux-Arts *(on your right)* has stood here since 1816. On the corner with rue Bonaparte at no **9** stands a 17C stone and brick house, visited by Manon Lescaut in the story by Abbé Prévost.
The writer Anatole France (1844-1924) was born at no **19** (plaque on no **15**), which also served George Sand between 1832 and 1836, when she wrote *Lélia.*

Pont des Arts – The bridge dating from 1803 was the first to be built of iron and the first to be exclusively for pedestrians. Chairs were made available between orange trees in pots for people to pause and watch the river. Access was subject to a toll of one *sou* as for most of the Paris bridges, levied until 1849. Its success was immediate: 65 000 Parisians paid to walk over it the day it opened. The present construction is of steel and has only seven arches instead of the original eight.
The **view★★★** is outstanding, encompassing the full length of Pont Neuf and the Île de la Cité including Notre-Dame; downstream the Louvre, the Grand Palais and the Carrousel Bridge.

Quai de Conti – It begins at rue Dauphine and extends past the Mint and the Institut de France. Bookstalls line the opposite side.

Les INVALIDES★★★

Michelin plan 10: H 10, J 10, K 10
Ⓜ *Invalides (line 13), Varenne (line 13), St-François-Xavier (line 13) –*
Buses: 28, 48, 49, 69, 82, 92, 93

This fine neighbourhood elbowing the Faubourg St-Germain is endowed with elegant buildings that include the most outstanding single monumental group in Paris: the noble Dôme church that houses the tomb of **Napoleon** and the adjacent Army Museum endowed with its rich and spectacular collections.

Nearby neighbourhoods: FAUBOURG ST-GERMAIN, MUSÉE D'ORSAY, SÈVRES-BABYLONE, CHAMPS-ÉLYSÉES, TOUR EIFFEL.

Barracks for 4 000 men – Before Louis XIV's reign, old or invalid soldiers, were, in theory, looked after in convent hospitals. In reality, most were reduced to beggary.
In 1670 the Sun King founded the Invalides on the edge of what was then the Grenelle Plain. Funds were raised in part by a levy on serving soldiers' pay over a period of five years. Construction of the vast edifice capable of providing quarters for 4 000 took five years (1671-76). The original plans were by **Libéral Bruant**; a dome designed by **Jules Hardouin-Mansart** was added in 1706, lifting the overall effect from the strictly utilitarian to the monumental.

Pillage – On the morning of 14 July 1789 rebels advanced on the Invalides in search of arms. They crossed the moat, disarmed the sentries and entered the underground rifle stores. As further crowds blocked the stairs fierce fighting broke out in the semi-darkness. The mob finally made off with 28 000 rifles and hurried towards the Bastille.

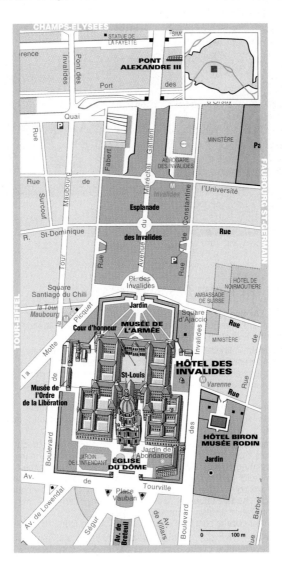

Napoleon's return – In 1793, the Revolution transformed the two churches, which were still adjoined, into a Temple to Mars, and had the captured enemy standards transferred there from Notre-Dame. When Napoleon had Marshal Turenne (d 1675) interred in the church in 1800, it became a military mausoleum, receiving further countless trophies from the imperial campaigns.

In 1840, the Dôme accommodated Napoleon's tomb. The coffin lay under the cupola and in St Jerome's Chapel until the tomb, designed by Visconti, was completed. The transfer took place on 3 April 1861.

The institution's revival – After the two World Wars the institution reverted to its original purpose in providing shelter and care to the war wounded with modernised hospital facilities. The buildings today are occupied by military administration and the Army Museum.

To celebrate the bicentenary of the French Revolution in 1989 the Dôme was re-gilded, using 12.65kg/27.8lb of gold leaf. The four statues representing Faith, Hope, Charity and Religion, which surround the lantern, were replaced.

Hôtel des Invalides

WITHIN THE HOTEL DES INVALIDES

★★★**Musée de l'Armée** ⊘ – 🔲 The galleries of one of the world's richest army museums, containing over 500 000 exhibits, lie on either side of the main courtyard, on several floors. Five main themes are illustrated.

Arms and armour – *West side*. Attractively displayed, they illustrate the evolution of methods of defence and attack from prehistoric times. In the Arsenal, reconstructed suits of armour alternate with paintings of military exploits. Note the sword and armour of King François I *(François I room)* and Charles V of Spain's pistol *(Pauilhac room)*.

The **Salle orientale** exhibits arms and armour from Persia, India, Japan; among the helmets are those of the Ottoman sultan Bajazet II and of a Slav ruler (Russia, 16C).

Ancien Régime and 19C – *East side*. This section presents a rich collection of weapons and uniforms from the 17C to the Second Empire. There are many uniforms and souvenirs relating to Napoleon, including the Emperor's arab steed, Vizir, and the dog he took with him to the island of Elba; both animals were stuffed.

Banners and artillery – A series of cannon is displayed around the courtyard, on different floors. The **Salle Gribeauval** *(west side)* contains nearly 200 models tracing the evolution of French artillery from 1550 to 1914.

The **ground-floor galleries** contain French banners dating from 1619 to 1953.

First World War – *West side*. Animated maps and maps showing troop movements show the development of the First World War.

Second World War, Free French and Resistance movement – *West side; start on the third floor*. Three floors are devoted to the Second World War *(red explanatory panels)*, the Free French and General de Gaulle's role in it, and the Resistance movement *(blue explanatory panels)*. The displays follow a chronological order from the 1940 defeat and General de Gaulle's radio appeal to the French people on 18 June 1940 to the concentration camps and the capitulation of Japan in 1945. Personal objects, weapons, models, video films, photos and documents illustrate the role each party played in this worldwide conflict.

★★ **Musée des Plans reliefs** ⊙ – *4th floor, west side.* An audio-visual presentation *(10min)* traces the history and manufacture of relief maps and three-dimensional models.

A collection of scale models of towns, harbours and fortresses (1:600) from the time of Vauban (17C) to the present illustrates the evolution of fortifications in France over the last 300 years. Many of them are in the process of restoration. A 10min film describes the history of their fabrication.

★★★ **Église du Dôme** ⊙ – The church is one of the major masterpieces of the age of Louis XIV, reaching new heights in the French Classical style.

Louis XIV commissioned **Hardouin-Mansart** to design a church that would complement the Invalides buildings of Libéral Bruant and embody the full splendour of his reign. In 1677, work began on the royal church oriented towards the north and joined to the Soldiers' Church by a common sanctuary. It was completed by Robert de Cotte in 1735.

Dome – The overall effect is one of graceful dignity. Forty engaged columns surround the drum, supporting a balustrade that encircles the dome base. At this level, pilasters frame the round-arched windows between consoles, rising to 12 gently arched panels with gilded sections that define the dome. Decorated with trophies, garlands and other ornaments, the dome is capped by an elegant gold lantern. Four Virtues seem to anchor the corners of the spire which rises 107m/351ft into the sky. The dome roof consists of lead sheeting, attached by copper nails to a wood frame. It was first given its golden splendour in 1715.

Interior – The decoration is sumptuous: painted cupolas, walls adorned with columns and pilasters framing low-relief sculptures by the greatest contemporary artists. The 19C saw various modifications. In 1842, two years after the return of Napoleon's body, Visconti enlarged the high altar (**1**), replaced the original baldaquin and had the crypt dug to receive the 'Eagle's' sarcophagus. The big window dates from 1873. These alterations disturbed the harmonious proportions of the interior, but its grandeur survives. By the entrance to the crypt are the tombs of Generals Duroc (**2**) and Bertrand (**3**).

Making the most of the museums

The Invalides are comprised of three museums: Army, Relief maps and the Order of Liberation. The ticket provides access to all three, together with the Dôme Church and Napoleon's tomb. The ticket is valid all day and it is possible to come and go at will.

Shopping

Androuet – *83 rue St-Dominique - 7th arr -* Ⓜ *Latour-Maubourg or Invalides -* ☎ *01 45 50 45 75 - Mon 4-8pm, Tue-Fri 9am-1.30pm, 4-8pm, Sat 9am-8pm - closed public holidays.* Since 1909 this family of master cheese merchants has excelled in the production of fine cheeses, and continues to work with the same producers. This loyalty has earned them a perfect understanding of their products and the time required for each one to mature.

Pétrossian – *18 blvd de Latour-Maubourg - 7th arr -* Ⓜ *Latour-Maubourg -* ☎ *01 44 11 32 22 - Mon, Sat 9.30am-8pm - closed Mon in Aug.* In this magnificent 1920s shop, Paris' caviar and smoked fish specialists introduce their customers to real Scottish and Norwegian salmon, smoked for five days over a fire of different wood essences, as well as wild white salmon from the Baltic. Their foie gras is also delicious.

Eating out

Turn back to the Selected restaurants section at the beginning of the guide for a list of restaurants, bistros, cafés etc. This neighbourhood is in the 7th *arrondissement*. The Hôtel des Invalides has its own cafeteria with free access independent of the museum.

"I used to say of him [Napoleon] that his presence on the field made the difference of 40 000 men."
Philip Henry, Earl of Stanhope: Conversations with the Duke of Wellington 1888.

Napoleon's tomb – The majesty of the setting perfectly befits the Emperor's image. In order to preserve the design of the church and a view of the altar, **Visconti** dug a circular crypt for the red porphyry sarcophagus on its base of green granite from the Vosges. Work was completed in 1861. Two massive bronze statues stand guard at the crypt entrance, one bearing an orb, the other the Imperial sceptre and crown; 12 statues by Pradier surround the crypt.

The Emperor's body is placed in six coffins, one contained inside the other: the innermost is of tin-plate; the second of mahogany; the third and fourth of lead; the fifth of ebony; the last of oak. When Napoleon's coffin was exhumed on St Helena and opened, the Emperor's body, dressed in his guardsman's uniform, was found to be in perfect condition, despite having been laid to rest 19 years before.

★ **Musée de l'Ordre de la Libération** ⓥ – *Pavillon Robert-de-Cotte, 51 bis boulevard de la Tour-Maubourg (or enter via the Musée de l'Armée).*

The Order of Liberation, created by Général de Gaulle at Brazzaville in 1940, honoured as companions those who made an outstanding contribution to the final victory. The list, which was closed in 1946, consists of service personnel and civilians, a few overseas leaders including King George VI, Winston Churchill and General Eisenhower, and several French localities (Paris, Nantes, Grenoble, Vassieux-en-Vercors, Sein Island). The museum also perpetuates the memory of French heroes from the African campaigns, major operations of the Resistance and the concentration camps. Displays include documents, trophies and relics.

Napoleon's Tomb

EXPLORING THE NEIGHBOURHOOD

★★ Pont Alexandre III – This bridge was built for the 1900 World Exhibition and is an example of the popular steel architecture and ornate style of the period. The armorial bearings of Russia and France evoke the memory of Alexander III, father of Nicholas II of Russia who laid the foundation stone. It has a splendid single-span, surbased arch; it affords a fine view of the Invalides.

Esplanade – The Esplanade, designed and constructed between 1704 and 1720 by Robert de Cotte, Mansart's brother-in-law, affords a spectacular vista 500m/0.3mi long and more than 250m/820ft wide, ending of course in the symmetrical, Classical buildings. The expanses of green lawn are bordered by avenues of lime trees.

★★★ Hôtel des Invalides – *Access from esplanade des Invalides.*

Garden – Fronting the Invalides are a series of gardens, bordered by a wide dry moat, ramparts lined with 17C and 18C bronze cannon and an 18-piece triumphal battery used to fire salutes on such occasions as the Armistice (11 November 1918) and the Victory March (14 July 1919).

★★ Façade – The façade is majestic in style and line, and in proportion and size – 196m/645ft long. The central block is dominated by a magnificent doorway, flanked by twin pavilions. An equestrian statue shows Louis XIV supported by Prudence and Justice in the rounded arch above the entrance.

★ Cour d'honneur – *Access through the gate.* Napoleon took great pleasure in reviewing his veterans here, before the perfect proportions of the Classical building with its regimented double tier of superimposed arches.

A central bay projects slightly from each side, its carved pediment breaking the regular architectural lines as do sculpted horses, trampling the attributes of war, at the corner angles of the roof. The dormer windows are decorated with trophies.

The most ornate pavilion on the main axis of the complex serves as a frontage to the church of St-Louis-des-Invalides. At the centre is the Seurre statue of Napoleon, known as the Little Corporal, which stood for some years at the top of the column in place Vendôme.

An impressive series of cannon are laid around the courtyard: note the *Catherina* (1487) and the *Württemberg culverin* (16C); there is a Renault tank and one of the Marne taxis used to carry soldiers to the front in the First World War.

From the main courtyard, walk up one of the corner staircases to see the small enclosed courtyards which can also be seen from the Musée de l'Armée.

★ Église de St-Louis-des-Invalides – The church, also known as the Soldiers' Church, was designed by Libéral Bruant and built by Mansart, who later added the dome to the group. Its design seems cold and functional, the only relief being the captured enemy banners overhanging the upper galleries. A window behind the high altar provides a glimpse of the baldaquin in the Dôme Church.

The magnificent 17C organ is enclosed in a loft designed by Hardouin-Mansart. It was here that **Berlioz**'s *Requiem* was first heard in 1837.

On your way out of the church, follow either the right-hand or left-hand corridor leading to the Église du Dôme.

On the right of the Dôme, behind Mansart's original trench, the **Intendant's Garden** has been replanted with formal beds round an oval pool.

Leave the Invalides via place Vauban and follow avenue de Breteuil which offers a magnificent view of the Invalides complex.

JARDIN DES PLANTES ★★

Michelin plan 10: L 16
Ⓜ/RER: Gare d'Austerlitz (lines 5 and 10/C) – Buses: 24, 57, 61, 63, 65, 91 –
See plan under JUSSIEU

The Jardin des Plantes is an Ali Baba's cave that manages to combine culture and pleasure, thus making science accessible to all. Together, the complex encompasses the Botanical Gardens and its menagerie of 1 200 animals, the Natural History Museum, and various other study collections of minerals and fossils.

Nearby neighbourhoods: JUSSIEU, MOUFFETARD, QUARTIER LATIN, MAUBERT, GOBELINS.

A royal garden – In 1626 Hérouard and Guy de la Brosse, physicians to Louis XIII, were granted permission to move the Royal Medicinal Herb Garden from the tip of the Île de la Cité to the St-Victor district. This was to evolve into a school for botany, natural history and pharmacy. In 1640 the garden was opened to the public.

First Fagon, Louis XIV's first physician, then the botanist Tournefort and the three Jussieu brothers journeyed afar to enrich the Paris collection.

Jardin des Plantes

It was during the curatorship of Buffon (1739-88) however, assisted by Daubenton and Antoine-Laurent de Jussieu, nephew of the earlier brothers, that the gardens were at their greatest. Having published his 36 volume *Natural History*, Buffon extended the gardens to the banks of the Seine, planted avenues of lime trees and the maze, built the amphitheatre and galleries... He was so greatly revered that he lived to see a statue erected in his honour.

★★ MUSÉUM NATIONAL D'HISTOIRE NATURELLE

★★★ Grande Galerie de l'Évolution ⊙ – *36 rue Geoffroy-Saint-Hilaire*.

This is one of the world's greatest conservatories in the field of natural science. At the Revolution **Bernardin de Saint-Pierre** was nominated curator of the Royal Botanic Gardens, renamed by the Convention (10 June 1793) the National Museum for Natural History. This body was to be dedicated to investigation, preservation and instruction. The same year a menagerie was instituted with animals from zoos, often privately owned by princes and circus performers. This enabled astounded Parisians to discover such animals as elephants (brought from Holland in 1795), bears (each one to have occupied the pit has been called Martin after the first one), giraffes (1827) etc. In 1870, however, when Paris was under siege, the citizens' hunger exceeded their curiosity and most of the animals were killed for food. With **Géoffroy-Saint-Hilaire**, **Lamarck**, **Lacépède**, **Cuvier**, **Becquerel** and many other great names, the institute won through its teaching and research in the 19C the international recognition which it maintains today.

The great story of evolution – The theory of evolution is one of the most important in scientific development. It draws together a large number of disciplines which, without it, would have remained isolated. Here, it serves as a constant theme throughout the Gallery presentations.

The diversity of living species – *Levels 0 and 1.* On the first level there is a children's discovery room.
As an introduction to the great show of life, visitors are invited to perceive the diversity of living species according to their environment. Confronted by the two whale skeletons, one example of a land-based mammal which reverted to the ocean, the visitor enters the marine world to encounter the fauna of the great deep (including the impressive cast of a giant squid), hydrothermal springs, coral reefs, the coastline and the high seas. Infinite diversity is most apparent in the realms of the minute, where thousands of micro-organisms live among grains of sand – illustrated with a scale model enlarged 800 times.
The polar regions are illustrated by polar bears, walruses and an enormous sea elephant; the African savannah by its famous caravan of zebras, giraffes, buffalo, lions and antelopes; the rain forest by magnificent display cases of gorgeous insects, and a steel ladder as a perch for monkeys and birds.

Human action on evolution – *Level 2.* This room shows the effects of human action on evolution: intensive farming or the displacement of species, domestication, changes in habitat and pollution. The most extreme case – hunting and extermination – is illustrated by the magnificent **Galerie des Espèces menacées ou disparues★★** (Gallery of Endangered or Extinct Species). Note, among the extinct species, the Cape lion with its black mane, turtles from the Seychelles and Rodriguez, and the blue hippotragus.

The evolution of life – On the **third floor** is the museum's oldest stuffed animal, a rhinoceros from Asia which belonged to Louis XV and Louis XVI. This leads to an historical display introducing the scientists who questioned the origin of the diversity of living beings and whose ideas paved the way for the theory of evolution, in particular Charles Darwin (1809-82) and his theory of natural selection.

The role of reproduction and natural selection is explained, together with how the cell works, that single unit of the living world, the notion of genesis, the nature of DNA.

Ménagerie ⓥ – Large reptiles, birds and wild animals are presented in a somewhat old-fashioned but serene setting; many appear tame. The rotunda, the oldest building in this section, houses a **Micro Zoo** ⓥ. Microscopes and special audio-headwear help visitors to discover the world of minute creatures and microcosms that proliferate unseen in our environment.

★**Galerie de Minéralogie et de Géologie** ⓥ – This gallery possesses exceptional examples of **minerals**, meteorites and **precious stones** and a collection of **giant crystals**, many of which come from Brazil. In the basement are shown the most precious stones, objets d'art and jewels from Louis XIV's collection. Evolutionary trends of flora **(Palaeobotany)** over 3 billion years are illustrated here, together with rare specimens of fossilised plants which are the origin of oil and coal.

Galerie de Paléontologie et Anatomie comparée ⓥ – The ground-floor gallery presents the **comparative anatomy** of vertebrates with 36 000 specimens. **Fossils** are displayed on the first and second floors among reproductions of large prehistoric animals and extinct species. A small room on the second floor is devoted to the **geology** of the Paris region.

★★ JARDIN DES PLANTES *Entrance on place Valhubert*

Botanic gardens – In the 17C a large accumulation of public waste occupied the site, over which Buffon laid a **maze** ⓥ; at the heart a small kiosk overlooks the rest of the gardens from the highest point.

The famous cedar of Lebanon is one of two planted by Bernard de Jussieu in 1734; these were brought back, so the story goes, in the scientist's hat, from England. The truth is that Jussieu got the two plants from Kew Gardens; on his way back to the gardens, the pot fell and broke, he therefore scooped the plants up into his hat and presented them thus to the gardener!

One of the oldest trees in Paris is a Robinia or false acacia planted here in 1636, near allée des Becquerel. The oldest (1601) stands in square Viviani.

Les Grands Serres ⓥ **(hothouses)** – The winter garden glasshouse contains an important collection of tropical plants. Opposite, the Australian hothouse contains Mediterranean and Australian species. The Mexican hothouse displays a collection of cacti.

Jardin alpin ⓥ – The Alpine Garden groups its high-altitude plants by soil type and orientation of the sun: Corsica, Morocco (south face), the Alps and the Himalayas (north face).

School of botany ⓥ – Over 10 000 species of flora, edible and/or medicinal herbs, are classified by family in the botanical study beds.

Rose garden – A ravishing collection of 180 varieties, in close competition with the garden at Bagatelle.

Iris garden – Irises are combined with perennial and climbing plants to create a colourful display.

Visiting tips

Please note that there is an admission charge to each gallery and it is not possible to buy a combined ticket; in addition, admission times vary from one gallery to the next. A multimedia library, a cafeteria and an interactive educational area are located near the Grande Galerie de l'Évolution; below are an auditorium and a temporary exhibition hall.

Eating out

Turn back to the Selected restaurants section at the beginning of the guide for a list of restaurants, bistros, cafés etc. This neighbourhood is in the 5th *arrondissement*.

JAVEL

This former industrial quarter was famous for manufacturing Citroën cars and bleach, (*eau de javel* means bleach). Today a magnificent contemporary garden named after André Citroën has replaced the factories.

Nearby neighbourhoods: PASSY, AUTEUIL, VAUGIRARD.

As you come out of the Javel metro station, (facing the river), turn left along the Port de Javel Bas.

★★ PARC ANDRÉ-CITROËN

André Citroën (1878-1935) went into manufacturing during the First World War when he built a factory here for producing shells. It was converted into a Citroën manufacturing plant in 1919; it operated here until the mid-1970s.

◉ The vast 14ha/35 acre site left by the closure of the Citroën factory has been transformed into a modern park where vegetation merges with stone, glass and above all water, which is omnipresent.

Suitable for all ages. The main lawn is a pleasant spot to stop and rest. The striking mirrored forms of the Ponant complex contrast with the rhythm of the fountains, the water-lilies in the still stretches of water; solid granite towers provide two raised look-out points, whereas the huge transparent glasshouses appear weightless. The orangery houses exhibitions during the summer; another contains native shrubs from the Australian subcontinent. Between the two extends a water peristyle where 100 water fountains enact their synchronised dance. Despite the signs prohibiting such play, on hot days children are wont to kick off their shoes and dance with the cooling sprays.

The symbolism of each thematic garden is fascinating – the white and black gardens, the restless garden and the serial gardens in which each of the six senses is associated with a metal and a colour.

The park draws upon traditional French formal garden design for its inorganic features, dark colours, right angles and symmetry (canal, water-lilies), upon English garden design for the glasshouses and the restless garden, whereas the smaller enclaves (serial and black and white gardens) recall Japanese prototypes.

The white garden – *On the other side of rue Balard, at the entrance to the park.* High walls enclose a small square planted with white-flowering perennials. To the north, water tumbles over a series of striated granite blocks.

★ **The black garden** – Here, connoisseurs will recognise spirea, reeds, bear's breech, rhododendrons, poppies, irises, amid the bushy, dark-leafed vegetation. Magnificent clipped conifers recall bonsai. A circuitous path leads into an open space with 64 fountains.

★ **The serial gardens** – A series of six beds is bisected by stretches of cascading water. Ramps and walkways provide a bird's-eye view over the whole area including its most secret nooks. Each garden is a concept – yellow is associated with gold and the sixth sense, silver with sight, red with bauxite and taste, orange with rust and touch, green with oxidised copper and hearing, blue with mercury and smell. Paths paved in stone or over wooden ramps thread their way through open space or dense foliage, under a pergola or through the air.

The restless garden – Clumps of rustling bamboo and random trees punctuate this man-made wilderness where apparently wind-sown plants are left to grow in the uncut grass, ever changing with the seasons.

NEARBY

Aquaboulevard – *4-6 rue Louis-Armand (Porte de Sèvres)* – Ⓜ *Balard* – Buses: 42, PC, 169.

◉ This semi-indoor, water-world complex includes a swimming pool with jacuzzi, wave machine and giant slide, set among trees and greenery. Additional fun is provided by mini-golf, bowling lanes, tennis and squash courts exercise and body-building rooms, restaurants and shops.

JUSSIEU ★

This area is bordered by the banks of the Seine, the Latin Quarter and the Gare d'Austerlitz. The neighbourhood is a rich cultural oasis: it stands upon the remains of the Gallo-Roman city, it is home to university buildings where students learn about science and natural history, to the Institute of the Arab World and the Paris Mosque, and has an attractive riverside contemporary sculpture park.

Nearby neighbourhoods: MAUBERT, QUARTIER LATIN, JARDIN DES PLANTES, MOUFFETARD.

EXPLORING THE NEIGHBOURHOOD

★ **La Mosquée** ⊘ **(The Mosque)** – *Place du Puits-de-l'Ermite*. It is almost disconcerting to enter this exotic walled compound with its white Hispano-Moorish buildings overlooked by a minaret, erected between 1922 and 1926. Three holy men oversee the enclave: the *muphti*, a lawyer, administrator and judge; the *imam* who looks after the mosque; and the *muezzin* or cantor who calls the faithful to prayer five times a day from high up in the minaret. This centre functions not only as a religious institution but also as a cultural centre with facilities for learning Arabic and Arab civilization (library and conference centre).

La Mosquée

Most of the interior decoration and courtyard design was entrusted to craftsmen from Muslim countries: Persian carpets, North African copper and brass, Lebanese cedar. The courtyard encloses a garden – symbol of Muslim Paradise. At the heart of the religious buildings is a patio surrounded by finely carved arcades, modelled upon the Alhambra in Granada. The prayer chamber is outstanding for its decoration and magnificent carpets.

On the corner of rue Daubentaon and rue Geoffroy-St-Hilaire, a North-African café serves delicious cakes and mint tea.

Follow rue Quatrefages to reach rue de Navarre.

Arènes de Lutèce - *Off rue de Navarre*. This, and the Cluny public bath house *(see QUARTIER LATIN – Hôtel de Cluny)* are the only two Parisian monuments to survive from the Gallo-Roman period. The arena, the exact date of whose construction remains unknown, was destroyed in 280 by the Barbarians and lay buried for 1 500 years before being rediscovered by accident when rue Monge was laid in 1869. The site was methodically excavated and restored only at the beginning of the 20C.
The arena seems to have been designed for circus and theatrical presentations; although many of its stone tiers have now vanished, the stage and layout of the dressing rooms survive. Propped against a wall in square Capitan are the engraved stones which indicated the seats reserved for the notables of the period.

Pierre and Marie Curie University – *Place Jussieu*. The former wine market was moved from this site when the Halles were reorganised. The site is now lined with the modern high-tech buildings of the university, although these are in need of a facelift *(work in progress)*. During term-time, this precinct in France's biggest university campus contrasts sharply with the quiet streets in the immediate vicinity.

Before taking rue des Fossés-St-Bernard towards the river, turn left up rue du Cardinal-Lemoine.

Hôtel Charles Le Brun – *49 rue Cardinal-Lemoine*. Now used as offices, this fine building was built by Boffrand in 1700 for Charles II Le Brun, nephew of the famous painter at the court of Louis XIV. Watteau lived here in 1718, as did **Buffon** in 1766; it was here that he completed his treatise on Natural History in several volumes. Fine Classical façade with large carved triangular pediment.

Take rue des Fossés-St-Bernard and walk along quai St-Bernard.

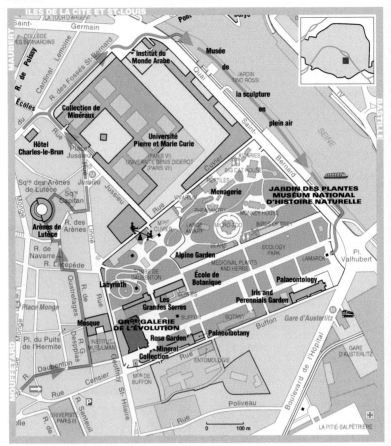

Musée de Sculpture en plein air – *Square Tino-Rossi*. The riverside garden was initiated by Gilioli César in 1980 and contains contemporary sculpture by Brancusi, Stahly, Zadkine, César, Rougemont etc.

MUSEUMS AND OTHER ATTRACTIONS

★**Institut du Monde arabe** ⊙ – *1 rue des Fossés-Saint-Bernard*. The aim of the Institute set up by France in conjunction with 20 Arab countries is to promote Islamic culture, cultural exchanges and cooperation. The building enclosed in a mantle of glass and aluminium and cored by a sheath of translucent alabaster, was conceived by the architect **Jean Nouvel** and the Architecture Studio.

The curved upper north face of the building is etched with a photographic impression of the buildings opposite on Île St-Louis; diametrically opposite, a rectilinear south-facing façade winks its 240 mechanical occuli shuttering out unwanted light. The multitude of hexagonal diaphragms recall the patterns in Islamic tiling. On the western side, behind the glass frontage, the cylindrical white-marble Book Tower borrows the form of the Samarra mosque minaret.

The institute houses a museum, library, reference section and audio-visual facilities.

Museum – On display are works of art from the 9C to the 19C from countries ranging from Spain to India illustrating Arab history: cut and over-painted glass, lustre ware, chased bronze, wood and ivory sculpture, geometric or floral carpets. Palace and mosque architecture and scientific achievements in the fields of medicine, astronomy and mathematics are also featured. There is a fine collection of astrolabes: these instruments were used to observe and calculate the position of heavenly bodies before the invention of the sextant.

On the lower level, exhibitions of art from the Arab world since 1950 are held comprising painting, sculpture, calligraphy and the graphic arts, and photography.

From the terrace there is a fine view of the east end of Notre-Dame, Île St-Louis and the Bastille neighbourhood.

★**Collections des Minéraux** ⊙ - *Pierre and Marie Curie University, 34 rue Jussieu*. This geology museum presents its superb study collections of stones, rocks and dazzling crystals – ranking perhaps among the best collections in the world.

Le grand LOUVRE★★★

Michelin plan 10, H 13
Ⓜ *Palais Royal-Musée du Louvre (lines 1 and 7)*

For eight centuries the Louvre was the seat of kings and emperors. Constant alterations by successive rulers made it into a vast royal palace. Today it is famous for one of the richest collections of art and antiquities in the world. If time allows, it is best to visit a selection of galleries at any one time and return on another occasion for others.

Nearby neighbourhoods: JARDIN DES TUILERIES, PLACE DE LA CONCORDE, PALAIS-ROYAL, CHÂTELET-HÔTEL DE VILLE, INSTITUT DE FRANCE, MUSÉE D'ORSAY.

THE HISTORY OF A GRAND DESIGN

Philippe Auguste (1180-1223) lived in the Palais de la Cité. In 1190 he had the Louvre fortress built on the north bank of the Seine, at the weakest point in his capital's defences against its English neighbours. A **keep** surrounded by a moat, the symbol of royal power, stood at the centre. This fortress was located on the south-west quarter of the present Cour Carrée.

Louis IX, also known as St Louis (1226-70), and **Philip the Fair** (1285-1314) both lived in the Palais de la Cité. The former had a great hall and a **lower hall** built; the latter installed his arsenal and the royal treasury in the Louvre, where they were to remain for the next four centuries.

Charles V (1364-80) transformed the old fortress into a comfortable residence, without changing its dimensions. In it, he installed his famous **library** of 973 books, the largest in the kingdom. A miniature in the *Very Rich Hours* of the Duke of Berry depicts this attractive Louvre, surrounded by new ramparts which put an end to its military career. After Charles V, the Louvre was not to be inhabited by royalty for the next century and a half.

François I (1515-47) lived mainly in the Loire Valley or the Marais. In 1528, in desperate need of money, he prepared to demand contributions from the Parisian population. To soften them up, he announced his intention to take up residence in the

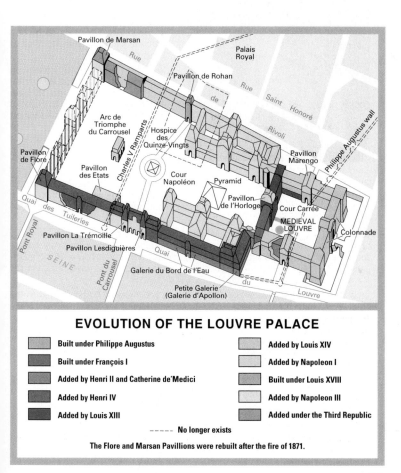

EVOLUTION OF THE LOUVRE PALACE

Built under Philippe Augustus		Added by Louis XIV	
Built under François I		Added by Napoleon I	
Added by Henri II and Catherine de'Medici		Built under Louis XVIII	
Added by Henri IV		Added by Napoleon III	
Added by Louis XIII		Added under the Third Republic	

- - - - - No longer exists

The Flore and Marsan Pavillions were rebuilt after the fire of 1871.

Le Grand LOUVRE

Louvre. Rebuilding began: the keep, a bulky form which cast a shadow over the courtyard, was razed, and the advance defences were demolished; however, orders for a new palace for the King of France to be built on the foundations of the old fortress, were not given to **Pierre Lescot** until 1546. Lescot's designs in keeping with the style of the Italian Renaissance which had found such favour on the banks of the Loire, were new to Paris. By 1547, at the death of the king, construction was barely visible above ground level.

Henri II (1547-59) took up residence in the Louvre and retained Lescot as chief archi-tect. The old great hall was transformed into the **Salle des Caryatides**; on the first floor, the Salle des Cent-Suisses reserved for the Palace Guard, preceded the royal suite in the south wing (that of the Queen was on the ground floor). The coffered vaulting over the Henri-II-style staircase leading to the two rooms was carved by Jean Goujon. Royalty never occupied the other buildings around the Cour Carrée. The Louvre gateway, 2m/6.6ft wide opened between two large towers to the east. Visitors arriv-ing on foot were permitted access as long as they were properly dressed; pages and footmen hung about the courtyard and around the gateway, playing dice, arguing and catcalling after passing *bourgeois*.

Catherine de' Medici (1519-89) withdrew to the Hôtel des Tournelles, her residence in the Marais, after the accidental death of her husband Henri II. Once declared Regent, she decided to take up residence in the Louvre, on the floor since known as the Logis des Reines (Queens' Lodging), but was not at all happy living in the middle of Lescot's building site. In 1564, she ordered **Philibert Delorme** to build her a residence of her own on the site known as Les Tuileries, in which she would have greater freedom of movement.

Between the two palaces, the Queen Mother planned to have a covered passage built to enable people to walk the 500m/547yd unnoticed, under shelter from inclement weather. The connecting galleries – the **Petite Galerie** and the **Galerie du Bord de l'Eau** (or Grande Galerie), along the banks of the Seine were duly begun, but work was brought to a halt by the Wars of Religion. The old Louvre was to keep its two Gothic and two Renaissance wings until the reign of Louis XIV.

Henri IV

Henri IV (1589-1610) continued work on the Louvre on his arrival in Paris in 1594. **Louis Métezeau** added an upper floor to the Galerie du Bord de l'Eau; **Jacques II Androuet Du Cerceau** completed the Petite Galerie and built the **Pavillon de Flore**, with another gallery leading off at right angles to link it with the Tuileries Palace, while seeing to the interior decoration of the Tuileries. The scale of construction on the Louvre site reflected the high status that the monarchy was once again enjoying at this time.

Louis XIII (1610-43) enjoyed living at the Louvre, but the Court endured severely cramped conditions. Urged by Richelieu, Louis undertook to enlarge the Louvre fourfold. Lemercier built the Clock Pavilion, and the north-west corner of the court-yard, a Classical statement in response to Lescot's design. The Royal Mint and the Royal Press were accommodated in the Grande Galerie.

Louis XIV (1643-1715). After the death of Louis XIII, Anne of Austria moved to the Palais-Royal with the under-age Louis. Nine years later, they moved to the Louvre having found the Palais-Royal less than secure, intimidated by the Fronde uprisings. Louis XIV turned to **Le Vau** to resume work on the extension of the Louvre; he had him build the **Galerie d'Apollon** and requested a worthy façade be designed to close off the Cour Carrée (the **Colonnade**). In 1682, the king moved his court away from the capital to Versailles. Construction was brought to a halt; Le Vau's and Perrault's buildings were left without roofs.

18C-19C – By now, the Louvre was so run down as to prompt talk of pulling it down altogether. After the brief interval of the Regency (1715-22), Louis XV lived at Versailles, whence Louis XVI was brought to Paris on 6 October 1789, briefly occupying the Tuileries until his incarceration at the Temple prison.

The Convention used the theatre and the Committee of Public Safety installed itself in the royal apartments of the Tuileries, until appropriated by Bonaparte, the Premier Consul.

The Louvre, centre for the arts

The city of Paris gradually engulfed the area around the Louvre site. The abandoned palace apartments were let to a wide variety of people. A Bohemian colony of artists set up camp in the galleries, organising living quarters on the mezzanine level, the floor above was used as a passageway (in which the King touched those afflicted with scrofula on five occasions a year). Resident artists included **Coustou, Bouchardon, Coypel** and **Boucher**; the palace lanterns were tended by **Hubert Robert's** wife. The space along the Colonnade was divided into apartments; rows of stove chimneys pierced the wonderful façade; shacks were erected in the courtyard; cabarets and taverns accommodated lean-tos along the outside façade. The royal apartments became occupied by the *Académies* – the Académie Française, having been installed there before Louis XIV moved out of the Tuileries, attracted other academic bodies dedicated to writing and literature, architecture, science, painting and sculpture. The fine arts academy began organising exhibitions of members' work in 1699, an event held around the feast of St Louis (25 August) which was to become a regular feature in the Salon Carré from 1725, and which lasted until the 1848 Revolution. Diderot, followed by Baudelaire, became critics of these *salons*, at which taste in art during the 18C and early 19C was formulated.

Napoleon I (1799-1814) while living in the Tuileries, took great interest in the Louvre; his first undertaking was to expel its lodgers. The emperor commissioned the architects **Percier** and **Fontaine** to complete the Cour Carrée, to enlarge place du Carrousel so that he might review his troops there, and to build the Arc de Triomphe du Carrousel. The fall of the emperor stopped work in 1814.

Napoleon III (1852-70), also resident in the Tuileries, oversaw the completion of the Louvre. He entrusted first **Visconti**, then **Lefuel** with the task of closing off the Grande Cour to the north. The latter compensated for the difference in levels of the two arms of the Louvre by rebuilding the **Pavillon de Flore★** in an exaggeratedly grandiose style (high relief by **Carpeaux, The Triumph of Flora★**) and by modifying the western section of the Galerie du Bord de l'Eau. It was at this time that the Carrousel entrance gates *(guichets)* were inserted.

The Republic – The uprising of the Paris Commune (a week of bloodshed from 21 to 28 May 1871) resulted in the Tuileries Palace being burned down; its collections however were saved at the last minute. In 1873 the Presidency of the Third Republic installed itself in the Palais de l'Élysée.

In 1875, **Lefuel** undertook the restoration of the Louvre, proposing along with others that the Tuileries be rebuilt. In 1882 the Assembly after due deliberation, had the ruins removed, thereby obliterating any political significance or association with the past regime.

The **Grand Louvre** project was implemented by **François Mitterrand** from 1981 onwards. Most of the work was finished by 1993, with the opening of the Richelieu wing. A fashion museum has been created in the Rohan wing.

Brief history of the museum – Product of the Age of Enlightenment and its thirst for universal knowledge, the Louvre has recently celebrated its bicentenary. The new-born French Republic wished to transform the royal collections into a museum for everyone (1793). The inauguration of the Richelieu wing (1993), a major milestone in the Grand Louvre development project (1981-97), is entirely in keeping with this aim.

François I was the first eminent patron of Italian artists of his day. Twelve paintings from his original collection, including the *Mona Lisa* by Leonardo da Vinci, *La Belle Jardinière* by Raphael and a *Portrait of François I* by Titian, are among the most important works presently in State hands. By the time Louis XIV died, over 2 500 paintings hung in the palaces of the Louvre and Versailles.

The idea of making the collection accessible to the public, as envisaged by Marigny under Louis XVI, was finally realised by the Convention on 10 August 1793 when the doors of the Grande Galerie were opened to visitors.

Napoleon subsequently made the museum's collection the richest in the world by exacting a tribute in works of art from every country he conquered; many of these were reclaimed by the Allies in 1815.

In turn, Louis XVIII, Charles X and Louis-Philippe all further endowed the collections: scarcely had the *Venus of Milo* been rediscovered when she was brought to France by Dumont d'Urville. Departments for Egyptian and Assyrian art were opened.

Gifts, legacies and acquisitions continue to enrich the collections of the Louvre, with over 350 000 works now catalogued.

Since the Grand Louvre project, the palace and museum have become one and the same.

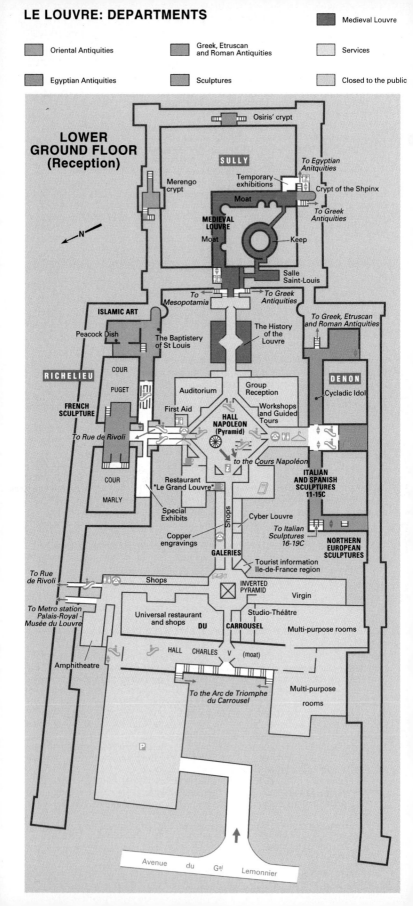

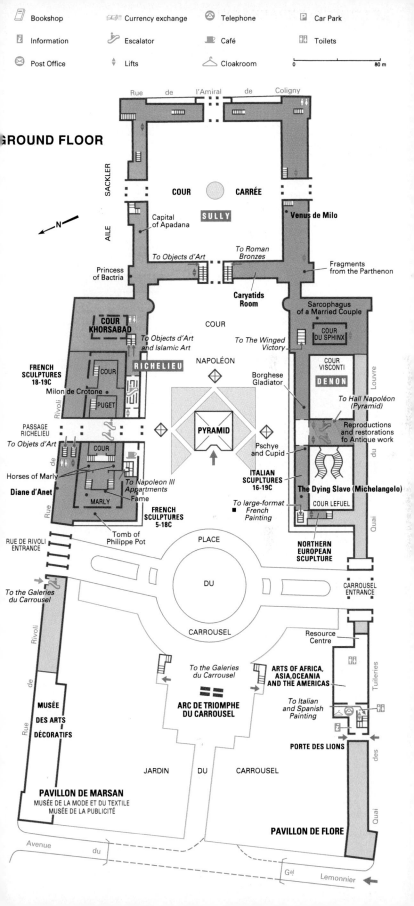

📖 Bookshop	💱 Currency exchange	☎ Telephone	🅿 Car Park	
ℹ Information	Escalator	☕ Café	🚻 Toilets	
✉ Post Office	Lifts	Cloakroom		

0 _____ 80 m

GROUND FLOOR

Rue   de   l'Amiral   de   Coligny

SACKLER

COUR   CARRÉE

SULLY

AILE

N

Capital of Apadana

Venus de Milo

To Objects d'Art   *To Roman Bronzes*

Fragments from the Parthenon

Princess of Bactria

Caryatids Room

Sarcophagus of a Married Couple

COUR KHORSABAD

COUR

COUR DU SPHINX

To Objects d'Art and Islamic Art

To The Winged Victory

COUR VISCONTI

FRENCH SCULPTURES 18-19C

RICHELIEU

NAPOLÉON

Borghese Gladiator

DENON

COUR

Rivoli

PUGET

Milon de Crotone

PYRAMID

To Hall Napoléon (Pyramid)

Reproductions and restorations fo Antique work

PASSAGE RICHELIEU

COUR

To Objets d'Art

de

Horses of Marly

To Napoleon III Appartments

Diane d'Anet

Fame

Pschye and Cupid

ITALIAN SCULPTURES 16-19C

The Dying Slave (Michelangelo)

Rue

MARLY

COUR LEFUEL

FRENCH SCULPTURES 5-18C

To large-format French Painting

Quai

RUE DE RIVOLI ENTRANCE

Tomb of Philippe Pot

PLACE

NORTHERN EUROPEAN SCULPTURE

To the Galeries du Carrousel

DU

CARROUSEL ENTRANCE

Rivoli

de

CARROUSEL

Resource Centre

Tuileries

Rue

MUSÉE DES ARTS DÉCORATIFS

To the Galeries du Carrousel

ARTS OF AFRICA, ASIA, OCEANIA AND THE AMERICAS

ARC DE TRIOMPHE DU CARROUSEL

To Italian and Spanish Painting

PORTE DES LIONS

JARDIN   DU   CARROUSEL

des

PAVILLON DE MARSAN
MUSÉE DE LA MODE ET DU TEXTILE
MUSÉE DE LA PUBLICITÉ

PAVILLON DE FLORE

Quai

Avenue   du

G^al   Lemonnier

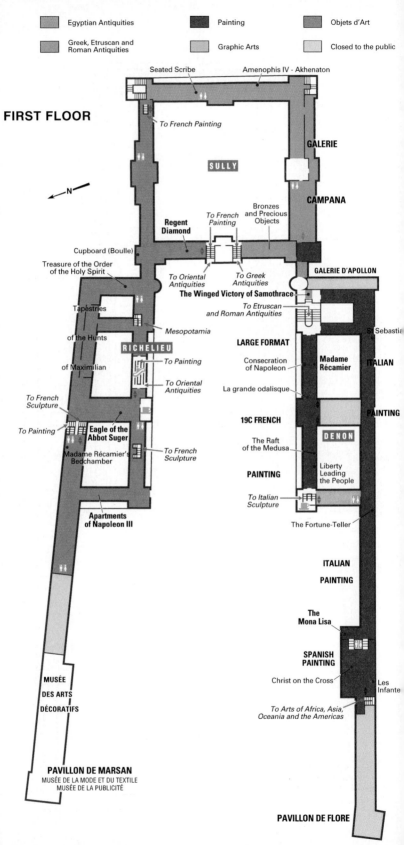

LE LOUVRE: DEPARTMENTS

- Egyptian Antiquities
- Greek, Etruscan and Roman Antiquities
- Painting
- Graphic Arts
- Objets d'Art
- Closed to the public

FIRST FLOOR

N

Seated Scribe
Amenophis IV - Akhenaton

To French Painting

SULLY

GALERIE

CAMPANA

Regent Diamond
To French Painting
Bronzes and Precious Objects

Cupboard (Boulle)

Treasure of the Order of the Holy Spirit

To Oriental Antiquities
To Greek Antiquities

GALERIE D'APOLLON

The Winged Victory of Samothrace

To Etruscan and Roman Antiquities

St Sebastia

Tapestries

of the Hunts

Mesopotamia

RICHELIEU

To Painting

LARGE FORMAT

Consecration of Napoleon

Madame Récamier

ITALIAN

of Maximilian

To Oriental Antiquities

La grande odalisque

PAINTING

To French Sculpture

To Painting

Eagle of the Abbot Suger

Madame Récamier's Bedchamber

To French Sculpture

19C FRENCH

The Raft of the Medusa

DENON

Liberty Leading the People

PAINTING

To Italian Sculpture

The Fortune-Teller

Apartments of Napoleon III

ITALIAN

PAINTING

The Mona Lisa

SPANISH PAINTING

MUSÉE

DES ARTS

DÉCORATIFS

Christ on the Cross

Les Infante

To Arts of Africa, Asia, Oceania and the Americas

PAVILLON DE MARSAN
MUSÉE DE LA MODE ET DU TEXTILE
MUSÉE DE LA PUBLICITÉ

PAVILLON DE FLORE

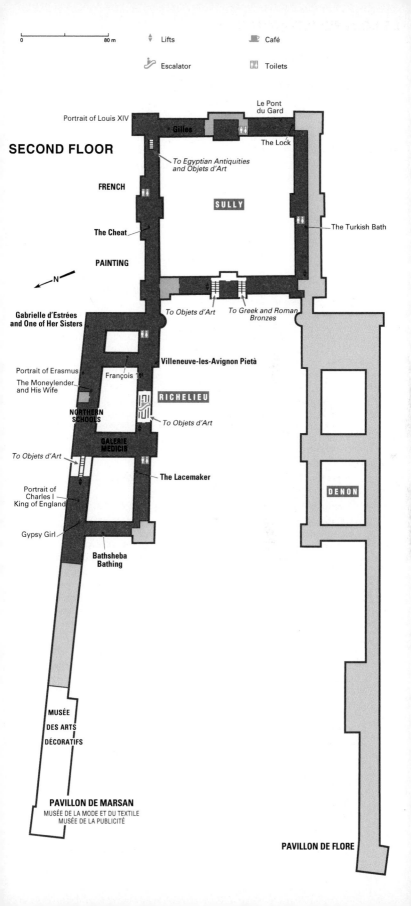

SECOND FLOOR

0 ─────── 80 m

Lifts

Escalator

Café

Toilets

Le Pont du Gard

Portrait of Louis XIV

* Gilles

The Lock

To Egyptian Antiquities and Objets d'Art

FRENCH

SULLY

The Cheat

The Turkish Bath

PAINTING

N

To Objets d'Art

To Greek and Roman Bronzes

Gabrielle d'Estrées and One of Her Sisters

Villeneuve-les-Avignon Pietà

Portrait of Erasmus

François 1er

The Moneylender and His Wife

RICHELIEU

NORTHERN SCHOOLS

To Objets d'Art

GALERIE MEDICIS

To Objets d'Art

The Lacemaker

Portrait of Charles I King of England

DENON

Gypsy Girl

Bathsheba Bathing

MUSÉE DES ARTS DÉCORATIFS

PAVILLON DE MARSAN
MUSÉE DE LA MODE ET DU TEXTILE
MUSÉE DE LA PUBLICITÉ

PAVILLON DE FLORE

Le Louvre

Access – The main entrance is via the **Pyramid**. Direct access to the **Carrousel du Louvre** shopping centre is possible via the **Palais-Royal Musée du Louvre** metro station, on either side of the **Arc du Carrousel** or at no 99 rue de Rivoli.

The Carrousel-Louvre car park – *Daily 7am-11pm.* It has space for 80 coaches and 620 cars. Access via the underground passage avenue du Général-Lemonnier, then enter the shopping centre through the old Charles V fortifications.

Hall Napoléon

Under the Pyramid, this hall is the nerve centre of the visitor network designed by the architect Pei. Visitors are immediately oriented towards one of three wings of the museum: Denon, Richelieu or Sully. This vast reception hall also houses a certain number of other services: bookshop, Le Grand Louvre restaurant, group facilities and an auditorium.

Information

General information can be obtained by calling or consulting the following:
☎ *01 40 20 51 51 (answering machine),* ☎ *01 40 20 53 17 to speak to someone at the desk (6 languages). Internet: www.louvre.fr.*
Fourteen video screens in the hall provide information about events on a daily basis in the museum. There is also a general activity programme (6 languages) available at the main information desk which comes out every 3 months.
Audio-guides can be hired (6 languages) on the mezzanine level in the various wings.

Shopping

Carrousel du Louvre – *Rue de Rivoli – 1st arr –* ☎ *01 43 16 47 10.* The combination of a museum with a shopping gallery of some 16 000sq m/19 135sq yd, including a performing arts centre (Studio-Théâtre), many brand name shops and a variety of multi-purpose halls (congresses, exhibitions etc) is one of the more original ideas invented by the Grand Louvre. The shops are selected for their quality and/or the link they may have with the museum.

Île-de-France Tourist Centre – *Daily 10am-7pm (except Tue).* Information and brochures on Paris and the Île-de-France region.

Boutique des Musées Nationaux – Reproductions, books, games etc.

Boutiques du Musée du Louvre – **Chalcographie** (prints and engravings), **postcards** (hundreds of postcards of the museum's main works of art, reproductions of paintings), **posters** and a **bookshop** (including an extensive art history section). Upstairs is a wide choice of **reproductions**, **plaster casts**, **jewellery** and **children's books**.

Other shops – Virgin (music shop and bookshop focused on 20C arts – cinema, photography, architecture), Nature et Découvertes (nature-oriented objects and activities), Lalique (crystal), Flammarion (books), Courrèges and Esprit (fashion), a bank and currency exchange bureau, Les Minéraux (minerals) together with shops devoted to home decoration and a post office.

How the museum is organised

The collections have been divided into three main regions: **Denon**, **Richelieu** and **Sully**, which make up two wings and Cour Carrée.

Sully
History of the Louvre: *Entresol.*
Medieval Louvre: *Entresol.*
Egyptian Antiquities: *Ground and 1st floors.*
Greek Antiquities (Cariatides room, Hellenic period): *Ground floor.*
Oriental Antiquities (Iran and art of the Levant): *Ground floor.*
Greek Antiquities (Bronze room, Campana gallery): *1st floor.*
17C-18C objets d'art: *1st floor.*
17C-19C French painting, including Graphic arts: *2nd floor.*
Beistegui collection (room A): *2nd floor.*

Denon
Italian sculpture: *Entresol and Ground floor.*
Scandinavian sculpture: *Entresol.*
Roman and Coptic Egypt: *Entresol (rooms A, B and C).*
Greek Antiquities: *Ground and 1st floors.*

Etruscan and Roman Antiquities: *Ground floor.*
Italian painting: *1st floor.*
Spanish painting: *1st floor.*
19C French painting (large sizes): *1st floor.*
Objets d'art (Apollon gallery): *1st floor.*

Richelieu
Exhibitions-documents: *Entresol.*
Islamic art: *Entresol.*
French sculpture *(Marly and Puget rooms)*: *Ground floor.*
Oriental Antiquities (Mesopotamia): *Ground floor.*
Objets d'art (including Napoleon III's apartments): *1st floor.*
14C-17C French painting: *2nd floor.*
Scandinavian schools: *2nd floor.*

Going out

Angelina – *226 rue de Rivoli – 1st arr – ☎ 01 42 60 82 00 – Mon-Fri 9am-7pm, Sat and Sun 9am-7.30pm.* This charming, very genteel tearoom just opposite the Tuileries, is known throughout Paris for its mouth-watering cakes and pastries and its unctuous (and very filling) chocolate called l'Africain.

Café Marly – *93 rue de Rivoli – 1st arr – ☎ 01 49 26 06 60 – daily 8am-2am.* Located in the Richelieu wing of the Louvre Museum, this haven of peace and good taste has a worldly, cosmopolitan, arty aura. Ideal to take tea or to meet special friends or customers. From the terrace under the arcades, it provides a view over Pei's pyramid.

Le Fumoir – *6 rue de l'Amiral-de-Coligny – 1st arr – ☎ 01 42 92 00 24 – www.lefumoir.com – daily 11am-2am – closed late Dec.* A library, a bar which achieved its fame during the Prohibition years, an excellent cocktail menu, a few sofas and wide bay windows overlooking the Louvre and the Église Saint-Germain l'Auxerrois: the stage is set for a quiet afternoon or evening.

Eating out

Turn back to the Selected restaurants section at the beginning of the guide for a list of restaurants, bistros, cafés etc. This neighbourhood is in the 1st *arrondissement.* The Louvre's shopping complex *(see above)* also has a wide range of cafés and restaurants.

THE LOUVRE PALACE EXTERIOR

As well as being a museum, the Louvre is a palace steeped in history. A stroll around the outside helps one appreciate the scale of the buildings. Visiting the exhibition on the History of the Louvre and the excavations discovered below ground also provides an understanding of how the construction has evolved. *For this you will need an entrance ticket.*

Start from the church of St-Germain l'Auxerrois, near the Louvre-Rivoli metro station. Coming from rue de Rivoli, head towards the Seine. Opposite is the immense colonnade of the Louvre Palace.

★★**Colonnade** – In 1662, Louis XIV decided that the palace exterior on the side facing Paris was still not quite grand enough for a royal residence. He therefore summoned **Bernini**, the great master of the Italian Baroque, to design plans for a new one. Bernini suggested demolishing the existing palace: work was begun but was suspended a year later in favour of plans by three French architects: **Perrault**, **Le Vau** and **D'Orbay**.
The central pediment, carved during the Empire, featured a bust of Napoleon I, which was replaced at the time of the Restoration by one of the Sun King, who is thus crowned rather inappropriately by a Minerva in imperial dress. The true height and Classical harmony of the structure can be fully admired now that moats have been cleared to a depth of 7m/23ft around the rusticated base, in accordance with the original 17C plans.

Head towards the river and turn right. Opposite the Pont des Arts, cross the Jardin de l'Infante to gain access to Cour Carrée.

★★★**Cour Carrée** – The fine elegant Renaissance façade between the Clock Pavilion and the south wing is the work of **Pierre Lescot**. The graceful, expressive sculpture of the three avant-corps (projecting bay) and the upper storey are by the master **Jean Goujon**, depicting allegorical scenes in high relief, animated figures in niches, friezes of children and garlands. At night, a new system of illuminations sets off the most impressive remnant of the old Louvre to full effect.

The Louvre, Cour Napoléon

Leave the courtyard by passing under the Clock Pavilion.

The **pavillon de l'Horloge** *(see illustration p 93)* was built in 1640 during the reign of Louis XIII by **Lemercier**, who was also responsible for the north-west wing, a replica of Lescot's façade.

Enter Cour Napoléon and head for the Pyramid.

★★**Pyramid** – The pyramid, 21m/69ft high and 33m/105ft wide at the base, was designed by the architect **Ieoh Ming Pei**; it is built of sheet glass supported on a framework of stainless-steel tubes. The extravagantly decorated façades overlooking Cour Napoléon make a majestic backdrop to the sharply contrasting, rigidly geometric form of the glass pyramid at the centre of the courtyard.

It is from directly below the pyramid, in the museum reception area over which it forms a huge vault, that one can fully appreciate the originality of design and materials used.

An **equestrian statue of Louis XIV**, a copy of a marble statue by Bernini, stands on the axis leading to the Champs-Élysées, slightly at an angle with the old Louvre.

Cross the road that traverses place du Carrousel, in the direction of the Tuileries Gardens.

★**Arc de Triomphe du Carrousel** – This delightful pastiche, inspired by the Roman triumphal arch of Septimus Severus, was built from 1806 to 1808. The six bas-relief sculptures commemorate the Napoleonic victories of 1805. On the platform, where Napoleon placed the four horses removed from the basilica of San Marco in Venice (until they were returned there in 1815), **Bosio** sculpted an allegorical goddess, representing the Restoration of the Bourbons, accompanied by Victories and driving a quadriga.

The square takes its name from the lavish equestrian and theatrical tournament held there in honour of the birth of the Dauphin in 1662.

From directly beneath the arch there is a magnificent **view**★★★ along the axis that runs from the Louvre through the Tuileries, place de la Concorde, the Champs-Élysées, the Arc de Triomphe and avenue de la Grande-Armée, as far as the Grande Arche at La Défense.

Descend one of the flights of stairs near the Carrousel, or go through the Pyramid and the main entrance.

La Galerie Carrousel du Louvre – Michel Macary's architectural style blends well with the original design by Ieoh Ming Pei. The inverted crystalline pyramid provides a well of light in the central area of the arcade; concrete masonry, rows of windows and subdued lighting combine to give the main arcade the appearance of a large entrance hall. On the site of Charles V's moats, the pillars and floor in Burgundy stone exude a certain polished frigidity.

Go back towards the main entrance via the underground passage.

THE MUSEUM ⊘

★ History of the Louvre – The two galleries on each side of the rotunda, decorated with stone reliefs by Jean Goujon, present the architectural and decorative evolution of the Louvre building during its transformation from fortress to royal residence and finally to museum. Numerous documents, paintings and relief models recall the rulers and architects who contributed to the present physiognomy of the palace.

★★★ Medieval Louvre – *Carry on from the rotunda into the Sully crypt.* Here, a dark line on the floor indicates the location of one of the 10 towers which made up part of the old Louvre. Further on, the visitor encounters the impressive surroundings of the **fortress** built by Philippe Auguste in the early 13C.

The wooden walkway follows the line of the north and the east moats. On the left is the counterscarp wall, a simple façade showing visible signs of repair work; on the right is the 2.6m/7ft-thick curtain wall.

On the east side, a trapezoidal construction indicates the location of the foundations of the residence added by Charles V in 1360. In the middle of the ditch, the supporting pier of the drawbridge is framed by the twin towers of the **east gate** of Philippe Auguste's castle. Its rectangular stones are evenly placed and feature put-log holes and heart-shaped engravings carved by the stonemasons.

A modern gallery leads to the moat around the circular keep or **Grosse Tour** built for Philippe Auguste between 1190 and 1202. The moat, with an average width of 7.5m/23ft, was once paved with enormous stones.

The tour of the Medieval Louvre ends with two galleries. The first contains the earthenware items discovered during the excavation of Cour Carrée. The second, the **Salle Saint-Louis** with mid-13C vaulting, has a display of royal items found at the bottom of the well in the keep. These include a replica of Charles VI's parade helmet, the **chapel doré**.

★★★ Egyptian antiquities

The department of Egyptian Antiquities is the legacy of **Jean-François Champollion**, who drew on the work of the English physicist Thomas Young (1773-1829) for help in unravelling the mysteries of hieroglyphics in 1822, thus founding Egyptology. A consistent policy of purchasing, collecting and acquiring excavated material continued until the Second World War, endowing the Louvre with thousands of artefacts.

There are two ways of visiting the Egyptian Antiquities: either via the Oriental galleries in the Richelieu wing, turning right at the end of the Sackler wing, or by the Sully entrance on the ground floor, through the Medieval Louvre section, which brings you to the Crypte du Sphinx and follows a themed circuit. Take the staircase up on the left. The descriptions given follow the second route.

Sphinx – *In the crypt.* This colossal monolith in pink granite, 4.8m/16ft long, was found at Tanis in the Nile delta, the capital of Egypt during its decline.

Themed circuit

Through works of art and ordinary objects, 19 galleries illustrate the everyday life and culture of ancient Egyptian society. Wall panels and plastified information boards help to enhance the presentation of this fascinating collection.

Agriculture, hunting and fishing – *Galleries 2 to 5.* The small statues in gallery 2 represent the fauna found in the all-important Nile: hippopotami, crocodiles, frogs. Agricultural practices and food are evoked by means of statues and models destined for furnishing tombs, along with stelae and samples of food (bread dating from 3 500 years ago), and bas-relief sculptures, particularly those in the **Mastaba of Akhout-Hetep★★**. The upper chamber of a Fifth Dynasty (c 2350 BC) civil tomb was used in the cult of the deceased. The inside walls are adorned with carved and painted scenes of the hunt, of banquet preparations and of navigation illustrating the wishes of the deceased to have a beautiful tomb (corridor), to enjoy plenty of good food (bearers of offerings) and to survey by boat the lands which would have yielded such luxuries.

Art and Crafts – *Galleries 6 and 7.* The principles of hieroglyphic writing are exhibited along with the materials used and the gods who protected the scribes. Egyptian art used a wide variety of materials: wood, stone, semi-precious stones, metals, glass and pottery. Examples of these are found here, in both finished and unfinished works: statues, vases and bas-relief sculptures, whereas explanatory displays reconstruct the methods used. Notice the rare bronze statue of the god Horus, on a pedestal which is rather too high.

Domestic life – *Galleries 8 to 10.* Furniture, pottery, clothes, musical instruments and toys evoke the decor of wealthy homes; jewels and toilet articles (including spoons used for offerings in the form of women swimming or decorated with animals) are evidence of a sophisticated lifestyle. Terracotta models give an idea of urban architecture.

Temples – *Galleries 11 and 12.* This is the beginning of the section where monumental works are displayed. Egyptian temples were reached via avenues of sphinxes, and this idea is evoked in the corridor leading to the Henri IV gallery, whose majestic proportions and high ceiling set off the imposing works exhibited here: statues of gods and goddesses, portraits of dignitaries, engraved historical records of a pharaoh's reign. Note the extreme elegance of the boat in the goddess Anouket's procession in the central showcase.

Funerary rites – *Galleries 13 to 17.* Much has been learned of everyday life in ancient Egypt from the reconstitution of the living world in tombs. The ritual content of a tomb included Canopic jars containing the organs of the defunct, statues of funerary servants who would have been charged with menial duties for the deceased in his or her after-life and protective amulets placed on the mummy.

Starting from the Crypt of Osiris and the **royal tomb of Ramses III**, is an impressive series of shaped mummy cases, from carved granite sarcophagi to those in wood or cloth, covered in paintings.

Divinities – *Galleries 18 and 19.* The gods and goddesses of ancient Egypt are displayed in alphabetical order, listing the appearance, role, and attributes of each one next to a collection of metal, pottery and stone statues. The role of magic and the animal kingdom in religion is also specified: mummified cats and crocodiles and sarcophagi for animals, and the cult of the bull-god Apis.

Chronological circuit

First floor. Go up the stairs at the end of the themed circuit. In this display, information panels give the main dates of Egyptian civilization. Most of the major pieces of the Louvre's collection are on this floor. The galleries date from the time of Charles X, when they first received the antiquities collection, and the ceilings of some rooms (27 to 30) have preserved their original decoration.

Nagada period (late prehistoric) – *Gallery 20.* Stone vases, pottery and sculpted painting palettes.

★★ **Knife of Gebel-el-Arak** – This small exhibit, one of the earliest known to feature low-relief carving dates from the end of the Prehistoric Era in Egypt (c 3200 BC). The engraved rhinoceros-horn handle bears a figure and animals from the sub-desert region of Middle Egypt on one side and, on the other, a river battle scene. One side of the polished flint blade has also been finely worked.

Stele of the Serpent King – *Gallery 21.* This primitive work (Thinite Period) depicts King Djet, one of the first Pharaohs, identified by his symbol the serpent, beneath his protector, a falcon, against the backdrop of the façade of his palace, which frames the whole image.

Old Kingdom (2700-2200 BC) – *Gallery 22.* Some of the earliest examples of Egyptian statuary, including the couple **Sepa and Nesa** (Third Dynasty) and the **Head of King Didoufri** (Fourth Dynasty, 2570 BC). This work is a contemporary of the Great Pyramids and one of the first to be adapted to fit a sphinx. It is crowned with the royal headdress.

★★★ **Seated Scribe** – This famous statue in painted limestone from the Fifth Dynasty (c 2500 BC) was excavated at Sakkara. Strikingly realistic, the facial expression is alert, the hands poised as if ready to commit to papyrus what he hears, the eyes, inlaid with coloured rock crystal and the eyelids outlined in copper seem to engage the viewer.

Middle Kingdom (2000-1700 BC) – *Gallery 23.* Tomb of Chancellor **Nakhti**. The beautiful statue in acacia wood depicts the chancellor life-size, dressed in a fringed loincloth. Note also some of the items buried with the chancellor

Rameses II's breast-plate (Sakkara, c 1290-1220 BC)

to accompany him in the afterlife: models of a granary, of ships, and blue faience hippopotami.

The lintel and statues of Sesostris III show this Twelfth-Dynasty sovereign at two different stages of life. The expressive portrait of the ageing king is particularly striking. The highly stylised female figurine bearing offerings of food to the deceased wears a body-clinging strapped shift. Note also the beautiful nude figure of the woman with broken thumbs.

New Kingdom (1550-1200 BC) – *Galleries 24 to 27.* This period saw several famous pharaohs, one known for his power (Ramses II, whose funeral temple is depicted in a model in gallery 26), another for the riches discovered in his tomb (Tutankhamun). The busts and statues from the reign of Amenophis III reflect this ideal of preciosity: **the lady Touy**, priestess of the god Min; a green enamelled stone statuette of **Queen Tiy**, wife of Amenophis III. The magnificent **Bas-relief of King Sethi I and the goddess Hathor** in colourfully painted limestone comes from the Valley of the Kings. The sumptuously dressed goddess of the Thebes mountain presents the king with a magic collar. The exquisite royal **Jewels of Rameses II**, the son and heir of Sethi I, includes a ring with horses, Rameses II's great breast-plate, a gold goblet and a gold cloisonné bracelet decorated with griffins and winged lions.

Akhenaton and Amarnian art (c 1370-1350 BC) – *Room 25.* Amenophis IV changed his name to Akhenaton in deference to the sun god Aton and, together with his queen, Nefertiti, introduced monotheism. Among the Royal portraits from their reign note in particular the bust of a princess, a teenage dignitary with the hint of a sulky pout, and the extraordinarily sophisticated features of the **bust of Akhenaton★★** with its highly developed realism and the inward-looking expression on the face.

The last pharaohs (1000-30 BC) – *Galleries 29 and 30.* The end of pharaonic Egypt was interspersed with a number of intermediate periods when the kingdom was subject to exterior rule (Persians, Greeks). Some refined works of art date from this period, such as the statue of **Queen Karomama** in bronze inlaid with gold and silver, and the precious **Osorkon Triad**, in gold and laps-lazuli, regrouping Osiris, seated on an altar, his wife and sister Isis and their son Horus, protector of the monarchy.

The Egyptian department's collection continues in the entresol Denon, with the late antiquities of the Roman period (gallery A) and Coptic Christians (galleries B and C).

Roman Egypt – *Room A.* Attractively displayed in a vaulted gallery, this collection illustrates a new influence from the Roman and Hellenist world of the Mediterranean, as expressed in funerary customs. There are a number of painted plaster death masks for men, women and children, shrouds decorated with portraits of the defunct, and votive stelae. Note the **mummy** dating from the Roman Period with its painted portrait inserted in the swaddling over the face.

Walk through the gallery devoted to pre-Classical Greece.

Coptic Egypt – *Gallery B.* Egypt succumbed gradually to the influence of Christianity, and particularly Byzantine art. Here is a large collection of colourful **textiles**, a domain in which Coptic art flourished in the 5C-6C AD, as well as sculpture, including a fragment of the Annunciation.

Monastery of Bawit – *Gallery C.* The fragments of the monastery of St Apollo (6C-7C AD) come from the village of Bawit in Middle Egypt. The parts of the basilical chapel arranged as found include panels and friezes in carved limestone or painted wood; the **capitals** are particularly eye-catching. In the chancel, a 7C distemper painting shows Abbot Mena carrying a marvellously embossed book of the Gospels under the protection of Christ.

★★★ Greek antiquities

The Greek Antiquities section is one of the jewels in the Louvre's collection.

To visit the collection in chronological order, start with gallery 1 in the entresol of the Denon wing.

Pre-classical Greece – *This gallery has recently been refitted and presents Cycladic (Idol's Head, c 2500 BC), Minoan and Mycenaean art before coming to the pre-Classical age.*
The limestone statue of the **Lady of Auxerre** is one of the earliest examples of Greek sculpture (c 630 BC), a gauge for the austere Dorian style, with its rigid, full-frontal pose (the face in line with the body). Although dating from only two generations later, the **Kore of Samos** from the Temple of Hera, is more Ionian in style; it is more sophisticated with its stylised draperies. The **Rampin Horseman** (named after its donor) exemplifies the refined detail of mid-6C BC Attic style, notably in the rendering of hair and beard; the rider's face lit by a slight smile.
This severe style is also evident in the **stele depicting the Exaltation of the Flower** (note the graceful gesture of the hands) which is from Pharsalus.
In gallery 2 are examples of Greek inscriptions.
Take the stairs up to the ground floor.

Classical Greece – The **metopes** from the Temple of Zeus (c 460 BC) are shown off to advantage by a new presentation in gallery 4.
Cross gallery 6.

Gallery 7 contains sculptural fragments from the **Parthenon**, a Doric temple built in honour of Athena on the initiative of Pericles c 445 BC on the Athens Acropolis at the height of the great period of Hellenistic Classicism.

The **fragment of the frieze★★★** (a large part of which is in the British Museum, London) depicts the young girls who embroidered the veil offered to the city's patron goddess during the Panathenaic procession (every four years). The slow, dignified procession, the different expressions and the graceful bearing of the figures testify to the skill of **Phidias**.

Replicas of statues, 5C-4C BC – *Galleries 14 to 16*. Very few great Greek original bronze statues survive, since this material has been melted down and put to other uses over the centuries. However, many marble copies were made to satisfy the eclectic tastes of the Romans. Several statues recall the severe style, notably the *Apollo Citharoedus* and the torso of a discus thrower.
The most important works exhibited here are by **Polyclitus** (*Diadumenus and the Wounded Amazon*, badly restored in the 17C) and **Phidias** (*Apollo* of the Kassel type – of which the best copy is the head of *Athena Parthenos*).
Classicism evolved a freer, less severe style: the *Borghese Ares* still conforms to a conventional pose, but the facial expression is more human. The late 5C BC is punctuated by Praxiteles' *Adonis* or *Narcissus*, his clinging draperies moulding the contours and forms of their female wearers. By the early 4C BC there is a return to realism *(Discus-Bearer of Naucydes, Athena Pacifica)*.
Apart from the muse *Melpomene* from the Theatre of Pompeii (1C BC), gallery 16 is devoted to replicas of works by the great sculptor **Praxiteles** (active 370-330 BC), who breathed life into the marble he sculpted, his figures having a fluid and careless grace yet charged with spirituality. *Apollo the Lizard-Slayer* poses informally, a youth poised on one leg, his weight carelessly swung on one hip; **Diana of Gabies★** embodies all the femininity and modesty of Artemis, the huntress, goddess of the moon, as she fastens her cloak, qualities shared by *Venus of Arles* and the **Cnidian Aphrodite★★**, the most prized female statue of Antiquity. Nearby, a copy of the face of Aphrodite known as the *Kaufmann Head* after its former owner, is both alert and serene.
Among the original works from the Classical period is the Piombino Apollo, which came from the workshops of the Greek empire in Sicily and southern Italy, and was found in the sea off Tuscany.

At gallery 16, turn left and walk back to gallery 12.

Original statues, 2C BC. – *Gallery 12*. The natural, serene beauty of the **Venus of Milo★★★** (or more properly, the Aphrodite of Milo), twisted in a graceful spiral of movement echoed in the draperies around her body, make this statue one of the masterpieces of Antique statuary.

★★ **Salle des Caryatides** – *Gallery 17*. This gallery was once the great hall of the old Louvre Palace modified by Pierre Lescot. It is named after the four monumental draped female **statues** by Jean Goujon which support the minstrels' balcony. The *Nymph of Fontainebleau* above the minstrels' balcony is a copy of the work by the Florentine, **Benvenuto Cellini** (16C), the original of which is found in the sculpture department.
The sculptures displayed are copies dating from the Hellenistic Period (4C BC), harmonising well with the Renaissance decor. Figures with elongated proportions attributed to be after **Lysippus** are almost Mannerist in style, caught at the point of action: *Hermes tying his sandal, Crouching Aphrodite* of Vienna, *Artemis* known as **Diana of Versailles**, *The Three Graces*, and **Sleeping Hermaphrodite** (on a mattress by Bernini).

The collection continues on the 1st floor, up the Escalier Daru.

★★★ **Winged Victory of Samothrace** – Early 2C BC. From its pedestal at the top of the Escalier Daru, designed especially for it, this statue seems on the point of taking flight. This masterpiece of Hellenistic art, the figurehead on a stone ship's prow, commemorates a naval victory at Rhodes. The treatment of draperies sculpted as if blown in a strong wind mould the contours of the winged figure. The suggestion of free movement and powerful action make this work of art particularly impressive.

Pass to the right of the Winged Victory.

Roman and Greek glassware – *Galleries 34 to 38*. In Louis XIV's former Grand Cabinet, designed by Le Vau, a hundred or so pieces of 6C BC glassware are exhibited for the first time. Following on from the Salle Clara (gallery 35) three rooms display Ancient and Classical Greek **terracotta** pieces. Nearly 2 000 vases and figures are on show.

★★ **Galerie Campana** – *This occupies the wing facing the Seine, galleries 39 to 47*.
The collection of the **Marquis Campana**, an enthusiastic antiquarian who excavated the Etruscan necropolises of northern Latium *(see below – Etruscan Antiquities)*, in particular that at Cerveteri (1840s), was bought almost in its entirety in 1861 by Napoleon III. It included numerous Greek vases, which were discovered in the same region.

The different forms and functions of Greek vases are presented firstly, with a panorama of the different subjects found in their decoration, from everyday life to legends and from religion to love *(gallery 39)*.

After the decadence of the Cretan and Mycenaean civilizations, the Geometric Period (10C-8C BC) seems to evolve towards frieze decoration. New vase forms develop in Corinth and eastern Greece, decorated with black figures. The same type of ornamentation was used by the Master of the Caere Hydria and by the painter of Amasis. The conventions of standard black-figure vase painting seem to have been first contradicted by the potter of Andokides c 530 BC, who painted-in the background and details of his figures in black,

Krater representing a purification rite
(Apullian style c 390-380 BC)

leaving the main profiles in red biscuit. The technique was perfected in c 500 BC by **Euphronios** and Douris *(gallery 40)*. The final gallery displays the delicate and graceful Myrina and **Tanagra figurines** so full of movement.

★★ **Salle des Bronzes et objets précieux** – *Gallery 32*. Antique bronzes and jewellery are displayed alongside examples of Archaic pitcher handles with Gorgon head masks. A fascination for apparently unidealised human features, at times even bizarre ones, are most characteristic of this period; portrayals of infancy or old age, stunted growth and deformity are most remarkable: note in particular *Eros and Psyche* with the faces of young children; a black adolescent with his hands tied behind his back; a giant. The handsome **bust of a young man from Beneventum** draws inspiration from the works of Polyclitus.

The *Effigy of a kneeling black slave* (2C-3C AD) dates from the Roman period. A polygonal display case holds jewellery. At the end of the room is the large gilded *Apollo of Lillebonne*.

Take the Daru staircase down to the ground floor.

Original statues, 2C to 1C BC – *Gallery B*. The Greek collection finishes with the Gallerie Daru, on the ground floor, among the statues and sarcophagi of the Roman empire, with the **Borghese Gladiator★★** (c 100 BC), a statue of the fighting warrior, exemplifies the standardisation of attitude and expression typical of this period.

★★ Etruscan antiquities

This collection is found on the ground floor of the Denon wing, beginning with gallery 4 (Olympie) and continuing through galleries 18 to 20.

The origins of the Etruscan people remain uncertain: some claim them to be descended from tribes indigenous to central Italy west of the Apennines, some from Aeneas' men from Troy... What is undisputed is their civilization drawn in part from Ancient Greece, and absorbed completely by Ancient Rome. In 265 BC Etruria ceded its independence becoming a part of the Roman Empire. Many of the finest artefacts have been recovered from tombs; these include domestic utensils in bronze and terracotta, jewels in gold and precious stones, frescoes, sculpted sarcophagi and funerary urns, bronze toys and devotional objects. Undoubtedly, Etruscan art is most original seeming to exude happiness, humour and sophistication.

Villanovian articles *(gallery 18)* made of iron or bronze are inscribed with geometric patterns (throne in laminated bronze); Etruscan terracotta includes the three Campana painted plaques, impasto pottery and antefixes (decorative tiles

Gabies Head (c 425– 400 BC)

211

for the ends of roof joints) in the shape of women's heads. The main exhibit, however, is the famous painted terracotta **Sarcophagus of the Married Couple★★★** (6C BC) found at Cerveteri as was its pair now at the Villa Giulia in Rome. The strikingly life-like sculpture of a couple serenely participating at the Divine Banquet seems moulded directly from a Greek vase painting.

Bucchero black earthenware *(gallery 19)* fashioned to imitate metal is typical of the Orientalising Period (mid-7C). Simple forms with engraved textures gradually ceded in the 6C BC to more complicated designs (deeply grooved lines, details in relief). Much of this pottery was copied from Greek prototypes, first the black-figure painting (early 6C) and later the red (5C-4C).

The Etruscans were also highly skilled goldsmiths, here shown in the sophisticated and elaborate applications of granulation and filigree, culminating in *repoussé* work.

Classical and Hellenistic phases – *Gallery 20.* The **Gabies head**, an oenochoë (wine pitcher) in the shape of a human head; alabaster cinerary urns and terracotta sarcophagi from Volterra and Chiusi epitomise the artistic originality of this period. The bronze mirrors with wooden handles often decorated with scenes from Greek mythology, were produced in large quantities by the Etruscans.

★★ Roman and palaeo-Christian antiquities

Through the Salle du Manège (copies after the Antique) pass round the rotunda (ground floor, gallery 5) and turn right into the former apartments of Anne of Austria.

★★ **Appartement d'été d'Anne d'Autriche** – *Galleries 22 to 26.* Anne of Austria's summer suite with ceilings painted by **Romanelli** displays two of the most original genres in Roman art: the portrait (a cold and idealised *Marcellus*, posed in the nude, by Cleomenes the Athenian; four effigies of *Augustus* at different stages of his life; bust in basalt of *Livia Drusilla*, wife of Augustus); and the relief carving, whether historical (fragment of the *Ara Pacis*, the Altar of Peace consecrated by Augustus) or mythological (sarcophagus of the *Nine Muses*, sarcophagi from Saint-Médard-d'Eyrans in the Galerie Daru).

Galleries 27 to 31 – 3C-4C AD portraits *(Gordian III; Auriga)* surround the *Pillars of the Incantada* (enchanted palace), the remains of a portico from Thessalonika *(gallery 27).*

The opulent residences were adorned with magnificent **mosaics★** *(The Phoenix, The Judgement of Paris, Preparations for a banquet)*, as were the floors of churches in north Africa and the Middle East (Kabr Hiram, near Tyre in the Lebanon). Note also the fragments of frescoes from Pompeii *(Winged Spirit).*

The old Cour du Sphinx *(gallery 31)* contains the great frieze from the Temple of Artemis at Magnesia on the River Maeander. The marvellous **mosaic floor** depicting the seasons comes from a villa in Antioch.

★★ **Boscoreale Treasure** – *Salle Henri II (gallery 33) on the 1st floor, Sully wing.* Its blue and black ceiling was painted by Braque in 1953 *(The Birds).*

This splendid collection was found at the heart of a vine growing area, in a place called Boscoreale, in the ruins of a Roman villa destroyed by the eruption of Mount Vesuvius in AD 79. The treasure trove consisted of coins, jewellery and **silver tableware**, all of which had been put into a wine tank for safe keeping. It gives a good indication of the sophisticated tastes of the wealthy and cultured social class. The most beautiful silver items were displayed on special stands for visitors to admire.

★★★ Near-eastern antiquities (Antiquités Orientales)

Ground floor of the Richelieu wing.

In 1843, **Paul-Émile Botta**, the French Consul in Mosul (Iraq), excavated the remains of the city built by Sargon II of Assyria – now the site of Khorsabad – thereby discovering a lost civilization.

The first Assyrian museum opened at the Louvre in 1847. Further digging was actively undertaken by **Victor Place**, until the 1930s when the Oriental Institute of Chicago took charge. The new Louvre galleries house the oldest treaties, laws and representations of historical scenes known to man.

An urban civilization evolved between 3300 and 2800 BC in the swampy region of the lower reaches of the River Tigris and River Euphrates (modern Iraq). The land of Sumer was divided among rival cities before the first empires arose.

Mesopotamia – *Galleries 1 to 6.* The Sumerian site of **Telloh** (ancient Girsu) was home to the famous **vultures stele** (c 2450 BC – *fragments displayed straight ahead of entrance*), immortalising the victory of the King Eannatum of Lagash over the rival city of Umma. On the side nearest the entrance, the guardian god of the city is seen capturing the enemy in a net; round on the other side, the prince is seen in a war chariot at the head of his foot soldiers.

On display by the entrance to gallery 1b, note the votive relief of Ur-Nanshe *(to the left)*, the founder of the Lagash dynasty, and the silver and copper vase dedicated by King Entemena of Lagash to the god Ningirsu *(to the right)*. Documents in the form of engraved terracotta cones are also exhibited.

The Sumerian culture spread northwards to what is now Syria (site of **Mari**); one custom was to offer small statues of worshippers intended to perpetuate the prayers of the faithful. The Louvre has an impressive collection of these statuettes dedicated to Ishtar; the most memorable of these being that of the **Intendant of the palace of Ebih-II**★ (middle of the 3rd millennium BC), with beautiful blue (lapis lazuli) eyes, and clothed in a voluminous, fluffy sheepskin skirt.

The Semitic dynasty of Akkad (2340-2200 BC) succeeded in uniting Mesopotamia around the ancient Babylonian city of Agade. Wonderful artefacts dating from this dynasty include the marvellous **stele of Naram-Sin** (2250 BC) in pink sandstone, which depicts the victorious king climbing a mountain over the dead bodies of enemy soldiers. Towards 2130 BC, the striking group of about a dozen fairly large **statues of Prince Gudea** and those of his son Ur-Ningirsu were produced in Lagash. This region regained its independence after the decline of the Akkad dynasty. The sovereign, wearing a robe on which there is a long prayer of dedication to the gods, is sometimes represented with an architect's materials.

At the beginning of the 2nd millennium BC, **Babylon** made its first impact on history: the Babylonian king destroyed Mari and conquered Mesopotamia. In the centre of the gallery stands the famous **Code of Hammurabi**★ (1792-50 BC), a black basalt stele 2.5m/8ft high; at the top, the king is depicted receiving from the sun god Shamash (who carries measuring instruments − ruler, surveyor's cord − symbolising justice) 282 laws which are engraved below in the Akkad language *(gallery 3)*.

The Babylonian Empire was succeeded by the Assyrian Empire in the 8C-7C BC. After the 6C BC, when Babylon reached the height of its power under King Nebuchadnezzar (*Passing Lion*, a relief in green and gold coloured glazed bricks adorned the triumphal route of the palace of Nebuchadnezzar II), the Eastern world, from the Mediterranean to India, was united under the rule of the Persian Empire.

★★ **Cour Khorsabad** − The large Assyrian reliefs from the palace of Sargon II at Dur-Sharrukin (modern Khorsabad) greet visitors at the same height as they would have been during the Assyrian era. Two **winged bulls** with five legs, so that two legs are visible when viewed from the front and four when in profile, reconstitute part of the decoration of the third doorway of the Khorsabad palace complex. The wall opposite is a reconstruction of the façade of the throne room (the bull on the left, with its head turned to look at the viewer, is a cast of the original now in the Oriental Institute, Chicago). Other wall space is taken by the frieze of marvellous bas-relief scenes *(Transporting Lebanese wood; Medes tributaries; (opposite) Bearers of the wheeled throne and the king's furniture)* interspersed with *Winged Genies giving blessing* and several images of a *Hero overcoming a lion*.

The Hittites, who brought the Hammurabi dynasty of Babylon to ruin, settled on the Anatolian plateau (at the heart of modern Turkey) in the middle of the 2nd millennium BC. Their hieroglyphic script can be seen on the **stele of the god of the storm**, Tahunda *(gallery 5)*.

The palace of the provincial capital **Til Barsip** was decorated with frescoes, rather than carving. Here, the fragments have been complemented by reconstructions of the original works *(gallery 6)*.

Arslan-Tash was another provincial capital with sites that yielded spoils of war from Phoenician or Armenian cities including some wonderful **ivories** *(Cow suckling calf)*. The central display case contains fragments of the bronze door from the palace of King Salmanasar III at Balawat (9C BC).

Reliefs from the palace of Ashurnasirpal II depict winged spirits, some with the heads of birds, giving blessing in front of the sacred tree. Further on, King Ashurnasirpal II (883-859 BC) is shown with his armour bearer.

The **reliefs**★★ from the palace of Ashurbanipal at **Nineveh** are numbered among the masterpieces of world sculpture. The site was excavated by British archaeologists. Note the stages of the Elamite campaign: the capture of a city; deportation of its population; view of the city of Arbeles with its many towers. On the far wall, Ashurbanipal II is shown in his chariot. In the last series of reliefs, note in front of the guards a marvellously detailed horse's head near the figure of a knight.

Iran − *Galleries 7 to 16*. Transhumance between the Fars mountains (to the east, on the mountainous plateau where Persepolis was later to be built) and the Susa plain perpetuated the Mesopotamian influence, and gave rise to the first Iranian state: **Elam**. From the end of the 5th millennium, Elamite potters (the capital of Elam was Susa) were becoming renowned for their beautiful, highly stylised animal (large vase with ibex) or geometric decoration.

Among the furniture from tombs and temples in the 3rd millennium is the statue of the goddess Narundi (c 2100 BC), and the painted terracotta **secret-compartment vase** (labelled *vase à la cachette*) found containing various objects including alabaster vases, weapons and copper tools *(gallery 8)*.

Princess of Bactria (early 2nd millennium BC)

The unusual open-work circular *standard* (with little linked human figures) supported by two bulls *(display case to the left, rue de Rivoli side)* belongs to **Luristan** culture, a region in the north-west of Elam widely reputed for its metalwork. Within the bounds of central Asia, a great civilization was flourishing in **Bactria** (Afghanistan). The figurine known as the **Princess of Bactria★★** wears a marvellous blue robe with full sleeves and a crinoline-like skirt, in a fleecy textile reminiscent of that on the statue of the *Intendant Ebih-Il (see gallery 1b above)*. Immediately to her right, **Le Balafré** (Scarface – he has also lost an eye) is the nickname given to the statuette of a mountain spirit.

The art of bronze reached its apogee during this period: see the **Statue of Queen Napirasu** in the centre of the gallery (note in particular the embroidery on her robe). Panels of cast bricks *(along the wall to the right)* depict alternately half-bull-half-man figures protecting a palm tree and Lama goddesses. These would once have adorned a temple *(gallery 10)*.

From the 6C to the 4C BC Susa reached its apogee under the Achaemenid kings. Gold- and silversmiths produced outstandingly delicate works of art (bracelets and goblets, winged ibex). The enormous **Apdana capital★★** from the palace of Darius at Susa gives some indication of the gigantic scale of the palaces of Persian rulers, which were decorated with enamel brick friezes.

The **mosaics** from the palace of Bichapur (3C AD) date from the Sasanian period and mark the transition to Muslim art.

Levantine art – *This collection is divided between the west wing of Cour Carrée, for the part representing the earliest evidence up to IC BC (starting from gallery 10) and the final galleries in the Sackler wing.*

Palestine and Transjordania – *West wing, galleries D to A.* On the **stele of Mesha**, King of Moab (9C BC) commemorates his victory over the kings of Israel and the Omri dynasty. Its reference to the Hebrew state is the earliest known.

Central Syria – Terracottas (vase bases, models of houses with storeys) and statuette of a seated god.

Excavation of Ugarit (modern Ras Shamra) has uncovered Phoenicia, the crossroads of the Ancient world: Egyptian-influenced **breast-plate** decorated with the royal falcon (2000-1600 BC); **stele of Baal with a Thunderbolt** (god of the storm), a beautiful **patera** depicting a royal hunting scene in repoussé gold (14C-13C BC). For the first time, c 1300 BC, the cuneiform alphabet is used in place of syllabic script.

Sackler wing – *Galleries 17 to 21.* Among the Phoenician tombs, the **sarcophagus in the form of the mummy of Eshmunazar II★★**, King of Sidon (5C BC) betrays Egyptian influence in Syria. It is engraved with the text of a curse. Marble sculptures from Sidon evoke the cult of Mithra, and bronzes that of Jupiter from Heliopolis (modern Baalbek) in Syria, during the Roman era.

There are astonishingly intense funeral portraits from Palmyra, as well as a lovely **Aphrodite with a Tortoise★**.

The colossal Basin of Amathus in limestone was made in the 5C BC, probably to collect the water supply necessary for the ceremonies of the city's temple *(gallery 21)*.

Cult statues from the island of Cyprus (7C-3C BC) and funerary strips in gold leaf.

★★ Islamic art

Richelieu wing, entresol, first staircase on the right, then straight ahead.

Exhibits from Spain, Egypt, Iran, Syria and India *(those from the Maghreb are displayed in the Museum of African and Oceanian Art at Vincennes)*. Because of their fragility and sensitivity to light, the miniatures are displayed in the environmentally controlled galleries of the entresol. Each exquisite exhibit displays the height of sophistication and refined stylisation.

The first gallery (A) is devoted to architecture (mosques, madrasas, Topkapi Palace).

The dawn of Islam – From Iran, seek out the dish inscribed with a partridge (Sasanian silverwork, 7C-9C), and the stone relief panel bearing two ibex face to face (7C-8C), a recurrent decorative motif, and the strange zoomorphic vase, made of blue and white glass.

The Abassidian world – The intricate fragment of cenotaph or chest (Egypt, late 9C-early 10C) is a rare early example of marquetry, an art form that was to become popular from the 12C: wooden door panel with plant ornamentation from the palace of Djawsaq al-Khaqani (Iraq, 836).

Islam in the West (10C-15C)

The contribution made by the civilizations of Islam to Western philosophy, art and science is considerable *(gallery 3)*. The kingdom of Granada in Spain flourished until 1492. Note the *Peacock aquamanile* (Spain, 13C), the work of a Muslim craftsman in the service of a Christian prince; marvellous caskets and ivory pyxes (sculpted cylindrical boxes) from Spain and Sicily, in particular the **pyx called after Al-Mughira** (10C, with a domed lid); the *Lion with an articulated tail* (Spain, 12C-13C) with a very large, wide-open mouth, possibly once part of a fountain.

Notice the 11C-12C dish decorated with an epigraphic inscription *(gallery 4, at the top of the display case by the entrance)* which reads: "The taste of knowledge is bitter at first, but is ultimately sweeter than honey. Health to him who possesses it."

Seljuq Iran (11C-13C) – *Gallery 5*. Ceramics include a ewer with an animal's head *(in the centre of the first display case)*. Scientific and technological instruments comprise astrolabes, celestial spheres, pestle and mortar, magic mirrors, a scale pan with beautifully intricate engraving (signs of the zodiac etc) and a **goldsmith's box of tools**. The glass case at the far end of the gallery displays writing tools (a knife with a coral handle was used to carve the calami). Gallery 6 accommodates a chandelier with ducks from Khurasan (12C-13C, *in the centre of the far end display case*) with decoration symbolising the idea of light and an open-work ceramic ewer with a cock's head *(to the right in the same display case)*.

Peacock dish (Iznik, 16C)

The Mamelukes (1250-1517) – *Galleries 8 and 9*. Here are some really marvellous exhibits in copper inlaid with gold and silver, carved with intricate patterns. The **Saint-Louis font** (1300), was used to baptise French children (decorated with fleur-de-lis, a frieze of knights and animals). Blue-glazed ceramics, lamps in blown glass, a Koran desk. Near the entrance, hanging from the wall, is the salver named after a Sultan of Yemen, a 14C work from Cairo.

Mongol Iran (13C-14C) – *Gallery 10*. The large dish with rings of fish *(at the far end of the display case along the left wall)* recall Chinese celadon ware (pale grey-green porcelain or earthenware) which was exported in large quantities during the Song and Yuan dynasties.

Safavid Iran (1501-1736) – *Gallery 11*. This was a period of magnificence for Iran, during which the capital, Ispahan, was one of the greatest cities in the world: decorative wall panel in painted tiles and, in the display case beyond it, a book-binding decorated with scenes of royal entertainment out of doors.

The portrait of the second sovereign of the Qajar dynasty (1779-1924) was offered to Napoleon I's ambassador to Persia. In the display case next to it, note two 19C cat figurines inlaid with gold and silver.

Mughal India (1526-1858) – Collection of weapons *(daggers)* and armour *(15C Iranian helmets)*; hookah bases (water pipes) – note the delicate inlaid work; dagger with a horse's head (with a rock crystal handle) and its sheath; early-18C floral stand. In the centre of the gallery, the **Mantes carpet** (so-called as it once adorned the floor of a church in this town) is a splendid late-16C Iranian work.

The Ottoman world (14C-19C) – *Gallery 12*. It was in the Imperial workshops, especially in **Iznik**, a suburb of Istanbul, that painters and draughtsmen produced the distinctive motifs that adorn these ceramics and tiles.

Various colours, including the famous Iznik red, were added to under-glaze blue and white during the 16C. Note the **saz** style of long, flowing flowers with frilly edges (saz), among the open leaves and real flowers (tulips, carnations and hyacinths). The masterpiece of this style is the **peacock dish** with its original bird motif *(in the middle display case on the right on entering)*.

The red and midnight blue carpet with the central medallion (18C, Turkey, Ushak) belongs to a type that was destined for the Court or for mosques.

To the left of the entrance, note the beautiful **scribe's table** (a little chest with legs) in wood, mother-of-pearl and tortoiseshell marquetry (Istanbul, 16C-17C). In the little bay tucked behind this display case, jade and rock crystal **cupels** (assay dishes) inlaid with gold wire and precious stones are displayed with two **archer's rings** designed to protect the archer's thumb from the rubbing of the bowstring. Two ceramic plaques in an alcove on the wall to the right depict the holy mosques of Mecca (Ka' ba veiled in black) and Medina.

The Art of the Book – *Gallery 13*. Bookbindings and miniatures (note the marvellously subtle use of colour on those from Mughal India).

★★★ Italian School: painting

Denon wing; first floor, to the left of the Winged Victory of Samothrace.

The collection of Italian paintings, one of the glories of the Louvre, was carefully acquired as a result of a passion harboured by the kings of France for the art of that peninsula. Renaissance masterpieces include such key works as the *Mona Lisa*, *The Wedding at Cana* and *The Man with the Glove*, but it is the Baroque pieces, favoured by Louis XIV, that are most especially unique. Numerous 19C and 20C bequests and acquisitions have since filled the gaps with works by the Primitives, who were unrepresented in the royal collections, and the Mannerist painters, who had not featured very significantly in them.

The collection is presented in chronological order.

Primitives and Quattrocento (15C) – In the *Salle Percier* and *Salle Fontaine*, by way of introduction to Italian painting, are the frescoes from the *Villa Lemmi* by **Botticelli** commemorating the marriage of Lorenzo Tornabuoni (surrounded by allegories of the Liberal Arts) with Giovanna degli Albizzi (offering her bridal veil to Venus and her attendants the three Graces). Fra Angelico's *Crucifixion* is found in the Salle Duchâtel.

Salon Carré – Thirty of the large-format Florentine **Primitives** hang where the former salons of the Académie des Beaux-Arts were held.

The large altarpiece, the *Virgin and Angels*, by the Tuscan **Cimabue** (c 1280) shows a move away from Byzantine conventions towards an attempt to portray movement, three-dimensional volume and space.

During the early part of the 14C, it is **Giotto** who maintains the momentum to greater realism. Narrative scenes are reduced to the essentials: in the large portrait of *Saint Francis of Assisi receiving the stigmata*★★, the saint is depicted in a rugged landscape of monumental proportions. Note the direct appeal in predella scenes of St Francis rebuilding the tottering church in *The Dream of Innocent III* and the charming *Saint Francis talking to the birds*.

A Dominican monk, **Fra Angelico** the Blessed, the painter of the convent of San Marco in Florence, evoked life in Paradise as serenely mystical. Saints and angels crowd round in the *Coronation of the Virgin*, painted in 1435 for the church of San Domenico at Fiesole outside Florence. The supernatural light illuminates the faces, the clothes in celestial hues of pink and blue, and the colourful patterns on the stairs leading up to the throne.

The *Virgin and Child* provides a constant inspiration explored by Fra Filippo Lippi, Botticelli, Perugino...

Intrigued by the problems of portraying perspective, **Paolo Uccello** painted the *Battle of San Romano*, in which the forces of Florence beat those of Siena in 1432 (the other panels, painted for the Medicis, are in Florence – Uffizi – and London – National Gallery): lances articulate the background space into regular stripes; the captain Michelotto Attendoli's black charger suggests depth; the surging crowd of armed warriors in magnificent plumed helmets are depicted ready to advance or retreat, accentuating the theatrical effect of movement and action.

Salle des Sept-Mètres – *Gallery 6*. In Siena, the jewel-like art of **Simone Martini** (small panel of the *Way to Calvary*) recalls the art of illumination.

The Quattrocento was a period of quest and rationalisation: how should space and volume be represented on a two-dimensional plane? Portraiture provided an opportunity for detailed observation and sensitive analysis: the medallion portrait in profile of *A Princess of the House of Este* by **Pisanello**; the authoritarian and enigmatic *Sigismondo Malatesta* by **Piero della Francesca**.

Grande Galerie – The immense cyma displays 13C to 15C works in its first part, as far as the famous Salle des États, and in the second part 16C and 17C works.

Subject matter, physiognomy and pose evolve. *Saint Sebastian* by **Mantegna** is so precisely observed as to be almost sculptural; the sorrowful *Resurrected Christ giving Blessing* by **Giovanni Bellini**. The *Portrait of an Old Man and a Young Boy* by **Ghirlandaio** combines Florentine elegance with Flemish realism, featured also in the strong, proud features of *Il Condottiere* and the face of the suffering *Christ at the column* by **Antonello da Messina**.

The High Renaissance – *Grande Galerie (second part devoted to the 16C and 17C)*. The fulfilment of objectives and the successful application of ideal principles marked a new phase of the Renaissance, this time concentrated in Rome and nurtured by a reformed Papacy. When the city was sacked in 1527, Venice became the power-base and ultimate patron of the Arts, a possession guarded until the end of the 16C.

Leonardo da Vinci (1452-1519), acclaimed as a universal genius, ranks in pride of place among the artists of this period. *The Virgin of the Rocks*, a mature work in which the play of the hands is particularly remarkable, strengthening the harmonious pyramidal arrangement of the figures against the rather menacing rocky crags of the background landscape; *The Virgin and Child with St Anne*, analysed by Sigmund Freud as suggesting Leonardo's childhood inhibitions: brought up by his grandmother and then his mother, he suffered recurrent nightmares about being attacked by a ravening vulture (seen in the folds of the Virgin's robes).

The portrait of **Mona Lisa★★★**, wife of the Florentine Del Giocondo, is displayed in room 13 *(at the western end of the Grande Galerie)*, in a special display case.

From the Grande Galerie, turn right and walk through rooms 9, 10 and 11 then turn right again and cross the gallery devoted to large French paintings to reach room 76.

The Fortune-Teller, Caravaggio

It contains the **Wedding at Cana★★★** by **Veronese**, executed in 1563 for the refectory of a convent in Venice, which covers one entire wall. The painter uses the scene from the Gospel as a pretext for painting the Golden Age of Venice the Serenissima with its majestic architecture and sumptuous lifestyle in a composition of consummate skill. The 130 figures in this enormous painting (66m²/710sq ft), recently restored, are mainly portraits of contemporary figures (Emperor Charles V, Suleiman the Magnificent, Titian, Bassano, Tintoretto and the artist himself playing the viola).

Return to the Grande Galerie.

Raphael (1483-1520), the pupil of Perugino, imbues his paintings with gentleness, his landscapes reflect the soft undulating countryside around his native Urbino. **La Belle Jardinière★★** portrays a gentle Virgin watching over the Infants Jesus and John the Baptist, combining humanity and harmony with religious faith. In the *Portrait of Balthazar Castiglione*, the temperament of the gentleman who was a close friend of Raphael is economically portrayed.

Correggio, who was a keen observer of women's sensibilities, developed in Parma a style combining a delicate and slightly self-conscious sensuality with a romantic elegance that was to influence painting into the 18C: *The Mystical Marriage of St Catherine, Antiope Sleeping.*

After 1530, the rest of Italy – Florence, Mantua, Rome – embraced Mannerism, imitating the style (*maniera* in Italian) of Michelangelo and Raphael **(Giulio Romano)** or creating portraits of an aristocratic and glacial elegance **(Bronzino)**.

Counter-Reformation (late 16C) and Seicento (17C) – *Beyond the passage that leads to the Mollien wing, housing graphic works (cartoons for tapestries by Lodi di Cremona, gouaches by Correggio).*

This period is dominated by the Bolognese School, following the founding of the Accademia degli Incamminati (Academy of the Progressives) by the Carracci brothers. A *Circumcision* is on display by the revivalist **Barocci**. The Grand Manner of the Bolognese and Roman Baroque Schools was to have a significant influence on 17C and 18C French painting.

The canvases of the Aemilian School (from the Emilia Romana region) are eclectic, fusing a tendency towards the academic, a legacy from the study of the masters of the Renaissance (Domenichino's *Saints)*, with forward-looking realism. This provides for a bold and virtuoso style of composition using varied poses and expressions, magnificent landscape settings and subtle lighting effects. The school's main exponents were **Annibale Carracci** (who often drew in the country; *Fishing* and *Hunting* might be said to be among the best landscapes in the Louvre), **Guido Reni** (who tended more to an aristocratic, decorative style: *Deianeira and the Centaur Nessus; David holding the head of Goliath*) and **Il Guercino** (painter of marvellously accurate human figures: *The Resurrection of Lazarus*).

This realism was adopted even more forcefully by **Caravaggio**, who modelled his figures upon people drawn from the poorer walks of life *(The Fortune-Teller★★)*. The *Death of the Virgin*, one of his most powerful works, was rejected by the chapter of the Roman church which had commissioned it because of its unorthodox use of an ordinary woman as the model for the Virgin.

At the end of the Grande Galerie, in the Pavillon des États, 17C works are exhibited in the Salle Salvatore Rossa: **Pietro da Cortona**, who practised in Rome *(Romulus and Remus discovered by Faustulus)*; **Domenico Fetti** of Venice *(Melancholy)*; and **Luca Giordano** of Naples *(Portraits of Philosophers* dressed in the clothes of ordinary people).

Settecento (18C) – *Painting from this period is housed in the Piazzetta gallery and the small adjacent rooms.* The opulent lifestyle of the noble classes during the Age of Enlightenment is reflected in the works of Pannini *(Concert given in Rome on the occasion of the marriage of the Dauphin, son of Louis XV).* **Guardi** captured the atmosphere of the lagoon of Venice in the dazzling series **Ascension Day Ceremonies★**, during which the Doge, in a sumptuous state barge, celebrated the marriage of Venice with the Adriatic by throwing a ring into the sea.

The luminous religious and mythological compositions of **Giambattista Tiepolo** contrast strongly with the scenes of street life painted by his son, **Giandomenico Tiepolo** *(The Charlatan, Carnival).* The life of the common man is also portrayed in the work of **Pietro Longhi**, often with a humorous touch *(Presentation).* The *Flea*, by **Crespi** of Bologna, is reminiscent of Dutch painting.

Spanish paintings are also displayed in the Pavillon des États.

★★ Spanish School: painting

Spanish painting is characterised by realism and mysticism.

The collection of 15C **Spanish Primitives** including *The Flagellation of Saint George* by Martorell of Catalonia, *The Flagellation of Christ* by Jaime Huguet and *Man with a Glass of Wine* by a Portuguese master precede the Mannerist Domenikos Theotokopoulos, an icon painter of Cretan origin, pupil of Tintoretto in Venice, better known as **El Greco**. His *Christ on the Cross★★*, with its stretched figure out-lined against a dark, stormy, almost abstract background, appears almost expressionist.

José de Riberac took subjects which were the social antithesis of the Spanish Golden Age, for example the *Club-footed Boy*, depicting the unfortunate cripple armed with his crutch and a note begging for charity (to indicate he was dumb as well), none the less with an open smile. Note also *The Young Beggar★★* by **Murillo**, unusually lit transversely. The humane realism of such paintings contrasts with the spirituality of **Zurbarán** *(Funeral Ceremonies of Saint Bonaventura)*, the baroque exuberance of Carreño de Miranda *(Mass for the founding of the Trinitarian Order)* and the stiff court Infanta portraits by **Velasquez**. The delightful Madonnas painted by Murillo in muted colours have the quality of pastels. The **Beistegui Collection** *(Sully wing, 2nd floor, take the Escalier Henri II)* includes the portrait of the *Marquesa de la Solana*, one of *Goya*'s best, along with that of the *La Comtessa de Santa Cruz*.

★★★French School: 19C large-format painting

Through the ground floor of the Denon wing (Salle du Manège and Galerie Daru), go up the Escalier Daru, before reaching the Winged Victory of Samothrace, take the ramp opposite. The large-format works of the French Revolution, Empire and the early 19C are displayed in the Daru and Mollien galleries, parallel with the Grande Galerie. Access is also possible behind the Salle des États.

The rest of the French School (14C-19C) is in the Richelieu wing, 2nd floor.

Women of Algiers, Delacroix

The Oath of the Horatii, commissioned by Louis XVI, which **David** despatched from Rome for the Salon of 1785, embodies the main elements of neo-Classicism in painting. As a History painting it tells a story drawn from classical literature in an uncompromising way, bold in its statement of virtue; masculine strength is contrasted with female sensibility. It was immensely well received.

A preliminary sketch for the **Coronation of Napoleon I★** shows the new Emperor crown-ing himself; in the final composition, however, Napoleon is shown in the act of crowning Josephine. The unfinished *Portrait of Madame Récamier*, opposite, depicts Bonaparte's opponent at the age of 23, reclining in the style of Classical Antiquity on a day bed *(see also Objets d'art)*.

Ingres' overwhelming concern with the expressive and sensual use of line can be clearly seen in *La Grande Odalisque* and his *Portrait of Mademoiselle Rivière*, where the aesthetic prevails over anatomical Realism.

Théodore Géricault gave artistic expression to current political issues; *The Raft of the Medusa★★* (1819) drew its subject matter from a recent disastrous shipwreck thought largely to be the result of governmental incompetence. The effects of back-lighting and the positions of the unfortunate victims of the shipwreck of the

Medusa, only one of whom is facing the viewer, evoke the wild fluctuations between hope and despair among the ragged survivors, who have just caught sight of the flag of the Argus (the ship which was eventually to rescue them) on the horizon. **Eugène Delacroix**, the leading exponent of Romanticism, expressed his support for the cause of Greek independence in *The Massacres at Chios*, inspired by the brutal repression imposed on the inhabitants of that island. His reaction to the days of violence in the 1830 Revolution was ***Liberty leading the People★★***, which he exhibited at the Salon. *The Women of Algiers* was painted in the wake of his trip to Morocco and Algeria, and demonstrates Delacroix' use of contrasting colour (red for foreground, green for depth). In ***The Death of Sardanapalus★***, the East is portrayed in a mixture of magnificence and barbaric decadence, as the Sultan had ordered that everything and everyone he held dear should be destroyed in front of him, before he himself committed suicide.

★★★ Northern Schools: painting

In the Richelieu wing, take the main escalator to the 2nd floor. Turn left off gallery 3 (French Painting).

This section includes the painting of the German, Flemish and Dutch Schools from the 14C to the 17C. Light in these galleries filters through an overhead structure of cruciform beams, designed by Pei.

Flemish Primitives – The Flemish Primitives paint delicate, oval faces, carefully drawn folds of clothing and exquisite textures while paying close attention to domestic detail.

The most famous work on display is the ***Madonna with Chancellor Rolin★★*** by **Jan van Eyck**, the artist who, with his brother, pioneered the technique of painting with oils. The serious expressions of the subjects, the detailed observation of the town and landscape in the background are quite remarkable. Nicolas Rolin was the founder of the Hôtel Dieu in Beaune (Burgundy) and an adviser to the Duke of Burgundy, Philip the Good.

The **Braque Family Triptych** is an intensely spiritual work painted by **Roger van der Weyden** in his mature period. The *Annunciation* is depicted against the background of a luxuriously furnished interior.

Hans Memling lived in the peaceful surroundings of Bruges with its beguine convents. He formulated a type of woman in his works, serene and beautiful; in the magnificent **Triptych of the Resurrection** and the *Portrait of an Old Woman*, Realism is compromised by a mood of gentle meditation.

Hieronymous Bosch's sharp sense of ridicule is well portrayed in *The Ship of Fools*.

German School – The chronological presentation of panels enables a comparison of the Flemish Primitives with those of the German School. The general self-contained harmony of the former is succeeded by the more self-consciously disturbed style of the latter: the colours are harsh; magnificent draperies are as minutely described as are the textures of jewellery and weapons; facial expression is often hard and tormented. Idealisation as portrayed by the Cologne School is sometimes to the detriment of spatial depth.

In the centre of the gallery, an original **painted table top** by Hans Sebald Beham depicts scenes from the life of David. The small room adjoining the gallery houses the prize exhibits of the collection: *Portrait of the Humanist Erasmus* by **Hans Holbein the Younger**; *Venus standing in the centre of a landscape* by **Lucas Cranach the Elder**; Albrecht **Dürer**'s *Self-Portrait* with a thistle, the symbol of fidelity, intended for his fiancée.

16C and 17C Flanders – Flemish Renaissance art retained many medieval features from the International Gothic painting style for some time: *Altarpiece of the Lamentation of Christ* by **Joos van Cleve** (note the predella); interesting portraits by Jan Gossaert, known as **Mabuse** *(Carondelet Diptych)*.

The Moneylender and his Wife★★ is one of the most famous works by **Quentin Metsys**. It depicts the couple absorbed in weighing and counting money – note the exquisite rendering of the hands complete with their shadowy veins; a profusion of minutely observed detail characterises the attributes of their household, a veritable still-life study on the shelves behind including a manuscript and pearls. In the centre of the picture, a convex mirror testifies to the presence of a third character or witness to the scene; a window provides a landscape view of the world outside. To the right of the picture, two more figures confer behind a half-open door.

Bruegel the Elder is represented by the small picture, *The Beggars* (in the room on the side of rue de Rivoli) interpreted in several ways to show a parody of royal power (cardboard crown), military power (paper helmet) or ecclesiastical power (bishop's mitre); the fox tails pinned to the beggars' cloaks serve to allude to the poverty stricken.

The Flemish Mannerists adopted aesthetic principles for painting the human figure imported from Italy (*David and Bathsheba* by Jan Massys, but retained their preoccupation with minute detail. The miniaturist tradition continued through the work of Jan Brueghel (son of Bruegel the Elder), known as **Velvet Brueghel** *(Battle of Arbelles)*.

Rubens, master of the Baroque, seems to exalt life itself (*Portrait of Hélène Fourment*, his second wife; *The Village Fair*, gallery 21) with fleshy bodies and sumptuous attire *(Hélène Fourment in her Carriage)*. All these elements abound in the 24-panel cycle celebrating the *Life of Queen Marie de Medici*, now housed in the new **Galerie Médicis★★** (gallery 18) designed by Pei.

Jordaens, a pupil of Rubens, cultivated a highly coloured realism which verged on earthiness *(gallery 19, on the cour Napoléon side)*: *The King Drinks!*, *Jesus chasing the Merchants from the Temple*, *The Four Evangelists*.

Van Dyck was the portraitist to the Genoese and English aristocracy *par excellence (gallery 24)*, catching the refined elegance of both courts: *Charles I, King of England*, *The Marquessa Spinola-Doria*, *The Palatine Princes*.

17C Dutch School – The Netherlands, a maritime republic, fashioned its art to bourgeois taste depicting domestic scenes, portraiture and landscape *(galleries 28 to 39)*.

Frans Hals pioneered the character portrait with pictures such as the *Gypsy Girl* and the *Lute-player*. His robust style was to influence Fragonard *(see French Painting)* and Manet.

Wonderful landscapes are portrayed by **Jacob van Ruisdael** *(Ray of Sunlight)* and **Van Goyen**, his silvery river scenes stretching into far distances *(gallery 38)*.

Rembrandt gradually forsook *chiaroscuro* in favour of a more limited, but more subtle palette ranging through warm, rich, earthy tones of gold and brown; highlighted detail projects out of the darkness, giving a somewhat unreal but none the less highly emotive effect *(The Philosopher in Meditation)*. Frequent exploration of subject-matter drawn from the Bible enabled him to transcend the realms of reality and everyday life *(Pilgrims of Emmaus)* whilst never compromising the very human quality of his figures. Note the rendering of the nude in *Bathsheba bathing*, a portrait of his second wife, and of the problems and loneliness that beset the artist in his old age, painfully etched on the face in his poignant *Self-Portrait before an Easel* (gallery 31).

The Astronomer, Vermeer

Other masters of this period include **Ter Borch**, **Pieter de Hooch**, **Gerrit Dou** and **Adriaen van Ostade**, who were principally genre painters. **Vermeer van Delft** imbues his contemplative scenes of domestic activity with poetic peace *(The Lacemaker★★, The Astronomer★★)* a quality achieved by his use of indirect light and oblique shadows.

★★★French School: painting

Richelieu wing: take the main escalator to the 2nd floor. Large-format 19C French Painting is exhibited in the Denon wing.

It is difficult to define the particular characteristics of the French School of painting, despite the extensive collection of the Louvre spanning the 14C to the 19C. Categorised retrospectively into movements, stylistic development is punctuated by strong individual characters who often sought inspiration from abroad: Italy, Flanders, the Netherlands. A complete tour through 73 galleries is a huge undertaking. The collection is arranged chronologically by genre, each serving very well as the focus of a visit in itself (the Primitives, the Fontainebleau School, the Caravaggisti, 17C religious painting etc). Certain groups of works by particular artists are outstanding: Claude Lorrain, Poussin, Fragonard, Chardin and Corot.

14C – *Galleries 1 and 2*. **Jean le Bon**, soon to be King of France, posed for a **Portrait★** (1350) at a time when the subjects of painting were almost exclusively religious. The *Narbonne altarcloth*, with its beautiful Gothic decoration on silk, is a typical example of the art of the time.

15C – *Galleries 3 to 6.* The International Gothic tradition of portraying narrative subjects on a gold background was maintained by the Court of Burgundy *(Altarpiece of Saint Denis* by Henri Bellechose, *gallery 3).* The two Thouzon Altarpiece panels *(gallery 4)* are from a slightly earlier period. Provençal art, with its severe style and strong contrasts in light, is represented by the *Pietà of Villeneuve-lès-Avignon* by **Enguerrand Quarton**, a work of great poignancy: the tragedy of the scene is conveyed in the dislocated body of Christ, scarred by the flagellation, the paralysed rigid attitudes of the other, living figures and the despair of the bowed heads.

In central France, Jean Hey, known as the **Master of Moulins**, trained in Flanders, adds a French predilection for elegance to his meticulous drawings *(Portrait assumed to be of Madeleine of. Burgundy with Mary Magdalen).*

In the north, **Jean Fouquet** *(see also gallery 6: Objets d'art)*, a protégé of Agnès Sorel, created true and realistic portraits: **Charles VII**, on the day after his victory over the English; **Guillaume Jouvenel des Ursins**, Chancellor of France.

16C – *Galleries 7 to 10.* Renaissance artists were passionately interested in Humanism. Consequently, many works of art of this period focus on the individual, hence the profusion of portraits, such as those by **Jean Clouet** *(François I★)* and his son **François Clouet** *(The Botanist Pierre Quthe).*

The Italian artists summoned by François I during the construction of the Château de Fontainebleau introduced Mannerism into French decorative and applied arts. The First and Second Schools of Fontainebleau are represented respectively by *Diana the Huntress,* which has been thought to be the portrait of Diane de Poitiers, Henri II's mistress, and ***Gabrielle d'Estrée with one of her sisters★***, probably painted to celebrate the birth of one of Henri IV's illegitimate children.

17C – *Galleries 11 to 34.* This century opened with the Caravaggisti, painters often patronised by Cardinals who had served in Rome and who encouraged a taste for Caravaggio's distinctive use of *chiaroscuro* and the direct realism of his figures *(see Italian Painting, Denon).* Next to the magnificent collection of works by **Valentin de Boulogne** (*The Concert* bas-relief) is a charming work by **Claude Vignon**, *Young Singer,* remarkable for the freedom of its execution. During the reign of Louis XIII, the somewhat academic allegories of **Simon Vouet** *(Wealth)* contrast with the austere, controlled style of **Philippe de Champaigne**, who emphasises in his ***Portrait of Cardinal de Richelieu★*** the dignity and unbending will of the statesman. Galleries 20 to 23 are devoted to the graphic arts in France in the 17C *(Le Grand Siècle)*, in particular to drawings by **Le Brun** *(Horses of Dawn's Chariot)* intended for the decoration of Versailles and Sceaux, and to pastels. Paintings by this artist can be seen in galleries 31 and 32.

Georges de la Tour (1593-1652) is a famous master of the illuminated figure on a black background, as exemplified in ***The Cheat★***, where the card players exchange intriguing glances.

Nicolas Poussin (1594-1665), the artist-philosopher who settled in Rome is represented by a marvellous collection of canvases *(from gallery 12).* He is regarded as the most Classical of

The Cheat, Georges de la Tour

French academic painters, drawing from the formal canons of Beauty and yet remaining sensitive to the sensuality of colour inspired by Titian.

In later life, landscape in his painting becomes increasingly important, as composition is meticulously articulated by near, middle and far distance. Particular canvases to note include *Inspiration of the Poet; The Great Bacchanal; The Triumph of Flora;* and *Shepherds of Arcadia.* Platonic ideas of Nature as a nourishing force and of the cyclical progression of life and time are expressed in ***The Four Seasons★★***, in landscapes which are cold but harmonious.

Claude Gellée (1600-82), otherwise known as **Le Lorrain**, provides another high point. His canvases show land– and seascapes bathed in soft twilight: *Cleopatra's Arrival at Tarsus, View of a Seaport at Sunset.* He was perhaps the first painter to attempt to paint the sun as a direct light source, hence his influence upon the English painter Turner and later the Impressionists.

Galleries 25 to 29 – Numerous genre scenes and small-format still-life works were executed by painters inspired by Flemish artists working in Paris, such as **Lubin Baugin** *(behind the screen in gallery 27: Still life with wafers, Still life with chess board).*

Painting becomes a vehicle for portraying social reality in the works of **Le Nain brothers** where sober realism hints at the moderate wealth of a middle-class patron: *Peasant Family at home*★ (healthy faces, stemmed wine glass, *gallery 29*).

Eustache Le Sueur (1616-55) was both a painter of religious subjects *(Life of Saint Bruno, gallery 24)* and a sophisticated decorative artist influenced by Raphael (**The Muses** from the Hôtel Lambert, *gallery 25*).

Gallery 31 – Chancellor Séguier on horseback is a solemn, official portrait by **Le Brun** of his first patron, shown surrounded by his pages, exuding an awareness of the responsibility conferred on him by Louis XIII.

Gallery 32 – This gallery contains the huge compositions by Le Brun depicting scenes from the life of Alexander. In the same gallery, **Philippe de Champaigne** displays his talent for creating penetrating portraits of his contemporaries *(Portrait of Robert Arnault d'Andilly)*. He also painted the famous **ex-voto of 1662**, a reflection of the Jansenist spiritual ideal, in thanksgiving for the miraculous cure of his daughter, a nun at the convent of Port-Royal-des-Champs.

18C - *Galleries 34 to 54*. The *Portrait of Louis XIV* by **Rigaud** (1701) was so well received by the monarch that he kept the original for himself despite it having been commissioned as a present for his grandson, Philip V of Spain, who had to be content with a copy. Only a few years separate this image of the Grand Siècle from the dreamy, elegant canvases of **Watteau** (d 1721), heralding the spirit of the Age of Enlightenment. In the marvellous *Pilgrimage to Cythera*★★, the figures preparing to leave the island of Venus are portrayed in a gently curving line against a softly lit landscape. Theatre was another source of inspiration for painters as demonstrated in works by Watteau's teacher, **Claude Gillot** *(Quarrel of the Cabmen*, inspired by the *Commedia dell'Arte)*, and in those of Watteau himself, such as the strange and famous figure of **Gilles**.

Lancret's decorative scenes of light-hearted bantering *(The Music Lesson, Innocence)* were intended to be inserted in panelling. The hunting scenes by **Jean-François de Troy** and **Carle van Loo** were painted for the dining room in the Royal Suite at Fontainebleau.

Boucher often drew his subject matter from mythology, allowing him free licence to treat them with a delicacy not untinged with eroticism: **Diana resting after her bath** and **Odalisque** *(gallery 38)*, both painted in fresh, shimmering tones.

A more modest realism fashions the works of **Chardin** in both his still-life paintings *(The Ray*★, The Buffet, The Copper Cistern)* and his genre paintings *(Child with Top, The Purveyor, Child saying Grace)*.

Luncheon (gallery 40) by **Boucher** was the first during a short period in which the artist was strongly influenced by Dutch masters; in it he depicts his own family at table, thereby providing an insight into the customs and furniture of the period.

Galleries 41 to 45 – The collection of delicate pastels and miniatures in the Couloir des Poules and adjacent galleries by **Quentin de la Tour** *(Portrait of the Marquise de Pompadour*★*)*, Chardin and others surround the great religious and mythological paintings contained in gallery 43: *Pentecost* by **Restout**; *Meal at Simon's House* by **Subleyras**.

Galleries 46 and 47 – Landscapes, which until now had provided a setting for the main characters in the picture, now become the subject in the works of **Joseph Vernet** *(Toulon Roadstead)*.

Galleries 48 and 49 – **Fragonard**'s light touch and happy sense of movement are combined in *The Bathers* and his **fantasy figures** *(Portrait of Abbé de Saint-Non)*. *The Lock*★, while still light-hearted in spirit, is more formal in composition, succumbing to the neo-Classical influence of Jacques-Louis David.

Shortly before the Revolution, **Hubert Robert** undertook to paint a series of canvases for the apartment of Louis XVI at Fontainebleau, thereby initiating a taste for Romanticised Roman ruins, idealised and juxtaposed irrespective of topographical accuracy *(The Pont du Gard)*.

Elisabeth Louise Vigée-Lebrun (1755-1842)

Vigée-Lebrun was, in her time, one of Europe's most famous portraitists. As a woman, she was not allowed formal training, but through skill and drive she achieved admission to the Royal Academy. When her patrons were exiled or executed during the French Revolution, she began 12 years of travel in Europe with her young daughter and her paintbrushes (but without her husband). It is curious that she was both an ardent monarchist and defender of the social order, and a freedom-loving, single working mother. Her uncritical, flattering style of portraiture has been criticised, but recently art historians have taken a second look at this prolific artist (by her own account, 877 pictures), who now has her own room at the Louvre *(Gallery 52)*.

Gallery 51 – Note also, by the same painter, two canvases depicting the **Grande Galerie du Louvre**, one as a construction project, the other as a ruin.

Following Diderot's advice, **Greuze** began painting scenes with moral subjects (comparable perhaps with Hogarth's Harlot/Rake's Progress during the 1730s), thus formulating a new genre. Themes of family tensions in a rustic setting seemed to be ideal for extolling virtue *(The Father's Curse; The Punished Son)*. Gallery 52 is devoted to the delicate portraits of **Elisabeth Vigée-Lebrun**.

Neo-Classicism – *Gallery 54*. Devoted to **David** *(Portrait of Madame Trudaine)* and his pupils *(Bonaparte at Arcole*, by Gros), who mark the transition from the 18C to the 19C.

19C – *Galleries 55 to 73*. Works by **Prudhon:** *Marie-Marguerite Lagnier; Venus Bathing or Innocence*.

Ingres, pupil of David, best epitomises the softer neo-Classical taste of the Empire. Clarity of line and form are the main concerns of this artist who vigorously opposed those of the colourists Delacroix and Géricault, imposing a different interpretation of exotic subjects beloved to both factions of the Romantic School: *The Turkish Bath★*, painted 54 years after *The Valpinçon Bather★*, uses the same nude subject seen from behind. The *Portrait of Monsieur Bertin* draws inspiration from Flemish Realism. Ingres was Director of the Académie de France in Rome (Villa Medici) when his pupil **Hippolyte Flandrin** painted his study *Young Nude Man by the Sea* (1837 – *gallery 63*). **Géricault** regularly painted horses racing *(Epsom Derby★)*, thrilled by the latent power of the horse, just as his excellent portraits *(The Madwoman obsessed with Gambling – La Monomane du jeu)* show his fascination with personality through physiognomy. **Delacroix's** Romantic passion is apparent through his free and speedy brushwork notably in his *Self-Portrait★*; his *Landscape under a wide sky* prefigures the Impressionists *(gallery 62)*. Other notable works include his *Young orphan girl at the cemetery (gallery 71)*; the reworked study of the head of a young man in the *Massacres at Chios (see Large-Format 19C French Painting, Denon wing)*.

Jean-François Millet is remembered for his depictions of humble peasant life *(The Winnower)*.

The final galleries are devoted to **Corot**, who is recognised by his landscapes, often bathed in nostalgia, vibrant with scintillating light in the fresh, clear air *(Souvenir of Mortefontaine, Marissel Church, Bridge at Mantes)*. *Douai Belfry* was painted during his stay in northern France; a number of views, notably *Volterra, View of Florence from the Boboli Gardens* and decorative panels for a bathroom *(gallery 68)* resulted from three journeys made to Italy. He was also an accomplished portraitist *(The Lady in Blue, The Lady with the Pearl)*.

★ Beistegui Collection

Take the Escalier d'Henri II to the 2nd floor and turn left (the end of the tour of the galleries of French painting is to the right).

Go through the gallery next to the staircase which displays a different painting every month – the *tableau du mois* – a work which is currently of particular interest (a recent acquisition, restoration, commemorative work etc).

The entire **collection of Carlos Beistegui** (1863, Mexico-1953, Biarritz) consisting above all of portraits, is displayed in a special gallery.

Note the *Portrait of a young artist* and a scene of dissolute living *(Le Feu aux poudres)* by **Fragonard**; **David**'s famous *Unfinished Portrait of Napoleon; The Duchess of Chaulnes as Hebe* by Jean-Marc Nattier; *Dido's Suicide* by **Rubens**; and *The Marquesa de la Solana★* (1794), one of **Goya**'s best-known works.

★★ Italian School: sculpture

Denon wing: at entresol level. The collection continues on the ground floor directly above.

Donatello Gallery – 13C Italian sculpture is stylised and static *(Virgin* from Ravenna), produced at a time of instability often coined as the Dark Ages. A century later, artists and sculptors learnt to review Roman reliefs, re-interpreting their subject matter as Christian narrative. From Pisa (graceful *Virgin* by Nino Pisano) to 15C Siena (Jacopo della Quercia *seated Madonna*) and Florence, sculpture evolved to conform with Renaissance aesthetics, towards idealised form and calculated proportion (**Donatello** bas-relief of *The Virgin and Child★*, **Verrocchio** two delightful little angels). Other fine examples include a **bust** of a young lady in painted and gilded wood and the enchantingly delicate medallion by Desiderio da Settignano. Francesco Laurana is represented by a bust of the *Princess of Aragon*.

By the close of the 15C Florentine sculpture features a more mannered elegance (Agostino di Duccio bas-relief and the Della Robbia family vitrified lead-glazed terracottas).

Benvenuto Cellini's *Nymph of Fontainebleau* is well placed on the banister of the Mollien staircase.

Michelangelo Gallery – The two marble *Slaves*★★★ (1513-20) sculpted by **Michelangelo** for the tomb of Pope Julius II, although uncompleted are famous masterpieces as expressions of strength apparently breaking out of the rough stone.

Bernini's distinctive, lively modelling is evident in the modello for the *Angel bearing the Crown of Thorns*, whereas his bust of *Cardinal Richelieu* is both expressive and monumental.

The neo-Classical *Psyche Revived by the Kiss of Cupid*★★ (1793) is quite exquisite, contrived by **Canova** to blend the Antique with a Rococo lightness of touch.

★★ Northern Schools: sculpture

Denon wing: at entresol level, beyond the Italian sculptures, and continued on the ground floor above in the west wing of Cour Lefuel.

The brittle, deeply folded drapery of the *Virgin of Isenheim*, near Colmar, is typical of sculpture of the German School of the late Middle Ages, often executed in polychrome lime wood. Swabian sculptors imbue their figures with greater serenity (*Mary Magdalen* by Gregor Erhart), whereas the great Franconian master **Tilman Riemenschneider** produced more delicate pieces such as the marble **Virgin of the Annunciation**★.

In the Netherlands, large numbers of polychrome multi-panelled altarpieces composed of small picturesque scenes carved in wood were produced, and exported (*Coligny altarpiece* from Marne).

Along passage Richelieu, note the splendid glass panes designed by **Peter Rice** to provide an appropriate setting for the rich displays of the museum's new wing.

★★★ French School: sculpture

The collection dominates the ground floor of the Richelieu wing: Cour Marly, Crypte Girardon and Cour Puget together with surrounding galleries.

The inauguration of the Richelieu wing has provoked a re-appraisal of the Louvre sculpture collections. Sheltered by wonderful glass roofs, the sculptural groups which adorned 17C and 18C Royal parks may be surveyed in Cour Marly and Cour Puget. The Renaissance collection is very comprehensive; any gaps in medieval sculpture may be filled by a visit to the Cluny Museum *(see QUARTIER LATIN)*; neo-Classical sculpture, which had been languishing in storage, is at last enjoying the presentation it deserves.

High Middle Ages and Romanesque – *Galleries 1 to 3*. The fast evolution of Romanesque architecture enabled sculpture to flourish and develop in tandem, complete with its own regional differences.

Compare the stylised ornamentation of the 12C **Estagel priory doorway** (Gard region) with the three fine double capitals from an abbey in the Languedoc region.

The 12C **Courajod Christ**, once part of a Deposition, exemplifies the degree of skill attained in this art form at this time. Other particularly remarkable exhibits include: *Saint Michael vanquishing the dragon*, a marvellous triangular composition from Nevers; a *Virgin in majesty* from Auvergne; **capitals** from Burgundy and Poitiers *(David fights Goliath, Harvest scene)*; and finally, the **Carrières-sur-Seine altarpiece** *(gallery 3 on the side of Cour Marly)*, which marks the transition from Romanesque to Gothic art.

Virgin and Child

Gothic – *Galleries 4 to 9*. The Gothic Middle Ages, the age of cathedrals, produced figurative sculpture imbued with such grace, poise, sophistication and serene beauty on the one hand and such expressive realism on the other as to bear comparison with the best creations from Antiquity.

The rigid, linear style of the **statue columns** from the old church of Corbeil, Solomon and the Queen of Sheba, reflect the spirituality of nascent Gothic art.

In the 13C and 14C, sculpture progressed towards ever greater regional characteristics: delightful **smiling angels** in northern France; *Saint Matthew being dictated the Gospel by the Angel of God* from the rood screen of Chartres Cathedral; marble altarpiece fragments from the abbey of Maubuisson (Val d'Oise). Displayed in gallery 6 is the Javenant *Virgin of the Annunciation*, tinged with self-consciousness, a fine warrior's head, and a number of representations of the Virgin and Child.

Subsequent galleries accommodate fragments of funerary monuments: small **figures guarding the entrails** (symbolised by little bags) **of King Charles IV the Fair and Queen Jeanne d'Evreux** by **Jean de Liège**; the statues of *Charles V* and *Jeanne de Bourbon* which were once part of the Louvre's medieval ornamentation.

Late Gothic – *Galleries 10 to 12*. Funerary monuments become much larger in the 15C: the **tomb of Philippe Pot★★**, Seneschal of Burgundy, is particularly impressive with its famous hooded mourners; the tomb of Renée d'Orléans-Longueville has unusual Italianate decoration; the recumbent figure of Anne of Burgundy, resting on a black-marble slab, was made in a Paris workshop (note the quality of detail in the facial features of the deceased). In gallery 11, the *Saint George fighting the dragon*, a famous bas-relief by **Michel Colombe**, heralds the Renaissance.

Renaissance – *Galleries 13 to 19*. The *Mort-Saint-Innocent* gallery is named after the macabre effigy of death which once stood at the centre of the Parisian cemetery of this name *(see les HALLES)*. To the right of the entrance, note the **altarpiece of the Resurrection of Christ**, a delicately executed work in stone combining Flamboyant Gothic motifs with Renaissance ornamentation.

The influence of Italian art is tempered by ideals of grace and detail: the recumbent figure of Amiral Philippe de Chabot resting on its elbow, fashioned by the chisel of **Pierre Bontemps**; the delicate detail of the bas-relief sculptures by **Jean Goujon**, architect and sculptor of the old Louvre; the power and masterly skill in the works of Germain Pilon (*Resurrected Christ*, group of the **Three Graces** from the monument of the heart of Henri II, *Mater Dolorosa*). The distant sensuality of **Diana of Anet** echoes the tendencies of the School of Fontainebleau *(see French School: Painting-16C)*.

The works of **Jacques Sarazin** and **Simon Guillain** *(Monument from the Pont au Change)* point towards Classicism. The *Longueville pyramid* in the final gallery is decorated with beautiful reliefs in bronze gilt. Architectural form dominates over sculpture in the funerary monument of Jacques-Auguste de Thou.

The staircase, **Escalier Lefuel**, features an impressive array of arcades and banisters *(leading to the Objets d'art Department: medieval treasure, and 17C Flemish Paintings)*.

The 17C – French sculpture evolved little during the reigns of Henri IV and Louis XIII before enjoying a great vogue through the reign of Louis XIV. The new layout of this part of the Louvre into terraced courtyards provides the perfect setting for the magnificent figurative groups that once adorned the parks of royal residences at Marly, Versailles, Sceaux and the Tuileries.

★★ **Cour Marly** – The **Château de Marly**, sadly now demolished, was used by Louis XIV as a retreat from the restraints of Court etiquette, to be enjoyed in the company of a few carefully selected courtiers. The grounds were decorated with wonderful sculpture in the late 17C and 18C, only some of which is now here.

The most famous figures adorned the **Abreuvoir**, or horse pond: **Fame** by **Coysevox** comprises *Fame, setting a trumpet to her lips*, and *Mercury, messenger of the Gods*, was replaced in 1745 by the famous rearing **Marly horses★★** being restrained by horse tamers, by **Guillaume Coustou**, nephew of Coysevox.

Other statues ornamenting the fountains or the park included the charming running effigies *(Apollo and Daphne, Atlanta and Hippomenes)* and *Aeneas carrying Anchises* by **Pierre Lepautre** (1716).

★ **Crypte Girardon** – This area between the Marly and Puget courtyards houses an impressive relief by Pierre Puget of the meeting of *Diogenes and Alexander* against a background inspired by the Roman Forum.

Busts on display include *The Grand Condé*, a bronze by **Antoine Coysevox**, who captures the rough looks and lean physique of this great soldier while displaying his aristocratic rank (breast-plate decorated with griffins); the equestrian statue of *Louis XIV* by **François Girardon** is a smaller version of that which once adorned place Vendôme.

★★ Cour Puget – The first statues to catch the eye are the *Captives* from place des Victoires which, like those by the statue of Henri IV on Pont Neuf, once adorned the pedestal of the equestrian statue of Louis XIV; these were removed during the Revolution, along with all other Royal effigies.

The courtyard is named after the famous self-taught sculptor, painter, decorator and architect from Marseille, **Pierre Puget** (who drew up the designs for the Hôpital de la Vieille-Charité in the city of his birth). Profoundly impressed by Baroque Italy, Puget emerged as a highly individual figure in 17C French sculpture: *Milo of*

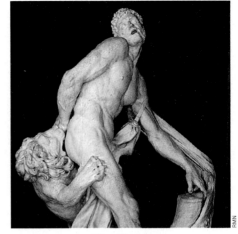

Milo of Croton

Croton★★ was displayed at the entrance to the Royal avenue in the gardens of Versailles; *Hercules the Gaul* (or *Hercules resting*) was bought by Colbert for his château at Sceaux. In his series of herms, note those from Colbert's residence *(to the left, rue de Rivoli side)* which include the extraordinary representation of *Winter*, muffled up to the ears and shivering with cold.

The middle level of terraces accommodates the charming *Duchess of Burgundy* by Coysevox and an impressive *Julius Caesar* by Nicolas Coustou. The bas-relief from the Hôtel de Bourbon-Condé *(on the wall)* exemplifies the delicate sculpture of **Clodion**.

The upper level is devoted to neo-Classical sculpture; notice *Roland in a frenzy*, a tormented bound figure in bronze by **Jehan Duseigneur**.

· The 18C – *Galleries along rue de Rivoli*. The smaller sculptures, especially the terracottas, are particularly captivating.

The exquisite *Cupid putting a finger to his lips*★ by **Falconet** *(gallery 22)* was commissioned by Madame de Pompadour to adorn the garden of her mansion, the Hôtel d'Évreux, now the Palais de l'Élysée. In a display case, there is a *Bather* stretching her foot towards the water of a fountain.

Cupid whittling a bow from Hercules' club★ by **Bouchardon** *(gallery 23)* was ill-received when presented to the Court in 1750, as Cupid was felt to be too realistic.

The *Effigy of Voltaire, nude* by **Jean-Baptiste Pigalle** (1776) is a bold study of the ageing philosopher. Note also the graceful *Bather* (or *Venus*) by **Christophe-Gabriel Allegrain** *(gallery 24)*.

Gallery 25 contains fragments of sculpture received by the Académie Royale de Peinture et de Sculpture: the version of **Pigalle**'s masterpiece *Mercury doing up his sandals (display case on the right)* is more sophisticated than that in bronze in the courtyard; *Dying Gladiator (on its own at the far end of the gallery)* by **Pierre Julien**; *Morpheus (display case opposite)* by **Houdon**.

The bust of the *Comtesse du Barry* by **Pajou** is a famous representation of the royal favourite; *Psyche abandoned* (because she had just looked on the face of her lover, Cupid, thereby disobeying his request that she should not see him) caused an uproar because of its complete nudity and stark realism *(gallery 27)*.

The marble **head of Voltaire** (1778), by **Jean-Anatole Houdon**, was sculpted shortly after the triumphant reception given to the defender of the oppressed on his arrival in Paris *(gallery 28)*.

The **gallery of great men** *(in the centre of gallery 29)* regroups a series of marble effigies between *Diana the Huntress* by Houdon, and *Peace*.

Among the neo-Classical sculpture note the lovely group of *Zephyr carrying off Psyche (near the window, gallery 31)*.

Mythological figures by **Jean-Jacques Pradier**, the official sculptor, adopt Mannerist poses *(Three Graces)*. *The Genius of Liberty* by Augustin Dumont is a replica of the statue which stands atop the column of the Bastille *(gallery 32)*.

The final gallery *(33)* is devoted to the work of **François Rude**, author of the *Marseillaise* on the Arc de Triomphe *(a model of the face in a display case)*, *Mercury doing up his sandals* and a graceful *Neapolitan Fisherman*, and **Antoine-Louis Barrye** who is famed for his observation of animals, sculpted in minute detail, effectively rendering the morphology of wild creatures: *Lion Hunt; Tiger devouring a gavial*.

★★★ Objets d'art

These are exhibited on the 1st floor of the Richelieu wing, and of the west wing of Sully. For a chronological visit, take the corridor on the right, then the escalator designed by Pei.

The galleries of the Richelieu wing were redesigned in 1993, replacing eight floors of offices conceived during the 1850s when the palace was completed. The department, however, already had a long history dating back to the Revolution when part of the treasure of St-Denis was deposited here in 1793. This basic collection was subsequently endowed with the Royal collections of bronzes and vases in precious stones *(see Galerie d'Apollon, Denon)*, with furniture from former Royal residences belonging, by the late 19C, to the State, and with many private donations, bringing the total number of pieces in the collection to 10 000.

Unlike the Museum of Decorative Arts next door, this department of the Louvre holds no copies or reconstructions of period pieces. The beautiful presentation cases are designed by **Jean-Michel Wilmotte**.

★★★ Medieval treasure of the Louvre

★★★ **Medieval treasure of the Louvre** – This is one of the high points of a visit to the Louvre. The most famous exhibits come from the Royal Abbey of St-Denis *(see EXCURSIONS)* which served the French monarchy as a mausoleum. The gold and silver plate and above all the ivories, some of which are over 1 000 years old, are quite astounding.

The entrance to gallery A is flanked by two pink porphyry columns with the bust of an emperor projecting from each just above head level. These columns are supposed to have been part of the atrium of the basilica of St Peter in Rome, built by Constantine in the 4C AD.

Byzantium – *Right as you enter gallery 1.* Many western churches have been embellished with the spoils of Constantinople, pillaged by the Crusaders (1204). **Ivories**, luxurious possessions, date mainly from the 10C and 11C, a period when the empire had reached the apogee of its splendour under the Macedonian dynasty.

Among the many ivories, note the **Harbaville triptych** (10C), named after the collector who acquired it shortly after its discovery; a casket decorated with rosettes enclosing scenes from mythology; the magnificent **Barberini ivory** *(to the left of the central aisle)* depicts a triumphant emperor (6C).

Charlemagne and the High Middle Ages – Opposite the entrance is displayed a 9C **equestrian statue of Charlemagne** or possibly of **Charles the Bald**, modelled on Antique equestrian statues *(the horse has been restored)*. The ivories are no less splendid than those in the Byzantine section.

The objects discovered in 1959 in the tomb of Queen Arnegonde, wife of Clovis' son Clothair I (511-561), at St-Denis testify to the talent of these so-called barbarian goldsmiths: large brooch, both parts of an **ornate belt buckle** and a pair of fibulae inlaid with garnets.

Romanesque and early Gothic art – Suger, the Abbot of St-Denis (1122-51), hoped to make his abbey one of the leading churches in Christendom. He experimented with a new type of construction, based on ogive vaulting, and enriched his treasury with liturgical vases. The most famous of these, the **Eagle of Abbot Suger★★**, incorporates an Antique porphyry vase *(display case opposite the entrance)*. To the right of the eagle *(same display case)*, note the beautiful **Aliénor crystal vase** which is thought to be a 6C or 7C Ancient Iranian work, and to the left, a 7C Byzantine **sard ewer**.

The display cases in the bay to the left of the central aisle contain some marvellous exhibits from Germany: an **aquamanile** (type of ewer) in the shape of a griffin; quadrifoil *Reliquary of Saint Henri* (Emperor Henri II, beatified in 1152); and the arm-reliquary of *Charlemagne*, from the treasury at Aix-la-Chapelle (Aachen). Ottonian art (Otto the Great founded the Holy Empire in 962) is represented by two interesting little **ivory plaques**: *The Miracle of the Loaves and Fishes* and *Christ pointing at a child*. Note *(in the display case opposite)* the magnificent **bookbinding** from the treasury of Maastricht Cathedral.

The central display case contains a **coronation sword** known as **Charlemagne's** or the **Joyeuse**. Next to it are the coronation spurs.

Displayed in the bay to the right is a lovely collection of **reliquary caskets, heads of bishops' croziers**, 12C and 13C Limoges plaques and, in a separate case, the **ciborium by Maître Alpais**.

Gothic art – *Gallery 3.* Opposite the entrance stands the exquisite ivory statue of the **Virgin and Child** made for the chapel of the palace of Saint Louis (now the Sainte-Chapelle). It follows the Rayonnant Gothic style for large statuary. In a case to the right, note an *Angel* and *Virgin of the Annunciation*, dating from the same period, but parts of different compositions, and displayed in the left case, a famous ivory *Deposition*.

The **polyptych-reliquary of the True Cross** was created for an abbey in the Ardennes. It is a monument in itself, complete with porch, pinnacles and ogive arches.

The striking silver gilt Virgin and Child group known as the **Virgin of Jeanne d'Evreux★** after its royal donor, Philip the Fair's widow, was given to the abbey of St-Denis in 1339. The statuette is unusually large, the Virgin's lily holds a relic.

In the bay to the right of the gallery, cases contain the arm-reliquaries of *Saint Louis of Toulouse* and of *Saint Luke*, a beautiful gilt and inlaid enamel cross from Siena, various **carved ivory mirror frames** (depicting scenes such as the *Siege of Amour's Castle*, or a *Game of Chess*) and some rather endearing tiny gilt and enamel diptychs.

In the bay to the left, the **reliquary of the True Cross of Jaucourt** consists of a Byzantine centre-piece resting on two kneeling angels.

Griffin aquamanile (Nuremberg, c 1400)

At the far side of gallery 4, against the magnificent backdrop of the monumental Italian **Embriachi altarpiece★★** made of wood and ivory, note the **sceptre of Charles V**, made for the coronation of his son; the statuette on top represents Charlemagne.

The display cases to the right of the sceptre of Charles V contain the most famous exhibits from the treasure of St-Denis: the large, diamond-shaped **ornamental clasp** decorated with a fleur-de-lis, and the beautiful **bookbinding** enclosing a 14C Parisian ivory.

Note also the **hand of justice**, made in 1804 for the coronation of Napoleon I and, like the *Charlemagne* crown, decorated with cameos from one of the reliquaries from St-Denis; next to this, an **aquamanile** (1400) from Nuremberg in the form of a griffin.

Gallery 6 – The tapestries were executed in Flanders or in the north of France. The display cases contain masterpieces of the art of gold– or silversmithing: the beautiful **Saint Louis chessboard and pieces** (late 15C and 17C) made of rock crystal; a wonderful salt cellar in agate and gold; a Venetian reliquary of the Flagellation; and, perhaps the most interesting exhibit, a copper plaque on which **Jean Fouquet** *(see French Painting)* painted his *Self-Portrait* (c 1450) – a background of black enamel highlighted with a dark grey-brown glaze and gold hatching. This same technique of enamel painting was to flourish in Limoges at the end of the 15C.

Renaissance - *Galleries 7 to 17*. This series of galleries encircle the gallery hung with the tapestries of The Hunts of Maximilian *(follow them round in a clockwise direction)*:

– painted enamels dating from the reign of Louis XII; particularly fine examples were produced by the workshop of the **Maître aux Grands Fronts** *(Pietà between St Peter and St Paul*, Limoges, c 1500*)*.

– marquetry panels from a church in Padua and a *Self-Portrait of Alberti (first display case on left)*, the great Renaissance theoretician (15C bronze).

– the **Riccio bas-relief sculptures**, which combine religious themes with the philosophical concepts of scholars at Padua University *(Sacrifice of Asclepius, Hell, Paradise)*.

– the **Pisanello** medallions *Lionel d'Este; Dante; Aretino* and *Mehmet II*, conqueror of Constantinople.

– lovely 16C Limoges enamels, many of which are almost monochrome and the beautiful, and colourful, collection by the **Master of the Aeneid** *(The Trojan Horse)*.

– the **Sauvageot Collection**, illustrates the art of glassmaking in Europe: compare the delicate Venetian glasses with the interesting 17C German embossed glasses. A painting depicts a view of the collection in 1856.

★★ **Tapestries of The Hunts of Maximilian** – *Gallery 19*. This series of sumptuous tapestries woven in silk, wool and gold thread used to belong to the Royal collections. The tapestries depicting 12 hunting scenes set in the forest of Soignes south-east of Brussels, where they were woven c 1530, are from cartoons by Bernard van Orley. Each scene corresponds to a month of the year and a sign of the zodiac. The figures featured include the Emperor Maximilian's grandchildren: Emperor Charles V-to-be, Ferdinand I-to-be and Maria of Hungary.

In the centre, typical Italian **majolica** from Urbino is decorated with grotesques, mythological, biblical and historical scenes.

★ **Galerie de Scipion** - *Gallery 20.* This series of tapestries, commissioned from the Gobelins workshops by Louis XIV, depict scenes from the life of Scipio Africanus; they are copied from one of the most famous series of tapestries from Renaissance Brussels known as **The Great Scipio** commissioned by François I.

Galleries 21 to 23 – Among the enamel work on display by **Léonard Limousin** the *Portrait of the Connetable Anne de Montmorency (directly opposite the entrance to gallery 21)* stands out amid other magnificent altarpieces. Gallery 23 has an amusing collection of **busts of 12 Caesars**, made in silver and semi-precious stones.

Gallery 24 *(off gallery 21)* – The walls are hung with splendid 16C Oudenaarde **tapestries** depicting *The Labours of Hercules* against a background of luxuriant foliage.

Gallery 25 – Adolphe de Rothschild's collection is displayed beneath a Renaissance woodwork **ceiling**. Among the 16C Florentine bronzes, note the monkey by Jean Boulogne which once adorned a fountain.

★ **Jean Boulogne Rotunda** – *Gallery 26.* This houses a number of bronzes by this master and his pupils. The walls are hung with beautiful tapestries from Ferrara depicting scenes of metamorphosis.

★★ **Treasure of the Order of the Holy Spirit** – *Galleries 27 and 28.* This, the most prestigious order of the Ancien Régime, was founded by Henri III while the Wars of Religion were raging, to secure the loyalty of the nobility to the crown. The honour's insignia is the blue sash. The monarch's choice of placing the Order under the patronage of the Holy Spirit came about because it was at Pentecost that he had both been crowned King of Poland (1573) and succeeded to the throne of France (1574). Note the marvellous gold– and silverwork: silver-gilt **Kiss of Peace** (north Italy, c 1500), and Charles IX's eye-catching **helmet and shield** decorated in gold and brightly coloured enamel.
In the reconstruction of the **chapel**, the resplendent robes of the knights and officers of the Order are displayed next to 17C gold-embroidered altar cloths.

Galleries 29 to 31 – French furniture from the latter half of the 16C shows how designs were influenced by contemporary architecture. The distinctive ceramics embossed with river animals are by **Bernard Palissy**; the dishes with a metallic sheen are known as lustre ware.

★ **Salle d'Effiat** - *Gallery 32.* Louis XIII furniture from the Château d'Effiat in the Puy-de-Dôme (Auvergne) appears somewhat severe in style.

The 17C, Louis XIV's reign – *Galleries 33 and 34. Return to the Jean Boulogne rotunda and turn left.* The very fine tapestry illustrating *Moses in the Bulrushes* is one of a series on themes from the Old Testament, designed by **Simon Vouet**, and destined for the Louvre. In the centre of gallery 33 is the ornate **gold Anne of Austria casket**. Gallery 34 is a rest room. On the pedestal table that once belonged to Louis XIV, the magnificent **Jupiter hurling thunderbolts at the Titans** is by **Alessandro Algardi** (1598-1654).

The 18C – *Galleries 35 to 61.* Note in the entrance *(display case on the right)* the sober lines and decoration of Marie-Antoinette's **travelling case**, in sharp contrast with the queen's infamous extravagant taste for ribbons and nosegay ornamentation. The Chinese cabinet contains the queen's elegant writing table, a sophisticated combination of materials (steel and lacquered panels, mother-of-pearl inlay and bronze gilt *or moulu*) by **Adam Weisweiler**. Seats by **Jacob**, one of the pioneers of the Empire style *(see Madame Récamier's Bedchamber below)*, are displayed alongside lacquer furniture by **Carlin**. The cylindrical writing desk by **Riesener**, a new type of furniture in 1770, stands in front of the splendid desk by **Benneman**, at which Napoleon worked when he was at the Tuileries.
The recently refurbished Rothschild gallery contains furniture ornamented with Sèvres porcelain plaques and pot-pourri vases, once the property of the Marquise de Pompadour. **Cressent**'s monkey commode illustrates the move from Grand Siècle formal design to the more fantastical Rococo, as decoration became more feminine in arrangements of asymmetrical, intertwining plant-like fronds.
The Gobelins **tapestries** with pink backgrounds *(Loves of the Gods)*, woven to designs by **Boucher**, the candelabra, andirons, wall clocks, console-tables, and cabinets all reflect the degree of artistic imagination of the times, testifying to the delicate tastes of one of the most sophisticated periods in French history.

The Restoration and Louis-Philippe periods (1815-48) – *Retrace your steps to gallery 34 and turn left, formerly the Salles du Conseil d'État, 62 to 65.* Note the elegant **dressing table and chair** from the **Escalier de Cristal**, a workshop specialising in bronze gilt furniture set with Baccarat crystal. *Charles X's bed* from the Tuileries and the delicately worked **grape harvest goblet** *(coupe des vendanges)* in silver gilt, enamel, agate and pearls by **Froment-Meurice** *(display case on the side of the Cour Carrée)*.
Gallery 64 displays what remains of the exquisite treasure of the kings of France. The **Regent diamond★★★** weighing 140 carats was purchased in 1717. Its exceptional clarity and perfect shape make it one of the most famous precious stones in the world, it having adorned among other things the coronation crown of Louis XV, the parade sword of Premier Consul Bonaparte and the diadem of the Empress Eugénie.

Other French Crown Jewels on display include the **Côte de Bretagne** ruby (107 carats), the pink diamond *Hortensia*, Queen Amélie's **sapphire jewellery set** and Empress Eugénie's crown and diadem. Other display cases contain Louis XIV's impressive collection of **semi-precious stone vases★**.

Empire style (1798-1815) – *Richelieu wing, first floor, access via the Lefuel staircase*. The monumental **table centrepiece** in bronze gilt and marble marquetry is by **Valadier** *(gallery 67)*. The sophisticated furniture from **Madame Récamier's Bedchamber★** *(gallery 69)* designed by the **Jacob** brothers (1798) epitomises Empire-style design, distinguished by elegant line. The young lady's salon was the hub of opposition to Napoleon *(see also Large-Format 19C French Painting, Denon)*. Gallery 71 contains porcelain.

The armoire, or **grand écrin** (large casket), for Empress Josephine's jewellery was designed by **Jacob-Desmalter** *(gallery 73)*; its elegant bronze ornamentation is based on designs by Chaudet *(see French Sculpture)*.

★★★ Napoleon III Apartments – *These are also accessible via Cour Marly, up the Escalier du Ministre (towards the Pyramid)*.

This majestic carpeted staircase, decorated with a very fine wrought-iron banister, leads the visitor into a stunning world of gold, crimson velvet and crystal. The architect **Lefuel**, having completed the Louvre, went on to design an opulent almost overwhelming decor best seen at night by the light of the chandeliers. It was normal at that time for the Louis XIV style to be applied to the state halls of official palaces.

There's no place like home... when you're Napoléon III

These apartments provide one of the few examples of great Second Empire decors to have survived complete with their original furnishings. They consist of an antechamber, a presentation hall, a *salon-théâtre* (used for musical entertainment), a great hall (with a capacity for 265 spectators), a boudoir or *salon de terrasse* (with a view of the gardens) and a small and a large dining hall. The latter contains an enormous sideboard in ebonised wood. Between the various allegorical paintings every opportunity to use *trompe-l'œil* has been exploited: mural paintings imitating Boulle marquetry; sculpted decor in reinforced papier maché; and imitation polychrome marble. The halls were inaugurated in 1861; some 10 years later, they were appropriated by the Ministry of Finance.

African, Asian, Pacific island and American art

If the Louvre has long been regarded as a museum of Western art and antiquities, its collection now includes ethnic art, or so-called primary art, with the creation in 2000 of these new galleries, next to quai des Tuileries. Access is via the Porte de Lions. A new museum devoted entirely to this type of art is currently being planned, and will be built on quai Branly.

Africa, Asia, Pacific Islands and the Americas – Four galleries present 120 sculptures and other masterpieces chosen for their artistic value and historic context. Among the pieces on display are a statue of a man from the Nagada II period of pre-dynastic Egypt (5-4 millennia BC); a superb Sokoto terracotta head from Nigeria; a stone sculpture which once belonged to André Breton, from the Indonesian island of Nias and a sculpture over 2000 years old from Chupicuaro in Mexico.

Le LUXEMBOURG★★

Michelin plan 10: K 13, L 13
Ⓜ️ *Odéon (lines 4 and 10), Cluny-La-Sorbonne (line 10) –*
RER: Luxembourg (line B) – Buses: 21, 27, 38, 82, 84, 85, 89

A historical green space in the midst of the Latin Quarter, the magnificent gardens of the Luxembourg Palace attract people of all ages, from all walks of life. The area's proximity to the Senate and to various university faculties (law school, art history and archaeology) means that the gardens are often full of students during term time. The neighbourhood is a popular place in which to sit a moment and absorb the atmosphere of Paris.

Nearby neighbourhoods: QUARTIER LATIN, ODÉON, ST-GERMAIN-DES-PRÉS, PORT-ROYAL, MONTPARNASSE.

Religious beginnings – At the beginning of the 13C the area was occupied by an old ruin nicknamed the Château de Vauvert, which was supposedly haunted. It was exorcised in 1257 by a community of Carthusians, with the help of St Louis. Having succeeded, they laid claim to the area and built a vast monastery with extensive grounds.

Marie de Medici's palace – After the death of Henri IV, his queen, Marie de Medici, who disliked living at the Louvre, decided to build her own palace modelled on the Palazzo Pitti in Florence where she had spent her childhood. In 1612 she bought the mansion of Duke François of Luxembourg together with various properties around: in 1615 her architect, Salomon de Brosse began construction; in 1621 **Rubens** was commissioned to paint a series of 24 large allegorical pictures representing the queen's life – these now hang in the Galerie Médicis in the Louvre.

The palace as parliament – In 1790 when the monastery was suppressed, the gardens were enlarged and the palace vista extended to the far end of avenue de l'Observatoire. Under the Terror the palace was used as a prison. The building successively became home to a parliamentary assembly for the Directory, the Consulate, the Senate and its successor the Peers' Chamber. Chalgrin, architect of the Arc de Triomphe and the Odéon, completely transformed the interior. Between 1836 and 1841 Alphonse de Gisors enlarged the complex on the garden side, by the addition of a new front to the main building and two lateral pavilions in keeping with the original style.
During the second half of the 19C, the surrounding streets were laid (boulevard St-Michel, rue de Médicis and rue Guynemer).
The building was occupied by the Germans during the Second World War. On 25 August 1944 it was freed by Leclerc's Division and the French Resistance. The palace is now the seat of the **Sénat** (the French Upper House) composed of 319 members.

Outdoor activities

In the summer, open-air concerts take place in the **Luxembourg Gardens** (boulevard St-Michel side). The **Gardens** also have two shady café-terraces which are very pleasant in fine weather.

Outdoor activities for children

🎠 On rue de Guynemer side, the **garden** is very well supplied with swings, merry-go-rounds, puppet shows etc. There is a fenced area where young children can play safely and sand pits for all ages. Given the neighbourhood, most of the paying activities are quite expensive.

Going out

Le Rostand – *6 pl. Edmond-Rostand – 6th arr –* ☎ *01 43 54 61 58 – daily 8am-2am*. This recently redecorated café has been popular with generations of students and professors from the Sorbonne for years. Wicker furniture and walls hung with paintings await the cinema-goer or walker who has strayed from the nearby Luxembourg Gardens.

Shopping

Christian-Constant – *37 rue d'Assas – 6th arr –* Ⓜ️ *Notre-Dame-des-Champs –* ☎ *01 53 63 15 15 – constant.christian@wanadoo.fr – 8.30am-9pm*. Inventor of the Appellation d'Origine Pur Cru, this chocolate, pastry and ice-cream maker is not only one of Paris' best craftsmen, he is also an adventurer of the palate. He creates the most amazing sweets and desserts which both astound and delight the taste buds.

Eating out

Turn back to the Selected restaurants section at the beginning of the guide for a list of restaurants, bistros, cafés etc. This district corresponds to the 5th and 6th *arrondissements*.

★★ LUXEMBOURG PALACE

Exterior – To give a Florentine quality to his design for the palace, Salomon de Brosse used bosses, ringed columns and Tuscan capitals, while keeping the typically French ground plan of a central block built around an arcaded courtyard, with a central domed gateway-pavilion. The Doric order, applied throughout the symmetrical ground floor lends the design a robust elegance. The south façade is enhanced by a domed central pavilion, a large pediment and a fine terrace edged with a balustrade.

Rooms in the basement are flooded with natural light permitted by the two inner courtyards below the level of allée de l'Odéon, laid with French *parterre* gardens.

The **Petit Luxembourg**, now the residence of the president of the Senate, comprises the original Hôtel de Luxembourg presented to Richelieu by Marie de Medici and also the cloister and chapel of a convent founded by the queen.

The **Musée du Luxembourg** houses temporary exhibitions during the summer months.

★★ GARDENS

The Luxembourg Gardens exert a great draw on Parisians probably ever since Napoleon decreed that they should be dedicated to children. They attract students and young mothers or nannies with children who stop to watch the tennis or *boules*, to see the *marionette* puppet shows or listen to the free concerts, to sail boats on the *grand bassin*, or play on the pedal-car circuit.

Overall the gardens conform to a formal layout, the only serpentine lines of the more English-style garden being along rue Guynemer and rue Auguste-Comte. The spirit of the monks lives on in the serious tending of trees and bees.

The **Medici Fountain** (1624) in its leafy setting at the far end of a long pool shaded by plane trees shows obvious Italian influence in its embossed decoration and overall design. Statues began to invade the lawns under Louis-Philippe and today have reached such numbers that they seem to stand around every corner. The queens of France and other illustrious women line the terraces.

Rue de Vaugirard – The Senate has extended its premises to a series of buildings across rue de Vaugirard, the longest street in Paris. In the ground-floor galleries can be seen exhibitions of coins and medals and Sèvres Porcelain.

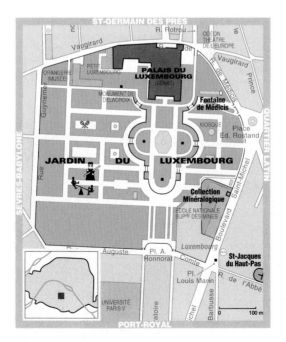

LA MADELEINE★★

Michelin plan 10: F 11, F 12, G 11, G 12
Ⓜ Madeleine (lines 8, 12 and 14) – Buses: 24, 42, 52, 84, 94

La Madeleine *(see illustration p 95)*, the church dedicated to St Mary Magdalen, is one of Paris' most familiar landmarks, familiar to all for its distinctively striking Greek temple appearance and its convenient position at the junction of the boulevards with an artery from place de la Concorde.

Few churches have had such a stormy history as La Madeleine. It was started by one architect in 1764 on plans based on the church of St-Louis-des-Invalides, a second razed what had already been erected to begin a building modelled on the **Panthéon**; all work ceased between 1790 and 1806 as various projects were considered. **Napoleon** announced that on this spot should be erected a temple to the glory of the Great Army and gave the commission to Vignon. Once more the existing structure was razed and building started on the Greek temple; work proceeded slowly. In 1814 **Louis XVIII** confirmed that the Madeleine should indeed be a church; during the reign of Charles X it was still surrounded by waste land; in 1837 the building was nearly selected for use as Paris' first railway terminal. The church's vicissitudes ended with its consecration in 1842, although its priest was shot by the Commune in 1871.

Nearby neighbourhoods: PLACE DE LA CONCORDE, FAUBOURG ST-HONORÉ, OPÉRA, ST-LAZARE.

EXPLORING THE NEIGHBOURHOOD

★ **Rue Royale** – The street runs from the Madeleine with its immense pediment raised high on its line of columns, to place de la Concorde, on an axis with the white mass of the Palais-Bourbon. The famous restaurant Maxim's, at no 3, was formerly the Hôtel de Richelieu. At the end of the 18C the writer Mme de Staël lived at no **6**, and Gabriel at no **8**.

As you walk up rue Royale towards the Madeleine, make a short detour along rue Saint-Honoré (to the right) as far as place Maurice-Barrès.

Rue St-Honoré – *see PALAIS ROYAL*

Église Notre-Dame-de-l'Assomption – *Place Maurice-Barrès*. This was the former chapel of the Convent of the Sisters of the Assumption (now the Polish Church in Paris). The circular building capped by a disproportionately large dome dates from the 17C. Above the main altar is an Annunciation by Vien (18C) and to its right an Adoration of the Magi by Van Loo. In the dome is a fresco of the Assumption by Charles de la Fosse (17C).

★★ **La Madeleine** – A majestic colonnade of Corinthian **columns** – 52 in all, each 20m/66ft tall – encloses the church on all sides and supports a sculptured frieze. A monumental flight of steps (28) leads to the imposing peristyle giving on to place de la Madeleine and a splendid **view★** down rue Royale, the obelisk at the heart of place de la Concorde and beyond to the Palais-Bourbon and the Invalides dome. The gigantic pediment is adorned with a sculpture by Lemaire of The Last Judgement and reliefs on the bronze doors represent the Ten Commandments.

La Madeleine

Shopping

Chanel – *31 rue Cambon – 1st arr –* Ⓜ *Madeleine –* ☎ *01 42 86 28 00 – Mon-Sat 10am-7pm.* Such is its fame, this legendary house needs no introduction, because it is now synonymous with France's reputation for elegance and luxury throughout the world. Leather sofas and an attentive staff continue to uphold Chanel's tradition of high-quality service and products.

Baccarat – *11 pl. de la Madeleine – 8th arr –* Ⓜ *Madeleine – other shop: 30 bis rue de Paradis, 10th arr –* ☎ *01 42 65 36 26 – www.baccarat.fr – Mon-Sat 10am-7pm – closed public holidays.* The flagship shop of this prestigious house could almost be a real museum of crystal. The simple design and discreetly luxurious surroundings enhance the shapes and forms of the objects on display: vases, jewellery, accessories, artist's creations etc.

Betjeman and Barton – *23 blvd Malesherbes – 8th arr –* Ⓜ *Madeleine –* ☎ *01 42 65 86 17 – Mon-Sat 9.30am-7pm – closed public holidays and 2 weeks in Aug.* This importer of high-quality teas will delight all tea-enthusiasts by the quality of its products and the elegance of their presentation. The welcoming, friendly shop also has a fine collection of Chinese teapots.

Fauchon – *26 pl. de la Madeleine – 8th arr –* Ⓜ *Madeleine –* ☎ *01 47 42 60 11 – 9.30am-7pm.* Delicatessen, pastry maker, high-class grocery and tearoom all rolled into one. Fauchon sells luxury goods from France and abroad. Very popular with the Parisian bourgeoisie and foreign visitors who come to admire the shop's sumptuous decorations at Christmas time.

Hédiard – *21 pl. de la Madeleine – 8th arr –* Ⓜ *Madeleine –* ☎ *01 43 12 88 88/76 – www.hediard.fr – Mon-Sat 9.30am-9.30pm – closed public holidays.* At the entrance, a delicious array of exotic fruits and spices invites gourmets to venture into this house of mouth-watering delicacies. The wine cellar, managed by a competent, young wine expert, is also worth a look.

Lalique – *11 rue Royale – 8th arr –* Ⓜ *Concorde or Madeleine – other address: Carrousel du Louvre, 1st arr –* ☎ *01 53 05 12 12 – Mon-Wed 10am-6.30pm, Thu-Fri 9.30am-6.30pm, Sat 9.30am-7pm – closed public holidays except 8 May, Ascension and 11 Nov.* Lalique's first creations are now owned by collectors from all over the world. Renowned for its specialist work in transparent-satin finishes, this prestigious house manufactures crystal in all shapes and sizes from the famous Bachantes vase to watches and perfume bottles.

Les Trois Quartiers – *23 blvd de la Madeleine – 8th arr –* Ⓜ *Madeleine – Mon-Sat 10am-7pm.* This shopping complex right in the centre of the Madeleine quarter is of course devoted to luxury: fashion, beauty, jewellery, gifts, home decoration, sport etc.

Rue Royale – *Rue Royale – 8th arr –* Ⓜ *Concorde or Madeleine.* Fashion (Adolfo Dominguez, Gucci...), jewellery (Poiray, Fred...), crystal (Christofle, Cristallerie Saint-Louis) or chinaware (Bernardeau), this wide avenue has the flagship shops of many of Paris' most prestigious and most luxurious brand names.

Eating out

Turn back to the Selected restaurants section at the beginning of the guide for a list of restaurants, bistros, cafés etc. This district corresponds to the 1st and the 8th *arrondissements*.

The single nave church has a vestibule and an apsed chancel. In the dark vestibule note at the far end on the right a *Marriage of the Virgin* by Pradier and on the far left a *Baptism of Christ* by Rude. The nave is crowned by three domes.
Chopin's funeral took place here in 1849. In 1858, Camille Saint-Saëns was hired to play the organ. It was here that he composed some of his most remarkable pieces.

Place de la Madeleine – Next to the church is a flower-market and behind it the most famous epicure *épiceries* or food stores Fauchon and Hédiard.

Le MARAIS★★★

Michelin plan 10: H 16, H 17, J 15, J 16, J 17
Ⓜ *Chemin-Vert (line 8), St-Paul (line 1) – Buses: 20, 29, 69, 76, 96*

The Marais district stretches between place de la Bastille and the Hôtel de Ville, the Seine and the **quartier du Temple**. It is unusual for its fine pre-Revolution residential architecture, including such gems as the oldest square in Paris, place des Vosges; and the Soubise, Salé and De Rohan mansions, many of which are now restored and converted into museums and municipal offices. Visitors should tour the area on a weekday when access to buildings is possible.

Business in the district grew up traditionally around tailoring: the rag trade and leather work have been in part revived by internationally successful young fashion designers. The Quartier du Temple is notable for jewellers and goldsmiths.

Nearby neighbourhoods: BEAUBOURG, CHÂTELET-HÔTEL DE VILLE, BASTILLE, ÎLE SAINT-LOUIS.

HISTORICAL NOTES

In the 13C marshland surrounding the raised rue St-Antoine, a highway since Roman times, was drained and converted into arable land.

Philippe Auguste's defensive wall, which also served as a dike, and the Charles V wall ending in the powerful Bastille fortress in the east, brought the Marais within the city limits. Royal patronage began after the flight of **Charles V** from the royal palace to the **Hôtel St-Paul**. Charles VI also took up residence there and the royal menagerie and park are recalled in rue des Lions-St-Paul and rue Beautreillis.

By the beginning of the 17C the then place Royale, now place des Vosges, built by Henri IV, had become the focal point of the Marais.

The Jesuits were the first to settle along rue St-Antoine, with members of the nobility and royal courtiers following after; splendid mansions were erected and decorated by the best contemporary artists. The *hôtel*, a discreet Classically designed private residence, standing between entrance court and garden, developed as a distinctive feature in French architecture. Women of the world attracted free-thinkers and philosophers through their *salons* – the brilliant conversational groups who frequented their houses. Two churches, St-Paul and St-Gervais, attracted famous preachers and musicians.

Then, gradually, the nobility began to move west to Île St-Louis, then Faubourg St-Germain and Faubourg St-Honoré. After the taking of the Bastille, the quarter was virtually abandoned.

In the 20C, the derelict quarter was essentially saved from complete destruction by **André Malraux**, Charles de Gaulle's Culture Minister.

EXPLORING THE NEIGHBOURHOOD

The Marais can be visited by following two walking tours: the **St-Paul circuit** and the **Marais circuit**.

The descriptions of museums and the collections found in the most attractive of the hotels are found at the end of the chapter, under the heading Museums and other attractions.

① St-Paul walk

This walk takes you through the southern part of the Marais.

Start from the St-Paul metro station.

Église St-Paul-St-Louis – *99 rue Saint-Antoine.* In 1580 the Jesuits established a community for ordained members. Louis XIII donated them land to build a new church (1627-41): this was modelled on the Gesù Church in Rome, but dedicated to St-Louis in the king's honour.

After the demolition of an old church dedicated to St Paul, the edifice in rue St-Antoine accommodated a larger parish, thereby becoming known as the church of St-Paul-St-Louis (1802).

Façade – The tall Classical orders of superimposed columns screen the dome, a feature favoured by the Jesuits but which was subsequently abandoned when the Sorbonne, Val-de-Grâce and Invalides churches were built.

Interior – It has a single aisle and inter-communicating barrel-vaulted chapels, a cupola with a lantern hovers above the transept crossing and tall Corinthian pilasters line the walls.

This well-lit, spacious church with its ornate decoration and sculptures, drew an elegant congregation attracted by musical excellence (directed by **Marc-Antoine Charpentier**) and eloquent preaching. Many of its rich furnishings were lost at the Revolution. Reliquaries holding the hearts of Louis XIII and Louis XIV were melted down, whereas the hearts were purchased by the painter Saint-Martin who ground the organs to mix with oil to varnish his paintings. Having used only a small part of Louis XIV's heart, the larger of the two, he gave the remainder to Louis XVIII, who rewarded the painter with a gold tobacco box.

Going out

Le Marais

This old district of Paris, saved by Malraux, is the centre of Paris' Jewish community and the HQ of its gay population. Hip, cool bars have sprung up everywhere (crossroads of rue Vieille-du-Temple and rue Sainte-Croix-de-la-Bretonnerie) and fashion shops line the pavements of rue des Francs-Bourgeois. Rue des Rosiers and the surrounding streets however still resemble a traditional, old Jewish neighbourhood. Long-established shops are grouped around the Marché des Blancs-Manteaux, rue Saint-Antoine and the neighbouring streets. The delightful place du Marché-Sainte-Catherine is surrounded by restaurants. At the back of the gardens of the Hôtel de Sully, a small passage leads to the arcades of place des Vosges, its fashion shops, antique dealers and art galleries. The northern part of the Marais is quieter and home to many museums. Even further north is the old district of the Temple, traditional home of leather goods dealers and also, more recently, of a few up and coming night-spots.

Au Petit Fer à Cheval – *30 rue Vieille-du-Temple – 4th arr – daily 9am-2am*. This delightful little bistro, now a very fashionable meeting place, owes its name to its old bar in the shape of a horse shoe. Very popular among the local gay crowd, it is most cosmopolitan. A few tables on the pavement. Often packed in the evening. The restaurant is behind the bar.

Bar de Jarente – *5 rue de Jarente – 4th arr – ☎ 01 48 87 60 93 – Mon-Sat 8am-10pm – closed Aug.* An old café in what is now one of Paris' trendiest and smartest districts. This relic of working-class Paris has belonged to the same owners for over 30 years. Handsome terrace overlooking place du Marché-Ste-Catherine.

L'Ébouillanté – *6 rue des Barres – 4th arr – ☎ 01 42 71 09 69 – ebouillante@wanadoo.fr – Tue-Sun noon-10pm in summer, noon-9pm in winter*. This little tearoom – possibly the smallest in Paris – has a pleasant terrace on a pedestrian street with a view of the church of Saint-Gervais-Saint-Protais. Pastries, salads and bricks (North African stuffed pancakes). First-floor room.

La Belle Hortense – *31 rue Vieille-du-Temple – 4th arr – ☎ 01 48 04 71 60 – daily 1pm-2am*. Named after a novel by Jacques Roubaud, this establishment's shelves are devoted to the marriage between wine and literature. Lively literary discussions liberally washed down with regional produce. At the rear, art exhibitions in the green room (non-smoking). Smart and popular with artists and writers.

La Tartine – *24 rue de Rivoli – 4th arr – daily 8.30am-10pm (except Tue, Wed morning) – closed 2 weeks in Aug, 1 Jan and 1 May*. This genuine Parisian bistro will appeal to those who appreciate the old-fashioned, worn smoky look. Taste one of the 100 gold prize winner wines awarded at the Paris Agricultural Show. Ideal meeting place or for a short break.

Le Loir dans la Théière – *3 rue des Rosiers – 4th arr – Ⓜ St-Paul – ☎ 01 42 72 90 61 – Boccia.Paul@wanadoo.fr – Mon-Fri 11am-7pm, Sat-Sun 10am-7pm*. For over 20 years, this elegant light-green tearoom, equipped with comfortable armchairs, serves good home-made snacks, cakes and pastries.

Les Étages – *35 rue Vieille-du-Temple – 4th arr – ☎ 01 42 78 72 00 – Mon-Fri 3.30pm-2am, Sat-Sun 11am-2am*. One almost wants to tiptoe into this four-storeyed bar, such is the intimate, almost private atmosphere inside. The succession of amusingly decorated little rooms provides a wide choice for a quiet rest in one of the well-worn sofas.

Les Marronniers – *18 rue des Archives – 4th arr – ☎ 01 40 27 87 72 – daily 8am-2am*. Many visitors to this café never get further than the pleasant terrace outdoors on rue des Archives, overlooking the reformed Billettes Church and the BHV department store. The colourful upstairs room is however well worth a visit. A quiet spot for an afternoon pause. Brunch on Sundays from 11am to 4pm.

Lizard Lounge – *18 rue Bourg-Tibourg – 4th arr – ☎ 01 42 71 73 63 – daily noon-1.30am – closed one week in August*. Warm, simple and intimate, this establishment clearly favours the English pub-style. It is both open and friendly, a contrast to many of the district's more selective, club establishments.

Ma Bourgogne – *19 pl. des Vosges – 4th arr – ☎ 01 42 78 44 64 – daily until 1am*. A very pleasant terrace under the arcades of place des Vosges. Wide selection of Beaujolais.

Mariage Frères – *30 rue du Bourg-Tibourg – 4th arr – ☎ 01 42 72 28 11 – www.mariagefreres.com – daily noon-7pm – closed 1 May.* An aura of gentility and good-breeding pervades this temple to tea, with its colonial-style decor and stylish waiters. This secular institution also sells biscuits, jams and chocolate, all tea-flavoured, together with teapots and crockery, without of course forgetting a selection of over 500 teas from some 20 countries.

Shopping

Antik Batik – *18 rue de Turenne – 4th arr – Ⓜ Bastille, St-Paul or Chemin-Vert – ☎ 01 44 78 02 00 – 11am-7pm – closed 10 days in Aug.* This ethnic style fashion shop sells the creations of designers influenced by Latin America, India and Indonesia. Always colourful, their originality has long found followers among Paris' youth.

Izrael Épicerie du Monde – *30 rue François-Miron – 4th arr – ☎ 01 42 72 66 23 – Tue-Fri 9.30am-1pm, 2.30-7pm, Sat 9am-7pm.* This grocery shop-cum-delicatessen, reminiscent of Ali Baba's cave, is one of the best known in Paris.

Sacha Finkelsztajn – *27 rue des Rosiers – 4th arr – Ⓜ St-Paul or Hôtel-de-Ville – ☎ 01 42 72 78 91 – laboutiquejaune@ club-internet-fr – Mon, Wed-Thu 10am-2pm, 3-7pm, Fri-Sun 10am-7pm.* Following in his father's footsteps, Sacha Finkelsztajn upholds the tradition of Yiddish gastronomy from Central Europe and Russia in his friendly yellow shop. Strange, foreign spices and flavours, delicious, mouth-watering pastries, cheeses, tarama and olive caviar await visitors.

Art

Galerie Vidal Saint-Phalle – *10 rue du Trésor – 4th arr – Ⓜ St-Paul – ☎ 01 42 76 06 05 – Tue-Sat 2-7pm – closed public holidays and Aug.* This modern art gallery exhibits the work of well-known artists, little seen in France, such as Rafols-Casamada.

Rue Vieille-du-Temple – *Rue Vieille-du-Temple – 3rd arr – Ⓜ Filles-du-Calvaire.* At the top of rue Vieille-du-Temple (from rue du Perche on) and in the surrounding streets (rue Charlot, rue de Poitou), there are a large number of art galleries. Each gallery has a brochure with map.

Eating out

Turn back to the Selected restaurants section at the beginning of the guide for a list of restaurants, bistros, cafés etc. This district corresponds to the 3rd and 4th *arrondissements*.

The twin shell-shaped stoups at the entrance were given by **Victor Hugo** who lived nearby in place des Vosges. In the transept three 17C paintings illustrate scenes from the life of St Louis. A fourth painting disappeared, and has been replaced by a painting of *Christ on the Mount of Olives* by Delacroix (1827). In the chapel to the left of the high altar there is a **Mater Dolorosa** in marble by **Germain Pilon** (1586) – the terracotta version is now in the Louvre.

Leave the church by the left-hand door, as you look towards the alter. A passageway leads to rue St-Paul.

Village St-Paul – The area bordered by rue des Jardins-St-Paul, rue Charlemagne, rue St-Paul and rue Ave-Maria has been restored; houses and antique shops crowd around the inner courtyards.

Rue des Jardins St-Paul – A long section of the **Philippe Auguste City Wall** (Enceinte de Philippe Auguste), intersected by two towers, can still be seen in this street. It linked the **Barbeau Tower** at 32 quai des Célestins to the St-Paul postern and is the largest surviving fragment.
It was in rue St-Paul that Rabelais died in 1553.
At the far end there is a view of the east end and dome of the church of St-Paul-St-Louis.

★ **Hôtel de Sens** – *1 rue du Figuier.* The Hôtel de Sens, Hôtel de Cluny and Jacques Cœur's house are the only great surviving medieval private residences in Paris.
The mansion was constructed between 1475 and 1507 as a residence for the archbishops of Sens of which Paris was a dependency until 1622. During the period of the **Catholic League** in the 16C it became a centre of intrigue conducted by the Cardinal of Guise. In 1594 Monsignor de Pellevé died of apoplexy within its walls while a *Te Deum* was being sung in Notre-Dame to celebrate Henri IV's entry into Paris.

In 1605, **Queen Margot**, Henri IV's first wife, came to live here after her long exile in Auvergne. At the age of 53, the former queen had a busy social life and many gallant callers.

From 1689 to 1743 the house was occupied by the Lyons Stage Coach Company which made a journey reputed to be so unsafe that passengers wrote their wills before setting out.

The old houses which originally surrounded the mansion have been pulled down.

The Flamboyant Gothic porch leads into the courtyard with a square battlemented tower enclosing a spiral staircase. Turrets and beautiful dormer windows adorn the external walls. The **Forney Library** ⊙ is devoted to the Decorative and Fine Arts, and industrial techniques. It has a large collection of posters and wall papers.

Hôtel d'Aumont - *7 rue de Jouy*. Built in the early 17C by Le Vau, it was later remodelled and enlarged by Mansart, and decorated by **Le Brun** and Simon Vouet. The formal garden is attributed to Le Nôtre. The inner courtyard and façades are almost severe in line. Four successive dukes of Aumont lived there until 1742, accumulating large collections of objects and entertaining lavishly. A large garden has since been created between the house and the river. It is presently occupied by the Paris administrative court.

Mémorial du Martyr juif inconnu ⊙ - *17 rue Geoffroy-l'Asnier*. It burns an eternal flame in memory of the Jewish victims of National Socialism. There is also a museum devoted to the Jewish struggle against Hitlerism.

Hôtel de Châlons-Luxembourg – *26 rue Geoffroy-l'Asnier*. Built in 1610, this mansion derives its name from two of its former proprietors, a merchant named Châlons and Madame de Luxembourg. It has a carved main gate and an interesting stone and brick façade.

★ **Église St-Gervais-St-Protais** – *Place St-Gervais*. The church stands on a low mound emphasised by steps leading up to the façade. A basilica dedicated to the brothers Gervase and Protase, Roman officers martyred by Nero, has stood on the site since the 6C. The main part of the present building, in Flamboyant Gothic, was completed in 1657.

The elm in the square was, according to medieval custom, a place where justice was dispensed as well as a place for wheeling and dealing, employment and rendezvous.

Exterior – The imposing façade (1616-21) with superimposed Doric, Ionic and Corinthian orders was the first expression of the Classical style in Paris, attributed to Métezeau or Salomon de Brosse.

Interior – The Flamboyant vaulting, 16C windows and 16C to 17C fine stalls carved with misericords representing various trades are from the original building. The organ built in 1601 and enlarged in the 18C is the oldest in Paris. The position of organ-master was held successively by members of eight generations of Couperins between 1656 and 1826.

In the third chapel of the north aisle, a 13C low relief altar-front depicts the Death of the Virgin. In the left transept hangs a beautiful 16C Flemish oil panel on wood of the Passion. At the crossing, against a pillar, stands a Gothic Virgin and Child in stone. A wooden Christ by Préault (1840) and a fine 17C wrought-iron grille adorn the sacristy exterior. In the Lady Chapel there is a remarkable Flamboyant keystone, hanging 1.5m/5ft below the vault and forming a circlet 2.5m/8ft in diameter. The adjoining chapel contains the tomb of Chancellor Michel Le Tellier (d 1686).

Window in the church of St-Gervais-St-Protais

Rue François-Miron – This road, once a Roman highway through the marshes, still bears the name of a local magistrate of the time of Henri IV. In the Middle Ages it was lined with the town houses of several abbots of the Île-de-France. The half-timbered and much restored nos **13** and **11** date back to the reign of Louis XI (15C). The beautiful Marie Touchet, mistress of Charles IX, is said to have lived at no **30**. Behind the front building *(access via no 22 rue du Pont-Louis-Philippe, at the end of the corridor)*, there is a tiny Renaissance courtyard remarkably decorated with carved wood panels.

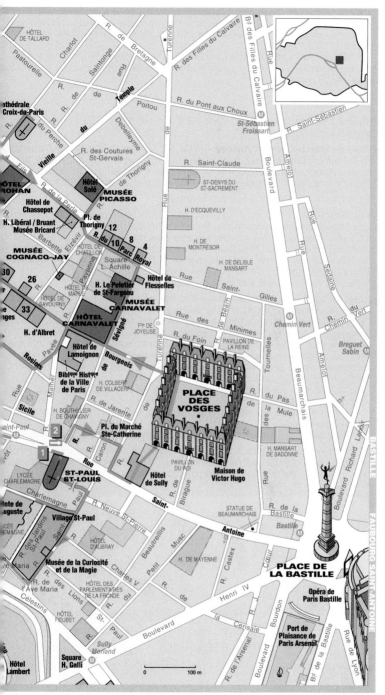

The association for the preservation of Paris' historic buildings has uncovered in the basements of nos **44-46** fine Gothic **cellars★** from the town house belonging to the Abbey of Ourscamp, north of Compiègne.

★ **Hôtel de Beauvais** – *No 68 (work in progress)*. In 1654 Catherine Bellier, known as One-Eyed Kate, first woman of the bedchamber to Anne of Austria, bestowed her favours on the 16-year-old Louis XIV and was rewarded with a fortune. In addition, for her services, her husband Pierre Beauvais and she were ennobled and acquired the site of the former (13C) town house of the abbots of Chaalis.

They commissioned the architect Lepautre, to build them a splendid mansion from the balcony of which Anne of Austria, the Queen of England, Cardinal Mazarin and dignitaries watched the triumphal entry of Louis XIV and Marie-Thérèse into Paris in 1660.

In 1763, when Mozart aged seven, came to Paris accompanied by his father and sister, he stayed in this house by courtesy of the Bavarian ambassador, for whom he gave several concerts.

2 Marais walk

Starting from the St-Paul metro station, follow rue de Sévigné, then turn first right along rue d'Ormesson.

★**Place du Marché-Sainte-Catherine** – In the 13C a priory dedicated to St Catherine du Val des Escoliers was built here. In the 18C the square was surrounded by large houses, harmonious in style, with mulberry trees planted in the middle. More recently it has become a pedestrian zone with outdoor cafés and restaurants.

To the south, rue Caron leads to rue St-Antoine.

Rue St-Antoine – From the 14C this unusually wide street became a popular setting for gatherings and celebrations. The area in front of the church was turned into a tilt-yard after the cobbles had been removed and the ground covered with sand. It was here that in 1559 **Henri II** received a fatal blow to his eye in a tourney with his Scots captain of the guard, Montgomery. The king died in the Hôtel des Tournelles. Montgomery fled but was executed in 1574.

In the 17C rue St-Antoine was the city's most elegant thoroughfare.

★**Hôtel de Sully** ⊙ - *62 rue St-Antoine.* This fine mansion was built in 1625 by Du Cerceau and bought 10 years later by the ageing Sully, former minister of Henri IV. Part of the building is presently given over to the Caisse Nationale des Monuments Historiques et des Sites (Ancient Monuments and Historic Buildings Commission).

The main gate, between massive pavilions, has been restored and opens into the inner courtyard, an outstanding Louis XIII architectural composition with ordered decoration, carved pediments and dormer windows; allegorical figures represent the Elements and the Seasons.

The main building retains its original painted ceilings (1661, restored); especially noteworthy is the painted decoration of the Duchess of Sully's rooms, in the garden wing. Temporary exhibitions are held in the main building and garden wing (ground floor and basement).

At the far end of the garden, the Orangery (1625) opens onto place des Vosges.

★★★**Place des Vosges** – This is Paris' oldest square. Today it is a peaceful place to sit, either near the fountains in the central garden or under the cool arcades. Small orchestras play on Sundays and the atmosphere is particularly pleasant at weekends.

Place des Vosges

Hôtel des Tournelles – The house, acquired by the Crown in 1407 on the assassination of the **Duke of Orléans** *(see below)*, was the residence of Charles VII where Louis XII ended his days and Henri II died; it was subsequently pulled down by **Catherine de' Medici.**

Place Royale – In 1605, Henri IV determined to transform the Marais into a splendid quarter with a vast square at its centre in which all the houses would be built to a like symmetry. On its completion in 1612, the Royal Square became the centre of elegance, courtly parades and festivities. Duels were also fought there in spite of **Cardinal Richelieu**'s ban. From 1800 it took the name of place des Vosges after the Vosges *département*, the first to pay its taxes.

The square today – The 36 houses retain their original symmetrical appearance: two storeys with alternate stone and brick facings are built over the ground-level arcade rising to steeply pitched slate roofs pierced by dormer windows.

Pavillon du Roi – The soberly decorated King's Pavilion on the south side and the largest house in the square, is balanced by the Queen's Pavilion (Pavillon de la Reine) to the north. Also of interest around the square are no **1bis** where Madame de Sévigné was born, no **17** where **Bossuet** lived, no **21** where Richelieu lived (1615-27), no **6** where Victor Hugo spent 16 years (1832-48) and no **8** occupied by both Théophile Gautier and Alphonse Daudet.

★ **Rue des Francs-Bourgeois** – This old street was originally known as rue des Poulies after the pulleys *(poulies)* on the looms of the local weavers' shops. It took its present name in 1334 when almshouses were built in it for the poor who were known as the men who pay no tax or *francs bourgeois.*

Hôtel d'Albret – *Nos 29 bis and 31.* Built in the 16C for the Duke of Montmorency, Constable of France, this mansion was remodelled in the 17C. It was in this house that the widow of the playwright Scarron, the future **Marquise de Maintenon**, became acquainted with **Mme de Montespan** to whose children Louis XIV appointed her governess in 1669; she later became the king's mistress. The unusual façade was altered in the 18C. The restored mansion houses the city's Cultural Affairs Department.

Hôtel Barbes, *no 33*, with its fine courtyard, was built around 1635.

Hôtel de Savourny at 4 rue Elzevir has an attractive courtyard.

Hôtel de Coulanges *nos 35-37* now Europe House, is 17C.

Hôtel de Sandreville *no 26* dating from 1586, has been converted into flats.

Hôtel d'Alméras, *no 30*, whose brick and stone façade is hidden behind a gateway featuring curious rams' heads.

Hôtel Poussepin, *no 34*, now serves as the Swiss Cultural Centre.

★ **Maison de Jean Hérouet** – *54 rue Vieille-du-Temple.* Built around 1510, it belonged to the treasurer to Louis XII; it still has its mullioned windows and an elegant corbelled turret.

Nearby stood, in the 15C, the **Hôtel Barbette**, the discreet residence of Queen Isabella of Bavaria who began the fashion for masked balls, while the king, Charles VI, resided at the Hôtel St-Paul.

Église de Notre-Dame-des-Blancs-Manteaux – The interior has remarkable woodwork – an inner door, organ loft, communion table and a magnificent Flemish **pulpit★** with marquetry panels inlaid with ivory and pewter, framed in gilded and fretted woodwork, typical of the period's Rococo style (1749).

Rue des Archives – A peaceful street which houses the national archives behind the façades of its fine mansions.

★★ **Hôtel de Soubise** – *No 58.* This is the oldest of the mansions, dating from the 14C. The **gateway★**, known as the **porte Clisson**, is flanked by a pair of corbelled turrets *(58 rue des Archives)*.

From 1705 to 1709 the mansion was remodelled into an elegant palace. The plans were entrusted to an unknown architect, Delamair, who retained the existing mansion, but built the main façade at right angles to it, and created a majestic horseshoe-shaped **courtyard★★**. The Musée de l'Histoire de France is housed in the building *(see description: Museums and other attractions).*

★★ **Hôtel de Guénégaud** – *No 60.* This mansion, built c 1650 by **Mansart**, was minimally remodelled in the 18C and has been beautifully restored in the 20C. With its plain harmonious lines, its majestic staircase and its small formal garden, it is one of the finest houses of the Marais. It contains the Musée de la Chasse *(see description: Museums and other attractions).*

Turn left onto rue des Quatre-Fils.

Note the garden and rear façade of the mansion.

★ **Cathédrale Ste-Croix-de-Paris** ⊙ – *Rue Charlot.* This much-restored church was erected in 1624 as a Capuchin monastery chapel and was attended by Mme de Sévigné. It is now the Armenian church.

1785: The Affair of the Diamond Necklace

Cardinal de Rohan had lost favour with Queen Marie-Antoinette. An unscrupulous adventuress, the Comtesse de la Motte, devised an elaborate ruse to persuade Rohan to act as the purchaser of a diamond necklace worth 1 600 000 livres. She convinced him that the Queen wanted to acquire the piece surreptitiously, even arranging a brief meeting in the gardens of Versailles one night, with a prostitute playing the role of the Queen! The plot came to light when the Cardinal was unable to make the payments, and it was discovered that the necklace had been broken up and sold in London. Rohan was tried and acquitted, but deprived of his offices. The Comtesse was sentenced to flogging, branding and life in prison, but instead fled to England and published her kiss-and-tell *Memoires*, vilifying the Queen.

The chancel is adorned with 18C gilded panelling from the former **Billettes Church**. To the left stands a remarkable **statue★** of St Francis of Assisi by Germain Pilon (16C).

Go back to rue de Quatre-Fils.

★★ Hôtel de Rohan – *87 rue Vieille-du-Temple.* In 1705 Delamair started work on the mansion simultaneously with the Hôtel de Soubise *(see above)*, for the

Soubise's son, the Bishop of Strasbourg who later became Cardinal de Rohan. It was successively the residence of four cardinals of the Rohan family, all of whom were bishops of Strasbourg. The last one lived there in grand style until his disgrace in the affair of the queen's necklace (1785). It was occupied by the state press (Imprimerie Nationale) under Napoleon and later in 1927 by the national archives.

Hôtel de Rohna, Horses of Apollo

The courtyard differs from that of the Soubise mansion as the main façade gives onto the garden which serves both properties *(see description: Museums and other attractions)*.

Follow rue de la Perle.

Place de Thorigny – This crossroads is a good place to sit down and admire the façades of the **Hôtel de Chassepot** at 3-5 rue de la Perle, and at no 1 in the same street, of the **Hôtel Libéral Bruant**. This elegant mansion has been restored to its original appearance and now houses a lock museum. In rue Thorigny, at no 5, is the **Hôtel Salé**, which contains the Picasso Museum *(see description: Museums and other attractions)*.

Rue du Parc-Royal – The 17C mansions lining the street opposite Léopold-Achille Square form a remarkable architectural group notwithstanding remodelling: **Canillac** (no **4**), **Duret-de-Chevry** (no **8**, extensively restored), **Vigny** (no **10**, a National Documentation Centre) and **Croisilles** (no **12**) which houses the library and archives of France's historic buildings commission.

Return to rue des Francs-Bourgeois via rue Payenne or rue de Sévigné.

Rue Payenne – Square Georges-Cain, lined by the orangery and the façade of the Hôtel St-Fargeau, is laid as a lapidary garden.

The **Hôtel de Châtillon** *(no 13)* has a paved courtyard and an interesting staircase.

The neighbouring **Hôtel de Marle** or **de Polastron-Polignac** *(no 11)* has a fine mask above the entrance and a keel-shaped roof attributed to Philibert Delorme; once owned by the Countess of Polignac, the governess of Marie-Antoinette's children, this house now accommodates a Swedish Cultural Centre.

The architect François Mansart died at no **5**. The old gateway was uncovered during restoration.

Rue de Sévigné – Beyond the Hôtel Carnavalet is the **Hôtel Le-Peletier-de-Saint-Fargeau** (no **29**) built by Pierre Bullet (1686-90) and named after its owner who was responsible for Louis XVI's death sentence. No **52**, the much-restored **Hôtel de Flesselles**, bears the name of Paris' last provost.

★★ Hôtel Carnavalet – *23 rue de Sévigné*. Construction was started in 1548 for Jacques des Ligneris, president of Parliament; the house was given its present appearance by **François Mansart** in 1655. The buildings surrounding the three garden courts are 19C.

Marie de Rabutin, the **Marquise de Sévigné**, who wrote the famous *Letters* which, with a light touch and quick wit give a lucid picture of day-to-day events, lived in the house from 1677 to 1696.

In 1866, the city of Paris acquired the mansion as a home for its historic collections *(see description: Museums and other attractions)*.

Exterior – **Jean Goujon** carved the lions at the main entrance which is 16C, and the keystone cornucopia. The supporting globe was later recarved into a carnival mask in allusion to the mansion's name.

The **statue** of Louis XIV in the courtyard by **Coysevox** was originally at the Hôtel de Ville. The building at the end is Gothic; only the four statues of the Seasons are Renaissance in style. The large figures on the wings are 17C; the cherubs with torches decorating the end of the wing are again by Jean Goujon.

Follow rue des Francs-Bourgeois to the right, and turn left onto rue Pavée.

★ Hôtel de Lamoignon – *24 rue Pavée*. The Hôtel d'Angoulême, which was built around 1585 for Diane of France, the legitimised daughter of Henri II, was bought in 1658 by Lamoignon, president of the first Parliament to sit in Paris. There he entertained Racine, Mme de Sévigné, the Jesuit preacher Bourdaloue, and the poet and critic Boileau. Malesherbes, the jurist and royal administrator who conducted Louis XVI's defence before the Convention, another Lamoignon, was also born here. In the 19C, Alphonse Daudet resided in the house.

Bibliothèque historique de la ville de Paris – Founded in 1763, the library is rich in French Revolution documents and has valuable collections of books, journals, manuscripts, maps, posters, photographs, cuttings etc. The **reading room** with its painted ceiling is one of the finest in Paris.

Rue des Rosiers – This street, together with the adjoining rue des Écouffes, which derives its name from a pawnbroker's shop sign, is the main axis of the **Jewish quarter** which has grown up in Paris' 4th *arrondissement*.
Rue Vieille-du-Temple (**Hôtel Amelot-de-Bisseuil** at *no 47*) and **rue du Roi-de-Sicilie** are full of small shops selling the latest fashions, jewellery and decorative items. Rue du Roi-de-Sicile ends in a small square, **place du Bourg-Tibourg**.

MUSEUMS AND OTHER ATTRACTIONS

★ Maison de Victor Hugo ⏱ – *6 place des Vosges*. A museum opened in 1903 in the former Hôtel de Rohan-Guéménée (early 17C) which was the home of the writer from 1832 to 1848. Drawings by Hugo himself are shown in rotation as part of temporary exhibitions on the first floor. On the second floor the displays evoke Hugo's various residences (the Chinese salon and the furniture from Juliette Drouet's house on Guernsey illustrate his talent as a decorator). There are also portraits, busts, photographs and mementoes of the poet and his family.

★ Musée de la Curiosité et de la Magie ⏱ – *11 rue Saint-Paul*.
⊡ The collection of ingenious accessories dispels some of the mystery from the art of magic, conjuring, legerdemain, prestidigitation and sleight-of-hand; a fascination that has been with us since Ancient Egyptian times. Midway through the museum, a stage, a few seats and a number of tiers provide the setting for regular magic shows *(about 30min; included in the entry fee)*.
Note the beautiful **turned objects**, so often made of boxwood in Nuremberg and fundamental to the magic boxes given to children in the last century: the **secret box** or **nest** (the piece of jewellery which disappeared was naturally found in the smallest box); **automatons**; objects fashioned in soft metal (brass, tin) made in Dinand (Belgium) whence their name *dinanderie*; a bottomless vase; a saucepan producing doves; balls full of scarves...
In the automaton room, above the door and display cases, are several **optical illusions**: one, a fairly long hollow box, appears to be a solid volume. A few metal bolts and a hollow bust of **Robert Houdin** (1805-71), the diplomat and ingenious clockmaker who elevated conjuring to the rank of an art in the 19C, are used to produce the same effect. Additional rooms contain further optical illusions and mirror games.

★★ Musée d'Art et d'Histoire du judaïsme ⏱ – *Hôtel de Saint-Aignan, 71 rue du Temple*. An ultra-modern museum in an historical setting, presenting both ancient and contemporary exhibits. Accompanying explicative notes provide the visitor with an in-depth view of Jewish culture.

The Jewish religion – The most important and unifying elements of the faith throughout the centuries are the Law (the Torah, gallery 1), religious teaching (gallery 7) and cultural festivals (galleries 4 and 7). The ceremonies associated with different festivals are explained by means of reconstructed synagogues and displays of religious objects. Belief in the Messiah and the subject of pilgrimages are also presented *(gallery 6)*.

The Diaspora – The history of the Jewish people is one of journeys and exiles. The first galleries (2, 3 and 5) illustrate the settlement of the Jews in France in the Middle Ages, and in Italy from the Renaissance to the 18C, through stelae, manuscripts and royal edicts, showing the integration of the Jewish community, the problem of discrimination and their everyday life (marriage certificates; jewels).

Two Jewish communities – As a result of contact with Muslim Spain, the Sephardic community evolved (gallery 8), whereas in Eastern Europe the Ashkenazic Jews (gallery 7) developed their own particular rites and clothing.

Contemporary Judaism – Under the First Empire, the Age of Enlightenment in the early 19C favoured the emancipation of the Jews in France, but by the end of the century modern anti-Semitism was all too present, with the Dreyfus affair and the Deportation (galleries 9 and 12) leading to the creation of Zionism. This remarkable exhibition finishes in galleries 11 and 13 with an illustration of Jewish influence on 20C art and the contemporary Jewish world (temporary exhibitions).

Musée de l'Histoire de France ⊙ – *Hôtel de Soubise, 60 rue des Francs-Bourgeois*. The building is a museum in its own right and has retained its original decor. During the renovation of the museum, exhibitions, lectures, concerts and educational workshops are organised.

★★ **The apartments** – Delamair's Classical architectural style, typical of Louis XIV's reign (simple façade, vast courtyard and suite of rooms), contrasts with Boffrand's extravagant Rococo decoration under Louis XV, when formal decor gave way to more intimate interiors. Between 1735 and 1740 the most gifted painters (Boucher, Natoire, Van Loo) and sculptors of the period worked under Boffrand, a pupil of Mansart, to decorate with all the delicacy and flourish of the Rococo style as was fashionable at Versailles.

The ground-floor apartments were the home of Hercule-Mériadec, the eldest son of the Prince de Soubise: the bedroom is decorated with mythological scenes, including *Aurora and Cephalus* by François Boucher and *Mars and Venus* by Carl Van Loo. The oval sitting room is decorated with high-relief carvings in plaster illustrating science and art.

On the first floor, beside the Guise Chapel is the Salle des Gardes (guard-room) which served as the League headquarters during the Wars of Religion. Note the two 17C Gobelin tapestries copied from 16C Belgian hangings woven for Charles V depicting Maximilian out hunting, together with the collection acquired from the Parlement de Paris archives (1847). This room is part of the circuit extended from the medieval display in the reading room that progresses through history to the present day.

The Assembly rooms, decorated with painted panels by Carl Van Loo *(Venus at her toilet)* and Boucher *(Venus bathing)*, contain a model of the Bastille made with stones from the fortress and a table and chairs originally belonging to the Paris Parliament.

Chambre de la Princesse – This spectacular, dazzling interior has survived intact. A large bed with baldaquin furnishes this splendid room fitted with white and gold panelling. Note the fine corner medallions in brushed gold depicting the Loves of Jupiter. Two superb paintings by Boucher *(The Cage or the obliging Clergyman* and *The Garland or the courteous Clergyman)* hang on either side of the bed.

Salon ovale de la Princesse – Masterful display of Rococo at its most refined, the sky-blue ceiling contrasts well with Nattier's feminine hues in his depiction of the *Story of Psyche*.

Petite chambre de la Princesse – Fine roundels illustrate the Elements, and panels by Van Loo, Restout, Trémolières and Boucher are set over the doors.

Musée de la Chasse et de la Nature ⊙ – *Hôtel Guénégaud, 60 rue des Archives*. The collection includes arms from prehistory to the 19C and trophies and souvenirs from big game expeditions. Tapestries, ceramics and sculptures on the theme of the hunt are also on view.

★★ **Hôtel de Rohan** ⊙ – *87 rue Vieille-du-Temple*. A staircase leads to the Cardinals' **apartments**★. Gobelin tapestries hang in the entrance hall. The first salons are adorned with Beauvais tapestries after cartoons attributed to Boucher.

The interior decoration dates from 1750. Also of interest are the Gold Salon and the amusing small Monkey Room with animal decorations by Christophe Huet, and the delicate panelling and wall hangings of the smaller rooms (Fable Room).

★★ **Musée Picasso** ⊙ – *Hôtel Salé, 5 rue de Thorigny*. The house was built from 1656 to 1659 for a salt tax collector, hence its name; it passed in the 18C to the De Juigné family, before becoming the École Centrale (1829-84) and subsequently the

Hôtel de Soubise, Salon de la Princesse

École des Métiers d'Art (1944-69). Recently restored and refurbished by the architect Simounet, the mansion now houses the Picasso Museum. Inside, the main **staircase★** with its spacious stairwell and splendid wrought-ironwork rises majestically to the first floor and a profusely carved ceiling.

The museum's origins – One of the dominant figures of 20C art, Pablo Ruiz Picasso (1881-1973) was born in Malaga. The young Picasso took courses in art at both Barcelona, where his father was a teacher, and Madrid. Aged only 23 he left his native country to settle in France, where he pursued his long and active career. Between 1936 and 1955, during his stay in Paris, Picasso lived at 7 rue des Grands Augustins (the 17C Hôtel d'Hercule) where he painted *Guernica* (1937).

Following his death at Mougins in 1973, Picasso's heirs donated an outstanding collection of the artist's works in lieu of estate duties. The collection comprises over 250 paintings, an excellent group of sculptures, collages, more than 3 000 drawings and engravings, 88 ceramics as well as illustrated books and manuscripts.

Tour – To follow the chronological order of the different phases *(explanatory notices)* of Picasso's prodigiously productive and long painting career, start on the first floor with his *Self Portrait* from the Blue Period. All the artist's styles and techniques are represented in his sketches for *Les Demoiselles d'Avignon, Still Life with Cane Chair* and *Pipes of Pan* and other favourite subjects such as female nudes, travelling acrobats and portraits of couples and of his own family (his son, *Paul as Harlequin*).

Also exhibited is Picasso's private collection of works by his friends and contemporaries (the Picasso Donation – *1st and 2nd floors*) such as Braque, **Cézanne** and **Rousseau**.

Films on the artist, his life and work are shown on the third floor.

Rue des Coutures-St-Gervais and **rue Vieille-du-Temple** skirt the gardens and afford glimpses of the imposing garden front. There is an unusual fountain by Simounet in the formal public garden beyond the museum's garden.

Musée de la Serrurerie Bricard ⓥ – *Hôtel Libéral-Bruand, 1 rue de la Perle.* In five well-lit rooms the art of the locksmith is traced from the Roman era to the Empire: collections of iron and bronze keys; wrought-iron Gothic locks; Venetian door knockers; gilded bronze locks from the Tuileries and Palais-Royal, combination lock etc as well as 20C ironwork and pieces from the Bricard workshops. To the right of the courtyard is a reconstruction of a locksmith's workshop.

★★**Cognacq-Jay Museum** ⓥ – *Hôtel Donon, 8 rue Elzévir.* This collection of 18C European art was bequeathed to the city of Paris by Ernest Cognacq (1839-1928), founder of the **Samaritaine department store**.

The **Hôtel Donon** has been refurbished to provide a worthy setting for the collection. The late-16C main part of the building with its tall roof is typical of Philibert Delorme's syle. The harmony and taste of both the mansion and the collection it houses give a good impression of the gallant and sophisticated lifestyle of the Age of Enlightenment.

MUSÉE CARNAVALET

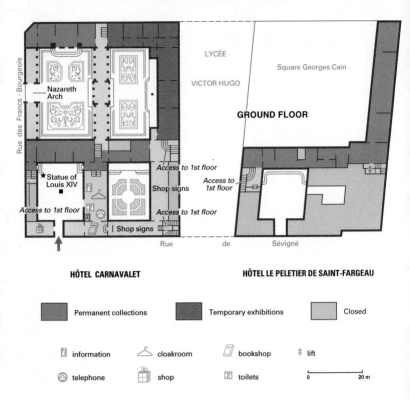

HÔTEL CARNAVALET   HÔTEL LE PELETIER DE SAINT-FARGEAU

- Permanent collections
- Temporary exhibitions
- Closed

- 🛈 information
- △ cloakroom
- 📖 bookshop
- ↕ lift
- ☎ telephone
- 🎁 shop
- 🚻 toilets
- 0 — 20 m

In the panelled ground-floor rooms is a selection of drawings by Watteau and paintings by Rembrandt, Ruisdael, Largillière and Chardin. Portraits bring to life some of the personalities of Louis XV's court: his queen, Marie Leczinska (1703-68), their daughter Madame Adélaïde, and Alexandrine, the daughter of **Madame de Pompadour**, Louis XV's mistress.

On the second floor, watercolours by Mallet illustrate the austere but elegant life of the Bourgeoisie under **Louis XVI** (1774-92). In the Oval Room Fragonard's portrayals of children and Rococo pastoral pictures contrast with terracottas by Lemoyen and paintings by Greuze. The sculpture gallery groups together works showing a strong Italian influence (Falconet, Houdon and Clodion) alongside paintings by Hubert Robert and Boucher.

The third floor is dedicated to Mme Vigée-Lebrun and her period, pastels including a self-portrait by La Tour, and British School paintings. In the carved oak-panelled salon are an oval table and *commode* signed RVLC by Roger Vandercruse, better known as Lacroix, and a pair of *commodes* by Martin Carlin. The study is hung with Venetian paintings, including Guardi's *St Mark's Square*. Showcases display Meissen and Sèvres porcelain, snuffboxes and *bonbonnières*.

★★ **Musée Carnavalet-Histoire de Paris** ◷ – *Hôtel Carnavalet, 23 rue de Sévigné*. The museum illustrating the history of Paris is housed in two separate mansions, the Hôtel Carnavalet and the Hôtel Le-Peletier-St-Fargeau: the variety of its exhibits make it one of the capital's most attractive museums.

Paris from its origins to the end of the Middle Ages is vividly depicted by means of archaeological finds such as the wooden **Neolithic canoes** found in Bercy in 1999; the oldest dates from 4400 BC.

The museum also brings back to life some of the main events of the capital's history, such as the French Revolution or the Commune.

The museum is particularly rich in decorative arts: painted and carved wood panelling and ceilings from other Parisian mansions have been reconstructed here (drawing rooms from the Hôtel de la Rivière painted by Lebrun, Belle-Époque decor of the Fouquet jewellery shop).

Literary history is illustrated by many portraits, pieces of furniture and souvenirs evoking famous writers (Marcel Proust's bedroom).

Maison européenne de la Photographie ⊘ – *5-7 rue de Fourcy*. This centre for contemporary photographic art houses an exhibition area, a large library, a video viewing facility and an auditorium. The mansion between rue François Miron and rue de Fourcy was built in 1704 for Hénault de Contobre, the royal tax collector. Selected as the site for the photography museum, the building was restored and completed by an additional wing on rue de Fourcy. The façade overlooking the street, the period ironwork and the central staircase are fine examples of Classical architecture. The centre exhibits in rotation works representing the cutting edge of photographic art (12 000 in all dating from 1958 onwards).

The Hénault-de-Cantobre hall is devoted to temporary exhibitions on historic and scientific themes.

The basement houses a library, video library and an auditorium.

MARCHÉ AUX PUCES★

Michelin plan 10: A 13, A 14
Ⓜ *Porte-de-Clignancourt (line 4) – Bus: 85*

Looking for old furniture, medals, uniforms, dolls or a hat that was once fashionable? The Saint-Ouen flea markets are a source of never-ending interest. They are open at weekends and on Mondays, but beware of pickpockets and of buying fake brand names. Turn north when leaving the metro station and go under the boulevard Périphérique to reach the markets.

EXPLORING THE NEIGHBOURHOOD

The flea markets are starting to look more like shops these days, although the neighbourhood retains the atmosphere of an unusual and picturesque village. Don't expect to find an Old Master, as it still might have been possible to do in the 1920s. But if you search long enough, and bargain carefully, you may still find something to treasure among the assorted bric-a-brac – a real collector's paradise.

Marché Vernaison – One of the oldest markets in Paris, which goes by the name of its original proprietor. In about 1885 he rented a part of his property to dealers, known as *chiff-tir* or *biffins* (rag-pickers), who resold the objects they collected. This is still true today: knick-knacks, furniture.

★**Marché Biron** – Founded in 1925 by 70 antique dealers. Don't be put off by appearances on seeing the first street, as the second is a treasure-trove of period furniture, reminiscent of grand châteaux. This is the smartest of the flea markets, with a warm, friendly atmosphere.

Marché Cambo – Furniture, paintings.

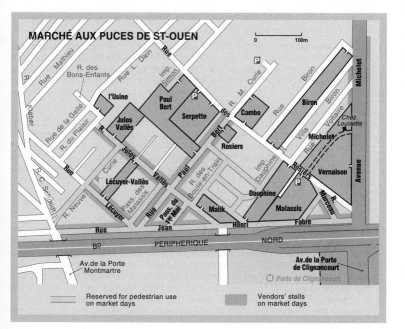

Marché des Rosiers – Furniture, knick-knacks, paintings. Nearly all antique dealers are specialists in glass paste jewellery and Art Nouveau furniture.

Marché Serpette – One of the most recent markets. Old and country furniture, knick-knacks, old weapons.

Marché Paul-Bert – Open-air bric-a-brac market.

Marché Jules Vallès – Rustic furniture. Has a reputation as the market with the most affordable prices.

Marché Malik – Second-hand clothes, glasses, records.

★ **Marché Dauphine** – Paintings, prints, furniture and bric-a-brac to suit every taste and from all periods. This is the most up-to-date market, not only the setting (metal-framed architecture on two floors with a glass roof), but also in the way it trades: a certificate is provided for buyers who request it (there is an independent valuation office in rue des Rosiers).

Mallassis – Antiques. Inside there is a restaurant, the Saint Framboise.

The adjoining streets are full of temporary markets selling clothes of all descriptions.

MAUBERT

Michelin plan 10: K 14, K 15
Ⓜ *Maubert-Mutualité (line 10) – Buses: 47, 63, 87*

This part of Paris has been a popular meeting place since the Middle Ages, and was also the place where mobs assembled and barricades were erected on more than one occasion. This neighbourhood is a fragment of medieval Paris threaded with narrow, winding streets and forms part of the Latin Quarter.
Its name is probably a corruption of Maître Albert or Albert the Great who taught theology from the square in the 13C. "La Maube" has recently been subjected to major restoration. President Mitterrand (1916-96) lived in rue de Bièvre for many years.

Nearby neighbourhoods: JUSSIEU, QUARTIER LATIN, NOTRE-DAME, ÎLE DE LA CITÉ, ÎLE ST-LOUIS, JARDIN DES PLANTES, BASTILLE.

EXPLORING THE NEIGHBOURHOOD

Start by walking along the river.

Quai de la Tournelle – Just before the Pont de l'Archevêché (1828) are a line of old houses with a splendid view★★★ of Notre-Dame from the bridge. Opposite Île St-Louis, the **Pont de la Tournelle** boasts a striking statue of St Geneviève by Landowski. No 15, opposite the bridge, is the very old Tour d'Argent restaurant where Henri IV is said to have discovered the use of a fork.

Quai de Montebello – In the Middle Ages, wood for building and heating was floated on rafts down to Paris and stored at the Port-aux-Bûches between the Petit Pont and the Pont au Double. In the 17C the **Pont au Double** linked two sections of the **Hôtel-Dieu** hospital on the Left Bank and island. The present bridge was built in 1885.

Just after the square, turn left.

Square René-Viviani – The small church close was enlarged in 1928 to its present size, care being taken to preserve the Robinia or false acacia planted in 1601, one of the two oldest acacias in Paris, and now supported with a prop (the species was introduced from the United States by the botanist, Robin, hence the name). The view★★★ is remarkable: the church of St-Julien itself stands out clear and white behind a curtain of trees; **rue St-Julien-le-Pauvre** bustles with life beneath a picturesque jumble of roofs; the Île de la Cité; and finally, above all, Notre-Dame is seen from its best angle in all its glory, massive in scale yet delicate in detail.

★ **Église St-Julien-le-Pauvre** – *1 rue St-Julien-le-Pauvre.* The present building was constructed at the same time as Notre-Dame between 1165 and 1220. It is named after Saint Julian the Confessor, the medieval Bishop of Le Mans, also known as the Poor because he gave so much away that his purse was always empty.
Inside, the Gothic vaulting of the aisles is original, whereas the nave was re-roofed with cradle vaulting in 1651. The chancel, the most beautiful part of the building, is screened off by a wooden iconostasis hung with icons or holy pictures.
Note the two pillars in the chancel with **capitals★** carved with acanthus leaves and harpies.

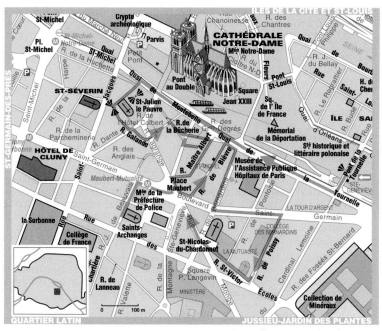

Square – The **view★★** of St-Séverin across the entrance to rue Galande is one of the most picturesque of old Paris, and still a popular subject for painters. An iron well-head, originally from inside the church, now stands against the doorway near two Roman paving stones from the old Orléans-to-Lutétia road (Lutétia being the Roman name for Paris).

No 14 rue St-Julien-le-Pauvre dates from the 17C and was at one time the house of the governor of the Petit Châtelet or lesser Barbican.

Rue Galande – At nos **54-46** cellars and pointed medieval arches have been unearthed; a carved stone above the door of no **42** shows St Julian the Hospitaller in his boat. Note the 15C gable of No **31**.

Cross rue Lagrange and take rue de l'Hôtel-Colbert, then turn right to reach place Maubert.

Rue du Fouarre – This was one of the places where, in the Middle Ages, public lectures were given by the university in the open air attended by students seated on bundles of straw *(fouarre)*. Dante is said to have attended lectures in this street in 1304.

Rue de la Bûcherie – The École d'Administration now occupies the premises of the first Medical School founded in the 15C.

Impasse Maubert – It was here that the Greek College was founded in 1206 – the first in Paris – and that the infamous Marquise de Brinvilliers concocted her poisons in the 17C.

Rue Maître-Albert – The old houses rise above a network of underground passages down to the banks of the Seine and to the adjoining alleyways that sheltered rogues and conspirators up until the 20C.

Place Maubert – Since the early Middle Ages, this square has been a traditional rallying point for university students; barricades have gone up here in times of popular uprising.

Rue des Anglais is named after the English students who lived there in the Middle Ages.

Follow boulevard St-Germain in a westerly direction, then take the first left.

Rue de Bièvre – The name is taken from that of a tributary of the Seine. The area around was particularly populated by boatmen and tanners. The entrance of the former St-Michel College at no **12** is surmounted by a statue of St Michael slaying the dragon. A garden opposite no **17** is a peaceful place for children to play.

Coming out onto quai de la Tournelle, turn right and then right again along rue des Bernardins until it joins boulevard St-Germain. Turn left along it, then right onto rue de Poissy.

Rue de Poissy – This street was laid through the gardens of the former **Bernardins College**, which was founded in 1246 to educate monks and taken over by the Cistercians in the 14C. Since 1845 the buildings have served as a fire station (nos 18-24 rue de Poissy). From the road, one can catch a glimpse of the upper part of the refectory with its three ogive-vaulted aisles divided into 17 bays. It is one of the finest Gothic halls in Paris. *Not open to the public.*

Turn right.

Église St-Nicolas-du-Chardonnet – A chapel was constructed in what was a field of thistles *(chardons)* in the 13C. In 1656 it was replaced by the present building oriented north-south; the façade was completed only in 1934. It is dedicated to St Nicholas, the patron saint of sailors. The **side door★** on rue des Bernardins has remarkable wood carving designed by Le Brun, a parishioner of the church. The interior is Jesuit in style, liberally decorated with paintings by Restout, Coypel, Claude, Corot and Le Brun (his funeral monument, by Coysevox, stands in an ambulatory chapel on the left near Le Brun's own monument to his mother). Note the interesting funerary monument by Girardon to the right of the chancel. The 18C organ loft is from the former Church of the Innocents.

Return to place Maubert via rue Monge. Turn left along rue Jean-de-Beauvais.

Église des Sts-Archanges – *9 bis rue Jean-de-Beauvais.* Purchased by the Romanian Orthodox Church in 1882, this much restored chapel is dedicated to the archangels Michael, Gabriel and Raphael. It was originally built in the 14C as part of the Beauvais College founded by Jean Dormous in 1370.

MUSEUMS AND OTHER ATTRACTIONS

Musée de l'Assistance publique – Hôpitaux de Paris ⊘ – *47 quai de la Tournelle.* The Hôtel Martin (1630) has variously served as a private residence, a hostel for young girls employed in good works, a bayonet forge (during the Revolution), and a General Dispensary turned museum.
The museum traces the evolution of the public health service in Paris from the Hôtel-Dieu (650), and its relationship with Church charity. On display are documents, paintings, engravings, drug jars, vaccination equipment and artefacts. There are temporary exhibitions on the ground floor.

Musée des Collections historiques de la préfecture de Paris ⊘ – *1 bis rue des Carmes.* The collection displays the evolution of the Paris police from the time of sentry watchmen in the early Middle Ages to the creation of the Guardians of the Peace Corps in 1870. There are also interesting legal documents on display such as *lettres de cachet* or royal warrants, decrees, prison registers, weapons and souvenirs of famous criminals and conspirators.

Plaine et parc MONCEAU★★

Michelin plan 10: D 9, D 10, E 9, E 10
Ⓜ *Monceau (line 2) – Buses: 30, 84, 94*

In 1778 the Duke of Chartres, the future Philippe-Égalité, commissioned the painter-writer Carmontelle to design a garden on the Monceau Plain. The artist created a land of dreams, scattered with follies in keeping with English and German landscaped gardens of the period.
Garnerin, the world's first parachutist, landed in the park on 22 October 1797. Major changes were involved at the time of the Second Empire in 1852 when part of the park was sold for the building of luxurious houses, some of which now house museums. The park has changed little since.

★ Parc Monceau – *Entrance via the rotunda (north, next to the metro station).* The rotunda, with its fine wrought-iron gates at the entrance, known as the Chartres Pavilion, is what remains of one of Ledoux's toll-houses built in the **Farmers-General perimeter wall**.
Many statues nestle among the greenery and mature trees with varied foliage. The oval **naumachia basin** is modelled on the Roman pools constructed for the simulation of naval battles, its decorative colonnade borrowed from the never completed mausoleum of Henri II at St-Denis. Nearby is a Renaissance arcade that once stood in front of the Hôtel de Ville.
On leaving the park, follow avenue Van-Dyck (south-east), then turn right onto rue de Courcelles and left onto rue Daru.

Cathédrale St-Alexandre-Nevski 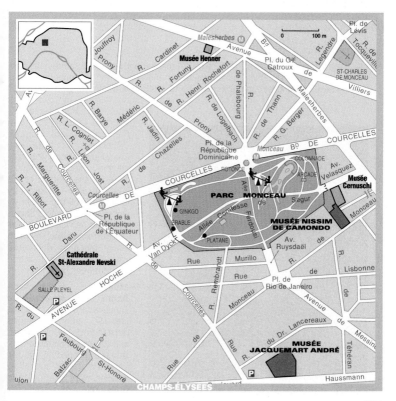 ⊘ – *12 rue Daru.* This, the Russian Orthodox Church of Paris, was erected in 1860 in the Russian neo-Byzantine style on a Greek cross plan. The main features of the exterior are gilded onion-shaped domes whereas the interior is decorated with frescos, gold and icons. Magnificently sung mass is celebrated in the tradition of Mother Russia.

On 12 July 1918, Pablo Picasso and Olga Khoklova were married here attended by their witnesses Max Jacob, Jean Cocteau, Guillaume Apollinaire and Serge Diaghilev.

MUSEUMS AND OTHER ATTRACTIONS

★ **Musée Cernuschi** ⊘ – *7 avenue Vélasquez. Closed for restoration.* The banker Henri Cernuschi bequeathed his house and extensive collection of Oriental art to the City of Paris in 1896.

Devoted to ancient Chinese art the collection includes Neolithic terracottas, bronzes (the famous *Tigress* – wine flask in the shape of an animal crouching protectively over the clan patriarch) and archaic jades, ceramics, some fine funerary statuettes and pen and ink drawings. Note the 5C stone Bodhisattva and 8C Tang silk scroll painting illustrating *Horses and their Grooms*.

Temporary exhibitions alternate with displays of traditional Chinese painting.

Musée Henner ⊘ – *43 avenue de Villiers.* Collected together in the Alsatian artist Jean-Jacques Henner's (1829-1905) house are over 500 paintings, drawings and sketches spread on three levels. Several portraits of members of his family and friends are realistically rendered. Landscapes full of clear, warm light evoke an early trip he made to Italy where he studied the works of Titian and Correggio. His larger canvases characterised by simple compositions and rigorous brushstokes, often depict languorous Romantic figures of nymphs. An audio-visual display describes the artist's work and its development.

★★ **Musée Nissim de Camondo** ⊘ – *63 rue de Monceau.* In 1936 Count de Camondo presented his house and 18C art collection to the nation in memory of his son Nissim, killed in the First World War. The house was built in 1863 and modified in 1911, and overlooks the adjoining Monceau Park at the rear. Although packed with exquisite furniture, the rooms appear quite uncluttered and retain much of the elegant yet intimate aura of a private 18C house.

Park and museums

Park Monceau – There are children's play areas scattered throughout the park, but most are on the east side: roller-skating, sand pits, merry-go-rounds.

Jacquemart-André Museum – An interactive audio guide is available (included in the entrance fee) in English, French, German, Japanese, Italian and Spanish. A pleasant way to find out more about this residence and the lives and works of the André couple.

Art and music

Galerie Lelong – *13 rue Téhéran – 8th arr –* Ⓜ *Miromesnil –* ☎ *01 45 63 13 19 – galerie.lelong@wanadoo.fr – Tue-Fri 10.30am-6pm, Sat 2-6.30pm – closed Aug.* One of Paris' most famous galleries. It displays work by several international artists: Alechinsky, Appel, James Brown, Chillida, Dibbets, Judd, Kounellis, Michaux, Miro, Monory, Pignon-Ernest, Rebeyrolle, Saura, Scully, Tàpies...

Salle Cortot – *78 rue Cardinet – 17th arr –* ☎ *01 47 68 85 72 – www.ecolenor malecortot.com – all year 8.30-11.30pm.* This handsome room with seating for 400, now a listed monument, was designed by Auguste and Gustave Perret in 1929. It is part of the Paris School of Music and puts on concerts of classical music, but also masterclasses with artists such as Rostropovitch, François-René Duchâble, Felicity Lott. Some of the best acoustics in Paris.

Eating out

Café Jacquemart-André – *158 boulevard Haussmann –* Ⓜ *Miromesnil or St-Philippe-du-Roule –* ☎ *0145 62 11 59 – 11.30am-5.30pm – 12/20€.* This non-smoker restaurant-cum-tearoom is housed in Édouard André and Nélie Jacquemart's former dining room which boasts a splendid ceiling by Tiepolo and large tapestries illustrating the legend of Achilles. On the menu: salads, quiche and cakes; brunch on Sundays. Terrace overlooking the courtyard. No reservation required but bear in mind that the place is crowded with locals at lunchtime.

Turn back to the Selected restaurants section at the beginning of the guide for a list of restaurants, bistros, cafés etc. This district corresponds to the 17th *arrondissement*.

The mansion preserves an elegant Louis XVI interior with panelled salons, furniture made by the greatest cabinetmakers (Riesener and Weisweiler), Savonnerie carpets and Beauvais tapestries, paintings by Guardi and Hubert Robert, gold and silver ornaments by the royal goldsmith, Roettiers and a selection of porcelain from the most famous factories (Vincennes, Meissen, Chantilly). Among the outstanding pieces are tapestries of the *Fables* of La Fontaine after cartoons by Oudry, a roll-top desk by Oeben and a splendid Sèvres porcelain service, known as the Buffon service, in which every piece is decorated with a naturalistic depiction of a different bird.

Galerie en ruine, Hubert Robert

★★ Musée Jacquemart-André ⊘ – *158 boulevard Haussmann.* This elegant late-19C house contains outstanding 18C European and Italian Renaissance art. On the ground floor the Louis XV period is vividly recalled with paintings and drawings by Boucher

(Venus Sleeping and *Venus at Her Toilet)*, Greuze, Chardin, Watteau, Fragonard *(Portrait of an Old Man)*; sculpture by Houdon, Lemoyne, Coysevox; Beauvais tapestries, furniture and objets d'art. Other 17C and 18C European Schools of painting are represented by Rembrandt, Van Dyck, Canaletto (two views of Venice), Reynolds and frescoes by Tiepolo (ceilings in rooms 4, 5, 13 and over the stairs). There are also fine 16C Limoges enamels and ceramics by Palissy. In the Italian rooms on the first floor are displayed a remarkable collection from the Florentine Quattrocento – Botticelli *(Virgin with Child)*, Della Robbia, Donatello – and the Venetian Renaissance – Mantegna *(Ecce homo)*, Tintoretto, Titian). Among the most noteworthy are Uccello's famous *St George Slaying the Dragon* and a fine bronze bust by Bernini.

MONTMARTRE★★★

Michelin plan 10: C 12 – C 14, D 12 – D 14
Ⓜ *Anvers (line 2), Abbesses (line 12), Lamarck-Caulaincourt (line 12) – Buses: 30, 54, 67, Montmartrobus*

The Butte, as it is known locally, meaning the hillock or mound, is the part of Paris most full of contrasts – anonymous boulevards run close to delightful village streets and courts, steep stone steps lead to open terraces, pilgrims tread the streets beside nightclub revellers. On the southern side, a funicular provides access to one of Paris' most famous landmarks, Sacré-Cœur.

Nearby neighbourhoods: PIGALLE.

HISTORY OF MONTMARTRE

Martyrs' Mound – In Roman times, Montmartre had two hill-top temples dedicated to Mercury and Mars. Later on, a local legend dating from the 8C led it to be known as the martyrs' mound after **St Denis**, first **Bishop of Lutetia**, the priest Rusticus, and the deacon Eleutherius. Having undergone torture by the grill in the Cité in about AD 250, they were brought here to be decapitated, after which, it is said, St Denis picked up his gory head and walked north to the place now known as St-Denis.

The early days of the Commune – In 1871, after the fall of Paris, the people of Montmartre collected 171 cannon on the hill to prevent their capture by the Prussians. The battery was declared government property, and on 18 March the military were sent to seize the weapons but were unable to remove them, whereupon the crowd seized the generals and shot them – a bloody episode which was to mark the beginning of the Commune. Montmartre remained under Federal control until 23 May.

Bohemian life – Throughout the 19C, artists and men of letters were drawn to the free-and-easy way of life as lived on the Butte.
The composer **Berlioz** (buried in the Montmartre cemetery) and the writers and poets Nerval, **Murger** and Heine, were the precursors of the great 1871-1914 generation; young painters sought inspiration on place Pigalle, artists' models and seamstresses led a Bohemian existence. In the early days, groups of poets (Le Chat Noir) congregated in cafés enlivened with songs by **Aristide Bruant**, poems by Charles Cros and

Going out

Au Virage Lepic – *61 rue Lepic – 18th arr – ☎ 01 42 52 46 79 – daily 7pm-2am (except Tues)*. This typical Montmartre bistro is equally pleasant for a quick drink or for dinner.
La Bohème du Tertre – *2 pl. du Tertre – 18th arr – ☎ 01 46 06 51 69 – daily 7am-5am*. Small ball-musette on Sunday.
Le Sancerre – *35 rue des Abbesses – 18th arr – ☎ 01 42 58 47 05 – daily 7am-2am*. This traditional café is one of the best-known in Montmartre, as busy by night as by day.

Shopping

Marché St-Pierre – *Sq. Willette – 18th arr*. In addition to a pleasant walk, this colourful, lively market provides an excellent choice of cut-price fabric and clothes.

Eating out

Turn back to the Selected restaurants section at the beginning of the guide for a list of restaurants, bistros, cafés etc. This district corresponds to the 18th *arrondissement*.

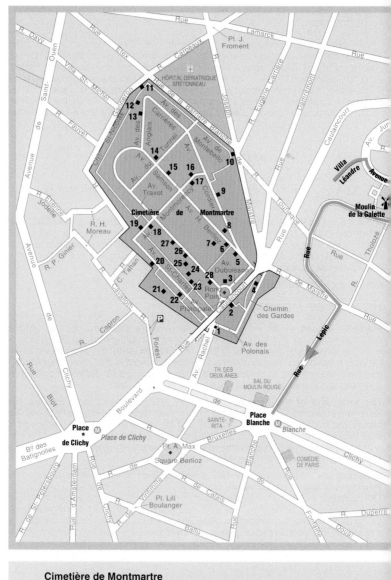

Cimetière de Montmartre

1 - Lucien and Sacha Guitry

2 - Eugène Labiche

3 - Émile Zola
(transferred to the Panthéon in 1908)

4 - Dalida

5 - Hector Berlioz

6 - Greuze

7 - Heinrich Heine

8 - François Truffaut

9 - Théophile Gautier

10 - Edgar Degas

11 - Léo Delibes

12 - Poulbot

13 - Jacques Offenbach

14 - Charles Fourier

15 - Nijinsky

Jehan Rictus, humour, drawings by Caran d'Ache, André Gill and **Toulouse-Lautrec**. These evolved into the *caf' conc'* (café-concert) with programmed entertainment: the Moulin Rouge opened in 1889 with Yvette Guilbert, Valentin le Désossé, Jane Avril and Louise Weber nicknamed *La Goulue*. The Butte, thanks to the **Lapin Agile** café and **Bateau-Lavoir** studios, remained until the outbreak of the Great War the capital's literary and artistic centre.

As the next generation of artists and émigrés congregated in Montparnasse, Montmartre abandoned itself to its nocturnal entertainments. Today, although still run-down, Montmartre draws tourists from far afield in search of the spirit of the Belle Epoque, or more simply to enjoy the view over the city.

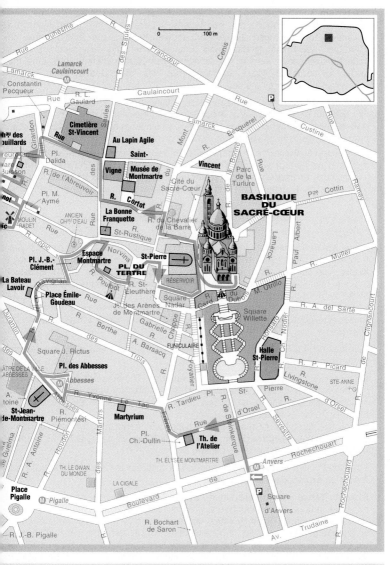

EXPLORING THE NEIGHBOURHOOD

From boulevard de Rochechouart to Sacré-Coeur

Take rue de Steinkerque for a fine view of Sacré-Coeur, then turn left onto rue d'Orsel.

Place Charles-Dullin – An attractive shady little square. The small theatre nestling among the trees was founded in the early 19C as the Théâtre de Montmartre; it grew to fame between the wars when Charles Dullin founded the **Théâtre de l'Atelier** in 1922.

Take rue Trois-Frères, then turn left onto rue Yvonne-Le-Tac.

Martyrium – *11 rue Yvonne-Le-Tac.* A chapel has replaced the medieval sanctuary built to mark the site where St Denis and his companions are presumed to have been decapitated. It was here in the former crypt on 15 August 1534, that **Ignatius Loyola**, Francis Xavier and their six companions undertook apostolic vows in the service of the Church thereby instituting the Society of Jesus. Six years later the order was recognised by Pope Paul III, subsequently known as the Jesuit Order.

★**Place des Abbesses** – This animated little square is the very heart of the community, with its distinctive original **Hector Guimard** Art Nouveau entrance to the metro station (the only other is at Porte Dauphine), which leads down 280 spiralling steps past a continuous mural painted by 20 local artists.

Église St-Jean-de-Montmartre – *South side of the square.* This unusual church designed by Baudot was the first to be built of reinforced concrete (1904); it continues to impress structural engineers on account of its audacious use of the material, especially given the slenderness of supporting beams and piers.

Leave square Jean-Rictus by rue des Abbesses and turn right onto rue Ravignan.

★**Place Émile-Goudeau** – This high point in artistic and literary realms was frequented from 1900 by the pioneers of modern painting and poetry; **Picasso**, Van Dongen, Braque, and Juan Gris, evolved Cubism – with Picasso's famous *Demoiselles d'Avignon*, whereas Max Jacob, **Apollinaire** and Mac Orlan broke away from traditional poetic form and expression. They met at no 13, **Le Bateau-Lavoir**, a rickety wooden building which burnt down in 1970 just as it was to be restored. Now rebuilt, the block continues to provide artists' studios and apartments.

Continue up rue Ravignan to place Jean-Baptiste-Clément and along rue Norvins past a former water tower.

Carrefour de l'Auberge de la Bonne-Franquette – The **crossroads** with rue Norvins, rue des Saules and rue St-Rustique was often painted by **Utrillo**, son of the artist Suzanne Valadon, and it is his renderings that best evoke the spirit of Old Montmartre for us today.
During the latter half of the 19C, this haunt was frequented by Pissarro, Sisley, Cézanne, Toulouse-Lautrec, **Renoir**, **Monet** and **Émile Zola**. *La Guinguette*, the painting by Van Gogh was inspired by its garden.

Take rue Poulbot on the right, leading to the minute place du Calvaire which commands an exceptional view over Paris.

★★**Place du Tertre** – This simple, shaded square fronted with small houses is a peaceful village in the early morning hours; later, invaded by sightseers, it becomes a busy tourist attraction animated by cafés, restaurants, art galleries, the bustle of street artists offering their canvases, a personalised charcoal portrait or paper cut-outs.
No **21** (formerly no 19 bis) is the seat of the Free Commune founded in 1920 by Jules Dépaquit to preserve the imaginative and humorous traditions of the Butte; it now houses the Tourist Information Centre.
No **3**, once the local town hall, is now Poulbot House to commemorate local children (P'tits Poulbots), popularised in the artist's delightful line drawings and illustrations from the early 20C.
The first petrol-powered motor car to have reached the top of the Butte was driven by its designer Louis Renault on 24 December 1898.

★**Église St Pierre-de-Montmartre** – *2 rue du Mont-Cenis.* The church of Saint Peter is the last surviving vestige of the great abbey of Montmartre and one of the oldest churches in the capital, dating back to 1134. The nave was revaulted in the 15C; the west front dates from the 18C. The three bronze doors showing St Denis, St Peter and the Virgin, are by the Italian sculptor, **Gismondi** (1980).

Interior – The oldest pointed arches in Paris (1147) meet in the single bay of the apse. In places, the worn Romanesque capitals have been replaced. The apse and aisles are lit by modern stained glass designed by Max Ingrand (1953).
The high altar is adorned with enamelled panels by Froidevaux (1977). The Way of the Cross is by Gismondi.

★★**Basilique du Sacré-Cœur** – *Place du Parvis-du-Sacré-Cœur.* The tall white silhouette of the basilica is a feature of the Paris skyline, with its pointed cupolas dominated by the 80m/262ft campanile. Internally, this pilgrim church is decorated with mosaics; the chancel vault designed by Luc-Olivier Merson depicts France's devotion to the Sacred Heart.

Sacré-Cœur atop Montmartre

Construction – After the disastrous Franco-Prussian War of 1870, a group of Catholics vowed to raise money by public subscription to erect a church to the Sacred Heart on Montmartre hill. The proposal was declared a State undertaking by the National Assembly in 1873.

The architect **Paul Abadie** (1812-84) based his designs for a neo-Romano-Byzantine basilica on the old church. Building began in 1876 and concluded in 1914. The church was consecrated in 1919 and has attracted countless pilgrims ever since.

The dome ⊘ – From inside there is a bird's-eye view down into the church and from the external gallery a **panorama★★★** extending for over 30km/18mi may be glimpsed on a clear day.

La Savoyarde – Hanging in the belfry, this is one of the heaviest bells in the world (19t). It was cast in 1895 at Annecy, and offered as a gift from the dioceses of Savoy.

The church plate is visible in the **crypt** ⊘, as is an audio-visual display on the history and cult of the basilica.

The terrace – From the church steps there is a remarkable **view★★** over the capital. Immediately below is square Willette laid out in 1929 (a funicular train shuttles up the steep hill thereby saving a steep climb for the price of a metro ticket).

From Sacré-Cœur to rue Lepic

Follow rue Chevalier-de-La-Barre and turn right onto rue du Mont-Cenis.

Rue Cortot – No **12** boasts of having put up Renoir, Othon Friesz, Utter, Dufy, Émile Bernard, Suzanne Valadon and her son **Utrillo**, and the radical poet Pierre Reverdy over the years. It is now the entrance to the Montmartre Museum.

Descend rue des Saules on the right.

The vineyard – On the first Saturday in October, the grapes are harvested – always a most festive event.

Rue St-Vincent – The junction with rue des Saules is one of the most delightful corners of the Butte: flights of steps drop away mysteriously straight ahead while another road rises steeply beside the **cemetery**... the picturesque charm is further enhanced by the famous **Lapin Agile**, half-hidden by an acacia. Between 1900 and 1914 it attracted a host of often penniless writers and artists (Francis Carco, Roland Dorgelès, Pierre Mac Orlan, **Picasso**, Vlaminck...). A traditional cabaret show still draws a crowd *(9pm, except Mondays)*.

Hector Berlioz once lived in the house on the corner with rue du Mont-Cenis, where he composed *Harold in Italy* and *Benvenuto Cellini*.

Cimetière St-Vincent – This modest cemetery is the resting place of the musician Honegger, the painter Utrillo, the writer Marcel Aymé, and Émile Goudeau the founder of the Club des Hydropathes.

Nearby *(52 rue Lamarck)*, the most fashionable restaurant in Montmartre, the **Beauvilliers**, was named after Antoine Beauvilliers, a famous chef at the court of Louis XVIII; note the exuberant late-19C decor (sculptures, paintings...).

Walk up the steps on the left then turn right onto a narrow lane.

Château des Brouillards – This was built in the 18C as a folly; it was later used as a dance hall; Gerard de Nerval lived there for a time. Its grounds have become square Suzanne-Buisson (a statue of St Denis stands on the spot where he is said to have washed his decapitated head).

Avenue Junot – Opened in 1910, this wide peaceful thoroughfare gave onto the Montmartre *maquis*, an open space of ill repute where mills still turned their sails to the wind. Among the artists' studios and private houses is the **Hameau des Artistes** (no 11) and the **Villa Léandre★** (no 25). There is a view of the windmill from no 10.

Moulin de la Galette – The dance hall which enjoyed such a rage at the turn of the 20C, inspired many painters including **Renoir** *(see ORSAY)*, **Van Gogh** and Willette. The windmill which has topped the hill for more than six centuries is the old *Blute-fin* which was defended against the Cossacks in 1814 by the heroic mill-owner Debray whose corpse was finally crucified upon the sails.

Rue Lepic – The old quarry road that winds gently down the steep hill is the scene each autumn of a veteran car rally. Van Gogh lived with his brother at no **54**.

Go down rue Lepic which joins boulevard de Clichy at place Blanche.

MUSEUMS AND OTHER ATTRACTIONS

Musée de Montmartre ⊙ – *12 rue Cortot*. The museum houses a rich collection of mementoes evoking the quarter's Bohemian life, its nightclubs and personalities, and hosts interesting temporary exhibitions. Besides the many topographical paintings there are reconstructions of the Café de l'Abreuvoir where Utrillo was a frequent visitor, and of the composer **Charpentier**'s studio.

Halle St-Pierre – *2 rue Ronsard*. Part way up the hill and off to the right stands a fine 19C cast-iron textile market that has been transformed into an exhibit hall. The ground floor hosts temporary year-long exhibitions. On the first floor, the **Musée d'Art naïf Max Fourny** ⊙ displays paintings and sculpture by contemporary artists from some 30 countries.

Cimetière de Montmartre ⊙ – *Avenue Rachel-plan p 256-57*. Many famous people, among them artists and writers are buried here, including author Émile Zola (whose body was later transferred to the Panthéon), the dramatist Labiche, painter Edgar Degas, the great dancer Nijinski, actor Louis Jouvet, composer Jacques Offenbach, and film director François Truffaut.

MONTPARNASSE★★

Michelin plan 10: L 11, L 12, M 11, M 12
Ⓜ *Montparnasse-Bienvenue (lines 4, 6, 12 and 13), Edgar-Quinet (line 6), Vavin (line 4), Gaîté (line 13) and Raspail (lines 4 and 6) –*
Buses: 28, 48, 58, 82, 89, 91, 92, 94, 95, 96

Although this neighbourhood has changed since the days when artists and philosophers made it their own, from the early 1900s through to the 60s, and although chain restaurants now vie for space with the famous cafés, Montparnasse is still a great place to spend an evening, have a drink, see a film, enjoy a meal, listen to music in an after-hours club, and tune into the high energy of the crowd.

Mount Parnassus – The debris from age-old quarries formed a deserted rough-grass-covered mound. For students, chased away from the Pré-aux-Clercs by Queen Marguerite, it became a favourite haunt where they could freely declaim poetry. They named this wild place Mount Parnassus after the sacred mountain where Apollo entertained his Muses.

A pleasure ground – At the time of the Revolution, cafés and cabarets mushroomed on the city's outskirts. Revellers congregated at the Montagnes-Suisses and Élysée-Montparnasse gardens and the Arc-en-Ciel and Grande Chaumière dance halls. It was here that the polka and the cancan were introduced to Paris. The Bullier Dance Hall once stood on carrefour de l'Observatoire where the **Closerie des Lilas** was later established; crowds gathered at the Constant Dance Hall and in the drinking dens of the village of Plaisance to dance the mazurka between sips of rough Suresnes wine.

As the sprawl continued, Haussmann intervened, ordering the area into confined neighbourhoods around the villages Plaisance, **Vaugirard** and Montrouge, accessed by rue de Rennes, boulevard Arago and boulevard d'Enfer (now boulevard Raspail).

Bohemian Montparnasse – At the turn of the 20C avant-garde artists, poets and writers, moved to the Left Bank and to Montparnasse in particular, following a lead set by Alfred Jarry, **Douanier Rousseau** (who worked locally at a customs-house) and **Henri Murger** who had already described the Bohemian lifestyle in his *Scenes of Bohemian Life*. The newcomers included **Apollinaire**, Max Jacob and Jean Moréas.

The former Wine Pavilion from the 1900 Exhibition was reconstructed at no 52 **rue de Dantzig**. The main pavilion, circular in shape, with a cubist roof, accommodated 24 painters in narrow cells or coffins on two floors thereby earning ts name **La Ruche**, meaning Beehive. This rabbit warren replaced the **Bateau-Lavoir** *(see MONTMARTRE)* by providing lodging and studios to impoverished, often foreign, artists, notably Modigliani, **Soutine**, Chagall, **Zadkine** and Léger. It was from such cramped quarters that the Expressionist movement emerged.

Discussion and debate were animated by the Russian political exiles (Lenin, Trotsky), composers (Stravinsky, Satie and the Six), foreign artists and writers (Hemingway, Foujita, Picasso, Eisenstein, Blasco Ibañez, **Man Ray**, Cendrars, Fargué, André Breton, **Cocteau**). This was the golden age of the **Paris School** lasting into the mid-1930s, and ending with the outbreak of war in Spain and Western Europe.

This former international Bohemian quarter became entirely Parisian; in the frenzy of materialism and exhibitionism prevalent after the war whichdrove the pace of fashion (as observed by Fernand Léger), the Vavin crossroads became the navel of the world: it came to be frequented by the trendy set, sporty 'stylish' hatchback cars. At the Dingo, the Viking, the Caméléon bars, crazy concoctions and cocktails began to replace the old-time cafés-crèmes, late-night opening stretched ever further into the morning: such was the American influence of the 1950s.

During the 1960s, the pace became too much; Aragon, Cocteau, **Braque**, **Sartre**, De Beauvoir continued to be glimpsed, but already the likes of Foujita, Picasso, Chagall had moved on.

Since redevelopment the Maine-Montparnasse complex has become the nucleus of a business area, although along boulevard du Montparnasse, Parisians and out-of-towners are drawn to the shops, cafés, cinemas and nightclubs, keeping up a lively hubbub day and night.

EXPLORING THE NEIGHBOURHOOD

Montparnasse has two faces: the modern tower, train station and place de Catalogne, and the more traditional aspect, where cafés and theatres are a reminder of the area's bohemian life during the 1920s.

Place du 18-Juin-1940 – Until 1967 this site was occupied by the old railway station, which will be remembered as General Leclerc's headquarters at the time of the liberation of Paris. It was also where, on 25 August 1944, the German military governor signed his garrison's surrender. Today the square is lined with cinemas and cafés.

In the cube-shaped building of the **International Textile Centre** (CIT) are over 200 companies on 12 floors. The Centre Commercial tower houses department stores (Galerie Lafayette, Habitat, C & A), and luxury shops selling the latest in fashion, cafés and restaurants.

Going out

L'Utopia – *79 rue de l'Ouest – 14th arr –* Ⓜ *Pernety –* ☎ *01 43 22 79 66 – daily 9.15pm-dawn – closed 10 days in Aug and 25 Dec.* Rock and blues feature prominently on the Utopia's programme, with concerts which set this somewhat abandoned district swinging.

La Coupole – *102 blvd du Montparnasse – 14th arr –* ☎ *01 43 20 14 20 – Sun-Thu 8.30pm-1am, Fri-Sat 8.30pm-1.30am.* Originally a wood and coal depot, this café, opened in 1927, owes its name to the glass dome which formerly hung over the restaurant. Its 33 pillars and pilasters were decorated by a large number of artists, many of whom were students of masters such as Matisse and Léger. It played a key role in the capital's literary world in the 1930s and was frequented by Faulkner, Giacommetti, Sartre and Beckett. Revamped in 1988, it is as busy and popular with Parisian night-owls as ever it was. The downstairs dance floor is famous for its salsa evenings, there is a *thé-dansant* on Sundays and an old-fashioned ball at the weekend.

La Rotonde – *7 pl. du 25-Août – 14th arr –* ☎ *01 45 40 40 20 – daily 5am-11pm.* Lenin was a waiter here for a few months, Trotsky was a regular for a time. Picasso, Derain, Modigliani, Matisse and Vlaminck would meet here for heated discussions. Open since 1903, it is a symbol of modern 20C history, full of souvenirs – it is still popular with some of Paris' foreign communities (Russia and South America).

Le Dôme – *108 blvd du Montparnasse – 14th arr –* ☎ *01 43 35 25 81 – daily noon-3pm, 7pm-12.30am – closed Sun and Mon in Aug.* Opened in 1906, it was the haven for writers and painters, and much in vogue with bohemian Americans in the 1920s and post-war. Today it is frequented by the neighbourhood locals, often from the fashionable worlds of show-biz or politics.

Le Rosebud – *11 bis rue Delambre – 14th arr –* ☎ *01 43 35 38 54 – daily 7pm-2am – closed Aug, Christmas and New Year.* Located in a smart street. The corporate business look is not at all out of place in this chic bar, with a literary and cinema flavour to it (decorated with posters of Mistinguett).

Le Sélect – *99 blvd du Montparnasse – 14th arr –* ☎ *01 45 48 38 24 or 01 45 44 56 45 – daily 8am-3am.* It was the place to be when it first opened in 1924. Next door to other flashier brasseries, the Select has retained a quiet, intimate feel.

Shopping

Centre commercial Maine-Montparnasse – *Pl. du 18-Juin-1940 – 14th arr.* The various levels of this gigantic shopping complex house department stores such as Galeries Lafayette, C & A and Habitat, together with some 60 shops, most of which are devoted to fashion.

Marché parisien de la Création - *Boulevard Quinet.* Around 100 artists exhibit their works on Sundays from 10am to 7pm.

Jean-Paul Hévin – *3 rue Vavin – 6th arr –* Ⓜ *Vavin or Notre-Dame-des-Champs – other shops: 231 rue St-Honoré, 1st arr; 16 av. de la Motte-Picquet, 7th arr –* ☎ *01 43 54 09 85 – www.jphevin.com – Mon-Sat 10am-7.30pm, Sun 10am-2pm, 3pm-6pm – closed 3 weeks in Aug and public holidays.* One of the capital's four best chocolate makers. For over 10 years, this master craftsman has been delighting us with his bitter *ganaches* made from a variety of cocoa beans. Don't miss his delicious macaroons or his legendary chocolate *millefeuille*.

Eating out

Turn back to the Selected restaurants section at the beginning of the guide for a list of restaurants, bistros, cafés etc. This district corresponds to the 6th, 14th and 15th *arrondissements*.

★★Tour Montparnasse ⊘ – Completed in 1973, this 209m/688ft-high tower dominates the whole quarter, adding a modern landmark to the Paris skyline. It is perhaps the most spectacular and controversial feature of the complex as a whole. The strictly geometric lines of the façades are softened by their gently curved surfaces. The foundations are sunk to a depth of 70m/230ft, bearing 120 000t of masonry and shafts. It takes 40 seconds to reach the 56th floor air-conditioned observatory which affords a magnificent **panorama★★★** of Paris and its suburbs. By night Paris is a wonderland, truly living up to its name, City of Lights. There is also a bar and panoramic restaurant at this level. From the open roof terrace (59th floor) the view can extend as far as 50km/31mi.

Gare Montparnasse – Trains run south-westwards from a U-shaped terminus surrounded on three sides by immense 18 storey glass, steel and concrete blocks. The station proper, on five levels, connects with the metro and supplies every amenity, even a small chapel to St Bernard *(entrance at no 34)* – the lectern was carved from a railway sleeper.

Porte Océane, the main entrance, is a vast glass-clad arch linking the city to the station. A massive concrete slab suspended over the tracks has been laid with a large expanse of garden and tennis courts. The **Jardin Atlantique★** is typical of Paris' modern green oases, appealing to all the senses, with textured walkways, fountains, colourful flowers, and rustling and fragrant plants.

Place de Catalogne – The two, six-storey, strikingly modern yet neo-Classical buildings were designed by Ricardo Bofill around oval squares. The continuous semicircular façades of the stone Amphithéâtre provide an effective design around a vast sunken disc-shaped fountain in the centre, which in turn leads into the Les Colonnes residential development (1986), where glass surfaces ripple with reflections around an open green space.

Walk beneath the arch formed by the façade.

Église Notre-Dame-du-Travail – This unusual church (1900) appears uninteresting from the outside. Internally, however, it shows an audacious use of metal structures at a time when industrial techniques were radically changing building methods. Here the bare iron girders are meant to honour the combined ideals of work and worship.

Walk along rue de l'Ouest and avenue du Maine to rue de la Gaîté.

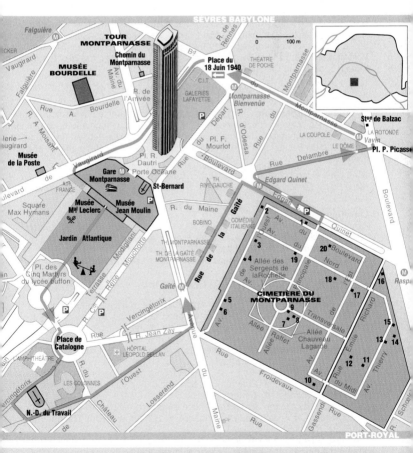

Cimetière du Montparnasse

1 - J.-P. Sartre	6 - Zadkine	11 - César Franck	16 - The kiss, by Brancusi
2 - Soutine	7 - Jussieu	12 - Guy de Maupassant	17 - Sainte-Beuve
3 - Baudelaire (Aupick tomb)	8 - Rude	13 - Bartholdi	18 - Saint-Saëns
4 - H. Laurens	9 - Serge Gainsbourg	14 - Kessel	19 - H. Langlois
5 - Tristan Tzara	10 - Henri Poincaré	15 - André Citroën	20 - Léon-Paul Fargue

Montparnasse cemetery, with the tower in the background

Rue de la Gaîté – This old country road has, since the 18C, been lined with cabarets, dance halls, restaurants and other pleasure spots – hence its name. The street's reputation began with the Mère Cadet, the Veau qui Tète and the Gigoteurs dance halls, and is maintained today by the **Montparnasse** Theatre (no **31**), the **Gaîté-Montparnasse** Theatre (no **26**), the famous **Bobino** Music Hall (no **20**), the **Comédie Italienne** (no **17**) and the **Rive-Gauche** Theatre (no **6**).

Walk away from the Tour Montparnasse along boulevard Edgar-Quinet which leads to the Cimetière Montparnasse.

Cimetière Montparnasse ⊘ – This is a tranquil spot traversed by shaded avenues of lime trees. Among the famous people whose final resting place is here are Baudelaire, Maupassant, Bourdelle, Soutine, Desnos, the actress Jean Seberg, author Samuel Becket, and the unfortunate Captain Dreyfus, of the affair that bears his name.

Walk back along boulevard Edgar-Quinet towards the Tour Montparnasse as far as place Edgar-Quinet, then turn onto the charming rue Delambre leading to carrefour Vavin.

Carrefour Vavin – *Place Pablo-Picasso.* This crossroads, originally the summit of the Parnassus Mound, continues to bustle with life at the heart of the old quarter. All around, the famous café-restaurants Le Dôme, La Rotonde, Le Sélect, La Coupole serve oysters and other specialities late into the night.
In 1939 the famous statue of **Balzac** by **Rodin** was placed on its island site.

MUSEUMS AND OTHER ATTRACTIONS

★★**Musée Bourdelle** ⊘ – *16 rue Antoine-Bourdelle.* Antoine Bourdelle's (1861-1929) house, garden and studio have been converted to display the artist's sculptures, paintings and drawings. Having studied under Rodin, his work evolved from an animated naturalistic figurative style to a more stylised and archaic one modelled on Romanesque, Byzantine and Gothic examples. It remained monumental throughout.
In the great hall are the original plaster prototypes for his huge sculptures cast in bronze – the Champs-Élysées Theatre panels *France,* **Heracles the Archer★★**, *Monument to General Alvear,* flanked by the four virtues *(Victory, Eloquence, Liberty and Strength).* This monument, erected to the glory of one of the leaders of Argentine independence, was inaugurated in Buenos Aires in 1926.
The most outstanding items among his immense output include the huge bronzes now in the garden (the *Virtues,* various animals) and his portrait busts of his contemporaries (**Rodin**, Anatole France).
His studio and his apartment are as he left them. In the kitchen, above the sink hangs a self-portrait (1925); on the street side is the workbench of the artist's father.
Don't miss the second series of studios with light pouring in through large window panes; displayed here are the bronze **Head of Apollo★**, *Rodin working* and the **portraits of Beethoven★** of whom he made 21 different studies.

The extension to the museum, designed by Christian de Portzamparc and completed in 1992, presents all the studies and fragments relating to the *Monument to Adam Mickiewicz*, erected near place de l'Alma, and the 1870 *War Monument* in Montauban (including *Howling Figures* and the *Roland Column*).

★ **Musée de la Poste** ⊙ – *34 boulevard de Vaugirard*. The museum presents an attractive account of the postal services through the ages (incised clay tablets from 2500 BC, medieval manuscripts on parchment). The development of the postal communication network in France encompasses changes from the early relay posts for mounted carriers, via carrier pigeons, to the 18 000 post offices of today and the modern services provided.
Of particular note are the stamp printing and franking machines displayed, a complete collection of French stamps since the first issue in 1849 and displays of other national collections, shown in rotation.

Musée du Montparnasse– *21 avenue du Maine*. The ivy covered artists' studios exude a charm from another era. The little museum is set up in the former studio of Maria Vassilieff, a Russian painter who founded her own academy. Exhibits are changed every four months. A 50min film recounts the history of the district and its artists.

Mémorial du maréchal Leclerc de Hautecloque et de la Libération de Paris – Musée Jean Moulin ⊙ – *North side of the Jardin Atlantique*. Exhibitions are dedicated to documents, photographs and artefacts commemorating two French heroes of the Second World War, one a symbolic figure for the Free French, the other a hero of the Resistance. Several films are presented, including one on the liberation of Paris.

Parc MONTSOURIS ★

Michelin plan 10 – fold 55: R 13 – S 13, S 14
Ⓜ *Porte d'Orléans (line 4) – RER: Cité Universitaire (line B) –*
Buses: 21, 67, 88, PC

The Montsouris Park forms a large green open space to the south of the city, a real haven of peace: a lake, multicoloured flower beds, birds singing... even the noise of the RER overhead cannot break the spell! And what a delight it is to wander through the surrounding streets, lined with quaint small houses looking like seaside bungalows! Sadly, like many of the city's parks, Parc Montsouris lost many trees in the great storm of 26 December 1999.

Nearby neighbourhoods: DENFERT-ROCHEREAU.

★ PARC MONTSOURIS

The park – Following **Haussmann's** instructions, Adolphe Alphand began work on this area undermined by quarries and capped by dozens of windmills, in 1868. By 1878 he had turned it into a park: the 16ha/50 acres were landscaped in the English-style with paths snaking up the mounds and circling the cascades, and a large artificial lake (the engineer specifically involved in the construction committed suicide, when the lake suddenly dried out on opening day).
The park is dominated by the **South bearing** *(mire du Sud)* of the Paris **meridian**. The municipal meteorological observatory is housed in a building nearby.

Shopping

Fil'O Fromage – *4 r. Poirier-de-Narçay – 14th arr* – Ⓜ *Porte-d'Orléans –* ☎ *01 40 44 86 75 – Tue-Fri 9am-1pm, 4-7.45pm; Sat 9am-7.30pm – closed public holidays and Aug.* People come from afar such is the reputation of this magnificent cheese shop and its legendary façade. For over 10 years, Mrs Boubrit, a perfectionist, has been providing impeccable cheeses.

Eating out

Turn back to the Selected restaurants section at the beginning of the guide for a list of restaurants, bistros, cafés etc. This district corresponds to the 14th *arrondissement*.

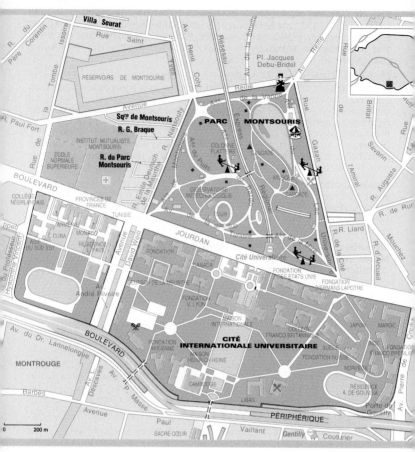

Beyond the park – At the turn of the 20C, painters attracted by the park's peace and its proximity to Montparnasse came to live here, notably **Douanier Rousseau** and Georges Braque, who had a studio (west of the park) in a street which now carries his name. Explore **rue du Parc Montsouris**, **rue Braque** and **square de Monsouris** before heading north along rue Saint-Yves to Villa Seurat.

During the inter-war period famous residents of the **Villa Seurat** included the artist Gromaire, Lurçat, Orloff the sculptor, Henry Miller (installed in Artaud's studio at no 18 by Anaïs Nin), Dalì and **Soutine**.

No **2** avenue Reille was designed by Auguste Perret and no **53** by Le Corbusier.

Villa Seurat

In the 1930s American novelist **Henry Miller** immortalized this tranquil cul-de-sac (fictionalised as the Villa Borghese) in his controversial novel *Tropic of Cancer* (published in Paris in 1934 and banned in the USA and England until the 1960s).

...The whole street is given up to quiet, joyous work. Every house contains a writer, painter, musician, sculptor, dancer or actor. It is such a quiet street and yet there is such activity going on, silently...

EXPLORING THE NEIGHBOURHOOD

The avenues Reille and René-Coty are overlooked by the **Montsouris reservoirs** with grass-covered sides and roofs. Collected here in these 100-year-old reservoirs are the waters of the Vanne, Loing and Lunain. Trout in aquaria vouch for the purity of the water which provides half the city of Paris' supply.

★ **Cité internationale universitaire** – *Main entrance: 19-21 boulevard Jourdan.* The city on the edge of Montsouris Park spreads over an area of 40ha/100 acres, housing over 5 500 students from 120 different countries in its 37 halls of residence. Each hall forms an independent community, its architecture and individual character frequently inspired by the country which founded it. The very first hall to be built was the **E-and-L-Deutsch-de-la-Meurthe Foundation**, inaugurated in 1925, built with funds provided by a French financier of the same name. The Maison Internationale (1936) with a swimming pool, theatre and vast rooms was sponsored by John D Rockefeller Jr. The Fondation Suisse and Fondation Franco-Brézilienne were designed by **Le Corbusier**.

Église du Sacré-Cœur ⊘ – Built between 1931 and 1936 on the edge of the city parish boundary, it now stands on the far side of the boulevard Périphérique in Gentilly, and is reached by a footbridge. Its façade has a relief by Saupique, dominated by a great bell-tower.

MOUFFETARD ★

Michelin plan 10: L 15, M 15
Ⓜ *Censier-Daubenton (line 7) – Buses: 47, 89*

This area on the fringe of the Latin Quarter is dotted with small restaurants and clothes shops catering for the many students that permanently throng the neighbourhood.

Nearby neighbourhoods: QUARTIER LATIN, JUSSIEU, JARDIN DES PLANTES, GOBELINS, PORT-ROYAL.

EXPLORING THE NEIGHBOURHOOD

Start from the Censier-Daubenton metro station and follow rue Daubenton. A gate and passage lead from no **41** rue Daubenton to a small side entrance to the church.

Église St-Médard ⊘ – *141 rue Mouffetard.* The church, started in the mid-15C, was completed in 1655. The Flamboyant Gothic nave has modern stained glass; the unusually wide chancel is Renaissance-influenced with asymmetrical semicircular arches and rounded windows. In 1784 the pillars were transformed into fluted Doric columns. There are paintings of the French School, a remarkable 16C triptych *(behind the pulpit)* and, in the second chapel to the right of the chancel, a *Dead Christ* attributed to Philippe de Champaigne.

Going out

Connolly's Corner – *12 rue de Mirbel – 5th arr –* ☎ *01 43 31 94 22 – www.liam.connolly@wanadoo.fr – daily 4pm-2am.* Slightly off rue Mouffetard itself, this friendly Irish pub proudly displays its trophies of cut-off ties. Concerts on Saturday evenings at 10pm. Darts.

Finnegans Wake – *9 rue des Boulangers – 5th arr –* ☎ *01 46 34 23 65 – www.irishfrancefinneganswake.com – Mon-Fri 11am-2am, Sat-Sun 6pm-2am.* One of the capital's oldest Irish pubs. Quiet atmosphere and excellent Guinness. Concerts on Fri evenings.

Le Requin Chagrin – *10 rue Mouffetard – 5th arr –* ☎ *01 44 07 23 24 – Mon-Thu 4pm-2am, Fri-Sat 4pm-5am.* One of the most discreet pubs in the neighbourhood.

Place de la Contrescarpe – *Pl. de la Contrescarpe – 5th arr.* This square is lined with cafés and is always full of rue Mouffetard's colourful, motley crowd who invade the pretty terraces of the numerous cafés. The Café Contrescarpe and La Chope have the largest terraces, but the nearby Irlandais, Café des Arts, Teddy's Bar and the Mayflower are also very pleasant.

Shopping

La Maison des trois thés – *5 rue du Pot-de-Fer – 5th arr –* ☎ *01 43 36 93 84 – www.maisondestroisthes.com – Tue-Sun 1-8pm.* This establishment can boast international renown thanks to the master of tea, Tseng Yu Hui, who has set up shop here. It sells close to 450 teas, and some of the finest and rarest China teas, which can reach several hundred thousand francs a kg. Tasting between 7.5 and 686€. Can be closed due to expeditions to Asia.

Eating out

Turn back to the Selected restaurants section at the beginning of the guide for a list of restaurants, bistros, cafés etc. This district corresponds to the 5th *arrondissement.*

★**Rue Mouffetard** – The *Mouffe*, as it is known, winds downhill to St-Médard, lined with old houses and crowded most mornings with market shoppers in search of a bargain; on Sundays, street musicians play jazz adding further touches of colour to the area. Picturesque painted signs are a reminder of past times, like that at no **69** where a carved oak tree once topped the sign for *Le Vieux Chêne* and At the Clear Spring at no **122**.

Nos **104** and **101** mark the entrances to passage des Postes and passage des Patriarches. The **Pot-de-Fer Fountain** like others in the district, runs with surplus water from the Arcueil Aqueduct which **Marie de Medici** had constructed to bring water to the Luxembourg Palace. Almost opposite, at no **53** a cache of 3 350 gold coins bearing the head of Louis XV was discovered when the house was demolished (1938), presumably left there by Louis Nivelle, the king's bearer and counsellor.

Other streets in the vicinity – During the Middle Ages the area abounded in student colleges. One of the rare examples is the **Scottish College**.

Denis Diderot (1713-84) lived at **3 rue de l'Estrapade** between 1747 and 1754 while overseeing the publication of his famous Encyclopaedia. There is a striking view to be caught over the dome of the Panthéon.

The Convulsionnaries

In 1727 a Jansenist deacon with a saintly reputation died at the age of 36 of mortification of the flesh and was buried in St-Médard churchyard beneath a raised black marble stone. Sick Jansenists came to pray before the tomb, to lie upon and underneath it giving rise to a belief in miraculous cures which led to massive scenes of collective hysteria.

In 1732, Louis XV decreed an end to the demonstrations; the cemetery was closed. The inscription nailed to the gate meant:

By order of the King, let God
No miracle perform in this place!

Rue Lhomond is lined with flights of steps – an indication of the former height of the hill. At no **30** stands the chapel serving the Séminaire du Saint-Esprit built in 1780 by **Chalgrin**. **Passage des Postes** starts level with no 55.

At **10 rue Vauquelin**, **Pierre and Marie Curie** isolated radium in October 1898 and discovered the principles of radioactivity.

★**Place de la Contrescarpe** – An inscription at no **1** recalls the Pinecone cabaret, La Pomme-de-Pin, described by Rabelais. René Descartes lived at **14** rue Rollin during his stay in Paris (1644-48).

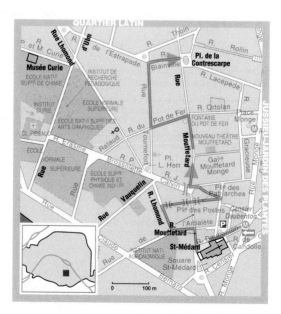

La MUETTE-RANELAGH ★

Michelin plan 10: H 4, H 5, J 4, J 5
Ⓜ La Muette (line 9) – RER: Boulainvilliers (line C) – Buses: 22, 32, 52

The original Muette Estate was developed as an elegant quarter. Today it enjoys the green open space of the Ranelagh Gardens and the attraction of the Marmottan Museum with its rich collection of art.

Historical notes – It was here that Charles IX (1550-74) had a hunting lodge where he kept his falcons when in moult (French *en mue* hence Muette). The name was preserved when Philibert Delorme built a château set in a park extending to the Bois de Boulogne.

The château had many royal residents: Marguerite de Valois, first wife of Henri of Navarre **(Queen Margot)**; Louis XIII; Duchesse de Berry – whose stay until she died aged 24, was 'short and sweet' as per her motto; Louis XV used the château as a clandestine meeting place during his affair with the **Marquise de Pompadour**; the future Louis XVI and Marie-Antoinette spent the first years of their married life here.

At the Revolution the estate was divided up. In 1820 the piano maker Sébastien Erard purchased the château and part of the park bordering on the Ranelagh. A century later the property was sold off in lots for development.

EXPLORING THE NEIGHBOURHOOD

Square Lamartine – This peaceful district grew up around the Passy artesian wells dug in 1855. Residents collect their supply of sulphur-rich water at a temperature of 28°C/82°F from a depth of 600m/1 970ft.

At the point where the elegant **avenue Henri-Martin** (formerly avenue de l'Empereur) cuts avenue Victor-Hugo has been placed **Rodin's** statue *Victor Hugo and the Muses*. The monumental bronze sculpture was cast after the Occupation from a plaster prototype.

Avenue Victor Hugo is lined with prestigious jewellery and fashion houses.

Avenue Henri-Martin leads to place de Colombie; bear left along avenue Raphaël.

Jardin du Ranelagh – Originally, Parisians came to the area to dance in the open air. In 1774 a café was built, named the Petit Ranelagh after Lord Ranelagh's very fashionable pleasure gardens outside London, and extended to accommodate a dance-hall-cum-stage. The present gardens were laid out by **Haussmann** in 1860.

Allée Pilâtre-de-Rozier – On 21 November 1783, the famous aeronaut accomplished the first free flight in a hot-air balloon.

The marble relief at the end of the avenue honouring Victor Hugo is entitled *The Poet's Vision*.

Rue André-Pascal – André Pascal was the pen-name used by Baron Henri de Rothschild to publish his writings; it was for this same banker that the adjacent sumptuous mansion was built. Since 1948 the mansion has been classified as international territory and houses the seat of the Organisation for European Cooperation and Development *(closed to the public)*.

Shopping

Pascal Le Glacier – *17 rue Bois-le-Vent – 16th arr* – Ⓜ *La Muette* – ☎ *01 45 27 61 84 – Tue-Sat 10.30am-7pm – closed public holidays and Aug.* Pascal and his wife are quite obsessed – with quality. Each sorbet is prepared in small quantities with fruits of the season, Evian water and a great deal of love and care. Their current success has not altered the attention to quality or high standards of this remarkable duo.

Réciproque – *95 rue de la Pompe – 16th arr* – Ⓜ *Rue-de-la-Pompe* – ☎ *01 47 04 30 28 – Tue-Fri 11am-7pm, Sat 10.30am-7pm (except Aug Tue-Sat noon-7pm) – closed public holidays.* Fashion, accessories, jewellery... The 800m sq of this second-hand shop are more than worth a glance. Nicole Morel selects only luxury goods in excellent condition, which are displayed by designer. From an Hermès scarf to a Vuitton bag, it's all there.

Eating out

Turn back to the Selected restaurants section at the beginning of the guide for a list of restaurants, bistros, cafés etc. This district corresponds to the 16th *arrondissement*.

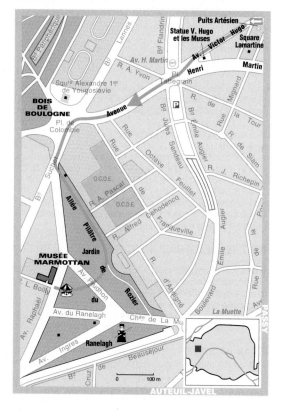

MUSEUMS AND OTHER ATTRACTIONS

★★ **Musée Marmottan-Monet** ⊙ – *2 rue Louis-Boilly*. In 1932 the art historian **Paul Marmottan** bequeathed his private house and collections of Renaissance tapestries and sculpture, Consular and First Empire portraits (26 of Boilly), medallions, paintings (Vernet) and furniture (Desmalter *commode*) to the Académie des Beaux-Arts. In 1950 Mme Donop de Monchy donated a part of her father's collection, including works by the Impressionists befriended and treated by Dr de Bellio (*Impression – Sunrise* which gave the Impressionist movement its name). In 1971, Michel Monet left 65 of his father's painted canvases to the museum which has been further endowed by the Wildenstein legacy of 228 13C-16C illuminated manuscripts from various European schools.

The collection of **Claude Monet** paintings, probably the most important known body of work by the Master of Impressionism, is accommodated by a special purpose-built underground gallery; many of the works were painted at the artist's Normandy home at Giverny, depicting his beloved water-lilies, wistaria, iris, rose-garden, weeping willows and Japanese bridge. Other panels show the painter's preoccupation with light (*The Houses of Parliament – London, The Europe Bridge, Rouen Cathedral*).

Bouquet de Fleurs, Gaugin

The Duhem Bequest of about 60 paintings, drawings and watercolours includes **Gauguin**'s splendid *Bouquet of Flowers* painted in Tahiti and an interesting pastel by **Renoir**: *Seated Girl in a White Hat*. Exceptional pictures by Albrecht Bonts (*Christ on the Cross* – 16C), Fragonard and Renoir provide interesting points of comparison.

Institut des arts de l'écriture: Musée du Stylo ⊙ – *3 rue Guy-de-Maupassant*, Ⓜ *Rue-de-la-Pompe*. A collection of some 1 500 examples of pens, from the 19C onwards.

Cathédrale NOTRE-DAME★★★

Michelin plan 10: J 15, K 15
🅜 Cité (line 4), St Michel (line 4) – RER: St-Michel Notre-Dame (line B) –
Buses: 21, 38, 47, 85

At the heart of Paris and in the heart of the Parisians, the cathedral of Notre-Dame has witnessed some of the greatest moments of the capital's history. This magnificent religious edifice is one of the supreme masterpieces of French art. It has been a source of visual and literary inspiration over the centuries, and is a living myth that always holds one more secret.

See also: ÎLE DE LA CITÉ, CONCIERGERIE, SAINTE-CHAPELLE. *Nearby neighbourhoods*: ÎLE ST-LOUIS, QUARTIER LATIN, MAUBERT.

HISTORY

Construction – *See illustration p 92.* For 2 000 years prayers have been offered from this spot: a Gallo-Roman temple, a Christian basilica, a Romanesque church preceded the present sanctuary founded by Bishop **Maurice de Sully**. A man of humble origin, he had become a canon at the cathedral and supervisor of the diocese by 1159 and, shortly afterwards, undertook to provide the capital with a worthy cathedral to rival the basilica built at St-Denis by Abbot Suger.

Construction began in 1163, during the reign of Louis VII. To the resources of the church and royal gifts were added the toil and skill of the common people: stonemasons, carpenters, ironsmiths, sculptors, glaziers, moved with religious fervour, worked with ardour under **Jean de Chelles** and **Pierre de Montreuil**, architect of the Sainte-Chapelle. By about 1300 the building was complete – the original plans had not been modified in any way.

Notre-Dame is the last large galleried church and one of the first to be supported by flying buttresses here prolonged by gargoyles intended to protect the foundations from the effects of rainwater.

Ceremonial Occasions – Long before it was completed, Notre-Dame had become the setting for major religious and political ceremonies. **St Louis** entrusted it with the Crown of Thorns in 1239 pending the completion of the Sainte-Chapelle. In 1302 **Philip the Fair** formally opened the kingdom's first Parliament. Celebrations, thanksgivings, state funerals have followed each other down the centuries: high points in French history include the coronation of young Henry VI of England (1430); the re-trial of Joan of Arc (1455); the crowning of **Mary Stuart** as Queen of France following her marriage to François II; the unusual marriage ceremony of Marguerite of Valois to the Huguenot, Henri of Navarre (1572), when she stood alone in the chancel and he by the door, although he came later to agree that "Paris is well worth a mass" and attended subsequent ceremonies inside the cathedral; and the marriage of Henrietta Maria by proxy to Charles I of England (1625).

The east end (chevet) of Notre-Dame

J.-P. Clapham/MICHELIN

It has also been subjected to radical maltreatment: the destruction of the rood screen by **Mansart** and **Robert de Cotte** (1699), the replacement of the medieval stained glass by plain glass (18C), the vandalism of the main doorway by Soufflot to make way for an ever more grandiose processional dais (1771). During the Revolution, the statues of the kings of Judea and Israel were decapitated, the building became a Temple of Reason and then of the Supreme Being. All but the great bell were melted down and the church interior was used to store forage and food.

On 2 December 1804 the church, decked with hangings and ornaments to mask its dilapidation, received Pope Pius VII for the coronation of the Emperor *(see the picture by David in the Louvre)*.

Restoration – As a result of **Victor Hugo**'s novel *The Hunchback of Notre-Dame* (1831) and a general popular feeling roused by the Romantic Movement, the July Monarchy ordered in 1841 that the cathedral be restored. Entrusted to **Viollet-le-Duc** and Lassus, the restoration program lasted 23 years: statuary and glass checked, extensions and appendages removed, the roof and upper sections repaired, doors and chancel restored, a spire added and a sacristy erected.

Today as before – Notre-Dame emerged virtually unscathed from the Commune of 1871 and the Liberation of 1944, and continues to participate in major historical events, happy or sad: the magnificent Te Deum of 26 August 1944 during which an assassination attempt was made on **General de Gaulle**, the moving Requiem Mass in his honour on 12 November 1970 and the magnificat followed by a solemn mass celebrated on the parvis by Pope John-Paul II on 31 May 1980.

TOUR ⊘

Notre-Dame was damaged by the severe storm which swept across France on 26 December 1999: the sacristy collapsed into the garden and four pinnacles fell onto part of the terraces.

Exterior

Place du Parvis – The cathedral can be seen in all its radiant glory from the parvis or square Viviani. A bronze plaque in the centre of the square marks the zero point from which all road distances in France are measured.

The square was quadrupled in size as cramped surrounding buildings were cleared away by Haussmann in the 19C; it is now dominated by the grandiose façade of Notre-Dame. In the Middle Ages, when **mystery plays** were enacted before churches and cathedrals, the porch was often used to represent the door to paradise *(paradis)* – hence the evolution of the name parvis.

★ **Crypte archéologique** ⊘ – Excavations beneath the parvis have revealed traces of buildings and monuments spanning the 3C to 19C. Of particular interest are two Gallo-Roman rooms heated by hypocaust *(to the left on entering)*, fragments of the Late Roman Empire rampart, medieval cellars, and the foundations of a documented orphanage designed by Boffrand.

The **Cathedral Museum** *(10 rue du Cloître-Notre-Dame)* catalogues the long sequence of restoration work and the major moments in the cathedral's history since the 17C. Pottery uncovered from under the parvis is also displayed.

The west front – The overall design is majestic and perfectly balanced despite being asymmetrical: the central doorway is the largest of the three, the left gabled. This medieval concept was to avoid monotony in design and intended to symbolise the lack of perfect order on earth.

The portals – In the Middle Ages the portals would have looked completely different: brightly coloured statues stood out against a gold background. Designed to be read like a Bible in stone, the scriptures and the legends of the saints are graphically retold for an illiterate congregation. Scenes tend to be read upwards, from an earthly level towards Heaven.

The six, wooden door panels have splendid wrought-iron strap-hinges. Legend has it that the side doors were worked by Satan himself to whom the locksmith, Biscornet, had forfeited his soul; the central door hinges, however, are 19C replacements.

Portal of the Virgin *(left)* – The fine tympanum has served as prototype to stonemasons throughout the Middle Ages. It shows the *Ark of the Covenant* flanked by three prophets who spoke of the glorious destiny of the Mother of God and three Kings from whom she is descended; above, a moving depiction of the *Death of the Virgin* with Christ and the Apostles; at the apex, the *Coronation of the Virgin* with Christ handing a sceptre to his mother who is crowned by an angel.

Consecutive bands of bead moulding, leaves, flowers and fruit run between the ranks of angels, patriarchs, kings and prophets at the celestial court. The trumeau (stone mullion) *Virgin and Child* is modern. Small low-relief carving representing the labours of the months and the signs of the Zodiac fill the sections on either side of the doorway.

The statues in the embrasures, were added by Viollet-le-Duc and include St Denis attended by two angels, John the Baptist and St Stephen.

Portal of the Last Judgement *(central)* – The main theme of this sculptural composition is the struggle of Good over Evil. It is far removed from its original condition: the tympanum was breached by Soufflot in 1771 and Viollet-le-Duc has substantially restored the two lower lintels.

Above a depiction of the *Resurrection* is the *Weighing of the Souls*, in which the good are led up to Heaven by angels, the damned by demons to Hell; at the apex, a seated *Christ in Majesty* is flanked by the kneeling Virgin and St John, interceding for the lost souls.

The six archivolts represent the celestial court. At the lowest level, Abraham receives the beautiful righteous *(left)* and demonic condemned *(right)* symbolising Heaven and Hell separated by the Word of God. The trumeau figure of Christ is 19C, the original having been removed by Soufflot. The columnar figures of the Wise and Foolish Virgins, differentiated by open *(left)* and closed *(right)* doors to paradise, are modern. In the embrasures, Viollet-le-Duc's Apostles stand over medallions representing the Virtues *(upper tier)* and Vices *(lower tier)*.

Portal to St Anne *(south)* – The cathedral's oldest statues fill the two upper levels of the tympanum; c 1165, they pre-date the building by some 60 years and were evidently intended for a narrower door. A rather formal *Virgin in Majesty with the Infant Christ* draws on Romanesque prototypes; she is attended by two angels and the cathedral patrons: Bishop Maurice of Sully *(standing, left)* and Louis VII *(kneeling, right)*. The 12C lintel shows scenes from the Life of the Virgin, and below, from her parents, St Anne and St Joachim (13C).

The ranks of angels, kings and patriarchs at the celestial court decorate the four tympanum archivolts. The central pier carries a 19C slender, elongated figure of St Marcellus, the 5C Bishop of Paris who is meant to have delivered the capital from a dragon. Kings, queens and saints frame the doorway.

Abutting the piers between portals are additional 19C statues *(from left to right)* of St Stephen, the Church, the Synagogue (blindfolded) and St Denis.

Gallery of Kings *(above the portals)* – The 28 kings of Judea and Israel represent the Tree of Jesse, Christ's forebears. The original figures were destroyed in 1793 by the Commune who took them for the kings of France *(see QUARTIER LATIN – Musée Cluny)*; these were replaced by Viollet-le-Duc.

Rose window – The central great rose, nearly 10m/30ft across, is so perfectly designed that its elements have not moved in over seven centuries. From outside, it provides the standing statue of the Virgin and Child, flanked by two angels with a vast halo, the aura of Heaven.

At the same level, in the lateral bays, stand the figures of Adam *(left)* and Eve *(right)*, against stone masonry separating the window lights. Together, the group (restored by Viollet-le-Duc) portrays Redemption after the Fall from Grace.

Great gallery – A superb row of delicate arches articulate the transitional tier between the main building and the base of the towers, between solid masonry and open sky. At the corners of each buttress, Viollet-le-Duc placed fantastic birds, monsters and demons, which although large, are scarcely visible at ground level, obscured by the projecting balustrade.

Towers – The twin towers soar to a height of 69m/226ft, pierced by slender 16m/50ft lancets. Emmanuel, the great bell in the south tower *(right)* weighs 13t, its clapper nearly 500kg/9.75cwts. The perfect pitch of its toll (F sharp) is said to be due to the gold and silver jewellery cast into the molten bronze by *Parisiennes* when the bell was restruck in the 17C.

Ascent ⊘ – Steep steps climb to a platform in the south tower providing a splendid **view★★★** of the spire and flying buttresses; the Cité and Paris beyond. Note the famous chimeras (carved wild beasts) and great bell above the great gallery. In the chapel, a museum-video retells the story of Notre-Dame *(15min)*. This is where Quasimodo lived: the hunchback who was beguiled by the charms of Esmeralda, the gipsy dancer he kidnapped from the Cour des Miracles.

North side – A canons' cloister, now destroyed, flanked the north side giving its name to the street that replaced it.

The magnificent **Cloister Portal** was built by Jean of Chelles (c 1250), who applied experience gained from building the Sainte-Chapelle (completed 1248) to maximise the amount of light permeating the interior. The large intricate rose perfectly integrates with the clerestory to form an unprecedentedly tall opening (18m/58ft high), slightly larger in diameter (13m/43ft).

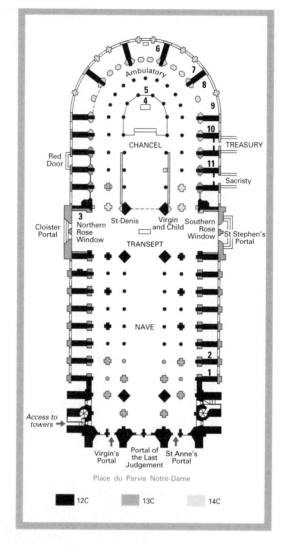

Below, the many gabled, carved doorway is markedly more ornate than the doors of the west front, installed 30 years before. The three-tiered tympanum illustrates events from the *Life of the Virgin* and above, from the story of Théophile selling his soul to the Devil, the subject of a popular mystery play at the time.

The fine trumeau figure of the **Virgin** lost its Christ Child at the Restoration.

The **Red Door**, built by Pierre of Montreuil was reserved for exclusive use by members of the cathedral chapter. Its tympanum illustrates the Coronation of the Virgin attended by King Louis IX and his Queen, Margaret of Provence; the archivolts carry scenes from the Life of St Marcel.

Seven 14C **bas-relief sculptures** inlaid into the foundations of the chancel chapels depict the Death and Assumption of the Virgin.

East end – At the beginning of the 14C, the cathedral's east end was reinforced by the adjunction of a series of superb flying buttresses designed by Jean Ravy, which form a 15m/49ft arch to counteract the thrust of the vaulting.

Splendid vistas of the east end and the Seine can be enjoyed from the small, verdant, south-facing John XXIII Square which is always very crowded.

From here can be seen a 13C section of roof which retains the original timberwork, and the 90m/295ft-high spire reconstructed by Viollet-le-Duc who included himself among the decorative copper figures of Evangelists and Apostles!

South side – Beyond the 19C sacristy is the magnificent **St Stephen's** doorway, similar to the cloister door but richer in sculpture. Initiated by Jean of Chelles (1258), and completed by Pierre of Montreuil, it has a remarkable tympanum illustrating the life and stoning of St Stephen, to whom the former church that pre-dated the cathedral had been dedicated. St Stephen, St Marcel and most of the lateral figures date from the 19C.

At the base of the buttresses, eight small 13C low-relief sculptures depict street and university scenes.

Interior

Transitional Gothic – The ordered elevation and precise overall design of the internal space is as impressive today as it must have been in the 13C. The sheer size (130m/427ft long x 48m/158ft wide) and soaring height (35m/115ft) mark a turning point in the development of Gothic architecture and building techniques on a grand scale (accommodating a congregation of up to 6 500 souls).

Besides the elevation, the floor plan also breaks new ground: the nave is given double aisles and the chancel a double ambulatory, separated in the middle by transepts that project only slightly from the outer aisles, thereby producing a homogenous, unified space.

The windows – In the 13C and 14C, the clerestory windows were enlarged to allow extra light to permeate the chapels across the aisles. In so doing, not only was the wall mass reduced and lightened, the gallery was lowered; the weight and thrust of the vault therefore had to be diffused across the aisles and down to solid masonry at gallery level: the problem was ingeniously resolved with the invention of the flying buttress. A section of the 12C elevation can still be seen at the transept crossing (small rose and tall lancet windows).

The medieval stained glass was replaced by clear glass inscribed with fleur-de-lis in the 18C and by *grisaille* glass in the 19C. The modern glass by Le Chevalier, installed in 1965, returned to medieval manufacturing processes and colours.

Note the massive piers measuring 5m/16ft across, supporting the towers, and the organ (restored in 1992) which boasts the largest number of pipes of any organ in France *(concerts: Sundays at 5.45pm)*.

Chapels – Notre-Dame is edged with a continuous ring of chapels built between the buttresses in the 13C in response to demand from an increasing number of guilds and noble families; even the transepts were extended in order to maintain proportions.

In keeping with a tradition renewed in 1949, the Goldsmith's Guild of Paris endowed the cathedral with a work of art annually in May. Among the most beautiful are *Mays* by Le Brun (**1, 2**) and Le Sueur (**3**).

On the left are the tombstones of a 15C canon, and of Cardinal Amette.

Transept – The **windows**, remarkable for their sheer size and weight, are testimony to the technical skill of the medieval masons.

The north rose, which has survived almost intact since the 13C, depicts Old Testament figures around the Virgin; in the restored south rose Christ is surrounded by saints and angels.

At the entrance to the chancel, a statue of St Denis by Nicolas Coustou complements the beautiful 14C

Virgin and Child – Our Lady of Paris, previously in St-Aignan Chapel. On the south-west pier is a plaque commemorating the deaths of the million or so British citizens lost in the First World War, many of whom are buried in French soil.

The nearby inscription in the pavement recalls the conversion of the 20C poet Paul Claudel.

G. Boullay/MICHELIN

The transept

Chancel – In front of the high altar lies Geoffrey Plantagenet, son of Henry II of England (d 1186). The chancel was redecorated by Robert de Cotte (1708-25). Seventy-eight original stalls remain from the embellishment, as do a *Pietà* by Guillaume Coustou (**4**), Louis XIII by Coustou and Louis XIV by Coysevox. It was at this time that the stone chancel screen was removed; the only remarkable 14C **low-relief** scenes to survive pertain to the Life of Christ and His Apparitions. These were restored by Viollet-le-Duc.

Tombstones for the bishops of Paris who are buried in the crypt, line the ambulatory (**5-11**).

Treasury ⊘ – The sacristy built by Viollet-le-Duc contains manuscripts, ornaments and church plate from the 19C. The Crown of Thorns, the Holy Nail and a fragment of the True Cross are displayed on Fridays during Lent and on Good Friday in the main area of the cathedral.

ODÉON ★

Michelin plan 10: J 13, J 14, K 13, K 14
Ⓜ *Odéon (lines 4 and 10), Mabillon (line 10) – Buses: 58, 70, 86, 96*

Bordering upon the Latin Quarter and the St Germain-des-Prés neighbourhood, this area is permanently animated by young students, university staff, publishers at work and at play.

Nearby neighbourhoods: QUARTIER LATIN, ST-GERMAIN-DES-PRÉS, INSTITUT DE FRANCE, MAUBERT, LUXEMBOURG.

EXPLORING THE NEIGHBOURHOOD

③ **Quartier de l'Odéon** *see map p 32.*

Carrefour de l'Odéon – This great junction marked by place Henri-Mondor is dominated by a bronze statue of Danton (1759-94). Full of movement, it was erected at the end of the 19C on the site of the famous Revolutionary leader's house.

★**Cour du Commerce-St-André** – *Entrance via 130 boulevard St-Germain, opposite Danton's statue.* This courtyard was opened in 1776 on the site of a **real tennis court** *(jeu de paume)*. It was here in a loft in 1790 that Dr Guillotin perfected his philanthropic decapitating machine using sheep. At no **8**, **Marat** printed his paper L'Ami du Peuple *(The People's Friend)*. In the first alleyway (gated) to the right, one of the towers of the Philippe Auguste city wall can be seen on the corner.

Cour de Rohan – A series of three courtyards once (15C) formed part of a mansion owned by the archbishops of Rouen (Rohan is a corruption of Rouen). The middle one is overlooked by a fine Renaissance house belonging to Diane de Poitiers.
The peaceful rue du Jardinet, built on the site of former gardens, runs onto rue de l'Éperon where the Lycée Fénelon stands, the first girls' school to be opened in Paris (1893).

Rue de l'Ancienne-Comédie – Formerly rue des Fossés-St-Germain, this street was renamed in 1770, the date the Comédie-Française moved out. On the brink of financial ruin the company went to the Tuileries Palace Theatre before finally moving to the Odéon.

Carrefour de Buci – In the 18C the Buci crossroads was the focal point of the Left Bank. It boasted a sedan chair rank, a corps of 20 sentries, a gibbet and a pillar to which miscreants were attached by an iron collar.
There were a number of **real tennis courts** in the area, three in rue de Buci alone. This archaic form of tennis, as we know it, was a very popular game: until the 15C the ball was thrown by hand (hence the name *jeux de paume*), then a glove was used and finally the racket was introduced. In 1687, the best players received a fee for appearing in public – an early example of sport being played professionally!
The area around the Buci crossroads is particularly lively on Saturdays *(rue Grégoire-de-Tours, rue de Bourbon-le-Château)*; there are many fashion boutiques and restaurants as well as antique shops along rue Mazarine and rue Dauphine leading to the river.

Return to carrefour de l'Odéon.

Rue de l'École-de-Médecine – At no **5** the long-gowned Brotherhood of Surgeons, founded by St Louis in the 13C, performed anatomical operations of every kind until the 17C.

Going out

Birdland Café – *20 rue Princesse – 6th arr – ☎ 01 43 26 97 59 – tibird@cara-mail.com – Mon-Sat 7pm-dawn, Sun 9pm-dawn – closed 25 Dec.* Both the name and the walls decorated with photos of jazz musicians evoke the original New York Birdland. In the summer, the doors stay open onto the street lined with bars and restaurants.

Bob Cool – *15 rue des Grands-Augustins – 6th arr – Ⓜ Odéon and Saint-Michel – ☎ 01 46 33 33 77 – daily 6pm-2am.* A camouflage net hangs over the central room, adding an original flavour to the lively evenings organised here once a month. Regular painting and photography exhibitions. Ideal for a cocktail after having been to see one of the classics shown at the nearby Studio Christine.

La Palette – *43 rue de Seine – 6th arr – ☎ 01 43 26 68 15 – daily (except Sun) 8am-2am – closed 3 weeks in Aug, 1 week in Feb and all public holidays.* This is one of St-Germain's best-known bistros: its pleasant provincial Parisian terrace has somewhat invaded the pavement. Decorated with paintings and palettes, the influence of the nearby art school is obvious. One of the waiter's, whose painting hangs on the wall of the large room, has become a celebrity of sorts over the years.

Le Comptoir du Relais – *9 carrefour de l'Odéon – 6th arr – ☎ 01 43 29 12 05 – Mon-Thu noon-midnight, Fri-Sat noon-2am, Sun 1-10pm.* Perfect for a break after the cinema or while strolling through the Latin Quarter. Regional wines served by the glass in tasteful surroundings. The terrace is very popular, slightly off the main road. Small, gloomy, dungeon-like basement.

Le Dix – *10 rue de l'Odéon – 6th arr – ☎ 01 43 26 66 83 – daily 5pm-2am.* The meeting place of the district's students, decorated with Belle Epoque theatre posters. In the basement, mirrors have replaced the tubes of the splendid 1901 organ from Northern France.

Le Procope – *13 rue de l'Ancienne-Comédie – 6th arr – ☎ 01 40 46 79 00 – daily 11am-1am.* Founded in 1686, it is the oldest existing café in Paris and renowned for its former popularity with literary giants such as La Fontaine, Voltaire, or later on, Daudet, Oscar Wilde and Verlaine. Now it is a restaurant, more popular with tourists than writers, but it is still possible to stop by for tea or coffee in the afternoon, between 3-5pm.

Les Étages Saint-Germain – *5 rue de Buci – 6th arr – ☎ 01 46 34 26 26 – daily 11am-2am.* This amazing establishment nicely fills out the two floors of an old house, leading visitors through a maze of tiny rooms, all decorated differently. From the second floor, there is a good view of rue de Buci and rue Grégoire-de-Tours. Young clientele, but more conventional than its sister establishment in the Marais.

Shopping

Le Coupe Papier – *19 rue de l'Odéon – 6th arr – Ⓜ Odéon – ☎ 01 43 54 65 95 – Mon 1-7pm; Tue-Fri 10am-7pm, Sat 11am-7pm – closed public holidays.* A bookshop devoted to theatre, cinema, opera and dance. It publishes a full reference catalogue. Specialised in contemporary arts, it also has a selection of English and Italian language works not translated into French. A few videos and CDs.

Le Moniteur – *7 pl. de l'Odéon – 6th arr – Ⓜ Odéon – ☎ 01 44 41 15 75 – www.editionsdumoniteur.com – Mon-Sat 10am-7pm – closed public holidays.* Designed by Wilmotte, this publishing house bookshop is specialised in architecture and urban planning and is always packed with students and tourists. Some books about Paris in English and a large number of international magazines and reviews.

Eating out

Turn back to the Selected restaurants section at the beginning of the guide for a list of restaurants, bistros, cafés etc. This district corresponds to the 6th *arrondissement*.

At no **15** stood the **couvent des Cordeliers** – a Franciscan monastery of high repute in the Middle Ages for its teaching. In 1791, the revolutionary group formed by Danton, Marat, Camille Desmoulins and Hébert, known as the Cordeliers, took over both the monastery and its name; opposite, lived Jean-Paul **Marat** (1743-93) the pamphleteer who was stabbed in his bath by Charlotte Corday on 13 July 1793. The present buildings, now part of the university (Paris VI), were built between 1877 and 1900 to house the School of Practical Medicine. Of the vast monastic buildings, only the monks' Flamboyant Gothic refectory dormitory remains, off the courtyard.

The central part of the former Medical School (no 12), now known as the **René Descartes University** (Paris V), dates back to 1775.

Musée d'Histoire de la médecine ⊘ – *Université René-Descartes, 12 rue École-de-Médecine*. This museum houses the College of Surgeons' collections of surgical instruments from Ancient Egyptian to modern times.

Take rue Dupuytren, then rue Delavigne.

Place de l'Odéon – This semicircular square has remained essentially unchanged since its creation in 1779.

At no **1**, the Café Voltaire was frequented by the Encyclopaedists and, at the turn of the 20C, by famous writers and poets: Barrès, Bourget, Mallarmé, **Verlaine**, **Gide**, **Hemmingway**...

Théâtre de l'Odéon – In 1782 a theatre was built in the gardens of the former Condé mansion to accommodate the French Comedians who for the past 12 years had been confined to the Tuileries Palace Theatre. The new theatre, built in the popular Antique style of the day, was given the name Théâtre Français.

Beaumarchais' *Le Mariage de Figaro* was particularly well received in 1784.

With the advent of the Revolution, the actors split between Royalists and Republicans disbanded in 1792. In 1797 the theatre was taken over and renamed the Odéon, after the building used by the Greeks to hold musical competitions. Concerts and dances were generally popular before works began to be staged with disastrous results. In 1807 the building was rebuilt to its original plans after a fire. In spite of the great success of Alphonse Daudet's play, *L'Arlésienne*, set to music by **Bizet**, the theatre's audience dwindled, migrating to theatres on the Right Bank.

Between 1946 and 1959, known first as the Salle Luxembourg and then as the Théâtre de France, it began to specialise in 20C plays, achieving pre-eminence in 1968 under Jean-Louis Barrault and Madeleine Renaud. Inside, the ceiling is painted by André Masson (1963).

In 1983, the theatre became the Théâtre de l'Europe, first on a part-time basis, then completely assuming this identity in 1990.

West of place de l'Odéon, rue Régnard leads to rue de Condé.

Rue de Condé is lined with old houses; at no 26, Beaumarchais wrote *Le Barbier de Séville* in 1773.

Turn left then right and right again to walk down rue de Tournon.

Rue de Tournon contains mostly luxury boutiques, but offers a fine view of the Sénat.

OPÉRA★★

Michelin plan 10: F 12, F 13, G 12, G 13
Ⓜ *Opéra (lines 3, 7 and 8)* – Buses: *20, 21, 22, 27, 42, 52, 53, 66, 81, 95*

This district, encompassing the distinctive Palais Garnier Opera House with its long avenue stretching down to the Palais-Royal and the splendid place Vendôme, is at the hub of theatre land. Home to many of the more classic contemporary fashion designers, the streets are thronged with elegantly attired people day and night.

Nearby neighbourhoods: GRANDS BOULEVARDS, MADELEINE, ST-LAZARE, PALAIS-ROYAL.

EXPLORING THE NEIGHBOURHOOD

Start from the intersection of rue de Rivoli and rue de Castiglione, Ⓜ Tuileries.

Rue de Castiglione – This street was known formerly as passage des Feuillants after the Benedictine monastery which it skirted. The crossroads of rue de Castiglione and rue St-Honoré affords a view of the place and Colonne Vendôme.

★★ **Place Vendôme** – Place Vendôme *(see illustration p 94)* epitomises the full majesty of 17C French design. It is named after the Duke of Vendôme, the illegitimate son of Henri IV and Gabrielle d'Estrées. In c 1680, on land north of rue St-Honoré earmarked for development, Louvois, Superintendent of Buildings, conceived the idea

Place Vendôme

B. Kaufmann/MICHELIN

of designing a square lined with splendid buildings around a monumental statue of Louis XIV. **Jules Hardouin-Mansart** was commissioned to design the square. In 1699 the equestrian statue of the king by Girardon was unveiled in the square defined by a mere painted semblance of beautiful façades. Only gradually were the plots of land purchased by speculators between 1702 and 1720.

The column – During the Revolution the royal statue was destroyed and in 1810 **Napoleon** erected the Austerlitz column at its centre. The column's stone core, 44m/132ft high, is encased in a bronze spiral cast from 1 250 cannon captured at the Battle of Austerlitz (1805), and decorated with military scenes in imitation of Trajan's column in Rome.

The original statue mounted on the column was of Napoleon as Caesar; in 1814 it was replaced by one of Henri IV, removed for the 100 Days (1815) when Napoleon attempted to regain power. Louis XVIII then had a colossal fleur-de-lis hoisted there; Louis-Philippe re-established Napoleon, this time in military uniform, and Napoleon III substituted a replica of the original. The Commune tore down the column in 1871 – an incident for which the painter Gustave Courbet was blamed and exiled.

The layout – A continuous line of arches rings the square at ground level supporting a giant order of pilasters up to a steeply pitched roof with dormer windows.

Each house around the square evokes a memory or a name: no **19** is the former Hôtel d'Évreux (1710) owned by the governor of the Crédit Foncier de France; no **15** now houses the **Ritz Hotel**; nos **13** and **11**, occupied by the Ministry of Justice, were formerly the Royal Chancellery – the official measure for the metre was inlaid in the façade in 1848; no **9** was the house of the military governor of Paris at the end of the 19C; **Chopin** died at no **12** in 1849; no **16** was the home of the German, Dr Mesmer, founder of the theory of Mesmerism.

The square and its surrounding area collect together all the great names in jewellery design: Van Cleef & Arpels, Boucheron, Mauboussin... At a stone's throw, in rue Cambon, is the house from which **Coco Chanel** reigned over the fashion world for half a century, while living at the Ritz Hotel nearby.

Rue de la Paix – In the French version of Monopoly, this is the most expensive street in Paris. Jewellers and goldsmiths, **Cartier** (no **11**) among others, have brought it international fame making its name synonymous with elegance and luxury.

★★ **Place de l'Opéra** – Haussmann envisaged place de l'Opéra not simply as a setting for the National Music Academy but also as a circus from which a number of roads should radiate. This vision was criticised for being too grandiose: the square seemed enormous at that time, whereas today, choked with traffic, it barely seems big enough! The square is presently lined with luxurious shop-windows proffering elegant leather goods (Lancel) and jewellery (Clerc) whereas the Café de la Paix terraces provide an enticing break to the foot-weary.

Turn left onto boulevard des Capucines.

Boulevard des Capucines – This street takes its name from a Capuchin monastery that once stood between the present boulevard and place Vendôme.

No 27 has a splendid façade embellished with brass and copper panels by Frantz Jourdain, maestro of the Art Nouveau decorative style. Originally intended for a de luxe branch of the Samaritaine department store, it is now occupied by a finance house.

Turn right onto rue Scribe.

Rue Scribe – Named after Eugène Scribe (1791-1861), who directed the Théâtre Comique Français for 30 years. At no 4, the **Le Grand-Hôtel** is a grand vestige from the era of Napoléon III (1862); the Opéra salon has been converted into a restaurant.

Take rue Auber to return to boulevard des Capucines, and turn right onto rue de la Michodière.

Place Gaillon – The original fountain was erected in 1707 but remodelled by Visconti in 1827. The **Restaurant Drouant** is probably best-known as the place from which the winners of the much acclaimed Goncourt Literary Prize are announced each autumn. Previous winners have included Marcel Proust, André Malraux, Henri Troyat, Robert Merle, Simone de Beauvoir, Romain Gary and Tahar Ben Jelloun.

Rue Gaillon leads to avenue de l'Opéra.

★Avenue de l'Opéra – This luxurious thoroughfare was begun simultaneously at either end by Haussmann in 1854 and completed in 1878. The avenue quickly became one of Paris' prestige streets and most animated thoroughfares. For the tourist the avenue is the ideal shopping centre for perfumes, scarves, gifts and *articles de Paris* (fancy souvenirs). It is also a thriving commercial centre.

MUSEUMS AND OTHER ATTRACTIONS

★★L'Opéra-Garnier ⊘ – *Place de l'Opéra*. The celebrity of France's first home of opera, the prestige of its ballet company, the architectural magnificence of the great staircase and foyer, the sumptuous decoration of the auditorium, make attending a performance a gala event. Even if you can't get a ticket, it is well worth taking the tour of the Opera, which has recently been completely restored, inside and out.

The Opéra Company – The Paris Opéra has successively been based at the Palais-Royal Theatre (1673), at the Salle des Machines in the Tuileries Palace (1764), then back at the Palais-Royal for the great performances of Rameau *(Zoroastre)* and Gluck

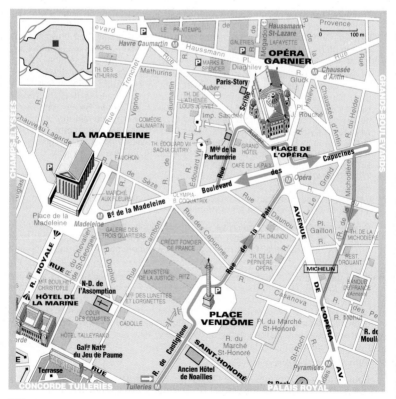

phée), the Salle Favart (1820) – [th]e of the *opéra-comique* – the [th]e Le Peletier (1821) – and the [Palai]s Garnier (1875) before being [final]ly transferred to the Opéra-[Bas]tille in 1990. Since 1994 the [Palai]s Garnier and the Opéra Bastille [hav]e been collectively known as the [Opé]ra National de Paris (ONP).

[Balle]t – The ballet company reper-[toir]e is extensive, with programmes [that] include contemporary music and dance as well as classical pieces. Recent modifications have equipped it with 20C high-tech facilities. The ONP has its own ballet school.

The Opera House – The site of Garnier's Opera House was determined by Haussmann's town planning schemes. In 1820 the idea for a pur-pose-built opera house was born. It took 40 years before a competition was held to find an architect: 171

Opéra Garnier

submitted plans. **Charles Garnier**, a 35-year-old unknown architect, winner of the Rome prize in 1848, was awarded the contract. It is perhaps the most successful monument of the Second Empire.

It is a large theatre with a total area of over 11 237m²/120 955sq ft with a vast stage that will hold up to 450 performers, and a central chandelier that weighs 8t: but given the huge space allowed in the wings for stage changes etc the auditorium seats only 2 200.

Going out

Bar Hemingway, Hôtel Ritz – *15 pl. Vendôme – 1st arr – ☎ 01 43 16 30 30 – www.ritzparis.com – Tue-Sat 6.30pm-2am – closed 1-25 Aug.* Hemingway, introduced by F Scott Fitzgerald, was a client of this cosy, little bar, now decorated with photographs of the writer and complete with a library. Cigar evenings with cocktails specially designed for the event (Wednesdays). Smart dress.

Harry's New York Bar – *5 rue Daunou – 2nd arr – ☎ 01 42 61 71 14 – www.harrys-bar.fr – daily 10.30am-4am – closed 24-25 Dec.* Forever popular with Parisian expatriate Americans and all those keen on Bloody Mary's and Blue Lagoons.

Café de la Paix – *12 blvd des Capucines – 9th arr – ☎ 01 40 07 30 20 – www.cafedelapaix.com – daily 9am-1am.* Opened in 1862, it is located on one of Haussman's most successful examples of urban planning and what is also one of the capital's busiest crossroads. Many artists ate here: Maurice Chevalier, Josephine Baker, Mistinguett, Serge Lifar to name but a few.

Shopping

Espace Michelin – *32 avenue de l'Opéra – 2nd arr - ☎ 01 42 68 05 20 – Mon noon-7pm, Tue-Sat 10am-7pm.* Maps, travel guides and objects illustrating Bibendum, the Michelin mascot.

Goyard – *233 rue St-Honoré – 1st arr – Ⓜ Tuileries – ☎ 01 42 60 57 04 – goyard@free.fr – Mon-Sat 10am-7pm – closed public holidays.* This reputable luggage-maker has recently changed hands but has retained its former spirit. At the back of the shop, an impressive early-20C mahogany staircase leads up to a room where the establishment's first creations are displayed, including a trunk-desk designed for Conan Doyle.

Place Vendôme – *Pl. Vendôme – 1st arr – Ⓜ Opéra, Madeleine or Tuileries.* The classic architecture of this legendary square provides a perfect backdrop for the world's leading jewellery houses.

Eating out

Turn back to the Selected restaurants section at the beginning of the guide for a list of restaurants, bistros, cafés etc. This district is in the 9th *arrondissement*.

The building – The main façade overlooks place de l'Opéra. At raised ground level, between the arched entrances into the theatre are a series of sculpted figures that Garnier wished to commission exclusively from Carpeaux. His allegorical group **Dance** has been replaced by a **Paul Belmondo** copy.

A projecting bay and side entrance were originally reserved for subscribers, who were able to drive their carriages into the courtyard lit by lanterns borne by statues of women by Cartier-Belleuse. The so-called Emperor's Pavilion, on rue Scribe, has a double ramp for the sovereign's carriage, facilitating direct access to the royal box.

★★★**Interior** – A feature of the building's originality is Garnier's use of multicoloured marbles quarried in different parts of France: white, blue, pink, red and green. The magnificent **Great Staircase** and the **Grand Foyer** are conceived for sumptuous occasions. The ceiling in the **auditorium**, which may be visited outside rehearsals, is painted with figures taken from the realms of opera and ballet by **Marc Chagall** (1964).

Bibliothèque-musée *(tickets from the ticket office in the left hall, access on the first floor, Baignoires / Orchestre level)* – The library was started in 1866. Documenting living memories of the house and its companies since 18C, it contains every score performed since 1669 and over 80 000 books and prints relating to dance, the singing voice, music and the theatrical arts. All exhibitions are presented in the rotunda.

Garnier's architectural drawings hang up the stairs to the second-floor library with its fine period wooden furnishings, the models gallery (three-dimensional stage set designs), and painting collection (Hubert Robert, Renoir, Van Dongen, Perroneau...).

Musée de la Parfumerie Fragonard ⊘ – *9 rue Scribe.* All kinds of paraphernalia relating to perfume making are collected together in this museum, explaining the history of perfume making over 3 000 years, from Ancient Egypt to the Grasse factories of today.

Paris-Story ⊘ – *11 bis rue Scribe.* Every hour a film of the history of Paris, from the Lutetia of 250 BC to the modern day, is shown on a panoramic screen.

Coco Chanel's headquarters

At the end of 1910, Gabrielle Chanel (1883-1971), the descendant of a family of stall holders from the Cévennes, and well versed in financial dealings and horse racing, set up shop as a milliner in a basement at no 21 rue Cambon. Ten years later she moved to no 31.

Her essential talent was in fabric cutting and dressmaking, applied with skill in the use of humble fabrics such as jersey, tweed and plaid. She had an expert eye for colour and designed clothes that relied on line rather than ornament for effect, austere but graceful. Her tailored outfits were often based on the British Sporty Look designed for comfort and ease of movement, popular among modern, independent and career-minded women after the First World War. It is to Chanel that we owe the little black number – that prerequisite element of the female wardrobe, versatile enough to be dressed down if worn with flat court shoes or up with stilettos and large imitation jewels, and the tailored suit. Survival of Chanel's business during the war was ensured by the launch of the famous Number 5 perfume (1920), a stable, indefinable scent blending animal and vegetable extracts with artificial stabilisers.

Naturally thin, Coco wore her hair short, often under simple hats. Impressed and forever interested in the ballet and the theatre, Chanel shaped the trends in fashion – she even made the sun-tan fashionable!

Musée d'ORSAY ★★★

Since 1986, the immense space of the former Gare d'Orsay has served as a fine arts museum, whose collection covers the years 1848 to 1914. Everything is wonderful about it, both the setting and the masterpieces it contains. A new footbridge across the Seine links the museum with the Tuileries opposite.

From railway station to museum – At the end of the 19C the Orléans rail company acquired the site of the ruined Orsay Palace, which had been set ablaze in 1871 during the Commune, on which to build a new rail terminus. The company commissioned Victor Laloux (1850-1937), the winner of the Prix de Rome in 1878 and professor of architecture at the École des Beaux-Arts, to design a station which would harmonise in style with the buildings of this elegant quarter facing the Louvre and the Tuileries across the Seine. He designed an iron and glass structure screened on the outside by a monumental façade modelled on the Louvre and on the inside by a coffered ceiling with stucco decoration. He also planned an adjoining hotel. Two years later the building was inaugurated, on 14 July 1900.

For nearly 40 years Orsay station, the terminus for the southwest region and the first to be purpose-built for electric traction, handled about 200 trains daily. As electrification spread to the rest of the network, longer trains came into service and the platforms at Orsay station proved inadequate. In 1939 progress outpaced the building's capabilities; the main-line station functioned briefly for suburban traffic before succumbing to closure. It was put to a number of uses: as reception centre for prisoners at the Liberation, a film-set for Kafka's *The Trial* filmed by Orson Welles in 1962, a theatre for the Renaud-Barrault Company in 1973, temporary **auction-rooms** during the refurbishment of the Hôtel Drouot in 1974.

Shortly after the station closed, a plan was mooted to convert it into a museum for 19C art. A conclusive decision was taken in 1977 by President V Giscard d'Estaing. Gae Aulenti, the architect who had carried out the renovation of the National Museum of Modern Art in Paris and of the Palazzo Grassi in Venice, was entrusted with the museum's interior design and decoration. The museum was inaugurated by President F Mitterrand on 1 December 1986.

Musée d'Orsay

62 rue de Lille – ☎ *01 40 49 48 14. Information, reception:* ☎ *01 40 49 48 48; answering machine:* ☎ *01 45 49 11 11 or* ☎ *01 45 49 49 49 for group bookings; Minitel: 3615 ORSAY; Internet: www.musee-orsay.fr.*

Making the most of the Musée d'Orsay – Either consult the theme cards at the entrance to each room or request a guided tour (general, theme, monographic etc); detailed programme at the information desk.

Shopping in the musée d'Orsay – The book, card and gift shops are open 9.30am-6.30pm (9.30pm on Thu). Direct access off quai Anatole-France for the book and card shop. Cross the esplanade in front of the museum to get to the gift shop.

Eating out

Moderate

Le Restaurant du Musée d'Orsay – *Median level –* ☎ *01 45 49 47 03 – restaurant.orsay.rv@elior.com – daily (except Mon) and Thu evening – no reservations – 22.87/30.40€.* After a pleasant stroll past Van Gogh and Gaugin, you may want to stop for a bite to eat. The beautiful frescoes, gilt work and mouldings never fail to impress visitors to the striking dining room of the former Palais d'Orsay. Unpretentious cuisine with either a buffet or set meal. Tearoom in the afternoon.

If you turn back to the Selected restaurants section at the beginning of the guide, there is also a list of restaurants, bistros, cafés etc. This district is in the 7th *arrondissement*.

Shopping

Richart – *258 bd St-Germain – 7th arr –* Ⓜ *Solférino – other shop: 36 av. de Wagram, 8th arr –* ☎ *01 45 55 66 00 – www.richart.com – Mon-Sat 10am-7pm.* This master craftsman excels in the art of producing chocolates which delight both the eye and the palate. His assortments, which resemble miniature paintings, are composed of exquisitely decorated *ganache* chocolates.

★★★MUSÉE D'ORSAY ⓥ *62 rue de Lille.*

Permanent exhibitions – The collections are presented in chronological order and by theme. Each major artistic movement from the period 1848 to 1914 is represented, and the collection is divided into four major categories: painting, sculpture, architecture and decorative arts.
The permanent collection begins on the ground floor, continues on the uppermost level, and finishes on the middle floor. There are frequently changing temporary exhibitions.
A free plan of the museum is available at the reception desk, showing the exact content of the galleries. This will help the visitor to relate to the main artistic movements mentioned here.

Bal du Moulin de la Galette, Auguste Renoir

Painting and sculpture

Neoclassicism – This movement, which was inspired by the works of Antiquity, dates from the end of the 18C and reached its height in the early to mid-19C.
The artists: the sculptors Cavelier, Guillaume and **Pradier**; the painter **Jean-Auguste-Dominique Ingres** (1780-1867), who placed particular emphasis on line and contours. His portrayal of naked flesh in *The Spring* (1856) was particularly praised by Gautier.

Romanticism – Running parallel with Neoclassicism, Romanticism developed first in England and Germany and concentrated on colour and movement. It was still popular in 1860.
The artists: the sculptors Barye, Rude and Préault; the painters Chassériau and **Eugène Delacroix** (1798-1863), whose expressive style is illustrated by The *Tiger Hunt* (1854), painted after the artist had visited Morocco.

Realism – From 1830 until the end of the 19C these artists started painting from their observations of everyday life and of nature, abandoning contemporary academic practice.
The artists: the sculptor Meissonnier; the painters Rosa Bonheur, Antigna, Fantin-Latour, **Honoré Daumier** (1808-79), Jean-François Millet (1814-75) and Gustave Courbet (1819-77), whose paintings caused a scandal, especially *The Origin of Life*. Daumier's *Busts of Parliamentarians* portrayed a satirical view of the social and political life of the period. *The Angelus* earned Millet much scorn from the contemporary critics who saw the work as condescendingly moralising. In fact, the painter was merely expressing his personal understanding of country people and rural life, in this case the importance of work and faith.
The Burial at Ornans (1849) is perhaps the first real expression of Realism. Likened to his contemporary Émile Zola who developed the Realist novel, Courbet here depicts the real life of ordinary people from his home village, full of dignity and reverence while attending the funeral of a working man. The scale of the figures,

standing upright against the horizontal elements of the composition, makes a bold statement to the glory of common people, 13 years before Victor Hugo was to do the same in literature.

The Barbizon School – The development of industrial towns prompted some artists to rediscover the countryside. **Camille Corot** (1796-1875) moved to Barbizon in 1830, favouring dark earthy hues of colour, muted tones of twilight, inspired by the wooded landscapes around Fontainebleau. Théodore Rousseau (1812-67) is considered as the leader of the Barbizon School of painters, skilfully catching the effect of fleeting light.

Eclecticism – This broad movement, covering the second half of the 19C, and corresponding to the Second Empire in France, was followed by official painters. It no longer favoured only Antiquity, but a mixture of all previous styles. Note the harmonious marble sculpture *Sleeping Hebe* (1869) by Carrier-Belleuse, in the central alley, as well as Carpeaux's *Ugolin* (1862) and *The Dance* (1869), which was created for the façade of the Opéra Garnier.
The artists: the sculptors Debois, Barrias, Clésinger, Cordier and Jean-Baptiste Carpeaux (1827-75); the painters Winterhalter, Couture, Fromentin and Guillaumet.

Academism – This label regroups all the artists who continued to work in the established academic tradition throughout the second half of the 19C.
The artists: the sculptors Fremiet, Mercié and Albert Carrier-Belleuse (1824-87); the painters Blanche, Cabanel, Duran and Gérôme.

Symbolism – Between 1855 and 1900 there was a reaction towards expressionism and against naturalism and impressionism. These artists rejected reality and sought to explore hidden worlds by graphic means.
The artists: the sculptors Bartholomé, Camille Claudel and **Auguste Rodin** (1840-1917), who dominated the last years of the 19C; the painters Burne Jones, Hodler, Homer, Mucha, Doré, Detaille, Levy-Dhurmer, Degouve de Nuncques, Munch, Klimt, Carrière, Puvis de Chavannes, Gustave Moreau (1826-98), whose poetic mysterious vision is suffused with languid sensuality (*Orpheus*, 1865) and Odilon Redon (1840-1916), who portrays his fantastical world of Symbolism with *The Buddha* (1906). Of his many works displayed here, Rodin felt that *Balzac* (1897) was a true expression of his own art, representing the great novelist in an abstracted pose that contrasts with the brilliance of his creative genius.

The origins of Impressionism – The new generation of artists, in reacting against the sombre shades used by their predecessors, set out to render the vibrations of light and to capture impressions of colour; hence their choice of subjects: sunlit gardens, snow, mist and flesh tones. Despite being open to the advice proffered by the Barbizon group, they remained independent of them.
The artists: Boudin, Bazille, Cézanne, Renoir, Monet, Edgar Degas (1834-1917) and Edouard Manet (1832-83), who broke with studio convention by the boldness of their colours and compositions.
Le Déjeuner sur l'herbe was shown at the 1863 Salon des Refusés. Despite having been inspired by Raphael's *Judgement of Paris* and recalling Giorgione's *Concert champêtre* in the Louvre, Manet's naked Bourgeois figures depicted in a harsh uncompromising light scandalised contemporary audiences. Two years later, Manet was further to affront his public with *Olympia* who unlike her idealised nude Renaissance counterparts is depicted with realism, unashamedly naked.

Impressionism – The 1870 war prompted artists to disperse and to regroup in the Île-de-France region: Pontoise, Auvers-sur-Oise. As the official Salons repeatedly rejected their paintings, they decided to show their work independently: the first exhibition was held in 1874 at the studio of the photographer **Nadar** where the contemptuous term impressionists was first coined after Monet's *Impression-Sunrise* (see La MUETTE-RANELAGH: Musée Marmottan-Monet).
The artists: the sculptors Degas and Rosso; the painters **Degas**, **Sisley**, **Cézanne**, **Manet**, **Berthe Morisot Pissarro**, Gustave Caillebotte (1848-94), who was also renowned as a patron of the arts, **Pierre-Auguste Renoir** (1841-1919), painter of nudes, and **Claude Monet** (1840-1926), whose work epitomised this new relationship between the artist and nature. Note the five canvasses of *Rouen Cathedral* (1892-93), part of a series of 30 painted at different times of day, examining the play of light on the cathedral's façade.
Among the best-known works from this group of artists are *Planing the floor* (1875) by Caillebotte (gallery 30), Renoir's *Le Moulin de la Galette* (1876) (gallery 32), and the bronze *Little 14-Year-Old Dancer* (1881) (gallery 31) by Degas.

Naturalism – This movement lasted from 1870 to 1920 and continued the tradition of Realism, this time as expressed by official or academic artists.
The artists: the sculptors Aubé, Dalou and Constantin Meunier (1831-1905); the painters Breitner, Bashkirtseff, Bastien-Lepage and Cormon.

Musée d'Orsay, EDIMEDIA

L'Église d'Auvers-sur-Oise, Vincent van Gogh

The Pont-Aven School – The charming Breton village of Pont-Aven attracted artists from 1885 to 1895, who together formulated a new style by eliminating detail, simplifying forms and using flat, bright colours.

The artists: the painters Lacombe, Paul Sérusier (1864-1927), who painted *The Talisman (1888)*, Émile Bernard (1868-1941) and **Paul Gauguin** (1848-1903), who later moved to Tahiti in search of a mythical Eden. His *Self-portrait with the yellow Christ* (1889) (gallery 43) was painted at Pouldu, in Brittany.

Neo-Impressionism – 1886 marks the official end of Impressionism, but research into the nature of light continued with Divisionism or Pointillism, suggesting light by means of dabs of pigment. Here small dots of pure colour are painstakingly juxtaposed to evoke shimmering light.

The artists: the painters **Matisse**, Renoir, Cross, Paul Signac (1863-1935), Paul Cézanne (1839-1906), Georges Seurat (1859-91), **Henri de Toulouse-Lautrec** (1864-1901), who so accurately portrayed the nightlife of Montmartre, and **Vincent Van Gogh** (1853-90), whose tormented temperament was reflected in the anguished movement of his work. He only took up painting in 1880 after visiting the Borinage countryside. Influenced by Impressionism, he lightened his palette and discovered the luminosity of Provence. His disturbed mind led him to suicide at Auvers-sur-Oise despite the friendship of Dr Gachet and his intense correspondence with his brother Theo. *Self-portrait* (1889) and *The church at Auvers-sur-Oise* (1890) (gallery 39) betray the mental anguish of the artist in the bold lines and almost violent colour contrasts.

The Circus was left incomplete at Seurat's death in 1891. It clearly demonstrates the scientific use of spectrum colours to achieve luminosity and movement. Note the contrasts between the texture of the swinging acrobats and that of the mesmerised spectators.

Note Signac's *The Red Buoy* (1895) (gallery 46), Cézanne's *Apples and Oranges* (1895) (gallery 36), and Toulouse-Lautrec's *La Toilette* (1896) (gallery 47).

The Nabis – This group of painters whose name is derived from the Hebrew for prophet, devised the Nabis pictorial manifesto under the direction of Gauguin in October 1888 at Pont-Aven. The movement continued until 1910. All the artists involved were concerned as much with easel paintings as with large decorative panels, book illustration, prints and stage sets. Post 1900 the group tended towards softer colours and more complex composition on a larger scale.

The artists: the painters Roussel, Valloton, Édouard Vuillard (1868-1940), Pierre Bonnard (1867-1947), who was strongly influenced by Japanese prints, and Maurice Denis (1870-1943), who published pamphlets outlining the group's aspirations. Note Bonnard's *Game of Croquet* (1892), *The Muses* (1893) by Denis and Vuillard's *Public Garden* (1894) (gallery 70).

Architecture

This section is limited to the architecture of the Second Empire period (1852-70). Among the architectural models is a fascinating study of the Opéra district, with a cross-section through the Opéra Garnier showing the foyer, auditorium, the stage and its machinery, as well as its sumptuous decor.

The decorative and applied arts

1850-80 – The key quality inherent in the exhibits of this period is versatility, as fashion and taste succumbed to the influence of colonisation, foreign travel, the universal exhibitions, in particular that of 1867 which revealed Japanese art. New industrial businesses employed artists who combined good design with practicality, able to produce one-off pieces as well as the mass-produced. **Christofle** radically changed their orientation as electro-plating processes enabled mass production of silver-plate without losing the fine art of crafting quality in solid silver. Certain pieces like the **Vase depicting the Education of Achilles** were made for the universal exhibitions. The cabinetmaker **Diehl**, famous for his boxes fashioned in different styles and materials, and for occasional furniture, also made ornate showpieces. The **medal cabinet**, regarded as one of the most original pieces of the 1867 exhibition, is decorated with scenes from Merovingian history (low relief in silver-plated bronze by Frémiet).

French Art Nouveau – A desire for change and for a new form of expression away from the past swept through Europe in around 1890, most notably affecting architecture and the applied arts, namely Art Nouveau or the Modern Style. This movement associated with industrial progress is characterised by serpentine lines and organic decoration. Art in everything, a fundamental concept to the style, broke down distinctions between artist and craftsman, painter and decorator, to achieve the most complete design.

In France Art Nouveau was launched by the Nancy School, an association of artists and craftsmen founded by master glass craftsman Émile Gallé. After studying sculpture and painted wallpapers, Lalique (1860-1945) turned his hand to moulded glass and jewellery. Inspired by the natural shapes of plants, his distinctive designs fuse gold with silver, ivory, enamel, polished stone and glass in combinations of colour and surface texture. Other artists include Majorelle, Gruber, Carabin and Charpentier.

International Art Nouveau – From 1880 the first examples of Art Nouveau appeared in England and soon spread to other parts of Europe (Glasgow, Vienna) and to the United States.

The artists: the Belgians Van de Velde and Victor Horta (1861-1947), whose furniture from the Hôtel Aubecq, Brussels, can be seen in gallery 61, the Austrians Loos and Thonet, known for his curved wooden furniture, the American Frank Lloyd Wright and the Scot, Charles Rennie Mackintosh, pioneer of Functionalism.

PALAIS-ROYAL★★

Michelin plan 10: G 13, G 14, H 13
Ⓜ Palais-Royal-Musée du Louvre (lines 1 and 7) – Buses: 21, 27, 69, 76, 81, 95

In this part of Paris the grandiose setting of the Palais-Royal and the church of St-Roch reminds one vividly of the city's past, in contrast to rue de Rivoli and rue St-Honoré which seem to epitomize the present with their bustling shops.

Nearby neighbourhoods: LES HALLES, FAUBOURG ST-HONORÉ, LE LOUVRE, LES TUILERIES, PLACE DES VICTOIRES.

The Cardinal's Palace – In 1624, **Richelieu**, having just become Prime Minister, acquired a mansion near the Louvre with grounds extending to the Charles V perimeter wall. In 1629 he commissioned the architect **Jacques Lemercier** to build the huge edifice known as the Cardinal's Palace.

The Royal Palace – On his deathbed in 1642 the Cardinal left his mansion to Louis XIII who soon followed him to the grave. The king's widow, Anne of Austria, with her young son, the future Louis XIV, then left the Louvre for the beautiful mansion, which was smaller and more comfortable, and which henceforth became known as the Royal Palace. The Fronde in 1648 forced their hasty departure. When Louis XIV returned to Paris he settled back in the Louvre, lodging **Queen Henrietta** Maria of France, widow of Charles I of England, and then their daughter, Henrietta, in the Palais-Royal.

The Orléans – After a sudden fatal illness had struck Henrietta, the palace was given in apanage to her husband **Philippe of Orléans**, brother of Louis XIV. He was followed by his son, Philippe II of Orléans, Regent during the minority of Louis XV, a highly gifted but also highly dissolute man whose palace suppers were notorious.

Palais-Royal

S. Sauvignier/MICHELIN

287

In 1780 the palace passed to Louis-Philippe of Orléans, who being forever short of money undertook to redevelop the site: around three sides of the garden he commissioned the architect **Victor Louis** to build uniformly fronted blocks of apartments over arcades of shops at ground level. Three new streets were called after the younger Orléans brothers: Valois, Montpensier and Beaujolais. The palace precinct became the favourite idling place for Parisians. Between 1786 and 1790 Victor Louis was also commissioned by Philippe-Égalité to build the Théâtre Français (now the **Comédie-Française**) and the Palais-Royal Theatre at the corner of rue de Montpensier and rue Beaujolais (also still in operation).

After the Revolution, the palace became a gambling house until, in 1801, Napoleon converted it into offices, and in 1807 into the Exchange and Commercial Court.

Louis XVIII returned the mansion to the Orléans family and it was from there that Louis-Philippe set out for the Hôtel de Ville, in 1830, to be proclaimed king.

EXPLORING THE NEIGHBOURHOOD

Place des Pyramides – Just off rue des Pyramides in rue d'Argenteuil was where Corneille died in 1684. The equestrian statue of **Joan of Arc** is by the 19C sculptor, Frémiet. It was here that she was wounded on 8 September 1429 when leading her attack on the capital.

Commemorating this, the only known historical link between France's best-loved saint and the capital city.

There are four statues of Joan in the city, including the splendid golden equestrian model nearby (the others: 16 rue de la Chapelle, place St-Augustin and 21 boulevard St-Marcel).

★ **Rue de Rivoli** – It was Napoleon who, in 1811, had the part of the avenue between rue de Castiglione and place des Pyramides constructed, although it was not to be completed until nearly the middle of the century. The houses facing the Tuileries are of uniform design above arcades lined with both luxury and souvenir shops.

Place du Palais-Royal – The façade of the Palais-Royal overlooking the square consists of a central block (occupied by the Conseil d'État) with two recessed lateral wings, the whole decorated with restrained, 18C carvings of military trophies and allegorical figures by Pajou. The square is also flanked by the **Louvre des Antiquaires**, consisting of 250 antique shops.

★ **Place André-Malraux** – From this crossroads there is a splendid view up avenue de l'Opéra. Created in the time of Napoleon III and ornamented with modern fountains, it was formerly known as place du Théâtre-Français, taking its present name from the writer and Minister of Culture under De Gaulle.

Comédie-Française – *2 rue de Richelieu*. The best way to appreciate the interior of one of the finest theatres in Paris is to attend a performance. The repertoire is mainly classical, although the works of more modern authors are now included.

In the foyer are Houdon's famous bust of **Voltaire**★★ and the chair in which **Molière** was sitting when taken fatally ill on stage in 1673 in a performance of *Le Malade imaginaire*.

A turbulent history

In 1680 Louis XIV combined Molière's company with the troupe at the **Hôtel de Bourgogne** and granted it the sole right of performance in the capital. The new company took the name Comédie-Française.

The company, caught up in endless quarrels with the authorities at the Sorbonne, was constantly on the move. During the Revolution a dispute broke out in the company between players who supported the Republicans and those favouring the Royalists. In 1792 the former, led by Talma, took over the present theatre. Napoleon showed a great interest in the Comédie-Française, and also in the leading lady, Mlle Mars. In 1812 he decreed that the company should consist of an association of actors, active associates, apprentice players and retired players on pension. Today the theatre continues to be managed by a director nominated by the State.

★ **Palais Royal** – Richelieu's palace now accommodates the Ministry of Culture and the Council of State *(closed to the public)*. The east wing accommodated Richelieu's theatre, for which Molière created several of his major plays.

Main courtyard – Enter by the covered passage. Enclosed within a continuous arcaded gallery, it is dominated by an impressive central façade, surmounted by allegorical statues. A monumental modern composition (280 black and white columns of

Palais-Royal Gardens

S. Sauvignier/MICHELIN

unequal height) by **Daniel Buren** fills the central space. Separating the courtyard from the garden is a double colonnade, the Orléans Gallery, built at the time of the Restoration (1814-30) and formerly covered by an iron and glass roof. It presently accommodates two sculpture-fountains by Pol Bury.

The Valois side gallery is known as the Prow Gallery because of its nautical decoration (Richelieu was Minister for the Navy).

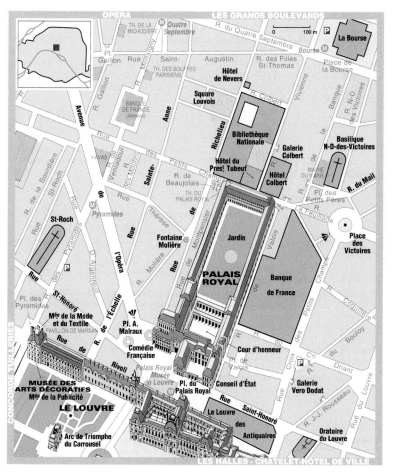

Going out

Bar de l'Hôtel Costes – *239 rue St-Honoré – 1st arr – ☎ 01 42 44 50 25 – daily noon-1am.* In what is one of the capital's smartest addresses, a maze of little rooms provides a variety of styles, ranging from Second Empire to Mediterranean. The Italian-style patio is popular in the fine weather. In favour with the capital's cosmopolitan jet-set, who flock here to listen to the latest hit tunes.

Bar anglais de l'Hôtel Régina – *2 pl. des Pyramides – 1st arr – Quartier Louvre-Palais royal – ☎ 01 42 60 31 10 – www.regina-hotel.com – daily noon-midnight.* This is one of the nicest bars to be found in the luxury hotel bracket: sober, very English, with wood panelling, small armchairs and an experienced barman. Particularly cosy and ideally situated 2min from the Louvre and the Tuileries.

Café Ruc – *159 rue St-Honoré – 1st arr – ☎ 01 42 60 97 54 – booking recommended – 28.97/40.40€.* This purple-coloured café/restaurant is a favourite among tourists and members of the Comédie Française's troupe, who meet here for tea, a glass of wine or a late supper. Served in a tasteful, but unpretentious decor. It owes its name to one of its early owners.

La Scala – *188 bis rue de Rivoli – 1st arr – ☎ 01 42 60 45 64 – www.lascala-paris.com – Tue-Sun 10.30pm-6.30am.* This ultra-modern dance complex has three floors, with bars, laser beams and a giant screen. The clientele are in their 20s and 30s.

Shopping

Le Louvre des Antiquaires – *2 pl. du Palais-Royal – 1st arr – Ⓜ Palais-Royal – ☎ 01 42 97 27 00 – www.louvre-antiquaires.com – Tue-Sun 11am-7pm, Tue-Sat in July and Aug.* 250 antique dealers have set up shop in this vast building. Paintings, archaeology, jewellery, furniture etc. This gallery of beautiful objects displayed in superb show cases is worthy of a museum. Ask for a map at the entrance.

Les Salons du Palais Royal Shiseido – *142 gal. de Valois – 1st arr – Ⓜ Bourse or Palais-Royal – ☎ 01 49 27 09 09 – www.salons-shiseido.com – Mon-Sat 10am-7pm – closed public holidays.* Serge Lutens, the former artistic director of Shisheido, now creates his own perfumes. Based on the night and day theme, this fan of Morocco has designed a setting full of mystery to present his fragrances of rare essences.

Verlet – *256 rue St-Honoré – 1st arr – Ⓜ Palais-Royal – ☎ 01 42 60 67 39 – www.verlet.com – Mon-Sat 9am-7pm, 1 May-1 Oct: Mon-Fri – closed 3 weeks in Aug.* The pleasant smell of freshly ground coffee seeps out of the establishment of this coffee shop-cum-tearoom. Since 1880, the house has stocked a wide variety of coffees, teas and in the winter, preserved fruits, to the delight of the faithful regulars of this genuine craftsman.

Eating out

Turn back to the Selected restaurants section at the beginning of the guide for a list of restaurants, bistros, cafés etc. This district is in the 1st *arrondissement*.

★★ Jardin du Palais-Royal – The quiet garden has retained its 18C atmosphere. It is overlooked by the elegant façades designed by the architect Victor Louis. The shops along the gallery are rather quaint and often a bit dusty.

The writer and analyst of the feminine mind Sidonie **Colette** (1873-1954) died at the age of 81, at 94 Galerie de Beaujolais. **Jean Cocteau** (1889-1963), poet, playwright and film-maker, lived for 20 years in an apartment overlooking the gardens, at 36 rue de Montpensier.

Rue de Richelieu – The 19C **Molière** fountain by Visconti with statues by Pradier stands just before no **40**, the site of Molière's house, to which he was taken after collapsing on stage on 17 February 1673 at the age of 51. No **61** served as home to Henri Beyle (1783-1842), more commonly known as **Stendhal**, where he wrote his novels *Le Rouge et le Noir* and *Promenades dans Rome*.

Rue Ste-Anne – No **47** is the house the composer **Lully** had built in 1671, borrowing 11 000 *livres* from Molière to do so. Note the music masks and motifs ornamenting the façade.

Rue de l'Échelle – So called after the ladder or flight of steps leading to a scaffold which stood on the site during the Ancien Régime. The ecclesiastical courts then sent polygamists, perjurers and blasphemers to the steps where they were exposed in shame before the public.

★ **Rue St-Honoré** – The windows of the section of rue St-Honoré between rue Royale and rue de Castiglione are a window-shopper's paradise.

Under the Ancien Régime, before rue de Rivoli was laid, this road was the main route out of Paris towards the west. Its reputation goes back many years to the pre-Revolution era when members of the royal court, nobility and financiers, all came to do their shopping.

★ **Église St-Roch** – Some idea of the scale of Baron Haussmann's earth-moving undertakings can be gained from the fact that to enter the church nowadays you have to walk up 13 steps, whereas before the construction of the Opera Avenue, you had to go down seven.

On 5 October 1795 St-Roch was the scene of bloody fighting. A column of royalists leading an attack on the Convention, then in the Tuileries, aimed to march through rue St-Roch. Bonaparte, who was in charge of the defence, however, mowed down the men massed on the church steps and perched on its façade with gunfire. The bullet holes can still be seen.

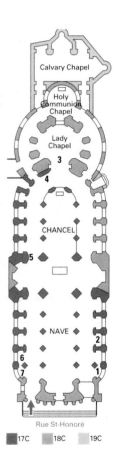

The foundation stone of the church was laid by Louis XIV in 1653. The elevated Moulins site compelled the architect, Lemercier, to orientate the church on a north-south axis rather than the more usual east-west.

Funds quickly ran dry but work was able to continue as a result of a lottery organised in 1705. Instead of completing the nave however, a series of chapels was constructed beyond the apse, so that the church's original length (80m/262ft) was extended to 125m/410ft. This effectively destroyed the unity of design.

The **Lady Chapel**★ by Jules Hardouin-Mansart, with its tall, richly decorated dome, leads into a Communion Chapel with a flat dome and finally a Calvary Chapel, *(closed for restoration)* rebuilt in the 19C.

In 1719 a gift of 100 000 *livres* from **John Law**, who had recently converted to Catholicism, enabled the nave to be completed. Robert de Cotte's Jesuit-style façade dates from 1736.

Among those buried in St-Roch in the Lady Chapel and side chapels are the playwright Corneille, the garden designer **Le Nôtre**, the Abbot de l'Épée, the philosophers **Diderot** and d'Holbach, and **Mme Geoffrin**, hostess of a famous 18C *salon*. The 17C mariner, Duguay-Trouin, has been transferred to Saint-Malo.

Works of Art:

1) Tomb of Henri of Lorraine, Count d'Harcourt by Renard (17C) and bust of the 17C Marshal de Créqui by **Coysevox** (17C).

2) Tomb of Duke Charles de Créqui.

3) *The Triumph of the Virgin*★ painted by J B Pierre on the dome. The *Nativity* at the altar by the Anguier brothers, was brought from the Val-de-Grâce.

4) *Resurrection of the Son of the Widow of Naïm* by Le Sueur (17C).

5) Le Nôtre bust by Coysevox and funerary inscription.

6) *Baptism of Christ* by Lemoyne.

7) Baptismal Chapel: frescoes by Chassériau (19C).

MUSEUMS AND OTHER ATTRACTIONS

★ **Musée de la Mode et du Textile** ⊘ – *107 rue de Rivoli*. The collection encompasses over 20 000 outfits, 35 000 accessories and 21 000 fabric samples dating from the 18C to the present day, displayed in changing exhibitions. Famous names include Poiret, Lanvin, Schiaparelli, Dior and Paco Rabanne.

★★ **Musée des Arts décoratifs** ⊘ – *111 rue de Rivoli*. The numerous exhibits provide a broad cross-section of the evolution of design and taste in the decorative and applied arts in France from the Middle Ages to the 20C: sculpture, painting, ceramics, furniture, jewellery, glass and tableware. Most of the paintings and sculptures come from churches and monasteries.

Musée de la Publicité ⊙ – *107 rue de Rivoli.* Permanent and frequently changing temporary exhibitions. A **database★** composed of thousands of posters and advertising films is available for consultation.

Oratoire du Louvre – *4 rue St-Honoré.* The Oratorian Congregation founded by Cardinal Pierre de Berulle, a secular priesthood dedicated to teaching and preaching later to rival the Jesuits, had a church built by Lemercier (1621-30). This became the royal chapel in the reigns of Louis XIII, Louis XIV and Louis XV. At the Revolution the chapel became an arms depot. Napoleon ceded the church to the Protestants in 1811 before the seminary was re-established in 1852. The façade is 18C.

PASSY

Michelin plan 10: H 5, H 6, J 5, J 6
Ⓜ *Passy (line 6) – RER: Kennedy-Radio France (line C) – Buses: 22, 32, 52, PC*

In the 13C Passy was a woodcutters' hamlet; in the 18C it became known for its ferruginous waters and in 1859 it was incorporated into the city of Paris.

The Fellows of Chaillot or *bonshommes* was the familiar name by which the Minim Friars, whose monastery stood on the hill until the Revolution, were known, presumably because of the red wine produced by the community and still recalled in the names of rue Vineuse and rue des Vignes.

Today some of the houses and gardens that used to make up the peaceful residential quarter remain, although many are being replaced by large blocks of flats.

Nearby neighbourhoods: TROCADÉRO, AUTEUIL, JAVEL, BOIS DE BOULOGNE.

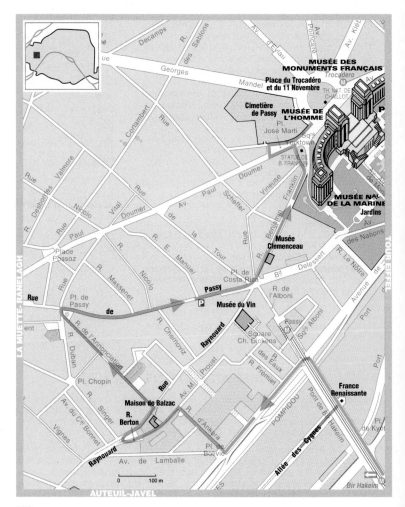

EXPLORING THE NEIGHBOURHOOD

Start from Bir-Hakeim metro station.

Allée des Cygnes – From half way across the Bir-Hakeim Bridge there is access down to the man-made islet in the Seine. Allée des Cygnes, or Swans' Walk, built at the time of the Restoration, provides a good view of the Maison de Radio-France *(see AUTEUIL)* on the right and of the modern development **Front de Seine** on the left with the **Beaugrenelle** mall. The figure of *France Renaissante* looking upstream is by the Danish sculptor, Wederkinch (1930); a bronze replica of the **Statue of Liberty** faces downstream, rising tall above weeping willows.

At the end of Pont de Bir-Hakeim, turn left along avenue du Président-Kennedy, then turn right along rue d'Ankara.

★ **Rue Berton** – Rue Berton, on the left, is one of the most unusual in Paris, its ivy clad walls and gas-light brackets giving it an old country town atmosphere. No 24 was the back entrance to Balzac's house.

Rue Raynouard – This street is full of historical interest. Many famous people have lived in this street named after an obscure academician of the Restoration, including Louis XIV's powerful financier Samuel Bernard, the Duke of Lauzun, **Jean-Jacques Rousseau**, and the song-writer Béranger. It was at no 66 that **Benjamin Franklin** resided during his visit to France to negotiate an alliance with Louis XVI on behalf of the new Republic of the United States; he erected France's first lightning rod over his house.

The modern blocks of flats in reinforced concrete at nos 51 to 55 show a confident application of the new material by Auguste Perret who lived here from 1932 to his death in 1954.

Rue de Passy is lined with exclusive boutiques.

Cimetière de Passy ⊘ – *2 rue du Commandant-Schloesing*. Passy Cemetery, above place du Trocadéro, contains the graves of many famous figures, deceased since 1850, from the worlds of literature (Croisset, T Bernard, Giraudoux), painting (Manet, Berthe Morisot), music (Debussy, Fauré), aviation (Henry Farman) and film (Fernandel).

MUSEUMS AND OTHER ATTRACTIONS

Maison de Balzac ⊘ – *47 rue Raynouard*. Down its original metal stairway, half-hidden in a garden, is the house occupied illicitly by Honoré de Balzac, under the pseudonym of his governess Mme de Breugnol between 1840 and 1847; often on the run from his creditors, he was able to make use of the back route out of the house. Manuscripts, caricatures and engravings pertaining to the author of La Comédie Humaine (the Human Comedy) described in his novels complement an adjoining library.

Musée du Vin – Caveau des Échansons ⊘ – *5-7 square Charles-Dickens*. No 5 rue des Eaux marks the original entrance to the former quarries. Under the Empire they were converted into France's first sugar beet refinery. The underground galleries now house a wine museum with waxwork figures and implements recalling the days when monks produced wine there.

Musée Clemenceau ⊘ – *8 rue Franklin. Closed for restoration*. The great man's apartment is as it was on the day of his death in 1929. Mementoes in a gallery on the first floor recall Georges Clemenceau's career as a journalist and statesman: the Montmartre mayoralty, the **Treaty of Versailles** and the premiership. Note the extraordinary horseshoe-shaped desk.

Cimetière du PÈRE-LACHAISE ★

Michelin plan 10: H 20, H 21
Ⓜ *Père-Lachaise (lines 2 and 3) – Buses: 26, 60, 61, 69*

Paris' largest cemetery spreads over 40ha/99 acres of sloping ground, and is the final resting place of many famous figures. A pleasant place for a stroll, Père-Lachaise is exceptional, not only for its size, but also for the quality of its statuary.

The name – In 1626 the Jesuits bought a piece of land in the open countryside to build a retreat for retired priests. One frequent visitor to the place was Louis XIV's confessor, Father La Chaise, who gave generously to the house's reconstruction in 1682. The Jesuits were expelled in 1763. Forty years later, the city acquired the property for conversion to a cemetery. It was designed by Brongniart.

Cemetery ⊘ – The Père-Lachaise cemetery has several entrances. Plans are available from the Porte des Amandiers and Porte Gambetta.

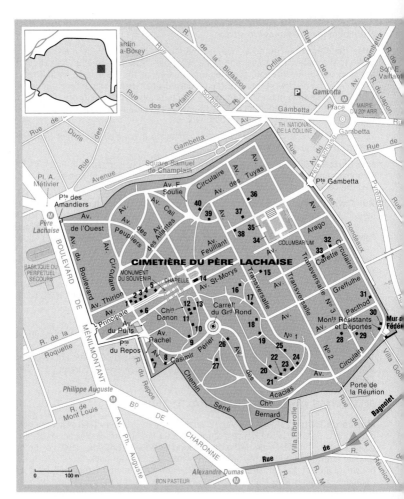

Cimetière du Père Lachaise

1 · Colette

2 · Rossini (cenotaph)

3 · Alfred de Musset (under a willow, at his request)

4 · Baron Haussmann

5 · Generals Lecomte and Thomas

6 · Arago

7 · James de Rothschild

8 · Abelard and Heloise

9 · Miguel Angel Asturias

10 · Chopin

11 · Cherubini

12 · Boieldieu (cenotaph)

13 · Bellini

14 · Thiers

15 · Sarah Bernhardt

16 · Corot

17 · Molière and La Fontaine

18 · Alphonse Daudet

19 · Hugo Family

20 · Bibesco Family (Anna de Noailles)

21 · Maréchal Ney

22 · Beaumarchais

23 · Maréchaux Davout, Masséna, Lefebvre

24 · Murat and Caroline Bonaparte

25 · David d'Angers

26 · Auguste Comte

27 · Jim Morrison

28 · Modigliani

In order to preserve the romantic funerary statues, most of the cemetery has been designated a heritage site. There are over 3 000 trees, creating an attractive setting for the tombs. The cemetery is a popular place of pilgrimage, where tourists mingle with Parisians and those who have come to lay flowers on the tombs of family members or famous figures; among them are Chopin, Balzac, Proust, Oscar Wilde, Jim Morrison...

Le Mur des Fédérés (Federalists' Wall) – On the evening of 27 May 1871 the last insurgents of the Paris **Commune**, having shot their hostages in Belleville, rallied in the cemetery. It was there among the tombstones that bitter fighting ensued with the arrival of the men of Versailles. At dawn on 28 May, the 147 survivors were stood against the wall in the south-east corner and shot. They were buried where they fell in a communal grave – a place of pilgrimage for many ever since.

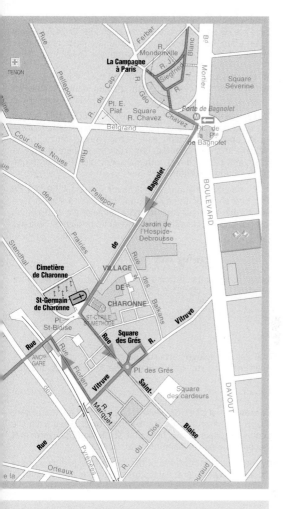

Perhaps the most moving monument is the one next to the wall, dedicated to the resistance movement and deportees of the Second World War.

EXPLORING THE NEIGHBOURHOOD

The village of Charonne – The countryside in Paris.

From the cemetery, go to place Gambetta, then to Porte de Bagnolet via rue Belgrand. From the metro (Porte-de-Bagnolet), head for the north-east corner of the square with the same name, then take the steps in rue Géo-Chavez.

The village of Charonne kept its country atmosphere until recently, and still provides a haven of peace and quiet, not far from the busy Paris ring-road. Once surrounded by vineyards, some houses in this district served as country retreats for wealthy

Going out

La Flèche d'or – *102 bis rue de Bagnolet – 20th arr –* ☎ *01 43 72 04 23 – Mon 1pm-2am, Tue-Sun 10am-2am.* Paris' parallel underground culture reigns over this abandoned station, which used to be situated just outside the capital's frontiers. A wide range of concerts (world music, French, rock, reggae) are held here for a varied public, but which is predominantly young and cool. You can brunch, drink, dine and dance here (every evening, with themed dance parties on Sundays from 5pm).

La Maroquinerie – *23 rue Boyer – 20th arr –* ☎ *01 40 33 30 60 – daily (except Sunday) 11am-1am – closed public holidays.* Located in a former leather workshop, this alternative café operates primarily as a public reading centre, but it also puts on shows and concerts (world music, jazz, rock etc). There is a pleasant interior terrace where you can sit down with a book or glance through one of the manuscripts left by budding authors.

La Mère Lachaise – *78 blvd de Ménilmontant – 20th arr –* ☎ *01 47 97 61 60 – daily 11am-2am.* This peaceful, but trendy café has opted for a Buffon-style decor with a 1909 herb garden, a herbal cabinet and a jungle of plants. Fine terrace close to Père-Lachaise. Chess and newspapers available; brunch on Sundays (noon-5pm).

Eating out

Turn back to the Selected restaurants section at the beginning of the guide for a list of restaurants, bistros, cafés etc. This district is in the 20th *arrondissement.*

Parisians. A pleasant stroll can be enjoyed around the more working-class area, along rue du Père-Prosper-Enfantin, rue Irénée-Blanc, rue Mondonville and rue Jules-Seigfried.

Take rue de Bagnolet.

★ **Église St-Germain-de-Charonne** – *4 place St-Blaise.* The church and square were the focal point of the village of Charonne. The stunted bell-tower dates from the 13C and has interesting carved capitals. It was here that St-Germain-d'Auxerre met Geneviève, who was to become the patron saint of Paris, in 429.

Rue St-Blaise – Formerly the main thoroughfare of the village, this is now a pretty little street, partly pedestrianised, where carefully restored houses mingle with more modern buildings.

An Américaine in Paris

"Paris was where the twentieth century was"

American expatriates Gertrude Stein and Alice B Toklas lived just minutes from the Luxembourg Gardens at no 27 rue de Fleurus.

From 1903 to 1937, their courtyard apartment and atelier with its famed collection of paintings by contemporary masters hosted Paris' most avant-garde expatriate *salon*; their guest list reads like a Who's Who of the early-20C art and literary world: Picasso, Juan Gris, Matisse, Erik Satie, Hemingway, Pound, Sherwood Anderson... Although Gertrude Stein significantly influenced numerous expatriate writers (the term Lost Generation is attributed to her), international recognition for her own experimental works came only in 1933 with the publication of *The Autobiography of Alice B Toklas.*

In 1938 the two women moved nearby to no 5 rue Christine (in the Odéon quarter). Gertrude died in 1946 and was buried in Père Lachaise Cemetery. Alice joined her in 1967.

PIGALLE

Centre of Parisian nightlife, Pigalle is universally known yet has no important monuments. A century ago, the area was home to painters' studios and literary cafés, including the influential Nouvelle Athènes. Today, the cosmopolitan crowd which throngs its pavements is attracted by the neon lights of cabarets, nightclubs, bars and sex shops. The area is well depicted in the **Georges Simenon** detective novels.

Its name comes from the sculptor **Jean-Baptiste Pigalle** (1714-85), admired in his own lifetime for the tomb of Marshal Saxe and the nude figure of Voltaire (in the Louvre).

Nearby neighbourhood: MONTMARTRE.

EXPLORING THE NEIGHBOURHOOD

Place de Clichy – The bustling square was the site of one of Ledoux's toll-houses, where in March 1814 Marshal Moncey's troops put up a spirited defence against the Allied army. Today it is lined with brasseries and a cinema complex.

Boulevard de Clichy – The boulevard runs along the line of the Farmers General wall. Restaurants, cinemas, theatres and nightclubs make it a centre of Paris nightlife. The **Deux-Anes Theatre** at no 100 maintains the Parisian cabaret tradition.
Raoul Dufy lived at no 5 (Villa de Guelma) between 1911 and 1953 at the peak of his painting career.

Going out

Chao-Ba Café *– 22 blvd de Clichy – 18th arr – ☎ 01 46 06 72 90 – Sun-Wed 8.30pm-2am, Thu 8.30pm-4am, Fri-Sat 8.30pm-5am – closed 24, 25 Dec.* Fans, bamboo, parasols, cane furniture; the stage is set of this Asian-style bar. The two floors of this bar provide a short escape from the nearby bustle of the neighbourhood shops and bars.

La Locomotive *– 90 blvd de Clichy – 18th arr – ☎ 01 53 41 88 88 – www.laloco.com – daily 11pm-dawn.* Just next door to the Moulin-Rouge, the Loco as it is known, is always packed with tourists and night-owls. Several dance floors provide a variety of musical styles (disco, funk, rock). Live rock every Tuesday or Wednesday.

MCM café *– 92 blvd de Clichy – 18th arr – ☎ 01 42 64 39 22 – daily 9am-dawn.* This music café, belonging to the cable TV music station, is one of the capital's fashionable places. Spacious room, large bar, pleasant surroundings, varied concerts (pop, rock, blues, soul, gospel, hip-hop, even techno). Private events (film releases) are also held here.

Shopping

À l'Étoile d'Or *– 30 rue Fontaine – Ⓜ Blanche – ☎ 01 48 74 59 55 – Mon 2.30-8pm, Tue-Sat 11am-8pm – closed Aug and public holidays.* The finest confectionery in France can be found in this elegant 1900-style boutique.

Eating out

Turn back to the Selected restaurants section at the beginning of the guide for a list of restaurants, bistros, cafés etc. This district is in the 9th *arrondissement*.

Place Blanche – This square owes its name to the former chalk quarries. The neon sails of the **Moulin Rouge** identify the famous music hall renowned for the French can-can as immortalised in **Toulouse-Lautrec**'s posters depicting the singers and dancers of his time: Valentin le Désossé, Jane Avril, La Goulue....

Place Pigalle – At the end of the 19C the square and its adjoining streets were lined with artists' studios and literary cafés, of which the most famous was the **Nouvelle Athènes**.

Boulevard de Rochechouart – The dance halls and cabarets of years gone by (La Boule Noire, 1822, Le Chat Noir, 1881) have disappeared, although the façade of the Élysée-Montmartre is still visible (no 72). La Cigale (no 120) and other modern clubs have recently brought new life to the district with rock and techno music.

MUSEUMS AND OTHER ATTRACTIONS

Musée de la Vie romantique ⊙ – *Maison Renan-Scheffer, 16 rue Chaptal.* The charming house set back from the street with its garden was where **Ary Scheffer** (1795-1858) lived and worked for nearly 30 years. This artist of Dutch origin was influenced by the Romantics and greatly admired by Louis-Philippe. On Friday evenings his home was the meeting place for a group of painter and literary friends (Delacroix, Ingres, Liszt, Chopin, George Sand and Ernest Renan who married Ary's niece).

Aurore Lauth-Sand's bequest of paintings, jewellery and drawings evokes memories of her grandmother **George Sand**, her family and friends *(ground floor)*. Ary Scheffer's works are exhibited on the first floor except during temporary exhibitions. The studio-annexe has been refurbished with a collection of his furniture, easel, paintings and photographs.

Musée de l'Érotisme ⊙ – *72 boulevard de Clichy.* Opened in 1997, this unusual museum traces the fascination that eroticism has exerted on artists since the beginning of time, over many continents (South America, Africa, India, China, Europe). Erotic art, whether sacred or profane, is illustrated here in all its forms: painting, sculpture, graphics, decorative art and objects. A unique permanent collection of over 2 000 pieces, with changing temporary exhibitions. Seven floors of exhibits, open until late every night.

Faubourg POISSONNIÈRE★

Michelin plan 10: E 14-E 16, F 14-F 16
Ⓜ *Gare de l'Est, Poissonnière, Cadet –*
Buses: 30, 31, 32, 38, 39, 46, 47, 56, 65

Up until 1750, the street was known as rue Ste-Anne, taking its name from a chapel that stood at no 77. It became known thereafter as rue du Faubourg-Poissonnière as it was the last leg of the fish-traders' journey from the coast to the wholesale markets at Les Halles. Today it is a pleasant place for a stroll.

EXPLORING THE NEIGHBOURHOOD

Église St-Laurent ⊙ – *68 boulevard de Magenta.* The belfry is all that remains of the 12C sanctuary. The nave was rebuilt in the 15C and the church altered in the 17C (chancel sculpture and woodwork). The west front and spire date from the Napoleon III period.

Walk north along boulevard de Magenta to square A.-Satragne (on the left).

Ancienne maison St-Lazare – *107 rue du Faubourg-St-Denis.* In the Middle Ages this was the capital's leper house. St Vincent de Paul, the founder of the Priests of the Mission (known today as Lazarists), died here in 1660.

At the time of the Revolutionary troubles the building became a prison and the poet André Chénier, one of its most industrious inmates, was here prior to his execution. Changed to a women's prison, it reverted to being a hospital in 1935.

Follow rue du Faubourg-St-Denis to rue de Paradis and turn right.

Shopping

Furet – *63 rue de Chabrol – 10th arr – Ⓜ Poissonnière – ☎ 01 47 70 48 34 – Mon-Sat 8am-8pm – closed Aug and public holidays.* This 1947 sweet shop sells legendary *Tanrade* jams, still prepared using cottage-industry techniques and fruits of the season. Don't miss the black chocolate jam called Cahua!

Eating out

Turn back to the Selected restaurants section at the beginning of the guide for a list of restaurants, bistros, cafés etc. This district is in the 9th and 10th *arrondissements.*

Rue de Paradis – The street is known today for its shops of fine tableware. These are chief points of sale for the French glass, china and porcelain factories located here because of their proximity to the Gare de l'Est and the rail links with Lorraine where the industry is concentrated.

Continue to the intersection with rue d'Hauteville and turn right; the street leads to place Franz-liszt.

Église St-Vincent-de-Paul – *Pl. Franz-Liszt.* The church was built by the architect **Hittorff** (1824-44) who was also responsible for the final decoration of place de la Concorde. Basilical in form, the church has a columned portico and two tall towers. Inside, Flandrin's fresco runs around the nave, dividing the elevation in two. A bronze calvary by Rude stands on the high altar.

MUSEUMS AND OTHER ATTRACTIONS

Hôtel Bourrienne ⊙ – *58 rue d'Hauteville (at the back of the courtyard).* Located at the heart of the Nouvelle-France quarter, this 18C house was owned by Fortunée Hamelin, a friend of Joséphine de Beauharnais. In 1801, crippled by debts, this famed *Merveilleuse* ceded her house to Louis-Antoine Fauvelet de Bourrienne, secretary and confidant of the First Consul. There, between 1813 and 1824, the witty Mme de Bourrienne established one of Paris' most brilliant *salons*. The façade overlooking the gardens is enhanced by three central arcades.
Decorated under the Empire and Restoration, the ground floor boasts a small sitting room, a dining room (furniture by Jacob and Aubusson carpet), a study, a sitting room (Savonnerie carpet, Directoire chandelier), a bedroom and a **bathroom** in blue and gold reflecting the sumptuous taste of the times.

★**Musée Baccarat** ⊙ – *30 bis rue de Paradis.* **Baccarat**, the glassmakers who have supplied royal palaces and state residences throughout the world for the last 150 years display some of their workshops' finest pieces (chandeliers, vases, perfume bottles).

★**Musée de la Franc-Maçonnerie** ⊙ – *16 rue Cadet.* A large room in this modern building accommodates a collection of documents (Constitution of Anderson from 1723), badges, and portraits that encapsulate the history of this organisation, one of the main Masonic lodges of France.

PORT-ROYAL

Michelin plan 10: L 13, L 14
RER: Port-Royal (line B) – Buses: 38, 83, 91

The Port-Royal neighbourhood is centered around the crossroads of boulevard de Port Royal and avenue de l'Observatoire, where traffic lanes are separated by a pretty garden.

Nearby neighbourhoods: MONTPARNASSE, LUXEMBOURG, GOBELINS.

EXPLORING THE NEIGHBOURHOOD

Avenue de l'Observatoire – The wide avenue with its central flower borders runs on an axis with the Luxembourg Palace. It is lined with buildings belonging to the Paris V University. The **Observatory Fountain★** (1873) by Davioud is known for its famous four quarters of the globe by Carpeaux.
There is a fine view across Luxembourg Gardens towards Montmartre.

Take rue du Val-de-Grâce off the avenue to the right as you face Luxembourg Gardens.

★★**Val-de-Grâce**– The 17C buildings of the former abbey remain.
The first half of the 17C saw the establishment of religious communities: in 1605, the Carmelites; in 1612, the Ursulines; in 1622, the Feuillantines founded by Anne of Austria; in 1626, the Visitandines. The same year, Mother Angélique Arnauld ordered the construction of Port-Royal, the dependency of the Jansenist Port-Royal-des-Champs.
Anne of Austria visited the community frequently to pray and discreetly to intrigue against Richelieu. At 37, Anne, who had been married 23 years, was still childless; she promised the gift of a magnificent church if her prayers were answered, and kept her vow on the birth of Louis XIV in 1638. The plans for the church of Val-de-Grâce were drawn by **François Mansart**.
The foundation stone was laid by the young king himself in 1645. Anne, finding Mansart too slow, employed **Lemercier** to oversee the execution of his predecessor's designs, until his death. The building was at last completed by Le Muet in 1667 and consecrated in 1710 (Louis XIV was 72).
Val-de-Grâce became a military hospital in 1793.

Going out

Le Bistro Irlandais – *15 rue de la Santé – 13th arr* – ☎ *01 47 07 07 45 – Mon-Fri noon-2.30pm, 7.30pm-2am, Sat 7.30pm-2am – closed public holidays.* Posters extolling the benefits of Guinness abound in this pub, as in any pub the world over. This one also has a liberal sprinkling of charm, friendliness, good cooking and is generally a nice place to be. A little corner of Ireland spirited away to Paris.

La Closerie des Lilas – *171 blvd du Montparnasse – 6th arr* – ☎ *01 44 27 00 30 – daily 9am-1.30am.* This institution may at first seem intellectual, snobbish or intimidating, but it is in fact quite charming. Its wood panelling and sheltered terrace exude a warm, intimate atmosphere. Although all that remains of Sartre or Hemingway are their names carved into their favourite tables, it continues to be popular with some of Paris' literary names of today.

★★ **Church** ⊘ – The church, probably the most Roman-looking in France, was erected in the Jesuit style after the Sorbonne and before the Invalides. Its façade framed between consoles is articulated by pilasters supporting a double triangular pediment. The dome, shouldered by 16 pilasters is encrusted with carved elements (garlands, statues, composite capitals).

Inside, the Baroque influence is apparent in the polychrome floor, the bold entablature between arcade and deeply coffered vault and the altar baldaquin with its six twisted barley-sugar columns. The **dome★★** is frescoed by Mignard with 200 figures three times life-size. It inspired Molière to write his only poem: *La Gloire du Val de Grâce.*

The sculpture is by Michel Anguier and Philippe Buyster.

Former convent – Beyond the porch *(right of the church)* is the Classical cloister, with two superimposed tiers of bay and a mansard roof. The gardens, through the courtyard's second arch, are overlooked by the convent's majestic rear façade. The pavilion used by Anne of Austria is distinguished by its porch with ringed columns.

Musée du Service de santé des Armées ⊘ – Displays include documents and mementos of the great military physicians and the French Health Service. Models and equipment indicate treatment meted out to the wounded during the Empire and the First World War and show the progress of medical research.

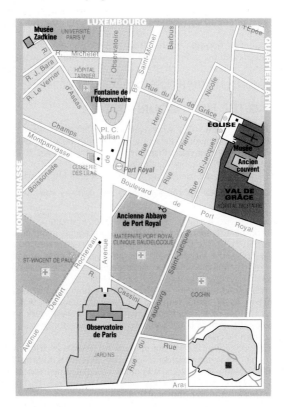

MUSEUMS AND OTHER ATTRACTIONS

PARIS MERIDIEN
2°20'17" east of Greenwich

Ancienne abbaye de Port-Royal ⊘ – *123 boulevard de Port-Royal.* The convent became in turn a prison, a home for abandoned children, and finally the Baudelocque maternity hospital in 1818. All that remains of the former abbey are the Hôtel d'Atry, the cloisters, the chapel (built by Lepautre in 1646) and the chapter-house which has retained its period wood-work.

Walk to the end of avenue de l'Observatoire.

*Observatoire de Paris ⊘ – *61 avenue de l'Observatoire.* The construction, on orders from **Colbert** and to plans by **Claude Perrault**, was begun at the summer solstice, on 21 June 1667, and completed in 1672.

Important milestones in the history of the Observatory include the calculation of the true dimensions of the solar system (1672), the exact determination of longitudinal meridians (Louis XIV remarked that the Academician's calculations had considerably reduced the extent of his kingdom), a calculation of the speed of light, the production of a large map of the moon (1679), the discovery by mathematical deduction of the planet Neptune by **Le Verrier** (1846), and the invention of new instruments (astrolabe, electronic camera).

The building – The four walls are oriented towards the cardinal points of the compass, the south side of the building determines the capital's latitude, and its median plan is bisected by the **Paris Meridian**, calculated in 1667. This determined 0° longitude until 1884 when Greenwich Mean Time was adopted generally, (with the exception of France and Ireland – 1911). The meridian is marked by 135 bronze discs laid into the street and into the floor of buildings, a memorial to **François Arago** (1786-1853) designed by Jan Dibbets for the Millennium celebrations.

A small **museum** displays old instruments in one of the garden pavilions.

Musée Zadkine ⊘ - *100 bis rue d'Assas.* Russian by birth and French by adoption, the sculptor Ossip Zadkine (1890-1967) came to Paris in 1909, after a stay in London. His works in wood and stone express anguish and anxiety. This house, now presented as a museum, was his home from 1928 to his death.

The works on display include the *Woman with a Fan*, from his Cubist period, the elm-wood sculpture of *Prometheus* and the model of his memorial to the destruction of Rotterdam *(The Destroyed City)*. Also exhibited are works from the last years of the artist's life, several busts and portraits of Van Gogh, including a plaster cast of his statue now in Auvers-sur-Oise.

QUARTIER LATIN★★★

Michelin plan 10: J 14, K 14, K 15, L 13-L 15
Ⓜ St-Michel (line 4), Cluny-la-Sorbone (line 10) or Cardinal-Lemoine (line 10) –
RER: St-Michel-Notre-Dame (lines B and C), Luxembourg (line B) –
Buses: 21, 27, 38, 82, 83, 84, 85, 86, 87, 89

This part of the Left Bank is built on the Roman – hence Latin – origins of Paris. It is here that the University has grown with its famous schools, the Sorbonne, the Panthéon and the church of St-Étienne-du-Mont as the principal landmarks. Despite being steeped in history, it is a busy and lively district and a popular meeting place.

Nearby neighbourhoods: ST-GERMAIN-DES-PRÉS, ODÉON, INSTITUT DE FRANCE, LUXEMBOURG, MAUBERT, JUSSIEU, MOUFFETARD.

Gallo-Roman Lutetia – In the 3C Lutetia was a small town of some 6 000 inhabitants: Gauls occupied the Île de la Cité, while Romans settled around the top and slopes of the rise that was later known as Montagne Ste-Geneviève. The Romans provided their community with all the usual amenities: an aqueduct stretching 15km/9mi brought water to the public baths from the Rungis plain, and a network of paved roads was built to serve the first Latin Quarter.

The medieval Alma Mater – In the 12C teachers, clerks and scholars threw off the tutelage of the bishops of the Ancien Cloître and migrated to the area around the monastic communities of Ste-Geneviève and St-Victor on the Left Bank. With authority from Pope Innocent III (1215) the group was incorporated leading to the founding of the University of Paris, the first in France.

Students were drawn from the provinces and abroad, and registered according to discipline – theology, medicine, the liberal arts, canon law – or by nationality into colleges: the Sorbon College (1257), Harcourt College (1280), the Coqueret College, the Scottish College, Clermont College (1550), Ste Barbe, Navarre and some 10 others.

Latin, as the language of educated men and lingua franca among the different nationalities, continued to be spoken by scholars and teachers in the area until the Revolution in 1789.

Place St-Michel, a favourite meeting point for students

From tutelage to autonomy – In 1793 the Convention disbanded all the universities in France. Latin ceased to be the official written language.

In 1806 Napoleon founded the Imperial University of France, with academies being made responsible for education by the State.

Gradually, the enormous influx of students made the system unworkable, and new buildings were erected (rue des Saints-Pères, Halle aux Vins, Censier) in order to decentralise the faculties (Orsay, Nanterre, Châtenay-Malabry) but this did not prevent unrest.

In **May 1968** the tension came to a head, provoked by the forced evacuation of the Sorbonne on 3 May and the closure of the main faculties on 6 May. Demonstrations and street violence left 945 injured as the area was barricaded and the students declared the Sorbonne to be a *commune libre*. Trade unions led large-scale strikes, bringing chaos to the national car industry and public transport. On 30 May President de Gaulle was forced to dissolve his government.

October 1970 saw the disappearance of the University of Paris as such and the creation, in its place of 13 autonomous universities in the Paris region, each with a full range of disciplines, its own curricula and examinations; by 1992, these had grown to 17, with a student population of 329 000.

EXPLORING THE NEIGHBOURHOOD

Quai St-Michel – No stroll along the Seine would be complete without a quick scan of the *bouquiniste* stalls – an integral part of the Paris scene. Their distinctive dark green boxes have changed little over the years, and among the second-hand books, engravings and drawings there is always a bargain to be found.

Place St-Michel – This is a popular meeting point for students and young people. The present square dates from the reign of Napoleon III, as does the fountain by Davioud. Pont St-Michel, dating from the 14C, was restored at that time. In August 1944 a number of violent scuffles broke out when students allied to the Resistance confronted German soldiers.

Around St-Séverin – This is perhaps one of the oldest quarters of Paris. **Rue de la Harpe** was the main north-south Gallo-Roman road; **rue de la Parcheminerie** (Parchment Street) was once lined with public scribes, letter-writers and copyists. Today, the bustle continues with local residents, students and tourists attracted by experimental cinemas and nightclubs, foreign-food restaurants, in search of entertainment late into the night.

Going out

La Fourmi Ailée – *8 rue du Fouarre – 5th arr – ☎ 01 43 29 40 99 – daily noon-1am (except lunch times in July and Aug)*. Two minutes from Notre-Dame, this charming tearoom is located in a former bookshop. In addition to the cakes and pastries, it also serves salads and very filling meals in a room complete with fire-place, books, old paintings and knick-knacks.

Les Trois Maillets – *56 rue Galande – 5th arr – ☎ 01 43 54 00 79 – daily 5pm-dawn*. A warm friendly feeling emanates through this former wine cellar where you can stop for a drink, dinner or even get up on the tables and dance to the sounds of world music, salsa, pop or Middle-Eastern music.

Short break

There are many cafés around place St-Michel and along the lower part of boulevard St-Michel; in springtime, place de la Sorbonne and its lively pavement cafés is the favourite haunt of students and lecturers of the nearby university.

Eating out

Turn back to the Selected restaurants section at the beginning of the guide for a list of restaurants, bistros, cafés etc. This district is in the 5th and 6th *arrondissements.*

★★ Église St-Séverin – *1 rue des Prêtres-St-Séverin*. In the 6C a hermit by the name of Séverin lived in this area, who persuaded Clodoald, grandson of King Clovis, to take holy orders. An oratory, raised to his memory, was burned down by the Normans. It was replaced first by a chapel and later by a church dedicated not to the original Séverin but to a Swiss namesake, St Severinus.

Exterior – *See illustration p 91*. Building of the present church began in the first half of the 13C. The west door dates from this era, whereas above, windows, balustrades and rose window are all 15C Flamboyant Gothic, as are the tower superstructure and spire. Work concluded in 1530.

Interior – The width of the building compared to its length is immediately striking. The extra breadth dates from the 14C and 15C when expansion was possible only laterally. The first three bays of the nave are far superior to the rest with tracery typical of the Late Gothic Rayonnant style. In the later bays, columns are reduced to shafts devoid of capitals and the tracery becomes more angular and complicated. In the chancel, the five arches around the apse stand taller than those of the nave, reaching up to the well-articulated Flamboyant vaulting. The double **ambulatory★★** encircling the chancel is a spectacular further expression of Flamboyant architecture with its bouquets of ribs rising from elegant shafts, faceted with straight or spi-ralling surfaces. Piers in the chancel are faced with marble and wood.

★ Windows – The beautiful stained glass in the upper windows is late 15C; the west end bay partly hidden by the organ illustrates a Tree of Jesse (16C); modern glass in the chevet is by Bazaine.

Boulevard St-Michel – The Boul' Mich, as it is known, is the heart of the area with its café terraces, publishing houses and bookshops – some highly specialised (arts, sciences, languages, philosophy).

Rue des Écoles – Dating from the 19C, this street takes its name from the Quartier des Écoles. The main entrances of the **Collège de France** and the **Sorbonne** are found here.

Place de la Sorbonne – Lined with cafés, bookstores and other shops, this square serves as a recreation area for students. The statue of philosopher Auguste Comte has to endure not only the ravages of time, but also the indignity of graffiti.

La Sorbonne – *47 rue des Écoles*.

History – In 1257 a college for 16 poor students who wished to study theology was founded by King Louis IX, at the instigation of his confessor, a Paris canon, Robert de Sorbon (named after his native village of Sorbon in the Ardennes). From such a simple beginning was to develop the Sorbonne, the centre of theological study in pre-Revolutionary France and the seat of the University of Paris.

Under pressure from Philip the Fair, the theological faculty condemned the Knights of the Templar which resulted in their dissolution under Clement V in 1314. During the Hundred Years War, the Sorbonne sided with the Burgundians and the English: recognising Henry V of England as King of France, they dispatched one of their most eminent members, Bishop Pierre Cauchon to Rouen as prosecutor in the trial of Joan of Arc. The Sorbonne steadfastly opposed all Protestants in the 16C and, in the 18C, all philosophers.

In May 1968, the Sorbonne was the starting point of the student uprising.

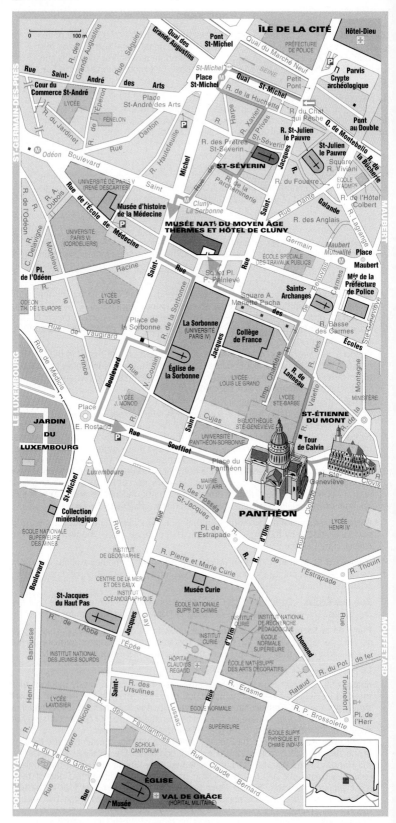

The buildings – Richelieu, elected Chancellor of the Sorbonne, put in hand the first phase of reconstruction by restoring buildings and the church (1624-42). It was well after Napoleon re-instituted the University, however, that the Sorbonne was rebuilt and expanded to become the most important university in France (between 1885 and 1901).

The complex has to accommodate 22 lecture halls, two museums, 16 examination halls, 22 seminar rooms, 37 tutorial rooms for teaching staff, 240 laboratories, a library, a physics tower, an astronomy tower, administration offices, and the chancellor's lodge. The rooms, halls and corridors are hung with historical or allegorical paintings.

The Colleges of the Latin Quarter

Whether ancient or more recent, these represent the height of the academic humanist tradition in France. A certain amount of rivalry exists between them.

Collège des Écossais – *65 rue du Cardinal-Lemoine*. The **Scottish College**, a building with a noble façade which has belonged to the Roman Catholic Church of Scotland since the 14C. It is one of the oldest colleges of the University of Paris.

Collège de Navarre - *1 rue Descartes*. Several important academic bodies have been based at this address. First founded in 1304 by Jeanne of Navarre, wife of Philip the Fair, it was originally intended for 70 poor scholars, among whom, at different times, Henri III, Henri IV, Richelieu and Bossuet were numbered! In 1794 the Convention initiated the École Polytechnique to replace a deficit in engineers. The college was transferred to Palaiseau on the outskirts of Paris, in 1977.

Collège de Montaigu – *10 place du Panthéon*. This college was known for its teaching, its austere discipline and its squalor – its scholars were said to sleep on the ground amid lice, fleas and cockroaches.

College Ste Barbe – *Rue Valette*. The last surviving building of the Latin Quarter colleges, dating from 1460.

Collège de France – *11 place Marcelin-Berthelot*. With its great past and an equal present-day reputation, this college offers free public lectures. 19C building reorganisations have been replaced in the 20C by vast additions. The college retains complete academic autonomy but has been dependent financially on the State since 1852.

★ **Église de la Sorbonne** ⊘ – The church *(see illustration p 92)* was designed by **Lemercier** between 1635 and 1642 in the Jesuit style, although here the proportions of the façade do not overwhelm the rest of the building and two, instead of three, orders are superimposed. Inside, in the chancel is the white-marble **tomb★** of Cardinal Richelieu, designed by Le Brun, and magnificently carved by **Girardon** (1694). The cupola pendentives painted with Richelieu's coat of arms, angels and Church Fathers are by Philippe de Champaigne.

Rue St-Jacques – *Behind the Sorbonne*. This street got its name from the pilgrims on their way to Compostela in Spain, who were lodged in a hostel on this site in the 14C. Today it houses the **Institut national de jeunes sourds**.

Église St-Jacques-du-Haut-Pas – *252 rue St-Jacques*. The church, built in the Classical style between 1630 and 1685, became a Jansenist centre.

Rue Soufflot – This street and the semicircular square are lined with the symmetrical block of the former Law Faculty (by Soufflot 1772) – now the offices of Paris I, Paris II and Paris V Universities – and buildings by Hittorff dating from 1844.

★★ **Église St-Étienne-du-Mont** ⊘ – *Place Ste-Geneviève*. It is in this quite unique church, known for its **rood screen★★**, the only one in existence in Paris, that St Geneviève is particularly venerated. The servants of the abbey of St Geneviève attended services in the church crypt, until their community grew to such numbers that a parish church, dedicated to St Stephen, was built adjoining the abbey church; by the end of the 15C their number had also outgrown St Stephen's. Rebuilding began with the belfry tower and apse in 1492; in 1610 the foundation stone for the new façade was laid, and in 1626 the new church was consecrated.

The **façade★★** is highly original. Three superimposed pediments stand at the centre, their lines emphasised by the upward sweep of the belfry.

Despite its date (16C) the structure is Gothic. Tall aisle walls allow for large windows; an elegant line of balusters cuts the height of the tall pillars. The Flamboyant vaulting above the transept is most eye-catching. The stained glass, which for the most part dates from the 16C and 17C, is particularly unusual in the ambulatory and chancel.

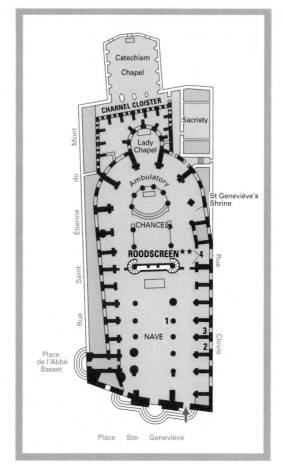

1) 1650 **pulpit★** supported by a figure of Samson.
2) **Stained-glass window★** of 1586 illustrating the parable of those invited to the feast.
3) 17C Entombment.
4) The epitaphs of Racine (by Boileau) and Pascal.

Cloisters – Also known as the Charnel Cloisters. At one time the church was bordered to the north and east by two small burial grounds. The cloisters are built off the right side of the ambulatory at the church's east end, and may at one time have been used as a charnel house. The small Catechism Chapel was added by Baltard in 1859.

Tour Calvin – *19-21 rue Valette*. This hexagonal tower (1560) stands in the courtyard of the building. It is all that remains of Fortet College where, in 1585, the Duke of Guise founded the Catholic League which was to expel Henri III from Paris.

Rue de Lanneau – *By the entrance to impasse Chartière*. Note the picturesque 16C houses.

You may continue walking to rue des Écoles to visit the Musée de Cluny.

MUSEUMS AND OTHER ATTRACTIONS

★★ Le Panthéon ⓥ – *Place du Panthéon*. The Panthéon's situation, intended function and architecture secure its popularity as a national monument and tourist attraction.

A royal vow – Louis XV, when desperately ill in Metz in 1744, vowed that should he recover he would replace the semi-ruined church of the abbey of Ste-Geneviève with a magnificent edifice built on the highest point on the Left Bank. He entrusted the fulfilment of his vow to his new Surintendant des Bâtiments, the Marquis of Marigny, brother to the Marquise de Pompadour. The project was given to his protégé, Jacques Germain **Soufflot** (1713-80), who planned a vast church 110m/361ft long by 84m/276ft wide by 83m/272ft high. The massive scale of such intentions won the architect contempt from all sides.

Foundations were laid in 1758 but a lack of funds and cracks in the structure caused by the movements of the ground meant that construction was completed only after Soufflot's death (1780) by his pupil Rondelet, in 1789.

The Temple of Fame – In April 1791 its function as a church was suspended by the Constituent Assembly in order to "receive the bodies of great men who died in the period of French liberty" – thus it became a Pantheon, where the gods of Antiquity would have lived. Voltaire and Rousseau are buried here, as were Mirabeau and Marat for a short while.

1) Saint Denis' prediction (Galand).
2) Scenes from the life of St Geneviève (Puvis de Chavannes).
3) Charlemagne crowned Emperor, and protector of the Humanities (H Lévy).
4) Miraculous Cure of Quiblinf and procession of the reliquary of St Geneviève (Maillot).
5) Battle of Tolbiac and Baptism of Clovis (J Blanc).
6) Death and funeral of St Geneviève (J-P Laurens).
7) Towards Glory (Ed. Detaille).
8) St Geneviève watching over Paris and St Geneviève bringing food to the town (Puvis de Chavannes).
9) Story of Joan of Arc (J-E Lenepveu).
10) The Concept of Fatherland, Plenty, Home and Plague (Humbert). Monument to the Unknown Heroes (Landowski).
11) The life of St Louis (Cabanel).
12) St Geneviève encourages and reassures the Parisians (Delaunay).
13) Martyrdom of St Denis (Bonnat).

Successively the Panthéon has served as a church under the Empire, a necropolis in the reign of Louis-Philippe, a church under Napoleon III, the headquarters of the Commune and finally as a lay temple to receive the ashes of Victor Hugo in 1885.

The **dome★★**, strengthened with an iron framework, can be best surveyed from a distance. Eleven steps rise to the peristyle composed of fluted columns supporting a triangular pediment, the first of its kind in Paris. This is inscribed with its dedication 'To the great men, the nation is grateful' in gold letters. Above, sculptured figures (1831) by David d'Angers represent Liberty handing crowns of laurel to the Nation to distribute among her great men: civilians on the left, the military led by Napoleon on the right. Low-relief carvings beneath the peristyle illustrate Public Education (by Lesueur, *on the left*) and Patriotic Commitment (by Chaudet, *on the right*).

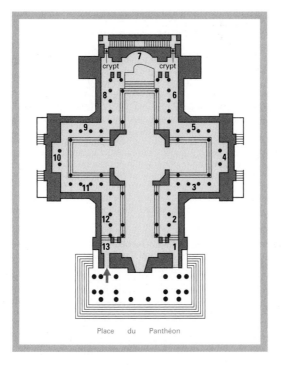

Place   du   Panthéon

Le Panthéon

Interior – Greek-cross in plan, the nave is divided from the aisles by a line of columns supporting a frieze, cornice and balustrade, roofed with flattened domes. Soufflot designed the great central dome as supported on free-standing columns but these have been substituted with heavy piers, thereby reducing the effect of weightlessness. The upper section has a fresco commissioned from Baron Antoine Jean Gros (1771-1835) by Napoleon in 1811, depicting *St Geneviève's Apotheosis*.

The walls are decorated with **paintings★** dating from 1877 onwards. The most famous are by Puvis de Chavannes and depict scenes from the life of St Geneviève. Stairs lead up to the dome from where there is a fine **view★★** over Paris.

Crypt - *Access from the east end.* The crypt extends under the full length of the building. Although strangely eerie and empty, it contains the tombs of great men in all walks of life throughout France's history: La Tour d'Auvergne, Voltaire, Rousseau, Victor Hugo, Émile Zola, Marcelin Berthelot, Louis Braille (inventor of a system of writing for the blind), Jean Jaurès, the explorer Bougainville. More recent heroes to be so honoured are the Nobel Prize winners Pierre and Marie Curie (who is also the first woman), the Resistance leader Jean Moulin and the Father of Europe Jean Monnet.

From abbots' residence to museum

About 1330, Pierre of Châlus, Abbot of Cluny-en-Bourgogne, the influential Burgundian Abbey, bought the ruins and the surrounding land to build a residence for abbots visiting Paris and for a college yet to be founded near the Sorbonne. Jacques of Amboise, Bishop of Clermont and Abbot of Jumièges in Normandy, rebuilt the house to its present design between 1485 and 1500. Hospitality was offered to many guests, including in 1515 Henry VIII's sister, Mary, widowed at 16 by the death of Louis XII of France, a man in his 50s who survived the marriage only three months. The white queen – as royal widows endured their period of mourning dressed in white – was closely watched over by Louis' cousin and successor, François I, lest she should bear a child which might cost him his throne. Indeed, when Mary was discovered one night in the company of the young Duke of Suffolk, the king compelled her to marry the Englishman in the chapel there and then before despatching her to England.

In the 17C the house accommodated the papal nuncios, the most illustrious being Mazarin.

At the Revolution the residence classed as State property was sold, passing to a variety of owners including a surgeon who used the chapel as a dissecting room, a cooper, a printer and a laundress. The City of Paris acquired the baths in 1819 and agreed to cede their rights to the land on condition that the whole be opened as a museum. In 1833 Alexandre Du Sommerard came to live in the house, installing his substantial collection of artefacts from the Middle Ages and the Renaissance. At his death in 1842 the mansion and its contents were purchased by the State; Edmond du Sommerard, son of the former owner was appointed as curator in 1844. The gardens were eventually opened to the public in 1971.

Foucault's Pendulum – In 1851 **Léon Foucault** took advantage of the dome's height to repeat publicly his experiment that proved the rotation of the earth – a discovery he had made in 1849.

His brass pendulum (28kg/62lb) hung from a steel cable (67m/220ft), deviated from its axis during oscillation in a circular movement. The direction of this movement was reversed if the experiment was conducted in the northern or southern hemisphere, hence proving his theory of the earth's rotation. The extent of the motion – nil at the Equator, 36hr at 45° latitude and 24hr at the pole – proved that the earth was spherical.

The pendulum can now be seen at the Musée National des Techniques *(see RÉPUBLIQUE)*.

★★ **Musée national du Moyen Âge – Thermes et Hôtel de Cluny** ⊘ – *6 place Paul-Painlevé.* The old residence of the abbots of Cluny, the ruins of the Roman baths and the museum's wonderful treasures, make a thoroughly interesting group.

Hôtel de Cluny – This mansion, together with the Hôtel de Sens, is one of only two large 15C private houses in Paris. Despite much restoration, original medieval details survive in features such as the wall crenellations and turrets, but it is the suggestion of a comfortable lifestyle and refined decoration that is particularly evocative.

In the main courtyard there is a fine 15C well kerb. The left wing is articulated with arches; the central building has mullioned windows; a frieze and Flamboyant balustrade, from which gargoyles spurt, line the base of the roof, ornamented with picturesque dormer windows swagged with coats of arms. A pentagonal tower juts out from the central building to contain a wide spiral staircase. There are other staircases in the corner turrets.

Concerts of medieval and baroque music are sometimes held here.

★ **Les Thermes** – Excavations have determined the plan of these **Gallo-Roman public baths** dating from AD 200. The present ruins cover about one third of the vast complex ransacked and more or less destroyed at the end of the 3C by the barbarians.

The best-preserved area is the frigidarium *(Room 12)*. Vault ribs rest on consoles carved as ships' prows – an unusual motif suggesting the idea that the building was constructed by the Paris guild of boatmen. It was this same guild that, in the reign of Tiberius (AD 14-37), dedicated a pillar to Jupiter, discovered beneath the chancel of Notre-Dame: known as **le pilier des Nautes** (Boatmen's Pillar), it is Paris' oldest existing sculpture.

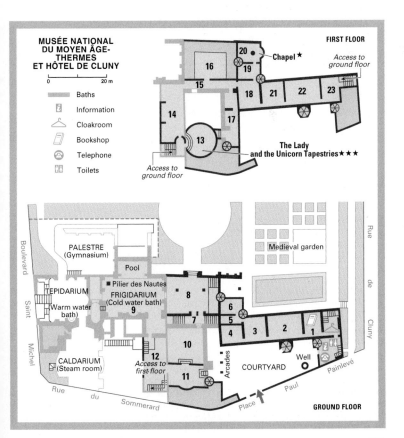

★ **Chapel** – *Room 20*. The chapel, on the first floor, was designed as the abbots' oratory. It has an elegant Flamboyant vault supported by a central column. Twelve statues of members of the Ambrose family would have stood in the niches, each with its console and carved canopy.

★★ **Museum** – The museum's 24 galleries are devoted to the Middle Ages, displaying the richness and skill of the applied arts of the period. Most of the art treasures collected evoke aspects of everyday life, notably in religious communities. These include illuminated manuscripts, furniture, arms and armour, church plate, ironwork, and stained glass.

Room 8 contains fragments of figurative sculpture from the façade of Notre-Dame: notably 21 heads of the kings of Judah from the Gallery of Kings, vandalised during the Revolution. These heads date from the mid-12C to mid-13C, and have an air of unexpected freshness and surprising intensity despite their condition.

Some of the finest masterpieces of the late Middle Ages are grouped in Room 14: the Tarascon *Pietà*, a tapestry depicting the story of the Prodigal Son; and sculptures in stone, marble and wood including two Flemish altarpieces.

La Dame à la Licorne★★★ (The Lady and the Unicorn *Room 13, 1st floor*) panels are the most exquisite examples of 15C and early-16C tapestries of the *mille-fleurs* or thousand flower design, woven in the south of the Netherlands, suggesting a love of nature, a taste for harmony and freshness of colour in the grace of the figures and animals portrayed. The six tapestries, armorial bearings of the Le Viste family from Lyon, portray the lion (chivalric nobility) and the unicorn (bourgeois nobility) on either side of a richly attired lady. Five are thought to be allegories of the senses with the sixth, to my heart's desire, showing the young woman depositing a necklace in a casket, symbolising a renouncement of such earthly, sensual pleasures.

Jardin medieval – ⊡ This garden presents medieval plants and their symbolic meaning. A clearing has been specifically designed for children.

★★ **Musée de Minéralogie** ⊘ – *60 boulevard St-Michel* The museum is in the École Supérieure des Mines, founded in 1783, which moved to its present site, the former Hôtel de Vendôme, in 1815. The **mineralogical collection** is among the world's richest: precious stones, minerals, crystals and meteorites.

Musée Curie ⊘ – *11 rue Pierre-Marie-Curie*. On the ground floor of the Physics and Chemistry Departments of the Curie Institute in the former Radium Institute, this museum collects together the Nobel Prize, papers, documents and photographs relating to the husband-wife Curie team, their daughter Irène and her husband Frédéric Joliot, and the apparatus used in their discovery of naturally occurring radioactivity, and its artificially produced counterpart (1934).

In Marie Curie's office is the lead casket which held one gram of radium presented to the scientist by women of the United States of America in 1921.

Centre de la Mer et des Eaux ⊘ – *195 rue St-Jacques*.
⊡ The centre is part of the Oceanographic Institute founded at the beginning of the 20C by Albert I of Monaco. It is devoted to marine biology, the ocean and its role and resources, presented via thematic exhibitions, films, aquaria and video games.

RÉPUBLIQUE

Michelin plan 10: G 16, G 17
Ⓜ *Temple (line 3), Réaumur-Sébastopol (lines 3 and 4), Arts-et-Métiers (lines 3 and 11), République (lines 3, 5, 8, 9 and 11)* – Buses: *20, 54, 56, 65, 74*

This neighbourhood encompasses the bustling place de la République, on the periphery of the Marais and Beaubourg, the Temple, and the Oberkampf district which, with its many bars, is a popular place for an evening out.

Nearby neighbourhoods: CANAL ST-MARTIN, FAUBOURG POISSONNIÈRE, LE MARAIS, GRANDS BOULEVARDS.

Place de la République – In 1854 **Haussmann** incorporated the small square into his grand anti-revolutionary urban scheme. The square was completed by 1862 and the **Statue to the Republic** by Morice erected in 1883. This work was favoured over Dalou's bolder composition, now at place de la Nation, who also designed the bronze low-relief sculptures around the base, representing the great events in the history of the Republic from its inception to the first 14 July national celebration in 1880.

Going out

Café Charbon – *109 rue Oberkampf – 11th arr* – ☎ *01 43 57 55 13 – daily 9am-2am – DJ from 10pm and concerts on Sunday evening – closed 1 May*. This former early-20C theatre café (which also used to sell coal – hence the name) has become one of the district's most popular venues. In a high-ceilinged room, with tall mirrors and a long bar, a young, arty crowd flocks here for a drink or brunch, to the sounds of the latest hits and world music.

Le Blue Billard – *111 rue St-Maur – 11th arr* – ☎ *01 43 55 87 21 – daily 11am-2am and every last Fri-Sat of the month 11am-4am*. Even before the Oberkampf neighbourhood had reached its current fashionable status, the Blue Billard was catering to the capital's snooker and billiards fans. Today it still provides some 20 or so French and American billiard tables, delicious cocktails and pleasant relaxed atmosphere. Louisiana restaurant with Cajun specialities.

Le Cithéa – *114 rue Oberkampf – 11th arr* – ☎ *01 40 21 70 95 – daily 10pm-5.30am – closed 1 Jan and 25 Dec*. This former cinema-theatre has become one of the trendiest places in town. A predominantly young and cool clique meets here to drink, dance and listen to live music every night: acid jazz, house, funk, soul or world music. Packed at the weekend.

Le Gibus – *18 rue du Fg-du-Temple – 11th arr* – ☎ *01 47 00 78 88 – Tue-Sat and the day before public holidays midnight-dawn*. This former rock temple is now devoted to techno and house music and every week a succession of the best DJs around ensure that a half-gay, half-straight clientele spend their nights in feverish dancing. Trendy but not exclusively clubby, it is focused first and foremost on dance in a low-ceilinged, concrete setting (for some it is a suffocating garage atmosphere, for others, pure heaven).

Le Scherkhan – *144 rue Oberkampf – 11th arr* – ☎ *01 43 57 29 34 – daily 5pm-2am – closed 1 Jan and 25 Dec*. In homage to *The Jungle Book*, a stuffed tiger stands threateningly at the entrance of this bar. This dark, trendy bar is nonetheless calm and peaceful and decorated in a pleasant pseudo-exotic style. Perfect to meet friends for a quiet drink, to the sound of jazz.

Web Bar – *32 rue de Picardie – 3rd arr* – ☎ *01 42 72 66 55 – Mon-Fri 8.30pm-2am, Sat and Sun 11am-1am*. This former jeweller's workshop is now the gem of Paris' cyber-cafés, thanks to some 20 computers connected to the web. In addition, under a large glass ceiling with metal beams, there is always a wide range of activities going on: salsa lessons, funk, jazz or theme evenings, exhibitions, shows and of course, direct broadcasts of Internet events. An unexpected, magical place that is quite delightful.

Shopping

La Bague de Kenza – *106 rue St-Maur – 11th arr* – Ⓜ *Parmentier* – ☎ *01 43 14 93 95 – 9am-9pm*. This Algerian pastry shop, quite unique in Paris, sells high-quality, subtly flavoured cakes and pastries, together with a wide range of breads, some of which are exclusive to the house. Particularly in vogue with the press and fine gourmets, famous and otherwise.

Rougier and Plé – *13 blvd des Filles-du-Calvaire – 3rd arr* – Ⓜ *Filles-du-Calvaire* – ☎ *01 44 54 81 00 – Mon-Sat 9.30am-7pm – closed public holidays*. Arts and crafts galore! Three floors with everything you could need for bookbinding, printing, drawing, graphics, modelling etc. If you are looking for a bag of colourful feathers to adorn your hat, or a glass-paste gem to repair your favourite brooch, this is the place.

Eating out

Turn back to the Selected restaurants section at the beginning of the guide for a list of restaurants, bistros, cafés etc. This district is in the 3rd and 11th *arrondissements*.

Oberkampf: one of the trendiest parts of Paris

From place de la République, go up avenue de la République to rue Oberkampf (7th road on the left). Rue Oberkampf and the surrounding streets (rue Saint-Maur, rue Jean-Pierre-Timbaud) are a long string of bars, some styled to recreate the atmosphere of Ménilmontant at the turn of the 20C, others with more modern decor. Greatly in favour with young, cool Parisians.

The Knights Templars

In 1140 the religious and military order, founded in 1118 in the Holy Land by nine knights to protect pilgrims and known as the **Order of Knights Templars**, established a house in Paris. Independent of any ruling monarch, they were soon entrusted with great wealth, underpinning a substantial and unrivalled international banking system. By the 13C their property investments counted almost one quarter of the land area of Paris – including all the Marais neighbourhood.

Philip the Fair decided to suppress this state within a state. On 13 October 1307, all the Templars in France were arrested, including the leader, Jacques de Molay, and 140 knights were imprisoned in Paris. Having been granted authority by the Pope, the king dissolved the order and had Molay together with 54 knights burnt at the stake. Two-thirds of the estates were confiscated by the Crown, the rest was given to the Knights of St John of Jerusalem, later known as the Knights of Malta.

Quartier du Temple – This quarter was once the domain of the Knights Templars and the Benedictines from St Martin-des-Champs. Today it is a busy business district: shops and restaurants; garment wholesale, retail and manufacture; and a renowned technical training school.

The Temple Prison – On 13 August 1792, the royal family were all imprisoned in the Temple Tower. On 20 January 1793, Louis XVI was condemned by the Convention and sent to the guillotine. On 2 August, the queen was transferred to the Conciergerie; she left only to go to the guillotine on 16 October.

EXPLORING THE NEIGHBOURHOOD

Start from Réaumur-Sébastopol metro station.

★★ **Conservatoire national des Arts et Métiers** – *292 rue St-Martin*. This former Benedictine priory dedicated to St-Martin-des-Champs became the Conservatoire, created by the Convention in 1794, and installed in the priory in 1799. It is an institution for technical instruction, a considerable industrial museum and a laboratory for industrial experiment.

In rue du Vertbois, a **watchtower** *(échauguette)* and fragments of the medieval (1273) priory wall can be seen.

In the courtyard, on the right, the present library, once the monastery **refectory★★**, was designed by **Pierre de Montreuil** (13C). Inside, seven slender columns run down the centre bisecting the space, articulated into perfect proportions with elegant Gothic lines. The doorway half way down the right side has delightful carvings on the outside.

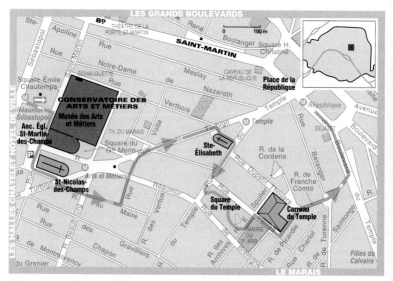

Turn left in rue de Turbigo to approach the former **Église St-Martin-des-Champs★** with its Romanesque east end (1130 – restored), fine capitals, belfry, and Gothic nave.

★ **Église St-Nicolas-des-Champs** – *252 bis rue St-Martin.* The church was built in the 12C by the priory of St Martin-des-Champs for the monastery servants and neighbouring peasants. It was rebuilt in the 15C and enlarged in the 16C and 17C. The façade and belfry are Flamboyant Gothic, the south door is Renaissance (1581).

Inside, in the chancel and chapels hang a considerable number of 17C, 18C and 19C paintings; on the double-sided altar is a retable by Simon Vouet (16C) and four angels by the 17C sculptor, Sarrazin. The fine Paris-made organ was rebuilt in the 18C.

Place de la République

Walk along rue au Maire, then turn left onto rue Volta and right onto rue de Turbigo which leads to the back of Ste-Élisabeth, walk round the church.

Église Ste-Élisabeth – This former monastic chapel (1628-46) dedicated to St Elisabeth of Hungary is now the church of the Knights of Malta. Of particular interest are the 100 early-16C Flemish low-relief sculptures depicting biblical scenes around the ambulatory.

Square and Carreau du Temple ⊙ – To the left of the town hall is the Carreau, a street market which is lined, like the surrounding Picardie, Corderie and Dupetit-Thouars streets, with clothes, costume and fancy clothes shops, and stalls and stores selling household linens.

MUSEUMS AND OTHER ATTRACTIONS

★★ **Musée des Arts et métiers** ⊙ – The museum illustrates technical progress in industry and science. Extensive collections of period pieces include full-scale machines and reduced scale models.

The visit begins with instruments used to explore the **infinitesimal** and **infinitely remote**. Next come **machines** which turn out daily life objects but also works of art. One floor below, models show **building techniques**. The next theme is **communication** illustrated through printing, television, photography, computing etc. The theme of **energy** is represented by mills, a model of the Marly machine (1678-85), turbines, boilers and various engines, whereas **locomotion** explores all means of transport: cycles, cars, aircraft (including Blériot's with which he crossed the channel) and 19C railways.

Back to the ground floor and the chapel with its magnificent vaulting. Displayed here are the first steam buses, a model of the Statue of Liberty, of the engine of the European rocket Ariane and of Foucault's pendulum that proved the rotation of the earth.

The finest exhibits include **Pascal's arithmetic machine** (1642), **Edison's phonograph** (1878), the **magic lantern** used by the **Lumière brothers** in 1895, Volta's battery (1800), an **automata theatre** which brings back to life Marie-Antoinette's dulcimer-playing puppet of 1784, Clément Ader's plane...

Faubourg SAINT-ANTOINE

Ⓜ *Bastille (lines 1, 5 and 8), Ledru-Rollin (line 8), Faidherbe-Chaligny (line 8)
or Nation (lines 1, 2, 6 and 9) – RER: Nation (line A)
Buses: 20, 65, 69, 76, 86, 87, 91*

The old densely populated streets around the Faubourg St-Antoine have been the centre of the cabinetmaking industry for centuries, and today they retain the charm of their former days. St-Antoine is also the name of a succulent pastry.

Nearby neighbourhoods: BASTILLE.

History – The neighbourhood grew up round the fortified Royal Abbey of St Antoine, founded in 1198. Louis XI further added to the abbey's privileges by giving it power to dispense justice locally and allowing the craftsmen in the vicinity to work outside the established powerful and highly restrictive guilds. From 1657, the cabinetmakers of St-Antoine were licensed by Colbert to replicate or adapt pieces from the royal workshops, to employ exotic woods such as mahogany and ebony instead of being bound to oak, and to develop the decorative use of bronze and marquetry.

At 31 rue de Montreuil, **Réveillon** pioneered the production of painted wallpapers. Soon his workshop employed 400 people. Crowded conditions provoked social unrest that erupted into violence on 28 April 1789, forcing the industrialist to flee.

In the workshop courtyard on 19 October 1783 **Pilâtre de Rozier** made the first lift-off in a paper balloon inflated with hot air and tethered by a cable.

Incorporated guilds were abolished at the time of the Revolution. In the face of mechanisation and labour-saving industrial processes, traditional multi-skilled craftsmen had to evolve specialised trades to survive. Small workshops abounded, but still in June 1848 when the national workshops were disbanded, the unemployed rallied to build numerous barricades in protest, leading to further violence in the Faubourg.

EXPLORING THE NEIGHBOURHOOD

Start from place de la Bastille.

Rue du Faubourg-St-Antoine – The street is lined with furniture shops and the surrounding area honeycombed with courtyards and arcades, often with picturesque names (Le Bel-Air, l'Étoile d'Or, les Trois-Frères, l'Ours, la Bonne-Graine).

Passage de la Boule Blanche at no 50 opens onto the entrance of the **Quinze Vingts Hospital** (Fifteen Twenty Hospital) at no 28 rue de Charenton. St Louis founded the hospital for 300 destitute blind people near the Louvre. It was later transferred to these 18C buildings which formerly served as barracks, erected by Robert de Cotte. **Fontaine Trogneux**, on the corner with rue de Charonne, is an attractive fountain from 1710.

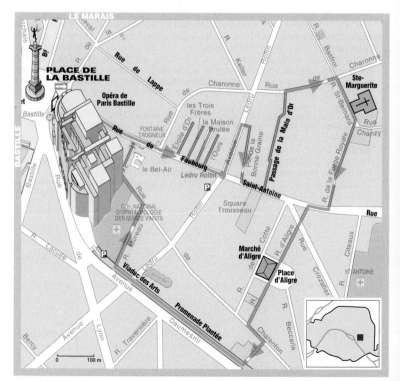

Going out

China Club – *50 rue de Charenton – 12th arr –* ☎ *01 43 43 82 02 – china-fum@imaginet.fr – Sun-Thu 7pm-2am, Fri-Sat 7pm-3am – closed 1 Jan, 25 Dec and Aug.* After a 1930s Shanghai-style facelift, this former workshop of the Faubourg St-Antoine sets out to recreate the exotic, sophisticated atmosphere of a past colonial era, even in the toilets. The effect is on the whole very pleasing. A traditionally hip, young crowd of Bastille night-birds gathers here in one of three areas: upstairs, the *fumoir* (smoking room), down in the basement is the Sing-Sang bar, very cosy with concerts at the weekend and, on the ground floor, a restaurant with a long bar and roomy Chesterfield sofas.

Sanz Sans – *49 rue du Fg-St-Antoine – 11th arr –* ☎ *01 44 75 78 78 – www.sanzsans.com – daily 9am-2am – closed Sun lunch and 25 Dec.* If you were planning on slipping in unnoticed here, forget it! A camera films all those who pass the threshold and projects them up on a giant screen in the handsome rear room. Kitsch decor, drapes, armchairs, loud music (hip hop, soul and dance) and DJs: it is fashionable, often noisy, but nonetheless worth a visit and good fun.

Market

Marché d'Aligre – *Pl. d'Aligre – 12th arr –* Ⓜ *Ledru-Rollin – daily except Mon.* Large, noisy, colourful market.

Shopping

L'Arbre à Lettres – *62 rue du Fg-St-Antoine – 12th arr –* Ⓜ *Ledru-Rollin – other shops: 33-35 blvd du Temple 3rd arr; 2 rue Édouard-Quenu 5th arr; 14 rue Boulard 14th arr –* ☎ *01 53 33 83 23 – Mon-Sat 10am-8pm, Sun 2.30-7pm – closed public holidays.* A little chain of bookshops that has acquired a following of faithful regulars. An efficient and extremely well-read staff, presentations of new books, together with a selection of the house's favourite authors. Excellent children's section.

Eating out

Turn back to the Selected restaurants section at the beginning of the guide for a list of restaurants, bistros cafés, etc. This district is in the 11th and 12th *arrondissements.*

Passage de la Main-d'Or – *133 rue du Faubourg-St-Antoine.* Typical of the old quarter, this arcade comes out onto rue de Charonne.

Walk to the rue de Charonne exit, turn right, continue to rue St-Bernard and turn right again.

Some of the great Ébénistes

Associated with the Louis XV and Louis XVI style are the following:

André Boulle (1642-1732): furniture supplier to the court, the most distinctive feature is the exquisite quality of brass and tortoiseshell inlay. His style enjoyed a revival during the Second Empire.

Charles Cressent (1685-1768): his bureaux and commodes are perhaps the most elegant of the Regency style, embellished with curvilinear ornamental ormolu (gilded bronze) mounts.

Jean-François Oeben (1720-63): the master of Riesener and Leleu, marks the transition between the Louis XV and Louis XVI styles. His intricate geometric marquetry and furniture with hidden mechanisms are particularly famous.

Jean-François Leleu (1729-1807): the master of the Louis XVI style at its most grandiose, rich in ormolu *appliqués* to complement overall design.

Jean Riesener (1734-1806): 30 workshops and retail outlets on rue St-Honoré. He was one of the innovators of the Louis XVI style and highly successful. His mahogany chests of drawers and *bureaux* with bronze mounts are distinctively sober in form and line.

Georges Jacob (1739-1814): established near Porte St-Martin, he dominates furniture design between Louis XVI and the First Empire. Renowned for his armchairs, he is credited with the invention of the *fauteuil à la reine.*

Église Ste-Marguerite – *36 rue St-Bernard.* The interior of this church, built in the 17C and enlarged in the 18C, is disparate in style; the low basket-arch vaulted nave contrasts with the tall and bright chancel. The marble *Pietà* (1705) behind the high altar is by Girardon, a fragment of a tomb intended for his wife; to the left of the chancel, the chapel dedicated to the Damned Souls has unusual *trompe-l'œil* frescoes (1765) by Brunetti. Both transept chapels contain large 18C canvases depicting St-Vincent-de-Paul.

Follow rue de la Forge-Royale, cross rue du Faubourg-St-Antoine and continue along rue d'Aligre.

Place d'Aligre – A daily market is held here *(mornings only)* for vegetables, cheap clothes and bric-a-brac.

Continue along rue d'Aligre, cross rue de Charenton and walk along rue Malot which leads to the Viaduc des Arts and Promenade plantée.

★**Promenade Plantée** – *Avenue Daumesnil, above the Viaduc des Arts. Access by stairs.* The railway has been transformed into a walkway with trees, gardens and shaded arbours, running all the way to the Bois de Vincennes. Lime trees, hazelnut trees, climbers, rose bushes and aromatic plants create a rural setting.

★**Viaduc des Arts** – *Avenue Daumesnil.* This stone and pink-brick viaduct used to carry the old suburban railway from the Bastille. Recently restored, its 60 vaulted archways accommodate a wide variety of businesses – silver and **goldsmiths**, cabinetmakers, fine art and sculpture restorers, designers of contemporary furniture, wrought-ironwork, interiors and soft-furnishings, and computer shops.

NEARBY

Place de la Nation – This was originally named the Throne Square in honour of the state entry made by Louis XIV and his bride, the Infanta Maria-Theresa, on 26 August 1660, when a throne was erected at which the King received due homage from the City of Paris. It was renamed place du Trône-Renversé (the Overturned Throne) by the Convention in 1794, when a guillotine was erected there, and it was here that the throne of Louis-Philippe was ceremoniously burnt in July 1848. It was given its present name on 14 July 1880, the first anniversary celebrations of the Revolution. It had been Napoleon's original intention to extend the Triumphal Way from the Arc de Triomphe to place de la Nation, but this was not to be.

★**Le Triomphe de la République** – *At the centre of the square.* **Dalou** (1838-1902), recently returned from England, took 20 years to perfect the composition of his monumental bronze group, 11m/36ft high and 38t in weight. Originally intended for place de la République, the sculpture seems out of proportion with its context. An allegory of the Republic borne by a chariot drawn by lions, is flanked by Work and Justice. Peace, perhaps the best-rendered figure, is slightly set back.

The two columns on either side of avenue du Trône were designed by Ledoux, and were subsequently topped with statues of Philippe Auguste and St Louis.

Cimetière de Picpus – In 1794, the guillotine installed in place de la Nation claimed 1 306 victims, including the poet André Chénier. The bodies were placed in two communal graves located in a sand quarry nearby. Later on, the families of the victims bought the surrounding ground and turned it into a cemetery. Most of the graves are inscribed with names from the French aristocracy. The *champ des martyrs* (martyrs' field), planted with cypress trees, can be seen through a railing.

Faubourg SAINT-GERMAIN★★

Michelin plan 10: H 10 – H 12, J 10 – J 12
Ⓜ *Assemblée-Nationale (line 12), Solférino (line 12), Varenne (line 13)*
RER: Musée d'Orsay (line C) – Buses: 73, 83, 84, 94

The Faubourg St-Germain was originally, as its name implies, the suburb *(faubourg)* of the town which developed round the abbey of St-Germain-des-Prés. The Revolution closed its sumptuous town houses and the quarter never fully regained its status. Only through a half-open door will you glimpse the beautiful façades erected by Delisle-Mansart, Boffrand or other 18C architects.

Nearby neighbourhoods: ST-GERMAIN-DES-PRÉS, MUSÉE D'ORSAY, INVALIDES, SÈVRES-BABYLONE.

History – Until the end of the 16C the surrounding countryside was used for farming and hunting; except for a strip of meadow at the river's edge finally won from the abbey of St-Germain-des-Prés by the university and rebaptised the Pré aux Clercs (Scholars' Meadow).

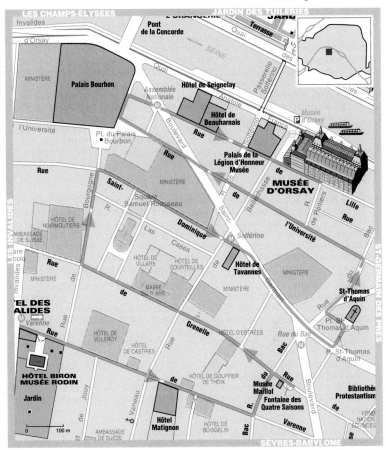

In the 17C Marguerite of Valois, first wife of Henri IV, took the east end of the meadow from the university as part of the grounds in which to build a vast mansion with a garden running down to the Seine. The acquisition was made so casually that the embankment came to be called the *Malacquis* (distorted to *Malaquais*) or Misappropriated Quay. On the death of Queen Marguerite in 1615 the university tried to reclaim the land but, after 20 years of legal proceedings, succeeded only in having the main street of the new quarter named rue de l'Université.

The district was at its most fashionable in the 18C. Noble lords and rich financiers built houses which gave the streets an individual character: one monumental entrance followed another, each opening onto a courtyard closed at the far end by the façade of an elegant mansion, beyond which lay a large garden.

The Revolution closed these sumptuous town houses and although they reopened their doors at the Restoration, fashionable society had migrated to the Champs-Élysées at the time of Louis-Philippe and Napoleon III.

Several mansions were pulled down when boulevard St-Germain and boulevard Raspail were opened. The finest houses remaining now belong to the State or serve as ambassadorial residences. Something of the quarter's great days can, however, still be recalled in rue de Lille, rue de Grenelle and rue de Varenne.

EXPLORING THE NEIGHBOURHOOD

This area includes the buildings that house the French Government headquarters, the Assemblée Nationale and several sumptuous 18C residential houses, now mainly serving official functions.

Rue de Varenne – The street was laid along a rabbit warren (*garenne* which evolved, in time, to Varenne) belonging to the abbey of St-Germain-des-Prés. There are several attractive old houses in this street: at no 73 the great Hôtel de Broglie (1735); nos 78-80, the Hôtel de Villeroy (1724), now the Ministry of Agriculture; no 72, the large Hôtel de Castries (1700). No 56, the Hôtel de Gouffier de Thoix, has a magnificent doorway ornamented with a shell carving. No 47, the Hôtel de Boisgelin is now the Italian Embassy.

The most famous house, of course, is the **Hôtel Matignon** at no 57, built by Courtonne in 1721 but since considerably remodelled. Talleyrand, diplomat and statesman to successive regimes, owned it from 1808 to 1811, then Madame Adelaïde, sister to Louis-Philippe. Between 1884 and 1914 it housed the Austro-Hungarian Embassy, in 1935 it became the office of the President of the Council of Ministers (as the prime minister was known at the time) and in 1958 the Paris residence of the prime minister. **Edith Wharton** (1862-1937), author of **The Age of Innocence**, lived at both no 53 and no 58 rue de Varenne for 13 years (1907-20) before moving north to the Pavillon Colombe near the Montmorency Forest. At the heart of literary circles that included Morton Fullerton, Henry James, André Gide, she entertained the upper-class Faubourg society in the manner of a Belle Epoque salon hostess. She is buried in the city of Versailles.

★★ Hôtel Biron – *77 rue de Varenne*. The mansion dates from the 18C. Among its proprietors was the poet Rainer Maria Rilke, a friend of Rodin. Later, the premises was used by a convent for the education of young girls from good families. After the Congregation Law of 1904, under which many convents were disbanded, the educational buildings and part of the gardens were given to the Lycée Victor-Duruy. The house was made available by the State to artists. Thus Auguste Rodin came to live there until his death in 1917, leaving much of his work to the Nation in lieu of rent.

Rue de Grenelle – The beautiful **Fontaine des Quatre-Saisons★** stands outside nos 59-61. Carved by **Bouchardon** between 1739 and 1745, this grand fountain was commissioned by Turgot, the dean of the local merchants' guild and father of Louis XVI's minister, in answer to complaints that the stately quarter was almost totally without water.

A seated figure of Paris looking down onto reclining personifications of the River Seine and River Marne adorn the ornate Ionic pillared fountain front. The sides are decorated with figures of the Seasons and delightful low-relief sculptures showing cherubs performing the seasons' labours.

Behind the fountain is the house where **Alfred de Musset**, the Romantic poet, lived from 1824 to 1839, during which time he wrote most of his plays and dramatic poetry.

At no 79 stands the great **Hôtel d'Estrées** (1713); no 85 is the **Hôtel d'Avaray** (1728), the Royal Netherlands Embassy; the **Pentémont Temple** with its Ionic cupola of 1750 was at one time a convent chapel, the nuns were replaced by the Imperial Guard and these, by the civil servants of the Ministry of War Veterans; no 110, the **Hôtel de Courteilles** (1778), dominating the street with its massive façade, is now the Ministry of Education; no 116 was built in 1709 for Marshal de Villars and considerably remodelled; no 118 is the much smaller **Hôtel de Villars**, built in 1712 and extremely elegant with twin garlanded, oval windows; no 136, the **Hôtel de Noirmoutiers** (1722), at one time the army staff headquarters was the house in which Marshal Foch died on 20 March 1929. The mansion now serves as the official residence of the *préfet* of the Île-de-France region.

Turn right onto rue de Bourgogne, then right again along rue St-Dominique towards boulevard St-Germain.

Hôtel de Tavannes ⏱ – *5 rue St-Dominique*. This mansion has a fine round arched doorway surmounted by a scallop and crowned by a triangular pediment. It housed a literary salon held by a Russian, Madame Swetchine, in the early 19C. The artist, Gustave Doré, died in the house in 1883. Inside there is a fine stairwell with a wrought-iron balustrade.

Turn right onto boulevard St-Germain then left along rue St-Thomas-d'Aquin.

Église St-Thomas d'Aquin – *Place St-Thomas-d'Aquin*. The church, formerly the chapel of the Dominican noviciate monastery, was begun in 1682 in the Jesuit style to plans by Pierre Bullet. The façade was completed only in 1769. Inside are 17C and 18C paintings and a ceiling (apsidal chapel) painted by Lemoyne in 1723 of the Transfiguration. The sacristy has Louis XV panelling.

Rue du Bac – At no 44 lived **André Malraux**, who in 1933 wrote *La Condition humaine*, the novel for which he received a Nobel Prize for Literature.

Rue de l'Université – The main thoroughfare through the old quarter. At no 51 is the Hôtel de Soyecourt built in 1707, no 78 was built in 1687 and no 82 is where the poet Lamartine resided between 1837 and 1853.

Rue de Lille – This street, named after the town of Lille, is typical of the old noble *faubourg*. Nos 80 and 78 were designed by the architect Boffrand in 1714. The first, the **Hôtel de Seignelay**, occupied by the Ministry of Commerce and Tourism, was owned originally by Colbert's grandson, then by the Duke of Charost, tutor to the young Louis XV and aristocrat philanthropist who was saved from the guillotine by his own peasants. By 1839 it had passed to Marshal Lauriston, a descendant of John Law, the Scots financier.

The **Hôtel de Beauharnais**, next door, received its name when Napoleon's stepson bought it in 1803 and redecorated it sumptuously for his own and his sister Queen Hortense's use. Since 1818 the house has been the seat of first the Prussian, and later, the German diplomatic missions to France. Now restored, it is the residence of the German ambassador. Other buildings of interest include no **71** the Hôtel de Mouchy (1775), and no **67** the Hôtel du Président Duret (1706). The writer **Jules Romain** lived at no **6** rue de Solférino from 1947 to his death (1972).

Going out

Café des Lettres – *53 rue de Verneuil – 7th arr – ☎ 01 42 22 52 17 – Mon-Fri 9am-midnight, Sat 11am-midnight, Sun noon-4pm – closed 1 May and 1 week at Christmas.* Located in the 18C Hôtel d'Avejan, headquarters of the House of Writers and of the National Book Centre, this little café has a terrace in the hotel's inner courtyard where you can stop for a drink in the summer outside the normal restaurant hours. Scandinavian brunch on Sundays.

Shopping

Barthélémy – *51 rue de Grenelle – 7th arr – Ⓜ Rue-du-Bac – ☎ 01 45 48 56 75 – Tue-Fri 8am-1pm, 3.30-7.15pm, Sat 8am-1.30pm, 3-7.15pm – closed Aug and public holidays.* Barthélémy is not only one of the best cheese merchants in town, he is also a man who adores sharing his love of cheese. This magnificent shop has retained its original 1900 decor.

Eating out

Les Jardins de Varenne du Musée Rodin – *77 rue de Varenne – 7th arr –* Ⓜ *Varenne - ☎ 01 45 50 42 34 – rodin@soustart-horeto.com – closed evenings and Mon – 15.25/22.87€.* The museum's lovely gardens conceal a pavilion with a charming shaded terrace where visitors can enjoy a mixed salad and a choice of sandwiches... a delightful break!

Turn back to the Selected restaurants section at the beginning of the guide for a list of restaurants, bistros, cafés etc. This district is in the 7th *arrondissement*.

MUSEUMS AND OTHER ATTRACTIONS

★★★**Musée d'Orsay** – *see Musée d'ORSAY.*

★★**Musée Rodin** Ⓥ – The house and garden enable one to see Rodin's sculptures in a perfect residential setting.

Rodin's sculpture, primarily figurative in terracotta, bronze and white marble, is immensely striking, vital and lifelike. Creation, in the guise of restless figures emerging from the roughly hewn rock, was a favourite theme **(Hand of God)** although it was his renderings of the nude that demonstrated his true technical genius **(St John the Baptist)** and won him public acclaim in 1879.

On the ground floor are some of his most expressive works: **The Cathedral, The Kiss, The Walking Man** and **The Man with a Broken Nose** – which was rejected from the Salon of 1864. At either end of the gallery, in corresponding rotundas which have kept their fine panelling, are **Eve** and the **Age of Bronze**. One room is devoted to drawings by the artist which are exhibited in rotation.

La Cathédrale, Rodin

Musée Rodin/B. JARRET

At the top of the beautiful 18C staircase, on the first floor, are smaller works: the plaster *maquettes* for the large groups and for the statues of **Balzac** and **Victor Hugo**. It is in the **garden**, however, that the most famous sculptures which established Rodin's reputation as a grand master during his own lifetime are to be seen: **The Thinker**, **The Burghers of Calais**, **The Gates of Hell** and the **Ugolin group**.

Personal artefacts and collections of furniture, pictures and antiquities belonging to the artist are displayed throughout the house and in the former chapel *(temporary exhibitions)*.

The latest acquisition to be made by the museum is Camille Claudel's **The Wave**, a composite work in onyx and bronze. The museum also houses three works by Van Gogh.

★ **Musée Maillol** ⊙ -*59 rue de Grenelle.* This museum draws from the private collection of Dina Vierny, once model of Maillol and eminent art dealer. It comprises not only the paintings and sculptures of her Catalan mentor, **Aristide Maillol** (1861-1944), but those of several of his contemporaries: Bonnard, Cézanne, Degas, Duchamp, Dufy, Gauguin, Kandinski, Renoir, Rousseau, Poliakoff.

This small body of important 20C art is complemented by a contemporary Soviet collection including the Communal Kitchen re-created by Ilya Kabakov. Russian by origin, Dina Vierny was instrumental in introducing Soviet artists to the European art markets during the early 1970s.

This foundation is also responsible for the donation in 1964 of 18 magnificent female nude bronze sculptures by Maillol now in the Tuileries Gardens. Two additional figures have recently been given.

★ **Palais Bourbon** ⊙ – 33 *quai d'Orsay.* In 1722 the Duchess of Bourbon, daughter of **Louis XIV** and **Mme de Montespan**, acquired land on which to build a house fronting onto rue de l'Université. By 1728 the palace and terraced gardens running down to the Seine were complete.

Twenty-eight years later Louis XV bought the property so that it could be altered to form part of the general scheme of place de la Concorde; in 1764, however, Louis XVI sold it to the Prince of Condé who enlarged and embellished it. Finally, the adjoining **Hôtel de Lassay** was added and renamed Le Petit Bourbon.

Work was almost finished when the Revolution broke out. The palace was confiscated to serve as a chamber for the Council of the Five Hundred. Next it was used to house archives, before serving as accommodation for the École Polytechnique. In 1807 Napoleon commissioned Poyet to design the present façade overlooking place de la Concorde in harmony with the Greek plan of the Madeleine Church. At the Restoration the palace was returned to the Condé family, only to be bought back in 1827 and converted for use by the Legislative Assembly.

Exterior – The Antique-style façade with a portico is decorated with an allegorical pediment by Cortot (1842), statues *(copies)*, on high, of Minerva by Houdon and Themis by Roland, and below, among other figures, those of Henri IV and Louis XIV's ministers, Sully and **Colbert**. The allegorical low-relief sculptures on the wings are by Rude *(right)* and Pradier *(left)*.

Interior – Among the most impressive of the many rooms decorated with paintings and sculpture, are the lobby, with its ceiling by Horace Vernet, the Council Chamber and the **Library★★**. This is a fine room in itself; added to which it is magnificently decorated with a History of Civilization, painted by **Delacroix** between 1838 and 1845. Houdon's portrait busts of Voltaire and Diderot are also in the library.

Salle des Séances (Council Chamber) – Proceedings are conducted by the President of the **National Assembly** from the *bureau* formerly used for the Council of the Five Hundred *(see above)*. He faces the deputies – 577 when all are present – seated on benches arranged in a semicircle. Government members occupy the front bench below the speaker's stand (note – the political right and left are as viewed by the president and therefore the reverse as seen from the gallery).

Palais de la Légion d'honneur – 2 *rue de Bellechasse. Closed for restoration.* The **Hôtel de Salm** was built in 1786 and was owned by various people until it was acquired by Napoleon, who made the mansion the Palace of the Legion of Honour in 1804. It was burnt during the Commune of 1871 and rebuilt, in 1878, by the members of the Legion to the original plans.

At the back of the palace, overlooking the river, there is a delightful semicircular pavilion in complete contrast to the severe lines of the main building.

★ **Musée de la Légion d'honneur** ⊙ – The museum presents original documents, decorations, pictures, uniforms and arms illustrating the orders of chivalry and nobility of pre-Revolutionary France (the Star, St Michael, the Holy Spirit, St Louis); the creation of the Legion of Honour by Napoleon on 19 May 1802, its rapid expansion during the Empire (personal decorations of Bonaparte and his brothers, educational establishments) and its subsequent history. Further galleries show other French civil and military decorations: academic prizes, the Military Medal, Military Cross, the Cross of the Liberation, Order of Merit, Order of Malta.

SAINT-GERMAIN-DES-PRÉS★★

Michelin plan 10: J 13
Ⓜ *St-Germain-des-Prés (line 4) – Buses: 39, 63, 70, 86, 87, 95, 96*

This old quarter on the Left Bank is known for its beautiful church as well as for its narrow streets, antique shops, restaurants, cafés and jazz clubs. Musicians, artists and intellectuals frequented the district in the post-war years.

Nearby neighbourhoods: ODÉON, QUARTIER LATIN, INSTITUT DE FRANCE, FAUBOURG ST-GERMAIN, SÈVRES-BABYLONE, ST-SULPICE, MONTPARNASSE, MUSÉE D'ORSAY.

A powerful abbey – Founded in the 8C, St-Germain-des-Prés was a link in the prodigious chain across Europe of 17 000 Benedictine abbeys and priories. It became sovereign ruler of its domain, answerable in spiritual matters to the Pope alone. The monastery was sacked four times in 40 years by the Normans but each time it was rebuilt and enlarged. In the 14C, when Charles V enclosed the city, the abbey fortified itself with crenellated walls, towers and a moat linked to the Seine.

From 1674 the abbey was used as a State prison, and at the Revolution it was finally suppressed: the rich library was confiscated, the church, from which the royal tombs disappeared, was turned into saltpetre works, whereas other buildings were sold, demolished or burnt.

EXPLORING THE NEIGHBOURHOOD

① An afternoon in St-Germain-des-Prés

Place du Québec – Charles Daudelin's fountain reproduces the effect of the snowmelt breaking up great layers of ice, reminiscent of Canadian winters.

Famous jewellers (Cartier) and fashion houses (Armani) set up sumptuous boutiques in the area in 1998. This could mean a page is being turned in the history of this one-time literary mecca.

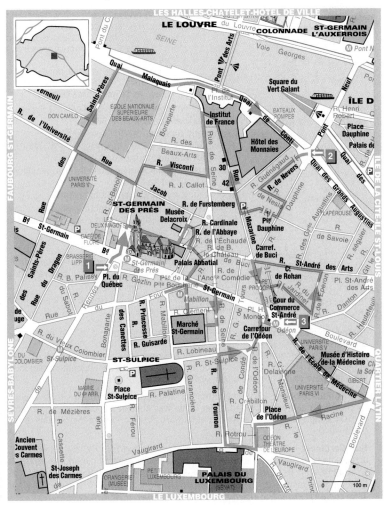

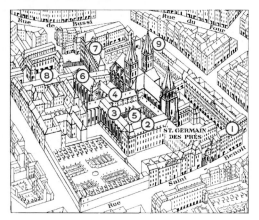

Abbey of Saint-Germain-
des-Prés in 1734
1 Annexe.
2 Guest rooms.
3 Refectory.
4 Chapter-house.
5 Main cloister.
6 Lady Chapel.
7 Abbatial palace.
8 Stables.
9 Prison.

★★Église St-Germain-des-Prés ○ – *Boulevard St-Germain* The church, the oldest in Paris, and the abbatial palace are all that remain of the famous Benedictine abbey.

Exterior – *See illustration p 91.* The 11C Romanesque church has altered considerably in appearance. The chancel flying buttresses are contemporary with Notre-Dame; of the three original bell-towers only one remains; it was restored in the 19C when it was crowned with its present pitched roof. The original porch is hidden by an outer doorway added in 1607.

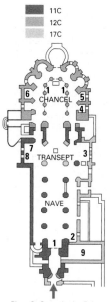

11C
12C
17C

Place St-Germain des Prés

Interior – The church's small dimensions are explained by the fact that it was built as a monastery chapel and not as a parish church. Grand scale restoration work in the 19C has left vaults, walls and capitals painted in garish colours. The chancel and ambulatory survive more or less from the 12C.

Off to the right of the cradle vaulted porch, is the Merovingian sanctuary with the tomb of St Germanus, known as **St Symphorian's Chapel.**

1) Modern wrought-iron grille by Raymond Subes.

2) Our Lady of Consolation (1340).

3) Tomb by Girardon (17C).

4) Mausoleum of James Douglas, a 17C Scottish nobleman attached to the court of Louis XIII.

5) **Descartes**' and the learned Benedictines, Mabillon's and Montfaucon's tombstones.

6) Boileau, the poet and critic's tombstone.

7) Statue of St Francis Xavier by N Coustou.

8) Tomb of John Casimir, King of Poland, who died in 1672, Abbot of St-Germain-des-Prés.

9) St Symphorian Chapel.

Rue de l'Abbaye – A Picasso sculpture, *Homage to Apollinaire*, has been placed in a small square on the corner of place St-Germain-des-Prés.

Abbatial Palace – *No 5.* The impressive brick and stone former abbatial palace was built in 1586 by the Cardinal-Abbot Charles of Bourbon.
The palace was remodelled in 1699 by Abbé de Fürstenberg and sold in 1797 as State property.
The angle pavilion and the Renaissance façade have been restored to their original appearance. The severity of the façade is tempered by the twin-casement windows with alternate round and triangular pediments.

★Rue de Furstemberg – This old-fashioned street with its charming square shaded by paulownia and white-globed street lights was built by the cardinal of the same name, through the former monastery stableyard. Nos **6** and **8** are the remains of the outbuildings.

Rue Cardinale – Twisting and turning, it was created in 1700 by Fürstenberg, across the long monastery tennis court. Still partially lined by old houses (nos **3-9**) it extends to a picturesque crossroads with rue de l'Échaudé (1388) and rue Bourbon-le-Château.
Take rue de l'Échaudé to reach boulevard St-Germain then turn right.

Boulevard St-Germain – Just off place St-Germain-des-Prés are the **Café des Deux-Magots** and the Café de Flore, the famous meeting spots for Left Bank intellectuals and artists. Opposite, the Brasserie Lipp (no 151) is a popular venue with politicians, writers and celebrities. Further on, two 18C mansions survive (nos **159** and **173**).

Follow boulevard St-Germain towards the Odéon.

The antiquarian quarter – The numerous art galleries and antique shops in the streets (rue des Saints-Pères, rue Jacob, rue Bonaparte, rue de Seine) between the boulevard and the river attract connoisseurs and collectors.

The old St-Germain Fair – Rue de Montfaucon at one time gave access to the St-Germain fairground. The fair, founded in 1482 by Louis XI for the benefit of the abbey, had until the Revolution (1790) a considerable effect on Paris' economy: a forerunner of International Exhibitions and world-trade fairs today. In 1818 the covered **St-Germain market** was built on part of the site.

MUSEUM

Musée Eugène-Delacroix ⊙ – *6 place de Furstemberg.* A museum dedicated to Delacroix, leader of the Romantic painters, has been made of the colourist's last studio-home where he lived from 1858 to 1863. Works by Delacroix and his friends, with changing exhibitions. The studio and garden are a haven of peace.

Going out

Café de Flore – *172 blvd St-Germain – 6th arr – ☎ 01 45 48 55 26 – daily 7am-2am.* Opened during the Second Empire, the Café de Flore has become one of the capital's most prestigious establishments, primarily due to the renown of some of its former literary regulars, including Apollinaire, Breton, Sartre and Simone de Beauvoir, Camus, and Jacques Prévert.

Les Deux Magots – *6 pl. St-Germain-des-Prés – 6th arr –* Ⓜ *Saint-Germain-des-Près – ☎ 01 45 48 55 25 – daily 7.30am-1.30am – closed one week in early Jan.* Like its neighbour, the Café de Flore, this establishment was frequented by the capital's intellectual elite from the end of the 19C onwards. Since 1933 a literary prize, named after it, is awarded every year in January.

Brasserie Lipp – *151 blvd Saint-Germain – 6th arr – ☎ 01 45 48 53 91 – www.brasserie-lipp.fr – daily 10am-2am.* Opened in 1880, it has always been a meeting place for men and women of letters and politics: Verlaine, Proust, Gide and Malraux used to meet here and Hemingway wrote *A Farewell to Arms* here. This superb 1900 and 1925 establishment is now a listed monument.

Café Mabillon – *164 blvd St-Germain – 6th arr – ☎ 01 43 26 62 93 – Daily 7.30am-6am.* This old Saint-Germain-des-Prés café has recently been renovated and is now in vogue with the neighbourhood's trendy clan who flock here to listen to the ear-splitting music.

La Rhumerie – *166 blvd St-Germain – 6th arr – ☎ 01 43 54 28 94 – www.larhumerie.com – daily 9am-2am. – closed Christmas eve and morning.* As might be expected, this establishment specialises in rums of all sorts: ti'planteur, coconut etc.

Bar du marché – *75 rue de Seine – 6th arr – ☎ 01 43 26 55 15 – Mon-Sun 8am-2am.* The Bohemian atmosphere of this café has become its trademark. Young people from near and far, a few pop-stars and a host of tourists come here to have a drink, fun and meet each other in a lively atmosphere. The staff's dress-style and relaxed attitude, which is supposed to evoke traditional Paris, accentuate the nostalgic style of this bistro.

Shopping

Emporio Armani – *149 blvd St-Germain – 6th arr –* Ⓜ *St-Germain-des-Prés – other shop: 25 pl. Vendôme 1st arr – ☎ 01 53 63 33 50 – Mon-Sat 10.30am-8.30pm – closed public holidays.* The sober, sophisticated style of this designer appeals to the young and the not so young. The shop, in line with the designs, is a tasteful blend of luxury and modernism. It also boasts an Italian tea shop which is very popular with its well-heeled clientele.

La Hune and L'Écume des Pages – *170 and 174 blvd St-Germain – 6th arr –* Ⓜ *St-Germain-des-Prés –* ☎ *01 45 48 35 85/45 48 54 48 – Mon-Sat 10am-11.45pm – closed public holidays.* These two bookshops both close late and are also keen contributors to the neighbourhood's cultural life (book signings, presentations, themes etc).

Marché Saint-Germain – *Rue Clément – 6th arr –* Ⓜ *Mabillon –* ☎ *01 43 29 80 59 – Mon-Sat 10am-8pm.* This pleasant covered market houses a number of fashion shops such as Gap and Somewhere, beauty institutes, home decoration shops and a large food hall.

Rue de Furstemberg – *Rue de Furstemberg – 6th arr –* Ⓜ *Mabillon.* Jac Dey, Pierre Frey, Verel de Belval, Taco and Manuel Canovas – this discreet little street is almost entirely devoted to home decoration. It is also home to Yveline, a charming antiques dealer who has a wonderful collection of articulated models.

Sonia Rykiel – *175 blvd St-Germain – 6th arr –* Ⓜ *St-Germain – other address: 70 rue du Fg-St-Honoré 8th arr –* ☎ *01 49 54 60 60 – soniarykiel.com – Mon-Sat 10am-7pm – closed public holidays.* The designs of this legendary, extremely talented designer are often inspired by her other passions: literature, cinema or food. Each new collection is feverishly awaited and always an event.

Le Carré Rive Gauche – *7th arr –* Ⓜ *Rue-du-Bac or St-Germain-des-Prés –* ☎ *01 42 61 31 45.* This association houses some 120 art galleries and antique dealers spread out through rue des Saints-Pères, rue de l'Université, rue du Bac and along quai Voltaire. Each one has a brochure in which their various specialities and addresses are indicated.

Debauve et Gallais – *30 rue des Sts-Pères –* ☎ *01 45 48 54 67 – Mon-Sat 9am-7pm – closed public holidays.* This chocolate maker established in 1800 counted the kings of France among his customers. The shop is officially listed as a historic monument.

Michel Chaudun – *149 rue de l'Université – 7th arr –* Ⓜ *Invalides –* ☎ *01 47 53 74 40 – Tue-Sat 9.45am-7.15pm – closed public holidays and Aug.* The talent of this would-be sculptor should not distract you from the roots of his work, he is first and foremost one of the capital's best chocolate makers. However visitors to his shop never tire of asking him if his African sculptures are really in chocolate!

Art

Marine Biras – *5 rue Lobineau – 6th arr –* Ⓜ *Mabillon –* ☎ *01 43 25 01 64 – Tue-Sat 11am-7pm – closed public holidays and Feb.* Marine Biras left the world of fashion some 10 years ago to open this quite unique textile gallery in Paris. From the artist's designs to the traditional fabrics from all over the world, everything in this tiny shop is exquisite.

Eating out

Turn back to the Selected restaurants section at the beginning of the guide for a list of restaurants, bistros, cafés etc. This district is in the 6th *arrondissement.*

Faubourg SAINT-HONORÉ ★

Michelin plan 10: E 8, E 9, F 9, F 10, F 11
Ⓜ *Madeleine (lines 8, 12 and 14), Concorde (lines 1, 8 and 12),
St-Philippe-du-Roule (line 9), Ternes (line 2) – Buses: 24, 42, 52, 80, 84, 94*

This old *faubourg* or neighbourhood imparts a leisured elegance with its luxury shops, art galleries, antique shops and haute couture boutiques particularly around rue Royale and rue de l'Élysée. For much of its length rue du Faubourg-St-Honoré runs parallel with the Champs-Élysées; it is also where the president of the Republic lives.

Nearby neighbourhoods: PALAIS-ROYAL, TUILERIES, PLACE DE LA CONCORDE, MADELEINE, CHAMPS-ÉLYSÉES, ST-LAZARE.

Going out

Water bar, Colette – *213 rue St-Honoré – 1st arr – ☎ 01 55 35 33 90 – Mon-Sat 10.30am-7.30pm.* This fresh water bar, located in the ultra-chic fashion shop, Colette, proposes simply dozens of varieties of water, sparkling or flat, from all over the world. More than worth a trip for those who can't wait to wet their appetites with the red Carola, the Pedras Salgadas or the Splitrock.

Bar de l'Hôtel Bristol – *112 rue du Fg-St-Honoré – 8th arr – ☎ 01 53 43 43 42 – Mon-Fri 8am-1.30am, Sat and Sun 10.30am-1.30am.* The muted, sophisticated ambience of this bar has all the charm of a grand palace frequented by celebrities from the worlds of fashion, the media, politics or business. Both rooms are decorated with paintings purchased from the Louvre. The inner courtyard has a delightful flowered terrace.

Shopping

Hermès – *24 rue du Fg-St-Honoré – 8th arr – Ⓜ Concorde – other shops: 42 av. Georges-V 8th arr; Hôtel Hilton, 18 av. de Suffren 15th arr – ☎ 01 40 17 47 17 – Mon 10am-1pm, 2.15-6.30pm, Tue-Sat 10am-6.30pm – closed public holidays.* Since it first began as a harness maker when Thierry Hermès opened the first shop in 1837, this family business has never ceased to grow, while retaining its original founding spirit. The equestrian influence remains strong in this establishment dedicated to quality before all else.

La Maison du Chocolat – *225 rue du Fg-St-Honoré – 8th arr – Ⓜ Ternes – other addresses: 52 rue François-Iᵉʳ 8th arr; 8 blvd de la Madeleine 9th arr; 19 rue de Sèvres 6th arr; 89 av. Raymond-Poincaré 16th arr – ☎ 01 42 27 39 44 – www.lamaisonduchocolat.com – Feb-Oct, Mon-Sat 10am-7pm, Nov-Jan 9.30am-7.30pm.* Robert Linxe's chocolate is one of the best in town. Treat yourself to the elegantly presented *ganaches* and pastries and don't forget to sample the delicious hot chocolate, the reputation of which has spread much further afield than the walls of this temple to chocolate.

Les Caves Taillevent – *199 rue du Fg-St-Honoré – 8th arr – Ⓜ Ch.-de-Gaule-Étoile, Ternes or St-Philippe-du Roule – ☎ 01 45 61 14 09 – www.taillevent.com – Mon 2-8pm, Tue-Fri 9am-8pm, Sat 9am-7.30pm – closed public holidays and 3 weeks in Aug.* Whether on the shelves or hung on the walls, all the bottles on display are dummies, the real ones are kept in a ventilated cellar. In addition to the best vintage wines, they also stock a fine selection of regional wines. Friendly and efficient staff.

Rue du Faubourg-Saint-Honoré – *Rue du Fg-St-Honoré – 8th arr – Ⓜ Concorde or Madeleine.* From rue Royale to place Beauvau, rue du Faubourg-Saint-Honoré is entirely devoted to fashion and luxury goods. All the leading brand names are there: Lolita Lempika, Lanvin, Hermès, Cartier, Guy Givenchy, Versace, Laroche, Dior, L Ferraud etc.

Eating out

Turn back to the Selected restaurants section at the beginning of the guide for a list of restaurants, bistros, cafés etc. This district is in the 8th *arrondissement*.

EXPLORING THE NEIGHBOURHOOD

★**Rue du Faubourg-St-Honoré** – Empress Eugénie was certainly superstitious, for she would not allow any building on the street to bear the number 13, and this is still true today. At no 252 is **Salle Pleyel**, built in 1927 and renovated in 1981. This classical concert hall is renowned for the quality of its acoustics and its concert posters.

Maison Paul Poiret once occupied no 107. This couturier (1879-1944) was one of the first modern clothes designers, banning the whale-bone corset and launching a taste for strong theatrical styles and colours. He integrated exotic features into dress design (harem-inspired *jupes-culottes*, Japanese-style kimono sleeves and long ankle-clinging hobble skirts) and may have been responsible for the revival of huge plumed hats. After the First World War he employed **Raoul Dufy** to paint his fabrics; his fashion house was the first to launch its own perfume.

Église St-Philippe-du-Roule ⊘ – *154 rue du Faubourg-St-Honoré*. The church designed by **Chalgrin** in imitation of a Roman basilica was erected between 1774 and 1784. The ambulatory was added around the apse in 1845. A fresco over the chancel of *The Deposition* is by Chassérieu.

Palais de l'Élysée – *55 rue du Faubourg-St-Honoré. Not open to the public*. The mansion was constructed in 1718 for the Count of Évreux. It was acquired for a short time by the Marquise de Pompadour and then by the financier Beaujon who enlarged it. During the Revolution it became a dance hall. It was home to Caroline Murat, Napoleon's sister, then Empress Josephine who redecorated it; it was here that Napoleon signed his second abdication after his defeat at Waterloo, on 22 June 1815, and that the future **Napoleon III** lived and planned his successful *coup d'état* of 1851.

Palais de l'Élysée

Since 1873 the Élysée Palace has been the Paris residence of France's president. The Council of Ministers meets on Wednesdays in the Murat Salon.

La Cour aux Antiquaires – *54 rue du Faubourg-St-Honoré*. The noble elegance of this gallery of shops, founded by Marie Laure Le Duc in 1969, is complemented by the trade in the fine and decorative arts.

No 6 rue d'Anjou – Here lived Marie-Joseph de La Fayette (1757-1834), the great champion of the causes of Liberty, American Independence and Franco-American alliance.

Turn right onto rue Boissy-d'Anglas and right again on avenue Gabriel.

Avenue Gabriel – Shaded gardens on the northern side, running parallel to the Champs-Élysées, stretch along the back of smart mansions lining the Faubourg St-Honoré. Note the Elysée Palace's fine wrought-iron gate with gilded cockerel, dating from 1905.

Avenue Matignon – This street is lined with art galleries dedicated to contemporary Fine Art: Maurice Garnier, Taménaga, Daniel Malingue, Bernheim-Jeune.

Place Beauvau – A fine wrought-iron gate (1836) marks the entrance to the 18C mansion built for the Prince of Beauvau, occupied by the Ministry of Home Affairs since 1861.

Michelin plan 10: E 11, E 12, F 11, F 12
Ⓜ St-Lazare (lines 3, 12 and 13) –
Buses: 20, 21, 24, 26, 27, 28, 29, 32, 43, 53, 66, 80, 84, 94, 95

Those who dislike crowds should avoid this district! Every morning and evening, thousands of commuters pass through the Gare St-Lazare on their way to and from the suburbs. The major department stores in the area attract yet more people, and the café terraces are a good place to sit and watch the world go by.

Nearby neighbourhoods: OPÉRA, MONCEAU, GRANDS BOULEVARDS, MADELEINE.

QUARTIER SAINT-LAZARE

The neighbourhood – The St-Lazare main-line **railway station** links north-west France (Dieppe, Caen, Le Havre) with Paris, shuttling people from the suburbs to town or out to the coast and seaside. The exciting development of the railway was especially well captured by the Impressionist painter **Claude Monet**. The area around was developed in the 19C to accommodate a middle-class society in standardised, comfortable apartment blocks served by convenient large department stores.

Place de l'Europe – The major intersection of six important roads straddles the railway lines north of St-Lazare; the bridge was last rebuilt in 1930. It also marks the boundary between the *bourgeois* neighbourhood to the west and a more popular quarter to the east, as defined at the time of the Restoration and the Second Empire.
The radiating axes were named after the grand European metropolises – London, Madrid, Amsterdam, Vienna, Stockholm, Milan, Moscow – to attract the right kind of residents.

Shopping

Augé – *116 blvd Haussmann – 8th arr* – Ⓜ *St-Augustin* – ☎ *01 45 22 16 97 – Mon 1-7.30pm, Tue-Sat 9am-7.30pm – closed public holidays*. Founded in 1850, this family enterprise has the oldest cellar in Paris. Venture into its authentic surroundings and discover the best of what France's vineyards have to offer. Foreign wines also available. All are selected with love and care. Reasonable prices.

Galeries Lafayette – *40 blvd Haussmann – 9th arr* – Ⓜ *Chaussée-d'Antin or Havre-Caumartin* – ☎ *01 42 82 34 56 – www.galerieslafayette.com – Mon-Wed, Fri-Sat 9.30am-7pm, Thu 9.30am-9pm – closed public holidays*. It would be impossible to go on a shopping spree in Paris without envisaging a trip to this major department store, where all the brand names have an outlet.

Printemps – *64 blvd Haussmann – 9th arr* – Ⓜ *Havre-Caumartin RER Auber* – ☎ *01 42 82 50 00 – www.printemps.fr – Mon-Wed, Fri-Sat 9.35am-7pm, Thu 9.35am-10pm*. This temple to fashion features the work of all the world's leading design houses. Divided into three buildings which are linked by passageways. A large panorama terrace overlooks the Printemps de la Maison.

EXPLORING THE NEIGHBOURHOOD

⋆**Église St-Augustin** – *Place St-Augustin*. The church was designed by Baltard between 1860 and 1871 and was the first ecclesiastical building to consist of a metal infrastructure clad in stone. The innovative means of construction meant that the traditional Gothic design could be retained without any need for external buttressing. It was here that Charles de Foucault was converted in October 1886.

From place St-Augustin, turn left on boulevard Haussmann, and continue until you reach square Louis-XVI on the right. Pass by rue Anjou and turn on rue Pasquier.

Chapelle Expiatoire ⊙ – *Square Louis-XVI (entrance at 29 rue Pasquier)*. The cemetery, opened in 1722, was used as a burial ground for the Swiss Guards killed at the Tuileries on 10 August 1792, and for the victims of **the guillotine** which stood in place de la Concorde. These last numbered 1 343 and included Louis XVI and Marie-Antoinette, whose remains were disinterred and transported to the royal necropolis at St-Denis in 1815.
The tombs of Charlotte Corday (who stabbed Marat in his bath to avenge the Girondins) and Philippe-Égalité are on either side of the steps leading into the chapel.

Boulevard Haussmann

Le Printemps – *64 boulevard Haussmann.* This store was founded in 1865 and owed its immediate success to its proximity to the station. It was the first to install lifts, and boasts fine window displays for children at Christmas.

Galeries Lafayette – *40 boulevard Haussmann.* A tiny haberdasher's founded in 1895 by Alphonse Khan is the origin of this modern-day chain. Its dome and balustrades were designed by Ferdinand Chanut in 1910. On 19 January 1919, the aviator Védrines landed his Caudron G3 on the shop's roof terrace.

Marcel Proust (1871-1922), spent 12 years at 102 boulevard Haussmann. The second-floor bedroom has recently been restored and opened, by appointment, to the public.

The author of *À la recherche du temps perdu (Remembrance of Things Past)* chose to live in his aunt's flat for the macabre reason that he had witnessed his uncle die there, and this memory might provide inspiration for his writing.

Being very susceptible to noise, Proust tended to work at night and struggled to sleep by day through the noise of the boulevard below; to this end he had the bedroom muffled with cork tiles and heavy curtains. There he would spend days on end shut-up in bed, brewing various vapours to help his chronic asthma.

His main distraction, other than occasionally venturing out to socialise with the upper classes at the **Ritz**, was the *théâtrephone* which relayed live performances of opera down an early version of the telephone, at some exorbitant expense.

When *Du côté de chez Swann*, the first volume of the collection, was submitted to the Gallimard publishers, it was turned down by André Gide who subsequently admitted that his decision had been the "gravest mistake ever made".

MUSEUM

★ **Musée Gustave-Moreau** ⊘ – *14 rue de La Rochefoucauld.* Gustave Moreau (1826-98) bequeathed his house and collection from a life's work to the French nation with specific instructions that it should remain intact: 850 paintings, 7 000 drawings, 350 watercolours and wax sculptures. Moreau was greatly influenced by the Colourist techniques of Delacroix and the neo-Mannerist Chassériau; he delighted in the fantastical, biblical and mythological subjects, reworking such figures as Sappho, Salome, Orpheus and Leda throughout his life. Among his students rank Rouault, Matisse and Desvallière.

An especially designed cabinet with wings holds many of his drawings, whereas another curious piece of furniture contains watercolours.

The cramped and cluttered living quarters were situated on the first floor: note a working sketch by Poussin and a photograph of the pre-Raphaelite work by Burne-Jones in the corridor.

Other personal possessions on view include Bernard Palissy and Moustiers ceramics (dining room), furniture, a rare portrait of the artist by Degas, the effects of Alexandrine Dureux, his close and intimate friend for 25 years who died in 1890.

The second and third floors of the family house were considerably altered by the artist to accommodate his paintings in a large, airy space.

Île SAINT-LOUIS ★★

Michelin plan 10: J 15, J 16, K 15, K 16
Ⓜ *Pont Marie (line 7) – Buses: 24, 63, 67, 86, 87, 89*

Calm quays and unpretentious Classical architecture make Île St-Louis one of the most attractive places in Paris. The most fulfilling way to explore the island is to wander over the Pont St-Louis from Île de la Cité and follow a circuit along the river and through its streets.

Nearby neighbourhoods: ÎLE DE LA CITÉ, CONCIERGERIE, SAINTE-CHAPELLE, NOTRE-DAME, MAUBERT, JARDIN DES PLANTES, LE MARAIS, BASTILLE.

Île aux Vaches and Île Notre-Dame – Originally there were two islands where in the Middle Ages judicial duels, known as the Judgements of God, were held. Early in the reign of Louis XIII, the contractor Christophe Marie obtained permission from the king and chapter of Notre-Dame to conjoin the islets and construct two stone bridges for access. In return he was to be allowed to develop the land for resale in lots. Work began in 1627 and lasted until 1664, resulting in a regular layout of intersecting streets and a homogenous Classical style of architecture. What makes Île St-Louis unique is its atmosphere of old world charm and provincial calm. Bankers, lawyers and nobles accounted for the first residents, now replaced by writers, artists and those who love old Paris.

On the island there is a 17C house at almost every step: nobly proportioned façades, many with tablets inscribed with historical or anecdotal information, wrought-iron balconies and tall brick chimneys. Behind massive panelled doors, studded with bosses and nails, lie secluded courtyards where the stone sets and mounting blocks have not changed since the days of horse-drawn carriages.

Going out

Berthillon – *31 rue Saint-Louis-en-l'Île – 4th arr –* ☎ *01 43 54 31 61 – Wed-Sun 10am-8pm – closed during school holidays.* Paris' most famous ice-cream maker, renowned for his unctuous ice creams and delicious sorbets.

Le Flore en l'Île – *42 quai d'Orléans – 4th arr –* ☎ *01 43 29 88 27 – daily 8am-2am.* With a superb view of the apse of Notre-Dame.

Eating out

Turn back to the Selected restaurants section at the beginning of the guide for a list of restaurants, bistros, cafés etc. This district is in the 4th *arrondissement*.

EXPLORING THE NEIGHBOURHOOD

② Tour of the island *See map p 157*

Pont St-Louis – This modern (1970) metal arched bridge links the two Parisian islands. It replaces the former Pont St-Landry (1630). Traffic is forbidden, making it a peaceful place to appreciate the views of Notre-Dame, the Hôtel de Ville and the Panthéon.

Quai de Bourbon – From the picturesque tip of the island with chain linked stone posts and canted 18C medallions, there is an altogether delightful **view**★ of the church of St-Gervais. A little further on are two magnificent town houses (nos **19** and **15**) which once belonged to parliamentarians – steep mansard roofs, mascarons, spacious stairwells encircled by wrought-iron balusters suggest their former splendour. At no **19** the sculptress **Camille Claudel** had her studio *(ground floor)* between 1899 and 1913.

★**Pont Marie** – Constructed by Christophe Marie in 1635 and rebuilt in 1670.

Quai d'Anjou – At no **29**, in a former wine cellar, Ford Madox Ford established his journal *The Transatlantic Review* in collaboration with John Quinn, Ezra Pound and **James Joyce**. The Marquise de Lambert, hostess of a famous literary salon, lived at no **27** (Hôtel de Nevers). The famous painter, sculptor, caricaturist and political satirist **Honoré Daumier** lived at no **9** between 1846 and 1863.

Ph. Gajic/MICHELIN

Hôtel de Lauzun – *No 17 (Closed to the public)*. The mansion was erected in 1657 by Le Vau for Gruyn, a military supplier who was imprisoned shortly afterwards for corruption. It belonged for only three years to the Duke of Lauzun, Saint-Simon's brother-in-law, who nevertheless left it his name. The poet, Théophile Gautier, lived there during the 1840s when he founded his Club des Hachischins, experimenting first with Baudelaire and later with Rilke, Sickert and Wagner. The house now belongs to the City of Paris.

Square Barye – This small garden at the tip of the island is the last trace of the terraced estate of a house that once belonged to the financier, Bretonvilliers.

Pont de Sully – This bridge, which dates from 1876, rests on the tip of Île St-Louis. From the first section there is a good **view★** of Notre-Dame, the Cité and Île St-Louis.
In the 17C there was a bathing beach here that was popular with the Court and the aristocracy; even Henri IV and his son are said to have been happy to join in the swimming.
Follow quai de Béthune then turn right onto rue de Bretonvilliers which leads to rue St-Louis-en-l'Île.

★ **Hôtel Lambert** – *No 2*. The mansion of President Lambert de Thorigny, known as Lambert the Rich, was built in 1640 by Le Vau and decorated by Le Sueur *(sketches now at the Louvre)* and Le Brun.

★ **Église St-Louis-en-l'Île** ⊙ – *No 19 bis*. The church is marked outside by an unusual iron clock and its original pierced spire. Designed by Le Vau, who lived on the island, building began in 1664, but was completed only in 1726. The ornate interior, in the Jesuit style, is highly decorated: woodwork, gilding and marble of the Grand Siècle (17C), statuettes and enamels.

Hôtel de Chenizot – *No 51*. A very fine doorway surmounted by a faun mask and a majestic balcony mark this house which, in the middle of the 19C, accommodated the archbishop.

Quai d'Orléans – There is a splendid **view★★** of the east end of Notre-Dame and the Left Bank.

MUSEUM

★ **Société historique et littéraire polonaise** – *6 quai d'Orléans*. A 17C building houses three museums.

Adam-Mickiewicz Museum ⊙ – The small museum has portraits, mementoes, manuscripts, documents relating to the poet (1798-1855) and his family. Note the busts by Bourdelle and David d'Angers.

Salle Chopin – A permanent exhibition devoted to Chopin, featuring the original manuscripts of his *Polonaises* and other compositions as well as portraits of his close friends and family. The collection includes sculptures of Berlioz and Beethoven by Boleslas Biegas (1877-1954), whose work is the subject of the third museum, along with other Polish artists.

Canal SAINT-MARTIN★

Michelin plan 10, folds 21 and 33: E 17, F-K 17
Ⓜ *République (lines 3, 5, 8, 9 and 11), Jacques Bonsergent (line 5),*
Goncourt (line 11), Jaurès (lines 2, 5 and 7b)

This peaceful, old-fashioned canal, dug at the time of the Restoration to link the Ourcq Canal at La Villette with the Seine via the Arsenal, is still navigated by numerous barges. The raised level of the watercourse straddled with iron footbridges, its nine locks and rows of trees, make for an unusual, serene Paris landscape.
Nearby neighbourhoods: RÉPUBLIQUE, LA VILLETTE, BUTTES-CHAUMONT.

EXPLORING THE NEIGHBOURHOOD

Along St-Martin Canal

Starting from place de la République, take rue du Faubourg-du-Temple as far as boulevard Jules-Ferry. Turn left onto square Frédéric-Lemaître.

Square Frédéric-Lemaître – From here there is an attractive view of one of the canal's locks. The canal disappears into an underpass beyond quai Valmy from square Frédéric-Lemaître, resurfacing beyond place de la Bastille as the Arsenal Basin. The basin has been developed as a pleasure boat harbour, the **Arsenal Marina** (Port de Plaisance de Paris-Arsenal), to accommodate over 200 boats.

The walk follows the canal, climbing with it as it passes through its nine locks. The tiny squares give way to metal footbridges which offer charming views of the canal.

Now and then a barge gliding along the still waters has to negotiate a lock and the canal suddenly comes to life.

Take avenue Richerand to visit the Hôpital St-Louis.

St-Louis Hospital – *Entrance on rue Bichat*. One of the oldest Parisian hospitals, **St-Louis** pioneered the science of dermatology. The brick and stone buildings, reminiscent of place des Vosges and place Dauphine with their steeply pitched roofs and dormer windows, are separated by flower-decked courtyards.

St-Martin Canal

Retrace your steps to St-Martin Canal.

Square des Récollets – A **swing bridge** crosses the canal, connecting rue de Lancry and rue de la Grange-aux-Belles. Between two smaller footbridges nestles the square named after a Franciscan convent which stood nearby, at 150 rue des Récollets, whose foundation stone was laid by Catherine de' Médici in 1604.

Montfaucon Gallows – The canal, rue Louis-Blanc, rue de la Grange-aux-Belles and rue des Écluses-St-Martin delimit an area once dominated by gallows that could hang up to 60 condemned people at a time. Various finance ministers died by it, notably Marigny, who built the gibbet during the reign of **Philip the Fair**, Montaigu, who repaired it, and the unlucky Semblançay who had nothing whatsoever to do with it. After the assassination (1572) of Admiral Coligny, his body was displayed here. Although already in disuse during the 17C it was 1760 before the gallows were dismantled.

Hôtel du Nord – *102 quai de Jemmapes*. This building lent its name to a film made in 1938 by Marcel Carné, who reconstructed the canalside setting in his studio. Based on the novel *Hôtel du Nord* by Eugène Dabit (1928), it starred the popular Parisian actress Arletty. Today it is a café-restaurant with live shows and dancing on Sunday afternoons.

Continue along the canal to place Stalingrad.

Rotonde de la Villette – *Place de la Bataille-de-Stalingrad*. The rotunda, one of the ring of toll-houses designed by Ledoux serves as a storehouse for archaeological finds.

Follow the left-hand quay of the Bassin de la Villette.

The walk finishes with the impressive sight of the **transporter bridge** in rue de Crimée, which opens to let boats pass from the Bassin de la Villette to the Canal de l'Ourcq.

The Crimée metro station is a few steps away to the left. It is also possible to walk back along the other side of the Bassin as far as the Jean-Jaurès metro station.

Eating out

Turn back to the Selected restaurants section at the beginning of the guide for a list of restaurants, bistros, cafés etc. This district is in the 10th *arrondissement*.

Going out

Chez Prune – *36 rue Beaurepaire – 10th arr – ☎ 01 42 41 30 47 – Mon-Sat 7.30am-2am, Sun 10am-2am – closed 25 Dec and New Year's Day*. Situated on the edge of the Saint-Martin Canal, Chez Prune can provide a quiet or a noisy break, depending on the time, but is always pleasant. Popular with the local youth who come here for snacks or a drink. A selection of generally weird and unusual paintings hangs on the walls, giving the place a trendy feel.

Opus Jazz & Soul Club – *167 quai de Valmy – 10th arr – ☎ 01 40 34 70 00 – Tue-Wed 8pm-2am, Thu-Sat 8pm-5am*. Under the beams and lofty ceiling of this former British Officers' mess, music is the key word: funk, soul, groove, theme evenings and concerts (jazz, gospel) etc.

Boat trips

For detailed information on various boat trips along the canal, see Practical Information: Discovering Paris.

The canal is 4.5km/2.7mi in length, 2.2m/7ft deep, and passes through nine locks including four double locks, to achieve a difference in level of 25m/82ft. The finest lock is the Récollets.

Boat trips pass through the locks and take the tunnel built by Baron Haussmann in 1860, which is 1 854m/6 082ft long, lit and ventilated by openings at street level. Underneath place de la Bastille, at the base of the Colonne de Juillet, it is possible to see the grilles of the crypt where those killed in the uprisings of 1830 and 1848 are buried.

SAINT-SULPICE ★

Michelin plan 10: K 13

Ⓜ *St-Sulpice (line 4), Mabillon (line 10)* – Buses: 48, 63, 70, 84, 95, 96

The district has long been famous for selling religious trinkets, which became known as St-Sulpice art and often reached heights of kitsch. It has come under the influence of neighbouring St-Germain-des-Prés and its shops now include bookstores and fashion boutiques.

Going out

Castel – *15 rue Princesse – 6th arr – ☎ 01 40 51 52 80 – Tue-Sat 9pm-5am – closed Aug.* A combination of dance, high fashion and conversation much in vogue with Paris' wealthy and famous. Whether for dinner or just a drink, the elegant, opulent settings are very pleasant, for those who manage to get in. Smart dress only.

Chez Georges – *11 rue des Canettes – 6th arr – Tue-Sat noon-2am – closed in Aug and between Christmas and the New Year.* An old café with a somewhat anarchic look to it. It is probably one of the district's few remaining genuine (and cheap) addresses. Old posters on the walls, a bar, a few benches, stools and the traditional tiles. Regulars gather here to exchange gossip around a glass of red wine. Basement cellar with music.

Shopping

Christian-Lacroix – *2-4 pl. St-Sulpice – 6th arr – Ⓜ St-Sulpice – ☎ 01 46 33 48 95 – www.christian-lacroix.fr – Mon-Sat 10am-7pm – closed public holidays.* A designer, known for his flamboyant, flowery, even precious style who seeks to bridge the gap between haute couture and street fashion. Each garment is a celebration.

La Procure – *3 rue de Mézières – 6th arr – Ⓜ St-Sulpice. Bus nos 48, 83, 84, 95, 96. – ☎ 01 45 48 20 25 – Mon-Sat 9.30am-7.30pm – closed public holidays.* An institution! 750sq m/897sq yd, of which 400sq m/478sq yd are devoted to theology, religious history and biblical exegeses. From the rarest ancient document in Acadian to the latest translation of the gospels, this bookshop is a treasure trove of knowledge.

Village Voice – *6 rue Princesse – 6th arr – Ⓜ Mabillon or St-Germain-des-Prés – ☎ 01 46 33 36 47 – Mon 2-8pm, Tue-Sat 10am-8pm, Sun 2-7pm.* Run by an Englishman since 1981, this charming bookshop has a good range of English-language literature and reviews.

Yves Saint-Laurent – *6 pl. St-Sulpice – 6th arr – Ⓜ St-Sulpice – ☎ 01 43 29 43 00 – Mon 11am-7pm, Tue-Sat 10.30am-7pm – closed public holidays.* A living legend. 40 years of creativity have forged the style of this artist so loved by women and whose inventions have marked the history of fashion. This shop presents four of the Rive Gauche collections.

Eating out

Turn back to the Selected restaurants section at the beginning of the guide for a list of restaurants, bistros, cafés etc. This district is in the 6th *arrondissement*.

EXPLORING THE NEIGHBOURHOOD

Place St-Sulpice – Initiated in 1754, the square was designed as a semicircular space defined by uniform façades of the type at no **6** (at the corner of rue des Canettes), designed by Servandoni. But this did not materialise.

The central fountain was erected by Visconti in 1844 and is known as the Fontaine des Quatre Points Cardinaux after the sculpted portraits of Bossuet, Fénelon, Massillon and Fléchier, facing the cardinal points of the compass. The name, Fountain of the Cardinal Points or the Four Cardinals Who Never Were, is a play on words as none of the four churchmen ever was made a cardinal (*point* in French means both point and never).

Shops bearing famous names such as Yves Saint-Laurent and Christian Lacroix are found along the northern side of the square.

★★ Église de St-Sulpice – *Place St-Sulpice.* The church, dedicated to the 6C Archbishop of Bourges, St Sulpicius, was founded by the abbey of St-Germain-des-Prés as a parish church for peasants living in its domain. Rebuilding began in 1646 with the chancel. A succession of six architects took charge over a period of 134 years.

Exterior – In 1732 a competition was held for the design of the façade and won by a Florentine, Servandoni, who proposed a fine façade in the style of the Antique, in contrast to the rest of the edifice. The final façade differs considerably from Servandoni's original concept. The colossal pediment has been abandoned; the belfries are crowned not by Renaissance pinnacles but by balustrades; the towers are dissimilar, the left one being taller and more ornate than the other which was never completed. The transept façade is in the Jesuit style with two superimposed orders and heavy ornaments.

Interior – The interior is extremely impressive by its size. Of the 20 artists who worked on the internal paintings, Delacroix's genius dominates. His **murals★** in the first chapel on the right, were painted between 1849 and 1861. Full of Romanticism in colour, composition, movement and temperament, they illustrate *St Michael Killing the Demon* (ceiling), *Heliodorus Being Driven from the Temple* (Heliodorus, a minister of the King of Syria, coveting the treasures of the Temple was struck down by three avenging angels, one of whom is riding a horse – right wall), and *Jacob Wrestling with the Angel* (left wall).

The **Lady Chapel★** in the apse was painted under the personal supervision of Servandoni. The Virgin and Child group behind the altar is by Pigalle. The **organ loft★** was designed by **Chalgrin** in 1776. The organ, rebuilt in 1862, is the largest in France and considered one of the finest.

Two stoups abutting the second pillars of the nave are made from giant shells given to **François I** by the Venetian Republic and by Louis XV to the church of St-Sulpice in 1745. The artist **Pigalle** sculpted the rock-like bases.

In the transept, a copper band inlaid in the floor stretches from a plaque in the southern *(right)* transept to a marble obelisk in the northern *(left)* arm. At noon at the winter solstice, a ray of sunlight, passing through a small hole in the upper window in the south transept, strikes marked points on the obelisk in the far transept. At the spring and autumn equinoxes, at noon, the ray is caught by the metal plaque.

Take rue St-Sulpice, then turn left onto rue Mabillon.

Marché St-Germain – This covered market is an attractive shopping centre.

Rue Guisarde and rue Princesse – It is pleasant to wander these pedestrianised streets, pretty to look at by day and busy with activity at nightfall.

Rue des Canettes – Duckling Street takes its name from the low relief at no **18**. It is a lively place to go out in the evening with many bars, restaurants and nightclubs.

SAINTE-CHAPELLE★★★

Michelin plan 10: J 14
Ⓜ *Cité (line 4) – Buses: 21, 38, 85, 96*

Built in the 13C by St Louis in the centre of Île de la Cité, to house holy relics, the Sainte-Chapelle comes as close to perfection as any religious edifice anywhere. The chapel is a Gothic marvel, a symphony of stone and stained glass, and the deep glow of its windows is one of the great joys of a visit to Paris.

See also: ÎLE DE LA CITÉ, CONCIERGERIE, NOTRE-DAME. *Nearby neighbourhoods*: ÎLE ST-LOUIS, CHÂTELET-HÔTEL DE VILLE, QUARTIER LATIN.

A sacred shrine – Baudouin, a French nobleman who had been on the fourth Crusade before becoming Emperor of Constantinople, was forced to pledge the Crown of Thorns against a loan of money from the Venetians. Unable to meet his debts, he appealed to **St Louis** (Louis IX) who redeemed the payment and retrieved the Crown in 1239. Ultimately, the acquisition of other relics and the creation of suitable reliquaries would cost more than twice as much as the construction of the chapel.

This exceptional building, erected in only 33 months at the behest of King Louis IX, is attributed to **Pierre of Montreuil** (known also as Pierre of Montereau); it was consecrated in 1248. Consisting of two superimposed chambers, the upper level was used by the sovereign and his court, the lower by his household.

Originally the chapel would have stood in a courtyard with the palace walls, linked to St Louis' apartments by a small gallery. When the palace was remodelled in the 18C, a wing from the May Courtyard was extended up to the chapel.

During the Revolution the reliquary shrine was melted down; some of the relics were saved and are now in Notre-Dame; the 17C organ played by the Couperins is now at St-Germain-l'Auxerrois. Between 1802 and 1837 the building was used to archive judiciary papers that were stacked high against the lancet windows; restoration was undertaken by Duban and Lassus (1841-67).

★★★ Sainte-Chapelle ⓥ – *4 boulevard du Palais*

Exterior – The impact made by the Sainte-Chapelle is immediate. Completed just 80 years after Notre-Dame cathedral, it is perhaps the apogee of Gothic architecture. Its innovative great windows (15m/50ft high) encroach upon the wall space making it seem insubstantial, built of glass rather than masonry; its vault appears precariously supported by the slenderest piers, not reinforced with great flying buttresses, but rather anchored in place by a sculpted gable and balustrade. This remarkably delicate feat of balance and counter-balance was so perfectly engineered that no crack has appeared in seven centuries. The spire soars to 75m/246ft. Its lead-covered wooden roof, destroyed by fire and rebuilt three times, dates from 1854. The lead angel perched on the apse roof once revolved by clockwork to show the Cross it bears to all points of the compass. Level with the fourth bay is an extension made by Louis XI to accommodate a chapel *(ground level)* and an oratory *(above)*.

Interior – Access is through the **lower chapel** intended for the palace retainers. Forty columns, decorated in the 19C, carry the central vault (only 7m/23ft high and 17m/56ft wide), contained by the external buttresses. The floor is paved with tombstones.

A spiral staircase to the right leads to the **upper chapel**, a great bejewelled glass-house which seems to draw in the rays of sunlight.

Upper chapel

The chamber is encircled by blind arcading, its capitals delicately carved with stylised vegetation; attached to each shaft is a figure of an Apostle holding one of the Church's 12 crosses of consecration – the six original ones *(red on the plan)* are most expressive (the others are in the Musée Cluny). The painting is modern. Two deep recesses in the third bay were reserved for the king and his family. In the next bay, on the right, is the door to the oratory added by Louis XI: a grille enabled him to follow the service unnoticed.

The reliquary shrine would have stood at the centre of the apse on a raised platform surmounted by a wooden baldaquin. Of the two twisting staircases enclosed in the open-work turrets, the leftone is original. King Louis IX relished opening the shrine's doors, encrusted with stones, to show off his prized relics.

The porch onto the terrace dates from the 19C.

The **stained glass** is the oldest to survive in Paris. Of the 1 134 scenes represented over a glazed area of 618sq m/6 672sq ft, some 720 are original. The king summoned the best master-craftsmen from work recently completed at Chartres (1240) hence their similar treatments: roundel-scenes, brilliant use of colour eclipsing simplicity of composition. The principal theme is the celebration of the Passion, as foretold by the Prophets and John the Baptist. The design of the main rose is only known from an illumination in the *Très Riches Heures du duc de Berry* (1413-16).

The existing Flamboyant rose was commissioned by Charles VII and illustrates St John's vision of the Apocalypse.

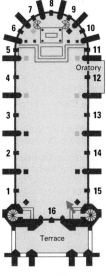

UPPER CHAPEL

The windows should be read from left to right and from bottom to top, with the exception of nos **6**, **7**, **9** and **11** which read lancet by lancet.
1) Genesis – Adam and Eve – Noah – Jacob *(damaged by the storm of December 1999)*.
2) Exodus – Moses and Mount Sinai.
3) Exodus – The Law of Moses.
4) Deuteronomy – Joshua – Ruth and Boaz.
5) Judges – Gideon – Samson.
6) Isaiah – The Tree of Jesse.
7) St John the Evangelist – Life of the Virgin – The Childhood of Christ.
8) Christ's Passion.
9) John the Baptist – Daniel.
10) Ezekiel.
11) Jeremiah – Tobias.
12) Judith – Job.
13) Esther.
14) Kings: Samuel, David, Solomon.
15) St Helena and the True Cross – St Louis and the relics of the Passion.
16) 15C Flamboyant rose window: the Apocalypse.

Le SENTIER

Michelin plan 10: G 14, G 15
Ⓜ *Bourse (line 3), Sentier (line 3), Bonne-Nouvelle (lines 8 and 9) – Buses: 67, 74, 85*

The Sentier quarter is the centre of the wholesale trade in fabrics and materials, trimmings, hosiery and ready-made clothes. It lies between the boulevards Montmartre, Poissonnière and Bonne-Nouvelle to the north, and rue Réaumur to the south, rue St-Denis to the east and rue Notre-Dame-des-Victoires to the west. Many of the streets are pedestrianised.

EXPLORING THE NEIGHBOURHOOD

Start from Ⓜ Étienne-Marcel (rue de Turbigo exit). Take rue de Turbigo, then rue St-Denis (left).

The Montorgueil-Saint-Denis area – The whole quarter stands on Mont Orgueil (the proud hill), a natural mound used as a redoubt and which, according to 16C chronicles, afforded a good view over the capital – hence the name of the nearby rue Montorgueil, which rates as one of the most lively streets in the area, along with rue St-Sauveur and rue des Petits-Carreaux.
Rue St-Denis is crossed by many small alleys, courtyards and passages. At no 145, **passage du Grand-Cerf**, a lovely arcade lined with boutiques, was built in 1835 on the site of the inn of the same name, a staging point until the Revolution.

Follow rue des Petits-Carreaux northwards to place du Caire (on the right).

Place du Caire – The former **cour des Miracles** (Courtyard of Miracles): a large courtyard, unpaved, stinking and muddy, lay hidden in a labyrinth of blind alleys, easily defensible passageways and darkened streets. Thousands of rogues, ruled by their own king, occupied the area which remained off-limits to any but their own. Victor Hugo's novel *The Hunchback of Notre-Dame* is a wonderful depiction of this wayward life. The neighbourhood was eventually cleared in 1667.

From rue du Caire walk through passage du Caire.

Shopping

Stohrer – *51 rue Montorgueil – 2nd arr –* Ⓜ *Les Halles, Sentier or Étienne-Marcel –* ☎ *01 42 33 38 20 – 7.30am-8.30pm – closed Aug.* Founded in the 18C by the pastry maker Stohrer, then decorated by Paul Baudry, creator of the Opéra Garnier's foyers, this house standing on the lively rue Montorgueil is reputed for its rum babas, macaroons and its *puits d'amour* (literally, wells of love – go ahead and fall in!).

Passage du Caire – A building decorated with Egyptian motifs (sphinx, lotus, hieroglyphs) marks the entrance of the passage intersected by three covered arcades. Napoleon's victorious campaign in Egypt in 1798 aroused great enthusiasm in Paris. A taste for the Egyptian style influenced all the decorative and applied arts, architecture and fashion included. Here street names reflect the craze, borrowed from campaigns against the Turks and the Marmalukes (rue du Nil, rue du Caire, rue d'Aboukir…).

Walk to rue de Cléry via rue d'Alexandrie and rue St-philippe.

Rue de Cléry – Fronted by clothes shops, this street is the old counterscarp of the Charles V perimeter wall.

Turn left onto rue des Degrés, where a stairway gives access to the former ramparts and leads to the back of the church of Notre-Dame-de-Bonne-Nouvelle.

Église Notre-Dame-de-Bonne-Nouvelle ⏱ – *25 rue de la Lune.*
The Classical belfry is all that remains of the church built by Anne of Austria – the rest of the building dates from 1823 to 1829. Inside numerous paintings decorate the walls. Note one by Mignard above the door in the south aisle of Anne of Austria and Henrietta-Maria, wife of Charles I of England; one at the end of the north aisle showing Henrietta of England and her three children before St Francis of Sales; an Annunciation by Lanfranco *(centre of the chancel, light switch on the right)*, and a painting by Philippe de Champaigne *(to the right)*. In the Lady Chapel there is a fine 18C Virgin and Child attributed to Pigalle.

Treasury – A small museum contains a 17C alabaster statue of St Jerome, two depictions of the Deposition and an 18C silk garment worn by the Abbot Edgeworth of Firmont who accompanied Louis XVI on his way to the guillotine.

SÈVRES-BABYLONE★

Michelin plan 10: K 11, K 12, L 11, L 12
Ⓜ *Rue-du-Bac (line 12), Sèvres-Babylone (lines 10 and 12), Vaneau (line 10) – Buses: 39, 68, 70, 83, 87, 94*

This neighbourhood dotted with interesting shops is a lively residential section of Paris. The origins of its name are obscure, although the first part refers to the manufacture of Sèvres porcelain.

Nearby neighbourhoods: FAUBOURG ST-GERMAIN, ST-SULPICE, INVALIDES, MONTPARNASSE.

EXPLORING THE NEIGHBOURHOOD

Start from boulevard du Montparnasse.

Rue du Cherche-Midi – This long street links Montparnasse with Sèvres-Babylone, and contains several fine town houses. At no 89 is the **Hôtel de Montmorency**, which today houses the Malian embassy, and nearby at no 85 is the Musée Hébert.
Make a short detour along rue Jean-Ferrandi to the right. Former artists' studios, nestling in narrow, flower-decked culs-de-sac, form an attractive picture.
On the corner of rue de l'Abbé-Grégoire is the Maison de Laënnec, once owned by René Laënnec (1781-1826), who invented the stethoscope and pioneered the use of auscultation. The **Hôtel de Rochambeau** at no 40 is named after Rochambeau who, in 1780, was empowered by Louis XVI to lead an army to assist the Americans in the War of Independence against the British.

Boulevard Raspail – The site of the former Prison du Cherche-Midi (1853-1954) at 52-54 boulevard Raspail is marked by roughly hewn square blocks of rock. This was where Captain Dreyfus was imprisoned (1894) and charged with selling military information to the Germans; the Dreyfus affair provoked impassioned debates regarding religious prejudice and human rights that were to lead to the establishment of a so-called left-wing party (1899). Later, the prison served as an interrogation centre during the Second World War.

Hôtel Lutétia – *45 boulevard Raspail.* Built in 1907 by the architects Louis Boileau and Henri Tanzin, the façade decoration was sculpted by Léon Binet and Paul Belmondo. Inside, the decor is elegantly old-fashioned with its Lalique chandelier; it was redone by the fashion designer Sonia Rykiel and Sybille de Margerie in 1983.

Carrefour de la Croix-Rouge – *Intersection of rue de Sèvres and rue du Cherche-Midi.* This crossroads was probably the site of a pagan temple dedicated to Isis predating the abbey of St-Germain. A red cross or calvary would have been installed in the 16C to rid the place of impious associations: hence the name. The present bronze Centaur statue is by César – the man who sculpted the famous figurines awarded annually to the film industry that bear his name.

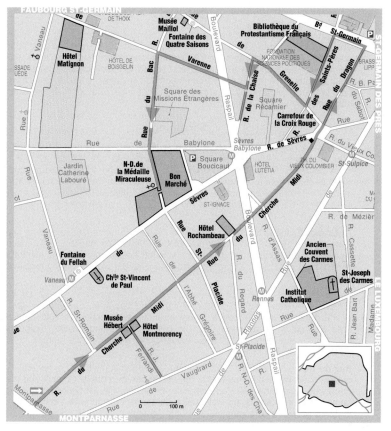

Rue du Dragon – This street, along with rue Bernard-Palissy and rue de Sabot nearby, captures the essence of a certain ineffable Parisian charm.

Turn left along boulevard St-Germain then left again onto rue des Saints-Pères.

Rue des Saints-Pères – The name is a distortion of St-Pierre to whom a chapel *(no 51)* belonging to a Charity hospital was dedicated in the 17C. It is now the Ukrainian Catholic church of St Vladimir the Great. The Engineering School is housed in the 18C mansions at no 28. Two other prestigious institutions are found here: the National Foundation for Political Sciences, and the French Protestant Library at no 54 *(see Museums and other attractions)*.

Rue de Grenelle – A street of old houses and elegant fashion shops with famous names.

Rue de la Chaise – Hôtel Vaudreuil *(no 5)* was given by Napoleon to the Borghese family, in-laws of his sister Pauline. Next door *(no 7)* stood the convent attached to the Abbaye aux Bois where Mme Récamier held her salons between 1819 and 1849, and received the novelist Chateaubriand (living at 120 rue du Bac) daily.

Turn right onto rue de Varenne and continue along rue du Bac.

Chapelle Notre-Dame-de-la-Médaille-Miraculeuse – *140 rue du Bac*. This is the chapel where the Virgin is said to have appeared to the novice Catherine Labouré from the convent of St-Vincent de Paul on 18 July 1830 – she was later beatified by Pius XII. This convent based at 95 rue de Sèvres is named after Monsieur Vincent who dedicated his life (1585-1660) to the destitute and orphans.

Le Bon Marché – *22 rue de Sèvres*. This department store, founded on the site of three former leprosy clinics, was the venture of Aristide Boucicault and his wife (1852). Success was achieved by several new practices we now take for granted: standardised price tagging, undercutting of competitors, offering a wide choice of quality products, maintaining stock levels, permitting an exchange of unwanted goods, discount sales and a mail-order service, prompt delivery of purchases outside Paris. Customer loyalty was encouraged by trained, courteous staff who, in turn were recompensed with free medical care and midday meals, uniforms, and facilities for evening language classes, choir practice and fencing! A tour of the *Épicerie* is a must.

Fontaine du Fellah – This unusual Egyptian-like figure in rue de Sèvres dates from 1806.

Going out

Bar Lutèce – *45 blvd Raspail* – *6th arr* – Ⓜ *Sèvres-Babylone* – ☏ *01 49 54 46 46* – *daily 9am-1am* – *Luté-Jazz evenings, Thu-Sat 10pm-1am and piano-bar daily from 7pm.* Two comfortable 1930s lounges welcome, in addition to its regulars, celebrities from the arts and letters. St-Germain-des-Prés is just down the road. In addition to the spacious room (adorned with an Arman sculpture), from 6pm onwards the Ernest Bar, a more intimate lounge, with its sculpture-cigar box signed by Hiquily, opens.

Shopping

Poilâne – *8 rue du Cherche-Midi* – *6th arr* – Ⓜ *Sèvres-Babylone or St-Sulpice* – *other address: 49 blvd de Grenelle 15th arr* – ☏ *01 45 48 42 59* – *www.poilane.fr* – *Mon-Sat 7.15am-8.15pm.* Not so long ago, penniless artists could be found here exchanging paintings for bread with this remarkable craftsman. The decoration has not changed since 1932, neither has the manufacturing method (6hr of preparation) of the bread which remains the best-known in Paris.

La Grande Épicerie de Paris – *38 rue de Sèvres* – *7th arr* – Ⓜ *Sèvres-Babylone* – ☏ *01 44 39 81 00* – *Mon-Sat 8.30am-9pm.* The handsome Art deco façade of this branch of the Bon Marché houses one of the capital's largest food halls: 30 000 products from all over the world! Equally excellent wine cellar.

Le Bon Marché – *24 rue de Sèvres* – *7th arr* – Ⓜ *Sèvres-Babylone* – ☏ *01 44 39 80 00* – *Mon-Wed, Fri 9.30am-7pm, Thu 10am-9pm, Sat 9.30am-8pm.* It was founded in 1852 by a highly inventive shopkeeper. His old French style and policy of selecting only the best products and fashion designers has led to the success of this exclusive department store spread over 32 000sq m/38 272sq yd.

Rue du Bac – *Rue du Bac* – *7th arr* – Ⓜ *Rue-du-Bac.* A multitude of home-decorators have grouped themselves in the streets between rue de Grenelle and rue de Sèvres: L'Occitane, MD Contemporain, Dîners en ville, Le Cèdre Rouge, the Conran Shop etc. A pleasant walk which can be finished off with a sorbet from the **Bac à glace** ice cream shop!

Eating out

Turn back to the Selected restaurants section at the beginning of the guide for a list of restaurants, bistros, cafés etc. This district is in the 6th *arrondissement.*

MUSEUMS AND OTHER ATTRACTIONS

Musée Hébert ⊘ – *85 rue du Cherche-Midi.* A fine 18C house accommodates a collection of the Romantic painter's work. He travelled widely in Italy, and his landscape paintings and attractive female portraits provide an insight into the tastes and social milieu of his lifetime (1817-1908).

★**Ancien couvent des Carmes** ⊘ – *70 rue de Vaugirard.* The Carmelite order, originally from Mount Carmel in Palestine, founded the House of the Carmelites in 1613. In the gardens, much altered by the building of rue d'Assas and rue de Rennes, the Carmelites cultivated the balm necessary for making their Eau des Carmes (a kind of herbal cordial drink) which provided them with substantial revenue. By the end of August 1792, during the troubled years of the Revolution, the monastery was turned into a prison; on 2 September, as the Prussians were advancing on Paris, churchmen and royalists were massacred (116 priests were killed in Les Carmes). Subsequently, 700 prisoners were held here. In 1796, under the Directory, peace returned; the buildings were secured in 1797 and returned to the Carmelites.

Église St-Joseph-des-Carmes – The church was built between 1613 and 1620 and is taken to be the first example of the Jesuit style in Paris. Inside, the chapels retain Louis XIII decoration. Note the **Bernini Virgin★** in the transept.

Bibliothèque du Protestantisme français ⊘ – *54 rue des Sts-Pères.* This discreet library, concealed at the end of a courtyard, is a good source of information on the Protestant religion in France. The decor evokes a studious atmosphere, with its long central table, wooden shelves, cast-iron pillars and glass roof. Note the names of famous Protestants inscribed on the balconies.

TROCADÉRO★★

Michelin plan 10: H 6, H 7
Ⓜ *Trocadéro (lines 6 and 9) – Buses: 22, 30, 32, 63, 82*

Set in the Trocadéro Gardens, the Chaillot Palace, with its broad terrace and powerful fountains, provides a raised view over the Seine, the Champ-de-Mars and the Eiffel Tower. It is this view, coupled with the rich and diverse museum collections that draws the visitor to this imposing architectural monument of the early 20C.

Nearby neighbourhoods: TOUR EIFFEL, ALMA, CHAMPS-ELYSÉES, INVALIDES, PASSY.

EXPLORING THE NEIGHBOURHOOD

Trocadéro – The name Trocadéro was given to the area in 1827 after a military tournament on the site had re-enacted the French capture four years previously of Fort Trocadéro, near Cadiz.

Place du Trocadéro et du 11-Novembre – The semicircular square was laid out in 1858. Today, dominated by an equestrian statue of Marshal Foch, it is a café-lined central point from which major roads radiate to the Alma Bridge, the Étoile, the Bois de Boulogne and the Passy quarter.

★★**Palais de Chaillot** – Built in 1939, the spectacular, low-lying palace of white stone, consisting of twin pavilions linked by a portico and extended by wings curving to frame the wide terrace, was the design of architects Carlu, Boileau and Azéma. The palace's horizontal lines along the brow of the hill make a splendid foil to the vertical sweep of the Eiffel Tower across the river. The pavilion copings, back and front, bear inscriptions in letters of gold by the poet Paul Valéry.

★★★**Terrace** – Looking across to the Champ-de-Mars, you get a wonderful **view**, in the foreground, of the Seine and the Left Bank and, rising above it all, the Eiffel Tower; at the end of the green swathe is the École Militaire, a handsome reminder of the 18C.

Eight gilded figures line the terrace along the wings – *Flora* by Marcel Gimont being the most famous. Before the left pavilion stands a monumental bronze of Apollo by **H Bouchard** balanced on the Passy side, with *America* by Jacques Zwoboda.

Art Deco statue,
Palais de Chaillot

★★★**Gardens** – *Avenue de New-York*. These were designed for the 1937 Exhibition. Beyond the walls on either side of the long rectangular pool on an axis with the Iéna Bridge, the final slopes of Chaillot Hill lead down, beneath flowering trees, to the banks of the Seine.

The pool, bordered by stone statues *(Youth* by Pierre Loison and *Joie de Vivre* by Léon Divier), is at its most spectacular at night when the powerful fountains are floodlit.

Théâtre national de Chaillot – Beneath the palace terrace is one of the capital's largest theatres *(access through the hall in the left pavilion)*. Firmin Génier created the TNP (Théâtre National Populaire) in 1920; one of its most famous directors was Jean Vilar (1951-63). In 1988, Jérôme Savary, of Grand Magic Circus fame, became the prolific and sometimes provocative director of the newly baptised Théâtre National de Chaillot.

MUSEUMS AND OTHER ATTRACTIONS

★★**Musée Nationale de la Marine** ⊙ – The Maritime Museum was founded in 1827 by order of Charles X.

⌖ **Chronology**: Scale models and important artefacts from the naval dockyards trace maritime history from the 17C to the present day. The models of galleys and sailing ships date from the 17C: *The Réale* (with decoration attributed to Puget). The **Ports of France★**, a series of canvases by the 18C artist, Joseph Vernet. The *Royal Louis* is a rare model from the Louis XV period. From the Revolution and the First Empire, there is the *Emperor's Barge* (1811), leading up to the Restoration, the Second Empire and the Third Republic.

Thematic: The scientific, technical, traditional and artistic evolution of navigation. The history of merchant shipping, steam ships and the navy is accompanied by film shows. The visit ends with two modern French warships: the nuclear submarine *Le Triomphant* (1996) and the *Charles-de-Gaulle* (1999).

★★ Musée des Monuments français ⊘ – This museum of France's monumental art and mural painting, comprising casts and replicas, was the brainchild of the Gothic Revival architect and restorer of medieval monuments Viollet-le-Duc. It was opened in 1879.

The exhibits are grouped by geographical region, by school and by period, making evolutions of style, themes, geographical and other influences, easy to follow.

Le Trocadéro

Jardin des TUILERIES ★

Michelin plan 10: G 11, G 12, H 11, H 12
Ⓜ *Concorde (lines 1, 8 and 12), Tuileries (lines 1 and 7)*
Buses: 42, 68, 72, 73, 84, 94

Stretching between the Louvre and place de la Concorde, the Arc de Triomphe and the Grande Arche at La Défense, the Tuileries Gardens were envisaged by **Colbert** as the first section of the road from the Royal Palace to the forest of St-Germain.

Nearby neighbourhoods: GRAND LOUVRE, PLACE DE LA CONCORDE, CHAMPS-ÉLYSÉES, PALAIS-ROYAL, FAUBOURG ST-HONORÉ.

The lost château – In the 15C the area was used as a rubbish tip by butchers and tanners of the Châtelet district. The local clay was dug for making tiles – *tuiles* – hence the name Tuileries. In 1563, Catherine de' Medici decided to have a château built next to the Louvre, a project she entrusted to **Philibert Delorme** in 1564. Work was abruptly halted when the Queen Mother learnt that her horoscope predicted that she would die near to St-Germain, and that the Tuileries depended upon St-Germain-l'Auxerrois. A house was therefore built in the lee of St-Eustache (the prediction nevertheless came true as 22 years later, Monsignor de St-Germain gave her the last rights).

In 1594, shortly after his arrival in Paris, Henri IV ordered work to proceed and the Pavillon de Flore was built. The riverside gallery designed to link the Louvre with the Tuileries followed, raised by a second storey.

Louis XIV extended the complex to accommodate a theatre (1659-61), named after the complicated scene-changing equipment, Salle des Machines. In 1664, the king moved to the Tuileries while building progressed on the Louvre. Le Vau revamped the exterior and constructed the Pavillon de Marsan. Parties, ballets and masques punctuated the three winters spent by the king at the Tuileries.

Walks

The Garden covers some 25ha from the two sphinxes which mount guard opposite the Pavillon de Flore (brought back from Sebastopol after the city was seized in 1855) to the national gallery of the Jeu de Paume, opposite the Hôtel Talleyrand on rue de Rivoli.

Fair

⊚ Every year a fair is held in the gardens from June 21 to Aug 25. The big wheel and other attractions can be seen from afar.

Children

⊚ Along rue de Rivoli, the Tuileries Garden has a wide range of activities for children with swings, merry-go-rounds, go-karts, roller-skating areas, horse and donkey riding and play areas. There is also a pond in the middle where small sailing boats can be rented (in the summer).

Going out

Café Véry – *Tuileries gardens – 1st arr – ☏ 01 47 03 94 84 – daily noon-11.45pm.* What better place to stop for a drink than under the leafy chestnut trees of the Tuileries Garden! Snacks and refreshments also available: salads, sandwiches and classic French dishes are served in the glass and blond-wood pavilion. Relaxed. In the evening, the entrance is via the gate from the Concorde.

Shopping

Galignani – *224 r. de Rivoli – 1st arr – Ⓜ Tuileries – ☏ 01 42 60 76 07 – galignani@gofornet.fr – Mon-Sat 10am-7pm – closed public holidays.* Founded in 1801, the bookshop is still run by the Galignani family. This prestigious firm is proud to have been the first English bookshop established on the continent. Excellent history, art and cooking sections.

Eating out

Turn back to the Selected restaurants section at the beginning of the guide for a list of restaurants, bistros, cafés etc. This district is in the 1st *arrondissement*.

The 18C – In 1715, on the death of the Sun King, the Regency installed the young Louis XV in the Tuileries. In 1722, he moved the court back to Versailles, and the palace was more or less abandoned as a residence.

Instead, Paris' first public concert-hall was set up in the Salle des Suisses in 1725. It drew many major composers and musicians, from home and other European courts, including **Mozart** (1778). Important performances of religious works lasted until 1789. Simultaneously, when fire devastated the Opéra Theatre in April 1763, the Company moved into the Salles des Machines, refurbished by Gabriel and Soufflot. The Comédie Française took over in 1770, staging **Beaumarchais'** *Barber of Seville* and Voltaire's *Irène* before 1782.

Troubled times – On 17 October 1789 the royal family were forced back to Paris by the angry mob; the queen and her children took flight on 20 June 1791. A year later, to the day, the palace was invaded by rioters who seized the king; two months later, on 10 August, the palace was attacked: 600 of the defending 900 Swiss guards were slaughtered and the palace was ransacked.

During the Convention, the buildings served as ministry offices.

Final decline – First Consul Bonaparte took up residence on 20 February 1800. In 1810, the Emperor Napoleon I celebrated his marriage to Marie-Louise in the Salon Carré of the Louvre. A year later, the king of Rome was born at the Tuileries which continued to serve as the Royal household to subsequent kings. Under **Napoleon III** the architects **Visconti** and Lefuel completed the Galerie Rivoli, thereby completing the union of the Tuileries and the Louvre.

During the week of Commune uprisings (1871), the Tuileries Palace was burnt down. In 1883, the stone ruins were purchased by a Corsican family who went on to use the stones to build a replica palace in Ajaccio (this too was burnt down in 1978).

The gardens – Catherine de' Medici envisaged an Italian-style park, complete with fountains, a maze, a grotto, populated with terracotta figures by **Bernard Palissy**, and a menagerie for her palace next to the Louvre. East of the octagonal basin stood a semicircular screen of trees famous for its echo. Henri IV later added an orangery and a silkworm farm. The park became a fashionable place for an outdoor stroll thereby

S. Sauvignier/MICHELIN

breaking new ground, for hitherto fashion and elegance had always been displayed indoors.

Le Nôtre French Garden – By 1664 the gardens required attention; Colbert delegated the work to Le Nôtre, born near the Marsan Pavilion and a gardener at the Tuileries, like his father and grandfather before him. He raised two terraces lengthways and of unequal height to level the sloping ground thereby creating the magnificent central axis; he hollowed out the pools and designed formal flower beds, quincunxes and slopes.

Colbert was so delighted that he intended the gardens to be kept for the royal family, but was subsequently persuaded by the author, Charles Perrault, to allow access to the public. In the 18C the gardens became ever more attractive and chairs were made available for hire and toilets installed. Louis-Philippe reserved a part of the gardens for the royal family. In 1783 the physicist, Charles, and the engineer, Robert, made one of the first hot-air balloon flights from the gardens.

EXPLORING THE NEIGHBOURHOOD

The Tuileries today – The gardens have recently undergone a substantial restoration programme. Parts designed by Le Nôtre remain unaltered, although some sculptures have been moved and others added, including the fine collection of **nudes★** by **Maillol** and Rodin's The Kiss. Other 20C works by Dubuffet, Ernst, Laurens, Moore, Calder, Giacometti, Arp and Picasso have recently been installed.

Steps and ramps afford access at several points to the terraces (the **Feuillants** on the north side, the **Bord de l'Eau** on the south) which run the length of the gardens and culminate in the Jeu de Paume and Orangery pavilions.

From the riverside terrace there is a splendid **view★★** over the gardens, the Seine and, in the background, the Louvre. This was the playground of the royal princes including the sons of Napoleon I and III. Below, an underground passage running the length of the terrace to place de la Concorde enabled Louis-Philippe to escape from the palace in 1848.

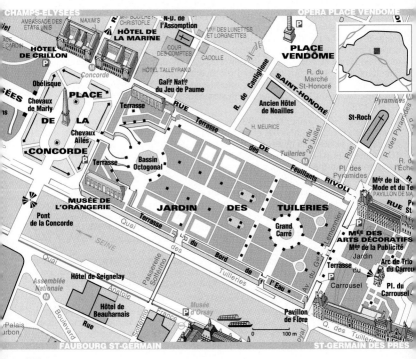

L'Arc de Triomphe du Carrousel

The **central alley** affords a magnificent **vista★★★**. On either side, the **quincunxes**, typical of formal French gardens (it is an arrangement of five objects, with one at each corner and one in the middle of a square or rectangle) are decorated with 19C and 20C statues.

The octagonal pool – Around the huge octagonal basin are arranged statues, terraces, slopes and stairways in one single architectural whole. Works are listed starting from the eastern side of the basin, going counter-clockwise.

The Seasons (N Coustou and Van Clève)
Arcade from the Tuileries Palace
Bust of Le Nôtre (Coysevox) – the original is in St-Roch *(see PALAIS-ROYAL)*.
The Tiber copied from the Antique
The Seine and *The Marne* (G Coustou)
The Loire and *The Loiret* (Van Clève)
The Nile copied from the Antique
Fame on a winged horse after Coysevox *(on the left of the main gate)*
Mercury on a winged horse after Coysevox *(on the right of the main gate)* – originals in the Louvre.

★ **Arc de Triomphe du Carrousel** – *see LE LOUVRE.*

Rue de Rivoli

Rue de Rivoli crosses the site of the former Tuileries **Riding School**. In 1789 the school was hastily converted into a meeting place for the Constituent Assembly. Sessions were subsequently held there by the Legislative Assembly and the Convention. On 21 September 1792, the day following the French victory over the Prussians at Valmy (commemorative tablet on a pillar in the Tuileries railings opposite no **230**), it became the setting for the proclamation of the Republic and the trial of Louis XVI (1792).
In 1944 the German General von Choltitz, Commandant of Paris, who had his headquarters at the **hôtel Meurice** (no **228**), took a momentous decision in the capital's own history by refusing to follow Hitler's orders to blow up the capital's bridges and principal buildings when the tanks of General Leclerc's division and the Resistance were known to be approaching. He surrendered on 25 August and Paris was liberated intact. At the far end by place de la Concorde several commemorative plaques record the heroism of those who fell during the Liberation.

MUSEUMS AND OTHER ATTRACTIONS

The two pavilions, the **Orangerie** and the **Jeu de Paume** were built during the Second Empire and have served as art galleries since the beginning of the 20C.

★★ **Musée de l'Orangerie** ⊘ – *Closed for restoration*. The horseshoe staircase with wrought iron-work by Raymond Subes leads to the first-floor galleries that accommodate the Walter-Guillaume Collection (Impressionists to 1930). This famous collection presents the work of many artists including Soutine, Picasso, Modigliani, Cézanne, Renoir, Derain, Matisse and Rousseau.

The two oval rooms on the ground floor are hung with panels from the water-lily series painted by **Monet** of his garden at Giverny, in Normandy known as the **Nymphéas★★★**.

Galerie nationale du Jeu de Paume ⊘ – Since its Impressionist collection was moved to the Musée d'Orsay, this gallery has been soberly refurbished to display to best advantage the most advanced elements in contemporary art.

VAUGIRARD

Michelin plan 10: N 8, N 9, P 8, P9
Ⓜ *Vaugirard (line 12)* – *Buses: 39, 70, 80, 88, 89*

The old village of Vaugirard used to be a rural dependency of the abbey of St-Germain-des-Prés; in the 18C it consisted of 700 people. In 1860 Vaugirard became a district of Paris with a population of 40 000 inhabitants. It is bisected by two principle streets: rue de Vaugirard and rue Lecourbe. It is a quiet residential area today, with a popular book market in Parc Georges-Brassens. The southern border is at the Porte de Versailles, where major trade fairs are held year-round.

Nearby neighbourhood: MONTPARNASSE.

EXPLORING THE NEIGHBOURHOOD

★ **Parc Georges-Brassens** - *Rue des Morillons*.

⊡ This is one of the largest parks created in Paris in the 19C. It occupies the site of the old Vaugirard abattoirs, of which a few vestiges survive – the horse hall, two bronze bulls by the animal sculptor Cain at the main entrance, and the auction belfry reflected in the central basin.

A wooded hill dominates the park with its children's play areas, a belvedere, a climbing rock and a vineyard harvested in early October with great fanfares.

An olfactory garden has been created for the blind, containing over 80 species of aromatic plants.

In rue Brancion there is a second-hand book fair every weekend.

Rue and villa Santos-Dumont – *Access via rue des Morillons*. Zadkine, Fernard Léger and Georges Brassens found inspiration for their work in the discreet charm of this corner of Paris.

Passage Dantzig – The three-storey wine pavilion designed by Eiffel for the Exposition Universelle of 1900 was salvaged from scrap by the socially successful sculptor Boucher, with the intention of adapting it for use as artists' lodgings and studios. Known as **La Ruche**, among its most famous lodgers were Fernand Leger (1905), Chagall (1910), Soutine, **Modigliani** and the Swiss novelist Blaise Cendras. The second generation included the sculptors Archipenko, Idenbaum, Lipchitz, **Zadkine**, **Brancusi** and Kisling.

Rue de Vaugirard – This is Paris' longest street, running between the Latin Quarter and the Porte de Versailles, where the major trade exhibitions are held. Shops tend to centre around intersections of rue de la Convention and rue de Vaugirard, rue Lecourbe, rue du Commerce and rue St-Charles.

Pasteur Institute ⊘ – *25 rue du Docteur-Roux*. A scientific foundation of international repute, the Pasteur Institute mainly comprises centres of basic and applied research, of teaching and documentation, of inoculation and screening with laboratories producing serums, vaccines and diagnostic tests, and a hospital specialising in infectious diseases.

The Institute has branches in Lille and Lyon, and 22 others worldwide, continuing pioneering research into such infectious diseases as Hepatitis and AIDS with international support. It was to this cause that Wallace Simpson bequeathed her famous jewellery collection when she died in 1993.

Émile Roux (1853-1933) had studied the toxins of diphtheria and discovered its antidote in the late 19C, when he was appointed director of the Pasteur Institute. He subsequently engaged researchers Albert Calmette and Camille Guérin who, from 1915 onwards, developed the vaccine against tuberculosis (BCG).

Going out

Planet Cyber Café – *173 rue de Vaugirard – 15th arr – Ⓜ Pasteur – ☏ 01 45 67 71 14 – Mon-Sat 10.30am-8pm – closed 1 Jan and 25 Dec*. One of the capital's tiniest cyber-cafés (10 computers), but one of the friendliest.

The living quarters of Louis Pasteur, including much scientific memorabilia, and the neo-Byzantine **crypt★** containing his tomb, are open to visitors.

Louis Pasteur (1822-95) is one of the greatest scientists ever to have lived. At the age of 25, in his laboratory at the École Normale Supérieure, he established the principle of molecular dissymmetry; at 35, that of fermentation; at 40, he laid the foundations for asepsis thus refuting preconceived ideas about spontaneous generations, and he studied the ruinous diseases affecting beer and wine production and of the silkworm; at 58, he studied viruses and vaccines. He isolated the rabies virus, researching its prevention, delivering an antidote for the first time on 7 July 1885.

Place des VICTOIRES★

Michelin plan 10: G 13, G 14
Ⓜ *Étienne-Marcel (line 4) – Buses: 29, 67, 74, 85*

Unusual shops, picturesque arcades and passageways – this is an elegant, peaceful district where it is pleasant to stroll and discover old Paris or, just simply, window-shop.

Nearby neighbourhoods: PALAIS-ROYAL, OPÉRA, LES HALLES, GRANDS BOULEVARDS.

EXPLORING THE NEIGHBOURHOOD

See plan PALAIS-ROYAL.

★Place des Victoires – In 1685 Marshal de la Feuillade, to curry favour with Louis XIV, commissioned a statue of the king from the sculptor **Desjardins**. The statue, unveiled in 1686, showed the king, crowned with the laurels of victory, standing on a pedestal adorned with six low-relief sculptures and four captives representing the vanquished Spain, Holland, Prussia and Austria. Surviving sections of the group are presently in the Louvre.

The main statue was melted down in 1792; a new figure by Desaix replaced it in 1806 only to be melted down in turn in 1815 (and reappear as Henri IV on the Pont Neuf). The present equestrian statue of the Sun King was sculpted by Bosio in 1822.

The side of the square with even numbers is the least damaged and gives some idea of the intended 17C elegance, although its harmony was impaired by the construction of rue Etienne-Marcel in 1883.

One of the façades of the **Banque de France**, founded at the instigation of **Napoleon** in January 1800, can be seen looking down rue Catinat, from the entrance of rue d'Aboukir.

Take rue Vide-Gousset, from the north side of the square, which leads to place des Petits-Pères. Make a brief detour up rue du Mail.

Rue du Mail – Note *(no 5)* the faun's mask and cornucopias adorning the doorway and at no 7 the capitals with interlaced snakes: these two 17C mansions make up the Hôtel Colbert, formerly owned by Louis XIV's minister (the grass snake is Colbert's emblem from *coluber* in Latin, *couleuvre* in French). At no 14, the 18C Hôtel de Berthault, lived Madame Récamier and Franz Liszt stayed at no 13 on several occasions between 1823 and 1878.

Basilique de Notre-Dame-des-Victoires – *Place des Petits-Pères*. The square occupies the site of an Augustinian monastery. The basilica (built 1629-1740) served as the Petits-Pères monastery chapel, dedicated in honour of the king's victories. It

Ph. Gajic/MICHELIN

Place des Victoires

served as the Stock Exchange from 1795 to 1809. Inside, the wood panelling in the chancel dates from the 17C, there are seven paintings by Van Loo (*Louis XIII dedicating the church to the Virgin*, and scenes from the *Life of St Augustine*), a fine 18C organ loft and a monument to the 17C composer, **Lully** *(2nd chapel on the left)*. The church is famous for its annual pilgrimage to the Virgin which goes back to 1836; some 35 000 ex-votos cover the walls.

Take passage des Petits-Pères to reach the Vivienne and Colbert galleries.

The Arcades – Built in 1823, the **Galerie Vivienne** is one of the busiest arcades in Paris. Light floods through the glass roof. Notice the half-moon windows on the mezzanine, and the mosaics designed by the Italian artist Facchina. There are old bookshops (nos 45 and 46, the Petit Siroux, was established in 1826), haberdashers and a tearoom. **Galerie Colbert** was opened in 1826 and has recently been renovated. Windows display the various activities of the National Library and the auditorium beneath the rotunda is used for concerts.

Passage Choiseul – This links rue des Petits-Champs to rue St-Augustin. Less lavish than those described above, this arcade opened in 1827. It was immortalised by the writer **Louis-Ferdinand Céline**, who lived at nos 64 and 67 as a child and gave a cutting description of it in his work *Mort à Crédit (Death on the Instalment Plan)*.

Shopping

E. Dehillerin – *18-20 rue Coquillière – 1st arr – ☎ 01 42 36 53 13 – Mon 8am-12.30pm, 2-6pm, Tue-Sat 9am-6pm – closed public holidays*. Pots and pans, knives of all shapes and sizes and other professional cooking utensils also sold to private customers.

Kenzo – *3 pl. des Victoires – 1st arr – Ⓜ Sentier – other addresses: 60-62 r. de Rennes, 6th arr; 16 blvd Raspail, 7th arr; 27 bd de la Madeleine, 8th arr; 18 av. George-V, 8th arr – ☎ 01 40 39 72 03 – Mon-Sat 10am-7.30pm – closed public holidays*. This spacious temple to ready-to-wear fashion is popular with men and women alike. The staff is charming and the service is personalised, in keeping with the collections of this Japanese designer who has combined Eastern and Western influences to create his own sober, elegant style.

Place des Victoires – *Pl. des Victoires – 1st arr – Ⓜ Sentier*. This square, devoted to fashion, has names such as Plein Sud, very popular with young women, Victoire, who cater to an elegant, international woman, Thierry Mugler, for men, and Cacharel and Kenzo. For smaller budgets, there is also Blanc-Bleu and Esprit.

Jean-Paul Gaultier – *6 rue Vivienne – 2nd arr – Ⓜ Bourse – ☎ 01 42 86 05 05 – Mon-Fri 10am-7pm, Sat 11am-7pm – closed public holidays*. Located in the former stables of the Palais-Royal, Jean-Paul Gaultier's shop is well worth a visit. Its extravagant design is a distinctive hallmark of this designer whose reputation is worldwide.

L. Legrand Filles and Fils – *1 rue de la Banque – 2nd arr – Ⓜ Bourse – ☎ 01 42 60 07 12 – www.caves-legrand.com – Mon 10am-7pm, Tue-Fri 9am-7.30pm, Sat 10am-1pm and 3-7pm*. This authentic wine cellar and fine grocery shop is the home of a reputed family of wine dealers. From the classical to the unusual, let yourself be guided by the master of the house and don't forget to take a look at their selection of regional goodies.

Ventilo – *27 bis rue du Louvre – 2nd arr – Ⓜ Les Halles – other addresses: 267 rue St-Honoré, 1st arr; 10 rue des Francs-Bourgeois, 3rd arr; 59 rue Bonaparte, 6th arr; 49-51 av. Victor-Hugo, 16th arr; 96 av. Paul-Doumer, 16th arr – ☎ 01 42 33 18 67 – www.ventilo.fr – Mon-Sat 10.30am-7pm – closed 1 week in summer, 1 May and Whitsun*. This highly elegant boutique with its oriental-style decor, also has a tearoom much appreciated by chic Parisians. Three floors of sportswear and classic clothes, but also beauty care products and decorative objects for the home.

The Hôtels – Look through the grille at no **8** rue des Petits-Champs for a glimpse of the courtyard and the sombre brick and stone façade of the **Tubeuf** mansion (1648-55). Opposite stands **Colbert**'s mansion (1665) now an annexe of the National Library.

The former **Hôtel de Nevers**, on the corner of rue Richelieu, was designed by Mansart and has served to accommodate in turn Mazarin's personal library, Mme de Lambert's literary salon (18C), and the royal medal collection.

Square Louvois – The square accommodates a fine fountain by Visconti (1884), whose four allegorical sculptures represent France's major four rivers: the Seine, the Rhône, the Loire and the Garonne.

In 1793, the Opéra Company moved into the **Hôtel Louvois**; it remained there until 1820, when the premises were burnt down following the murder of the Duc de Berry at the hands of a certain Louvel; it subsequently moved to rue Le-Peletier.

Bibliothèque nationale de France: site Richelieu – *58 rue de Richelieu.*

The Collections – In the Middle Ages the kings of France accumulated manuscripts in their palaces; Charles V mustered nearly 1 000 volumes in the Louvre Library, dispersed at his death; Charles VIII and Louis XII built their libraries at Blois.

The present national collection was founded upon François I's library from Fontainebleau, endowed with a copy of every book subsequently printed in France, as decreed in 1537. As of 1998, when printed works and periodicals were transferred to the new buildings at the François Mitterand site *(see BERCY)*, this part of the library has kept the specialised collections: manuscripts, engravings and photographs, maps and plans, musical scores, coins, medals and items from antiquity.

A home fit for a royal library – In the 17C the Hôtel Tubeuf was enlarged by Mansart and named after Cardinal Mazarin whose 500 pictures and personal decorative art collection it housed. Opposite, Colbert installed the Royal Library's 200 000 volumes (1666) in his own mansion in rue Vivienne. In 1720, this collection was moved in with the Mazarin collection. The Nevers and Chivry mansions were taken over in the 19C.

The east side of the main courtyard is by the 18C architect, Robert de Cotte. The reading room (1868) *(restricted access)* can be seen through a window. In the State Room is a plaster *model* for the marble bust of Voltaire by Houdon at the Comédie-Française (the philosopher's heart is enclosed in the base). On the floor above is the magnificent **Mazarin Gallery★** by Mansart *(access during temporary exhibitions)*. The great staircase leads to the **Medals and Antiques Museum★** ⊘ (mezzanine level): exhibiting objets d'art requisitioned or confiscated from royal collections at the time of the Revolution. Note the ivory chess sets, Dagobert's legendary throne, the Sainte-Chapelle Cameo and coins.

La Bourse (Stock Exchange) – The exchange building and the monumental square stand on the site of a Dominican convent which was secularised in 1795 and became the seat of the royalist faction responsible for the insurrection of 13 Vendémiaire – 5 October, 1795.

Paris' first exchange was John Law's bank. When it went bankrupt, the public got to learn so much about share dealing that a public exchange was founded (1724). It was located in the Palais Mazarin (now part of the Bibliothèque Nationale), before being transferred to the church of Notre-Dame des Victoires. Brongniart's building dates from 1808 to 1826; two wings were added between 1902 and 1907.

La VILLETTE★★

Michelin plan 10: B 20, B 21, C 20, C 21
Ⓜ *Porte de La Villette (north: Cité des Sciences et de L'Industrie – line 7) and Porte de Pantin (south: Cité de la Musique – line 5) – Buses: 75, 139, 150, 152*

The city's largest park extends between the Porte de La Villette and the Porte de Pantin. The vast green space is home to a modern museum complex dedicated to science and industry (La Cité des Sciences et de l'Industrie), and another devoted to music (La Cité de la Musique), as well as La Grande Halle and commodious concert venue, Le Zénith. The modern architecture in a green setting makes the park a place for both culture and relaxation. If you are travelling with children, be sure to include this in your itinerary, as there are plenty of things to interest them and a lot of room in the park for running and shouting.

★★★CITÉ DES SCIENCES ET DE L'INDUSTRIE ⊘

Designed by architect Adrien Fainsilber and opened in 1986, this interactive complex has three aims: to inform, to teach and to give pleasure. It succeeds in all three, in a setting where the elements of water, vegetation and light mould the building's inception.

The museums

Cité des Sciences et de l'Industrie – *30 av. Corentin-Cariou* – Ⓜ *Porte de La Villette*.

Information – *Answering machine* ☎ *01 40 05 80 00* – *Internet: www.cite-sciences.fr (in French)*.

Musée de la Musique – *221 av. Jean-Jaurès* – Ⓜ *Porte de Pantin* – ☎ *01 44 84 44 84* – *Internet: www.cite-musique.fr*.

PAYING ACTIVITIES

It is possible to purchase a combined ticket to both places. Audio-guide for Explora available (3.81€).

Explora and **Louis-Lumière cinema**: 7.50€. (Under 25s and adult accompanying an under 16: 5.50€; Under 7s free). Additional charge for the Planetarium: 2.50€.

Cité des Enfants (3-5 years or 5-12 years) and **Électricité**: 5€ per child for 1hr 30min. Reservations: ☎ 08 92 69 70 72.

Géode: 8.75€ per projection. Reservations: ☎ 08 92 68 45 40.

Cinaxe: 5.18€ at the Cinaxe. Not suitable for very young children.

FREE ACTIVITIES

Cité des métiers: Daily (except Sun and public holidays) 10am-6pm, Sat noon-6pm. Level – 1.

Médiathèque: Noon-6.45pm (7.45pm on Tue and Fri) – closed Mon. Levels – 1 and – 2 for adults; ground floor for children.

Salle Louis Braille: Computerised reading room for the blind. Level – 1, inside the Médiathèque, by appointment.

Cinéma Jean-Bertin: Documentaries, scientific and technical films. Ground floor; projection times available on location.

Mediterranean aquarium: Level – 2.

SOUVENIRS AND GIFT SHOP

Boutique Explorus – *Ground floor*. The shop sells games, gifts and other souvenirs, including lots of really fun toys which demonstrate scientific principles. A **book-shop** stocks catalogues of the exhibitions, together with guide books. Post cards and scientific reviews and books.

Eating out

Café de la musique – *221 av. Jean-Jaurès* – *19th arr* – ☎ *01 48 03 15 91* – *daily 8am-2am*. Conveniently located next to the Cité de la Musique, this café is modern and elegant, a charming place to sit and enjoy a cup of coffee or a fine meal. Inside, red and green armchairs alternate around little round tables. Outside, the terrace facing the green swathe of the park is a very inviting place to enjoy the late afternoon sun and a drink.

The Cité des Sciences et de l'Industrie has several bars, cafés, restaurants etc which are located on levels – 1, 0 and 1. You can also turn back to the "Eating out" section at the beginning of the guide for a list of restaurants, bistros, cafés etc. The museum and park are in the 19th *arrondissement*.

★★ **Explora** – ⌖ *Levels 1 and 2*. Explore today's and tomorrow's world by means of a variety of exhibitions and interactive shows, models and hands-on activities.

Space – *Level 1, south gallery and level 2, mezzanine*. A mystery that has fascinated man since the beginning of time. Surf in space, among the stars and the galaxies, in search of the answer.

The Earth's water – *Level 1, south gallery*. How does it become tap water? The purification, distribution and recycling of our drinking water.

Oceans – *Level 1, south gallery*. The Nautile, the most recent French submarine explores the wreck of the Titanic, forecasts earthquakes and studies underwater oases.

Hothouses, the gardens of the future – *Level 1, south gallery*. Learn how to grow plants without soil and create new varieties, but beware, tampering with nature is dangerous.

Cars – *Level 1, south gallery*. Witness the birth of a motor car, a simulated accident and watch the development of new engines.

Aeronautics – *Level 1, south gallery*. A mirage IV of the French air force welcomes you to this section illustrating the history of jet planes where you can fly the aircraft of your choice (flight simulator).

Energy – *Level 1, south gallery*. The Earth's resources (coal, gas, oil, water, etc) transformed by man into energy.

Images – *Level 1, north gallery.* How to transform what we see: photography, cinema, television, video films, digital images.

Computer science – *Level 1, south gallery.* Where would we be today without computers? Let us therefore follow the evolution of this marvellous tool and its varied applications.

Sounds – *Level 1, south gallery.* Visitors can listen to a multitude of sounds, from a rubbing noise to a buzzing noise, a whistling noise…

Mathematics – *Level 1 south gallery.* Geometric shapes, numbers, statistics….

Rocks and volcanoes – *Level 2, north mezzanine.* Earthquakes, volcanic eruptions, the formation of mountains and oceans… What is the centre of the Earth made of?

Planétarium – *Level 2, north mezzanine.* This is one of the prime visitor attractions. Astronomical phenomena are described with projections of actual real-life images, a simulator and triphonic sound.

Stars and galaxies – *Level 2, west mezzanine.* The solar system, the birth and death of a star, the instruments used by astronomers or rather astrophysicists.

Man and health – *Level 2, north and central mezzanine.* Being born, growing up, growing old, such is our life cycle and health is an integral part of it.

Medicine – *Level 2, north mezzanine.* What is medicine? Examine a dummy and determine its illness, take a trip through the human body and learn that drugs are not the only means of curing people.

Biology – *Level 2, north mezzanine.* It all starts with a single cell… Learn about some of the miracles accomplished by scientific research, in particular in the field of genetic diseases.

Light effects – *Level 2, north mezzanine.* Light plays an essential role in our perception of the world: it enables us to see in three dimensions, to perceive colours and even to see strange things (is it reality or an optical illusion?).

Cité des Enfants – 🎦 *Ground floor.* A hands-on interactive section reserved for 3 to 5 and 5 to 12 year-olds. Play, observation and experimentation in the world of science and technology. There is plenty to keep older children intrigued, as they find the answers to scientific and technical questions during sessions lasting 1hr 30min. How do you write software, or create a prototype?

Médiathèque – *Levels – 1 and – 2 for adults, ground floor for children.* This library provides not only books and printed data, but also access to externally held computerised published information in the form of video, CD-ROM and other educational material.

★★ **La Géode** ⊘ – *In the park just outside the museum. The most comfortable viewing is from the top of the hall.*
   🎦 The shining steel globe, 36m/118ft in diameter, seems to hover over a sheet of water; a brilliant feat of engineering in terms both of structure and technology. Inside, the auditorium is equipped with a hemispherical aluminium 1 000m²/11 000sq ft screen, perforated for sound. The wide-angle

La Géode

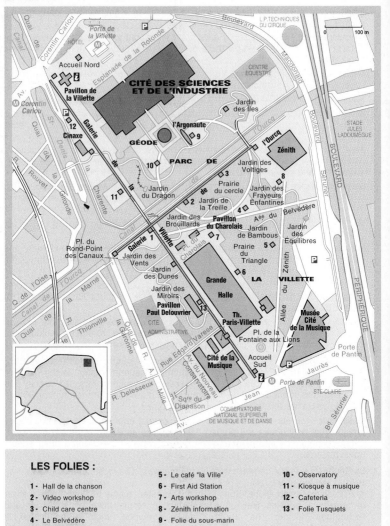

LES FOLIES :

1 - Hall de la chanson	5 - Le café "la Ville"	10 - Observatory
2 - Video workshop	6 - First Aid Station	11 - Kiosque à musique
3 - Child care centre	7 - Arts workshop	12 - Cafeteria
4 - Le Belvédère	8 - Zénith information	13 - Folie Tusquets
	9 - Folie du sous-marin	

lens encompasses a 180° field of vision, exceeding that of the human eye (140°), but similar to that of a bird's. The multimedia system projects films with scientific and cultural themes.

L'Argonaute – *Outside, next to the Géode*. This submarine was launched on 29 June 1957 at Cherbourg; it has covered 210 000mi, the equivalent of four times the circumference of the earth, and was submerged a total of 32 700hr before finally coming to rest beside the Géode. It now serves as an additional exhibition space dedicated to the submersible's technology.

Le Simulateur (Cinaxe) ⊘ – ⊚ *Outside*. The Cinaxe simulator enables up to 60 people to physically experience a particular film action – a flight through outer space, or driving round a motor-racing track, during a 4 to 5min ride. This sensation is in part achieved by the capsule's actual hydraulic motion, and partly through wearing 3-D glasses *(supplied)*.

CITÉ DE LA MUSIQUE

⊚ Located at the southern entrance to the park, near the Porte de Pantin, and on either side of the Lion Fountain, Music City, designed by Christian de Portzamparc, houses all the facilities needed to study dance and music in France today. The western part contains the **Conservatoire national supérieur de musique et de danse de Paris** (Paris National Conservatory of Music and Dance), whereas on the eastern side is a concert hall and a music museum.

★ **Musée de la Musique** Ⓥ – The museum contains around 900 musical instruments from the 17C to the present time. An audio-visual tour, taking the visitor through the history of Western music, includes Stradivarius and Amati violins, some 50 spinets, harpsichords, and pianos, guitars, recorders, bass viols and lutes. Also on display are tools used by stringed-instrument and piano makers, and instruments once owned by famous musicians (Berlioz, Chopin and Fauré, Adolphe Sax). Paintings, sculptures and models of the great European opera houses complete the exhibition.

★PARC DE LA VILLETTE

⌖ The park, which lies between the Cité de Sciences et l'Industrie and the Cité de la Musique, was designed by **Bernard Tschumi** around three principle sets of features: follies, galleries and play areas. It has become a favourite place to spend a summer evening in the park watching films projected on a giant outdoor screen; the ambience is friendly and relaxed. Chairs and mats are available for hire. *Check the programme in any events magazine, such as Pariscope.*

Red pavilions, built of enamelled iron over a concrete frame, punctuate the park every 120m/394ft on a grid pattern. **Follies**, more usually denoting 18C fanciful pavilions, are here designed with a particular function be it a slide, weather vane or viewing platform.

La Grande Halle – This former cattle market auction hall has been skilfully converted into a space for a variety of activities: concerts, circuses, theatre and dance productions, trade fairs and other assemblies.

Playing fields – One is triangular, one is circular; both are large, flat grassy spaces, eminently suitable for all kinds of ball games.

Gardens – There are 10 gardens in all in the park, with delightful play equipment for children. One favourite area (it is enclosed to control the number of visitors, but free of charge, and strollers can be checked) is designed around the theme of wind and dunes; parents sit on benches alongside while the children run, climb and swing in the different sections, according to their age group. The Dragon is also fun for kids of all ages, with its many steps, ladders and slides. The bamboo garden has been laid out in a 6m/19ft pit to create a micro-climate and encourage growth; it represents the second largest collection of bamboos in France, with 30 different varieties.

The galleries – These comprise two perpendicular covered galleries: Galerie de La Villette running north-south, and Galerie de l'Ourcq east-west.

Le Zénith – Inaugurated in 1984, this hall can accommodate 6 400 people, and is used mainly for variety and rock concerts.

Bois et château de VINCENNES★★

Michelin plan 10: N 22 – N 24, P 22 – P 24, R 23, R 24
Ⓜ *Château de Vincennes* – RER: *Vincennes*

Vincennes is mostly known for its vast woodland with its natural attractions, its famous zoo, beautiful flower garden and racecourse, which make it one of the capital's most popular recreation areas. However, the town also boasts a mighty fortress, once a royal residence and silent witness to some of the most dramatic events in French history.

Vincennes takes a day to discover and enjoy fully, whether by car or on foot.

HISTORY

The Royal Forest – Philippe Auguste enclosed the wood as a royal hunt with a wall 12km/7mi long and stocked it with game. **Charles V** built the small Beauté Château within it on a low hill overlooking the Marne.

In the 17C it became a fashionable place in which to go walking. Strollers gained access to the wood through six gates piercing the wall. The Pyramid monument commemorates the plantations which were carried out in Louis XV's reign.

A military firing range was opened in 1798, the first of a series of enclaves in the forest made exclusively for military and sporting purposes.

The forest in modern times – Napoleon III ceded the estate at Vincennes – excluding the château and military installations – in 1860 to the City of Paris, to be made into an English-style park, on the lines of London's Hyde Park. Haussmann created the Gravelle Lake with water diverted from the River Marne which, in turn, feeds the lakes and rivers throughout the wood. The National Sports Institute dominated by a modern covered stadium offers training facilities for athletics and swimming.

The Château – This medieval Versailles has two distinct features within its walls: a tall forbidding keep and a majestic group of 17C buildings.

The anor house – In the 11C the crown acquired Vincennes Forest from St Maur Abbey; in the 12C Philippe Auguste uilt a manor house within its confines to which Louis IX added a Holy Chapel. This king also forbade anyone to hunt the forest animals, preferring, instead, seated at the foot of an oak, to receive his subjects without ceremony.

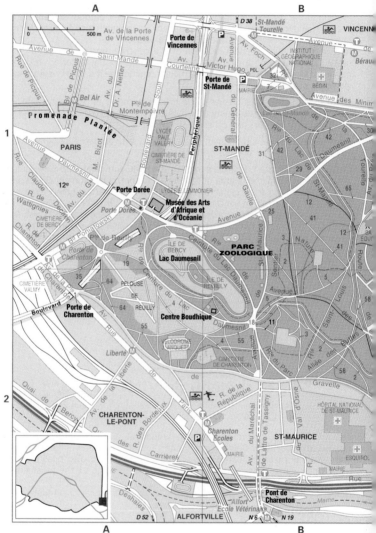

The fortified château – The castle was constructed by the Valois Philippe VI, John the Good and Charles V who completed it in 1396. Having built himself the Château de Beauté at Nogent, Charles imagined a royal city. To this end he invited his favourite nobles to build themselves houses within the huge estate but to no avail, for it was not until the reign of **Louis XIV** that the nobility sought to live in the king's shadow.

The classical château – Mazarin, appointed governor of Vincennes in 1652, had symmetrical royal pavilions designed and built by **Le Vau** to frame the main courtyard which faced south over the forest. In 1660, one year after the pavilions' completion, the young Louis XIV spent his honeymoon in the King's Pavilion.

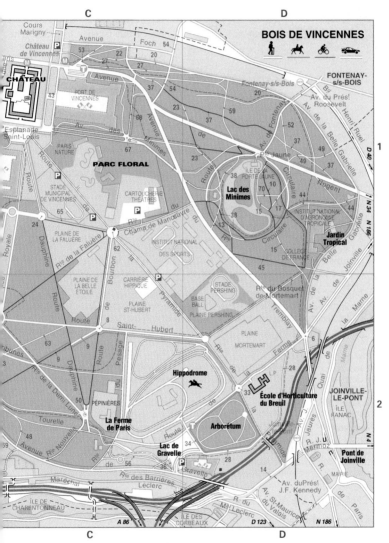

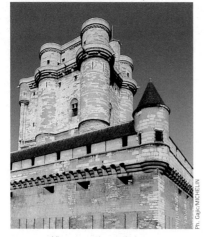

Vincennes, the castle keep

Ph. Gajic/MICHELIN

The prison – From the beginning of the 16C to 1784, the keep, no longer favoured as a royal residence, was used as a State prison to incarcerate supporters of the League, of Jansenism, of the **Fronde**, as well as libertine lords and philosophers. The disgrace of detention in Vincennes was far less than at the Bastille. Among the most famous were the Great Condé, the Prince de Conti, Cardinal de Retz, Fouquet (guarded by d'Artagnan), the Duke of Lauzun, **Diderot** and Mirabeau.

The porcelain factory – In 1738, quite by chance, the château became a porcelain factory when two craftsmen, dismissed from Chantilly, sought refuge at Vincennes and began to practise their trade.

A company was formed to produce soft-paste porcelain dinner and tea services, often decorated with sprays of flowers painted in natural colours. The factory was transferred to **Sèvres** in 1756.

The arsenal – Under Napoleon the château was converted into a formidable arsenal. The towers were reduced to the height of the perimeter wall and mounted with cannon, the rampart crenellations were removed, and the keep reverted to being a prison.

Daumesnil's refusals

In 1814 when the Allies called for the surrender of Vincennes, the governor, **General Daumesnil**, known as Peg Leg having lost a leg at the Battle of Wagram, retorted "I'll surrender Vincennes when you give me back my leg".

At the end of the Hundred Days, the castle was again called to surrender, and there came a second refusal. Five months later, however, the doors were opened to Louis XVIII.

In 1830 Daumesnil was still governor as insurgents attempted to attack Charles X's ministers imprisoned in the keep. The governor refused them entry, announcing that before surrendering he would blow himself and the castle sky-high.

The military establishment – Under **Louis-Philippe**, Vincennes was incorporated into the Paris defence system: a fort was built beside the château, the ramparts were reinforced with massive casemates, and the complex virtually buried below glacis.

On 24 August 1944 the Germans, before their departure from the castle, shot 26 resistance fighters, exploded three mines, breaching the ramparts in two places and damaging the King's Pavilion, and set fire to the Queen's Pavilion.

Restoration – The restoration of Vincennes was entrusted by **Napoleon III** to **Viollet-le-Duc**. Repair work carried out sporadically has lasted over a century and has only recently been completed. The main courtyard looks again much as it did in the 17C, the moat around the keep having been redug, the 19C casemates removed and the pavilions restored. The château ranks once more among the great historic royal houses of France.

CHÂTEAU DE VINCENNES ⊙

Outside the walls

A walk round the outside of the château, following the embankment around the moat provides a good sense of scale. On the western side, the walls are dominated by the impressive **keep**, erected in 1337, and a fine surviving example of medieval military architecture.

★★ **Donjon** – The 52m/170ft-tall tower, quartered by turrets, with a spur to the north for latrines, attiring room and a small oratory, was originally crowned with crenellated battlements and machicolations.

The keep proper was enclosed by a fortified wall and a separate moat. The base of the stone wall was reinforced to protect against sapping (breaching defences by undermining a wall), whereas turrets defended the corners. At sky level, a roofed sentry path, complete with battlements, and machicolations with gun embrasures below, ran right round the inner tower.

★ **Tour du Village** – This massive tower 42m/138ft high, which also survived the 19C alterations, served as the governor's residence in the Middle Ages. It was a good place from which to survey the entrance and supervise the defences of the fortress. Although the statues which graced the exterior have disappeared, some defensive features are still visible: slits for the drawbridge chains, groove of the portcullis, loopholes.

Cours des Maréchaux – Continue along the perimeter wall; the avenue was built in 1931 on the site of various outbuildings. It was in the penultimate of the five truncated towers along the east wall, the Tour du Diable, that the porcelain factory was established.

Tour du Bois – The arcades of the Classical Vincennes portico, overlooking the forest and closing the perimeter wall on the south side, come into view as you reach the château esplanade. The Bois Tower in the middle was reduced by Le Vau in the 17C when he transformed the gate into a state entrance (appearing as a triumphal arch from inside).

Duc d'Enghien

From the bridge over the moat can be seen, at the foot of the Tour de la Reine on the right, the column marking the spot where the Duc d'Enghien, Prince of Condé, was executed by a firing squad on 20 March 1804, accused of plotting against Napoleon (his body was exhumed on the orders of Louis XVIII and reburied in the Royal Chapel).

Within the walls

Cour Royale – The main courtyard is once more closed to the north by a portico, as Le Vau intended, and is framed by the two royal pavilions. Anne of Austria and Louis XIV's brother lived in the Pavillon de la Reine, where the governor, Daumesnil, died of cholera in 1832; the last royal occupant was the Duke of Montpensier, Louis Philippe's youngest son.

Mazarin died in the Pavillon du Roi in 1661 while awaiting the completion of his apartment in the Queen's Pavilion.

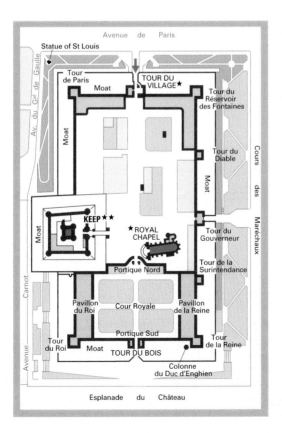

★★ Donjon – *Closed*. The ground floor served as the kitchens. The main room on the first floor originally served as a royal reception room hung with tapestries. Mirabeau was imprisoned for three years in one of the towers where he wrote a scathing condemnation of royal warrants.

A wide spiral staircase leads to the second floor and what was once the royal bedchamber. Henri V of England, Charles VI's son-in-law, died of dysentery in this room in 1422.

★ Chapelle Royale – The Royal Chapel, begun by Charles V in the 14C in place of the one built by **St Louis**, was completed only in the 16C in the reign of Henri II. The building, apart from the windows and some decoration, is pure Gothic; the façade with its beautiful stone rose windows is Flamboyant. The interior consists of a single elegant aisle with highly decorative consoles and a frieze running beneath the windows which, in the chancel, are filled with unusually coloured mid-16C **stained glass★** featuring scenes from the Apocalypse. The Duc d'Enghien's tomb is in the north chapel.

THE PARK

The **Lac Daumesnil★** *(to the west)*, the **Lac des Minimes** *(to the east)* and the **Lac de Gravelle** *(to the south)* are all popular focal points for walkers and boaters alike. The islands are accessible across bridges: Île de Reuilly has a café and Île de la Porte Jaune a restaurant.

Foire du Trône or foire aux Pains d'épice – The thousand-year-old Throne or **Gingerbread Fair** is held each spring *(Palm Sunday to Easter)* on the Reuilly Lawn near Lake Daumesnil. The fair recalls a concession obtained in 957 by the monks of St Antoine's Abbey to sell a piglet-shaped rye, honey and aniseed bread in memory of their saint during Holy Week. The followers of St Antoine used to ring bells to call the faithful, bells thus came to be hung around the necks of domestic animals to protect them. St Antoine's attribute, a small pig, is always portrayed with a bell. Nowadays, the yearly fun fair is better known for its flashy midway and stomach-churning rides.

Centre bouddhique du Bois de Vincennes ⊘ – *40 bis route de ceinture du Lac Daumesnil*. South of Lake Daumesnil is the Buddhist Temple of Paris, housed in one of the 1931 Colonial Exhibition buildings. The new roof with 180 000 tiles carved with an axe out of a chestnut tree is noteworthy. Inside is a monumental gilded statue of Buddha (9m/30ft).

THE ZOO AND OTHER ATTRACTIONS

★★ Le parc zoologique de Vincennes ⊘ – *Avenue Daumesnil*. Ⓜ *Porte Dorée.*

To the west of the park, 535 mammals and 600 birds of some 82 different species live in natural surroundings close to their familiar habitat. Around 120 births take place every year. At the centre is an artificial rock 65m/213ft high inhabited by wild mountain sheep.

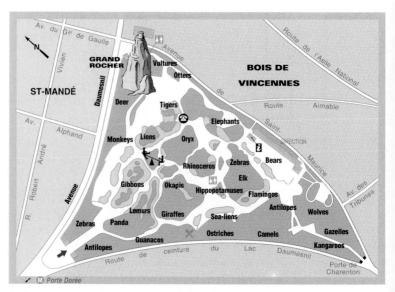

★★ **Parc Floral** ⊘ – *Route de la Pyramide.* The garden, landscaped by D Collin in 1969, extends over 30ha/75 acres and includes hundreds of species. The **Vallée des Fleurs** is delightful all year round. The pavilions tucked away amid pine trees around the lake, together with the Hall de la Pinède, house exhibitions and shows (photographs, dance, posters and horticulture).

Alleyways lined with modern sculpture (*The Tall Woman* by **Giacometti**, *Stabile* by **Calder**, the polished-steel *Chronos* by Nicolas Schöffer...) suggest an open-air museum.

The **Dahlia Garden** from Sceaux, south of Paris, has been recreated near the Pyramid *(in flower September-October)*. The **water garden** with its water-lilies and lotus is at its best from July to September. There are also a **Four Seasons Garden**, and gardens growing medicinal plants *(best seen from May to October)*, irises *(May)* and bamboo. Flower shows are held throughout the year: orchids *(early March)*, tulips *(from April)*, rhododendrons and azaleas *(from May)*.

★★ **Aquariums du Musée des Arts d'Afrique et d'Océanie** ⊘ – *293 avenue Daumesnil.* Ⓜ *Porte Dorée. This is the only section of the museum remaining open to the public.*

🔲 There are a tropical **aquarium★** and two **terrariums** (crocodiles and tortoises).

Arboretum de l'École du Breuil ⊘ – *Route de la Ferme. RER: Joinville-le-Pont.* This school specialises in horticulture and landscape design; it has beautiful gardens. The arboretum *(entrance on route de la Pyramide)* extends over 12ha/30 acres and includes 2 000 trees of 80 different species.

Excursions

Access – RER: (line A) Marne-la-Vallée-Chessy; by TGV from Lille, Lyon, Avignon, Marseille, Bordeaux, Nantes and Toulouse; by shuttle from Orly and Roissy-Charles-de-Gaulle airports; by car via motorway A4 direction Metz; exit at junction 14 and follow signs to Disneyland.

Standing on the Brie plain about 30km/18mi east of Paris is a unique development in Europe: Disneyland Paris.

Disneyland Paris theme park – The enormous site, which was conceived as a complete holiday resort and will continue to develop until the year 2017, already comprises the theme park and a resort complex offering accommodation and other recreational facilities.

The **Disneyland Hotel**, built in the style of a turn-of-the-20C American mansion from a seaside resort, stands at the entrance to the theme park. Five other hotels stand beside Lake Disney or along the Rio Grande, each bringing to life a different American theme: the **Hotel New York** (Manhattan), the **Newport Bay Club** (a 19C New England beach resort), **Sequoia Lodge** (the National Parks), **Hotel Santa Fe** (New Mexico) and the **Hotel Cheyenne** (a small western town).

Not far from the hotels, the main entertainment centre, **Disney Village**, recreates the American way of life with shops, restaurants and a nightclub. At a slight distance from the complex lies **Golf Disneyland Paris** with its 27-hole course. The **Davy Crockett Ranch** is a caravan and camp site in the woods 4.5km/3mi away, with wooden cabins recalling the life of the trappers.

A magician called Walt Disney – Walt Disney's name is linked to innumerable cartoon strips and animated cartoons which have entertained children throughout the world, and the heroes of his creations Mickey Mouse, Minnie, Donald, Pluto, Pinocchio, Snow White etc no one can forget.

He was born Walter Elias Disney in Chicago in 1901, the fourth child of Flora and Elias Disney. Walt soon showed great ability in drawing. After the First World War, in which he served as an ambulance driver in France, he returned to the United States where he met a young Dutchman called Ub Iwerks, who was also passionate about drawing. In 1923 the pair produced in Hollywood a series of short films called **Alice Comedies**. In 1928 Mickey Mouse, the future international star, was created. There next followed the era of the Oscar-winning, full-length animated cartoon films: **The Three Little Pigs** (1933), **Snow White and the Seven Dwarfs** (1937), **Dumbo** (1941). Disney productions also developed to include films starring real people, such as **Treasure Island** (1950) and **20 000 Leagues Under the Sea** (1954), and some mixing of the two, for instance **Mary Poppins** (1964) which won six Oscars.

On 15 December 1966 the man who had spent his life trying to bring dreams to life died; the Walt Disney Studios continued to make films, however, remaining faithful to Walt's ideas: **The Aristocats**, **Who Killed Roger Rabbit?** (which won four Oscars), **The Little Mermaid** (two Oscars), **Beauty and the Beast** (1991), **Aladdin** (1993) and **The Lion King** (1994), Pocahontas (1995), the Hunchback of Notre-Dame (1996), Hercules (1997), Mulan (1998), Tarzan (1999), Dinosaurs (2000), The 102 Dalmatians (2001) and Monsters & Co (2002).

General information

Hotel reservations – ☎ 01 60 30 60 30.

Internet – www.disneylandparis.com.

Booking a show – Entertainment programmes and booking facilities are available from City Hall, located in Town Square, just inside Disneyland Park.

Currency exchange – Facilities are available at the parks' main entrance.

Readmission – See Admission times and charges at the end of the guide.

Handicapped guests – A guide detailing special services available can be obtained from City Hall (Disneyland Park) or from the information desk inside Walt Disney Studios Park.

Lockers and storage – Near the main entrance and beneath Main Street Station.

Rental – Guests can rent cameras and video cameras from Town Square Photography, pushchairs and wheelchairs in Town Square Terrace (Disneyland Park) and in Front Lot (Walt Disney Studios Park).

Animals – They are not allowed in the theme parks, in Disney Village or in the hotels. The Animal Care Center is located near the visitors' car park.

Baby Care Center, Meeting Place for Lost Children, First Aid – Near the Plaza Gardens Restaurant (Disneyland Park) or in Front Lot (Walt Disney Studios Park).

Making the most of the theme parks

Tips – To avoid long queues at popular attractions, it is recommended to visit these attractions during the parade, at the end of the day or better still to get a **Fast Pass** issued by distributors outside the most popular attractions in both parks; this ticket bears a time slot of 1hr during which time you may have access to the attraction within a few minutes.
Disneyland Park: Indiana Jones (Adventureland); Space Mountain (Discoveryland); Peter Pan's Flight (Fantasyland); Big Thunder Mountain (Frontierland); Star Tours (Discoveryland).
Walt Disney Studios Park: Rock'n Roller Coaster (Backlot); Flying Carpets (Animation Courtyard); Studio Tram Tour (Production Courtyard).

Where to eat – Park maps include a list of eating places and their location within the parks, with symbols indicating those offering table service and vegetarian meals.

MODERATE: For a quick meal go to the **Bella Notte**, **Colonel Hathi's** or the **Plaza Gardens** in Disneyland Park, or to the **Backlot Express Restaurant** in Walt Disney Studios Park.

MID-RANGE: Take time and go to one of the following table service restaurants to enjoy a fine meal enhanced by an original decor (booking recommended, ☎ 01 64 74 28 82 or call at City Hall):
Silver Spur Steakhouse, **Blue Lagoon Restaurant**, **Walt's Restaurant** and **Auberge de Cendrillon** in Disneyland Park or **Rendez-vous des Stars Restaurant** in Walt Disney Studios Park.

Eating outside the theme parks

In Disney Village – This is the place to enjoy a culinary trip to the New World.

MODERATE: **Annette's Diner**, ☎ 01 60 45 70 37 – 13.72/19.82€.

MID-RANGE: **Rainforest Café**, ☎ 01 60 43 65 65 – 18.29/33.54€.
Los Angeles, ☎ 01 60 45 71 14 – 23.63€.
The Steakhouse, ☎ 01 60 45 70 45 – closed Sat lunch – 25.92/38.11€.

A few miles away – Fancy an old-world riverside restaurant?

MID-RANGE: *L'Ermitage, Allée Jean-de-La-Fontaine, écluse de Chalifert, 77144 Chalifert; 6km/3.7mi N of Disneyland Resort Paris along N 34 then D 45 – ☎ 01 60 43 41 43 – notrermitage.com – closed 29 Jul to 29 Aug – booking essential – 25/50€.* Founded in 1860, this riverside restaurant continues to offer its guests a lively convivial atmosphere, particularly at weekends (disco on Fri, cabaret on Sat and old-time dancing on Sun).

★★★ DISNEYLAND PARIS PARK ☉

This theme park, like those in the United States (opened in California in 1955 and in Florida in 1971) and Japan (Tokyo, 1983), is a realisation of Walt Disney's dream of creating a small, enchanted park where children and adults can enjoy themselves together. The large Disneyland Paris site (over 55ha/135 acres) is surrounded by trees and comprises five territories or lands, each with a different theme. As well as the spectacular shows featuring amazing automatons (Audio-Animatronics), each region has shops, bars, restaurants and food stalls.

Every day, the **Disney Parade★★**, a procession of floats carrying all the favourite Disney cartoon characters, takes place. On some evenings and throughout the summer the **Main Street Electrical Parade★★** adds extra illuminations to the fairytale setting. The **Fantasy in the Sky★** firework display rounds off an eventful day.

Listed below are descriptions of the main attractions.

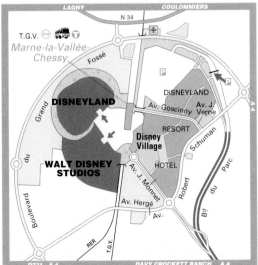

Main Street USA

The main street of an American town at the turn of the 20C, bordered by shops with Victorian-style fronts, is brought to life as though by magic. Horse-drawn street cars, double-decker buses, limousines, fire engines and Black Marias transport visitors from Town Square to Central Plaza (the hub of the park) while colourful musicians play favourite ragtime, jazz and Dixieland tunes. On each side of the road are **Discovery Arcade** and **Liberty Arcade** (exhibition on the famous Statue of Liberty at the entrance to New York harbour).

From Main Street station a small steam train, the **Euro Disneyland Railroad★**, travels across the park and through the **Grand Canyon Diorama**.

Frontierland

The conquest of the West, the gold trail and the Far West with its legends and folklore are brought together in Thunder Mesa, a typical western town, and Big Thunder Mountain which rises on an island washed by the rivers of the Far West. The waters here are plied by two handsome **steamboats★**, the *Mark Twain* and the *Molly Brown*.

★★★**Big Thunder Mountain** – In the bowels of this arid mountain lies an old gold mine which is visited via the mine train: this turns out to be a runaway train which hurtles out of control to provide a thrilling ride.

★★★**Phantom Manor** – A dilapidated house stands not far from Thunder Mesa, overlooking the rivers of the Far West. Inside, a strange atmosphere hangs in the air; a spine-chilling tour of the house reveals hundreds of mischievous ghosts...

  ★**The Lucky Nugget Saloon** – This horseshoe-shaped saloon – every western town had its saloon – is richly decorated. Dinner show: **Lilly's Follies**.

Adventureland

This is the land of exotic adventure: waterfalls, an oriental bazaar, African drumbeats, a treasure island, swashbuckling pirates... Access is from Central Plaza, through Adventureland Bazaar.

★★★**Pirates of the Caribbean** – In the tropical Caribbean seas, marauding pirates attack and loot a coastal fort and village in this famous action-packed encounter.

★★★**Indiana Jones et le Temple du Péril...à l'envers** – In the jungle lies a ruined temple; courageous archaeologists in wagons enter it and defy the laws of gravity. This is not for the faint-hearted.

  ★★**La Cabane des Robinson** – A giant tree (27m/89ft high) offering panoramic views serves as the ingeniously furnished home of the shipwrecked Swiss family Robinson from J D Wyss' novel.

Fantasyland

This area, based around Walt Disney's familiar trademark, Sleeping Beauty's castle, recalls favourite fairy tales by authors such as Charles Perrault, Lewis Carroll and the Brothers Grimm. Here familiar figures – Mickey Mouse, Pinocchio, Captain Hook – will happily pose for photographs.

  ★★**Le Château de la Belle au bois dormant** – The fairy tale castle with its blue and gold turrets crowned with pennants is at the very heart of Disneyland. Inside, Aubusson tapestries recount episodes from this famous story. Below, in the depths of the castle, a huge scaly dragon appears to be sleeping...

  ★★**It's a Small World** – The delightful musical cruise is a celebration of the innocence and joy of children throughout the world.

  ★**Alice's Curious Labyrinth** – At the end of this maze guarded by playing cards stands the Queen of Hearts' Castle where the queen from Lewis Carroll's classic story awaits those brave enough to visit...

  ★★**Peter Pan's Flight** – Fly in a boat through the skies above London and in Never-Never Land reliving the adventures of Peter Pan and the sinister Captain Hook who is relentlessly pursued by a hungry crocodile.

  ★**Les Voyages de Pinocchio** – Lively scenes based on Carlo Collodi's enduring tale present the lovable puppet Pinocchio and his friends.

  ★**Blanche-Neige et les Sept Nains** – Enjoyable tours lead through the mysterious forest in mining cars from the dwarfs' mine – just watch out for the wicked witch...

  ★**Le Carrousel de Lancelot** – This is an enchanting merry-go-round of brightly painted horses.

Discoveryland

This is the world of past discoveries and dreams of the future with great visionaries such as Leonardo da Vinci, Jules Verne and HG Wells and their wonderful inventions.

★★★ **Space Mountain – De la Terre à la Lune** – Fantastic journey through space, based on Jules Verne's novel *From the Earth to the Moon* (1873).

★★★ **Star Tours** – This is a breathtaking inter-planetary experience full of special effects inspired by the film *Star Wars:* voyage into space, piloted by a robot!

★★ **Honey I Shrunk the Audience** – In the Imagination Institute, Professor Wayne Szalinski demonstrates his famous shrinking machine. Hang on to your hat!

★★ **Le Visionarium** – A 360° screen reveals the wonders of Europe.

WALT DISNEY STUDIOS PARK

Inaugurated on 16 March 2002, this park is entirely dedicated to the wonders of the cinema. It offers its guests a chance to take a trip backstage and discover some of the secrets of filming, of animation techniques and of television. The park is divided into four production areas, each including an amazing variety of shows and attractions.

Front Lot

The park entrance is overlooked by a 33m/108ft-high water tower, a traditional landmark in film studios. In the centre of the Spanish-style courtyard, planted with palm trees, stands a fountain dedicated to Mickey.

Disney Studio 1 is the reconstruction of a famous Hollywood film set, Hollywood Boulevard, lined with restaurants and boutiques.

Animation Courtyard

This area offers a tribute to Walt Disney's invaluable contribution to the development of animation.

★★★ **Animagique** – This attraction celebrates Disney's full-length animation films; spectators find themselves at the centre of a 3D cartoon, next to Mickey, Donald Duck, Dumbo's pink elephants, Pinocchio....

★★ **Art of Disney Animation** – An interactive discovery of the secrets of animation.

★★ **Flying Carpets** – Guests wait backstage for instructions which direct them to the main film set where Aladdin's Genie guides them onto flying carpets!

Production Courtyard

Here spectators are allowed to see what happens in the usually out-of-bounds backstage areas of cinema and television studios: how film sets and special effects are created, how costumes are made...

★★★ **Cinémagique** – When fiction meets reality, spectators literally go through the screen and become the actors and heroes of the film.

★★ **Television Production Tour** – You are offered a guided tour of Disney Channel France and the possibility to watch the live filming of *Zapping Zone*.

★★ **Studio Tram Tour** – Sit back and enjoy this guided tour aboard a small tramway through amazing film sets... until you reach **Catastrophe Canyon★★★**!

Back Lot

Action, thrills and special effects!

★★ **Armageddon** – The Russian space station is threatened by meteorites... a thrilling (and particularly loud) experience!

★★★ **Rock'n Roller Coaster** – A unique musical experience awaits you inside a recording studio; be prepared to be propelled at full speed on a breathtaking journey... (not for the faint-hearted!).

★★★ **Moteurs...Action!** – A hero chasing some villains through a village in the south of France... an occasion to see some superb stunts.

★DISNEY VILLAGE

Situated just beside the theme parks and Disney Lake, the tall polished steel columns of Disney Village can be seen from afar. When night falls, the village seems covered with a web of lights.

In the main street of this American town it's always party time, with a happy, child-like atmosphere. On summer evenings, after the park closes, there is plenty going on here, and shops, restaurants and bars are always busy. In the street, onlookers applaud tightrope walkers and those on stilts, jugglers and musicians. Night-birds can round off the evening in the **Hurricanes** disco. The quality of the events, the increasing number of cinema screens at the **Gaumont multiplex**, and famous establishments such as **Planet Hollywood**, all add up to the success of this village, which continues to attract increasing numbers of local residents.

★★ **La Légende de Buffalo Bill** – The famous adventures of pioneer William Frederick Cody (1846-1917), alias Buffalo Bill, are the inspiration for this cabaret dinner, which evokes the story of the Wild West, complete with horses, bison, cowboys and Indians. The typically Texan menu is served on tin plates.

An evening of non-stop entertainment, filled with laughter and special effects.

Billy Bob's Country Western Saloon – An ideal place to continue the evening, this saloon bar where the beer flows freely is much frequented by cowboys. Music and country dancing complete the jolly atmosphere.

ST-DENIS★★

Michelin plan 20, maps 305: F-7, 101 fold 16, 106 folds 19 and 20
or 237 folds 17 and 18
Ⓜ St-Denis-Basilique (line 13) – RER: St-Denis (line D)

In 1840 the locality of St-Denis numbered a few thousand inhabitants; the industrial revolution brought this number to 100 000 and made the town one of the main manufacturing centres of the northern suburbs.

The inauguration of the Stade de France in 1998, gave this densely populated town new hopes for future prosperity. For visitors, however, the most interesting sight in St-Denis remains its basilica which houses the mausoleum of the kings of France. *For a quick visit allow 1hr.*

Monsieur St-Denis – Legend has it that after his beheading in Montmartre, the Evangelist St Denis, first bishop of Lutetia, got to his feet, picked up his severed head and walked north out of the city. He is said to have been buried where he was found by a passing woman. An abbey was built on the site of his tomb, which soon attracted streams of pilgrims.

In fact, vestiges of the Roman city Catolacus have been found to date from the 1C AD where it would have commanded views of the river and the main road out of Paris to Beauvais. It is believed that the man known as Monsieur (Monseigneur) St-Denis was secretly buried in one of the fields around the city after his martyrdom.

In 475 a large village church was erected on the site. Dagobert I had it rebuilt and

offered it to a Benedictine community who took charge of the pilgrimage. This abbey was to become the most wealthy and the most celebrated in France. Towards 750 the church was dismantled a second time and rebuilt by Pepin the Short, who set up a shrine under the chancel to receive the sacred remains of saints. The building as it stands today is principally the work of Abbot Suger (12C) and Pierre de Montreuil (13C).

Abbot Suger – The abbot's formidable personality dominates the history of the basilica. He was born of a peasant family and was given to the abbey at the age of 10. His remarkable gifts caused him to gain ascendancy over one of his fellow novices, a young boy whose destiny it was to become adviser to Louis VII. The king made friends with the monk, invited him to court and consulted him on numerous matters.

Window in the basílica

Elected Abbot of St-Denis in 1122, Suger personally drew up the plans for the abbey church. The minister of Louis VII, he was made Regent of France when the king took part in the Second Crusade. His wisdom and concern for public well-being were so great that when Louis VII returned, he gave him the name Father of the Homeland.

The Lendit Fair – Lendit was an important trade fair founded by the abbot in 1109. It was held on St-Denis plain and remained a major European event for over 600 years. A total of 1 200 booths were placed at the disposal of the participants. Every year the University of Paris would travel to Lendit to buy the parchment used in the Montagne Ste-Geneviève faculties.

★★★ BASILIQUE ST-DENIS

Mausoleum for the kings of France – Over a remarkable span of 12 centuries, most of the kings of France, from Dagobert I to Louis XVIII, were buried at St-Denis. In 1793 Barrère asked the Convention for permission to destroy the tombs. They were opened and the remains thrown into unmarked graves. Alexandre Lenoir salvaged the most precious tombs and moved them to Paris, entrusted to the Petits-Augustins, later to become the Museum of French Monuments. In 1816 Louis XVIII returned the tombs to the basilica.

Construction of St-Denis – This basilica marks a turning point in the development of French architecture: it was the first large church to feature a unity of design in plan and style. This, combined with its significance as a centre of pilgrimage proved to be the springboard for subsequent late-12C cathedrals and the evolution towards the Gothic style (Chartres, Senlis and Meaux).
Suger supervised the construction of the west front and the first two bays of the nave from 1136 to 1140, and the chancel and crypt between 1140 and 1144. The Carolingian nave was provisionally preserved and remodelled between 1145 and 1147. The amazing rapidity of the whole operation was due to Suger's dedication and to the help he received from his parishioners: they all teamed up to pull the wagons of stone from the limestone quarries of Pontoise.
In the early 13C the north tower was crowned by a magnificent stone spire. Work on the chancel was resumed and the transept, then the nave, were entirely restored. In 1247 **Pierre de Montreuil** was appointed master mason by St Louis: he remained in chargeof the work until his death in 1267.

Decline – The basilica subsequently fell into disrepair. The French Revolution caused further ravages and in his *Genius of Christianity*, Chateaubriand lamented the sorry state of the church. Napoleon gave orders to repair the damage and reinstated public worship in 1806.

Restoration – Debret, the architect who took over in 1813, aroused a wave of public indignation on account of his poor knowledge of medieval methods. For the spire, he used heavy materials which disrupted its gentle harmony. It collapsed in 1846 and had to be dismantled.
In 1847 Debret was succeeded by **Viollet-le-Duc**, who studied a number of original documents which guided him in his work. From 1858 up to his death (1879), he toiled relentlessly and produced the basilica that stands today. Essentially, the choir and west front (although much restored) provide some idea of the original. The rest must be gleaned from contemporary buildings (Chartres, Sens). Archaeological excavation of the crypt has revealed sections of the Carolingian martyrium and the remains of a Merovingian mausoleum (late-6C tomb of Princess Aregunde, the wife of Clotaire I, magnificent sarcophagi, splendid jewels). Foundations of earlier sanctuaries have also been uncovered.

Exterior

The absence of the north tower mars the harmony of the west front. In the Middle Ages the building would have been fortified from which some crenellation survives at the base of the towers.
The tympanum on the central doorway represents the Last Judgement, that on the right doorway depicts the Last Communion of St Denis and on the left the Death of St Denis and his companions.
All three doorways have been restored. The columnar figures of the doorways feature the Wise and Foolish Virgins *(centre)*, the labours of the months *(right)* and the signs of the Zodiac *(left)*.
On the north side of the basilica, the nave is supported by double flying buttresses. The transept, which presents a wonderful rose window, was initially to have had two towers but work stopped after the first floor. If the original plans had been carried out, the church would have had six towers altogether.

Interior ⊘

The basilica is marginally smaller than Notre-Dame: 108m/354ft long, 38m/125ft wide in the transept and 29m/95ft high.

The narthex, designed by Suger, in the two bays beneath the towers, would have had pointed vaulting throughout. The elegant nave is attributed to Pierre de Montreuil. The triforium elevation, open onto the exterior, was also innovative. The stained-glass windows in the nave are modern.

★★★ **Tombs** – St-Denis Basilica houses the remains of kings, queens and royal children, as well as those of leading personalities who served the French court, such as Bertrand du Guesclin (**1**). It is possible to date most monuments simply from their appearance, thus they serve as a chronological chart of French funeral art through the Middle Ages and into the Renaissance (79 recumbent figures). The tombs have been empty since the Revolution.

During the 14C it was customary to remove the heart and viscera from the bodies of French kings before embalming them. The inner organs, the heart and the body were all buried in different places. The bodies were taken to St-Denis.

Up to the Renaissance, the only sculpture to adorn tombs was in the form of **recumbent figures**. Note the 12C funeral slab of Clovis (**2**) and Fredegonde (**3**), worked in mosaic and copper, from the abbey of St-Germain-des-Prés.

Around 1260 St Louis commissioned a series of effigies of all the rulers who had preceded him since the 7C. The figures were mere allegories but they provide a telling example of how royalty was portrayed towards the mid-13C. They include the imposing tomb of Dagobert (**4**), with its lively, spirited scenes, the recumbent statues of Charles Martel (**5**) and Pepin the Short (**6**), and the female effigy carved in Tournai marble (**7**).

The tomb of Isabella of Arago and Philippe III the Bold (**8**), who died in 1285, shows an early concern for accurate portraiture imbued with a strong sense of personality. Towards the middle of the 14C, the wealthy oversaw the building of their tomb in their own lifetime. The effigies of Charles V by Beauneveu (**9**), Charles VI and Isabella of Bavaria (**10**) are therefore extremely lifelike.

During the Renaissance, **mausoleums** took on monumental proportions and were lavishly decorated. They had two tiers, representing life and death, each contrasting sharply with the other. On the upper level the king and his wife are featured kneeling in full regalia; on the lower level, the deceased were pictured lying down as naked cadavers. Admire the twin monument built for Louis XII and Anne of Brittany (**11**), and that of François I and Claude de France (**12**), executed by Philibert Delorme and Pierre Bontemps.

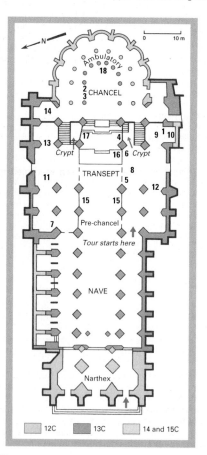

After commissioning the royal tomb, **Catherine de' Medici**, who survived her husband Henri II by 30 years, actually fainted in horror on seeing herself portrayed dead according to the standard convention; she therefore ordered a new effigy to be made showing her asleep. Both, by Primaticcio (**13**), and Germain Pilon (**14**), are here displayed.

Chancel – The beautiful pre-Renaissance stalls (**15**), in the pre-chancel were taken from the Norman Château at Gaillon. The splendid Romanesque **Virgin★** in painted wood (**16**) was brought from St-Martin-des-Champs. The episcopal throne opposite (**17**) is a replica of Dagobert's royal seat (the original lies in the Medals and Antiquities Gallery at the Bibliothèque Nationale in Paris – *see PLACE DES VICTOIRES*). At the far end, the modern reliquary of saints Denis, Rusticus and Eleutherius (**18**) stands at the edge of Suger's **ambulatory★**, with its wide arches and slim columns. The radiating chapels are decorated with several altarpieces and fragments of stained glass dating from the Gothic period.

12C   13C   14 and 15C

Praying figures of Louis XVI and Marie Antoinette

★★ **Crypt** – The lower ambulatory was built in the Romanesque style by Suger (12C) and restored by Viollet-le-Duc (acanthus capitals). In the centre stands a vaulted chapel known as Hilduin's Chapel (after the abbot who had it built in the 9C). Beneath its marble slab lies the burial vault of the Bourbon family, including the remains, among others, of Louis XVI, Marie-Antoinette and Louis XVIII. The communal grave in the north transept received in 1817 the bones of around 800 kings and queens, royal highnesses, princes of the blood, Merovingians, Capetians and members of the Orléans and Valois dynasty.

MUSEUMS AND OTHER ATTRACTIONS

Maison d'éducation de la Légion d'honneur – The former abbey, founded in the 7C, adjoins the basilica which was once the abbey church. The abbey was occupied until 1790 by some 100 Benedictines. The present monastic buildings date from the 18C and are the work of Jules Hardouin-Mansart, Robert de Cotte and Jacques Gabriel. The imposing staircase, the cloisters with their wide openings and the **wrought-iron railings★** testify to the importance of the abbey which welcomed the court when a royal funeral took place in the basilica. In 1809 Napoleon I made the abbey the seat of a college for the daughters of holders of the French order of merit, the Légion d'Honneur. Today the school looks after some 400 students.

Musée d'Art et d'Histoire ⊘ – *22 bis rue Gabriel-Péri.* The museum is set up in the former Carmelite convent, part of which has been restored. The convent was founded by Cardinal de Bérulle in 1625 and occupied by Louis XV's daughter Madame Louise de France between 1770 and 1787. The refectory and kitchen contain archaeological finds from St-Denis (medieval potsherds) or from the old hospital (17C and 18C ceramic apothecary phials and jars).
The former Carmelite chapel has a splendid Louis XVI dome. It was here that the prioress Louise de France died in 1787.
Other artefacts are displayed in the cells on the first floor, recalling the everyday life of the Carmelites. One room is dedicated to the work of post-Impressionist painter Albert André. On the second floor are drawings, paintings and documents relating to the Paris Commune of 1871.
The restored Louis XV pavilion presents works and mementoes of Paul Eluard.

Musée Bouilhet-Christofle ⊘ – *112 rue Ambroise-Croizat.* The continued success of the gold– and silversmiths Bouilhet-Christofle has been ensured by their perfecting of electroplating techniques. Nickel has been used as a base metal for electroplating since 1842; the museum, installed in a former nickel factory, built in 1874, exhibits more than 2 000 items including filigree sweetmeat dishes, pieces from the service designed for Napoleon III for his Château des Tuileries, an amazing tea urn dated 1873, the Art Deco service from the steamship *Normandie* and many contemporary creations.

★ Stade de France ⊘ – This huge yet elegant structure was designed by four architects: Zublena, Macary, Regembal and Costantini. It was the last major construction project of the 20C, built in a record 31 months, and inaugurated with great ceremony on 28 January 1998. It proved to be an appropriate setting for the 1998 World Cup, the largest event ever organised in France, which the French team won for the first time ever, beating the legendary Brazilian team 3-0.

The elliptical structure can be adapted to accommodate all kinds of sporting and entertainment events; thanks to a system of moveable seats, the number of spectators can be increased from 80 000 for matches to 100 000 for concerts. State-of-the-art technology makes the stadium's visual and acoustic qualities exceptional: the circular Teflon and aluminium roof covering the stands is extended by a glass area of 1ha/2.5 acres, which filters incoming light. There is also a sophisticated security system of grills which can be raised or lowered, and which is bound to pass into widespread use elsewhere.

Château de VERSAILLES★★★

Michelin plan 22, maps 311: I-3, 101 folds 22 and 23, 106 folds 17 and 18
or 237 folds 16 and 17

Access – *RER: (line C) Versailles Rive-Gauche – Château de Versailles; by commuter trains from St-Lazare (Versailles Rive-Droite) and Montparnasse (Versailles-Chantiers) rail stations; by car from the Porte de St-Cloud, take Motorway A13 to exit 1 and follow signs to Versailles-Château (16km/10mi). Average travel time: 30-45min.*

Symbol of absolute monarchy and the apogee of the arts in France during the reign of the Sun King, Versailles became the residence of the court and seat of government on 6 May 1682 and remained so until the Revolution.

Small beginnings – In 1624 **Louis XIII** gave orders to build a small hunting lodge around the present Marble Court. Philibert le Roy reconstructed the château in brick and stone in 1631. **Louis XIV** retained his father's château; from 1661 he had the gardens embellished for his splendid festivals. In 1668 the King's architect **Louis Le Vau** constructed a stone envelope, around the small château, building façades which concealed the old façades on the garden side of the château. Le Nôtre laid out the flower beds and park whereas Le Brun designed the sculptures for the park.

Grand schemes – **Jules Hardouin-Mansart** succeeded Le Vau and modified the palace with the Galerie des Glaces (Hall of Mirrors) and two wings in the south (1682) and the north (1689).

Under Colbert and Le Brun, the Gobelins factory and the artists of the Académie Royale designed the main furniture and decoration with the remarkable stylistic unity which defines Versailles Classicism.

Through a complex system of etiquette and magnificent feasts, Louis XIV managed to control the ever-dangerous nobility, thwarting their political ambitions by keeping them under surveillance.

Under **Louis XV** changes were limited mostly to the interior which he had restructured to create the Petits Cabinets.

When the **Revolution** drove Louis XVI from Versailles, a century of royal occupation came to a close. In the 19C, **Louis-Philippe** transformed part of the palace into a museum dedicated to French history. Since 1914 the State, supported by private patronage (including that of John D Rockefeller), has carried out important restoration work and refurbished the palace which is listed as one of UNESCO's World Heritage Monuments.

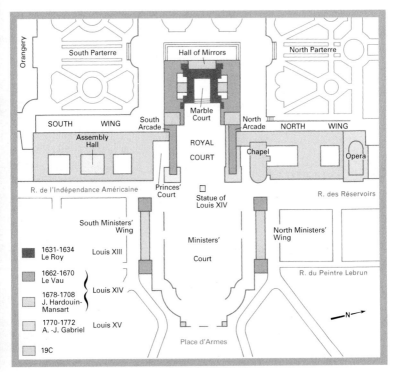

★★★ LE CHÂTEAU

A complete tour of the palace, park and the Grand and Petit Trianons takes two days. If you have only one day it is recommended that you begin with the interior of the château, where the most magnificent apartments are to be found.

The park and gardens are best enjoyed at leisure. For an unforgettable experience, visit them on one of the Jours des Grands Eaux Musicales, when all the fountains are turned on, to a musical accompaniment.

EXTERIOR ⊙

For a brief visit allow about 1hr

Set back from the château on **place d'Armes★★** are the **Écuries royales★** (Royal Stables) by Jules Hardouin-Mansart.

Courtyards – Beyond the palace's wrought-iron railings, created under Louis XVIII, lie three courtyards. In the centre of the forecourt, the **Cour des Ministres** (Ministers' Court) is a statue of Louis XIV commissioned by Louis-Philippe. Next is the **Cour royale** (Royal Court) which only persons of high rank were permitted to cross in horse-drawn carriages. The two bordering wings were furnished with a colonnade under Louis XV. Finally there is the **Cour de Marbre★★** (Marble Court) with its black and white marble pavement, the heart of Louis XIII's château.

★★★ **Garden front** – *Go through the north arcade, skirt the central part of the palace and step back for a good view.*
Designed by Le Vau in 1669, the façade is lined with pillars and Ionic columns rising from a bossaged base.

The balustrade crowning the façade bears trophies and vases and conceals the flat Italian-style roof. Le Vau created a terrace in the space in front of the building, but in 1678, Jules Hardouin-Mansart covered the space, and it became the Hall of Mirrors. This he extended with two wings.

Along the façade four metal casts of ancient statues are perched on the pedestals; these are the first works of the Keller brothers. Two giant Medici **vases★** representing War (by Coysevox) and Peace (by Tuby) stand under the windows of the War Salon and the Peace Salon located at either end of the Hall of Mirrors.

Statues of Apollo and Diana, surrounded by the Months of the Year, top the central building of the palace where the royal family lived.

INTERIOR ⊙

Below are three selected tours to help you make the most of your visit to Versailles.

Tour of the State Apartments

*From the visitors' entrance (**A**) go though the vestibule which houses the ticket office and up by the circular staircase to the Chapel Room (**a**) on the first floor.*

★★★**Chapelle royale** – The two-storey palatine chapel with a royal gallery is de dicated to St Louis. It was constructed by Jules Hardouin-Mansart, and finished in 1710 by his brother-in-law Robert de Cotte. The ceiling is the work of the painters Jouvent, Coypel and La Fosse. The marble altar sculpted by Van Clève is decorated in front with a gilded bronze low relief representing a *Pietà* by Vassé.

D. Hée/MICHELIN

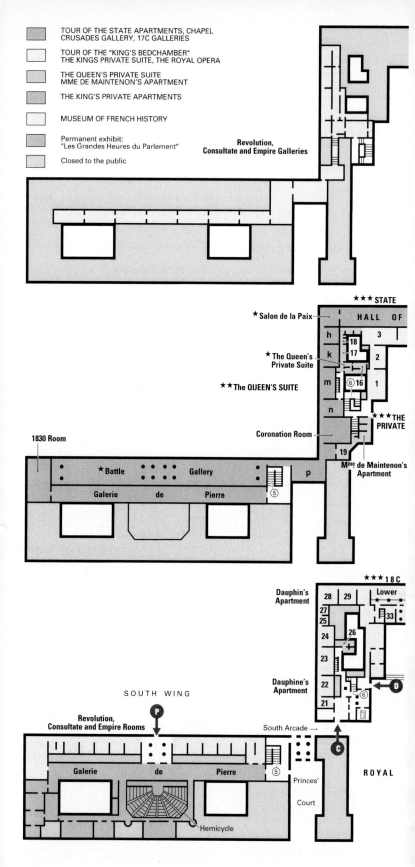

TOUR OF THE STATE APARTMENTS, CHAPEL
CRUSADES GALLERY, 17C GALLERIES

TOUR OF THE "KING'S BEDCHAMBER"
THE KINGS PRIVATE SUITE, THE ROYAL OPERA

THE QUEEN'S PRIVATE SUITE
MME DE MAINTENON'S APARTMENT

THE KING'S PRIVATE APARTMENTS

MUSEUM OF FRENCH HISTORY

Permanent exhibit:
"Les Grandes Heures du Parlement"

Closed to the public

Revolution,
Consultate and Empire Galleries

★★★ STATE

HALL   OF

★ Salon de la Paix

★ The Queen's
Private Suite

★★ The QUEEN'S SUITE

Coronation Room

★★★ THE
PRIVATE

Mᵐᵉ de Maintenon's
Apartment

1830 Room

★ Battle   Gallery

Galerie   de   Pierre

★★★ 18 C

Dauphin's
Apartment

Lower

Dauphine's
Apartment

SOUTH WING

Revolution,
Consultate and Empire Rooms

South Arcade →

Galerie   de   Pierre

ROYAL

Princes'

Court

Hemicycle

372

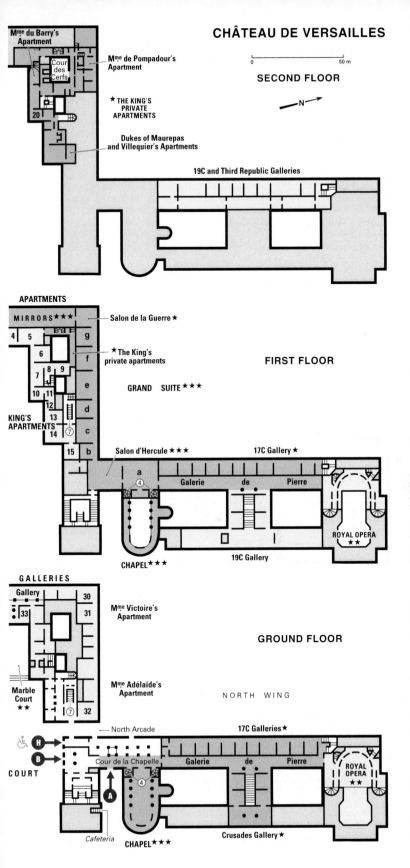

CHÂTEAU DE VERSAILLES

0 ————————— 50 m

SECOND FLOOR

N →

Mme du Barry's Apartment

Mme de Pompadour's Apartment

Cour des Cerfs

20

★ THE KING'S PRIVATE APARTMENTS

Dukes of Maurepas and Villequier's Apartments

19C and Third Republic Galleries

FIRST FLOOR

APARTMENTS

MIRRORS ★★★ — Salon de la Guerre ★

4 5
6
7 8 9
10 11
12
13
14 ⑦
15

★ The King's private apartments

GRAND SUITE ★★★

KING'S APARTMENTS

g
f
e
d
c
b

Salon d'Hercule ★★★

17C Gallery ★

a
④
Galerie   de   Pierre

ROYAL OPERA ★★

CHAPEL ★★★

19C Gallery

GROUND FLOOR

GALLERIES

Gallery
33
30
31
32

Mme Victoire's Apartment

Mme Adélaïde's Apartment

NORTH WING

Marble Court ★★

⑦

← North Arcade

17C Galleries ★

♿ H →
B →

COURT

Cour de la Chapelle

④

Galerie   de   Pierre

ROYAL OPERA ★★

A

Cafeteria

CHAPEL ★★★

Crusades Gallery ★

373

★★★**Grands Appartements** ⏱ – The State apartments consist of the reception rooms – the Salon d'Hercule, the Grand Appartement and the Galerie des Glaces – and the living quarters, of which the most interesting are the royal bedrooms.

★★ **Salon d'Hercule** – Known as Hercules' Salon, this room, begun in 1712 and completed in 1736, owes its name to the ceiling painted by Lemoyne. The artist needed three arduous years to cover the 480sq m/5 167sq ft ceiling with a painting of Hercules entering the Kingdom of the Gods. The artist committed suicide in 1737 shortly after finishing it. Two Veronese canvases occupy their original places: **Christ at the House of Simon the Pharisee★**, *Eliezer and Rebecca*.

★★★ **Grand Appartement** – The six-room suite with decoration by Le Brun was the king's apartment from 1673 to 1682. Then Louis XIV took up residence definitively at Versailles and had a new apartment designed around the Marble Court. Three times a week on Mondays, Wednesdays and Thursdays from 6pm to 10pm the king held court in the Grand Apartment.

One entered the rooms through the Royal Court by the Ambassadors' Staircase, sumptuously designed to impress visitors, but which was torn down by Louis XV in 1752.

Salon de l'Abondance (b) – When the king held court during the time of Louis XIV there were three buffets, one for hot drinks and two for cold. The ceiling painted by Houasse portrays all the royal magnificence and the gold ware collections of Louis XIV in *trompe-l'œil*.

Salon de Vénus (c) – The ceiling was painted by Houasse and like the ceilings of the following rooms it features decorated panels with gilt stucco borders.

Salon de Diane (d) – Billiard room under Louis XIV. Notice the bust of Louis XIV by Bernini (1665), a stunning example of Baroque workmanship. Paintings by La Fosse and Blanchard.

Salon de Mars (e) – Guard-room before 1682, this room was later used by Louis XIV for balls, games and music.

Two paintings have been restored to their 18C places: *Darius' Tent* by Le Brun and *The Pilgrims of Emmaüs* after Veronese. On the side walls, *Louis XV* by Rigaud and *Maria Leczczynska* by Van Loo occupy their original places. The ceiling with its martial scenes is by Audran, Jouvenet and Houasse. Above the fireplace hangs one of Louis XIV's favourite paintings, *King David* by Domenichino in which he is pictured playing the harp. It originally hung in the King's Bedchamber.

Salon de Mercure (f) – Formerly the antechamber, it occasionally served as a place where kings were laid in state. In 1715 Louis XIV in his coffin was kept here a whole week, with 72 ecclesiastics keeping vigil to ensure that four masses could be said simultaneously every day from five in the morning until noon without interruption. The ceiling is by JB de Champaigne.

Salon d'Apollon or **Salle du Trône (g)** – The throne stood on a central platform beneath a large canopy. The three hooks would have supported a canopy. It was here that ambassadors were received, and that dances and concerts were put on when the king held court.

The ceiling features *Apollo in a Sun Chariot* by La Fosse.

The entire width along the front of the palace overlooking the gardens is occupied by the Hall of Mirrors and its two wings, the Salon de Guerre and Salon de la Paix. Crossing the **Salon de la Guerre★** (War Salon), which links the Grand Apartment and the Hall of Mirrors, notice the large oval low relief by Coysevox representing Louis XIV triumphing over his enemies.

★★★**Galerie des Glaces** – Designed by Jules Hardouin-Mansart in 1687, the **Hall of Mirrors** was the showpiece under Louis XIV where court celebrations and elaborate receptions for foreign potentates took place.

The hall is 75m/246ft long, 10m/33ft wide, and it is 12m/40ft high, and it is illuminated by 17 large windows echoing 17 glass panels on the opposite wall. The 578 mirrors of glass which compose these panels are the largest that could be manufactured at that time. The hall enjoys the last rays of the setting sun.

On the ceiling **Le Brun** executed the most important cycle of his career as the king's chief painter. The cycle illustrates the life of Louis XIV and his military victories until the Treaty of Nijmegen in 1678.

The Hall of Mirrors was abundantly decorated with solid-silver furniture cast under Louis XIV.

The German Empire was proclaimed in this room on 18 January 1871 and the **Treaty of Versailles** was signed on 28 June 1919.

From the central windows one has a good **view★★★** of the Grand Perspective.

Entrance to the Queen's Suite is through the **Salon de la Paix★** which is decorated with a canvas by Lemoyne of Louis XV presenting peace to Europe.

** Appartement de la Reine – The Queen's suite was constructed for Louis XIV's wife Queen Marie-Thérèse who died here in 1683.

Chambre de la Reine (h) – Le Brun's original decoration for Marie-Thérèse was redone for Queen Maria Leczczynska between 1729 and 1735. The white and gold woodwork, the greyish tones of the ceiling by Boucher, and the doors decorated by Natoire and De Troy demonstrate the inclination towards the Rococo under Louis XV. Marie-Antoinette had other renovations made in 1770; the two-headed eagle and the portraits of the house of Austria recall the Queen's origins. The floral wall hangings were rewoven to the original pattern in Lyon, matching exactly the original hanging of the Queen's summer furnishings of 1786.

In France, royal births were public events: in this room 19 children of France were born, among them Louis XV and Philip V of Spain.

Salon des Nobles de la Reine (Peers' Salon) **(k)** – In this one-time antechamber presentations to the queen took place. This room was also where queens and dauphins of France lay in state. The room has been restored to the way it looked in 1789.

In the **antechamber (m)** note the painting by Madame Vigée-Lebrun of *Marie-Antoinette and her children* (1787). The **Salle de gardes de la Reine** (Queen's Guards-room) **(n)** protected her against intrusions such as that which occurred on the morning of 6 October 1789, when a rioting mob tried to invade the Queen's Suite and had to be fought off by the royal guard in a prolonged and bloody scuffle.

Salle du Sacre – The Coronation room was initially used as a chapel from 1676 to 1682; otherwise this large guard-room housed the sessions of Parliament which passed laws here. Louis-Philippe had the room altered to accommodate three enormous paintings: *Murat at the Battle of Aboukir* by Gros, *Champ de Mars Eagles* and *The Consecration of Napoleon* by David.

Salle de 1792 (p) – The walls of this large unfurnished room, situated at the angle of the central part of the palace and the south wing, are covered with portraits of warriors and battle scenes. Note Coignet's *The Paris National Guard Departs to Join the Army*, in which Louis-Philippe appears in the uniform of a lieutenant-general.

The **Galerie des Batailles★** (Battle Gallery) occupies the south wing. Designed in 1836 for Louis-Philippe by the architects Fontaine and Nepveu, it created a sensation. The 33 vast pictures evoke France's greatest military victories and include works by **Horace Vernet**, **Eugène Delacroix** and **Baron Gérard**.

The tour ends with the **Salle de 1830**, devoted to Louis-Philippe's accession to the throne.

Tour of the King's Bedchamber ⊘ *Entrance C*

*** Appartement du Roi or **Appartement de Louis XIV** – The king's suite stretches around the Marble Court. Designed between 1682 and 1701 by Mansart in Louis XIII's château, the decoration marks a clear break in the evolution of the Louis XIV style. The ceilings are not coffered but painted white; the white and gold panelling replaces the marble tiling; large mirrors adorn the fireplaces.

Escalier de la Reine – ⑥ The Queen's Staircase was the normal entrance to this apartment at the end of the Ancien Régime.

After the guard-room **(1)**, an antechamber **(2)** leads to the **Salon de l'Œil de bœuf (3)**. Here gentlemen attended the ceremonious king's rising *(le lever)* and retiring *(le coucher)*. The decoration marks the first flowering of the Louis XV style.

Chambre du Roi (4) – This was the bedroom of Louis XIV from 1701 and it was here that he died.

Above the bed, the alcove decoration represents France watching over the sleeping King and was sculpted by Coustou. The wall hangings are faithful reproductions of the summer furnishings of 1705. The paintings belonged to the King's personal collection.

Salle du Conseil (5) – Characteristic of Rococo, the Council Chamber was created under Louis XV by uniting two rooms. In this room decisions were made that involved the destiny of France, among them the decision to participate in the American War of Independence.

The tour ends with the **Dauphin** (the heir to the throne) and **Dauphine**'s (his wife) apartments on the ground floor.

Tour of the King's private apartments or Louis XV's apartments *Guided tour*

*** **Appartement intérieur du Roi** – The King's Private Suite served as private apartments to Louis XV, reserved for those closest to him. Here the king removed himself from the constraints of the Court. The rooms were designed by Gabriel and are decorated with carvings by Verberckt: shells, foliated scrolls and Rococo flower motifs are scattered everywhere.

Chambre à coucher (**6**) – Louis XV, and then Louis XVI, retired to this bedroom after they had performed the rising and retiring ceremonies which took place in the Grand Apartment. It was here that Louis XV died of smallpox on 10 May 1774.

Cabinet de la Pendule (**7**) – The Clock Room served as a gaming room when the king held court. Until 1769 it owed its name to the astronomical clock whose works were built by Passemant and Dauthiau with bronze embellishments by Caffiéri.

When crossing the **Antichambre des Chiens** (Dogs' Antechamber) (**8**) note the Louis XIV panelling. In the dining room called **Retours de chasse** (Hunters' Dining Hall) (**9**) Louis XV gave private dinners on hunting days.

Cabinet intérieur du Roi (**10**) – The Corner Room became a workroom in 1753. As an example of Verberckt's Rococo style, the furniture is remarkable; the medal cabinet is by Gaudreaux (1739), corner cupboards by Joubert (1755) and a roll-top **desk★** by Oeben and Riesener (1769).

Salles neuves – The new rooms were designed under Louis XV in the place of the Ambassadors' Staircase. In the **Cabinet de Mme Adélaïde** (**12**), the child **Mozart** played the harpsichord. The medal cabinet by Benneman is a masterpiece. The following rooms, Louis XVI's **Library** (**13**) and the **Porcelain Salon** (**14**) show the evolution of Versailles style towards the sober under neo-Classicism. The most notable is the **Salon des Jeux** (Louis XVI's Gaming Room) (**15**) as it appeared in 1775; corner cupboards by Riesener (1774), chairs by Boulard and gouache landscapes by Van Blarenberghe.

Go down the Louis-Philippe staircase ⑦ to leave via the north gallery.

** **Opéra Royal** – The opera house begun by Gabriel in 1768 was inaugurated in 1770 for the marriage celebrations of the dauphin, the future Louis XVI, and Marie-Antoinette.

The first oval hall in France, it received other exceptional technical touches from the engineer Arnoult: for festivals the floor of the stalls and circle could be raised to the level of the stage.

The balconies' low-relief sculptures, executed by **Pajou**, represent the gods of Olympus *(dress circle)* and the children and their signs of the zodiac *(upper circle)*.

Initially reserved for the court, the opera hosted sumptuous receptions on the occasion of visits from the King of Sweden in 1784, of Emperor Joseph II in 1777 and 1781, and of **Queen Victoria** in 1855. The National Assembly held session here from 1871 until 1875. On 30 January 1875 the adoption of the Wallon Amendment here laid the foundation of the Third Republic. A reception for **Queen Elizabeth II of England** in 1957 coincided with completion of the final restoration.

Other tours include **The milestones of the French Parliament's history**, **The Queen's Private Suite**, **Madame de Maintenon's Apartments**, **The King's Private Suite** and the **Museum** (17C-19C rooms).

***PARK AND GARDENS ⊙

Laid out principally by **Le Nôtre** during the years 1660 to 1670, the park and gardens are masterpieces of the art of French landscape gardening, in which nature is ordered geometrically according to the principles of Classicism. Sadly the park lost 7 492 trees (most of them rare species) in the storm of 26 December 1999.

The basins, fountains and statues are perfectly integrated with nature. The grand perspective or east-west axis symbolically retraces the path of the sun, from the **Latona Basin★** and fountain to the **Apollo Basin★**, continuing along the **Grand Canal★★**.

No trip to Versailles would be complete without visiting the **Grand Trianon** ⊙**★★** (1687), the **Petit Trianon** ⊙ **★★** (1768), where Marie-Antoinette spent much of her time, and the replica of a village, **le Hameau de la Reine ★★**, which was created for her between 1783 and 1786.

Making the most of Versailles

CHÂTEAU

Entrances – The various tours of the château start from different entrances:

Entrance **A**: State apartments (except groups)

Entrance **B**: State apartments (groups)

Entrance **C**: The King' and Dauphin's apartments (audio-guided tours, except groups)

Entrance **D**: Guided tours (same-day bookings, except groups)

Entrance **H**: Access reserved for handicapped visitors

Entrance **P**: The milestones of the French Parliament history

Music – Concerts of works by 17C and 18C French composers given by the Baroque Music Centre (October to December) in various venues: the Opéra Royal, the Chapelle Royale, the Salon d'Hercule, the Galerie Basse… Information and reservations, ☎ 01 39 20 78 10.

PARK

Fëtes de Nuit – These shows take place seven times during the summer around the Bassin de Neptune; they end with a fireworks display.

Grandes Eaux Musicales – Water displays reminiscent of those which took place during the reign of Louis XIV. Spectators are given an itinerary starting from the Bassin de Latone and ending at the Bassin de Neptune and Bassin du Dragon where a breathtaking finale takes place.

More information about these shows is available from the tourist office (see Admission times and charges at the end of the guide).

Eating out in town

MODERATE

Le Bœuf à la Mode – *4 r. au Pain (place du Marché-Notre-Dame) – ☎ 01 39 50 31 99 – closed Christmas weekend – 17.30/22.80€.* Guests will appreciate the convivial atmosphere of this 1930s style bistro serving tasty local specialities.

Le Baladin – *2 r. de l'Occident (St-Louis district) - ☎ 01 39 50 06 57 – sebat@wanadoo.fr – closed Sun and Mon in winter – booking recommended – lunch 16.50€ - 21/30€.* This pleasant restaurant in the old St-Louis district is appreciated for its refined cuisine; the terrace is sought after in fine weather.

MID-RANGE

Valmont – *20 r. au Pain – ☎ 01 39 51 39 00 – closed Sun evening and Mon – 17.99/24.39€.* This prettily restored old house on place des Halles will undoubtedly catch your eye… Venture inside and you will soon be conquered by the excellent service, charming decoration, a clever blend of tradition and modernity, elegantly laid tables and succulent dishes. Definitely something to look forward to.

Au Chapeau Gris – *7 rue Hoche – ☎ 01 39 50 10 81 – chapeaugris@wanadoo.fr – closed July, Tue evening and Wed – booking essential – 24.39/30.49€.* Au Chapeau Gris is literally an institution, said to date back to the Age of Enlightenment. A grand ambience and decor fit for Versailles are the setting for traditional French cuisine which never goes out of fashion. One of Versailles' most sought-after restaurants…

In the park

La Flotille – *Parc du Château, Grand Canal – ☎ 01 39 51 41 58 – closed evenings – booking essential Sun – 21/29€.* On the edge of the Grand Canal, in the château park, this small late-19C pavilion and its glass surround resembles an open-air café. It proposes two formulas, restaurant and brasserie, depending on your mood. The food is decent but the terrace makes all the difference in summer!

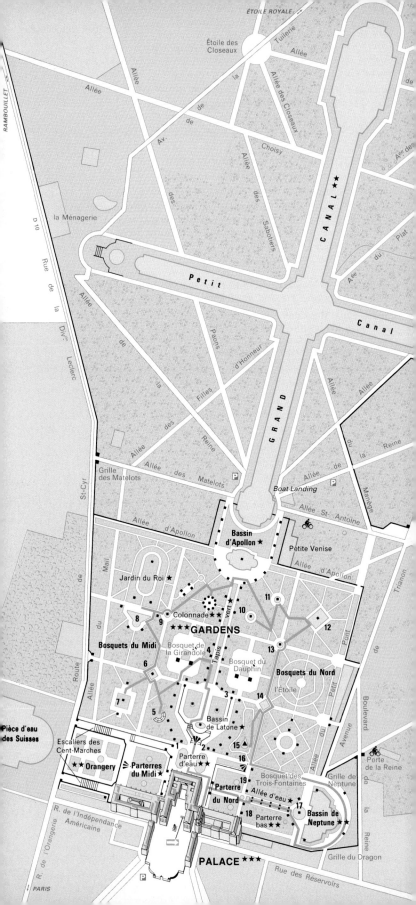

ÉTOILE ROYALE

Tuilerie

Étoile des
Closeaux

Allée

Allée

Allée des Closeaux

RAMBOUILLET

Allée

de

de

Av.

Choisy

Allée

Av. des

du Plat

de

des

des

Sabotiers

CANAL ★★

la Ménagerie

D 10

Rue

de

la

Allée

de

Petit

Canal

Paons

d'Honneur

G R A N D

Allée

Allée

Div.ᵉⁿ

Leclerc

la

Filles

Reine

de

des

Boat Landing

de

la

Manège

Allée

des

Reine

Allée

des

Matelots

P

Grille
des Matelots

St-Cyr

Allée

des

Matelots

P

Allée St- Antoine

Allée

d'Apollon

Bassin
d'Apollon ★

Petite Venise

Mail

Jardin du Roi ★

Colonnade ★★

de

11

10

12

Bosquets du Midi

★★★ GARDENS

8

9

Bosquet de
la Girandole

vert

Tapis

13

Bosquet du
Dauphin

Bosquets du Nord

6

du

Route

7

l'Étoile

14

Allée

Pont

Petit

de

Trianon

5

3

Pièce d'eau
des Suisses

Bassin
de Latone ★

15

Boulevard

Escaliers des
Cent-Marches

16

du

Porte
de la Reine

Grille
de Neptune

★★ Orangery

Parterres
du Midi ★

Parterre
d'eau ★★

Bosquet des
Trois-Fontaines

Allée

la

19

R. de l'Indépendance
Américaine

Parterre
du Nord ★

Allée d'eau

17

Bassin de
Neptune ★★

Reine

R. de l'Orangerie

18

Parterre
bas ★★

de

Grille du Dragon

PALACE ★★★

P

Rue des Réservoirs

PARIS

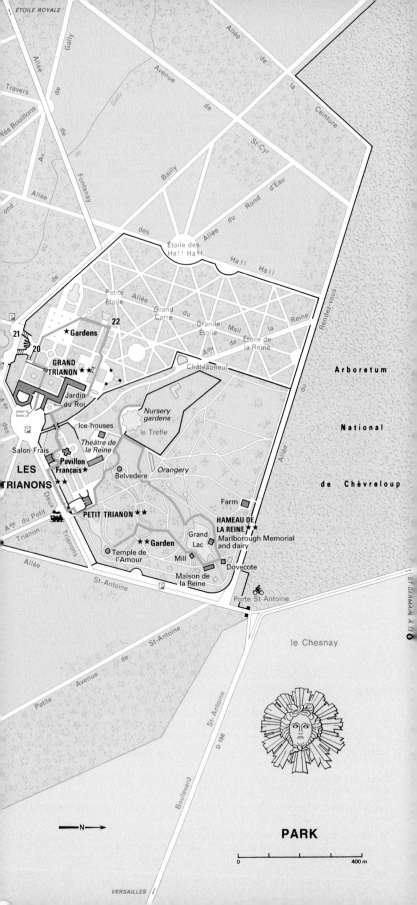

ÉTOILE ROYALE

Allée de Gally

Travers

rés Bouillons

Avenue de Gally

Allée de la Ceinture

St-Cyr

Allée du Rond d'Eau

Av. de Fontenay

Allée

ond

Bailly

des

de

Étoile des
Ha!! Ha!!

Ha!! Ha!! Ha!!

Petite
Étoile

Allée

Grand
Carre

du

Grande
Étoile

Grand Mail

la

Reine

Rendez-vous

Gardens ★

22

21

20

GRAND
TRIANON ★★

Étoile de la Reine

Châteauneuf

Arboretum

National

de Chèvreloup

Jardin
du Roi

Nursery
gardens

le Trèfle

Ice-houses

Salon Frais

Théâtre de
la Reine

Orangery

Belvedere

Pavillon
Français ★

LES
TRIANONS ★★

Farm

PETIT TRIANON ★★

HAMEAU DE
LA REINE ★★

Marlborough Memorial
and dairy

Grand
Lac

★★ Garden

Temple de
l'Amour

Mill

Dovecote

Allée

St-Antoine

Maison de
la Reine

Porte St-Antoine

ST GERMAIN A 13

le Chesnay

St-Antoine

de

Avenue

PARK

Petite

Boulevard

D 186

Allée St-Antoine

N →

0   400 m

VERSAILLES

Admission times and charges

The visiting times marked in the text with the clock-face symbol ⏱ *indicate the normal hours of opening and closing. These are listed here in alphabetical order. Admission times and charges are liable to alteration without prior notice and so the information given here should serve merely as a guideline. Museums, churches etc may refuse admittance during private functions, religious services or special occasions, and may stop issuing tickets up to an hour before the actual closing time.*

When **guided tours** *are indicated, the departure time for the last tour of the morning or afternoon will once again be prior to the given closing time.*
Most tours are conducted by French-speaking guides but in some cases the term 'guided tour' may cover group visiting with recorded commentaries. Some of the larger and more frequented museums and monuments offer guided tours in other languages. Enquire at the ticket office book shop.

The **admission prices** *indicated are the full rate for a single adult; reductions for children, students, seniors and groups should be requested on site and be endorsed with proof of ID. In some cases, admission is free (notably on Wednesdays, Sundays and public holidays).*

Churches and chapels *are usually open from 8am to noon and from 2pm to dusk. Visitors are not admitted during services and so tourists should avoid visiting at that time. As it is the norm for all churches to be open daily, only exceptional conditions are listed here. Although no fee is charged, donations towards upkeep are welcome.*

Travellers with special needs – *Some of the sights described in this guide are accessible to disabled people (marked* ♿ *). Some places may be accessible to wheelchair users, but have steps or stairways to contend with. Venues can provide assistance in giving wheelchair access to temporary exhibitions; it may be helpful therefore to check for recommended procedures, designated parking facilities and best times for by-passing long queues, before setting out.*
Detailed information on museum access is available from the Musées de France, Service Acceuil des Public Spécifiques, *6 rue des Pyramides 75041 Paris CEDEX* ☎ *01 40 15 35 88.*
Slow walkers, mature travellers and persons with various disabilities can find helpful trip-planning details on the Internet. Log in at www.access-able.com.

Paris Tourist Office   🛈 127, avenue des Champs-Élysées – 75008 – ☎ 01 49 52 53 54

Espace du tourisme d'Île de France – Pl. de la Pyramide-Inversée, Carrousel du Louvre, 99 r. de Rivoli, 1st arr – Ⓜ Palais-Royal-Musée-du-Louvre. ☎ 0 803 818 000. Internet site: www.paris-ile-de-france.com
Daily 10am-7pm. Tourist information on Paris and surrounding areas, hotel reservations, shows, bus-metro-regional express and train tickets.

A

ALMA

Musée National des Arts Asiatiques-Guimet – Daily except Tue 10am-6pm. Closed 1 Jan, 1 May, 25 Dec. 5.34€, no charge 1st Sunday in the month. 3.51€ other Sundays. ☎ 01 56 52 53 00. www.museeguimet.fr

Galerie du Panthéon Bouddhique de la Chine et du Japon – Daily except Tue 10am-6pm. Closed 1 Jan, 1 May, 25 Dec. No charge. ☎ 01 40 73 88 11.

Palais de Tokyo – Daily except Mon 10am-5.40pm, Sat-Sun 10am-6.45pm. Closed public holidays. No charge. ☎ 01 53 67 40 00.

Palais Galliera – During exhibitions: daily except Mon 10am-6pm. Closed public holidays. 7€. ☎ 01 56 52 86 00.

Musée des Égouts – ♿ May-Sep: daily except Thu and Fri 11am-5pm; Oct-Apr: daily except Thu and Fri 11am-4pm. Closed 2 weeks in Jan, 1 Jan and 25 Dec. 3.80€. ☎ 01 53 68 27 81.

Fondation Le Corbusier – Daily except Sat-Sun 10am-12.30pm, 1.30-6pm, Mon 1.30-6pm, Fri 1.30-5pm. Closed in Aug, 25 Dec-1 Jan and public holidays. 2.40€. ☎ 01 42 88 41 53.

Musée Bouchard – ♿ Wed and Sat 2-7pm. Closed public holidays (except Wed and Sat), from mid to end Mar, Jun, Sep and Dec. 3.81€. ☎ 01 46 47 63 46.

B

Opéra de Paris-Bastille – Guided tours (1hr15min). Day and time depending on performers' and technicians' work schedules. Call for information. 7.55€. ☎ 01 40 01 19 70.

Pavillon de l'Arsenal – ♿ Daily except Mon 10.30am-6.30pm, Sun and public holidays 11am-7pm. Documentation centre: Wed-Fri 2-6pm. Closed 1 Jan. No charge. ☎ 01 42 76 33 97.

Centre Georges-Pompidou – ♿ Pompidou centre: 11am-9pm (last admission 1hr before closing); museum and exhibitions: 11am-9pm, Thu 11am-11pm. Closed Tue and 1 May. Museum 5.5€, exhibitions 6.5€ or 8.5€ (under 18s: no charge, exhibitions 4.5€ or 6.5€), no charge for the museum 1st Sunday in the month. ☎ 01 44 78 12 33.

Église St-Merri – 3-7pm.

Musée de la Poupée – ♿ Daily except Mon 10am-6pm (last admission 45min before closing). Closed public holidays. 6€ (children: 3€). ☎ 01 42 72 73 11.

Maison de l'Air – Apr-Sep: daily except Mon 1.30-5.30pm, Sat-Sun and public holidays 1.30-6.30pm (last admission 30min before closing); Oct-Mar: daily except Mon 1.30-5pm. 3.35€. ☎ 01 43 28 47 63.

Bibliothèque Nationale de France François-Miterrand – Daily except Mon morning 9am-8pm, Sun noon-6pm. Guided tours by request. Closed public holidays and from 2nd to 4th Mon in Sep. Price information not provided. ☎ 01 53 79 49 49.

Shakespeare Garden – Daily 3-5pm (except during plays). No charge. ☎ 01 40 71 75 60.

Jardin d'Acclimatation – Jun-Sep: 10am-7pm; Oct-May: 10am-6pm. 2.3€. ☎ 01 40 67 90 82.

Musée en Herbe – ♿ Sun-Fri 10am-6pm, Sat 2-6pm (school holidays: 10am-6pm). Closed 1 Jan and 25 Dec. 3€. ☎ 01 40 67 97 66.

Jardin des Serres d'Auteuil – ♿ Daily 10am-5pm (Apr-Sep: 6pm). 1.52€. ☎ 01 40 71 75 60.

Parc de Bagatelle – ♿ Mar-Sep: 8.30am-6.30pm (8pm depending on the date); Oct-Feb: 9am-4.30pm (6pm depending on the date). 1.5€. ☎ 01 40 71 75 60.

Musée Arménien – Closed for renovation work.

Musée d'Ennery – Closed for renovation work.

Musée Dapper – ♿ Daily except Mon and Tue 11am-7pm. Closed early Aug to mid-Sep. 4.6€, no charge last Wed in the month. ☎ 01 45 00 01 50.

Musée National des Arts et Traditions populaires – Daily except Tue 9.30am-5.15pm (ticket office closes at 4.30pm). Depending on the type of exhibition: 3.35-4.57€ (children: 1.52€).

C

CHAMPS-ÉLYSÉES

Arc de Triomphe platform – Apr-Sep: 9.30am-11pm (last admission 30min before closing); Oct-Mar: 10am-10.30pm. Closed 1 Jan, 1 and 8 May (morning), 14 Jul (morning), 11 Nov (morning), 25 Dec. 7€. ☎ 01 55 37 73 77.

Musée du Petit Palais – The musuem is currently closed for restoration and should open again during 2004.

Palais de la Décourverte – Daily except Mon 9.30am-6pm; Sun and holidays 10am-7pm (last entrance 1hr before closing). Closed I Jan, 1 May, 14 Jul, 15 Aug and 25 Dec. 5.60€ (children: 3.65€). Planetarium 2.29€. ☎ 01 56 43 20 21.

Île de la CITÉ

Mémorial de la Déportation – Apr-Sep: 10am-noon, 1.15-7pm; Oct-Mar: 10am-noon, 1.15-7pm. No charge. ☎ 01 46 33 87 56.

Palais de Justice – Daily except Sun 8.30am-6pm. Visitors are normally allowed to attend a civil or criminal hearing. General public not admitted to the Galerie des Bustes Children's Court. Closed public holidays. ☎ 01 44 32 50 00.

La CONCIERGERIE

Apr-Sep: 9.30am-6.30pm; Oct-Mar: 10am-5pm. Closed 1 Jan, 1 May, 1 and 11 Nov, 25 Dec. 5.5€ (combined ticket with the Sainte-Chapelle: 8€). ☎ 01 53 73 78 50.

D

La DÉFENSE

La Grande Arche – Apr-Sep: 10am-8pm (last admission 30min before closing); Oct-Mar: 10am-7pm. 7€. ☎ 01 49 07 27 27. www.grandearche.com

Info-Défense – Apr-Sep: Mon-Fri 9.30am-5.30pm; Oct-Mar: Mon-Fri 10am-6pm. Closed public holidays. ☎ 01 47 76 37 13. Information office on site.

DENFERT-ROCHEREAU

Les Catacombes – Daily except Mon 9am-4pm, Tue 11am-4pm. Long stairways. It is advisable to take a torch with you. Closed public holidays. 5€. ☎ 01 43 22 47 63.

Fondation Cartier – &. Daily except Mon noon-8pm. Closed 1 Jan and 25 Dec. 5€. ☎ 01 42 18 56 51.

E

Tour EIFFEL

Lift: mid-Jun to end Aug 9am-midnight; early Sep to mid-Jun 9.30am-11pm. 3.70€ (1st floor), 6.90€ (2nd floor), 9.90€ (3rd floor). Stairs (1st and 2nd floor only): mid-Jun to end Aug 9am-midnight; early Sep to mid-Jun 9.30am-6.30pm. 3€. ☎ 01 44 11 23 23.

Village Suisse – &. Daily except Tue and Wed 10.30am-5pm. No charge. ☎ 01 45 66 00 09.

Maison de l'UNESCO – Daily except Sat-Sun and public holidays 9.30am-6pm. No charge. ☎ 01 45 68 10 60.

G

Les GOBELINS

Manufactures des Gobelins – Guided tours (1hr 30min) Tue-Thu at 2pm and 2.45pm. Closed public holidays. 8€. ☎ 01 44 54 19 33.

Les GRANDS BOULEVARDS

Musée Grévin – ♿ Daily 10am-7pm (last admission 1hr before closing). 15€ (under 14s: 9€). ☎ 01 47 70 85 05. www.grevin.com

Hôtel des Ventes Drouot-Richelieu – Daily 11am-6pm. Closed Sun (except one Sun in the month), public holidays and Aug. No charge. ☎ 01 48 00 20 52.

I

INSTITUT DE FRANCE

The Centre des Monuments Nationaux (National Monuments Centre) organises guided tours of the Institut de France one weekend a month. 8€ (under 25s: 6€). The tour includes the interior courtyards, the dome and Mazarin's tomb. Reservations: ☎ 01 44 54 19 30/35.

Hôtel des Monnaies et Médailles – Daily except Mon 11am-5.30pm, Sat-Sun noon-5.30pm. ☎ 01 40 46 55 33.

Les INVALIDES

Musée de l'Armée – ♿ Apr-Sep: 10am-6pm (last admission 30min before closing); Oct-Mar: 10am-5pm. Closed 1st Mon in the month, 1 Jan, 1 May, 1 Nov, 25 Dec. 6€. ☎ 01 44 42 37 72. www.invalides.org

Musée des Plans-Reliefs – ♿ Apr-Sep: 10am-6pm; Oct-Mar: 10am-5pm. Closed 1st Mon in the month, 1 Jan, 1 May, 1 Nov, 25 Dec. 6€. ☎ 01 45 51 92 45.

Église du Dôme – Apr-Sep: 10am-6pm; Oct-Mar: 10am-5pm. Closed 1st Mon in the month, 1 Jan, 1 May, 1 Nov, 25 Dec. 6€. ☎ 01 44 42 37 72.

Musée de l'Ordre de la Libération – Apr-Sep: 10am-5.45pm; Oct-Mar: 10am-3.45pm. Closed 1st Mon in the month except public holidays, 1 Jan, 1 May, 17 Jun, 1 Nov, 25 Dec. 6€. ☎ 01 47 05 04 10.

J

JARDIN DES PLANTES

♿ Apr-Sep: daily except Sat-Sun 8.15am-4pm. Closed public holidays. No charge. ☎ 01 40 79 30 00

Muséum national d'Histoire naturelle

Grande Galerie de l'Évolution – ♿ Daily except Tue 10am-6pm, Thu 10am-10pm. Closed 1 May. 6.10€. ☎ 01 40 79 30 00.

Menagerie – ♿ Summer: 9.30am-6pm; winter: 9.30am-5pm. 4.57€. ☎ 01 40 79 37 94.

Micro Zoo – Apr-Sep: 10am-noon, 2-5.15pm, Sun and public holidays 10am-noon, 2.30-5.45pm; Oct-Mar: 10am-noon, 1.30-4.30pm. Serve-yourself remote-controlled microscope equipment with sound effects is available. 4.57€. ☎ 01 40 79 38 88.

Galerie de Minérologie et de Géologie – Apr-Oct: daily except Tue 10am-5pm, Sat-Sun 10am-6pm; Nov-Mar: daily except Tue 10am-5pm. Closed 1 May. 4.57€. ☎ 01 40 79 30 00.

Galérie de Paléontologie et Anatomie comparée – Apr-Oct: daily except Tue 10am-5pm, Sat-Sun 10am-6pm; Nov-Mar: daily except Tue 10am-5pm. Closed 1 May. 4.57€. ☎ 01 40 79 30 00.

Jardin des Plantes: maze – ♿ From dawn to dusk. No charge.

Les Grandes Serres – Apr-Oct: daily except Tue 1-5pm, Sat-Sun 1-6pm; Nov-Mar: daily except Tue 1-5pm. Closed 1 May. 2.29€. ☎ 01 40 79 30 00.

Jardin Alpin – ♿ Apr-Sep: daily except Sat-Sun 8-11am, 1.30-5pm. Closed public holidays. No charge. ☎ 01 40 79 30 00.

School of Botany – ♿ Daily except Sat-Sun 8-11am, 1.30-5pm. Closed public holidays. No charge. ☎ 01 40 79 30 00.

JUSSIEU

La Mosquée – Daily except Fri 9am-noon, 2-6pm. Closed on Muslim feast days. 3€. ☎ 01 45 35 97 33.

Institut du Monde Arabe: musée – ♿ Daily except Mon 10am-6pm. Closed 1 May. 4€. ☎ 01 40 51 38 38.

Collections des Minéraux – Daily except Tue 1-6pm. Closed 1 Jan, Easter, 1 May, 14 Jul, All Saints, 25 Dec. 4.50€. ☎ 01 44 27 52 88.

L

Le Grand LOUVRE

Le Grand Louvre – **Opening times** – ♿ Daily except Tue and some holidays 9am-6pm. Some section open Wed and Mon until 9.45pm. Temporary exhibits under the Pyramid: 9am-6pm (9.45pm Wed).

Admission charges – Permanent collection and temporary exhibits (single ticket, except for temporary exhibits in the hall Napoléon): 7.50€ before 3pm, 5€ after 3pm and Sun all day. (no charge for visitors under age 18), no charge the 1st Sun of the month. Tickets valid all day long, even if you leave the museum. Ticket sales until 5.15pm (9.15pm Mon and Wed). Advance ticket purchase from the FNAC store ☎ 08 92 68 36 22 (1.10€ commission fee added to price), from Ticketnet ☎ 08 03 34 63 46 (0.91€ fee); tickets remain valid for an unlimited time.

Passes and discounts – The **Carte Musées et Monuments** (valid 1, 3 or 5 days for 70 museums and monuments) is for sale in the shopping gallery of the Carrousel du Louvre and allows you to enter the permanent collections immediately, without waiting. The "carte Louvre jeunes" pass (valid 1 year for those under age 26, for sale under the Pyramid or by mail) allows entrance to permanent collections and temporary exhibits as well as cultural activities reserved for museum members, discounts on events held in the auditorium and for guided tours, ☎ 01 40 20 51 04. The "**Carte des Amis du Louvre**" (valid 1 year, purchase from the Amis du Louvre booth between the Pyramid and the inverse Pyramid in the entrance area) allows entrance to the museum and temporary exhibits as well as discount prices for many other exhibits in the city, ☎ 01 40 20 53 74.

Temporary exhibits – In the Hall Napoléon (under the Pyramid): 9am-6pm (9.45pm Wed), or in the Richelieu and Sully wings (during opening hours).

Guided tours – Guided tours are available in English, and there are also activities in workshops. Tours are conducted daily except Tue and Sun and last 1hr30min. Individual visitors should buy their tickets at the window marked "Accueil des groupes" under the Pyramid, ☎ 01 40 20 52 09.

In many rooms, there are explanatory texts for consultation in several languages, placed at visitors' disposal in racks near the door.

LUXEMBOURG

Le Luxembourg – The park is open during daylight hours. The museum is open for temporary exhibits only, check the press for scheduled events.

M

MARAIS

Hôtel de Sens: Forney Library – Daily except Sun and Mon 1.30-8pm, Sat 10am-8pm. Closed public holidays. No charge (temporary exhibitions: 3.05€). ☎ 01 42 78 14 60.

Mémorial du Martyr Juif Inconnu – ♿ Daily except Sat-Sun 10am-1pm, 2-5.30pm (Fri 5pm). Closed on Jewish feast days. 2.30€. ☎ 01 42 77 44 72.

Hôtel de Sully – Tours of the courtyard and gardens: 8.30am-7pm. No charge. ☎ 01 44 61 21 50.

Cathédrale Ste-Croix-de-Paris – Tours available by appointment with the parish priest. ☎ 01 44 59 23 50.

Maison de Victor-Hugo – Daily except Mon 10am-6pm. Closed public holidays. No charge (except during temporary exhibitions). ☎ 01 42 72 10 16.

Musée de la Curiosité et de la Magie – Wed and Sat-Sun 2-7pm. Call for information during school holiday periods. 7€ (children: 5€). ☎ 01 42 72 13 26.

Musée d'Art et d'Histoire du Judaïsme – ♿ Daily except Sat 11am-6pm, Sun and public holidays 10am-6pm. Closed 1 Jan, 1 May, 25 Dec. 6.10€. ☎ 01 53 01 86 60.

Musée de l'Histoire de France – Daily except Tue 10am-5.45pm, Sat-Sun 1.45-5.45pm. Closed public holidays. 3.05 €. ☎ 01 40 27 60 96.

Musée de la Chasse et de la Nature – Daily except Mon 11am-6pm. Closed public holidays. 4.60€. ☎ 01 53 01 92 40.

Hôtel de Rohan – Open during temporary exhibitions.

Musée Picasso – 🚹 Apr-Sep: daily except Tue 9.30am-6pm; Oct-Mar: daily except Tue 9.30am-5.30pm. Closed 1 Jan and 25 Dec. 5.50€ (children: no charge), no charge 1st Sunday in the month. ☎ 01 42 71 25 21.

Musée de la Serrurerie-Bricard – Daily except Sat-Sun 2-5pm. Closed public holidays. 4.57€. ☎ 01 42 77 79 62.

Musée Cognacq-Jay – Daily except Mon 10am-5.40 pm (last entrance 30min befor closing). Closed public holidays. No charge. Gratuit. ☎ 01 40 27 07 21.

Musée Carnavalet-Histoire de Paris – Daily except Mon 10am-6pm. Closed some public holidays. No charge. ☎ 01 44 59 58 58. www.paris-france.org/musees/museecarnavalet

Maison Européenne de la Photographie – 🚹 Daily except Mon and Tue 11am-7.45pm. Closed public holidays. 5€. ☎ 01 44 78 75 00.

MAUBERT

Musée de l'Assistance Publique-Hôpitaux de Paris – Daily except Mon 10am-6pm. Closed public holidays. 4€, no charge 1st Sunday in the month. ☎ 01 40 27 50 05.

Musée des Collections historiques de la Préfecture de Paris – Daily except Sun 9am-5pm, Sat 10am-5pm. Closed public holidays. No charge. ☎ 01 44 41 52 50.

Plaine et parc MONCEAU

Cathédrale St-Alexandre-Nevski – Tue, Fri, Sun 3-5pm. ☎ 01 42 27 37 34.

Musée Cernuschi – Tue, Fri, Sun 3-5pm. ☎ 01 42 27 37 34.

Musée Henner – Daily except Mon 10am-noon, 2-5pm. Closed 1 Jan, 25 Dec. Price information not provided. ☎ 01 47 63 42 73.

Musée Nissim-de-Camondo – Daily except Mon and Tue 10am-5pm. Closed 1 Jan, 1May, 15 Aug and 25 Dec. 4.57€. ☎ 01 53 89 06 40/50.

Musée Jacquemart-André – 10am-6pm (last admission 30min before closing). 8€. ☎ 01 42 89 04 91.

MONTMARTRE

Basilique de Sacré-Cœur:

Dome – Daily 10am-5.45pm. 5€ (combined ticket for the crypt and dome). ☎ 01 53 41 89 90.

Crypt – Daily 10am-5.45pm. 5€ (combined ticket for the crypt and dome). ☎ 01 53 41 89 90.

Musée de Montmartre – Daily except Mon 10am-12.30pm, 1.30-6pm. Closed 1 Jan, 1 May, 25 Dec. 4.50€. ☎ 01 49 25 89 37.

Halle St-Pierre: Musée d'Art naïf Max-Fourny – 🚹 Daily 10am-6pm. Closed Aug, 1 Jan, 1May, and 25 Dec. 6€. ☎ 01 42 58 72 89.

Cimetière de Montmartre – Guided tours possible by appointment. ☎ 01 40 71 75 60.

MONTPARNASSE

Tour Montparnasse – Oct-Mar: Mon-Thu and Sun 9.30am-10.30pm, Fri, Sat and eve of public holidays 9.30am-11pm (last admission 30min before closing); Apr-Sep: 9.30am-11.30pm. 7.6€ (children: 5.2€). ☎ 01 45 38 52 56. www.montparnasse56.com

Cimetière Montparnasse – Guided tours possible by appointment. ☎ 01 40 71 75 60.

Musée Bourdelle – Daily except Mon 10am-6pm (last admission 30min before closing). Closed public holidays. No charge. ☎ 01 49 54 73 73.

Musée de la Poste – Daily except Sun 10am-6pm. Closed public holidays. 4.5€. ☎ 01 42 79 24 24.

Mémorial du Maréchal Leclerc-de-Hautecloque et de la Libération de Paris – Musée Jean-Moulin – 🚹 Daily except Mon 10am-6pm. Closed public holidays. No charge (exhibitions: 4€). ☎ 01 40 64 39 44.

MONTSOURIS

Église du Sacré-Cœur – Wed and Sat 2-7pm. ☎ 01 46 57 70 18.

MOUFFETARD
Église St-Médard – Daily except Mon.

LA MUETTE-RANELAGH
Musée Marmottan-Monet – Daily except Mon 10am-6pm (last admission 30min before closing). Closed 1 Jan, 1 May, 25 Dec. 6.50€. ☎ 01 44 96 50 33.

Institut des Arts de l'écriture: Musée du Stylo – Sun and public holidays 2-6pm. Mon-Sat by request. 2€. ☎ 06 07 94 13 21.

N

Cathédrale NOTRE-DAME
Guided tour – Guided tours at noon (additional tour Tue 4pm), Sat-Sun 2.30pm. In English: Wed and Thu noon, Sat 2.30pm. No charge. ☎ 01 42 34 56 10. www.cathedraledeparis.com

Crypte archéologique – Daily except Mon 10am-6pm. No charge. ☎ 01 43 29 83 51.

Towers: Ascent – Jul and Aug: 9am-7.30pm, Sat-Sun 9am-11pm; Sep: 9.30am-7.30pm; Oct and Nov: 10.30am-5.30pm; Dec-Mar: 10am-5pm. Access at the foot of the north tower (386 steps). Closed 1 Jan, 1 May, 25 Dec. 5.5€. ☎ 01 53 10 07 00.

Treasury – & Mon-Sat 9.30am-5.30pm, Sun 1.30-5.30pm. 2.5€ (children: 1€). ☎ 01 42 34 56 10.

O

ODÉON
Musée d'Histoire de la médecine – Mid-Jul to end Sep: daily except Sat-Sun 2-5.30pm; early Oct to mid-Jul: daily except Thu and Sun 2-5.30pm. Closed 25 Dec-1 Jan and public holidays. 3.50€. ☎ 01 40 46 16 93.

OPÉRA
L'Opéra-Garnier – Daily 10am-4.30pm (unless matinée or special event taking place). Guided tours of the public foyers and the museum at noon (arrive 15min in advance). 4.57€ (children under 10: no charge), guided tours 9.15€ (children under 10: 3.81€). Closed 1 Jan and 1 May. ☎ 01 40 01 22 63.

Musée de la Parfumerie Fragonard – Daily except Sun 9am-6pm. Closed public holidays. No charge. ☎ 04 93 36 44 65.

Paris-Story – & Daily 9am-7pm (every hour). 8€ (children: 5€). ☎ 01 42 66 62 06.

Musée d'ORSAY
& Mid-Jun to mid-Sep: daily except Mon 9am-6pm, Thu 9am-9.45pm, Sun 9am-6pm; mid-Sep to mid-Jun: daily except Mon 10am-6pm, Thu 10am-9.45pm, Sun 9am-6pm. Closed 1 Jan, 1 May, 25 Dec. 7€, no charge 1st Sunday in the month. ☎ 01 40 49 48 48.

P

PALAIS-ROYAL
Musée de la Mode et du Textile – & Daily except Mon 11am-6pm, Sat-Sun 10am-6pm. Closed 1 Jan, 1 May, 15 Aug and 25 Dec. 5.40€ (ticket combined with the Museum of Decorative Arts). ☎ 01 44 55 57 50.

Musée des Arts Décoratifs – & Same as for the Musée de la Mode et du Textile (Fashion and Textiles Museum). Only the collections covering the Middle Ages and the Renaissance are open to visitors. Those covering the 17C, 18C, 19C and 20C are closed due to renovation work until 2004.

Musée de la Publicité – & Same as for the Musée de la Mode et du Textile (Fashion and Textiles Museum). ☎ 01 44 55 57 50. www.museedelapub.org

Cimetière de Passy – Mid-Mar to early Nov: 7.30am-6pm, Sat 8.30am-6pm, Sun and public holidays 9am-6pm; early Nov to mid-Mar: 8am-5.30pm, Sat 8.30am-5.30pm, Sun and public holidays 9am-5.30pm. No charge (guided tours 2hr: 5.70€). ☎ 01 40 71 75 60.

Maison de Balzac – Daily except Mon 10am-6pm (last admission 30min before closing). Closed public holidays. 3.30€ (under 13s: no charge). ☎ 01 55 74 41 80.

Musée du Vin-Caveau des Échansons – ♿ Daily except Mon 10am-6pm (last admission 30min before closing). Closed 25 Dec-1 Jan. 6€. ☎ 01 45 25 63 26.

Musée Clemenceau – Closed for renovation work.

Mid-Mar to early Nov: 7.30am-6pm, Sat 8.30am-6pm, Sun and public holidays 9am-6pm; early Nov to mid-Mar: 8am-5.30pm, Sat 8.30am-5.30pm, Sun and public holidays 9am-5.30pm. No charge. ☎ 01 40 71 75 60.

Musée de la Vie Romantique – Daily except Mon 10am-6pm. Closed public holidays. No charge (temporary exhibitions: 4.50€). ☎ 01 48 74 95 38.

Musée de l'Érotisme – ♿ Daily 10am-2am 7€. ☎ 01 42 58 28 73.

Église St-Laurent – Daily except Sat-Sun.

Hôtel Bourrienne – ♿ Beginning to mid-Jul and Sep: guided tours (1hr, last admission 5.30pm) noon-6pm. 5€. ☎ 01 47 70 51 14.

Musée Baccarat – Daily except Sun 10am-6pm (last admission 30min before closing). Closed public holidays. 3€. ☎ 01 47 70 64 30.

Musée de la Franc-Maçonnerie – ♿ Daily except Sun and Mon 2-6pm. Closed public holidays and first 3 weeks in Aug. 2€. ☎ 01 45 23 74 78.

Val de Grâce:
Church – Guided tours Mon-Fri by request to the Conservation du Musée du Service de Santé des Armées.
Musée du service de santé des armées – Tue, Wed, Sat-Sun noon-5pm. Closed Aug. 4.6€. ☎ 01 40 51 51 92.

Ancienne abbaye de Port-Royal – Guided tours only. Contact the Réunion des Musées Nationaux, 6 av. Mahatma-Gandhi, 75016 Paris. ☎ 01 45 02 82 23.

Observatoire de Paris – Guided tours (2hr) 1st Sat in the month by written request (3 months in advance) to the Observatoire de Paris, service des visites, 61 av. de l'Observatoire, 75014 Paris. Closed Aug and public holidays. 4.5€. ☎ 01 40 51 21 74.

Musée Zadkine – Daily except Mon 10am-6pm. Closed public holidays. No charge. ☎ 01 55 42 77 20.

Q

La Sorbonne: Église de la Sorbonne – Open for temporary exhibitions and cultural events.

Église St-Étienne-du-Mont – Sep-Jun: 8.30am-6.45pm; Jul and Aug: daily except Mon 8.30am-noon, 4-6.45pm; school holidays: 8.30am-noon, 2-6.45pm. ☎ 01 43 54 11 79.

Le Panthéon – Apr-Sep: 9.30am-11pm; Oct-Mar: 10am-10.30pm. Closed 1 Jan, 1 and 8 May (morning), 14 Jul, 11 Nov (morning), 25 Dec. 7€. ☎ 01 55 37 73 77.

Musée National du Moyen Âge, Thermes et hôtel de Cluny – Daily except Tue 9.15am-5.45pm (last admission 30min before closing). Closed 1 Jan, 1 May, 25 Dec. 5.5€, no charge 1st Sunday in the month. ☎ 01 53 73 78 16.

Musée de Minéralogie – Daily except Sun and Mon 1.30-6pm, Sat 10am-12.30pm, 2-5pm. Closed public holidays. 5€. ☎ 01 40 51 92 90.

Musée Curie – Guided tours (45min) daily except Sat-Sun 1.30pm-5pm; Closed Aug and public holidays. No charge. ☎ 01 42 34 67 49.

Centre de la Mer et des Eaux – ♿ Daily except Mon 10am-12.30pm, 1.30-5.30pm, Sat-Sun 10am-5.30pm. Closed 1 Jan, 1 May, 14 Jul, 15 Aug and 25 Dec. 4.6€. ☎ 01 44 32 10 70.

R

RÉPUBLIQUE

Square and Carreau du Temple – ♿ Daily except Mon 9am-1pm, Sat 9am-6.30pm, Sun and public holidays 9am-1pm. Closed 14 Jul and 15 Aug. No charge.

Musée des Arts et métiers – Daily except Mon 10am-6pm (closes at 9.30pm Thu). Closed public holidays. 5.34€. ☎ 01 53 01 82 00.

S

Faubourg ST-GERMAIN

Hôtel de Tavannes – Mid-Aug to end Sep: guided tours (15min) daily except Sun 10am-noon, 2.30-6pm. No charge.

Musée Rodin – Apr-Sep: daily except Mon 9.30am-5.45pm (last admission 30min before closing); Oct-Mar: daily except Mon 9.30am-4.45pm. Closed 1 Jan, 1 May, 25 Dec. 5€, no charge 1st Sunday in the month. ☎ 01 44 18 61 24.

Musée Maillol – ♿ Daily except Tue 11am-6pm (last admission 45min before closing). Closed public holidays. 7€. ☎ 01 42 22 59 58.

Palais-Bourbon – ♿ Guided tours (1hr) Sat at 10am, 2pm, 3pm. Arrive 15min before and take an identity document with you. No charge. ☎ 01 40 63 64 08. www.assemblee-nationale.fr

Musée de la Légion d'Honneur – Closed for restoration.

ST-GERMAIN-DES-PRÉS

Église St-Germain-des-Prés – Open during religious services only. ☎ 01 43 25 41 71.

Musée Eugène-Delacroix – Daily except Tue 9.30am-12.30pm, 2-5pm (last admission 30min before closing). Closed 1 Jan, 1 May, 25 Dec. 4€, no charge 1st Sunday in the month. ☎ 01 44 41 86 50. www.musee-delacroix.fr

Faubourg ST-HONORÉ

Église St-Philippe-du-Roule – Tours available by appointment with the parish priest. ☎ 01 53 53 00 40.

SAINT-LAZARE

Chapelle Expiatoire – Thu-Sat: 1-5pm. Closed some public holidays. 2.5€. ☎ 01 44 32 18 00.

Musée Gustave-Moreau – Daily except Tue 10am-12.45pm, 2-5.15pm, Mon and Wed 11am-5.15pm. Closed 1 Jan, 1 May, 25 Dec. 3.35€. ☎ 01 48 74 38 50.

L'ÎLE SAINT-LOUIS

Église St-Louis-en-l'Île – Daily 9am-noon, 3-7pm, Mon 3-7pm. Guided tours on certain Sundays at 3pm. Contact the parish. ☎ 01 46 34 11 60.

Adam-Mickiewicz Museum – Closed for renovation work.

SAINTE-CHAPELLE

Apr-Sep: 9.30am-6.30pm; Oct-Mar: 10am-5pm. Closed 1 Jan, 1 May, 1 and 11 Nov, 25 Dec. 5.5€ (combined ticket with the Conciergerie: 8€).☎ 01 53 73 78 50.

LE SENTIER

Église Notre-Dame-de-Bonne-Nouvelle – Daily except Mon 8am-7pm, Wed 1-2.30pm, Sat noon-4pm, Sun noon-7pm. ☎ 01 42 33 65 74.

SÈVRES-BABYLONE

Musée Hébert – Daily except Tue 12.30-6pm, Sat-Sun 2-6pm (last admission 30min before closing). Closed 1 Jan and 25 Dec. 3€, no charge 1st Sunday in the month. ☎ 01 42 22 23 82.

Ancien Couvent des Carmes – Daily 7am-7pm, Sun and public holidays 9.15am-7pm. Closed 14 Jul. No charge. ☎ 01 44 39 52 84.

Bibliothèque du Protestantisme français – Daily except Sat-Sun 2-6pm. Guided tours by request to the Bibliothèque du Protestantisme français, 54 r. des Saints-Pères, 75007 Paris. Closed Aug and public holidays.

T

TROCADÉRO

Musée National de la Marine – ♿ Daily except Tue 10am-6pm (last admission 30min before closing). Closed 1 Jan, 1 May, 25 Dec. 7€. ☎ 01 53 65 69 53. www.musee-marine.fr

Musée des Monuments Français – Closed for restoration. ☎ 01 44 05 39 10.

Jardin des TUILERIES

Musée de l'Orangerie – Closed for renovation work. Reopening planned for 2004.

Galerie Nationale du Jeu de Paume – ♿ Daily except Mon noon-7pm, Tue noon-9.30pm, Sat-Sun 10am-7pm. Closed 1 Jan, 1 May, 25 Dec. 6€. ☎ 01 47 03 12 50.

V

VAUGIRARD

Pasteur Institute – Guided tours (1hr) daily except Sat-Sun 2-5.30pm. Closed Aug and public holidays. 3€. ☎ 01 45 68 82 83.

Place des VICTOIRES

Bibliothèque nationale de France: Site Richelieu:

Medals and Antiques Museum – Daily 1-6pm, Sat 1-5pm, Sun 10am-6pm. Closed 1 Jan, 15 Aug and 25 Dec. No charge. ☎ 01 53 79 83 30.

LA VILLETTE

Cité des Sciences et de l'Industrie – ♿ Daily except Mon 10am-6pm (Sun 7pm). Closed 1 May and 25 Dec. 7.50€ (under 25s and persons accompanying under 16s: 5.50€; children under 7: no charge). Extra charge for the Planetarium: 2.50€.

Le Cinaxe – Daily except Mon. 11am-5pm, film every 15min. 5.20€ (children: 4.50€) at the Cinaxe ticket window. Children under age 4 not allowed, not advisable for pregnant women and heart patients. Reservations ☎ 01 42 09 86 04; information 01 40 05 12 12.

La Géode – Check the schedule in the press or at the museum (www.lageode.fr); 8.75€ (children:6.75€) Reservations ☎ 08 92 68 45 40. Closed 1 May and Christmas.

Musée de la Musique – ⅄ Daily except Mon noon-6pm, Sun 10am-6pm. Closed some public holidays. 6.10€. ☎ 01 44 84 44 84. www.cite-musique.fr

Bois et Château de VINCENNES

Château – Summer: short tours (guided tours 45min: general presentation and the Sainte-Chapelle) at 10.15am, 11.45am, 1.30pm and 5.15pm; long tours (guided tours 1hr15min: general presentation, the moat, the watchpath and the Sainte-Chapelle) at 11am, 2.15pm, 3pm, 3.45pm and 4.30pm. Winter: short tours at 10.15am, 11.45am, 1.30pm and 4.15pm; long tours at 11am, 2.15pm, 3pm and 3.45pm. Closed 1 Jan, 1 May, 1 and 11 Nov, 25 Dec. Short tour 3.96€, long tour 5.49€ (under 18s: no charge), no charge 1st Sunday in the month (Oct-May). ☎ 01 48 08 31 20.

Centre Bouddhique – Apr-Oct: access to the temple on religious feast days. Call for information. ☎ 01 43 41 54 48.

Parc Zoologique – ⅄ Apr-Sep: 9am-6pm, Sun and public holidays 9am-6.30pm (last admission 30min before closing); Oct: 9am-6pm; Feb and Mar: 9am-5.30pm; Nov-Jan: 9am-5pm. 8€ (children: 5€). ☎ 01 44 75 20 10.

Parc Floral – ⅄ Apr-Sep: 9.30am-8pm; early Oct to mid-Oct: 9.30am-7pm; mid to end Oct and Mar: 9.30am-6pm; Nov-Feb: 9.30am-5pm. 1.5€ (children: 0.75€). ☎ 01 55 94 20 20.

Musée des Arts d'Afrique et d'Océanie – Daily except Tue 10am-5.30pm. Closed 1 May. 4.5€, no charge 1st Sunday in the month. The museum of Art from Africa and Oceania closed permanently on 31 Jan 2003. The aquarium remains open to the public. ☎ 01 44 74 84 80.

Arboteum de l'École de Breuil – Apr-Sep: 8am-4pm, Sat-Sun and public holidays 10am-7pm; Mar and Oct: 8am-4pm, Sat-Sun and public holidays 10am-6pm; Nov-Feb: 8am-4pm, Sat-Sun and public holidays 10am-5pm. 0.75 €. ☎ 01 53 66 14 00.

Excursions

DISNEYLAND PARIS

Early Jul to end Aug: 9am-11pm (9pm for Walt Disney Studios); Sep to mid-Jan: 10am-8pm, Sat-Sun and public holidays 9am-8pm; low season: 10am-8pm, Sat 9am-8pm. ☎ 01 60 30 60 30. For guided tours, contact the City Hall (Disneyland Park) on Town Square in Main Street, USA: 7.62€ (children: 4.57€). Parking: cars 6.86€, motorcycles 3.81€. Disneyland Passport in high season: 1 day: 36€ (children 3-11 years: 29€); 3 days: 99€ (children: 80€). The 3-day passport gives unrestricted access to both theme parks and can be used on non-consecutive days. All passports remain valid for 3 years. Readmission: to leave the park temporarily, visitors must have their hand stamped; visitors must keep passports and parking tickets.

ST-DENIS

🖪 1r. de la République, 93200 ST-DENIS, ☎ 01 55 87 08 70.

Guided tour of the town – Contact the tourist office.

Interior – Daily 10am-5.15pm, Sun and public holidays noon-5.15pm (Apr-Sep: 10am-6.15pm, Sun noon-6.15pm). Guided tours daily at 11.15am and 3pm. Closed 1 Jan, 1 May and 25 Dec. 5.5€. ☎ 01 48 09 83 54.

Musée d'Art et d'Histoire – Daily except Tue 10am-5.30pm, Thu 10am-8pm, Sat-Sun 2-6.30pm. Closed public holidays. 3.05€, no charge 1st Sun in the month. ☎ 01 42 43 05 10.

Musée Bouilhet-Christofle – Daily except Sat-Sun 9.30am-5.30pm. Closed public holidays. 7€. ☎ 01 49 22 40 40.

Stade de France – "First look" discovery visits 10am-6pm (ticket office closes at 5.30pm). 6€ (children: 4.5€). "Behind the scenes" guided tours (1hr 30min) at 10am, 2pm and 4pm. 14€ (children: 10€). It is advisable to enquire beforehand as visits are not allowed when shows are scheduled. ☎ 01 55 93 00 00. www.stadefrance.com

VERSAILLES

🖪 2bis av. de Paris, 78000 VERSAILLES, ☎ 01 39 24 88 88.

Guided tour of the town – Contact the tourist office.

Château

Le Château: Exterior – The courtyards of the château and of the Trianon, and the grounds (entrance fee 4.5€, for cars 5.5€ Sat-Sun and public holidays) can be visited freely every day from sunrise to sunset. An entrance fee is charged for visits to the château gardens from early Apr to end Oct and during the Musical Fountains event: 3€ (Musical Fountains: 5.5€). ☎ 01 30 83 77 88.

Le Château: Interior – Daily except Mon (last admission 30min before closing time) 9am-6.30pm (Oct-Apr: 5.30pm). 7.50€, (5.30€ from 3.30pm Tue-Sun). ☎ 01 30 83 76 20.

Tour of the King's bedchamber – Guided tours (1hr) daily except Mon 9am-4.30pm (Apr-Oct: 5.30pm). 4€ (children under 10: no charge), extra cost to be added to the entrance fee. ☎ 01 30 83 77 88.

Park and gardens

The Gardens – Guided pedestrian tours (1hr 30min) of the wooded areas daily except Sat-Sun during the Musical Fountains event 10am-3.30pm (summer: 9am-5pm). 5.5€ (summer: 7€), 10.5€ during the Musical Fountains event. ☎ 01 30 83 77 80.

Tourist train – Tour of the grounds (40min) with a stop at the Trianon and Grand Canal. Departure from the Parterre du Nord of the château. Mar and Oct: 10.30am-5pm; May-Aug: 10am-6.15pm; Apr and Sep: 10.30am-6.15pm; Nov: 11am-4.30pm; Dec-Feb: call for information. 5.1€ (children 3 to12 years: 3.20€). ☎ 01 39 54 22 00.

Bicycle hire – There are three rental points in the grounds from Feb to end Nov: near the Grand Canal daily (except in rainy weather) 10am-6.30pm. 5€ per hour; at the Grille de la Reine and Porte St-Antoine: Wed 1-6.30pm, Sat-Sun and public holidays 10.30am-6.30pm (Jul and Aug: 1-6.30pm, Sat-Sun and public holidays 10am-6.30pm). 4.4€ per hour. ☎ 01 39 66 97 66.

Boat hire – Mar to end Oct 10am-6pm. 11€ (1hr, boat for 4 people). ☎ 01 39 66 97 66.

Grand and Petit Trianon – Apr-Oct: noon-6.30pm (last admission 30min before closing); Nov-Mar: noon-5.30pm. 5€ (3€ after 3.30pm). ☎ 01 30 83 76 20.

Index

Notre-Dame .... Sights and monuments
Haussmann .... People, historical events and subjects

To find a museum, church or particular street, look for the proper name under the listings Museums, Churches or Streets. Bridges, boulevards, places etc are listed directly under their proper names, as are theatres, parks and gardens and *hôtels particuliers*.